Microsoft®

Visual Basic 6.0 Component Tools Guide

Microsoft® Press

PUBLISHED BY
Microsoft Press
A Division of Microsoft Corporation
One Microsoft Way
Redmond, Washington 98052-6399

Library of Congress Cataloging-in-Publication Data
Microsoft Visual Basic 6.0 Reference Library / Microsoft Corporation.
p. cm.
Includes index.
ISBN 1-57231-864-3
1. BASIC (Computer program language) 2. Microsoft Visual BASIC.
I. Microsoft Corporation.
QA76.73.B3M559 1998
005.26'8--dc21 98-14787
CIP

Printed and bound in the United States of America.

3 4 5 6 7 8 9 WCWC 3 2 1 0

Distributed in Canada by Penguin Books Canada Limited.

A CIP catalogue record for this book is available from the British Library.

Microsoft Press books are available through booksellers and distributors worldwide. For further information about international editions, contact your local Microsoft Corporation office or contact Microsoft Press International directly at fax (425) 936-7329. Visit our Web site at mspress.microsoft.com.

Acquisitions Editor: Eric Stroo
Project Editor: Maureen Williams Zimmerman

Part No. 097-0001956

Contents

Document Conventions

This manual uses the following typographic conventions.

Example of convention	Description
Sub, If, Case Else, Print, True, BackColor, Click, Debug, Long	Words with initial letter capitalized indicate language-specific keywords.
setup	Words you're instructed to type appear in bold.
event-driven	In text, italic letters can indicate defined terms, usually the first time they occur in the book. Italic formatting is also used occasionally for emphasis.
variable	In syntax and text, italic letters can indicate placeholders for information you supply.
[*expressionlist*]	In syntax, items inside square brackets are optional.
{**While** | **Until**}	In syntax, braces and a vertical bar indicate a choice between two or more items. You must choose one of the items unless all of the items also are enclosed in square brackets.

`Sub HelloButton_Click()`
`Readout.Text = _`
`"Hello, world!"`
`End Sub`
	This font is used for code.

ENTER	Capital letters are used for the names of keys and key sequences, such as ENTER and CTRL+R.
ALT+F1	A plus sign (+) between key names indicates a combination of keys. For example, ALT+F1 means to hold down the ALT key while pressing the F1 key.
DOWN ARROW	Individual direction keys are referred to by the direction of the arrow on the key top (LEFT, RIGHT, UP, or DOWN). The phrase "arrow keys" is used when describing these keys collectively.
BACKSPACE, HOME	Other navigational keys are referred to by their specific names.
c:\Vb\Samples\Calldlls.vbp	Paths and file names are given in mixed case.

Programming Style in This Manual

The following guidelines are used in writing programs in this manual. For more information, see Chapter 5, "Programming Fundamentals" in the *Microsoft Visual Basic 6.0 Programmer's Guide.*

- Keywords appear with initial letters capitalized:

```
' Sub, If, ChDir, Print, and True are keywords.
Print "Title Page"
```

- Line labels are used instead of line numbers. The use of line labels is restricted to error-handling routines:

```
ErrorHandler:
   Power = conFailure
End Function
```

- An apostrophe (') introduces comments:

```
' This is a comment; these two lines
' are ignored when the program is running.
```

- Control-flow blocks and statements in Sub, Function, and Property procedures are indented from the enclosing code:

```
Private Sub cmdRemove_Click ()
   Dim Ind As Integer

   Ind = lstClient.ListIndex    ' Get index.
   ' Make sure list item is selected.
   If Ind >= 0 Then
      lstClient.RemoveItem Ind ' Remove it
                               ' from list box.
      ' Display number.
      lblDisplay.Caption = lstClient.ListCount
   Else
      Beep                 ' If nothing selected, beep.
   End If
End Sub
```

- Lines too long to fit on one line (except comments) may be continued on the next line using a line-continuation character, which is a single leading space followed by an underscore (_):

```
Sub Form_MouseDown (Button As Integer, _
Shift As Integer, X As Single, Y As Single)
```

- Intrinsic constant names are in a mixed-case format, with a two-character prefix indicating the object library that defines the constant. Constants from the Visual Basic (VB) and Visual Basic for applications (VBA) object libraries are prefaced with a "vb"; constants from the data access (DAO) object library are prefaced with a "db"; constants from the Microsoft Excel object library are prefaced with an "xl." For example:

  ```
  vbTileHorizontal
  dbAppendOnly
  xlDialogBorder
  ```

  Throughout this book, user-defined constants are usually prefaced with "con" and are mixed case. For example:

  ```
  ConYourOwnConstant
  ```

  When using Windows API constants, however, the code examples still follow the same conventions as in previous versions of Visual Basic. For example:

  ```
  EM_LINESCROLL
  ```

PART 1

Using ActiveX Controls

This section provides an introduction and scenarios to help you get started with the ActiveX controls — formerly called OLE controls — included with the Microsoft Visual Basic 6.0 Professional Edition. Start here for general information and for suggestions and code to use when developing your applications. More detailed reference information, including links to properties, methods, and events associated with each control, is included in the *Microsoft Visual Basic 6.0 Language Reference* volume of the *Microsoft Visual Basic 6.0 Reference Library.*

Chapter 1 ActiveX Controls Overview

An introduction to ActiveX controls, including installation, upgrade, control class names, and distribution.

Chapter 2 Using the ActiveX Controls

Introduction to most of the ActiveX controls included with Visual Basic, along with many scenarios (including code) illustrating ways to use them.

CHAPTER 1

ActiveX Controls Overview

This chapter, "ActiveX Controls Overview," provides a starting point for each of the ActiveX controls, formerly called OLE controls, in the Microsoft Visual Basic programming system. Each ActiveX control is documented in its own section here with task-oriented overviews. These overviews are not meant to replace the language reference information, but to give the new user contexts for using the controls.

For language-specific information, search for the control's name.

Contents

What Is an ActiveX Control?

An ActiveX control is an extension to the Visual Basic Toolbox. You use ActiveX controls just as you would any of the standard built-in controls, such as the CheckBox control. When you add an ActiveX control to a program, it becomes part of the development and run-time environment and provides new functionality for your application.

ActiveX controls leverage your capabilities as a Visual Basic programmer by retaining some familiar properties, events, and methods, such as the Name property, which behave as you would expect. Then, however, the ActiveX controls feature methods and properties that greatly increase your flexibility and capability as a Visual Basic programmer.

For example, the Visual Basic Professional and Enterprise editions include the Windows Common controls that allow you to create applications with the look and feel of Windows 95 toolbars, status bars, and tree views of directory structures. Other controls allow you to create applications that take full advantage of the Internet.

Installing and Registering ActiveX Controls

At setup, the Professional and Enterprise Editions automatically install and register ActiveX controls in the \Windows\System or System32 directory. You are then able to use the ActiveX controls at design time to build your applications.

If you plan to create a setup program for your application, you'll need to include information on any ActiveX controls in the Setup.lst file. For more information, see Chapter 17, "Distributing Your Applications," in the *Microsoft Visual Basic 6.0 Programmer's Guide.*

> **Note** It is a violation of your license agreement to copy and distribute any information from the "Licenses" section of the system registry.

Upgrading VBX Controls to ActiveX Controls

If you have a project with VBX custom controls that you'd like to replace with ActiveX controls, Visual Basic can do this automatically. Conversion is only possible for VBX custom controls for which replacement ActiveX controls exist on your system. For more information, see Chapter 4, "Managing Projects," in the *Microsoft Visual Basic 6.0 Programmer's Guide.*

The following VBX custom controls are no longer supported in Visual Basic However, 32-bit ActiveX versions can be found as .ocx files in the \Tools\Controls directory of your Visual Basic CD-ROM:

- AniButton
- Gauge
- Graph
- KeyState
- MSGrid
- Outline
- Spin
- ThreeD

To install these controls, you will have to use the Regsvr32 and RegEdit applications, which are also available in the Tools directory. For instructions on how to use the Regsvr32 and RegEdit applications, consult the Readme.txt file in the \Tools\Controls directory.

Loading ActiveX Controls

ActiveX controls have the file name extension .ocx. You can use the ActiveX controls provided with Visual Basic or obtain additional controls from third-party developers.

You can use ActiveX controls and other insertable objects to your project by adding them to the Toolbox.

> **Note** Visual Basic ActiveX controls are 32-bit controls. Some third-party developers offer ActiveX controls which are 16-bit controls, and these can no longer be used in Visual Basic.

To add a control to a project's Toolbox

1. On the **Project** menu, click **Components** to display the **Components** dialog box, as seen in Figure 1.1.

   > **Tip** You can also display the dialog box by right-clicking on the Toolbox.

2. Items listed in this dialog box include all registered insertable objects, designers, and ActiveX controls.
3. To add an ActiveX control to the Toolbox, select the check box to the left of the control name.
4. Click **OK** to close the **Components** dialog box. All of the ActiveX controls that you selected will now appear in the Toolbox.

Figure 1.1 The Components dialog box

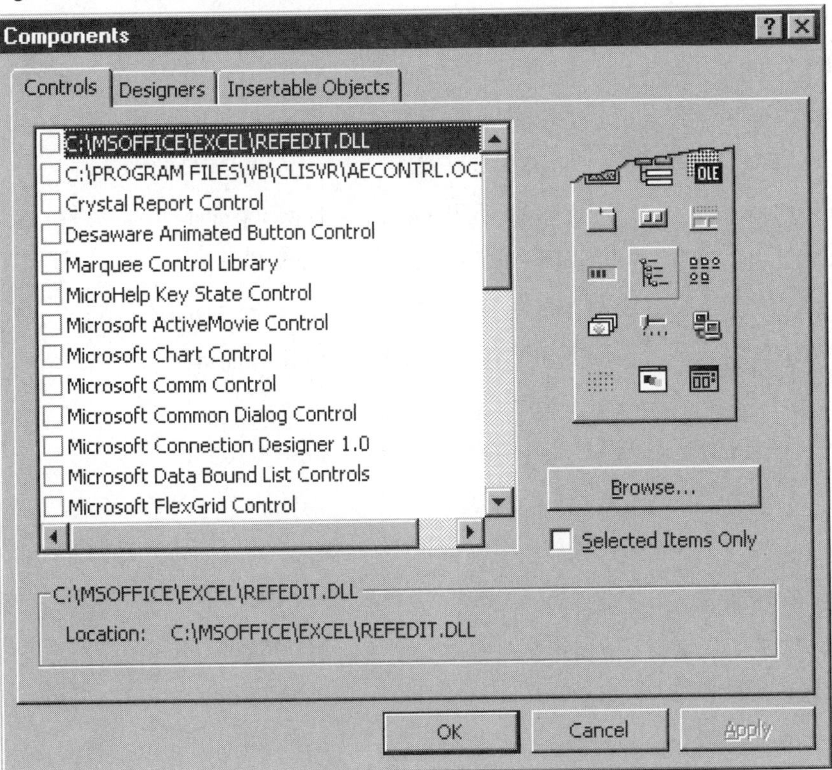

To add ActiveX controls to the Components dialog box, click the Browse button, and locate files with the .ocx file name extension. These files are commonly installed in your \Windows\System or System32 directory. When you add an ActiveX control to the list of available controls, Visual Basic automatically selects its check box in the Components dialog box.

ActiveX Controls File Names

To load an ActiveX control into the Toolbox, use the Components dialog box from the Project menu. The table below lists the names of components you will find in the dialog box along with the file name (.ocx) and the ActiveX controls contained by the component.

Note The presence or absence of components on your system depends upon which version of Visual Basic you are using.

Component Name	File Name	Control
Microsoft ADO Data Control 6.0	MSADODC.OCX	ADO Data Control
Microsoft Chart Control 5.5	MSCHART.OCX	Microsoft Chart
Microsoft Comm Control 6.0	MSCOMM32.OCX	MSComm
Microsoft Common Dialog Control 6.0	COMDLG32. OCX	CommonDialog
Microsoft Data Bound Grid Control 5.0	DBGRID32.OCX	DBGrid
Microsoft Data Bound List Controls 6.0	DBLIST32.OCX	DBList, DBCombo
Microsoft Data Repeater Control 6.0	MSDATREP.OCX	DataRepeater
Microsoft Data Grid Control 6.0	MSDATGRD.OCX	DataGrid
Microsoft Data List Controls 6.0	MSDATLST.OCX	DataList, DataCombo
Microsoft FlexGrid Control 6.0	MSFLXGRD.OCX	MSFlexGrid
Microsoft Grid Control	GRID32.OCX	Grid
Microsoft Hierarchical Flex Grid Control 6.0	MSHFLXGD.OCX	MSHFlexGrid
Microsoft Internet Transfer Control 6.0	MSINET.OCX	Internet Transfer control
Microsoft MAPI Controls6.0	MSMAPI32.OCX	MAPIMessages, MAPISession
Microsoft MaskedEdit Control 6.0	MSMASK32.OCX	MaskedEdit
Microsoft Multimedia Control 6.0	MCI32.OCX	Multimedia MCI
Microsoft PictureClip Control 6.0	PICCLP32.OCX	PictureClip
Microsoft RemoteData Control 6.0	MSRDC20.OCX	RemoteData
Microsoft RichTextBox Control 6.0	RICHTX32.OCX	RichTextBox

(continued)

Component Name	File Name	Control
Microsoft SysInfo Control 6.0	SYSINFO.OCX	SysInfo
Microsoft TabbedDialog Control 6.0	TABCTL32.OCX	Microsoft Tab Control
Microsoft Windows Common Controls 6.0	MSCOMCTL.OCX	TabStrip, Toolbar, StatusBar, ProgressBar, TreeView, ListView, ImageList, Slider, ImageCombo
Microsoft Windows Common Controls-2 6.0	MSCOMCT2.OCX	Animation, UpDown, MonthView, DTPicker, FlatScrollbar
Microsoft Windows Common Controls-3 6.0	COMCT332.OCX	CoolBar
Microsoft Winsock Control 6.0	MSWINSCK.OCX	WinSock

Data Bound ActiveX Controls

The following controls are *bound* controls. This means that they can be linked to a data control and can display field values for the current record in the data set. These controls can also write out values to the data set.

- DataCombo
- DataGrid
- DataList
- DataRepeater
- DateTimePicker
- Hierarchical FlexGrid
- ImageCombo
- Masked Edit
- Microsoft Chart
- Microsoft FlexGrid
- MonthView
- RichTextBox

For More Information For more on using bound controls, see in Chapter 7, "Using Visual Basic's Standard Controls," in the *Microsoft Visual Basic 6.0 Programmer's Guide.*

The About Property

Some ActiveX controls were developed by independent software vendors. If you would like more information about a control's vendor, click the control and press F4 to display the Properties window. Double-click the About property in the Properties window to open a dialog box that displays information about the vendor.

ActiveX Control Class

The class name for each ActiveX control is listed in the following table. (The class name for a control also appears in the Properties window.)

Control	Class name
Animation	Animation
Communications	MSComm
CoolBar	CoolBar
DataCombo	DataCombo
DataList	DataList
Data Repeater	DataRepeater
DateTimePicker	DTPicker
FlatScrollBar	FlatScrollBar
Hierarchical FlexGrid	MSHFlexGrid
ImageCombo	ImageCombo
ImageList	ImageList
Internet Transfer	Inet
ListView	ListView
MAPI	MapiSession, MapiMessages
Masked edit	MaskEdBox
MonthView	MonthView
MS FlexGrid	MSFlexGrid
Multimedia MCI	MMControl
Picture clip	PictureClip

(continued)

Control	Class name
ProgressBar	ProgressBar
RichTextBox	RichTextBox
Slider	Slider
Microsoft Tabbed Dialog Control	SSTab
StatusBar	StatusBar
SysInfo	SysInfo
TabStrip	TabStrip
Toolbar	Toolbar
TreeView	TreeView
UpDown	UpDown
Microsoft Chart	MSChart
Winsock	Winsock

Creating, Running, and Distributing Executable (.EXE) Files

To run your application under Microsoft Windows outside of Visual Basic, you need to create an executable (.exe) file. You create executable files for applications that use ActiveX controls the same as you would for any other application. There are a few issues to consider, however, when running such an application.

Visual Basic Executable (.EXE) Files

An ActiveX control file is accessed both by Visual Basic and by applications created with Visual Basic. When you run an executable file that contains an ActiveX control, the .ocx file associated with it must be registered in the system registry. Otherwise, the application will not be able to find the code needed to create the control.

If a control cannot be found, the Visual Basic run-time DLL generates the error message "File Not Found." If you want to distribute an application that uses ActiveX controls, it is recommended that your installation procedure copy all required .ocx files into the user's \Windows\System directory. Your installation procedure should also register the required controls in the system registry.

You can freely distribute any application you create with the Visual Basic to any Microsoft Windows user. The Package and Deployment Wizard included with Visual Basic provides tools to help you write setup programs that install your application. Users will need copies of the following:

- The Visual Basic run-time file.
- Any .ocx files.
- Additional DLLs, as required by your application or by ActiveX controls.

CHAPTER 2

Using the ActiveX Controls

The topics in this chapter provide introductions to most of the ActiveX controls provided with Microsoft Visual Basic. For many of these, you will also find scenarios — along with code — featuring the controls in sample applications.

Contents

- Using the Slider Control
- Using the StatusBar Control
- Using the SysInfo Control
- Using the Tabbed Dialog Control
- Using the TabStrip Control
- Using the ToolBar Control
- Using the TreeView Control
- Using the UpDown Control
- Using the Winsock Control

Using the Animation Control

The Animation control displays silent Audio Video Interleaved (AVI) clips. An AVI clip is a series of bitmap frames like a movie.

One example is the piece of paper that "flies" between folders when copying files in the Windows 95 system:

Although AVI clips can have sound, such clips cannot be used with the Animation control, and an error will occur if you try to load such a file. Only silent AVI clips can be used. To play .avi files with sound, use the Multimedia (MCI) control. See "Using the Multimedia Control," later in this chapter, for more information about the MCI control.

> **Note** A variety of soundless .avi files can be found in the \Graphics\AVI directory of the Visual Basic CD-ROM.

At run time, the Animation control does not have a visible frame.

The Animation control maintains a separate thread of execution while it is playing. Therefore, your application will not be blocked, and can continue to execute within its process.

Possible Uses

- To create dialog boxes that inform the user of the length and nature of an operation.
- To play silent instructional video clips about your application.
- To allow users to play files dropped onto the control.

Basic Operation: Open, Play, Stop, and Close Methods

When using the control, you open an .avi file using the Open method, play it using the Play method, and stop it with the Stop method. After a video has played, use the Close method to close the file. You do not need to close the file before opening a new one.

The following code uses two CommandButton controls, cmdPlay and cmdStop, and a CommonDialog control named dlgOpen. Set the caption of cmdPlay to "Open and Play." The caption of the CommandButton control cmdStop is set to "Stop."

```
Private Sub cmdPlay_Click()
   ' Configure a CommonDialog control to allow the
   ' user to find .avi files to play. The CommonDialog
   ' control is named "dlgOpen." The Animation control
   ' is named "anmAVI."
   dlgOpen.Filter = "avi files (*.avi)|*.avi"
   dlgOpen.ShowOpen
   anmAvi.Open dlgOpen.FileName
   anmAVI.Play
End Sub
```

This code stops the video playing:

```
Private Sub cmdStop_Click()
   anmAVI.Stop
End Sub
```

Play Method Arguments: Repeat, Start, and Stop

The Play method has three arguments — *repeat*, *start*, and *stop* — which determine how many times a file is played, at which frame to begin playing, and where to stop the file.

If the repeat argument is not supplied, the file will play continuously. For example, the following code will play a file continuously until the user clicks the cmdStop button:

```
Private Sub cmdPlay_Click()
   dlgOpen.Filter = "avi files (*.avi)|*.avi"
   dlgOpen.ShowOpen
   anmAVI.Open dlgOpen.FileName
   ' Play the file indefinitely.
   anmAVI.Play
End Sub
```

```
Private Sub cmdStop_Click()
   anmAVI.Stop
End Sub
```

The following code plays the file ten times, from the sixth to sixteenth frames (the first frame is frame 0):

```
anmAVI.Play 10, 5, 15
```

Play Files Automatically Using the AutoPlay Property

If the AutoPlay property is set to True, the control will begin playing a file as soon as it is loaded. Conversely, to stop a file from playing, set the AutoPlay property to False, as shown in the following code:

```
Private Sub cmdPlay_Click()
   ' Setting the AutoPlay property to True plays
   ' the file as soon as it is loaded. Thus there's
   ' no need for a Play method.
   dlgOpen.Filter = "avi files (*.avi)|*.avi"
   dlgOpen.ShowOpen
   anmAvi.AutoPlay = True
   anmAVI.File = dlgOpen.FileName
End Sub

Private Sub cmdStop_Click()
   ' Set AutoPlay to False to stop playing.
   anmAVI.AutoPlay = False
End Sub
```

Center the Play Area Using the Center Property

You can specify whether or not to center the video in the control by using the Center property. When the Center property is set to False, the control automatically sizes itself at run time to the size of the video. At design time, the left and top edges of the control define the area where the video will be displayed as seen:

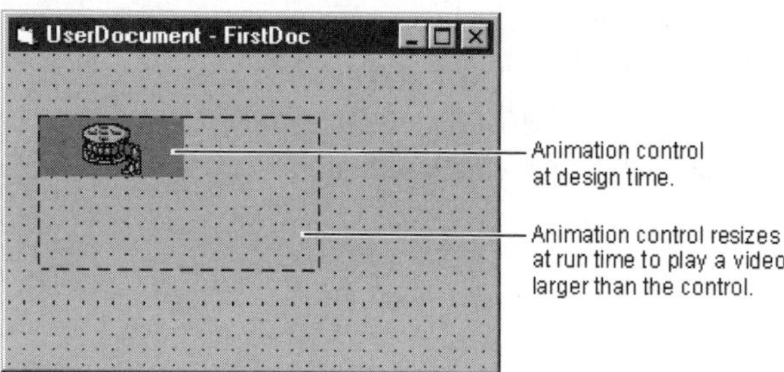
UserDocument - FirstDoc
Animation control at design time.
Animation control resizes at run time to play a video larger than the control.

When the Center property is set to True, the control does not resize itself. Instead, the video will be displayed in the center of the area defined by the control, as seen:

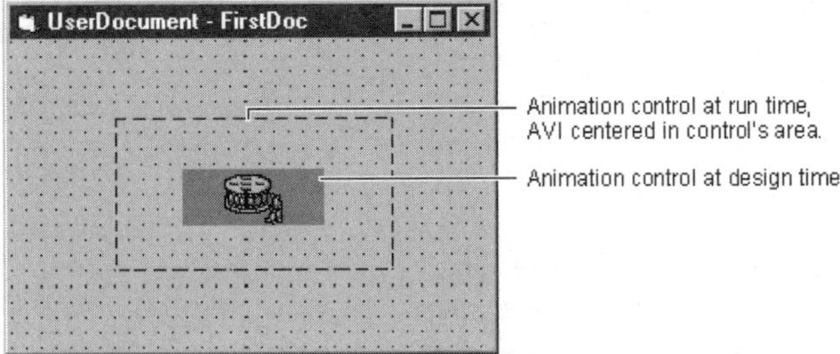

> **Note** If the area defined by the control at design time is smaller than the video, the edges of the video will be clipped.

> **Distribution Note** The Animation control is part of a group of ActiveX controls that are found in the MSCOMCT2.OCX file. To use the Animation control in your application, you must add the MSCOMCT2.OCX file to the project. When distributing your application, install the MSCOMCT2.OCX file in the user's Microsoft Windows System or System 32 directory. For more information on how to add an ActiveX control to a project, see the *Microsoft Visual Basic 6.0 Programmer's Guide*.

Using the Communications Control

The Communications control allows you to add both simple serial port communication functionality to your application and advanced functionality to create a full-featured, event-driven communications tool.

The Communications Control

The Communications control provides an interface to a standard set of communications commands. It allows you to establish a connection to a serial port, connect to another communication device (a modem, for instance), issue commands, exchange data, and monitor and respond to various events and errors that may be encountered during a serial connection.

Possible Uses

- To dial a phone number.
- To monitor a serial port for incoming data.
- To create a full-featured terminal program.

Sample Applications: Dialer.vbp and VBTerm.vbp

The Dialer.vbp and VBTerm.vbp sample applications which are listed in the samples directory, demonstrate simple and complex (respectively) programming techniques of the Communications control.

Basics of Serial Communications

Every computer comes with one or more serial ports. They are named successively: COM1, COM2, and so on. On a standard PC, the mouse is usually connected to the COM1 port. A modem may be connected to COM2, a scanner to COM3, etc. Serial ports provide a channel for the transmission of data from these external serial devices.

The essential function of the serial port is to act as an interpreter between the CPU and the serial device. As data is sent through the serial port from the CPU, Byte values are converted to serial bits. When data is received, serial bits are converted to Byte values.

A further layer of interpretation is needed to complete the transmission of data. On the operating system side, Windows uses a communications driver, Comm.drv, to send and receive data using standard Windows API functions. The serial device manufacturer provides a driver that connects its hardware to Windows. When you use the Communications control, you are issuing API functions, which are then interpreted by Comm.drv and passed to the device driver.

As a programmer, you need only concern yourself with the Windows side of this interaction. As a Visual Basic programmer, you need only concern yourself with the interface that the Communications control provides to API functions of the Windows communications driver. In other words, you set and monitor properties and events of the Communications control.

Establishing the Serial Connection

The first step in using the Communications control is establishing the connection to the serial port. The following table lists the properties that are used to establish the serial connection:

Properties	Description
CommPort	Sets and returns the communications port number.
Settings	Sets and returns the baud rate, parity, data bits, and stop bits as a string.
PortOpen	Sets and returns the state of a communications port. Also opens and closes a port.

Opening the Serial Port

To open a serial port, use the CommPort, PortOpen, and Settings properties. For example:

```
' Open the serial port
MSComm1.CommPort = 2
MSComm1.Settings = "9600,N,8,1"
MSComm1.PortOpen = True
```

The CommPort property sets which serial port to open. Assuming that a modem is connected to COM2, the above example sets the value to 2 (COM2) and connects to the modem. You can set the CommPort property value to any number between 1 and 16 (the default is 1). If, however, you set this value to a COM port that does not exist for the system on which your application is run, an error will be generated.

The Settings property allows you to specify the baud rate, parity, and the number of data bits and stop bits. By default, the baud rate is set at 9600. The parity setting is for data validation. It is commonly not used, and set to "N." The data bits setting specifies the number of bits that represent a chunk of data. The stop bit indicates when a chunk of data has been received.

Once you've specified which port to open and how data communication is to be handled, you use the PortOpen property to establish the connection. It is a Boolean value, True or False. If, however, the port is not functional, if the CommPort property is set incorrectly, or if the device does not support the settings you've specified, an error will be generated or the external device may not work correctly. Setting the value of the PortOpen property to False closes the port.

Working with a Modem

In most cases, you will use the Communications control to program your application to work with a modem. With the Communications control, you can use the standard Hayes-compatible command set to dial a phone number, or connect to and interact with another modem.

Once the serial port connection has been established using the CommPort, Settings, and PortOpen properties, you use the Output property to activate and interact with the modem. The Output property is used to issue commands which control the interaction between one modem and another. For example:

```
' Activate the modem and dial a phone number.
MSComm1.Output = "ATDT 555-5555" & vbCr
```

In the example above, the command "AT" initiates the connection, "D" dials the number, and "T" specifies touch tone (rather than pulse). A carriage return character (vbCr) must be specified when outputing to a terminal. You do not need to add the return character when outputing byte arrays.

When a command is successfully processed, an "OK" result code will be returned. You can test for this result code to determine if a command was processed successfully.

For More Information For a complete list of Hayes-compatible commands, check your modem documentation.

Setting Receive and Transmit Buffer Properties at Design Time

When a port is opened, receive and transmit buffers are created. To manage these buffers, the Communications control provides you with a number of properties that can be set at design time using the control's Property Pages.

Setting buffer properties at design time

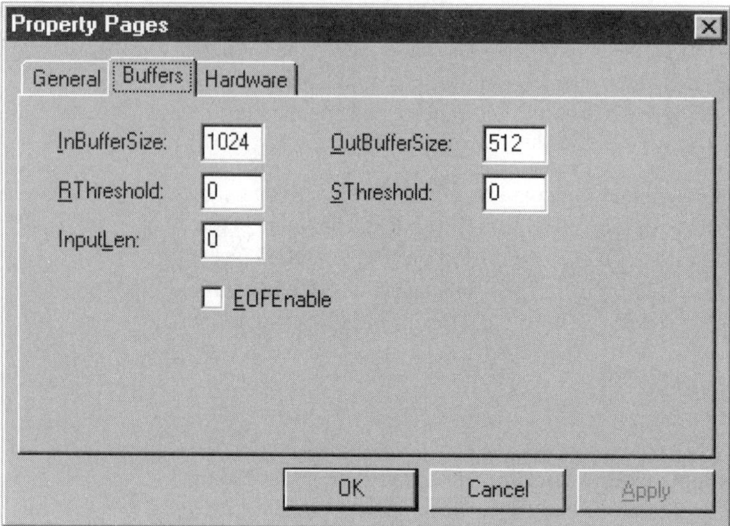

Buffer Memory Allocation

The InBufferSize and OutBufferSize properties specify how much memory is allocated to the receive and transmit buffers. Each are set by default to the values shown above. The larger you make the number, the less memory you have available to your application. If, however, your buffer is too small, you run the risk of overflowing the buffer unless you use handshaking.

> **Note** Given the amount of memory available to most PCs at this time, buffer memory allocation is less crucial because you have more resources available. In other words, you can set the buffer values higher without affecting the performance of your application.

The RThreshold and SThreshold Properties

The RThreshold and SThreshold properties set or return the number of characters that are received into the receive and transmit buffers before the OnComm event is fired. The OnComm event is used to monitor and respond to changes in communications states. Setting the value for each property to zero (0) prevents the OnComm event from firing. Setting the value to something other than 0 (1, for instance) causes the OnComm event to be fired every time a single character is received into either buffer.

For More Information See "The OnComm Event and the CommEvent Property" in this topic for more information on these properties.

The InputLen and EOFEnable Properties

Setting the InputLen property to 0 causes the Communications control to read the entire contents of the receive buffer when the Input property is used. When reading data from a machine whose output is formatted in fixed-length blocks of data, the value of this property can be set appropriately.

The EOFEnable property is used to indicate when an End of File (EOF) character is found during data input. Setting this to True causes data input to stop and the OnComm event to fire to inform you that this condition has occurred.

For More Information See "Managing the Receive and Transmit Buffers" and "The OnComm Event and the CommEvent Property," later in this chapter, for more information.

Managing the Receive and Transmit Buffers

As mentioned above, receive and transmit buffers are created whenever a port is opened. The receive and transmit buffers are used to store incoming data and to transmit outgoing data. The Communications control allows you to manage these buffers by providing you with a number of properties that are used to place and retrieve data, return the size of each buffer, and handle both text and binary data. Properly managing these buffers is an important part of using the Communications control.

The Receive Buffer

The Input property is used to store and retrieve data from the receive buffer. For example, if you wanted to retrieve data from the receive buffer and display it in a text box, you might use the following code:

```
TxtDisplay.Text = MSComm1.Input
```

To retrieve the entire contents of the receive buffer, however, you must first set the InputLen property to 0. This can be done at design or run time.

You can also receive incoming data as either text or binary data by setting the InputMode property to one of the following Visual Basic constants: comInputModeText or comInputModeBinary. The data will either be retrieved as string or as binary data in a Byte array. Use comInputModeText for data that uses the ANSI character set and comInputModeBinary for all other data, such as data that has embedded control characters, Nulls, etc.

As each byte of data is received, it is moved into the receive buffer and the InBufferCount property is incremented by one. The InBufferCount property, then, can be used to retrieve the number of bytes in the receive buffer. You can also clear the receive buffer by setting the value of this property to 0.

The Transmit Buffer

The Output property is used to send commands and data to the transmit buffer.

Like the Input property, data can be transmitted as either text or binary data. The Output property, however, must transmit either text or binary data by specifying either a string or Byte array variant.

You can send commands, text strings, or Byte array data with the Output property. For example:

```
' Send an AT command
MSComm1.Output = "ATDT 555-5555"

' Send a text string
MsComm1.Output = "This is a text string"

' Send Byte array data
MSComm1.Output = Out
```

As previously mentioned, transmit lines must end with a carriage return character (vbCr). In the last example, `Out` is a variable defined as a Byte array: `Dim Out() As Byte`. If it were a string variant, it would be defined as: `Dim Out() As String`.

You can monitor the number of bytes in the transmit buffer by using the OutBufferCount property. You can clear the transmit buffer by setting this value to 0.

Handshaking

An integral part of managing the receive and transmit buffers is ensuring that the back-and-forth transmission of data is successful — that the speed at which the data is being received does not overflow the buffer limits, for example.

Handshaking refers to the internal communications protocol by which data is transferred from the hardware port to the receive buffer. When a character of data arrives at the serial port, the communications device has to move it into the receive buffer so that your program can read it. A handshaking protocol ensures that data is not lost due to a buffer overrun, where data arrives at the port too quickly for the communications device to move the data into the receive buffer.

You set the Handshaking property to specify the handshaking protocol to be used by your application. By default, this value is set to none (comNone). You can, however, specify one of the other following protocols:

Setting	Value	Description
comNone	0	No handshaking (Default).
comXOnXOff	1	XOn/XOff handshaking.
comRTS	2	RTS/CTS (Request To Send/Clear To Send) handshaking.
comRTSXOnXOff	3	Both Request To Send and XOn/XOff handshaking.

The protocol that you choose depends upon the device to which you're connecting. Setting this value to comRTSXOnXOff supports both of the protocols.

In many cases, the communications protocol itself handles handshaking. Therefore, setting this property to something other than comNone may result in conflicts.

> **Note** If you do set this value to either comRTS or comRTSXOnXOff, you need to set the RTSEnabled property to True. Otherwise, you will be able to connect and send, but not receive, data.

The OnComm Event and the CommEvent Property

Depending upon the scope and functionality of your application, you may need to monitor and respond to any number of events or errors which may occur during the connection to another device or in the receipt or transmission of data.

The OnComm event and the CommEvent property allow you to trap and check the value of communication events and errors.

When a communication event or error occurs, the OnComm event is fired and the value of the CommEvent property is changed. Therefore, if necessary, you can check the value of the CommEvent property each time the OnComm event is fired. Because communications (especially over telephone lines) can be unpredictable, trapping these events and errors allows you to respond to them appropriately.

The following table lists the communication events that will trigger the OnComm event. The values will then be written to the CommEvent property.

Constant	Value	Description
comEvSend	1	There are fewer than SThreshold number of characters in the transmit buffer.
comEvReceive	2	Received RThreshold number of characters. This event is generated continuously until you use the Input property to remove the data from the receive buffer.
comEvCTS	3	Change in Clear To Send line.
comEvDSR	4	Change in Data Set Ready line. This event is only fired when DSR changes from 1 to 0.
comEvCD	5	Change in Carrier Detect line.
comEvRing	6	Ring detected. Some UARTs (universal asynchronous receiver-transmitters) may not support this event.
comEvEOF	7	End Of File (ASCII character 26) character received.

The OnComm event is also triggered, and a value is written to the CommEvent property, when the following errors are encountered.

Setting	Value	Description
comEventBreak	1001	A Break signal was received.
comEventCTSTO	1002	Clear To Send Timeout. The Clear To Send line was low for CTSTimeout number of milliseconds while trying to transmit a character.
comEventDSRTO	1003	Data Set Ready Timeout. The Data Set Ready line was low for DSRTimeout number of milliseconds while trying to transmit a character.
comEventFrame	1004	Framing Error. The hardware detected a framing error.
comEventOverrun	1006	Port Overrun. A character was not read from the hardware before the next character arrived and was lost.
comEventCDTO	1007	Carrier Detect Timeout. The Carrier Detect line was low for CDTimeout number of milliseconds while trying to transmit a character. Carrier Detect is also known as the Receive Line Signal Detect (RLSD).

(continued)

Setting	Value	Description
comEventRxOver	1008	Receive Buffer Overflow. There is no room in the receive buffer.
comEventRxParity	1009	Parity Error. The hardware detected a parity error.
comEventTxFull	1010	Transmit Buffer Full. The transmit buffer was full while trying to queue a character.
comEventDCB	1011	Unexpected error retrieving Device Control Block (DCB) for the port.

Using the CoolBar Control

The CoolBar control (Comctl332.ocx) allows you to create user-configurable toolbars similar to those found in Microsoft Internet Explorer. The CoolBar control is a container control, able to host child controls. It consists of a collection of one or more resizable regions known as bands. Each band can host a single child control.

Using the CoolBar control is the same as using most other ActiveX controls, with the following exceptions.

- Adding Controls to a CoolBar
- Displaying Pictures on a CoolBar
- Using Other Controls with the CoolBar

Note This version of the CoolBar control requires that Internet Explorer 3.0 or later be installed on both the development computer as well as any computer where the CoolBar control will be distributed.

At this time CoolBar is known to work in Visual Basic 5.0 Service Pack 2 or later, Internet Explorer 3.0 or later, Visual C++ 4.0 or later, and Visual FoxPro 5.0 or later. It should also work in any host container that supports the ISimpleFrame interface.

Adding Controls to a CoolBar

The method for adding child controls to a CoolBar control is slightly different from that of adding controls to other containers. The control must first be associated with a Band object; there is a limit of one child control per band.

To add a control to a CoolBar

1. With the CoolBar control selected, select a control from the ToolBox and draw it on the CoolBar.
2. Open the **Property Page** for the CoolBar and select the **Bands** tab.

3. Use the Index buttons to select the **index** of the Band object on which you want the control to appear.
4. Select the control from the **Child** list.

The child control will then move and resize along with the Band object at run time.

> **Note** If you simply add a control without associating it to a band, it will appear as a floating control over the CoolBar at run time. To avoid this situation, set the Visible property of the control to False.

You can have additional controls contained on a CoolBar and swap them in and out at run time using the Child property of the Band object.

Displaying Pictures on a CoolBar

The CoolBar control provides several properties that allow a great deal of flexibility in displaying pictures.

When you assign an image to the Picture property of the CoolBar control, that image will be tiled seamlessly across all bands, behind any child controls. By setting the FixedBackground property of a Band object to False, the Image will be tiled within that band.

The Band object has a Picture property that allows you to display a different background picture when the UseCoolbarPicture property is set to False. The Band object also has an Image property which can be used to display an icon to the right of the move handle.

The EmbossPicture property can be used to force an image to be displayed in two colors, similar to the Internet Explorer toolbar. The two colors to be used are determined by the EmbossHighlight and EmbossShadow properties.

When the EmbossPicture property is set to True, the image assigned to the Picture property will be dithered to the EmbossHighlight and EmbossShadow colors. The dithering process uses a fixed threshold to determine which colors in the image will be mapped to the highlight and shadow colors. Choose images with a good definition between dark and light colors for best results.

Using Other Controls with the CoolBar

There are certain limitations to the controls that can be used as child controls on a CoolBar control.

The CoolBar control can only host controls which expose a Window handle. Lightweight controls such as Label, Image, and Shape controls don't expose a Window handle and can't be used. Although you can place these controls on the CoolBar, they won't appear at run time and won't be listed in the Child list box on the Property Page.

Although each band in the CoolBar control can only host a single child control, you can get around this limitation by placing a container control (such as a PictureBox) on the band and hosting additional controls within that container. Keep in mind that if you do this, you will need to create the code to resize the nested controls in response to changes in the CoolBar.

Some controls may not behave as expected when contained within a CoolBar control. For example, a contained Toolbar control won't paint properly when its Wrappable property is set to True and the CoolBar is resized. To avoid this problem, set the Wrappable property to False.

Using the DataRepeater Control

The DataRepeater control functions as a data-bound container of any user control you create. For example, imagine creating a user control that contains three TextBox controls, and a CheckBox control. This user control is designed to show one record of an employee database — displaying name, birth date, employee number, and marital status of the employee.

After compiling the control into an .ocx, the DataRepeater control's RepeatedControlName property is set to the user control. The DataRepeater is then bound to a data source, such as the ADO Data Control, which sets up a connection between the user control and the employee database. At run time, the DataRepeater displays several instances of the user control—each in its own row, and each bound to a different record in the database. The result can resemble the figure below.

Employee Records Repeated in DataRepeater Control

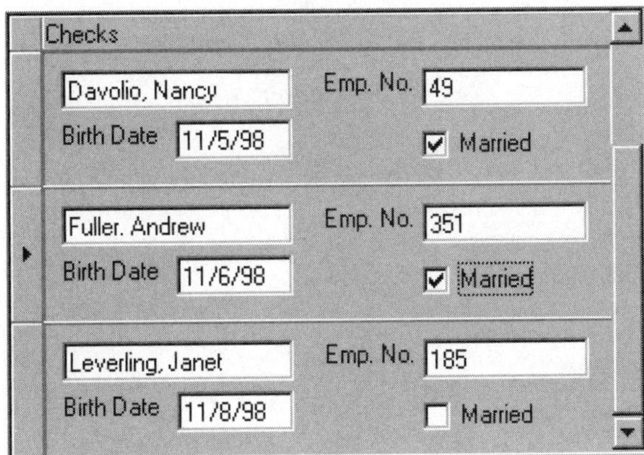

At run time, the user can scroll through a recordset using the HOME, END, PAGEUP, PAGEDOWN, and arrow keys.

Possible Uses

- To create a catalog that includes images of each product.
- To create a bankbook application to track personal finances.
- To create a custom data-bound grid that includes ComboBox controls.

Creating a Data-bound User Control for use in the DataRepeater Control

The first step when using the DataRepeater control is to create a data-bound user control. The procedure below creates a simple control that can be repeated in the DataRepeater.

For More Information Details about creating a data-bound user control can be found in "Binding a Control to a Data Source."

Creating a data-bound User control for use in the DataRepeater Control

1. Create a new **ActiveX Control** project.
2. In the Properties window, rename Project1 to **ProductsCtl**.
3. In the Properties window, rename UserControl1 to **ctlProducts**.
4. Add two **TextBox** controls and two **Label** controls to the form, and set their properties as shown in the table below.

Object	Property	Setting
Text1	Name	TxtProductName
Text2	Name	TxtUnitPrice
Label1	Caption	Product Name
Label2	Caption	Unit Price

Because the user control will be repeated, you may want to minimize its height; the simple user control described above looks like this:

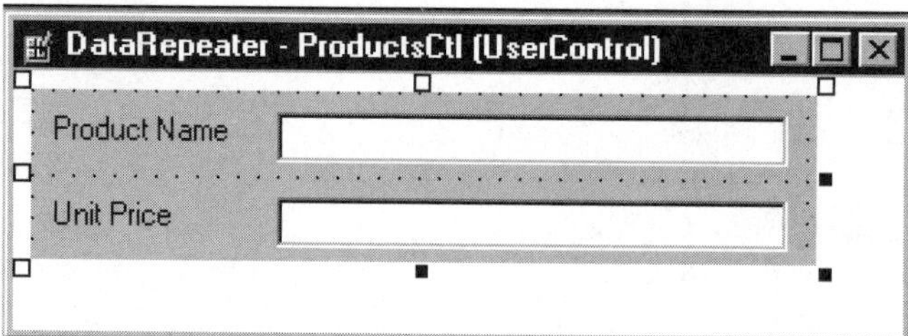

5. Add the code below to the control to create **Let** and **Get** properties of the user control.

```
Public Property Get ProductName() As String
   ProductName = txtProductName.Text
End Property
```

```
Public Property Let ProductName(ByVal newProductName As String)
   txtProductName.Text = newProductName
End Property

Public Property Get UnitPrice() As String
   UnitPrice = txtUnitPrice.Text ' Return a String!
End Property

Public Property Let UnitPrice(ByVal newUnitPrice As String)
   txtUnitPrice.Text = newUnitPrice ' NewUnitPrice is a String!
End Property

Private Sub txtProductName_Change()
   PropertyChanged "ProductName"
End Sub

Private Sub txtUnitPrice_Change()
   PropertyChanged "UnitPrice"
End Sub
```

Important Notice in the above code that the **UnitPrice** property is declared as a string. This is to allow the user of the DataRepeater control to use the DataFormat object to format the string as Currency. If you type the new value as Currency (what you might expect), the formatting supplied by the DataFormat object will be stripped.

6. Use the **Procedure Attributes** dialog box to make the properties data-bound.

   On the **Tools** menu click **Procedure Attributes**. On the **Procedures Attributes** dialog box, click **Advanced**. The **Name** box contains the property you want to make data-bound, and should contain **ProductName**. Click **Property is data bound**, then click **Show in DataBindings collection at design time**. Click the Name box and click **UnitPrice**. Once again, click **Property is data bound**, then click **Show in DataBindings collection at design time**. Click **OK** to close the dialog box.

7. Using the Windows Explorer, create a new folder on your hard disk named **ProductsCtl**.
8. On the **File** menu click **Save Project**. Save the project in the new folder using the names provided in the dialog boxes.
9. On the **File** menu click **Make ProductsCtl.ocx**. Save the .ocx to the same folder.

When you compile the user control into an .ocx, Visual Basic registers the control for you, allowing you to use it in the DataRepeater control.

Using the Data-bound User Control in the DataRepeater Control

Once you have built and compiled a data-bound user control, you can have it repeated in the DataRepeater control.

Using a data-bound user control in the DataRepeater control

1. Create a new **Standard EXE** project.
2. Set the following properties for the project and form:

Object	Property	Setting
Project1	Name	PrjRepeater
Form1	Name	FrmRepeater

3. Add the **DataRepeater** control and **ADO Data Control** to the **Toolbox**.

   On the Project menu, click **Components**. In the **Components** dialog box, click the **Controls** tab, and check **Microsoft Data Repeater Control** and **Microsoft ADO Data Control**. Click **OK** to close the dialog box.
4. Draw a **DataRepeater** control on the form. Make the control large enough to accommodate several "rows" of the control you want to repeat. One "row" is the height of the repeated control, as determined by the size of the UserControl object's designer.
5. Draw an **ADO Data Control** on the form, beneath the DataRepeater control.
6. Click the **ADO Data Control** to select it. Then, on the **Properties** window, click the **ConnectionString** property. Using the **ConnectionString** dialog box, create a connection string that accesses the Northwind database.
7. On the Properties window, click **Source**, and type the following SQL statement:

```
SELECT * FROM Products
```

8. Click the **DataRepeater** control to select it. On the Properties window, click **DataSource**, and click **ADODC1** to set the data source.
9. In the Properties window, click **RepeatedControlName** to display a drop-down list of all controls available on the computer. On the list, click **ProductsCtl.ctlProducts**. The selected control will be repeated in the DataRepeater control.

Binding the User Control Properties to the ADO Data Control

Once the user control is contained by the DataRepeater control, you must bind the user control's properties to the record source.

1. Right-click the DataRepeater control, and then click **DataRepeater Properties**. On the **Property Pages** dialog box, click the **RepeaterBindings** tab.
2. Click the **PropertyName** box to display a drop-down list of the data-bound properties of the repeated control. Click **ProductName**.
3. Click the **DataField** box to display a drop-down list of available data fields from the data source. Click **ProductName**.

4. Click the **Add** button to add the pair of property and data field to the **RepeaterBindings** collection.
5. Repeat steps 2 through 4 for the remaining property (**UnitPrice**).
6. Click the **Format** tab.
7. In the **Format Item** box, click **UnitPrice**.
8. In the **Format Type** box, click **Currency**. In the **Symbol** box, select a currency character appropriate to your country.
9. Click **OK** to close the dialog box.
10. Press **F5** to run the project. You can then use the scroll bar to scroll through the recordset, or click the ADO Data Control's navigation buttons.

Exposing User Control Events of the RepeatedControl

When you create a user control, it's common to create public events. When the user control is placed on a standard Visual Basic form, the custom events automatically appear in the form's code module.

With the DataRepeater control, however, exposing the user control's events is not an automatic occurrence. Because the user control is not put directly on a form, its events cannot be exposed in the code module. There is, however, a way of achieving the same end.

In brief, the major steps are:

1. Add a class module to the user control project, and name the module CtlEvents.
2. Add a public event to the module named ProductChange.
3. Add a public procedure to the module named FireControlChange that raises the ProductChange event (using the RaiseEvent statement).
4. Add a public property to the user control named Events that returns a reference to the CtlEvents object.
5. In the Change event of each constituent control of the user control, invoke the FireControlChange procedure to raise events.

   Note The following step-by-step procedure builds on the user control and DataRepeater control project built in "Using the DataRepeater Control" earlier in this chapter.

Creating events to be exposed by the user control

1. Add a **Class Module** to the ActiveX Control project.
2. Change the name of the class module from Class1 to **CtlEvents**.
3. Set the Instancing property to **6 – GlobalMultiuse**.
4. Add a public event declaration to the Declarations section of the class module. For demonstration purposes, the code below adds only one event declaration. In a real application, you would add one event declaration for every control on the user control.

```
Option Explicit
Public Event ProductChange()
```

5. Add a public procedure to the class module. In the procedure, add the **RaiseEvent** statement to raise the ProductChange event. This procedure is invoked in events of the UserControl, and its sole purpose is to raise the event.

```
Public Sub FireControlChange()
   RaiseEvent ProductChange
End Sub
```

   The ProductChange event is the event that will be exposed by CtlEvents when using the ProductsCtl user control in a DataRepeater control.

6. In the user control object's code module, declare a variable typed as the new class, as shown below:

```
Option Explicit
Dim EventsObj As New CtlEvents
```

7. Add a public Get procedure to the user control. In the procedure, use a Set statement to return the object reference.

```
Public Property Get Events() As CtlEvents
   Set Events = EventsObj ' returns the CtlEvents object reference
End Property
```

8. In the Change event of the control you want to monitor, invoke the class object's procedure:

```
Private Sub txtProductName_Change()
   PropertyChanged ("ProductName")
   EventsObj.FireControlChange
End Sub
```

9. Save and compile the project (make the .ocx).

To expose the events of the User Control in the container form

The following steps take place in the project that contains the DataRepeater control. In that project, a DataRepeater control contains the user control with the events created in steps 1 to 9 above.

1. In the project that contains the DataRepeater control, use the **Components** dialog box to add the **ProductsCtl** (ProductsCtl.ocx) to the **Toolbox**. This step is needed to ensure that the Visual Basic Package and Deployment Wizard will correctly include the necessary .ocx file with the project. It also allows access at design time to the **ProductsCtl** events in code.

2. In the **Declarations** section of the Form object's code module, paste the following code that declares an object variable with the **WithEvents** keyword:

   ```
   Option Explicit
   Dim WithEvents objRepCtl As CtlEvents ' Be sure to use WithEvents
   ```

3. In the DataRepeater control's RepeatedControlLoaded event set the variable to the **Events** property. You must set the variable using the DataRepeater control's **RepeatedControl** property, as shown below:

   ```
   Private Sub DataRepeater1_RepeatedControlLoaded()
      Set objRepCtl = DataRepeater1.RepeatedControl.Events
   End Sub
   ```

   Because you can set the RepeatedControlName property at run time, the RepeatedControlLoaded was designed to allow you to set control properties that can only be initialized after the control has been loaded.

4. The new object **objRepCtl** (with events) should now appear in the drop-down list of the **Object** box, in the upper left corner of the code module. Select the object from the list, and add code to the event of the object, as shown below.

   ```
   Private Sub objRepCtl_ProductChange()
      Debug.Print "objRepCtl_ProductChange"
   End Sub
   ```

5. Run the project. When you alter the Products field, the event will occur.

Adding Events to the Control

With a few simple additions of code, you can easily add more events to the user control. First add public events — one for each event you want to raise — to the class module:

```
Option Explicit
Public Event ProductChange()
Public Event UnitPriceChange() ' <- This is a new Event declaration.
```

Then add an argument to the class module's FireControlChange procedure. A Select Case statement is added to the procedure to distinguish which control is calling the procedure. Using that argument, the correct event is raised:

```
Public Sub FireControlChange(ctlName As String)
   Select Case ctlName
   Case "ProductName"
      RaiseEvent ProductChange
   Case "UnitPrice"
      RaiseEvent UnitPriceChange
   Case Else
      ' Handle other cases here.
   End Select
End Sub
```

Finally, switch to the UserControl object's code module. In the Change event of the controls you wish to monitor, invoke the procedure with the correct argument, as shown below.

```
Private Sub txtProductName_Change()
   PropertyChanged "ProductName"
   EventsObj.FireControlChange "ProductName" ' Invoke procedure.
End Sub

Private Sub txtUnitPrice_Change()
   PropertyChanged "UnitPrice"
   EventsObj.FireControlChange "UnitPrice" ' Invoke procedure.
End Sub
```

Maintaining a History of Clicked Records in the DataRepeater Control

A common task while using the DataRepeater control is to maintain a history of viewed records. The history can be displayed in a ListBox control. Any time the user clicks on an item in the history, the DataRepeater control displays that record in its client area. As with other data-aware controls (such as the DataGrid control), you (the developer) must store and retrieve bookmarks for each record you wish to track.

> **Important** Bookmarks are valid only for the life of a recordset, and are not persistable or interchangeable across recordsets.

The following step-by-step creates a history by first storing the bookmarks of viewed records in an array. A value associated with the record is also added to a ListBox control. When the user clicks an item in the ListBox control, the ListIndex of the clicked item is used to retrieve the bookmark of the record. Setting the VisibleRecords property to the bookmark causes the record to appear in the DataRepeater control.

The step-by-step builds upon the project created in "Using the DataRepeater Control" earlier in this chapter.

To create a history of viewed records

1. Add a Reference to the **Microsoft ActiveX Data Objects 2.0 Library**.

   On the **Project** menu, click **References** to open the **References** dialog box. Check **Microsoft ActiveX Data Objects 2.0 Library**, and click **OK** to close the dialog box.

2. In the Declarations section of the form's code module, declare an array of variants, and an object variable for the ADODB Recordset object. Use the ADODB recordset to navigate.

```
Option Explicit
Private varBookmarks() As Variant
Private rsProducts As ADODB.Recordset
```

3. In the form's Load event, use the **ReDim** statement to initialize the array. Set the recordset object variable to the recordset of the ADO Data Control.

```
Private Sub Form_Load()
   ReDim varBookmarks(0)
   Set rsProducts = adodc1.Recordset
End Sub
```

4. Draw a **ListBox** control on the form, and change its name from Listbox1 to **lstHistory**.

5. Add the following code to the DataRepeater control's CurrentRecordChanged event:

```
Private Sub DataRepeater1_CurrentRecordChanged()
   ' The CurrentRecordChanged event occurs immediately after the form
   ' is opened. At that point, the UBound(varBookmarks) = 0, and no
   ' records have been added. Thus you must add the first record to
   ' the history list, and its bookmark to the array. Then increment
   ' the array index to 1 and exit the sub. The next time a record is
   ' clicked, this code will be ignored.
   Dim iUpper As Integer ' Upper bound of bookmark array.
   Dim i As Integer      ' Counter for ListBox
   If UBound(varBookmarks) = 0 Then
      lstHistory.AddItem rsProducts!ProductName
      varBookmarks(0) = DataRepeater1.CurrentRecord
      ReDim Preserve varBookmarks(1)
      Exit Sub
   End If

   ' The code below now executes when the user clicks a record.
   ' First check the listbox to ensure the clicked record hasn't
   ' already been added to the history list. If so, exit.
   For i = 0 To lstHistory.ListCount - 1
   If lstHistory.List(i) = rsProducts!ProductName _
   Then Exit Sub
   Next I
```

```
        ' If no duplicates, then add the record to the history, and
        ' cache the bookmark in the array.
        lstHistory.AddItem rsProducts!ProductName
        varBookmarks(UBound(varBookmarks)) = DataRepeater1.CurrentRecord
        ' Increment the array.
        ReDim Preserve varBookmarks(UBound(varBookmarks) + 1)
    End Sub
```

6. The code below sets the **VisibleRecords** property to a cached bookmark. Paste the code into the form's code module.

```
Private Sub lstHistory_Click()
    Debug.Print lstHistory.Text, lstHistory.ListIndex
    DataRepeater1.VisibleRecords(1) = _
    varBookmarks(lstHistory.ListIndex)
End Sub
```

7. Run the project. Scroll through the recordset using the DataRepeater control's scrollbars. Click on any record to add it to the history. Click any item in the listbox to return to that record.

Using the DateTimePicker Control

The DateTimePicker control displays date and/or time information and acts as the interface through which users can modify date and time information. The control's display consists of fields that are defined by the control's format string. When the DateTimePicker is dropped down, a MonthView calendar is displayed.

The control has two different modes:

- Dropdown Calendar mode (default) — enables the user to display a drop-down calendar that can be used to select a date.
- Time Format mode — enables the user to select a field in the date display (i.e. the month, day, year, etc.) and press the up/down arrow to the right of the control to set its value.

You can use the control to display the date in various preset formats including Short Date (11/14/97), LongDate (Friday, November 14, 1997) and Time (7:00:00 P.M.). You can also specify custom formats using formatting strings, or create your own formats with callback fields.

DateTimePicker control in Dropdown Calendar Mode

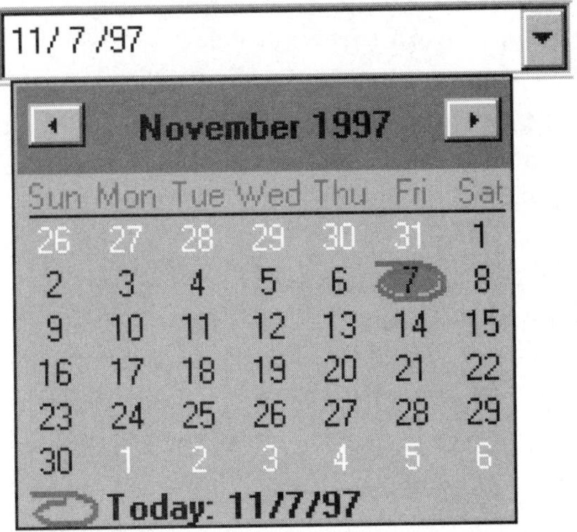

DateTimePicker control in Time Format Mode

Friday , November 07, 1997

Possible Uses

- To present date information where a restricted or specially formatted field is required, such as in a payroll or scheduling application.
- To give users the ability to select a date with the click of a mouse instead of typing a date value.

Using the Two Modes of the Control

The DateTimePicker operates as a masked edit control for entering date and time values. Each part of the date or time is treated as a separate field within the edit portion of the control. As the user clicks on each field, it is highlighted and they can use the up and down arrow keys to increment or decrement the value of the field. The user can also type values directly into the control, where applicable.

The UpDown property determines which mode the control is in. When UpDown is set to False, the control is in Dropdown Calendar mode. (The default value) When the UpDown property is set to True, the DateTimePicker is in Time Format mode.

In Time Format mode, two scroll arrows appear on the right side of the control. The user can click these arrows with the mouse to increment or decrement the value of the currently selected field. In Dropdown Calendar mode, the control drops down a calendar that the user can use to select dates.

The drop-down calendar has most of the features of the MonthView control later in this chapter. See "Using The MonthView Control" for more information on how to set up and format the Dropdown calendar portion of the DateTimePicker control.

Setting and Returning Dates

The currently selected date in the control is determined by the Value property. You can set the Value of the control before it is displayed (for example, at design time or in the Form_Load event) to determine which date will be initially selected in the control:

```
DTPicker1.Value = "10/31/97"
```

By default, the control's Value is set to the current date. If you change the DateTimePicker's Value in code, the control is automatically updated to reflect the new setting.

The Value property returns a raw date value, or a null value. The DateTimePicker control has several properties that return specific information about the displayed date:

- The Month property returns the integer value (1–12) of the month containing the currently selected date.
- The Day property returns the day number (1–31) currently selected.
- The DayOfWeek property returns a value indicating the day of the week the selected date falls on (values correspond to the values of *vbDayOfWeek* constants.)
- The Year property returns the year containing the selected date as an integer value.
- The Week property returns the number of the week containing the selected date.

Use the Change event to determine when the user has changed the date value in the control.

Using Checkbox to Select No Date

The CheckBox property makes it possible to specify whether the control returns a date. By default, CheckBox is set to False and the control always returns a date.

To enable the user to specify no date, set the CheckBox property to True (for example, if you are using the DateTimePicker to enter the completion date of a project but the project has not yet been completed).

When CheckBox is set to True, a small check box appears in the edit portion of the control to the left of the date and time. If the box is not checked, the Value property returns a null value. If the user checks this checkbox, the control returns the displayed date through its Value property.

Working with Date & Time Formats

The DateTimePicker gives you a tremendous amount of flexibility in formatting the display of dates and times in the control. You can use all the standard Visual Basic formatting strings, or you can create custom formats by using callback fields.

The Format property determines how the control formats the raw date value. You can choose from one of the predefined formatting options, or use the custom formatting feature of the control.

The CustomFormat property defines the format expression used to display the contents of the control. You specify a format string that tells the control how to format the date output. The DateTimePicker controls supports the following format strings:

String	Description
d	The one- or two-digit day.
dd	The two-digit day. Single digit day values are preceded by a zero.
ddd	The three-character day-of-week abbreviation.
dddd	The full day-of-week name.
h	The one- or two-digit hour in 12-hour format.
hh	The two-digit hour in 12-hour format. Single digit values are preceded by a zero.
H	The one- or two-digit hour in 24-hour format.
HH	The two-digit hour in 24-hour format. Single digit values are preceded by a zero.
m	The one- or two-digit minute.
mm	The two-digit minute. Single digit values are preceded by a zero.
M	The one- or two-digit month number.
MM	The two-digit month number. Single digit values are preceded by a zero.
MMM	The three-character month abbreviation.
MMMM	The full month name.
s	The one- or two- digit seconds.
ss	The two-digit seconds. Single digit values are proceeded by a zero.
t	The one-letter AM/PM abbreviation (that is, “AM” is displayed as “A”).
tt	The two-letter AM/PM abbreviation (that is, “AM” is displayed as “AM”).

(continued)

(continued)

String	Description
X	A callback field that gives programmer control over the displayed field (see below.) Multiple 'X' characters can be used in series to signify unique callback fields.
y	The one-digit year (that is, 1996 would be displayed as "6").
yy	The last two digits of the year (that is, 1996 would be displayed as "96").
yyy	The full year (that is, 1996 would be displayed as "1996").

You can add body text to the format string. For example, if you want the control to display the current date with the format "Today is: 05:30:31 Friday Nov 14, 1997." The format string you would use is "'Today is: 'hh':'m':'s ddddMMMdd', 'yyy". Body text must be enclosed in single quotes.

Creating Custom Formats with Callback Fields

One of the custom format fields described above is a callback field. A callback field allows you to customize the output of certain parts of a format string. To declare a callback field, you must include one or more 'X' characters (ASCII Code 88) anywhere in the body of the format string. Callback fields are displayed in left-to-right order.

When a new date is displayed in a format that includes one or more callback fields, The Format and FormatSize events are raised for each callback field. You can use the Format event to specify a custom response string, and the FormatSize event to determine the space needed to display the string. This behavior gives you complete control of how a callback field is displayed.

Each sequence of X's has a unique meaning. For example, X might mean "st/nd/rd/th" (for "1st" "2nd" "3rd" "4th" etc) and "XX" may mean "first" "second" "third" "fourth" etc. These fields do not format the users' text, they format the date into a displayable format.

For example, let's say you want to display the month in Spanish as well as English, using a format like this:

```
July (Julio) 29
```

You would create a format string that looked like this:

```
MMMM XXXX d
```

When processing the Format and FormatSize events, you can check which callback field is being called by comparing the input format sting with "XXXX." If the field string matches, an output string "(Julio)" can be built and the length of the output string can be supplied. The number of Xs is only used by an application to determine what text to supply for a callback field. When processing the FormatSize event, the size of the text can be programmatically calculated.

The Format event is called whenever the control needs to fill in the callback field, such as when the user selects a different date from that of the drop-down calendar. However, the FormatSize event is called only when there is a change to the format string (for instance, if you change it from "XX" to "XXXX.") This means that when you calculate the size of the callback field in the FormatSize event, you must take into account any possible value that can be returned by the Format event.

For example, you would use the following process to implement the callback field in the format string mentioned above.

1. In the (General)(Declarations) section of the form, declare an array variable to hold the lookup table for the names of the Spanish months:

```
Private sSpMonth(12) As String
```

2. In the Load event of the form, populate the lookup table and set the DTPicker to use the custom format string:

```
sSpMonth(0) = "Enero"
sSpMonth(1) = "Febrero"
sSpMonth(2) = "Marzo"
sSpMonth(3) = "Abril"
sSpMonth(4) = "Mayo"
sSpMonth(5) = "Junio"
sSpMonth(6) = "Julio"
sSpMonth(7) = "Agusto"
sSpMonth(8) = "Septiembre"
sSpMonth(9) = "Octubre"
sSpMonth(10) = "Noviembre"
sSpMonth(11) = "Diciembre"

DTPicker1.Format = dtpCustom
DTPicker1.CustomFormat = "MMMM (XXX) dd, yy"
```

3. In the **FormatSize** event, search through the list of possible return values to find the longest one. Specify this as the length of the formatted string. This will prevent clipping of the Spanish month name when the value in the control is changed.

```
Private Sub DTPicker1_FormatSize(ByVal CallbackField As String,
Size As Integer)
   Dim iMaxMonthLen As Integer
   Dim iC As Integer
      Select Case CallbackField
      Case "XXX"
         iMaxMonthLen = 0
         For iC = 0 To 11
            If iMaxMonthLen < Len(sSpMonth(iC)) Then
               iMaxMonthLen = Len(sSpMonth(iC))
            End If
         Next iC
      End Select
      Size = iMaxMonthLen
End Sub
```

4. In the **Format** event, return the appropriate value as the formatted string:

```
Private Sub DTPicker1_Format(ByVal CallbackField As String,
FormattedString As String)
   Select Case CallbackField
   Case "XXX"
      FormattedString = sSpMonth(DTPicker1.Month - 1)
   End Select
End Sub
```

You can create unique callback fields by repeating the 'X' character. Thus, the format string "XX dddd MMM dd,' 'yyy XXX" contains two callback fields. You can use Select or If statements to process multiple callback strings in the **Format** and **FormatSize** events.

Callback fields are treated as valid fields, so the application must be prepared to handle the **CallbackKeyDown** event. You can use this event to process individual keystrokes in the callback field and to provide keystroke validation or automated entry completion. For example, if the user was entering a month and they had typed the letter "D," you could use the **CallbackKeyDown** event to fill in the callback field with the word "December."

Formatting the Calendar Control

There are many options for formatting the calendar drop-down portion of the control. All the properties of the DateTimePicker that are preceded by the word "Calendar" affect the formatting of the calendar drop down. These properties correspond to properties in the MonthView control. For example, the DateTimePicker's **CalendarTitleTextColor** property is comparable to the **TitleTextColor** property of the MonthView. See the topic "Using The MonthView Control" for more information about calendar formatting issues.

Keyboard Interface

The Calendar control can be manipulated with the keyboard. The following table describes the different actions you can perform with the control at run time.

Key	Description
LEFT ARROW	Selects the next field to the left. If this key is pressed when the left-most field is selected, the selection wraps to the right-most field.
RIGHT ARROW	Selects the next field to the right. If this key is pressed when the right-most field is selected, the selection wraps to the left-most field.
UP ARROW	Increments the value of the selected field.
DOWN ARROW	Decrements the value of the selected field.
HOME	Changes the value of the selected field to its upper limit.

(continued)

Key	Description
END	Changes the value of the selected field to its lower limit.
UP ARROW	Increments the value for the selected field.
DOWN ARROW	Decrements the value of the selected field.
PLUS (+) on Numeric Keypad	Increments the value of the selected field.
MINUS (-) on Numeric Keypad	Decrements the value of the selected field.

The following table describes the different actions you can perform while the drop-down calendar is displayed.

Key	Description
LEFT ARROW	Selects the next day
RIGHT ARROW	Selects the previous day
UP ARROW	Selects the same day of week in the previous week
DOWN ARROW	Selects the same day of week in the next week
PAGE UP	Scrolls the display to past months.
PAGE DOWN	Scrolls the display to future months.
CTRL+PAGE UP	Scrolls the display to the previous year.
CTRL+PAGE DOWN	Scrolls the display to the next year.

Distribution Note The **DateTimePicker** control is part of a group of ActiveX controls that are found in the MSCOMCT2.OCX file. To use the DateTimePicker control in your application, you must add the MSCOMCT2.OCX file to the project. When distributing your application, install the MSCOMCT2.OCX file in the user's Microsoft Windows System or System32 directory. For more information on how to add an ActiveX control to a project, see the *Microsoft Visual Basic 6.0 Programmer's Guide.*

Using the FlatScrollBar Control

A **FlatScrollBar** control provides the same functionality as the standard Windows scroll bar, with the addition of an enhanced interface. The **FlatScrollBar** can appear in one of three ways: as the standard, three-dimensional (beveled) scroll bar; as a two-dimensional (flat) scroll bar; or, as a flat scrollbar with arrows that become beveled when the mouse pointer hovers over it.

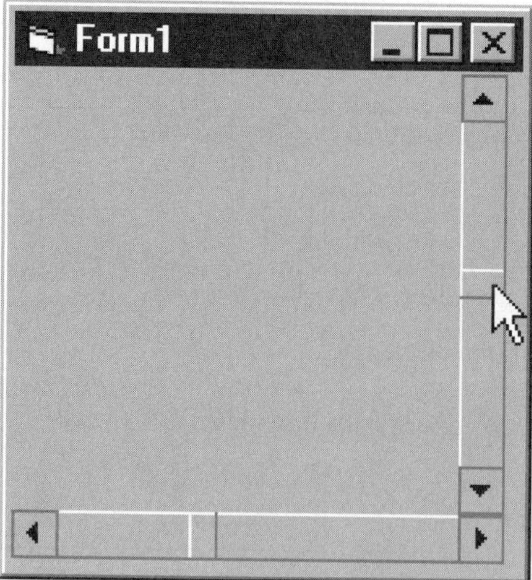

The **FlatScrollBar** can serve as either a horizontal or a vertical scroll bar. The Orientation property of the control determines how the scroll bar is used.

The **FlatScrollBar** also gives you the ability to disable either of the scroll arrows. Scroll arrows can be disabled by default, or toggled in response to program activity. For example, you can deactivate the downward scroll arrow when the thumb reaches the bottom of the scroll bar, informing the user that she can no longer scroll down.

Possible Uses

- To create an interface that is visually consistent with Microsoft Internet Explorer 4.0.
- To add a multimedia-style interface to existing applications.
- To provide a variety of interface styles to the user without adding new controls.

Set the Min and Max Properties at Design Time or Run Time

The Min and Max properties determine the upper and lower limits of a FlatScrollBar control; you can set these properties at either design time or at run time. At design time, change the value of either property using the property sheet. You can also right-click on the control and select Properties to invoke the Property Pages, and change the value of either property from there.

At run time, you can reset the **Min** and **Max** settings to accommodate different ranges. For example, if the size of a container changes, you can reset the **Max** value to reflect the container's new height or width.

SmallChange and LargeChange Properties

The SmallChange and LargeChange properties determine how the FlatScrollBar control increments or decrements its Value property when the user clicks the control. The SmallChange property specifies how many units the thumb will move when the user presses the up or down (left or right) scroll arrows. The LargeChange property specifies how many units the thumb will move when the user clicks inside the area of the control but not on a scroll arrow or the thumb.

Displaying Different Interface Styles Using the FlatScrollBar

The FlatScrollBar control has three different interface styles. The interface used is determined by the setting of the Appearance property. Use the interface that best complements the overall look and feel of your program's user interface.

You can set the Appearance property to fsb3D to have the FlatScrollBar appear as a standard Windows scroll bar. Set it to fsbFlat to give the scroll bar a 2-D appearance. A setting of fsbTrack3D will make the scroll bar appear 2-D, but the scroll arrows and thumb will become beveled in response to the mouse pointer.

Disabling Scroll Arrows in Response to Scroll Bar Movement

To give the user additional visual feedback when using the FlatScrollBar, you can disable scroll arrows in response to the Value of the control. This shows the user which scrolling options are available at any given time.

Arrows are specified according to their position, which changes based on the Orientation of the control. The left button of a horizontal scroll bar becomes the up button of a vertical scroll bar, and the right button becomes the down button. This relationship is reflected in the constant names used to specify the settings of the Arrows property.

Use the Arrows property to specify which of the control's scroll arrows are enabled. If you set the control to use only one arrow, the other will automatically be disabled. By default, both scroll arrows are enabled.

To disable the scroll arrows based on the control's Min and Max settings, enter the following code in the Change event of the FlatScrollBar control:

```
If FlatScrollBar1.Value = FlatScrollBar1.Min Then
   FlatScrollBar1.Arrows = fsbRightDown
ElseIf FlatScrollBar1.Value = FlatScrollBar1.Max Then
   FlatScrollBar1.Arrows = fsbLeftUp
Else
   FlatScrollBar1.Arrows = fsbBoth
End If
```

Using the ImageCombo Control

An ImageCombo control is similar to a standard Windows combo box control, with some important differences. The most visible difference is the ability to include pictures with each item in the list portion of the combo. By using graphic images, you can make it easier for the user to identify and choose items from a list of possible selections.

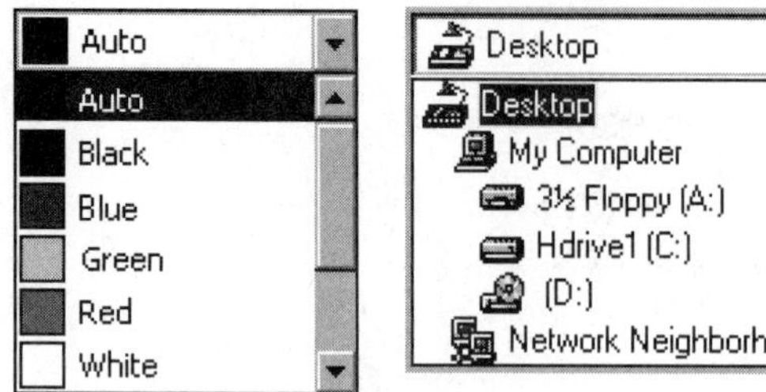

A less visible though equally important difference is the way the **ImageCombo** manages the list portion of the control. Each item in the list is a ComboItem object, and the list itself is the ComboItems collection of objects. This facilitates list management, making it easy to access items individually or collectively, and assign or change the properties that determine item content and appearance. This structure also makes it easier to deal with the images assigned to list items.

Because the items in the list are objects in a collection, certain properties found in the standard combo box (such as List, ListIndex, and ItemData) are no longer required. Therefore, these properties are not present in the ImageCombo control.

Each item in an ImageCombo list can have three pictures associated with it. The first picture, as specified by the Image property, appears in the drop-down portion of the control next to the text of the list item. The SelImage property specifies the list item's picture when it has been selected from the list. The SelImage picture appears next to the item in the edit portion of the combo box, as well as in the list portion.

To manage the images used for the list items, the **ImageCombo** uses the **ImageList** common control. Images are assigned to items in the ImageCombo through an index or key value that references a picture stored in the ImageList control.

The ImageCombo control also supports multiple levels of indentation. The amount of indentation is a property of the individual list item, so items maintain their level of indentation even if the list is reordered. Having items indented at different levels makes it possible to emphasize certain parts of the list or display hierarchical relationships.

Possible Uses

- To create a Windows Explorer style interface or create custom dialog boxes that resemble the common File Open and File Save dialogs.
- To create a list that uses different graphics and/or indenting to indicate the status of list items based on some external context, such as the state of other controls on the form.
- To present hierarchical information to the user in a drop-down list format.
- To add visual enhancements or indicators to standard drop-down lists.
- To display a combo box with a standard appearance that makes use of advanced object-based properties, methods and structures in code.

Adding Items to the ImageCombo

To add a new item to an ImageCombo, you use the **Add** method to create a new **ComboItem** object in its **ComboItems** collection. You can supply optional arguments for the **Add** method to specify many of the properties of the new item, including its **Index** and **Key** values, any pictures it will use, and the level of indentation it will have. The **Add** method returns a reference to the newly created **ComboItem** object.

The following code adds a new item called "Signal1" to the top of the list in an **ImageCombo**, as indicated by the supplied **Index** value of 1. The new item appears in the control as "Traffic," as specified in the object's **Text property**. The code then takes the reference to the new item returned by the **Add** method and uses it to change the item's ToolTip text.

```
Dim objNewItem As ComboItem

   Set objNewItem = ImageCombo1.ComboItems.Add(1, _
   "Signal1", "Traffic")

   objNewItem.ToolTipText = "Traffic Light"
```

Using Pictures with ImageCombo List Items

Images for the list items are supplied by an **ImageList** control associated with the **ImageCombo** control. For more information on using the **ImageList** control with other controls, see "Using the ImageList control."

To associate an ImageList Control with the ImageCombo at run time

1. Populate the ImageList control with the images that will be used in the ImageCombo control.
2. Right-click on the ImageCombo control and click **Properties** to open the **Property Pages** dialog box.
3. On the **General** tab, click the **ImageList** box and select the ImageList control you have populated.

To associate an ImageList control with the ImageCombo control at run time, simply set the **ImageList** property to the name of the ImageList control, as shown in the example below:

```
Private Sub Form_Load()
   Set ImageCombo1.ImageList = ImageList1
End Sub
```

Setting an Item's Picture

To specify the image that will appear next to a list item in the ImageCombo control, set the **Image** property of a ComboItem object equal to the **Index** or **Key** value of an image in the ImageList control. For example, if the first image in the ImageList control was assigned a **Key** value of "Stoplight," the following two lines of code accomplish the same thing:

```
ImageCombo1.ComboItems("Signal1").Image = 1
ImageCombo1.ComboItems("Signal1").Image = "Stoplight"
```

Alternatively, you can specify the image that will be associated with the ComboItem when you create it. Simply specify the **Key** or **Index** of the correct image as a parameter of the **Add** method, for example:

```
ImageCombo1.ComboItems.Add(1, "Signal1", "Traffic", _
"Stoplight")
```

The Selected Item Image

When you select an item from the list, the image specified by the ComboItem's **SelImage** property appears next to the item in the edit portion of the combo. The next time you drop down the combo box, the **SelImage** picture will appear next to the item in the list.

If your ImageList control contained a picture with a **Key** value of "Greenlight," you could use the following code to use that picture as the selected image for a list item:

```
ImageCombo1.ComboItems("Signal1").SelImage = _
"Greenlight"
```

Or you could specify the image to use as the selected image when the new item is added to the list. Pass the **Key** or **Index** value of the image as a parameter to the **Add** method:

```
ImageCombo1.ComboItems.Add(1, "Signal1", "Traffic", _
"Stoplight", "Greenlight")
```

Changing the Indentation of list items

The information in a combo list is often organized hierarchically. To facilitate this type of display, each ComboItem object has a specific level of indenting, as determined by the value of its **Indentation** property. Each level of indentation represents a space of ten pixels from the edge of the list, so a ComboItem with an **Indentation** of 3 would be indented by 30 pixels from a ComboItem with an **Indentation** of 0.

To set the default indentation of all items on the list, set the value of the ImageCombo control's **Indentation** property, either at design time using the property sheet, or through code.

Setting the Default Indentation of ComboItems

Select the **Indentation** property from the Property Sheet and change its value to an integer greater than zero. Each level of indentation represents ten pixels.

Setting the Default Indentation of ComboItems Through Code

Use the following code:

```
ImageCombo1.Indentation = 1
```

Setting the Indentation of Individual ComboItem Objects

To set the indentation of a particular list item, set the **Indentation** of the ComboItem object, specifying a **Key** or and **Index** value to identify the object. For example, the following code indents every third item in the list by 20 pixels:

```
For Each ComboItem In ImageCombo1.ComboItems
   If (ComboItem.Index / 3) = _
   (Int(ComboItem.Index / 3)) Then
      ComboItem.Indentation = 2
   End If
Next ComboItem
```

The following code indents the item with a **Key** value of “RightOn” by 40 pixels:

```
ImageCombo1.ComboItems("RightOn").Indentation = 4
```

Using the ImageList Control

An ImageList control contains a collection of images that can be used by other Windows Common Controls — specifically, the ListView, TreeView, TabStrip, and Toolbar controls. For example, the ImageList control can store all the images that appear on a Toolbar control’s buttons.

The ImageList control can also be used with controls that assign a Picture object to a Picture property, such as the PictureBox, Image, and CommandButton controls.

Using the ImageList control as a single repository saves you development time by allowing you to write code that refers to a single, consistent catalog of images. Instead of writing code that loads bitmaps or icons (using the LoadPicture function), you can populate the ImageList once, assign Key values if you wish, and write code that uses the Key or Index properties to refer to images.

The control uses bitmap (.bmp), cursor (.cur), icon (.ico), JPEG (.jpg), or GIF (.gif) files in a collection of ListImage objects. You can add and remove images at design time or run time. The ListImage object has the standard collection object properties: Key and Index. It also has standard methods, such as Add, Remove, and Clear.

For More Information Chapter 9, "Programming with Objects," in the *Microsoft Visual Basic 6.0 Programmer's Guide,* offers introductory information about working with objects and collections.

Finally, the control features the Overlay, Draw, and ExtractIcon methods, which allow you to create composite images, draw images on objects with an hDC property (such as the Form and Printer objects), and create an icon from a bitmap stored in the control.

Possible Uses

- To store the images that represent open folders, closed folders, and documents. These images can then be dynamically assigned to the TreeView control's Node object to represent its different states as it expands or collapses, or whether or not it is a document or a folder.
- To store images that represent common computer operations, such as saving, opening, and printing files. These images can then be assigned to Button objects on a Toolbar control used by your application.
- To store images for drag-and-drop operations, such as MousePointer icons, and DragIcons.

Managing ListImage Objects and ListImages Collections

The ImageList control contains the ListImages collection of ListImage objects, each of which can be referred to by its Index or Key property value. You can add or remove images to the control at design time or run time.

Adding ListImage Objects at Design Time

To add an image to at design time, use the ImageList control's **Property Pages** dialog box.

To add ListImage objects at design time

1. Right-click the ImageList control and click **Properties**.
2. Click the **Images** tab to display the ImageList control's Property Pages, as shown below.

ImageList control Property Pages dialog box

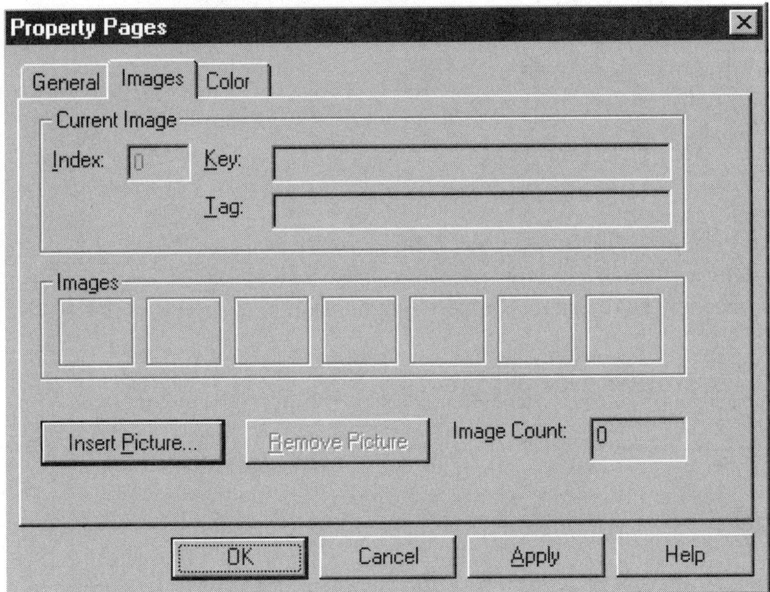

3. Click **Insert Picture** to display the **Select Picture** dialog box.
4. Use the dialog box to find either bitmap or icon files, and click **Open**.

   Note You can select multiple bitmap or icon files.

5. Assign a unique Key property setting by clicking in the **Key** box and typing a string.
6. Optional. Assign a **Tag** property setting by clicking in the **Tag** box and typing a string. The **Tag** property doesn't have to be unique.
7. Repeat steps 3 through 6 until you have populated the control with the desired images.

Adding ListImage Objects at Run Time

To add an image at run time, use the Add method for the ListImages collection in conjunction with the LoadPicture function. The following example occurs in a form's Load event; an ImageList control named "imlImages" is loaded with a single bitmap:

```
Private Sub Form_Load()
   ' Assuming the path is correct, the open.bmp
   ' picture will be added to the ListImages
   ' collection. The Key property will also be
   ' assigned the value "open"
   imlImages.ListImages. _
   Add ,"open", LoadPicture("c:\bitmaps\open.bmp")
End Sub
```

Assigning a unique Key property value to the ListImage object allows you to create code that is easier to read. When assigning the image to a property, you can use its Key value instead of its Index value. Thus, assigning an image to a property might result in code like the following:

```
' Assign an image to a TreeView control Node object.
' The unique key of the image is "open".
TreeView1.Nodes.Add , , ,"Folder1","open"
```

Determining Image Sizes

You can insert any size image into the ImageList control. However, the size of the image displayed by the second control depends on one factor: whether or not the second control is also a Windows Common control bound to the ImageList control.

When the ImageList control is bound to another Windows Common Control, images of different sizes can be added to the control, however the size of the image displayed in the associated Windows Common Control will be constrained to the size of the first image added to the ImageList. For example, if you add an image that is 16 by 16 pixels to an ImageList control, then bind the ImageList to a TreeView control (to be displayed with Node objects), all images stored in the ImageList control will be displayed at 16 by 16 pixels, even if they are much larger or smaller.

On the other hand, if you display images using the Picture object, any image stored in the ImageList control will be displayed at its original size, no matter how small or large.

> **Note** An exception is when you use an image from the ImageList control with the Image control. Setting the Image control's Stretch property to True will cause the image to resize to fit the control.

At design time, you can specify the height and width, in pixels, of images in the control by choosing a size from the General tab of the ImageList control's Property Pages dialog box. You can choose a predetermined size, or click Custom and set the image size by typing the size you desire in the Height and Width boxes. This can only be done when the ImageList contains no images. Attempting to change the size after the control contains images will result in an error.

Methods That Allow You to Create Composite Images

You can use the ImageList control to create a composite image (a picture object) from two images by using the Overlay method in conjunction with the MaskColor property. For example, if you have an "international no" image (a circle with a diagonal bar inside it), you can lay that image over any other image, as shown:

The syntax for the Overlay method requires two arguments. The first argument specifies the underlying image; the second argument specifies the image that overlays the first. Both arguments can be either the Index or the Key property of a ListImage object.

Thus the code to achieve the effect above is as follows:

```
' The composite image appears in a PictureBox
' control named "picOver". The Index value of
' the cigarette image is 2; the index value of the
' "no" symbol is 1.
ImageList1.MaskColor = vbGreen
Set picOver.Picture = ImageList1.Overlay(2, 1)
```

You could also use the Key property of the images, resulting in this code:

```
' Assuming the first image's Key is "smokes", and the
' second is "no".
Set picOver.Picture = ImageList1.Overlay("smokes","no")
```

The code example above also illustrates how the MaskColor property works. In brief, the MaskColor property specifies the color which will become transparent when an image is overlaid over another. The "no" image has a green background color. Thus, when the code specifies that the MaskColor will be vbGreen (an intrinsic constant), the green in the image becomes transparent in the composite image.

Using the ImageList with Other Controls

You can use the ImageList control as a repository of images for use by other Windows Common Controls and by controls with a Picture property.

Using the ImageList with Other Windows Common Controls

The ImageList control can be used to supply images for the following controls using certain of their properties, as listed in the following table.

Windows Common Control	Control Object	Properties Settable with ImageList Images
ImageCombo control	ComboItem	Image, OverlayImage, and SelImage
ListView control	ListItem	SmallIcon and Icon properties
TreeView control	Node	Image and SelectedImage properties
Toolbar control	Button	Image property
Toolbar control	Button	HotImageList property
Toolbar control	Button	DisabledImageList property
TabStrip control	Tab	Image property

For More Information For examples of using the ImageList with the ImageCombo, TreeView, ListView, Toolbar, and TabStrip controls, see the scenario topics for those controls. (For example, see "TreeView Control Scenario: Bind the TreeView to the Biblio.mdb Database" later in this chapter.)

To use the ImageList with these controls, you must first associate the ImageList with the other control, and then assign either the Key or Index property to one of the properties listed in the table above. This can be done at design time or run time. All of the Windows Common controls, except the ListView control (discussed in this topic), have an ImageList property that can be set with the name of the ImageList control you are using.

> **Important** You should populate the ImageList control with images before you associate it with another control. Once you have associated an ImageList with a control, and assigned any image to a property of the control, the ImageList control will not allow you to add any more images.

To associate the ImageList control with the TreeView, TabStrip, or Toolbar control at design time

1. Right-click on the control using images from the ImageList control and click **Properties** to display the **Property Pages** dialog box.
2. On the **General** tab, select the name of the ImageList control from the **ImageList** box.

To associate the ImageList control at run time, you might use the following code:

```
' Associate an ImageList named "imlImages" with a
' TreeView control named "tvwDB."
Set tvwDB.ImageList = imlImages
```

Once you have associated an ImageList control with another control, you can set properties for various objects using either the Key or Index property of an image in the ImageList control. For example, the following code sets the Image property of a TreeView control's Node object to an ImageList image with the Key property "leaf."

```
Private Sub Form_Load()
   ' The TreeView is named "tvwData."
   ' Add a node and set its Image property.
   ' The Key value of the image is "leaf."
   tvwData.Nodes.Add , ,"1 node","Top","leaf"
End Sub
```

Using the ImageList Control with the ListView Control

The ListView control can use two ImageList controls simultaneously. Instead of having a single ImageList property, the ListView control has an Icons and a SmallIcons property, each of which can be associated with an ImageList control. This can be done at design time or at run time.

To associate two ImageList controls with the ListView control at design time

1. Right-click on the ListView control and click **Properties** to display the **Property Pages**.
2. Click the **ImageLists** tab.
3. In the **Normal** box, select the name of an ImageList control.
4. In the **Small** box, select the name of another ImageList control.

You can also assign the ImageList controls at run time with code like that shown in the following example:

```
' Assuming the ListView control is named "lvwDB", the
' first ImageList is named "imlSmallImages," and the
' second is named "imlImages."
Set lvwDB.SmallIcons = imlSmallImages
Set lvwDB.Icons = imlImages
```

The ImageList control used depends on the display mode determined in the View property of the ListView control. When the ListView control is in Icon view, it uses the images supplied by the ImageList named in the Icons property. In any of the other views (List, Report, or SmallIcon), the ListView uses the images from the ImageList named in the SmallIcons property.

For More Information For details about the ListView control, see "Using the ListView Control" later in this chapter.

Assigning ListImage Objects by Index or Key Property

After you have associated the ImageList control with one of the Windows Common Controls, you can specify a particular image using the image's Index or Key property.

For example, if you are using the ImageList with a TreeView control, the following code will assign the third ListImage object (which has an Index value of 3) to a new Node object's Image property:

```
' The TreeView control is named "tvwDB."
' The fifth argument of the Add method
' specifies an image by either the ListImage
' object's Index or Key property.
tvwDB.Nodes.Add , , ,"node x", 3
```

On the other hand, you could use the Key property to achieve the same end:

```
' Assuming the Key property is "open."
tvwDB.Nodes.Add , , ,"node x", "open"
```

Because the ListImage object's Key property must be a unique string, at run time, you can then use the Key property instead of the Index property to reference the image. This results in code that is easier to read.

> **Tip** Because the Key must be a unique string, using a descriptive name for each ListImage object will make your code easier to read and debug.

Using the ImageList Control with Controls Not Part of the Windows Common Controls

You can also use the ImageList as an image repository for objects which have a Picture property. These include the following:

- CommandButton control
- OptionButton control
- Image control
- PictureBox control
- CheckBox control
- Form object
- Panel object (StatusBar control)

The ListImage object's Picture property returns a Picture object, which can be assigned to another control's Picture property. For example, the following code will display the third ListImage object in a PictureBox control named "picBox":

```
Set picBox.Picture = ImageList1.ListImages(3).Picture
```

ImageList Scenario: Add Open, Save, and Print Images to a Toolbar Control

Toolbars typically contain a row of buttons where each button performs a frequently used operation when pressed. Toolbar buttons often save screen space by using images to represent the operation. In this scenario, three common functions — opening, saving, and printing a file — are represented by images assigned to Button objects of a Toolbar control. The images and buttons commonly used to represent these functions are shown here:

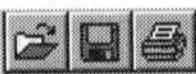

These objects are used in the following example:

- ImageList control named "imlTool"
- Toolbar control named "tbrStandard"

To add images to a Toolbar control

1. Add images to the ImageList and assign unique Key property values to each object.
2. Associate the ImageList with the Toolbar control.
3. Assign images to Button objects using the **Buttons** tab.

Add Images to the ImageList and Assign Unique Key Property Values

To add ListImage objects at design time

1. Right-click the **ImageList** control and click **Properties** to display the **Property Pages** dialog box.
2. Click the **Images** tab.
3. Click **Insert Picture** to display the **Select Picture** dialog box.
4. Use the dialog box to find the bitmap files in the following table. The bitmaps can be found in the samples directory.
5. After finding a file, click the file, and click **Open**, or double-click the file to open insert it into the ImageList control.
6. In the **Images** tab, click the **Key** box and type the Key property value, as found in the following table. The **Images** tab should resemble the figure below.

File	Key
open.bmp	open
save.bmp	save
print.bmp	print

Images tab with three ListImage objects

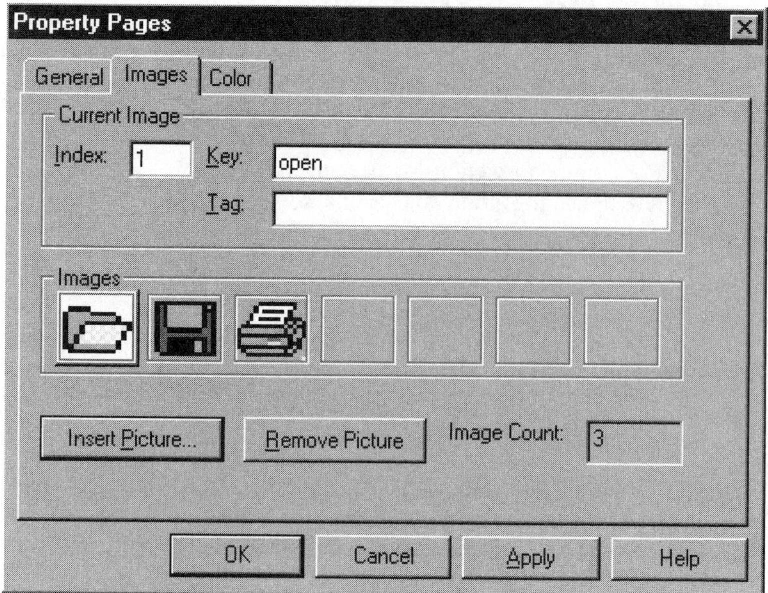

Associate the ImageList with the Toolbar Control

Before you can assign the images to Button objects, you must first associate the ImageList with the Toolbar control.

To associate an ImageList with a Toolbar control

1. Right-click on the **Toolbar** control and click **Properties** to display the control's **Property Pages**, as shown in the figure below.
2. On the **General** tab, select the name of the ImageList control from the **ImageList** box.

Associate an ImageList with a Toolbar control

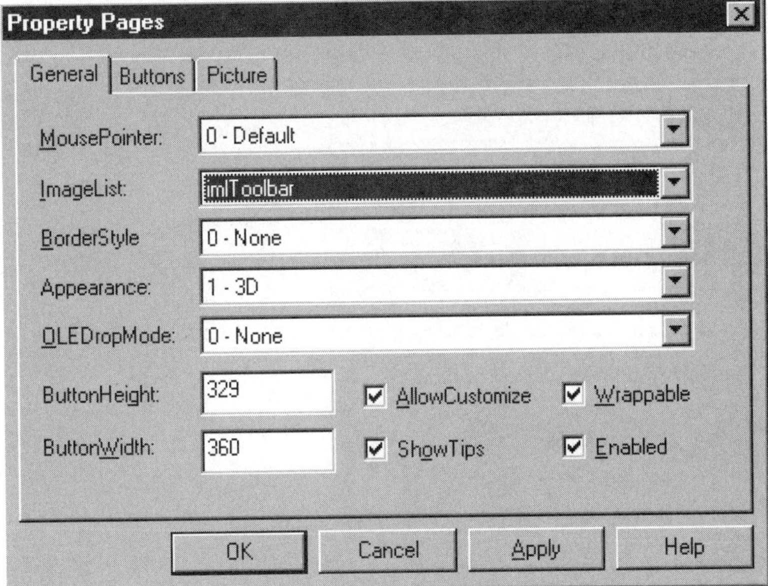

Assign Images to Button Objects Using the Buttons Tab

To assign an image to a Button object

1. Click the **Buttons** tab (on the Toolbar control's **Property Pages** dialog box) to display the **Buttons** tab, shown in the figure below.
2. Click **Insert Button** to insert a new Button object.
3. Click the **Image** box and type the Key value of a ListImage object.
4. Click **Apply**.
5. Repeat steps 2 to 4 to add more buttons, and assign images to the new Button objects.

Add Button objects and assign Images using the Buttons tab

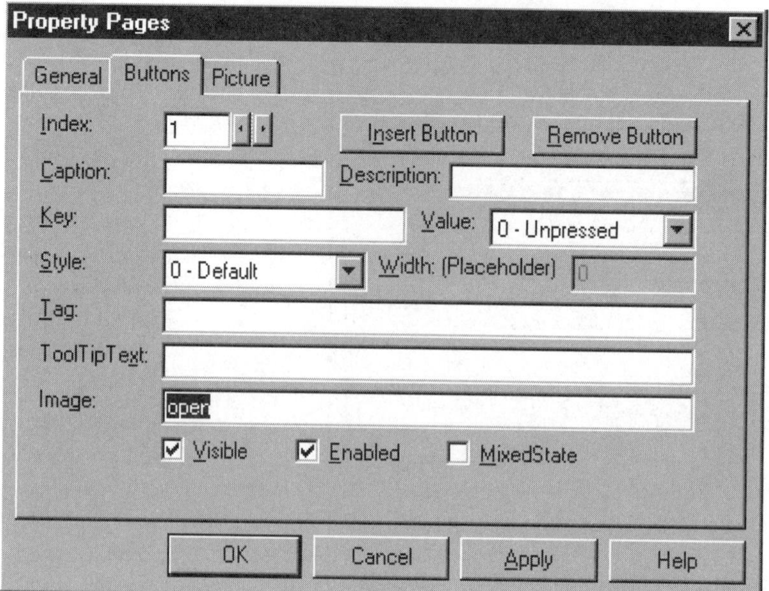

Using the Internet Transfer Control

The Internet Transfer control implements two widely-used Internet protocols: the HyperText Transfer Protocol (HTTP) and the File Transfer Protocol (FTP). Using the Internet Transfer control, you can connect to any site that uses one of these protocols, and retrieve files using either the OpenURL or Execute method.

Possible Uses

- To add an FTP browser to any application.
- To create an application that automatically downloads files from a public FTP site.
- To parse a World Wide Web site for graphics references and download the graphics only.
- To present a custom display of dynamic data retrieved from a Web page.

Basic Operation

The functionality of the Internet Transfer control depends on the protocol you wish to use. Because the two supported protocols work differently, the operations you can perform depend on which protocol you are using. For example, the GetHeader method only works with HTTP (HTML documents).

However, there are a few procedures that are common to both protocols. Basically, in order to use either protocol, you must:

1. Set the **AccessType** property to a valid proxy server.
2. Invoke the OpenURL method with a valid URL.
3. Invoke the Execute method with a valid URL and command appropriate to the protocol.
4. Use the GetChunk method to retrieve data from the buffer.

Setting the AccessType Property: Using a Proxy Server

In order to make any kind of connection to the Internet, you must determine how your computer is connected to the Internet. If you are on an intranet, you will probably be connected to the Internet via a proxy server.

In short, a *proxy server* is an intermediary between your computer and the Internet. All computers on an intranet that need to connect to the Internet must do so through a proxy server. Thus the proxy functions as a *firewall* between the intranet and the Internet, discarding invalid end-user and external requests, thereby protecting the intranet from hostile actions.

To find the proxy settings on your computer

> **Note** The following steps apply only to the Windows 95 and Windows NT 4.0 systems.

1. On the **Taskbar** of your computer, click **Start**.
2. On the **Settings** item, click the **Control Panel**.
3. Double-click the Internet icon.
4. On the **Internet Properties** dialog box, click **Connection**.
5. Under **Proxy Server**, confirm that the **Connect Through a Proxy Server** check box is selected.
6. If it is selected, click **Settings**. The name of proxy servers you use for various protocols will be found in the dialog box. If no proxy is defined, contact your system administrator for available proxy servers.

If you intend to use a proxy other than that named in the dialog box, set the AccessType property to icNamedProxy (2). Then set the Proxy property to the name of the proxy, as shown in the code below:

```
Inet1.Proxy = "myProxyName"
Inet1.AccessType = icNamedProxy
```

On the other hand, if you are content to use the default proxy (as determined by your computer's registry), ignore the Proxy property, and simply set the AccessType to icUseDefault (0).

The settings for AccessType are shown in the following table:

Constant	Value	Description
icUseDefault	0	(Default) Use Defaults. The control uses default settings found in the registry to access the Internet.
icDirect	1	Direct to Internet. The control has a direct connection to the Internet.
icNamedProxy	2	Named Proxy. Instructs the control to use the proxy server specified in the Proxy property.

Invoke the OpenURL Method

After you set the AccessType property, the most basic operation is to use the OpenURL method with a valid URL. When you use the OpenURL method, the result will depend on the target URL. For example, the following URL will return the HTML document found at www.microsoft.com:

```
' A TextBox control named Text1 contains the
' result of the method. The Internet Transfer
' control is named Inet1.
Text1.Text = Inet1.OpenURL("http://www.microsoft.com")
```

As a result, the TextBox control is filled with the HTML source, which may resemble the figure below:

```
<HTML>
<HEAD>
<TITLE>Microsoft Corporation</TITLE>
<STYLE>
<!-- ###### defines styles ###### -->
<!--
        A:link {color: 000000; font-weight:bold}
        A:visited {font: 9pt Arial; color: 0099cc; font-weight:bold}
        STRONG {font: 16pt Arial; color: 990000; text-decoration:none}
        BIG {font: 10pt Arial; background: cccc66}
        H1 {font: 24pt Arial; color: 000000}
-->
</STYLE>
<!-- ###### end defines styles ###### -->
```

In this case, the default action was to return the HTML document located at the URL. However, if the URL is modified to target a specific text file, the actual file would be retrieved. For example, the following code:

```
Text1.Text = Inet1. _
OpenURL("ftp://ftp.microsoft.com/disclaimer.txt")
```

would result in the actual text of the file, as shown below:

```
THE INFORMATION IS PROVIDED "AS IS" WITHOUT WARRANTY OF
ANY
KIND. MICROSOFT DISCLAIMS ALL WARRANTIES, EITHER
EXPRESSED
OR IMPLIED, INCLUDING THE WARRANTIES OF MERCHANTABILITY
AND
FITNESS FOR A PARTICULAR PURPOSE. IN NO EVENT SHALL
MICROSOFT CORPORATION OR ITS SUPPLIERS BE LIABLE FOR ANY
DAMAGES WHATSOEVER INCLUDING DIRECT, INDIRECT,
INCIDENTAL,
CONSEQUENTIAL, LOSS OF BUSINESS PROFITS OR SPECIAL
DAMAGES,
EVEN IF MICROSOFT CORPORATION OR ITS SUPPLIERS HAVE BEEN
ADVISED OF THE POSSIBILITY OF SUCH DAMAGES. SOME STATES
DO
```

Tip When you use either the OpenURL or Execute method, you need not set the Protocol property. The Internet Transfer control will automatically set itself to the correct protocol, as determined by the protocol portion of the URL.

Finally, you can use the OpenURL method with a URL that includes appended data. For example, many Web sites offer the ability to search a database. To search, send a URL that includes the search criteria. For example, the following code would use a search engine named "search.exe" with the criteria "find=Maui."

```
Dim strURL As String
strURL = _
"http://www.howzit.com/cgi-bin/search.exe?find=maui"
Text1.Text = Inet1.OpenURL(strURL)
```

If the search engine finds a match for the criteria, an HTML document would be assembled and returned with the appropriate information.

Saving to a File Using the OpenURL Method

If you wish to save the data retrieved through the OpenURL method to a file, use the Open, Put, and Close statements, as shown in the code below. This example streams a binary file into a Byte array before saving the data to disk:

```
Dim strURL As String
Dim bData() As Byte      ' Data variable
Dim intFile As Integer   ' FreeFile variable
strURL = _
"ftp://ftp.microsoft.com/Softlib/Softlib.exe"
```

```
intFile = FreeFile()        ' Set intFile to an unused
                            ' file.
' The result of the OpenURL method goes into the Byte
' array, and the Byte array is then saved to disk.
bData() = Inet1.OpenURL(strURL, icByteArray)
Open "C:\Temp\Softlib.exe" For Binary Access Write _
As #intFile
Put #intFile, , bData()
Close #intFile
```

A similar procedure can be used to write a text file to disk, except no Byte array is needed; the data is saved directly to the file:

```
Dim strURL As String     ' URL string
Dim intFile As Integer   ' FreeFile variable
IntFile = FreeFile()
strURL = "http://www.microsoft.com"
Open "c:\temp\MSsource.txt" For Output _
As #IntFile
Write #IntFile, Inet1.OpenURL(strURL)
Close #IntFile
```

Synchronous and Asynchronous Transmission

The OpenURL method results in a *synchronous* transmission of data. In this context, synchronous means that the transfer operation occurs before any other procedures are executed. Thus the data transfer must be completed before any other code can be executed.

On the other hand, the Execute method results in an *asynchronous* transmission. When the Execute method is invoked, the transfer operation occurs independently of other procedures. Thus, after invoking the Execute method, other code can execute while data is received in the background.

What does this mean for the user of the Internet Transfer control? In short, using the OpenURL method results in a direct stream of data that you can save to disk (as shown above), or view directly in a TextBox control (if the data was text). On the other hand, if you use the Execute method to retrieve data, you must monitor the control's connection state using the StateChanged event. When the appropriate state is reached, invoke the GetChunk method to retrieve data from the control's buffer. This operation is discussed in greater detail below.

Using the Execute Method with the FTP Protocol

The Execute method has four arguments: *url*, *operation*, *data*, and *requestHeaders*. FTP operations take only the *operation* argument and the *url* argument, which is optional. For example, to get a file from a remote computer, you could use the following code:

```
Inet1.Execute "FTP://ftp.microsoft.com", _
"GET disclaimer.txt C:\Temp\Disclaimer.txt"
```

If you are used to using FTP to retrieve files from anonymous FTP servers, you will be familiar with certain commands used to navigate through server trees, and to retrieve files to a local hard disk. For example, to change directory with the FTP protocol, you would use the command "CD" with the path of the directory you wish to change to.

For the most common operations, such as putting a file on a server and retrieving a file from a server, the Internet Transfer control uses the same or a similar command with the Execute method. For example, the following code uses the "CD" command as an argument of the Execute method to change directory:

```
' The txtURL textbox contains the path to open. The
' txtRemotePath textbox contains the path to change to.
Inet1.Execute txtURL.Text, "CD " & txtRemotePath.Text
```

> **Note** When using the Execute method with FTP commands, the *data* and *requestHeaders* arguments are not used. Instead, all of the operations and their parameters are passed as a single string in the *operation* argument; parameters are separated by a space. In the descriptions below, do not confuse the terms "file1" and "file2" with the *data* and *requestHeaders* arguments.

The syntax for FTP operations is:

operationName file1 file2

For example, to get a file, the following code includes the operation name ("GET"), and the two file names required by the operation:

```
' Get the file named Disclaimer.txt and copy it to the
' location C:\Temp\Disclaimer.txt
Inet1.Execute, _
"GET Disclaimer.txt C:\Temp\Disclaimer.txt"
```

The following table lists the supported FTP commands of the control:

Operation	Description	Example
CD *file1*	Change Directory. Changes to the directory specified in *file1*.	`Execute , "CD docs\mydocs"`
CDUP	Change to Parent. Same as "CD."	`Execute , "CDUP"`

(continued)

(continued)

Operation	Description	Example
DELETE *file1*	Deletes the file specified in *file1*.	`Execute , "DELETE discard.txt"`
DIR [*file1*]	Searches the directory specified in *file1*. If file1 isn't supplied, the current working directory is searched. Use the GetChunk method to return the data.	`Execute , "DIR /mydocs"`
GET *file1 file2*	Retrieves the remote file specified in *file1*, and creates a new local file specified in *file2*.	`Execute , _` `"GET getme.txt C:\gotme.txt"`
MKDIR *file1*	Creates a directory as specified in *file1*. Success is dependent on user privileges on the remote host.	`Execute , "MKDIR /myDir"`
PUT *file1 file2*	Copies a local file specified in *file1* to the remote host specified in *file2*.	`Execute , _` `"PUT C:\putme.txt /putme.txt"`
PWD	Print Working Directory. Returns the current directory name. Use the GetChunk method to return the data.	`Execute , "PWD"`
QUIT	Terminate current connection.	`Execute , "QUIT"`
RECV *file1 file2*	Same as GET.	`Execute , _` `"RECV getme.txt C:\gotme.txt"`

(continued)

Operation	Description	Example
RENAME *file1 file2*	Renames a file. Success is dependent on user privileges on the remote host.	`Execute , "RENAME old.txt new.txt"`
RMDIR *file1*	Remove directory. Success is dependent on user privileges on the remote host.	`Execute , "RMDIR oldDir"`
SEND *file1*	Copies a file to the FTP site. (same as PUT.)	`Execute , _ "SEND C:\putme.txt /putme.txt"`
SIZE *file1*	Returns the size of the file specified in *file1*.	`Execute "SIZE /largefile.txt"`

Important If your proxy server is a CERN proxy server, direct FTP connections (using the Execute method) are disallowed. In that case, to get a file, use the OpenURL method with the Open, Put, and Close statements, as shown in "Saving to a File Using the OpenURL Method" earlier in this chapter. You can also use the OpenURL method to get a directory listing by invoking the method and specifying the target directory as the URL.

Using the Execute Method with the HTTP Protocol

The HTTP protocol allows client machines to request data from the server using the GET, HEAD, POST, and PUT commands. These operations are shown in the following table:

Operation	Description	Example
GET	Retrieves the file named in *url*.	`Execute "http://www.microsoft.com & _ "/default.htm", "GET"`
HEAD	Retrieves only the headers of the file named in the URL property.	`Execute , "HEAD"`
POST	Provides additional data to support a request to the remote host.	`Execute , "POST", strFormData`
PUT	Replaces data at the specified URL.	`Execute , "PUT", "replace.htm"`

The Common Gateway Interface and the Execute Method

Many World Wide Web sites offer the ability to search a database. This is accomplished by using the HTTP protocol's ability to send queries using the Common Gateway Interface (CGI).

It is not in the scope of this topic to explain the CGI; however, if you are familiar with the CGI, you can use the Execute method to construct an application that simulates the behavior of World Wide Web sites. For example, the code below shows a typical CGI query string:

```
http://www.yippee.com/cgi-bin/find.exe?find=Hangzhou
```

This same query could be sent using the Execute method as shown below:

```
Dim strURL As String, strFormData As String
strURL = "//www.yippee.com/cgi-bin/find.exe"
strFormData = "find=Hangzhou"
Inet1.Execute strURL, "POST", strFormData
```

If you are expecting a result back from a server (as in the example above), you must use the GetChunk method to retrieve the resulting HTML document.

Using the State Event with the GetChunk Method

When you are downloading data from a remote computer, an asynchronous connection will be made. For example, using the Execute method with the operation "GET", will cause the server to retrieve the requested file. When the entire file has been retrieved, the State argument will return icResponseCompleted (12). At that point, you can use the GetChunk method to retrieve the data from the buffer. This is shown in the example below:

```
Private Sub Inet1_StateChanged(ByVal State As Integer)
   Dim vtData As Variant ' Data variable.
   Select Case State
   ' ... Other cases not shown.
   Case icResponseCompleted ' 12
      ' Open a file to write to.
      Open txtOperation For Binary Access _
      Write As #intFile

      ' Get the first chunk. NOTE: specify a Byte
      ' array (icByteArray) to retrieve a binary file.
      vtData = Inet1.GetChunk(1024, icString)
```

```
      Do While LenB(vtData) > 0
         Put #intFile, , vtData
         ' Get next chunk.
         vtData = Inet1.GetChunk(1024, icString)
      Loop
      Put #intFile, , vtData
      Close #intFile
   End Select
End Sub
```

Logging on to FTP Servers

FTP servers come in two flavors: public and private. Public servers, as suggested by the name, are open to anyone. Private servers, on the other hand, won't let you log on unless you are a bona fide user of the server. In either case, the FTP protocol demands that you supply a user name and a password. The two are used to authenticate a user and allow (or disallow) subsequent actions.

To log on to public servers the common practice is to log in as "anonymous," (UserName = "anonymous") and send your e-mail name as the password. However this process is simplified even further with the Internet Transfer control. By default, if you do not supply UserName and Password property values, the control sends "anonymous" as your UserName, and your e-mail name for the Password.

If you are logging on to a private server, simply set the UserName, Password, and URL properties as appropriate, and invoke the Execute method, as shown in the example below:

```
With Inet1
   .URL = "ftp://ftp.someFTPSite.com"
   .UserName = "John Smith"
   .Password = "mAuI&9$6"
   .Execute ,"DIR"' Returns the directory.
   .Execute ,"CLOSE" ' Close the connection.
End With
```

After you have invoked the Execute method, the FTP connection will remain open. You can then continue to use the Execute method to perform other FTP operations such as CD and GET. When you have completed the session, close the connection using the Execute method with the CLOSE operation. You can also close the connection automatically by changing the URL property, and invoking either the OpenURL or Execute method; such action will close the current FTP connection, and open the new URL.

Using the ListView Control

The ListView control displays data as ListItem objects. Each ListItem object can have an optional icon associated with the label of the object. The control excels at representing subsets of data (such as members of a database) or discrete objects (such as document templates).

Possible Uses

- To display the results of a query on a database.
- To display all the records in a database table.
- In tandem with a TreeView control, to give users an expanded view of a TreeView control node.

Four Different Views Available

The ListView control can display data in four different view modes (as shown in the following figures). How you program the control depends on which of the different views you want the user to see (or select).

Each of these views has a particular advantage over the others. Some of these are listed in the following table:

View	Advantage
Icon	Can be manipulated with the mouse, allowing the user to drag and drop the object and rearrange the objects.
SmallIcon	Allows more ListItem objects to be viewed. Like Icon view, objects can be rearranged by the user.
List	Presents a sorted view of ListItems object.
Report	Presents a sorted view, with SubItems allowing extra information to be displayed.

ListView in Icon view

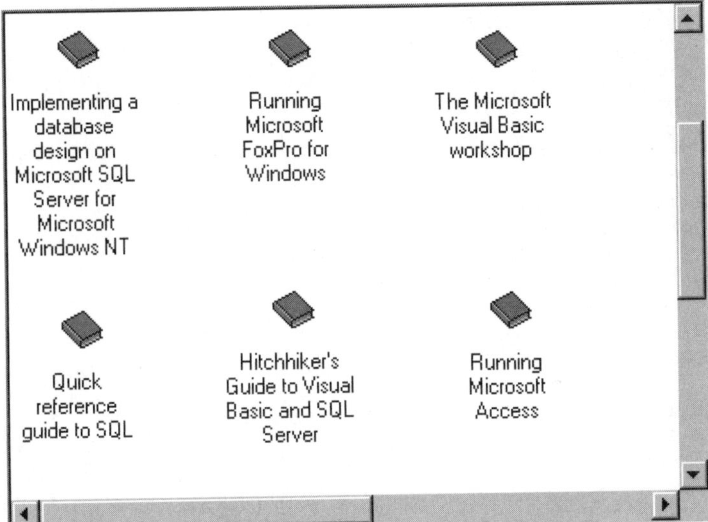

ListView in SmallIcon view

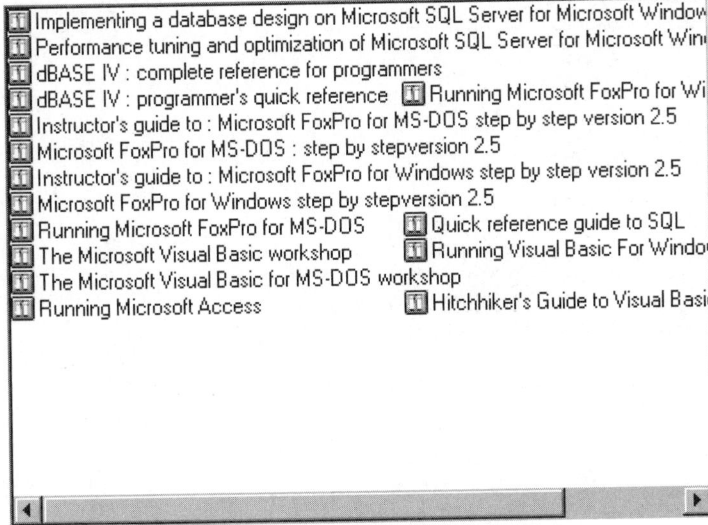

ListView in List view

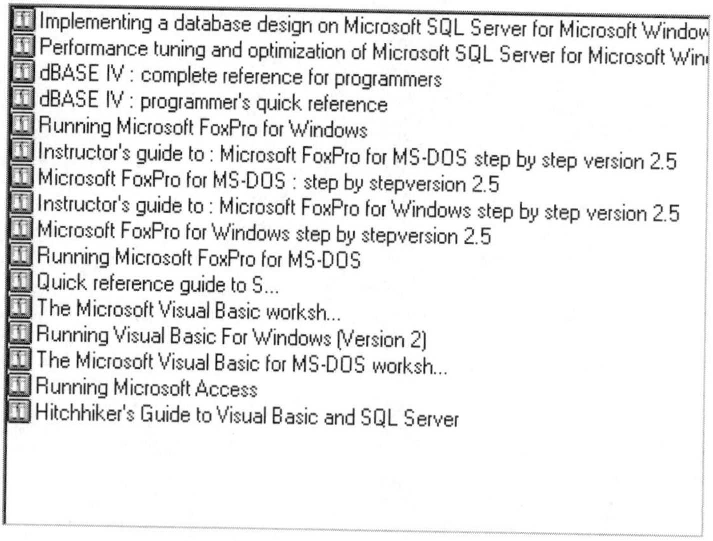

Implementing a database design on Microsoft SQL Server for Microsoft Window
Performance tuning and optimization of Microsoft SQL Server for Microsoft Win
dBASE IV : complete reference for programmers
dBASE IV : programmer's quick reference
Running Microsoft FoxPro for Windows
Instructor's guide to : Microsoft FoxPro for MS-DOS step by step version 2.5
Microsoft FoxPro for MS-DOS : step by stepversion 2.5
Instructor's guide to : Microsoft FoxPro for Windows step by step version 2.5
Microsoft FoxPro for Windows step by stepversion 2.5
Running Microsoft FoxPro for MS-DOS
Quick reference guide to S...
The Microsoft Visual Basic worksh...
Running Visual Basic For Windows (Version 2)
The Microsoft Visual Basic for MS-DOS worksh...
Running Microsoft Access
Hitchhiker's Guide to Visual Basic and SQL Server

ListView in Report view

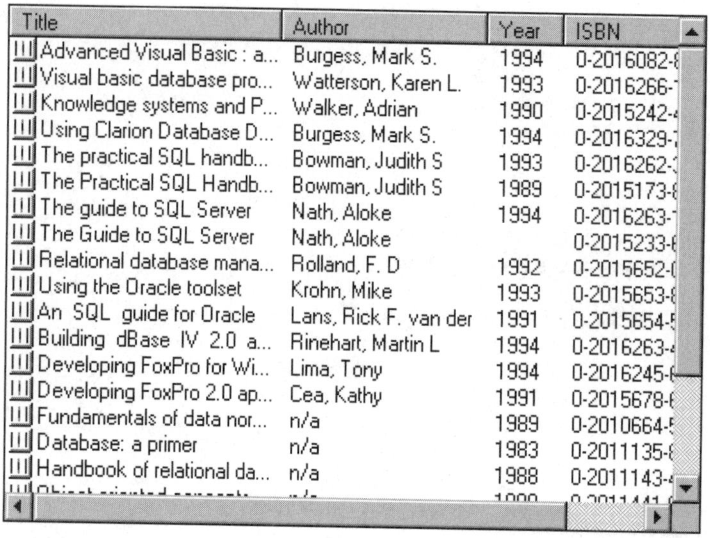

Title	Author	Year	ISBN
Advanced Visual Basic : a...	Burgess, Mark S.	1994	0-2016082-
Visual basic database pro...	Watterson, Karen L.	1993	0-2016266-
Knowledge systems and P...	Walker, Adrian	1990	0-2015242-
Using Clarion Database D...	Burgess, Mark S.	1994	0-2016329-
The practical SQL handb...	Bowman, Judith S	1993	0-2016262-
The Practical SQL Handb...	Bowman, Judith S	1989	0-2015173-
The guide to SQL Server	Nath, Aloke	1994	0-2016263-
The Guide to SQL Server	Nath, Aloke		0-2015233-
Relational database mana...	Rolland, F. D	1992	0-2015652-
Using the Oracle toolset	Krohn, Mike	1993	0-2015653-
An SQL guide for Oracle	Lans, Rick F. van der	1991	0-2015654-
Building dBase IV 2.0 a...	Rinehart, Martin L	1994	0-2016263-
Developing FoxPro for Wi...	Lima, Tony	1994	0-2016245-
Developing FoxPro 2.0 ap...	Cea, Kathy	1991	0-2015678-
Fundamentals of data nor...	n/a	1989	0-2010664-
Database: a primer	n/a	1983	0-2011135-
Handbook of relational da...	n/a	1988	0-2011143-

Change the View with the View Property

To change the display mode, use the View property. The following code sets the View property to the Report view (3), using the intrinsic constant lvwReport:

```
' The name of the control is "ListView1"
ListView1.View = lvwReport
```

Using the View property, you can allow the end user to dynamically change the view. In the Form's Load event, the ComboBox is populated with View choices:

```
Private Sub Form_Load()
   ' Populate the ComboBox control. The
   ' ComboBox control is named "cmbChooseView."
   With cmbChooseView
      .AddItem "Icon"       '0
      .AddItem "Small Icon"    ' 1
      .AddItem "List"       ' 2
      .AddItem "Report"    ' 3
   End With
End Sub
```

In the ComboBox control's Click event, the View of the control can then be reset, as shown:

```
Private Sub cmbChooseView_Click()
   ' The name of the ListView control is "lvwDB."
   lvwDB.View = cmbChooseView.ListIndex
End Sub
```

Two ImageList Controls for Icons and SmallIcons

A ListItem object consists of a label (the Text property) and an optional image which is supplied by an ImageList control. However, the ListView control, unlike other controls, can use *two* ImageList controls, which you set using the Icons and SmallIcons properties. Whether or not you use one or both ImageList controls depends on the intended display mode, as determined by the View property.

In the List, SmallIcon, and Report views, you can use a small icon to represent the ListItem object. One ImageList control (specified by the SmallIcons property) supplies the images for use in any of these three views. At design time or run time, set the SmallIcons property to the ImageList control that will supply these images. At design time, use the ListView control's Property Pages dialog box to set the ImageList for the SmallIcons. At run time, use the following code:

```
ListView1.SmallIcons = imlSmallIcons
```

In contrast, when the control is in Icon view, the control uses a different set of images supplied by a second ImageList control. Set the Icons property to this second ImageList control at design time using the Property Pages dialog box, or use the following code at run time:

```
ListView1.Icons = imlIcons
```

Note The size of the icons you use is determined by the ImageList control. The available sizes are 16 x 16, 32 x 32, 48 x 48, and Custom. For more information about the ImageList control, see "Using the ImageList Control" earlier in this chapter.

If you are planning to use more than one view, and you wish to display images, you must set the SmallIcon and Icon properties for each ListItem object. The following code first declares an object variable of type ListItem, then sets the object variable to a single ListItem object added to the collection using the Add method. The SmallIcon and Icon images are then set with the object variable reference:

```
Dim itmX as ListItem
Set itmX = ListView1.ListItems.Add()
' Assuming an image named "smallBook" exists in the
' ImageList set to the SmallIcons property.
itmX.SmallIcon = "smallBook"
' Assuming an image named "BigBook" exists in the
' ImageList that is set to the Icons property.
itmX.Icon = "BigBook"
```

After setting an image with the SmallIcon and Icon properties, the correct image will be displayed automatically when switching views using the View property.

ColumnHeaders Are Displayed in Report View

A unique feature of the Report view is ColumnHeader objects. The ListView control contains a collection of ColumnHeader objects in the ColumnHeaders collection.

A ColumnHeader

Title	Author	Year	ISBN
dBASE IV : complete reference for...	Hergert, Douglas.	1989	1-5561
dBASE IV : programmer's quick ref...	Viescas, John	1989	1-5561
Hitchhiker's Guide to Visual Basic ...	Vaughn, William R.	1996	1-5561

The ColumnHeader object has a Text property that displays text when the control is in Report view. You can also set the Width property of each ColumnHeader, as well as the Alignment property (which sets the alignment of the text displayed in the ColumnHeader object). The following example code creates four ColumnHeader objects and sets their Text and Width properties:

```
Dim colX As ColumnHeader ' Declare variable.
Dim intX as Integer ' Counter variable.
For intX = 1 to 4
   Set colX = ListView1.ColumnHeaders.Add()
   colX.Text = "Field " & intX
   colX.Width = ListView1.Width / 4
Next intX
```

Set Column Text with the ListSubItems Collection

Notice that in any of the views except Report view, the ListItem object displays only one label — the Text property. But in Report view, every ListItem object can have several other text items. For example, the "Hitchhiker's Guide to Visual Basic…" also has an author ("Vaughn, William R."), year (1996), and ISBN number associated with it. Each of these text items are members of the ListSubItems collection. To create a ListSubItem object, use the Add method for the ListSubItems collection. Thus, to set the author, year and ISBN number of a ListItem object, the code might look like this:

```
' The control is named lvwAuthors.
lvwAuthor.ListItems(23).ListSubItems.Add , , _
"Hitchhiker's Guide to Visual Basic and SQL Server"
lvwAuthor.ListItems(23).ListSubItems.Add , , _
"Vaughn, William R."
lvwAuthor.ListItems(23).ListSubItems.Add , , "1996"
lvwAuthor.ListItems(23).ListSubItems.Add , , "1-55615-906-4"
```

> **Note** The ListItems string array used in Visual Basic versions 4.0 and 5.0 has been supplanted by the ListSubItems collection.

SubItems Depend on ColumnHeaders Presence

Both the presence and number of ListSubItem objects depends on the presence and number of ColumnHeader objects. That is, you cannot create any ListSubItem objects if there are no ColumnHeader objects present. Further, the number of ColumnHeader objects determines the number of ListSubItem objects you can set for the ListItem object. And the number of ListSubItems is always *one less* than the number of ColumnHeader objects. This is because the first ColumnHeader object is always associated with the Text property of the ListItem object, as shown below:

First ColumnHeader and SubItems

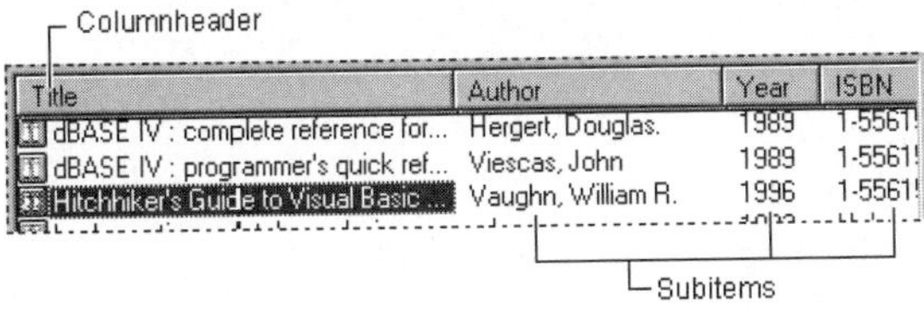

Thus, if the number of ColumnHeader objects in the above example is 4, then the maximum possible number of members of the ListSubItems collection is 3.

ListView Scenario 1: Using the ListView Control with the TreeView Control

The ListView control is often used in tandem with the TreeView control. (For more information on the TreeView control, see "Using the TreeView Control" later in this chapter.) The combination allows the end user to "drill down" through several hierarchical layers; the TreeView displays the larger structure, while the ListView displays the individual sets of records as each Node object is selected, as shown in the following illustration:

TreeView and ListView together

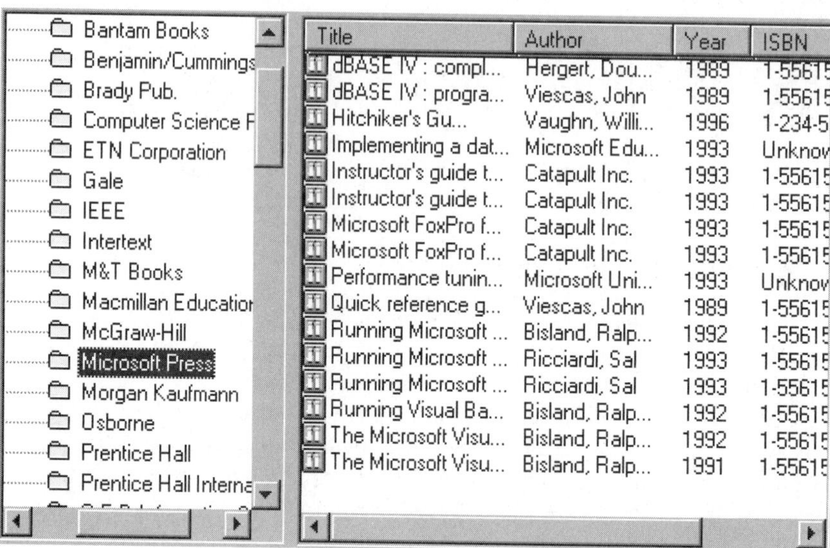

In this scenario, whenever a "Publisher" node on the TreeView control is clicked (the NodeClick event), the code populates the ListView control with the book titles owned by the publisher.

This scenario builds upon the scenario found in "Using the TreeView Control" by further binding the Biblio.mdb to the ListView control. The complete code for the four scenarios can be found in "ListView Scenarios: Complete Code" later in this chapter.

Sample Application: DataTree.vbp

The code examples in this topic are taken from the DataTree.vbp sample application, which is listed in the Samples directory.

The following procedure uses these objects:

- Form object named "frmDataTree"
- TreeView control named "tvwDB"
- ListView control named "lvwDB"
- ImageList control named "imlIcons"
- ImageList control named "imlSmallIcons"

To use a ListView control with the TreeView control

1. Add a reference to the Data Access Objects (DAO 3.5) to the project.
2. Declare module-level variables for the Database and ListItem objects.
3. Populate two ImageList controls with appropriate images.
4. Assign the ImageList controls to the Icons and SmallIcons properties of the ListView control.

   In the Form Load event:

5. Set the Database object variable to the Biblio.mdb database using the OpenDatabase statement.

   In the TreeView control's NodeClick event:

6. If the Node's Tag property is "Publisher" then call procedures to create ColumnHeaders and populate the ListView control.

Add a Reference to the Data Access Objects (DAO 3.5) to the Project

To bind a database to the ListView control, you must first add a reference to the current version of Data Access Objects (DAO).

Declare Module-Level Variables for the Database and ListItem Objects

Since you will want to access the Biblio.mdb database several times during a single session, it's more efficient to keep a single copy of the database open by creating a global Database object. Thereafter, you can access the database without reopening it. In the Declarations section of the form, write:

```
Private mDbBiblio As Database
```

(The variable is declared as Private, making it a module-level scope variable. If you want the database to be used by other modules, use the Public statement, and rename the variable to reflect its global status, i.e., `gDbBiblio`.)

When adding ListItem objects to the ListItems collection, you should use the Set statement with a variable of type ListItem.

```
Dim TempItem As ListItem
Set TempItem = lvwDB.ListItems.Add()
```

While you can declare the variable whenever you add ListItem objects, it is more efficient to declare a single module-level ListItem object variable once and use it to add all ListItem objects. Again in the Declarations section, write:

```
Private mTempItem As ListItem
```

Populate Two ImageList Controls with Appropriate Images

To use images in the ListView control, you must first populate two ImageList controls with images. Thereafter, at design time you can set the Icons and SmallIcons properties to the two ImageList controls. See "Using the ImageList Control," earlier in this chapter, for more information.

Assign the ImageList Controls to the Icons and SmallIcons Properties of the ListView Control

If you do not wish to set the Icon and SmallIcon properties at design time, you can set them at run time, as shown:

```
lvwDB.Icons = imlIcons
lvwDB.SmallIcons = imlSmallIcons
```

One reason for setting the ImageList controls at run time rather than design time would be to dynamically change the images for a different user. For example, a user with a monochrome screen may want icons that have a higher contrast of elements.

Set the Database object variable to the Biblio database using the OpenDatabase statement

The Form object's Load event can be used to initialize the Database variable. The code for this would be:

```
Set mDbBiblio = DBEngine.Workspaces(0). _
OpenDatabase("BIBLIO.MDB")
```

After you have successfully initialized the Database object variable, you can freely access it from anywhere within the code module.

If the Node's Tag property is "Publisher" Then Call Procedures to Create ColumnHeaders and Populate the ListView Control

When the TreeView control is populated (See "Using the TreeView Control" later in this chapter), the Tag property of every Node object is set to the name of the database table to which the Node belongs. In this scenario, if the Tag property's value is "Publisher," then the code invokes two user-designed procedures. The first, MakeColumns, creates columns for the ListView control.

The second function, GetTitles, populates the ListView control with ListItem objects. The function, however, requires an argument, the Key property of the Node object which contains the publisher's unique ID from the "Publishers" table. The GetTitles function uses the Key to search the "Titles" database to return all titles that belong to the publisher. The complete NodeClick code is shown:

```
Private Sub tvwDB_NodeClick(ByVal Node As Node)
   If Node.Tag = "Publisher" Then
      MakeColumns ' Create Columnheaders.
      GetTitles Val(Node.Key) ' Make ListItem objects.
End Sub
```

Tip The Key property value cannot be an integer, but must be a unique string. However, the string can be an integer followed by a string, for example "7 ID." The code above uses the Val function which returns only that part of the Key property value which is an integer. Therefore, when setting the Node object's Key property, use a string appended to the PubID field's value. For example:

```
tvwDB.Nodes(x).Key = rsPublishers!PubID & " ID"

Using the Val function will then return only the original PubID value.
```

Next Step: The MakeColumns Procedure

To see the MakeColumns function, see "ListView Scenario 2: Using a Procedure to Create ColumnHeaders."

ListView Scenario 2: Using a Procedure to Create ColumnHeaders

The code examples in this topic are taken from the DataTree.vbp sample application, which is listed in the Samples directory.

In the previous scenario, "ListView Scenario 1: Using the ListView Control with the TreeView Control," the ListView control and the TreeView control are showed working in tandem. In that scenario, the TreeView control's NodeClick event is used to call two procedures. The first procedure, "MakeColumns," which creates ColumnHeader objects, is outlined here.

The following example uses this object:

- ListView control named "lvwDB"

To create ColumnHeader objects

1. Clear the ColumnHeaders collection with the Clear method and create ColumnHeaders.
2. Use the Add method to create ColumnHeader objects.

Clear the ColumnHeaders collection with the Clear method and Create ColumnHeaders

The procedure first clears all members of the ColumnHeaders collection using the Clear method:

```
lvwDB.ListItems.Clear
```

This step is necessary if you intend to create different sets of ColumnHeader objects for different tables. For example, you may want to populate the ListView control not only when the Publisher nodes are clicked, but also when the user clicks the root of the tree. In that case, the ListView control would be populated with a different list.

Use the Add Method to Create ColumnHeader Objects

After clearing the ColumnHeaders collection, you use the Add method to add ColumnHeader objects to the collection, as shown:

```
Private Sub MakeColumns()
   ' Clear the ColumnHeaders collection.
   lvwDB.ColumnHeaders.Clear
   ' Add four ColumnHeaders.
   lvwDB.ColumnHeaders.Add , , "Title", 2000
   lvwDB.ColumnHeaders.Add , , "Author"
   lvwDB.ColumnHeaders.Add , , "Year", 350
   lvwDB.ColumnHeaders.Add , , "ISBN"
End Sub
```

Note that the Add method syntax allows you to set the Width property for each ColumnHeader object. In the above code, the Width property is set only for the "Title" and "Year" ColumnHeader objects.

ListView Scenario 3: Using a Procedure to Retrieve Titles from the Biblio.mdb Database

The code examples in this topic are taken from the DataTree.vbp sample application, which is listed in the Samples directory.

In ListView Scenario 1, "Using the ListView Control with the TreeView Control," the ListView control and the TreeView control are shown working in tandem. The TreeView control's NodeClick event is used to call two procedures, one to create ColumnHeader objects, and a second to populate the ListView control.

This scenario continues by developing the second procedure, called "GetTitles," that populates the ListView control with titles from the Biblio.mdb database.

The following example uses these objects:

- Form object named "frmDataTree"
- TreeView control named "tvwDB"
- ListView control named "lvwDB"
- ImageList control named "imlIcons"
- ImageList control named "imlSmallIcons"

To create a procedure that populates the ListView control

1. In the GetTitles procedure, clear the ListItems collection with the Clear method.
2. Use a query to create a "Titles" recordset.
3. Use the Do Until statement to create a ListItem object for each record in the recordset.

GetTitles Procedure: Clear the ListItems collection with the Clear method

Each time you invoke the GetTitles procedure, you will query the Biblio.mdb database to create a new collection of ListItem objects. The first thing to do, however, is to clear the old collection with the Clear method:

```
lvwDB.ListItems.Clear ' Clears all ListItems.
```

Use a query to create a "Titles" recordset

When the GetTitles procedure is invoked, the Key property's value of the Node property is passed to the procedure. Since the Key property contains the unique number that identifies the publisher (the PubID field), this value can be used to search the Titles table for all matches with the same PubID value.

The most efficient method to accomplish this is to create a query that finds only those records which have the same PubID value in the Titles table's PubID field. This query is:

```
Set rsTitles = mDbBiblio.OpenRecordset _
("select * from Titles where PubID = " & PubID)
```

Use the Do Until Statement to Create a ListItem Object for Each Record in the Recordset

Once the recordset is created, you can add to the ListItem collection. The following code iterates through this recordset to create a ListItem object for every record, setting the Text and SubItems properties with data from the recordset. The complete procedure is shown here:

```
Private Sub GetTitles(PubID)
   ' Clear the old titles.
   lvwDB.ListItems.Clear
   ' Declare object variable of type Recordset
   Dim rsTitles As Recordset
   ' While on this record, create a recordset using a
   ' query that finds only titles that have the same
   ' PubID. For each record in this recordset, add a
   ' ListItem object to the ListView control, and set
   ' the new object's properties with the record's
   ' Title, ISBN and Author fields.
   Set rsTitles = mDbBiblio.OpenRecordset _
   ("select * from Titles where PubID = " & PubID)

   Do Until rsTitles.EOF
   ' Add ListItem.
         Set mItem = lvwDB.ListItems.Add()
         mItem.Text = rsTitles!TITLE
         mItem.SmallIcon = "smlBook"
         mItem.Icon = "book"
         mItem.Key = rsTitles!ISBN
         ' Use a function to get the author and set
         ' the SubItems(1) property.
         mItem.SubItems(1) = GetAuthor(rsTitles!ISBN)
         If Not IsNull(rsTitles![Year Published]) Then
            mItem.SubItems(2) = _
            rsTitles![Year Published]
         End If
         mItem.SubItems(3) = rsTitles!ISBN
         rsTitles.MoveNext
   Loop
End Sub
```

ListView Scenario 4: Using a Function to Return an Author's Name from the Biblio.mdb Database

The code examples in this topic are taken from the DataTree.vbp sample application, which is listed in the Samples directory.

In the earlier scenario, "ListView Scenario 1: Using the ListView Control with the TreeView Control," the ListView control and the TreeView control are shown working in tandem. In that scenario, the TreeView control's NodeClick event is used to call a procedure called "GetTitles" to populate the ListView control. That procedure queries the "Titles" table to create a recordset, then creates a ListItem object for each record it finds.

One piece of information that is not contained in the "Titles" table is the name of the book's author. Instead, the "Titles" table contains a field named "ISBN" that stores the ISBN number of the book. The value of this field is also contained in a second table called "Title Author" which links the ISBN value with a field (Au_ID) that identifies the author.

To retrieve the author's name, the function must

1. Find the ISBN value in the "Title Author" recordset.
2. Find the AuthorID value in the Authors recordset.
3. Return the name of the author.

Setup

The scenario uses the following object:

- ListView control named "lvwDB"

Find the ISBN Value in the "Title Author" Recordset

The GetAuthor function uses the value of the ISBN field to search the "Title Author" recordset. As in other database operations, first declare an object variable of type RecordSet, then open the "Title Author" table and assign the reference to the object variable. However, since the code uses two recordsets, declare the object variables together, then open the recordsets, as shown.

```
Dim rsTitleAuthor As Recordset
Dim rsAuthors As Recordset

Set rsTitleAuthor = mDbBiblio. _
OpenRecordset("Title Author", dbOpenDynaset)
Set rsAuthors = mDbBiblio. _
OpenRecordset("Authors", dbOpenDynaset)
```

With the rsAuthors object variable and the value from the ISBN field, search the "Title Author" table:

```
Dim strQuery As String
strQuery = "ISBN = " & "'" & ISBN & "'"
rsTitleAuthor.FindFirst strQuery
```

Find the AuthorID value in the Authors recordset

The FindFirst method will return the first match that meets the criteria in the query. The other field in the "Title Author" table is the "Au_ID" field, which contains the ID of an author in the "Authors" table. Therefore, we can now use the value from the "Au_ID" field in the query, and search the "Authors" table, as shown:

```
' Reset query string.
strQuery = "Au_ID = " & rsTitleAuthor!AU_ID
' Search again using the FindFirst method.
rsAuthors.FindFirst strQuery
```

Return the Name of the Author

Finally, the "Authors" table has been entered, and the "Au_ID" field has been searched. Presuming no errors have been made, the current recordset should return the name of the author. The following code instructs the function to return the author's name to the calling code:

```
GetAuthors = rsAuthors!Author
```

The Complete GetAuthor Function

The complete function is shown:

```
Private Function GetAuthor(ISBN)
   ' Declare DAO object variables.
   Dim rsTitleAuthor As Recordset
   Dim rsAuthors As Recordset
   ' Set object variables to recordsets.
   Set rsTitleAuthor = mDbBiblio. _
   OpenRecordset("Title Author", dbOpenDynaset)
   Set rsAuthors = mDbBiblio. _
   OpenRecordset("Authors", dbOpenDynaset)
   ' Create query string.
   Dim strQuery As String
   strQuery = "ISBN = " & "'" & ISBN & "'"
   rsTitleAuthor.FindFirst strQuery
   ' If there is no author, return "n/a."
   ' Otherwise, return the name of the author.

   If rsTitleAuthor.NoMatch Then
      GetAuthor = "n/a"
      Exit Function
   Else
      ' Presume we have found the right recordset.
      ' Then reset the string query with Au_ID
      ' field value and search "Authors" table.
      strQuery = "Au_ID = " & rsTitleAuthor!AU_ID
      rsAuthors.FindFirst strQuery
      ' Return the name of the author from the Author
      ' field.
      GetAuthor = rsAuthors!Author
   End If
End Function
```

ListView Scenarios: Complete Code

The code discussed in the ListView scenarios 1 through 4, except for the procedure to populate the TreeView controls, is shown below. For code to populate the TreeView control, see "TreeView Control Scenario: Bind the TreeView to the Biblio.mdb Database" later in this chapter. For a working example of this code, see the sample application DataTree.vbp, which is listed in the Samples directory.

```
' General Declarations
Private mDbBiblio As Database ' Database variable.

Private Sub Form_Load()
   ' Open the Biblio.mdb and set the object variable
   ' to the database.
   Set mDbBiblio = DBEngine.Workspaces(0). _
   OpenDatabase("Biblio.mdb")

   ' Code to populate the TreeView control
   ' isn't shown here.
End Sub

Private Sub tvwDB_NodeClick(ByVal Node As Node)
   ' Check the Tag for "Publisher." If so, then
   ' call the MakeColumns procedure and then the
   ' GetTitles function.
   If Node.Tag = "Publisher" Then
      MakeColumns
      GetTitles Val(Node.Key)
   End If
End Sub

Private Sub MakeColumns()
   ' Clear the ColumnHeaders collection.
   lvwDB.ColumnHeaders.Clear
   ' Add four ColumnHeaders.
   lvwDB.ColumnHeaders.Add , , "Title", 2000
   lvwDB.ColumnHeaders.Add , , "Author"
   lvwDB.ColumnHeaders.Add , , "Year", 350
   lvwDB.ColumnHeaders.Add , , "ISBN"
End Sub

Private Sub GetTitles(PubID)
' Clear the old titles.
lvwDB.ListItems.Clear
' Declare object variable of type Recordset.
Dim rsTitles As Recordset
' While on this record, create a recordset using a
' query that finds only titles that have the same
```

```
' PubID. For each record in this recordset, add a
' ListItem object to the ListView control, and set
' the new object's properties with the record's
' Title, ISBN, and Author fields.
Set rsTitles = mDbBiblio.OpenRecordset _
("select * from Titles where PubID = " & PubID)

Do Until rsTitles.EOF
' Add ListItem.
      Set mItem = lvwDB.ListItems.Add()
      mItem.Text = rsTitles!TITLE
      mItem.SmallIcon = "smlBook"
      mItem.Icon = "book"
      mItem.Key = rsTitles!ISBN
      ' Use a function to get the author and set
      ' the SubItems(1) property.
      mItem.SubItems(1) = GetAuthor(rsTitles!ISBN)
      If Not IsNull(rsTitles![Year Published]) Then
         mItem.SubItems(2) = _
      rsTitles![Year Published]
      End If
      mItem.SubItems(3) = rsTitles!ISBN
      rsTitles.MoveNext
Loop
End Sub

Private Function GetAuthor(ISBN)
   ' Declare DAO object variables.
   Dim rsTitleAuthor As Recordset
   Dim rsAuthors As Recordset
   ' Set object variables to recordsets.
   Set rsTitleAuthor = mDbBiblio. _
   OpenRecordset("Title Author", dbOpenDynaset)
   Set rsAuthors = mDbBiblio. _
   OpenRecordset("Authors", dbOpenDynaset)
   ' Create query string.
   Dim strQuery As String
   strQuery = "ISBN = " & "'" & ISBN & "'"
   rsTitleAuthor.FindFirst strQuery
   ' If there is no author, return "n/a."
   ' Otherwise, return the name of the author.

   If rsTitleAuthor.NoMatch Then
      GetAuthor = "n/a"
      Exit Function
   Else
      ' Presume we have found the right recordset.
      ' Then reset the string query with Au_ID
      ' field value and search "Authors" table.
```

```
        strQuery = "Au_ID = " & rsTitleAuthor!AU_ID
        rsAuthors.FindFirst strQuery
        ' Return the name of the author from the Author
        ' field.
        GetAuthor = rsAuthors!Author
    End If
End Function
```

Using the MAPI Controls

The messaging application program interface (MAPI) controls allow you to create mail-enabled Visual Basic applications. MAPI is a set of core system components that seamlessly connect any mail-enabled or workgroup application to MAPI-compliant information services. For example, the Microsoft Exchange messaging system can be connected to most private or public e-mail systems through the use of MAPI drivers.

In Visual Basic, the MAPI controls are used to interact with the underlying message subsystem. To use these controls, you must first install a MAPI-compliant e-mail system like Microsoft Exchange. The underlying messaging services are provided by the workgroup environment — the Microsoft Exchange Server running under Windows 95 or Windows NT, for instance.

Using the MAPI controls involves two steps: establishing a MAPI session and then using various properties and methods to access and manage an individual Inbox. For example, create and send a message, include a file attachment, verify the recipient's address against the e-mail system's address book, etc.

The MAPISession control signs on and establishes a MAPI session. It is also used to sign off from a MAPI session. The MAPIMessages control contains all the properties and methods needed to perform the messaging system functions described above.

The MAPI controls are invisible at run time. In addition, there are no events for the controls. To use them you must set the appropriate properties or specify the appropriate methods.

Note If you attempt to run a program that uses the MAPI controls, make sure that you have the 32-bit MAPI DLLs installed properly or you may not be able to perform MAPI functions such as SignOn. For example, on Windows 95, you must install Exchange during the operating system setup, or install it separately from the control panel to correctly use MAPI functions.

Possible Uses

- To add messaging functionality to your application.
- To create a full-featured electronic mail application.

Using the MAPISession control

The MAPISession control is used to sign in and out of a MAPI session. Assuming that MAPI services are present, logging in with the MAPISession control is merely a matter of providing a registered user name and password. The MAPISession control will determine the electronic mail settings specified in the operating system and invoke the underlying message subsystem (the mail server).

The MAPISession control

Setting MAPISession Properties

You can set the MAPISession properties at design time using the MAPISession Property Pages. Right-click the MAPISession control and click **Properties** to display the **Property Pages** dialog box.

Setting the MAPISession properties at design time

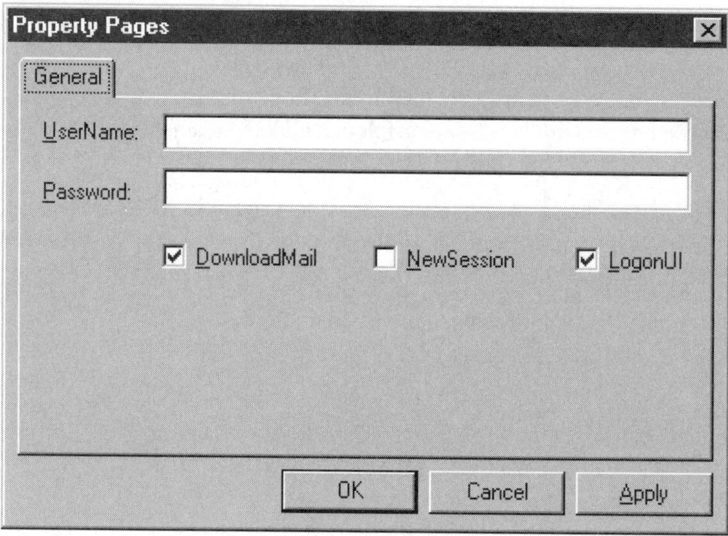

The UserName and Password properties are used to provide a valid sign-on to the underlying messaging system. You can either set these properties at design time or prompt the user at run time. Setting the LogonUI property to True will provide the user with the sign-on dialog box of the underlying mail system. If such a dialog box does not exist, this property will be ignored. You can create a custom dialog box to prompt the user for this information.

The NewSession property specifies whether a new mail session should be established. If a valid session is already established, setting the NewSession property will allow two sessions to run concurrently.

The DownloadMail property specifies whether the user's mail will be downloaded at the beginning of the current session automatically. Setting this value to True will download all the user's mail to their Inbox. Depending upon the mail system and the amount of incoming mail, this can be a processing-intensive operation. By setting this property to False, the user can choose to download mail at a later time or set the interval at which mail is automatically downloaded.

The SignOn and SignOff Methods

Once the UserName and Password properties have been set, use the SignOn method at run time to begin the MAPI session.

For example:

```
mpsSession.SignOn
```

When the session is established, the session handle is stored in the SessionID property. Depending upon the value of the NewSession property, the session handle may refer to a newly created session or an existing session.

To end the session use the SignOff method.

> **Note** The Action property can also be used to sign in and out of a MAPI session. It is recommended, however, that you use the SignOn and SignOff methods instead. The Action property is included for compatibility with earlier versions of Visual Basic.

The SessionID Property

When the SignOn method is used to successfully establish a messaging session, the SessionID property will return a unique messaging session handle. The SessionID value will be used by the MAPIMessages control to create an association with a valid messaging session. By default, this value is 0.

Using the MAPIMessages Control

Once you've logged into a messaging session using the MAPISession control, you use the MAPIMessages control to receive, send, or read messages from the Inbox which was specified at sign-on time.

The MAPIMessages control provides you with properties and methods to perform basic electronic mail tasks. For example, composing a message, addressing it to a recipient, verifying that the recipient's address is valid, or attaching a file.

The MAPIMessages control

In most cases, the MAPIMessages control is used to provide e-mail capabilities to certain functions within an application. For example, you may want to send a notification message to a workgroup alias after your application has automatically created a report. In other words, you can add e-mail capabilities to your application, without creating full-fledged e-mail applications.

You can, however, use the MAPI controls to create very powerful mail-enabled and workgroup applications.

Sample Application: VBMail.vbp

The examples in the following sections demonstrate the basic use of MAPI in Visual Basic. For more detailed use of the properties and methods of the MAPI controls refer to the VBMail.vbp sample application, which is listed in the Samples directory.

> **Note** You can also use the OLE Messaging technology to add MAPI functionality to your application. Information on OLE Messaging can be found in the *Microsoft Exchange Software Development Kit.*

Associating SessionID Properties

The SessionID property of the MAPIMessages control contains the messaging session handle returned by the SessionID property of the MAPISession control. To associate the MAPIMessages control with a valid messaging session, set this property to the SessionID of a MAPISession control that was successfully signed on. For example:

```
mpmMessage.SessionID = mpsSession.SessionID
```

This association to a valid MAPI session must be made before you can access messages and begin working with the MAPIMessages control.

Accessing Messages

Successfully logging into a MAPI session accesses the Inbox of the registered user specified by the UserName and Password properties of the MAPISession control. The Inbox is the message store. When the Inbox is opened two buffers are created: the *compose buffer* and the *read buffer.*

The read buffer is made up of an indexed set of messages fetched from the user's Inbox. The MsgIndex property is used to access individual messages within this set, starting with a value of 0 for the first message and incrementing by one for each message through the end of the set.

The message set is built using the Fetch method. The set includes all messages of type FetchMsgType and is sorted as specified by the FetchSorted property. The value of the FetchMsgType property is controlled by the underlying message system. The FetchSorted property can be set to add messages to the message set (read buffer) in the order they are received or in the order specified by the user's Inbox. Previously read messages can be included or left out of the message set with the FetchUnreadOnly property.

Messages in the read buffer can't be altered by the user, but can be copied to the *compose* buffer for alteration.

Messages are created or edited in the compose buffer. The compose buffer is active when the MsgIndex property is set to –1. Many of the messaging actions are valid only within the compose buffer, such as sending messages, saving messages, or deleting recipients and attachments.

Composing and Managing Messages

Managing messages is the primary function of the MAPIMessages control. Composing, sending, receiving, and deleting messages are performed by using methods that correspond to these basic functions (compose, copy, delete, etc.). The following table lists the MAPIMessages methods that specifically apply to messages:

Method	Description
Compose	Composes a new message
Copy	Copies the currently indexed message to the compose buffer
Delete	Deletes a message, recipient, or attachment
Fetch	Creates a message set from selected messages in the Inbox
Forward	Forwards a message
Reply	Replies to a message
ReplyAll	Replies to all message recipients
Save	Saves the message currently in the compose buffer
Send	Sends a message

To perform an action on an individual message, it must first be selected using the MsgIndex property. The message identified by the MsgIndex property is called the *currently indexed* message.

None of the other message properties can be set until a message is selected with the MsgIndex property. The index number can range from –1 to MsgCount –1 (the MsgCount property returns the total number of messages in the message set.) When a new message is created, the value of the MsgIndex property is set to –1.

Composing a Message

Use the Compose method to create a new message. When the Compose method is used, the compose buffer is cleared and the MsgIndex property is set to –1.

```
'Compose new message
mpmMessage.Compose
```

Completing a message involves several steps: determining the recipient of the message, choosing a subject title, and writing the message.

Addressing the Message

To set the recipient's name and address, use the RecipDisplayName and the RecipAddress properties. The RecipDisplayName is the proper name of the recipient, for example, "Richard Tull." The RecipAddress property contains the recipient's e-mail address: "richtull," for example.

```
'Address message
mpmMessage.RecipDisplayName = "Richard Tull"
mpmMessage.RecipAddress = "richtull"
```

Addresses for recipients outside the local workgroup (a message sent to someone at another company via the Internet, for example) require a complete Internet e-mail address: "richtull@littlemag.com."

Verifying the Recipient's Name

The recipient's name is verified when the message is sent by checking it against the list of registered users in the e-mail system, using the ResolveName method. Name verification for recipients outside the local workgroup is handled in various ways by the underlying message system.

The following example resolves the recipient's valid e-mail name by invoking the ResolveName method and setting the AddressResolveUI property to True.

```
' Resolve recipient name
mpmMessage.AddressResolveUI = True
mpmMessage.ResolveName
```

The AddressResolveUI property can be set to either display a details dialog box (True) or generate an error (False) when an ambiguous or invalid recipient address is encountered when the message is sent. The details dialog box will offer you an alternative address if a close match is found.

The Message Subject and Text

The MsgSubject property specifies the subject line for the message. You may enter up to 64 characters, including the Null character.

The body of the message is contained in the MsgNoteText property. For inbound messages, each paragraph is terminated with a carriage return-line feed pair (vbCrLf). Outbound messages can be delimited with a carriage return (vbCr), line feed (vbLf), or a carriage return-line feed pair.

```
'Create the message
mpmMessage.MsgSubject = "Status Report"
mpmMessage.MsgNoteText = "Build successful!"
```

Sending the Message

To send the message, use the Send Method. The Send method allows you to send a message with or without user interaction. Setting the value to True will display the compose message dialog box of the underlying e-mail system (Microsoft Exchange, for example). Setting it to False will send the message without displaying the compose message dialog. The following example sends the message without prompting for user interaction:

```
'Send the message
mpmMessage.Send False
```

Handling File Attachments

You can add file attachments to outgoing messages using the file attachment properties. These properties are listed in the following table:

Property	Description
AttachmentCount	Returns the total number of attachments associated with the currently indexed message.
AttachmentIndex	Sets the currently indexed attachment.
AttachmentName	Specifies the name of the currently indexed attachment file.
AttachmentPathName	Specifies the full path name of the currently indexed attachment.
AttachmentPosition	Specifies the position of the currently indexed attachment within the message body.
AttachmentType	Specifies the type of the currently indexed file attachment.

To add an attachment to an outgoing message, use the AttachmentPathName property to specify the name and path of the file. For example:

```
'Add attachment
mpmMessage.AttachmentPathName = "c:\Status _
Report.doc"
```

If the path name is incorrect or empty, an error will be generated.

Simply specifying the AttachmentPathName property will send the attachment with the message, use the name of the file to display in the message body, and position the attachment at the beginning of the message.

The AttachmentName property can be used to specify a different name for the attached file. If this property isn't set, the actual name of the file will be displayed in the message body.

The AttachmentPosition property is used to position the attachment within the message body. By default, the value is "0" and the attachment is located at the beginning of the message body. To position the attachment at the end of the message, count the number of characters in the message body. For example, in a message body that is five characters long, you could place an attachment at the end of the message by setting the value to 4. (The message body occupies character positions 0 to 4).

Two attachments can't be placed in the same position within the same message. You also can't place an attachment equal to or beyond the end of the message body. You can append an extra space or a vbCrLf character to the end of the message body and then set the AttachmentPosition property to one character less than the length of the MsgNoteText property.

Managing Messages

Many of the remaining properties and methods of the MAPIMessages control can be used to manage messages just as you would in a full-featured e-mail application.

By accessing messages in the read buffer you can sort, delete, or forward one or a number of messages. The following table lists the properties you can use to manage messages:

MsgConversationID	Specifies the conversation thread identification value for the currently indexed message.
MsgCount	Returns the total number of messages present in the message set during the current messaging session.
MsgDateReceived	Returns the date on which the currently indexed message was received.
MsgID	Returns the string identifier of the currently indexed message.
MsgIndex	Specifies the index number of the currently indexed message.
MsgOrigAddress	Returns the mail address of the originator of the currently indexed message.
MsgOrigDisplayName	Returns the originator's name for the currently indexed message.
MsgRead	Returns a Boolean expression indicating whether the message has already been read.

(continued)

Property	Description
MsgReceiptRequested	Specifies whether a return receipt is requested for the currently indexed message.
MsgSent	Specifies whether the currently indexed message has already been sent to the mail server for distribution.
MsgType	Specifies the type of the currently indexed message.

Working with the Address Book

The e-mail system's address book contains all of the addressing information for each registered user in the e-mail system. The address book is a dialog box which allows the user to look up or verify recipient addresses. The address book properties allow you to set or modify elements of the address book.

The Show Method

The e-mail system's address book is displayed using the Show method. The Show method can be set to show either the address book or the recipient details dialog box.

By default, the value is set to False and the address book dialog box is displayed when the Show method is used.

To display the details dialog box, set the value to True. The amount of information displayed in this dialog box depends upon the e-mail system. At minimum, the name and address of the recipient are displayed.

Address Book Properties

The address book properties allow you to set or modify elements of the e-mail system's address book. The following table lists these properties:

Property	Description
AddressCaption	Specifies the caption appearing at the top of the address book.
AddressEditFieldCount	Specifies which edit controls to display to the user in the address book.
AddressLabel	Specifies the appearance of the "To" edit control in the address book.
AddressModifiable	Specifies whether the address book can be modified by the user.
AddressResolveUI	Specifies whether a dialog box is displayed for receipt name resolution during addressing.

All of the address book properties can be set at design time using the MAPIMessages control's Property Pages dialog box.

Setting the MAPIMessages properties at design time

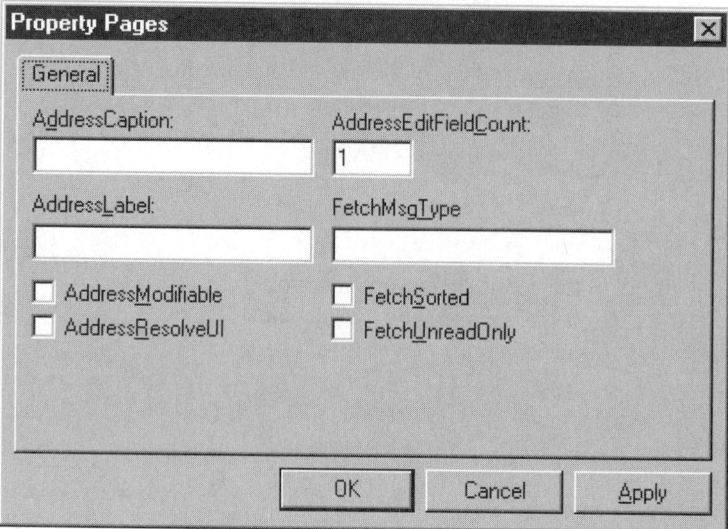

Setting the address book properties at design time allows you to specify options for the display and functionality of the address book dialog box. For example, you can modify the caption that appears in the address book dialog box using the AddressCaption property.

Using the MaskedEdit Control

The MaskedEdit control is used to prompt users for data input using a mask pattern. You can also use it to prompt for dates, currency, and time, or to convert input data to all upper- or lowercase letters. For example, to prompt the user to enter a phone number, you can create the following input mask: "(___) - ___ - ____." If you don't use an input mask, the MaskedEdit control behaves much like a standard text box.

When you define an input mask using the Mask property, each character position in the MaskedEdit control maps to a placeholder of a specified type, or to a literal character. Literal characters, or literals, give visual cues about the type of data being used. For example, the parentheses surrounding the area code of a telephone number are literals: (206).

The input mask prevents users from entering invalid characters into the control. If the user attempts to enter a character that conflicts with the input mask, the control generates a ValidationError event.

The MaskedEdit control is a bound control and can be used with a data control to display or update field values in a data set.

Possible Uses

- To prompt for date/time, number, or currency information.
- To prompt for custom mask formats such as a telephone number or any other input that follows a pattern.
- To format the display and printing of mask input data.
- To work with a data control to display and update field values in a data set.

The Mask Property

The Mask property determines the type of information that is input into the MaskedEdit control. The Mask property uses characters such as the pound sign (#), backslash (\), comma (,), and ampersand (&) as placeholders that define the type of input. The following table lists all the characters you can use to set the Mask property:

Mask character	Description
#	Digit placeholder.
.	Decimal placeholder. The actual character used is the one specified as the decimal placeholder in your international settings. This character is treated as a literal for masking purposes.
,	Thousands separator. The actual character used is the one specified as the thousands separator in your international settings. This character is treated as a literal for masking purposes.
:	Time separator. The actual character used is the one specified as the time separator in your international settings. This character is treated as a literal for masking purposes.
/	Date separator. The actual character used is the one specified as the date separator in your international settings. This character is treated as a literal for masking purposes.
\	Treat the next character in the mask string as a literal. This allows you to include the "#," "&," "A," and "?" characters in the mask. This character is treated as a literal for masking purposes.
&	Character placeholder. Valid values for this placeholder are ANSI characters in the following ranges: 32–126 and 128–255.
>	Convert all the characters that follow to uppercase.
<	Convert all the characters that follow to lowercase.
A	Alphanumeric character placeholder (entry required). For example: a z, A Z, or 0 9.

(continued)

(continued)

Mask character	Description
a	Alphanumeric character placeholder (entry optional).
9	Digit placeholder (entry optional). For example: 0 9.
C	Character or space placeholder (entry optional).
?	Letter placeholder. For example: a z or A Z.
Literal	All other symbols are displayed as literals; that is, as themselves.

To create an input mask, you combine mask characters with literal characters. Literal characters are characters which rather than representing some data type or format, are used as themselves. For example, to create an input mask for a phone number you define the Mask property as follows:

```
MaskEdBox1.Mask = (###) - ### - ####
```

The pound sign (a digit placeholder) is used with the left and right parentheses and the hyphen (literal characters). At run time, the MaskedEdit control would look like the following:

A MaskedEdit control with a phone number mask

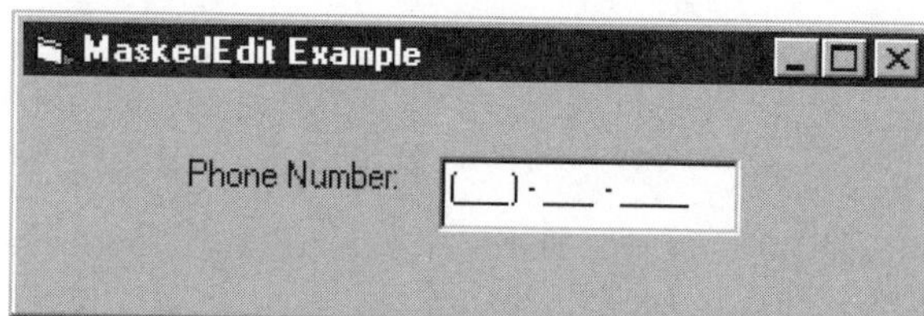

When you define an input mask, the insertion point automatically skips over literals as you enter data or move the insertion point.

The Text and ClipText Properties

All data entered in the MaskedEdit control is contained in and can be retrieved from the Text property. This is a run time only property and includes all the literal and prompt characters of the input mask. For instance, retrieving data from the Text property of the example above returns the string "(555) - 555 - 5555" — the phone number that was entered.

The ClipText property also returns data entered in the MaskedEdit control, but without the literal and prompt characters. Using the example above, retrieving data from the ClipText property returns the string "5555555555." The ClipText property is available only at run time.

Defining the Input Character

By default, all mask characters are underlined. This indicates to the user that the character is a placeholder for data input. When the user enters a valid character, the underline disappears. If you want the underline to remain, you can set the FontUnderline property of the MaskedEdit control to True.

You can also change the underline input character to a different character by using the PromptChar property. For example, to change the underline (_) character to the asterisk (*) character, you simply redefine the value of the PromptChar property:

```
MaskEdBox1.PromptChar = "*"
```

Using Mask Characters as Literals

If you want to use a mask character as a literal, you can precede the mask character with a backslash (\). For example, if you want the pound sign (#) to display, you set the mask as follows:

```
MaskEdBox1.Mask = "\##"
```

This would produce a mask that displays a pound sign (#) followed by a blank space for entering a number.

The Format Property

You can modify how the MaskedEdit control is displayed and printed using the Format property. The Format property provides you with standard formats for displaying number, currency, and date/time information.

The following table lists the standard formats you can use with the Format property:

Data type	Value	Description
Number	(Default) Empty string	General Numeric format. Displays as entered.
Number	$#,##0.00;($#,##0.00)	Currency format. Uses thousands separator; displays negative numbers enclosed in parentheses.
Number	0	Fixed number format. Displays at least one digit.
Number	#,##0	Commas format. Uses commas as thousands separator.
Number	0%	Percent format. Multiplies value by 100 and appends a percent sign.
Number	0.00E+00	Scientific format. Uses standard scientific notation.

(continued)

(continued)

Data type	Value	Description
Date/Time	(Default) c	General Date and Time format. Displays date, time, or both.
Date/Time	dddddd	Long Date format. Same as the Long Date setting in the International section of the Microsoft Windows Control Panel. Example: Tuesday, May 26, 1992.
Date/Time	dd-mmm-yy	Medium Date format. Example: 26-May-92.
Date/Time	ddddd	Short Date format. Same as the Short Date setting in the International section of the Microsoft Windows Control Panel. Example: 5/26/92.
Date/Time	ttttt	Long Time format. Same as the Time setting in the International section of the Microsoft Windows Control Panel. Example: 05:36:17 A.M.
Date/Time	hh:mm A.M./P.M.	Medium Time format. Example: 05:36 A.M.
Date/Time	hh:mm	Short Time format. Example: 05:36.

You use the Format property with the Mask property. For example, to create a mask that prompts for a Short Date input that displays in the Long Date format, you set the Mask and Format properties as follows:

```
MaskEdBox1.Mask = "##-##-##"
MaskEdBox1.Format = "dddddd"
```

When the user enters the date in the short format (06-27-96, for instance), the MaskedEdit control verifies that the entered data is valid, and then, when the focus passes to the next control, it is displayed as "Thursday, June 27, 1996."

> **Note** To automatically shift the focus to the next control when the data has been verified as valid, set the AutoTab property of the MaskedEdit control to True.

The Format property also allows you to specify custom formatting using the same format expressions defined by the Visual Basic Format function.

Setting Properties at Design Time

You can set the property values at design time using the MaskedEdit control Property Pages. Click the Custom option in the Properties window of the MaskedEdit control to bring up the Property Pages dialog box, as shown below:

Setting the Mask property at design time

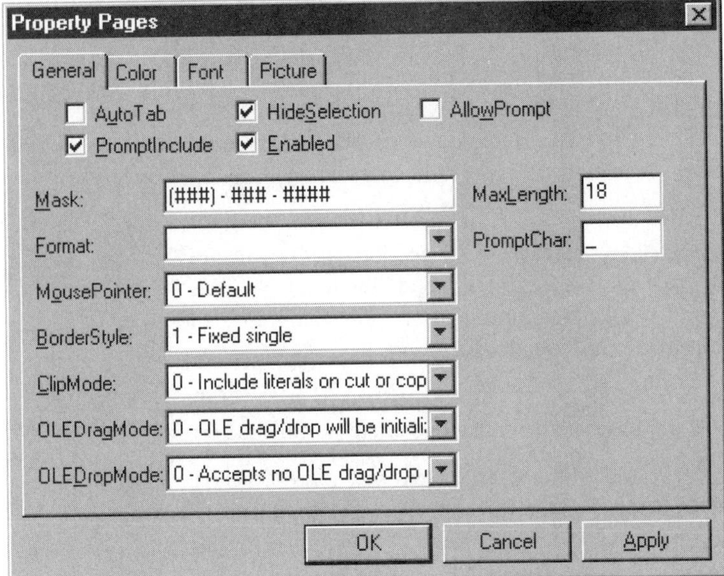

You enter the mask and format patterns as in the run time examples above. The Format drop down list allows you to select any of the predefined standard formats shown above. This dialog box also allows you to easily set such properties as PromptChar, ClipMode, and MaxLength.

A MaskedEdit field can have a maximum of 64 characters (the valid range is 1 to 64 characters). This includes literal characters as well as mask characters. You can set this value using the MaxLength property. At design time, this property is set automatically to the number of characters in the pattern when you enter a mask pattern.

The ClipMode property specifies whether or not literal characters are included when doing a cut or copy command. By default, when a selection in the MaskedEdit control is copied to the Clipboard, the entire selection, including the literals, is transferred. To limit the copy operation to only the data entered by the user, set the ClipMode property to True.

The ValidationError Event

The ValidationError event occurs when the MaskedEdit control receives invalid input, as determined by the input mask. For example, if you've defined an input mask that prompts for numbers, a ValidationError event will occur if the user attempts to enter a letter. Unless you write an event handler to respond to the ValidationError event, the MaskedEdit control will simply remain at the current insertion point — nothing will happen.

Mask characters are validated as they are entered and the insertion point is shifted to the right. When a character is entered or deleted out of sequence (when a digit is inserted or deleted after the phone number has been entered, for example), all nonliteral characters shift either to the right or left. When the shift occurs, if an invalid character replaces the position of a valid character, the ValidationError event is triggered.

For example, suppose the Mask property is defined as "?###," and the current value of the Text property is "A12." If you attempt to insert the letter "B" before the letter "A," the "A" would shift to the right. Since the second value of the input mask requires a number, the letter "A" would cause the control to generate a ValidationError event.

The MaskedEdit control also validates the values of the Text property at run time. If the Text property settings conflict with the input mask, the control generates a run-time error.

You can select text in the same way you would with a standard text box control. When selected text is deleted, the control attempts to shift the remaining characters to the right of the selection. However, any remaining character that might cause a validation error during this shift is deleted, and no ValidationError event is generated.

Using MaskedEdit as a Bound Control

The MaskedEdit control is a bound control. This means that it can be linked to a data control and display field values for the current record in a data set. The MaskedEdit control can also write out values to a data set.

> **Note** When the value of the field referenced by the DataField property is read, it is converted to a Text property string, if possible. If the recordset is updatable, the string is converted to the data type of the field.

The MaskedEdit control has three bound properties: DataChanged, DataField, and DataSource.

For More Information See "Using the ADO Data Control" in Chapter 7, "Using Visual Basic's Standard Controls," of the *Microsoft Visual Basic 6.0 Programmer's Guide* for information on using bound controls.

Using the MonthView Control

The MonthView control makes it easy for users to view and set date information via a calendar-like interface. Users can select a single date or a range of dates.

The control can be navigated using either the keyboard or mouse. Buttons at the top of the control are used to scroll months in and out of view.

In addition, the control has the ability to display up to 12 months at a time. This can be helpful when you want to give users the ability to view date information around the date of interest.

MonthView control

Possible Uses

- To present date information where a calendar representation of a date is easier to understand than that of a Label or Textbox control.
- To give users the ability to choose a date with the click of a mouse rather than typing a date value.
- To enable users to view multiple months as part of an advanced booking system such as those used by hotels and airlines.

Setting and Returning Dates

The currently selected date in the control is determined by the Value property. You can set the Value of the control before it is displayed (for example, in the form's Load event) to determine which date will be initially selected in the control:

```
MonthView1.Value = "10/31/97"
```

By default, the control's Value is set to the current date, and the current date is selected when the control first appears. If you change the MonthView's Value through code, the control will be updated immediately to reflect the new setting.

Certain events of the control can also be used to return date values. For example, the DateClick event is fired whenever the user clicks on a date in the control. The DateClick event returns a *DateClicked* value that evaluates to the date the user clicked. Similarly, the DateDblClick event returns a *DateDblClicked* value indicating the date that was double-clicked to cause the event. When using these events, you should refer to the value returned by the event, rather than the Value property of the control, as Value is not updated until after the event has occurred.

The Value property returns a date value that you can format in whatever manner you wish. The MonthView control also has several properties that return specific date information. The Month property returns the integer value (1–12) of the month containing the currently selected date. The Day property returns the day number (1–31) currently selected, and the DayOfWeek property returns a value indicating the day of the week the selected date falls on (values correspond to the values of *vbDayOfWeek* constants.) The Year property returns the year containing the selected date as an integer value. Finally, there is a Week property that will return the number of the week containing the selected date.

These properties can be set as well as read at run time, with varying effects on the currently selected date. For example, changing the value of the DayOfWeek property will select the date that falls on the specified day in the same week. This will change the value of the Day property, but depending on how the week falls, it may also change the value of the Month property. Changing the value of the Year property will cause the current date to be selected in the specified year, which may affect the value of DayOfWeek.

You should be especially careful when changing the value of the Week property. Setting a different week as the current week will not change the value of DayOfWeek, but will affect the value of Day, and possibly the values of Week, Month or even Year. For example, if the user has selected a Friday, and you set the value of Week to 52 in a year that ends on a Wednesday, the value of Week will become 1, and the values of Month and Year will also change. Weeks 1 and 52 will usually overlap.

Selecting a Range of Dates

You can use the MonthView control to display a contiguous range of dates, or to allow the user to select a date range. In order to extend the selection to more than one date, the MultiSelect property must be set to True. You can control the maximum number of days that may be selected by changing the value of the MaxSelCount property. By default, the maximum selection allowed is seven days.

The SelStart and SelEnd properties determine which days are selected. You can check the values of these properties to find out what range the user has selected. If only one date is selected, the two values will be the same. You can also set the values of these properties in code, which will cause a range of dates to become selected in the control. When setting the SelStart and SelEnd properties through code, you must observe the following rules:

- The SelStart date must occur before the SelEnd date.
- The selected range must contain the currently selected date. If necessary, you should set the Value property to one of the dates in the range before setting the SelStart and SelEnd values.
- The number of dates included in the range cannot exceed the maximum range size as specified by MaxSelCount.

For example, to select the week before Halloween through code, you would use the following:

```
MonthView1.Value = "10/31/97"
MonthView1.MaxSelCount = 7
MonthView1.SelStart = "10/25/97"
MonthView1.SelEnd = "10/31/97"
```

Formatting the Control's Appearance

The MonthView control allows you to customize its appearance in many ways. Various color attributes such as MonthBackColor, TitleBackColor, TitleForeColor and TrailingForeColor enable you to create a unique color scheme or the control. For example, TrailingForeColor determines the color of the dates that precede and follow the displayed month or months.

The font settings for the control determine the width and height of the control. Using larger fonts causes the control to grow to accommodate the increased font size. Conversely, you can set the font to a smaller size to shrink the control. Font size is set through the Font property.

Displaying More Than One Month

The MonthView control can display from one to twelve months at a time. You specify how many months will be displayed and how they will be arranged within the control. You do this by using the MonthRows and MonthColumns properties. For example, setting MonthRows to 2 and MonthColumns to 3 would result in a MonthView control that displayed six months at a time. Clicking on the arrow buttons at the top of the control would scroll the next six months or the previous six months into view.

Individual months are separated by a separator bar. The size of the separator is dependent on control size and display characteristics, but you can retrieve the dimensions used via the SeparatorHeight and SeparatorWidth properties. You can also retrieve the size of a single calendar by using the CalendarWidth and CalendarHeight properties. Together these properties are useful in determining how the control will change size if another row or column is added, and adjusting the size and position of your controls accordingly.

Other Formatting Settings

You can determine which day of the week will appear as the first day by changing the value of the StartOfWeek property. You can choose to display week numbers in the control by setting the ShowWeekNumbers property to True. Week numbers appear in a separate column to the left of the first day of the week. The display of the current date at the bottom of the control can be enabled or disabled using the ShowToday property.

Formatting Specific Days

Any day number on the MonthView control can also have its font set to bold. This capability can be used to draw attention to dates (i.e. holidays, vacations, etc.) or just distinguish them from ordinary dates. More than one date can be bolded at the same time. Although the bold information for a day is not preserved while scrolling from month to month, this behavior can be simulated using the GetDayBold event.

The following example makes all Sundays bold, even when new months are scrolled into view:

```
Private Sub MonthView1_GetDayBold(ByVal StartDate As Date, ByVal Count As Integer, State() As Boolean)
   Dim i As Integer
   i = vbSunday
   While i < Count
      State(i - MonthView1.StartOfWeek) = True
      i = i + 7
   Wend
End Sub
```

Keyboard Interface

The MonthView control can be manipulated using the keyboard. The following table describes the different actions you can perform with the control at runtime.

Key	Description
LEFT ARROW	Select the next day.
RIGHT ARROW	Select the previous day.
UP ARROW	Select the same day of week in the previous week.
DOWN ARROW	Select the same day of week in the next week.
PAGE UP	Scrolls the display to past months.
PAGE DOWN	Scrolls the display to future months.
CTRL+PAGE UP	Scrolls the display to the previous year.
CTRL+PAGE DOWN	Scrolls the display to the next year.

Navigating the MonthView

In addition to the two buttons at the top of the control, the MonthView control provides other ways to set the currently displayed month(s). You can display a particular month of any particular year.

To select a particular month

1. Click on the month name at the top of the calendar. A context menu will appear with the names of all the months.
2. From the menu, choose the name of the month you want to select.

The control will display the selected month in the current year.

To go directly to a particular year

1. Select the month you want.
2. Click on the year number at the top of the calendar. This will place it in edit mode.
3. Either click the up/down scroll buttons to scroll the year or type the year in the edit box.
4. Click anywhere outside the edit box or press the ENTER key when you are done.

The control will display the current month in the year you specified.

> **Distribution Note** The UpDown control is part of a group of ActiveX controls that are found in the COMCT232.ocx file. To use the UpDown control in your application, you must add the COMCT232.ocx file to the project. When distributing your application, install the COMCT232.ocx file in the user's Microsoft Windows System or System32 directory. For more information on how to add an ActiveX control to a project, see the *Microsoft Visual Basic 6.0 Programmer's Guide*.

Using the MSChart Control

The MSChart control allows you to plot data in charts according to your specifications. You can create a chart by setting data in the control's properties page, or by retrieving data to be plotted from another source, such as a Microsoft Excel spreadsheet. The information in this topic focuses on using an Excel worksheet as a data source.

Possible Uses

- To chart dynamic data, such as current prices of selected commodities.
- To plot stored data, such as product prices, for graphic analysis of trends.

Plot Data Using Arrays and the ChartData Property

The simplest way of plotting a chart is to create an array of numeric values, and then set the ChartData property to the array, as shown in the following example:

```
' This code might be pasted into the Load event
' of a Form that has an MSChart control named
' "MSChart1".
Dim arrPrices(1 to 10)
Dim i As Integer
For i = 1 to 10
   arrPrices(i)= i * 2
Next i
MSChart1.ChartData = arrPrices
```

The code above produces a simple, single-series chart. A "series" in a chart, is set of related data points. For example, a typical series might be the prices of a commodity over the course of a year. The chart below shows a single-series chart.

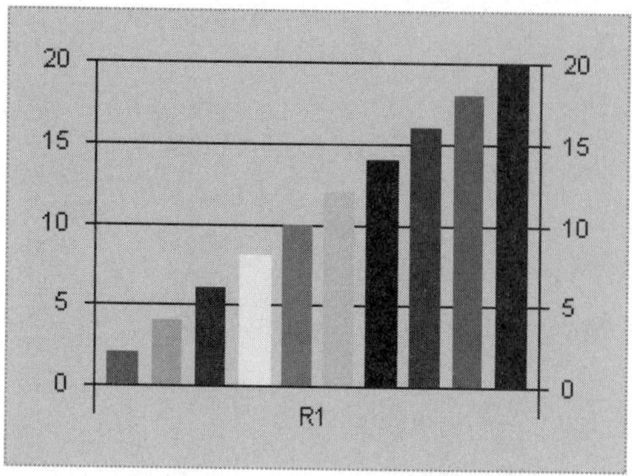

To create a more complex, multi-series chart, you must create a multi-dimensioned array, as shown in the following example:

```
' The number of series are determined by the second
' dimension. In this example, the chart will have two
' series, with five data points in each series.
Dim arrPriceQuantity(1 to 5, 1 to 2)
Dim i as Integer
For i = 1 to 5
   arrPriceQuantity(i, 1) = i ' Series 1
   arrPriceQuantity(i, 2) = 0 - i ' Series 2
Next i
MsChart1.ChartData = arrPriceQuantity
```

This will produce the following chart:

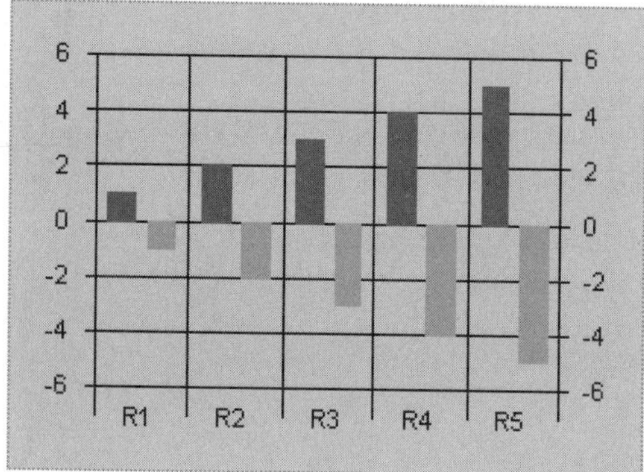

Adding Labels to the Chart

When you create a multi-dimensioned array, the first series can be assigned a string; when the array is assigned to the ChartData property, the strings become the labels for the rows. The following code shows this feature.

```
Dim arrValues(1 to 5, 1 to 3)
Dim i as Integer
For i = 1 to 5
   arrValues(i, 1) = "Label " & i ' Labels
   arrValues(i, 2) = 0 + i ' Series 1 values.
   arrValues(i, 3) = 2 * i ' Series 2 values.
Next i
MsChart1.ChartData = arrValues
```

The above code produces the chart shown below:

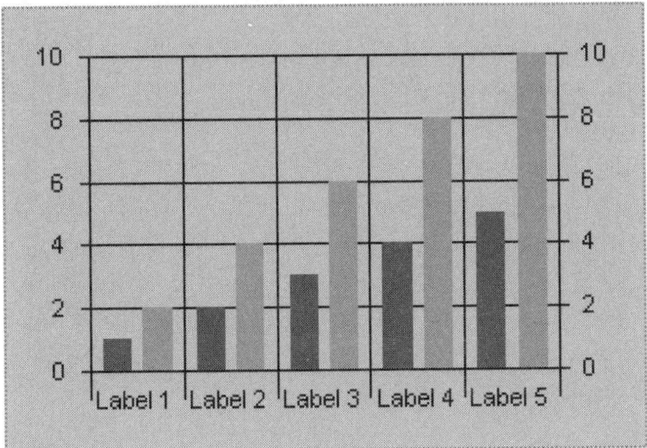

As you can see, creating a chart using the ChartData property can be quick and simple. However, the problem with using an array is getting the data into the array. Most users of this kind of data will probably prefer to use a spreadsheet program, such as Microsoft Excel, or perhaps a database program, such as Microsoft Access, to store and retrieve the data.

Setting or Returning a Data Point

Once you have created a chart, using an array from a spreadsheet or other data source, you may also want to set or return the value of a particular data point. This can be done by first setting the Row and (if applicable) Column properties, then setting or returning the Data property. For example, in a simple (single-series) chart, the following code would change the third data point.

```
With MSChart1
   ' Change third data point to 50.
   .Row = 3
   .Data = 50
End With
```

If the chart has more than one series use the Column property to designate the series, then set the Row and Data properties as above.

```
With MSChart1
   ' Set the second data point of the fourth series
   ' to 42.
   .Column = 4
   .Row = 2
   .Data = 42
End With
```

Using the PointActivated Event to Change a Data Point

If you've started to explore the MSChart control, you will notice that it has a large number of events. These events allow you to program the chart to respond to practically any action of the user. As an example of this programmability, the PointActivated event is used in the following example to show how a data point can be changed using the Series and DataPoint parameters. (The PointActivated event occurs whenever a data point is double-clicked.) The Series and DataPoint parameters correspond to the Column and Row properties, and can thus be used to set the Data property:

```
Private Sub MSChart1_PointActivated(Series As _
   Integer, DataPoint As Integer, MouseFlags As _
   Integer, Cancel As Integer)
   With MSChart1
      .Column = Series
      .Row = DataPoint
      .Data = InputBox _
      ("Change the data point:", , .Data)
   End With
End Sub
```

Data Binding the MSChart Control

The Microsoft Chart control is a data bound control, and allows you to graphically represent numeric data. Unlike other data bound controls, however, the Chart control cannot be used with the Remote Data Control, or the Data control. It can be used with the ADO Data Control, an ADO Recordset, and the Data Environment. This example will show how to open an ADO Recordset that contains the fields you want to display, and set the Chart control's DataSource property to the Recordset object. If the first field contains string data, that data will be used as the X axis labels.

The example below shows three series of data by first creating a Recordset object that has four fields; the first field contains the labels for the X axis, and remaining fields are displayed as series data.

```
Option Explicit
' Be sure to set a reference to the Microsoft ActiveX Data
' Objects 2.0 Library.
Private rsProducts As New ADODB.Recordset
Private cn As New ADODB.Connection

Private Sub Form_Load()
   Dim strQuery As String ' SQL query string.

   ' First change the path to a valid path for your machine.
   cn.ConnectionString = _
   "Provider=Microsoft.Jet.OLEDB.3.51;Data Source=" & _
   "C:\Program Files\Microsoft Visual Studio\VB98\nwind.mdb" ' <-Change this path.

   ' Open the connection.
   cn.Open

   ' Create a query that retrieves only four fields.
   strQuery = "SELECT ProductName, UnitPrice, " &_
   "UnitsInStock, UnitsOnOrder FROM Products WHERE SupplierID = 1"
   ' Open the recordset.
   rsProducts.Open strQuery, cn, adOpenKeyset
   ' Set the DataSource to the recordset.
   With MSChart1
      .ShowLegend = True
      Set .DataSource = rsProducts
   End With
End Sub
```

Using an Excel Worksheet to Populate an Array

If you have data stored in an Excel worksheet, you can use the GetObject method to get a reference to the workbook that contains the worksheet, then retrieve the values using the reference. To first get the reference, the only argument needed is the path to the workbook, as shown below:

```
' Place this code in the Declarations section.
Option Explicit
' If you are using Office 97, be sure to set a
' reference to Microsoft Excel 8.0 Object Library.
' If you are using Office 95, set a reference to
' Microsoft Excel 5.0 Object Library, and declare
' the variable as a Worksheet.
Dim wkbObj As WorkBook ' Declare an object variable.

Private Sub Form_Load()
   ' Then set the variable with the GetObject method.
   Set wkbObj = GetObject _
      ("C:\My Documents\MySpread.xls")
End Sub
```

Note In order to use Excel objects, you must set a reference to the Excel Objects library. To do this, click the Project menu, then click References. Search for the Excel Objects library and double-click it. Click OK. Also, note that if you're using GetObject with the Excel 5.0 Object Library, you must declare the variable as a WorkSheet; if you are using the Excel 8.0 Object Library, declare the variable as a WorkBook.

After setting a reference to the Excel object library, you can use the reference to walk through the Excel object model, populating the array with data from the worksheet. To do this, use the Range method in conjunction with the Value property to get the data from any single cell in a spreadsheet.

```
Dim arrPrices (1 to 7)
Dim i As Integer
For i = 1 to 7
   ' Fill the array with seven values from column B of
   ' the worksheet.
   arrPrices(i) = wkbObj.Worksheets(1) _
   .Range("B" & i + 1).Value
Next i
```

If you're not familiar with Excel spreadsheets, the following figure shows where the values are coming from.

Typical Excel Spreadsheet

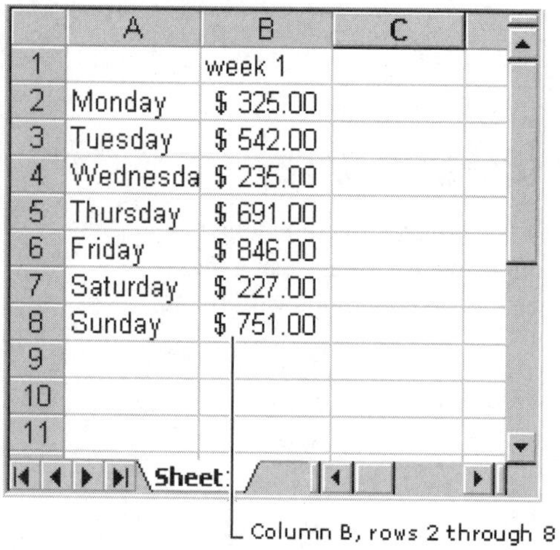

	A	B	C
1		week 1	
2	Monday	$ 325.00	
3	Tuesday	$ 542.00	
4	Wednesda	$ 235.00	
5	Thursday	$ 691.00	
6	Friday	$ 846.00	
7	Saturday	$ 227.00	
8	Sunday	$ 751.00	
9			
10			
11			

Sheet

Column B, rows 2 through 8

The layout of a spreadsheet, and the method used to refer to its cells, also maps conveniently to the method of referring to data points in the MSChart control. For example, a "column" in a spreadsheet (as in column "B" in the preceding illustration) corresponds to a "column" in the MSChart. And when you create a multi-series chart, each column corresponds to a series. Similarly, the "row" of a spreadsheet corresponds to the "row" in a "column" in the MSChart. For this reason, it helps to engineer a chart with a spreadsheet in mind.

For example, just as we first created a multi-series chart by increasing the dimensions of the array, we can now fill the array by using more than one column of the worksheet. In other words, to create a multi-series chart, we fill two (or more) columns of the spreadsheet with numbers, and use the columns to fill an array, as illustrated in the following code:

```
Dim arrData (1 to 7, 1 to 2)
Dim i As Integer
For i = 1 to 7
   ' Values from column A fill the first series of the
   ' array. If these values are strings, they become
   ' the labels for the rows.
   arrData(i, 1) = wkbObj.Worksheets(1) _
   .Range("A" & i + 1).Value

   ' Then values from column B fill the second.
   arrData(i, 2) = wkbObj.Worksheets(1) _
   .Range("B" & i + 1).Value
Next i
```

> **Tip** Use the CurrentRegion property to return the number of rows in an Excel column. You can then use this number to specify the upper bound of the array's first dimension.

The preceding code, used in conjunction with the spreadsheet shown in the figure above, will produce a chart that has each row labeled with the appropriate day of the week.

Manipulating the Chart Appearance

The MSChart control has many visible parts, all of which can be programmed. To get a grasp on how this is accomplished, it's useful to examine the following figure pointing out the parts of a chart.

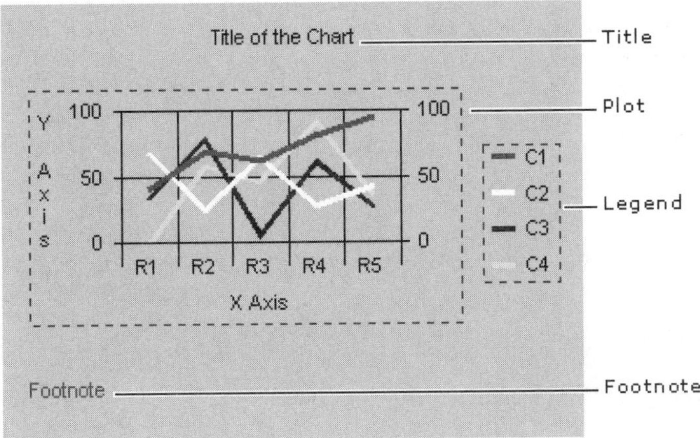

Each of these parts has a corresponding object in the MSChart control which can be used to change the format of practically any element of the chart. For example, the code below dramatically changes the look of a chart by changing the colors of the Plot object.

```
Private Sub cmdFormat_Click()
   ' First, change the chart type to a 3D chart to
   ' see all the parts of the plot.
   MSChart1.chartType = VtChChartType3dArea

   ' Color the backdrop light blue using
   ' the Plot object.
   With MSChart1.Plot.Backdrop
      ' No color will appear unless you set the style
      ' property to VtFillStyleBrush.
      .Fill.Style = VtFillStyleBrush
      .Fill.Brush.FillColor.Set 100, 255, 200
      ' Add a border.
      .Frame.Style = VtFrameStyleThickInner
      ' Set style to show a shadow.
      .Shadow.Style = VtShadowStyleDrop
   End With

   ' Color the wall of the plot yellow.
   With MSChart1.Plot
      ' Set the style to solid.
      .Wall.Brush.Style = VtBrushStyleSolid
      ' Set the color to yellow.
      .Wall.Brush.FillColor.Set 255, 255, 0
   End With

   With MSChart1.Plot ' Color the plot base blue.
      .PlotBase.BaseHeight = 200
      .PlotBase.Brush.Style = VtBrushStyleSolid
      .PlotBase.Brush.FillColor.Set 0, 0, 255
   End With
End Sub
```

Formatting Fonts

A very basic task with fonts might be to set the text of the chart's title. In order to do this, use the Title object's Text property:

```
MSChart1.Title.Text = "Year End Summary"
```

This is simple enough. The next question is how to change the font's attributes.

In order to format any text attribute on the chart, you must use the VtFont object. For example, to format the title, the following code will work:

```
With MSChart1.Title.VtFont
   .Name = "Algerian"
   .Style = VtFontStyleBold
   .Effect = VtFontEffectUnderline
   .Size = 14
   .VtColor.Set 255, 0, 255
End With
```

You can use the same technique with other parts of chart. The only difference lies in the object model. For example, to format the text attributes of the Legend area use the following code:

```
MSChart1.Legend.VtFont.Size = 18
```

Change the Scale Using the Type Property

To change the scale of the plot, you must specify that the y axis of the chart is going to be changed (changing the x axis has no visible effect). A convenient way to change the scale is to use a ComboBox control, as shown in the following code:

```
Private Sub Form_Load()
   ' Configure a ComboBox control named cmbScale.
   With cmbScale
      .AddItem "Log"
      .AddItem "Percent"
      .AddItem "Linear"
      .ListIndex = 0
   End With
End Sub

Private Sub cmbScale_Click()
   ' The ComboBox has three items: Log, Percent,
   ' and Linear (the default scale).

   Select Case cmbScale.Text
   Case "Log"
      MSChart1.Plot.Axis(VtChAxisIdY) _
      .AxisScale.Type = VtChScaleTypeLogarithmic

      ' You must specify a LogBase to be used when
      ' switching the scale to Log. The base can be
      ' set to any value between 2 and 200.
      MSChart1.Plot.Axis(VtChAxisIdY).AxisScale _
      .LogBase = 10

   Case "Percent"
      MSChart1.Plot.Axis(VtChAxisIdY).AxisScale _
      .Type = VtChScaleTypePercent
      ' Set the PercentBasis to one of six types. For
```

```
      ' the sake of expediency, only one is shown.
      MSChart1.Plot.Axis(VtChAxisIdY).AxisScale _
      .PercentBasis = VtChPercentAxisBasisMaxChart

   Case "Linear"
      MSChart1.Plot.Axis(VtChAxisIdY).AxisScale _
      .Type = VtChScaleTypeLinear
   End Select
End Sub
```

Change the Color of MSChart Objects Using the CommonDialog Control

You may wish to allow the user to pick the colors assigned to chart elements (such as the color of series) using the CommonDialog control. In that case, you can use the following functions that mask the bytes returned by the CommonDialog control's Color property to return individual red, green, and blue values required by the Set method.

```
' Paste these functions into the Declarations section
' of the Form or Code Module.
Public Function RedFromRGB(ByVal rgb As Long) _
   As Integer
   ' The ampersand after &HFF coerces the number as a
   ' long, preventing Visual Basic from evaluating the
   ' number as a negative value. The logical And is
   ' used to return bit values.
   RedFromRGB = &HFF& And rgb
End Function

Public Function GreenFromRGB(ByVal rgb As Long) _
   As Integer
   ' The result of the And operation is divided by
   ' 256, to return the value of the middle bytes.
   ' Note the use of the Integer divisor.
   GreenFromRGB = (&HFF00& And rgb) \ 256
End Function

Public Function BlueFromRGB(ByVal rgb As Long) _
   As Integer
   ' This function works like the GreenFromRGB above,
   ' except you don't need the ampersand. The
   ' number is already a long. The result divided by
   ' 65536 to obtain the highest bytes.
   BlueFromRGB = (&HFF0000 And rgb) \ 65536
End Function
```

Using the functions in the preceding examples, you can take the Long value returned by the CommonDialog object, and set the color of MSChart objects. The example below allows the user to change the color of a Series by double-clicking it:

```
Private Sub MSChart1_SeriesActivated(Series As _
   Integer, MouseFlags As Integer, Cancel As Integer)
   ' The CommonDialog control is named dlgChart.
   Dim red, green, blue As Integer
   With dlgChart ' CommonDialog object
      .ShowColor
      red = RedFromRGB(.Color)
      green = GreenFromRGB(.Color)
      blue = BlueFromRGB(.Color)
   End With

   ' NOTE: Only the 2D and 3D line charts use the
   ' Pen object. All other types use the Brush.

   If MSChart1.chartType <> VtChChartType2dLine Or _
   MSChart1.chartType <> VtChChartType3dLine Then
      MSChart1.Plot.SeriesCollection(Series). _
         DataPoints(-1).Brush.FillColor. _
         Set red, green, blue
   Else
      MSChart1.Plot.SeriesCollection(Series).Pen. _
         VtColor.Set red, green, blue
   End If
End Sub
```

Three-Dimensional Features of the MSChart Control

You can use the MSChart control's three-dimensional chart features to lend a certain sparkle to a report.

Rotate the Chart

You can manually rotate a 3D chart by using the CTRL key and the mouse. To do this, hold down the CTRL key, click on the chart, then hold down the mouse as you drag across the chart image. The following figures show the same chart, before and after rotation.

Before Rotation

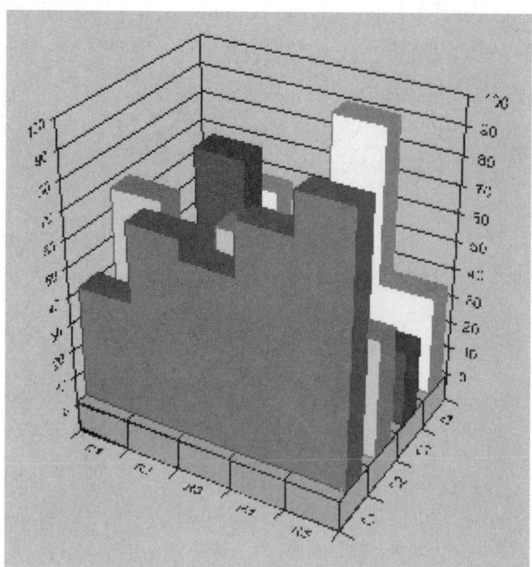

After Rotation

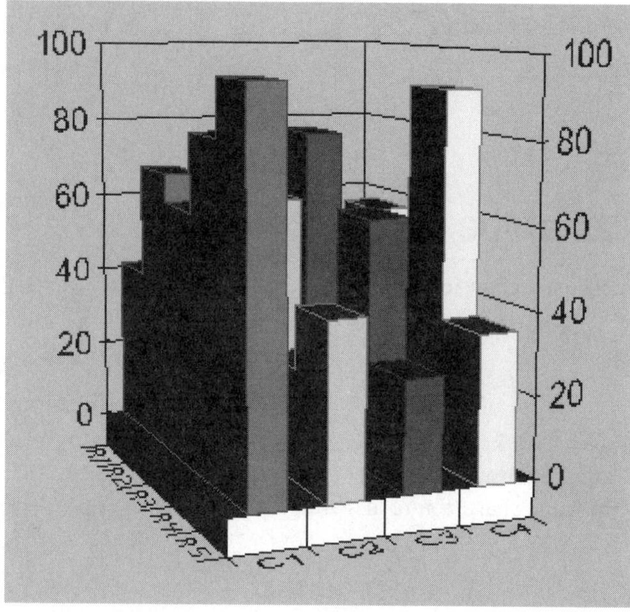

Rotating the Chart Programmatically

You can also rotate a 3D chart by using the Set method of the View3D object.

```
MSChart1.Plot.View3D.Set 10,100
```

Seeing the Light

In addition to rotating a 3D chart, you can also use the Light feature to control how a virtual light shines on the chart. In practice, the appearance of a chart changes as it rotates because its surfaces reflect steady light in continually changing angles.

By default, the chart comes with one LightSource. The following code will set the four parameters that affect the LightSource. These will be explained later. In the meantime, paste the code into a standard EXE project, and run it.

```
Private Sub Form_Load()
   With MSChart1
      .chartType = VtChChartType3dArea
      .Plot.Light.LightSources(1).Set 10, 10, 10, 1
   End With
End Sub
```

This code results in a chart that appears to have a light source shining on it from the lower left of the screen. As the chart is rotated, surfaces which face the light directly get brighter.

Light Basics

The LightSource feature is comprised of two parts:

- Ambient light: As its name suggests, this is light that has no specific source and thus no directionality.
- LightSources: a directional light that can be shone on the chart from any angle, with variable intensity. More than one light source can be created.

Ambient Light

Ambient light has a noticeable effect when you are using the LightSources. Ambient light simply bathes the chart evenly in a light that comes from no particular direction. You can set the AmbientIntensity property to any value between 0 and 1, with 0 turning off the light, and 1 increasing it to its maximum. For instance, to turn the ambient on to one quarter of its brightness, set the AmbientIntensity property to .25.

> **Tip** As you experiment with the LightSources, it is useful to set the property to 0. With no ambient light, the effect of the LightSource is accentuated.

The EdgeVisible and EdgeIntensity properties work together to highlight the edges of the chart. When the AmbientIntensity is set to a low value, you can set the EdgeIntensity property to a high value. The result is that the edges seem to glow, as shown in the following figure:

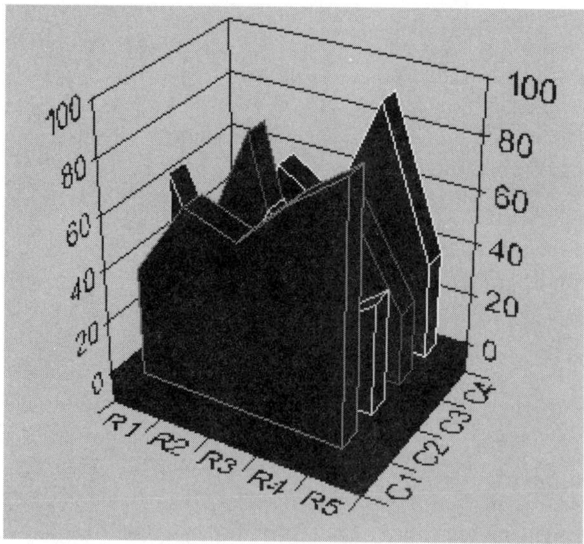

LightSources

Each LightSource in the LightSources collection has an Intensity property which — like the AmbientIntensity property — you can set to a value between 0 and 1. This property sets the brightness of the individual LightSource.

Each LightSource also can be positioned in the virtual space that surrounds the chart by setting the X, Y, and Z properties. By varying these properties, you can specify the direction from which the light will shine on the chart.

Using the Add Method to Add a LightSource

By default, the MSChart contains one LightSource member in the LightSources collection. You can, however, add LightSource members using the Add method, as shown below:

```
MSChart1.Plot.Light.LightSources.Add 10, 10, 10, 1
```

The parameters for the Add method include values for X, Y, and Z, which allow you to specify exactly the angle from which the light will shine, and a value for Intensity of the light.

Using the Multimedia Control

The Multimedia control allows you to manage Media Control Interface (MCI) devices. These devices include: sound boards, MIDI sequencers, CD-ROM drives, audio players, videodisc players, and videotape recorders and players.

This Multimedia control contains a set of push buttons that issue MCI commands which resemble the commands (functions) you would expect to see on a typical compact disc player or videotape recorder.

The Multimedia control

The buttons are defined, from left to right, as Prev, Next, Play, Pause, Back, Step, Stop, Record, and Eject.

Possible Use

- To manage the recording and playback of MCI devices.

Multimedia Requirements and Supported Device Types

Which buttons you use, and the functions provided to you by the Multimedia control, depend on the hardware and software configurations of a particular machine. For instance, if your application uses specific multimedia devices and drivers, they must be installed on the user's machine.

Driver support for many multimedia devices (audio and video files, for instance) is provided for in the Windows 95 and Windows NT operating systems. Other devices, such as digital audio tape players or image scanners require separate drivers, are usually provided by the manufacturer.

Devices are considered to be of two types: *simple* and *compound*. Simple multimedia devices do not require a data file for playback. For example, when Videodisc and CD audio players are opened, you play, rewind, or forward through "tracks." Compound devices, however, require a data file for playback.

The following table lists some of the devices supported by the Multimedia control and the string required by the DeviceType property to use the device. Those listing an accompanying file type are compound devices.

Device type	String	File Type	Description
CD audio	CDAudio		CD audio player
Digital Audio Tape	DAT		Digital audio tape player
Digital video	DigitalVideo		Digital video in a window (not GDI-based)
Other	Other		Undefined MCI device
Overlay	Overlay		Overlay device
Scanner	Scanner		Image scanner

(continued)

(continued)

Device type	String	File Type	Description
Sequencer	Sequencer	.mid	Musical Instrument Digital Interface (MIDI) sequencer
Vcr	VCR		Video cassette recorder or player
AVI	AVIVideo	.avi	Audio Visual Interleaved video.
Videodisc	Videodisc		Videodisc player
Wave audio	Waveaudio	.wav	Wave device that plays digitized waveform files

MCI Commands

The Multimedia control uses a set of high-level, device-independent commands, known as Media Control Interface commands, that control various multimedia devices. Many of these commands correspond directly to a button on the Multimedia control. For instance, the Play command corresponds to the Play button.

The Multimedia control is essentially a Visual Basic interface to this command set. Commands like Play or Close have equivalents in the MCI command structure of the Win32 API. For instance, Play corresponds to MCI_PLAY. The following table lists the MCI commands used by the Multimedia control, along with their Win32 equivalents:

Command	MCI Command	Description
Open	MCI_OPEN	Opens a MCI device.
Close	MCI_CLOSE	Closes a MCI device.
Play	MCI_PLAY	Plays a MCI device.
Pause	MCI_PAUSE or MCI_RESUME	Pauses playing or recording.
Stop	MCI_STOP	Stops a MCI device.
Back	MCI_STEP	Steps backward through available tracks.
Step	MCI_STEP	Steps forward through available tracks.
Prev	MCI_SEEK	Goes to the beginning of the current track using the Seek command. If executed within three seconds of the previous Prev command, goes to the beginning of the previous track or to the beginning of the first track if at the first track.

(continued)

Command	MCI Command	Description
Next	MCI_SEEK	Goes to the beginning of the next track (if at last track, goes to the beginning of the last track) using the Seek command.
Seek	MCI_SEEK	Seeks track forward or backward.
Record	MCI_RECORD	Records MCI device input.
Eject	MCI_SET	Ejects Audio CD from CD drive.
Save	MCI_SAVE	Saves an open file.

In Visual Basic, these commands are initiated using the Multimedia control's Command property. For example:

```
MMControl1.Command = "Open"
```

While the Multimedia control's implementation of the MCI command set is sufficient for most uses, directly utilizing the Win32 API can provide advanced programming functions and techniques.

For More Information For additional information on the MCI commands see the *Microsoft Multimedia Development Kit Programmer's Workbook* or the *Microsoft Windows Software Development Kit Multimedia Programmer's Reference*. These references, and a wealth of other information on the MCI commands, are available on the Microsoft Developer Network CD.

Programming the Multimedia Control

The Multimedia Control can be either visible or invisible at run time by setting the Enabled and Visible properties. By default, the Enabled and Visible properties are set to True and the control is visible at run time.

If you do not want the user to interact directly with the buttons on the Multimedia control but want to use the control for its multimedia functionality, set the Visible property to False. An application can control MCI devices with or without user interaction.

To enable or make individual buttons visible or invisible, you set each button's visible and enabled properties. For example, the Back button contains the properties BackEnabled and BackVisible. Each of the nine push buttons have corresponding properties.

In most cases, the default functionality of the individual buttons is sufficient to manage MCI devices. However, the Multimedia control contains run-time properties which allow you to augment or redefine the button commands.

The Notify, NotifyMessage, and NotifyValue properties provide valuable feedback on the failure or completion of a command.

Opening the MCI Device

After you place the Multimedia control on a form, whether it is set to be visible or not, the first step is accessing the MCI device. To do this, you set a number of run-time properties. For example:

```
'Set initial property values of the media device
MMControl1.Notify = False
MMControl1.Wait = True
MMControl1.Shareable = False
MMControl1.DeviceType = "CDAudio"
```

The Notify property, if set to True, generates a Done event when next command is completed. The Done event provides useful feedback indicating the success or failure of the command. The Wait property determines whether or not the Multimedia control waits for the next command to complete before returning control to the application. The Shareable property either restricts or allows use of the media device by other applications or processes. The DeviceType property is used to specify the type of MCI device.

Finally, the Open command is used to open the MCI device.

```
'Open the media device
MMControl1.Command = "Open"
```

When the control is visible, setting these properties and issuing the Open command enables the push buttons of the Multimedia control that are inherently supported by the MCI device. For instance, opening the cdaudio device enables the Prev, Next, Play, and Eject buttons. When Play is pressed, the Stop and Pause buttons are enabled.

Multiple instances of the Multimedia control can be added to a form to provide concurrent control of several MCI devices. You use one control per device.

Managing Multimedia Resources

To properly manage multimedia and system resources, you should close those MCI devices that are open before exiting your application. You can place the following statement in the Form_Unload procedure to close an open MCI device when the form containing the Multimedia control is unloaded.

```
Private Sub Form_Unload (Cancel as Integer)
   Form1.MMControl1.Command = "Close"
End Sub
```

Using the Error and ErrorMessage Properties

You can handle errors encountered by the Multimedia control using the Error and ErrorMessage properties. You can test for an error condition after each command. For example, following the Open command, you check the value of the Error property to test for the existence of a CD drive. If the CD drive is not available, an error message is returned. For example:

```
If Form1.MMControl1.Error Then
   MsgBox Form1.MMControl1.ErrorMessage,vbCritical, "CD Player not installed or not
working properly"
End If
```

For More Information See "ErrorMessage Property (Multimedia MCI Control)" and "Error Property (Multimedia MCI Control)" in the *Microsoft Visual Basic 6.0 Controls Reference* volume of the *Microsoft Visual Basic 6.0 Reference Library.*

Multimedia Control Scenario: Creating a Simple Audio CD Player

Using a few of the techniques discussed in the section, "Using the Multimedia Control," you can create a simple audio CD player application that illustrates features of the Multimedia control. This scenario uses one form and one instance of the Multimedia control and assumes that both an audio CD-compatible CD-ROM drive and a sound card are installed in the computer.

To begin, start a new project in Visual Basic. Add an instance of the Multimedia control to the form. In the form's Form_Load event procedure add the following code:

```
'Set initial property values of the media device
Form1.MMControl1.Notify = False
Form1.MMControl1.Wait = True
Form1.MMControl1.Shareable = False
Form1.MMControl1.DeviceType = "CDAudio"

 'Open the media device
Form1.MMControl1.Command = "Open"
```

Opening the MCI device in the Form_Load procedure initializes the device at run time. If an audio CD is loaded into the CD drive, the appropriate buttons on the Multimedia control are enabled.

A simple audio CD player

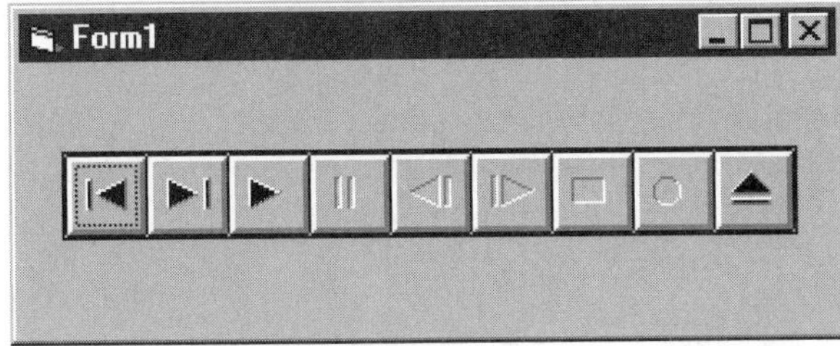

The Multimedia control recognizes what actions are relevant for the current state of a device. Therefore, the appropriate buttons are automatically enabled when supported MCI devices are opened with the Multimedia control. In this example, when the Play button is pressed, the Stop and Pause buttons are enabled. If the CD is removed from the CD drive while the application is running, all the buttons become disabled.

Sample Application: MCITest.vbp

The MCITest.vbp sample application, which is listed in the Samples directory, builds on this scenario and provides you with advanced programming techniques using the Multimedia control.

Using the PictureClip Control

The PictureClip control stores multiple images that can be used by other Visual Basic controls. All images are contained in a single bitmap. Selected regions can then be "clipped" from the bitmap and used with a PictureBox control to create animations, or with multiple PictureBox controls to create a toolbox, for instance.

The PictureClip control can be used with any control that assigns a Picture object to a Picture property, such as the PictureBox, Image, and CommandButton controls.

Storing multiple images in a single PictureClip control conserves Windows resources and speeds up retrieval of the images. The PictureClip control is similar to the ImageList control in this way; however, they differ in that all image resources in the PictureClip control must be contained in a single bitmap whereas the ImageList control is a collection of separate bitmaps.

Possible Uses

- To create an image resource bitmap which stores all the images needed for an animation or a toolbox.

Creating a PictureClip Image

The first step in using a PictureClip control is creating the image resource bitmap. The PictureClip control only supports 16-color bitmap (.bmp) images. When creating a set of images, collect all the separate images and cut and paste them into a single bitmap, as shown below.

A PictureClip control containing a resource bitmap

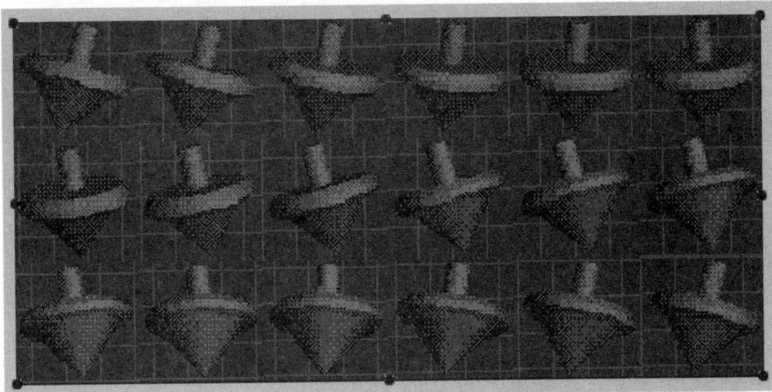

Note You need to make sure that each image is the same size as the others so that when individual images are retrieved into a PictureBox control, for example, they fill the space uniformly. In the example above, each image of the spinning top is a square of equal size.

Loading the Resource Bitmap into PictureClip

After creating an image resource bitmap, load it into the PictureClip control. The PictureClip control has a Property Pages dialog box which allows the bitmap to be loaded into the control and the grid set by specifying the number of columns and rows.

To load a resource bitmap into the PictureClip control at design time

1. Start a new project in Visual Basic.
2. Add a PictureClip control to the form.
3. From the Properties window of the PictureClip control select the **Custom** option or right-click on the control and select **Properties**. The **Property Pages** dialog box will open.
4. Select the **Picture** tab and then click the **Browse** button to locate the bitmap. The selected bitmap is displayed in the Preview window.

Loading a resource bitmap into the PictureClip control

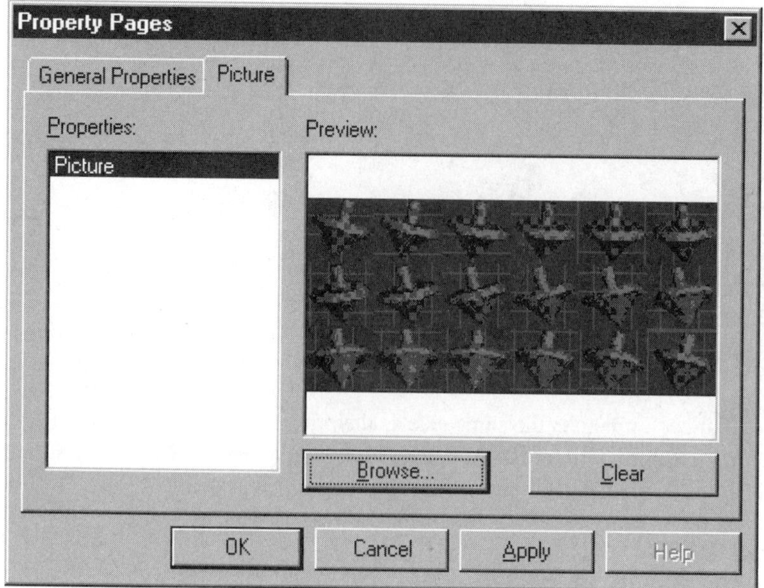

Loading the Resource Bitmap at Run Time

The resource image bitmap can also be loaded into the PictureClip control at run time using the Picture property, as in the following example:

```
PictureClip1.Picture = LoadPicture("c:\Program _
   Files\Microsoft Visual _
   Basic\Samples\PicClip\Redtop.bmp")
' If you have installed the Visual Basic sample applications, the PicClip
' project can be found in the \samples\VB98\ directory
```

Retrieving Images from the PictureClip Control

Once you've created and loaded an image resource bitmap into the PictureClip control, you can determine how you want to retrieve each image.

You can randomly select any portion of the image resource bitmap as the clipping region using the ClipX and ClipY properties to determine the upper-left corner of the clipping region and the ClipHeight and ClipWidth properties to define the area of the clipping region. The Clip property then contains the clipped region.

You can divide the image resource bitmap into a specified number of rows and columns. The rows and columns create cells which can then be accessed using an index number. The cells are indexed beginning at 0 and increase from left to right and top to bottom using the GraphicCell property.

Setting Rows and Columns at Design Time

Using the Property Pages dialog box, you can set the number of rows and columns at design time. In the example above, there are 18 red top images divided into 3 rows and 6 columns.

To set the number of rows and columns at design time

1. From the Properties window of the PictureClip control select the **Custom** option or right-click on the control and select **Properties**. The **Property Pages** dialog box will open.
2. Select the **General Properties** tab.
3. Select the number of rows and columns that correspond to the images in the resource bitmap. Click **OK**.

Setting the number of rows and columns

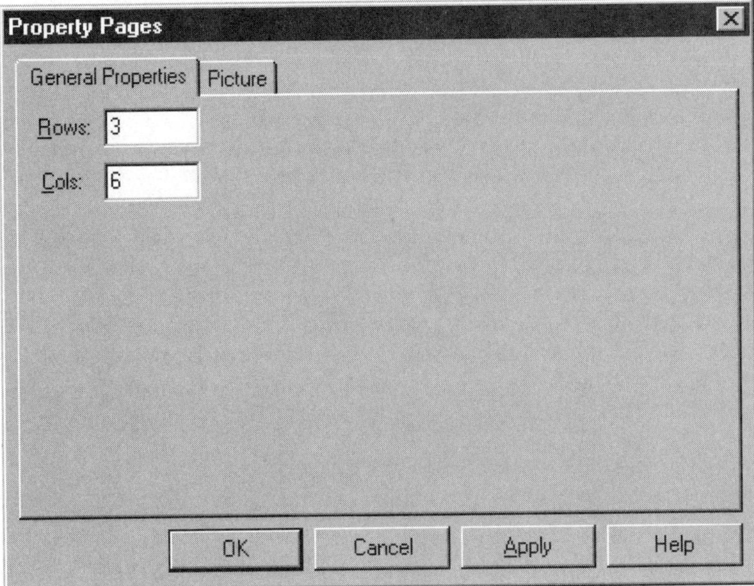

Selecting Cells at Run Time

You use the GraphicCell property to specify which cell in the image resource bitmap of the PictureClip control you want to load into a PictureBox control. The following example loads a single image (one cell) into a PictureBox control in the Form_Load event procedure:

```
Private Sub Form_Load()
   PictureClip1.Picture = LoadPicture("c:\Program _
      Files\Microsoft Visual _
      Basic\Samples\PicClip\Redtop.bmp")
   PictureClip1.Cols = 6
   PictureClip1.Rows = 3
   Picture1.ScaleMode = vbPixels
   Picture1.Picture = PictureClip1.GraphicCell(2)
End Sub
```

Note In Visual Basic, the default ScaleMode for forms and picture boxes is twips. Set ScaleMode to vbPixels for all controls that display pictures from a PictureClip control.

If you previously defined the numbers of rows and columns using the PictureClip Property Pages, you can simply load the image into the PictureBox control with the GraphicCell property. If not, you must specify the number of rows and columns by using the Cols and Rows properties. To use the GraphicCell property you must define at least one column and row.

Sample Application: Redtop.vbp

The Redtop.vbp sample application, which is listed in the Samples directory, builds on some of the examples shown above and demonstrates how to create a simple animation using the PictureClip control.

Using the ProgressBar Control

A ProgressBar control allows you to graphically represent the progress of a transaction. The control consists of a frame that is filled as the transaction occurs. The Value property determines how much of the control has been filled. The Min and Max properties set the limits of the control.

Use the ProgressBar whenever an operation will take more than a few seconds to complete. You must also know how long the process will take by using a known end point and setting it as the Max property of the control.

Tip Giving the user visual feedback on how much time remains on a lengthy operation gives the perception of improved performance.

Possible Uses

- To inform the user of progress as a file transfer occurs over a network.
- To reflect the state of a process that takes more than a few seconds.
- To inform the user of progress as a complex algorithm is being calculated.

Use the Value Property with the Min and Max Properties to Show Progress

To show progress in an operation, the Value property is continually incremented until a maximum — defined by the Max property — is reached. Thus the number of chunks displayed by the controls is always a ratio of the Value property to the Min and Max properties. For example, if the Min property is set to 1, and the Max property is set to 100, a Value property of 50 will cause the control to display 50 percent of the chunks, as shown:

Set the Max Property to a Known Limit

To program the ProgressBar, you must have a limit to which the Value property will climb. For example, if you are performing downloading a file, and your application can determine how large the files is in kilobytes, you can set the Max property to that number. As the file is downloaded, your application must also have some way of determining how many kilobytes have been downloaded; set the Value property to that number.

In cases where a Max property can't be determined in advance, you may want to use the Animation control to continuously show an animation until a Stop method is invoked in a terminate event.

For More Information For information on using the Animation control, see "Using the Animation Control" earlier in this chapter.

Hide the ProgressBar with the Visible Property

A progress bar usually doesn't appear until an operation has begun, and disappears again after the operation ends. Set the Visible property to True to show the control at the start of an operation, and reset the property to False to hide the control when the operation finishes.

ProgressBar Scenario 1: Inform User of TreeView Population Status

If you are using a TreeView control to view a database, populating the tree may take some time. In that instance, you can use the ProgressBar control to inform the user of the status of the operation.

In this scenario, the Biblio.mdb database is loaded into the TreeView control using a Do Until loop. Before the loop begins the ProgressBar control is unhidden. Through each iteration of the loop, the Value property of the ProgressBar control is updated with the PercentPosition property of the Recordset object. When the loop finishes, the ProgressBar control is hidden again.

Sample Application: DataTree.vbp

The code examples in this topic are taken from the DataTree.vbp sample application, which is listed in the Samples directory.

Objects Used

The following example uses the following objects:

- Form named "frmTreeView"
- ProgressBar Control named "prgLoad"
- TreeView control named "tvwDB"
- CommandButton control named "cmdLoad"

To show a ProgressBar while a TreeView control is being populated

1. In the Form object's Load event. hide the ProgressBar and set its Max property to 100.
2. In the TreeView population code, populate the tree with a Do Until statement.
3. When the loop ends, hide the ProgressBar.

In the Form Object's Load Event, Hide the ProgressBar and Set the Max Property to 100

A progress bar is most effective when it is visible only for the duration of the time-intensive process. To this end, you can use the Form object's Load event to set the Visible property of the control to False.

In this scenario, the Recordset object's PercentPosition property will be used. Since this property returns a number representing a percentage between 0 and 100, the Max property should be set to 100 when the form is initialized. (By default, the Min property is set to 0.) The following code hides the ProgressBar control and sets its Max property to 100.

```
Private Sub Form_Load()
   prgLoad.Visible = False
   prgLoad.Max = 100
End Sub
```

Populate the Tree with a Do Until Statement

Note The following code builds upon the code found in "TreeView Scenario1: Binding the TreeView to the Biblio.MDB Database." The working code can also be found in the DataTree.vbp sample application.

To populate a TreeView control from a database, you can use a Do Until loop. Schematically, the code might look like this:

```
' Presuming a Recordset object variable named
' "rsTitles" has been set to a valid database
' table.
Do Until rsTitles.EOF
   ' Using the current record, create a Node
   ' object.
   Set mNode = TreeView.Nodes.Add()
   ' Set properties of the Node.
   mNode.Text = rsTitles!Fields(1).Value
   ' Move to the next record.
   rsTitles.MoveNext
Loop
```

To update the ProgressBar control, use the PercentPosition property of the Recordset object. This property returns the position of the current recordset as a percentage of the total number of records. The code to update the ProgressBar should then be placed somewhere within the loop, as shown:

```
Do Until rsTitles.EOF
   ' Update the ProgressBar control.
   prgLoad.Value = rsTitles.PercentPosition

   Set mNode = TreeView.Nodes.Add()
   ' Set properties of the Node.
   mNode.Text = rsTitles!Fields(1).Value
   ' Move to the next record.
   rsTitles.MoveNext
Loop
```

When the Loop Ends, Hide the ProgressBar

Once the TreeView control has been entirely loaded with Node objects, you can hide the ProgressBar control, as shown:

```
Private Sub cmdLoad_Click()
   ' Show the ProgressBar control.
   prgLoad.Visible = True

Do Until rsTitles.EOF
      ' Update the ProgressBar control.
      prgLoad.Value = rsTitles.PercentPosition

      Set mNode = TreeView.Nodes.Add()
      ' Set properties of the Node.
      mNode.Text = rsTitles!Fields(1).Value
      ' Move to the next record.
      rsTitles.MoveNext
   Loop
   ' Hide the ProgressBar control.
   prgLoad.Visible = False
End Sub
```

ProgressBar Control Scenario 2: Using the ProgressBar to Show a TimeOut Interval

Applications that create processes over networks often have a "TimeOut" interval. This is a predetermined period of time after which the user will be presented with the choice of canceling a process, or continuing to wait. One way of graphically representing the TimeOut interval is with the ProgressBar control.

The following example uses the following objects:

- Form Object named "frmTimer"
- ProgressBar control named "prgBar1"
- Timer control named "tmrTimer"
- CommandButton control named "cmdBegin"

To create a progress bar that reflects a TimeOut interval

1. In the Form's Load event, set a Timer control's Interval property to 1000.
2. Set the ProgressBar control's Max property to the TimeOut Interval.
3. Begin the Timer with the Enabled property.
4. In the Timer control's Timer event, declare a Static variable to count the number of intervals.
5. Set the ProgressBar's value to the variable.
6. Test to see if the ProgressBar's value is the Max property.

In the Form's Load event, Set the Timer Control's Interval Property to 1000

In the Form object's Load event, configure the Timer control's Interval property. Because it's more useful to time a process in seconds, set the Interval to 1000 (milliseconds, or 1 second). Thus, at one second intervals, the ProgressBar control's Value property is updated.

```
tmrTimer.Interval = 1000
```

In the Form Load event, Set the ProgressBar Control's Max Property to the TimeOut Interval

The Load event is also where you set the Max property of the ProgressBar. The value of the Max property should be the number of seconds you want the Timer to continue before being disabled. However, to accurately reflect the number of seconds that must elapse, the ProgressBar's Min property should be set to 1.

The Load event can also be used to hide the ProgressBar by setting its Visible property to False. The following code shows the entire Load event with the previous code included.

```
Private Sub Form_Load()
    prgBar1.Visible = False
    tmrTimer.Interval = 1000
    prgBar1.Max = 10 ' Timer will go for 10 seconds.
End Sub
```

Begin the Timer with the Enabled Property

To start the timer, you must use the Enabled property. When you begin to time any process, you should also show the ProgressBar, as shown:

```
Private Sub cmdBegin_Click()
    prgBar1.Visible = True
    tmrTimer.Enabled = True
End Sub
```

In the Timer Event, Declare a Static Variable and Set it to 1

In the Timer event, declare a static variable. This allows you to efficiently increment the variable every time the Timer event occurs. But as we don't wish to count from 0, we must also set the variable to 1, using the IsEmpty function, as shown:

```
Static intTime
If IsEmpty(intTime) Then intTime = 1
```

Set the ProgressBar's Value to the Variable

Each time the Timer event occurs, the ProgressBar's Value property must be set to the value of the static variable:

```
prgBar1.Value = intTime
```

Test to See If the ProgressBar's Value is the Max Property.

After the ProgressBar's Value property has been updated, the variable must be tested to see if the TimeOut limit has occurred. If it has been reached, the variable must be reset to 1, the ProgressBar control hidden and its Value property reset to 1, and the Timer control disabled. If the limit hasn't been reached, then the variable is incremented by one. These steps are all implemented with an If statement, in the Timer event, as shown:

```
Private Sub tmrTimer_Timer()
    Static intTime ' Declare the static variable.
    ' The first time, the variable will be empty.
    ' Set it to 1 if it is an empty variable.
    If IsEmpty(intTime) Then intTime = 1
```

```
    prgBar1.Value = intTime ' Update the ProgressBar.

    If intTime = prgBar1.Max Then
       Timer1.Enabled = False
       prgBar1.Visible = False
       intTime = 1
       prgBar1.Value = prgBar1.Min
    Else
       intTime = intTime + 1
    End If
End Sub
```

The Complete Code

Here is the complete code for the example described in this topic:

```
Private Sub Form_Load()
   prgBar1.Visible = False
   tmrTimer.Interval = 1000
   prgBar1.Max = 10 ' Timer will go for 10 seconds.
End Sub

Private Sub cmdBegin_Click()
   prgBar1.Visible = True
   tmrTimer.Enabled = True
End Sub

Private Sub tmrTimer_Timer()
   Static intTime ' Declare the static variable.
   ' The first time, the variable will be empty.
   ' Set it to 1 if it is an empty variable.
   If IsEmpty(intTime) Then intTime = 1

   prgBar1.Value = intTime ' Update the ProgressBar.

   If intTime = prgBar1.Max Then
      Timer1.Enabled = False
      prgBar1.Visible = False
      intTime = 1
      prgBar1.Value = prgBar1.Min
   Else
      intTime = intTime + 1
   End If
End Sub
```

Using the RichTextBox Control

The RichTextBox control allows the user to enter and edit text while also providing more advanced formatting features than the conventional TextBox control.

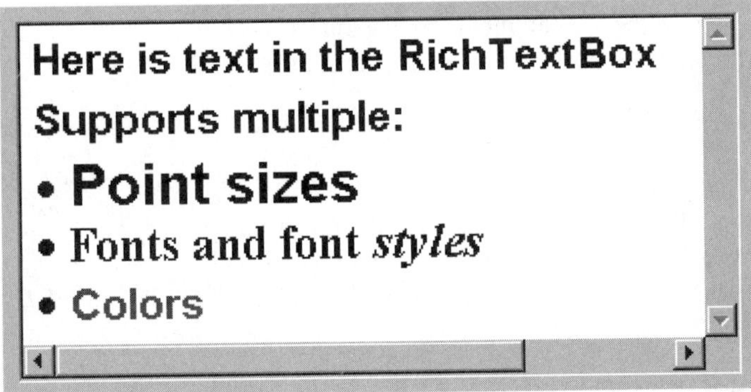

The RichTextBox control provides a number of properties you can use to apply formatting to any portion of text within the control. Using these properties, you can make text bold or italic, change its color, and create superscripts and subscripts. You can also adjust paragraph formatting by setting both left and right indents, as well as hanging indents.

Possible Uses

- As a "bottomless" text box, to allow an application to read extremely large text files.
- To implement a full-featured text editor into any application.

Features

- Open and save files in both the RTF format and ASCII text format. You can use methods of the control (LoadFile and SaveFile) to directly read and write files, or use properties of the control, such as SelRTF and TextRTF, in conjunction with Visual Basic's file input/output statements.
- Load the contents of an .rtf file into the RichTextBox control simply by dragging the file (from the Windows 95 Explorer, for example), or a highlighted portion of a file used in another application (such as Microsoft Word), and dropping the contents directly onto the control.
- Set the FileName property to load the contents of an .rtf or .txt file into the control.
- Print all or part of the text in a RichTextBox control using the SelPrint method.

- Bind the RichTextBox control with a Data control to a Memo field in a Microsoft Access database or a similar large capacity text field in other databases (such as a TEXT data type field in SQL Server).
- Programmatically add embedded objects such as bitmaps, icons, application icons into the control at run time using the OLEObject collection's Add method. At both design time and run time, drag and drop any embedded object, including documents such as Microsoft Excel spreadsheets and Microsoft Word documents, into the control.

Set Scrollbars at Design Time

By default, the RichTextBox doesn't include scrollbars. At run time, if a large file is loaded into the control, the end user will not be able to see all that is in the file. To allow the user to scroll easily, set the ScrollBars property to 1 (horizontal), 2 (vertical), or 3 (both). This must be done at design time, because the ScrollBars property is read-only at run time.

Open and Save Files with the LoadFile and SaveFile Methods

You can easily open or save an RTF file with the RichTextBox control by using the LoadFile and SaveFile methods. To open a file, use a CommonDialog control to supply the path name as shown:

```
Private Sub OpenFile()
   ' The RichTextBox control is named "rtfData."
   ' The CommonDialog is named "dlgOpenFile."
   ' Declare a String variable for file name.
   ' Show the Open File dialog box, and set the
   ' variable to the filename.
   Dim strOpen As String
   dlgOpenFile.ShowOpen
   strOpen = dlgOpenFile.FileName
   ' Use LoadFile method to open the file.
   rtfData.LoadFile strOpen
End Sub
```

To save a file is just as easy, using the SaveFile method:

```
Private Sub SaveFile()
   Dim strNewFile As String
   dlgOpenFile.ShowSave
   strNewFile = dlgOpenFile.FileName
   rtfData.SaveFile strNewFile
End Sub
```

Note If a file contains RTF codes that aren't supported by the control, the affected text only will not appear in the RichTextBox control.

Use the SelFontName, SelFontSize, and SelFontColor to Set Font Attributes

To change the font attributes of text in the RichTextBox control, use the SelFontName, SelFontSize, and SelFontColor properties.

The ComboBox control is often used to display a range of choices for these properties. Subsequently, the ComboBox control's Click event can be used to change the property. The following code first populates a ComboBox control named "cmbFonts" in the Form object's Load event. The Click event is then used to change the SelFontName property of a RichTextBox control:

```
Private Sub Form_Load()
   Dim i As Integer
   With cmbFonts
      For i = 0 to Screen.Fonts.Count - 1
      .AddItem Screen.Fonts(i).Text
   End With
End Sub

Private Sub cmbFonts_Click()
   rtfData.SelFontName = cmbFonts.Text
End Sub
```

> **Important** These properties only affect selected text, or, if no text is selected, the text that is typed after the current cursor location.

Format Indents, Hanging Indents, and Bulleted Paragraphs

Another feature of the RichTextBox control is its ability to create paragraphs with indents, hanging indents, and bulleted paragraphs. The three styles are shown here:

Indents and bulleted indents (rtf_3ind.bmp)

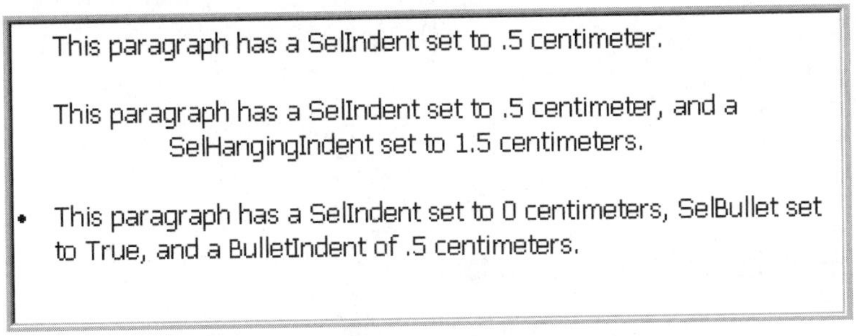

This paragraph has a SelIndent set to .5 centimeter.

This paragraph has a SelIndent set to .5 centimeter, and a SelHangingIndent set to 1.5 centimeters.

• This paragraph has a SelIndent set to 0 centimeters, SelBullet set to True, and a BulletIndent of .5 centimeters.

As with the SelFontName, SelFontSize, and SelFontColor properties, the end user must select a paragraph or range of paragraphs before applying these attributes. Thus, assuming the user had selected the second paragraph only, the code to create an indent and hanging indent would be as follows:

```
' Assuming the control is named "rtfData."
rtfData.SelIndent = .5
rtfdata.SelHangingIndent = 1.5
```

Note that the number used to set the SelIndent, SelHangingIndent, BulletIndent and other properties depends upon the ScaleMode property of the container of the RichTextBox control. For example, if the RichTextBox's container is a Form object, and you change the Form object's ScaleMode property from 7 (centimeters) to 1 (twips), the SelIndent property must change from .5 (centimeters) to 283 (twips). This is because one centimeter = 567 twips.

Also note that the SelBullet property of a paragraph must be set to True for a paragraph to have the bullet style.

Use the SelChange Event for Notification of Attribute Changes

To notify the user of the current attributes of any selected text, use the SelChange event, which occurs whenever the insertion point moves, or the selection has changed. The following example uses a Toolbar control to notify the user of changes in the SelBold property.

```
Private Sub rtfData_SelChange()
   ' Reset the Value property of a Toolbar
   ' Button object. The Toolbar control is
   ' named "tlbRTF."

   ' SelBold returns 0, -1, or Null. If it's Null
   ' then set the MixedState property to True.

   Select Case rtfData.SelBold
   Case 0 ' Not bold.
      tlbRTF.Buttons("bold").Value = tbrUnpressed
   Case -1 ' Bold.
      tlbRTF.Buttons("bold").Value = tbrPressed
   Case Else ' Mixed state.
      tlbRTF.Buttons("bold").MixedState = True
   End Select
End Sub
```

Use the SelPrint Method to Print the RichTextBox Contents

To print from the RichTextBox control, use the SelPrint method. This method requires one argument, the hDC property of the Printer object that will print the RichTextBox control's contents. If any text is selected by the user, only the selected text will be printed. If no text is selected, the entire contents of the control will be printed.

The following code uses the CommonDialog control to display a Printer dialog box when the user clicks a CommandButton control. The Flags property disables page numbers, and allows the user to choose various options on the dialog box:

```
Private Sub cmdPrint_Click()
   ' The CommonDialog control is named "dlgPrint."

   dlgPrint.Flags = cdlPDReturnDC + cdlPDNoPageNums
   If rtfData.SelLength = 0 Then
      dlgPrint.Flags = dlgPrint.Flags + cdlPDAllPages
   Else
      dlgPrint.Flags = dlgPrint.Flags + cdlPDSelection
   End If
   dlgPrint.ShowPrinter
   rtfData.SelPrint dlgPrint.hDC
End Sub
```

For More Information For more information on using the CommonDialog control, see Chapter 7, "Using Visual Basic's Standard Controls," in the *Microsoft Visual Basic 6.0 Programmer's Guide.*

Display Embedded Objects in the Control

At run time, the end user can drag and drop any embedded objects into the RichTextBox control. There are two kinds of objects that can be embedded into the control: objects which display as icons, and objects which display as data. As an example of the first type, the following figure shows a RichTextBox with an embedded file object.

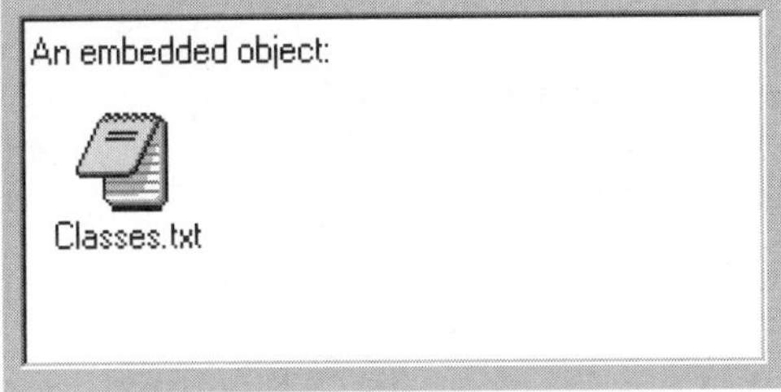

When clicked, the embedded object will behave as expected — starting up the application associated with the file. When the data in the control is saved as an RTF file (using the SaveFile method), the information in the embedded object will also be saved.

However, if the end user embeds a bitmap into the control, the bitmap itself will be displayed, not its icon, as shown:

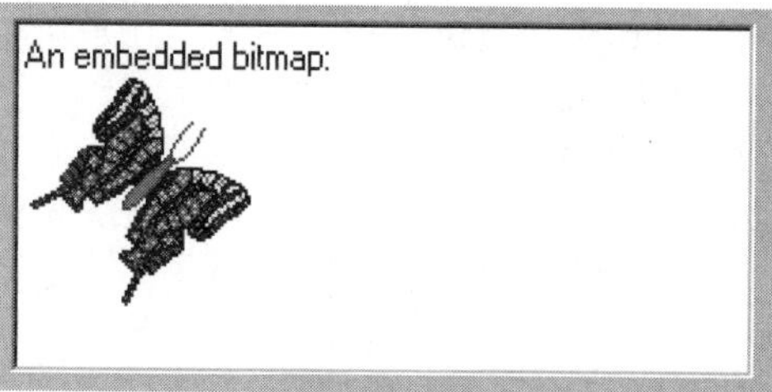

Clicking on the bitmap will start the Paint application, allowing the end user to edit the bitmap.

Add Embedded Objects Using the OLEObjects Collection's Add Method

You can programmatically add embedded objects to the control using the OLEObject collection's Add method, as shown:

```
Private Sub cmdAddObject_Click()
   ' Add the butterfly bitmap to the control.
   RichTextBox1.OLEObjects.Add , , , "bfly.bmp"
End Sub
```

Using the Add, Clear, and Remove methods, you can dynamically populate the control with embedded objects at run time.

RichTextBox Scenario: Change Fonts, FontSize, and FontColor

With the RichTextBox control the end user can change various attributes of text such as font, font size, and font color. In this scenario, three ComboBox controls appear on an application's toolbar to show attributes of text in the RichTextBox control:

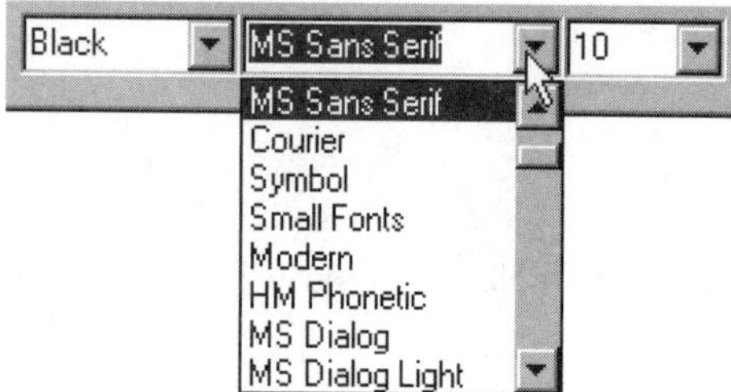

Using these ComboBox controls, the user can select a font, font color, and font size to apply to selected text.

The following objects are used in this scenario:

- Form object named "frmRTF"
- Toolbar control named "tlbRTF"
- ComboBox control named "cmbFontColor"
- ComboBox control named "cmbFontName"
- ComboBox control named "cmbFontSize"
- RichTextBox control named "rtfData"

Note The following steps are a general outline of the creation process. Each step is explained in greater detail later in this topic.

To create three combo boxes that display attributes

1. Set the Form object's ScaleMode to centimeters.
2. Create a Toolbar control.
3. Create three ComboBox controls on the Toolbar control.
4. In the Form object's Load event, populate the ComboBox controls.
5. In the ComboBox controls' Click event, set the SelFontName, SelFontColor, or SelFontSize property.
6. In the RichTextBox control's SelChange event, use the SelFontName, SelFontColor, or SelFontSize property to change the appropriate ComboBox control's List property.

Set the Form Object's ScaleMode to Centimeters

The Form object's ScaleMode property determines which measurement unit is used for certain properties. On the RichTextBox control, the SelIndent. SelHangingIndent, and other properties, use the ScaleMode unit. For these properties, it's more convenient to use centimeters rather than twips. In addition, when creating Button objects with the PlaceHolder style, the ScaleMode property determines how the Button object's width is measured.

To set the form object's ScaleMode property to centimeters

1. Click the Form object.
2. Press F4 to display the Properties window.
3. Click the ScaleMode property and select 7 (centimeters).

Create a Toolbar Control

On the Toolbox, double-click the Toolbar control icon. In the Properties window, double-click **Name** and change the name of the control to tlbRTF.

Create Three ComboBox Controls

Three ComboBox controls will be placed on the Toolbar. Each ComboBox control will be populated with font attributes.

To create three ComboBox controls

1. On the Toolbox, click the ComboBox control icon.
2. Draw a ComboBox control on the Toolbar control.
3. Set the Name property for each of the three ComboBox controls according to the following table:

ComboBox	Property	Value
ComboBox1	Name	cmbFontName
ComboBox2	Name	cmbFontSize
ComboBox3	Name	cmbFontColor

Populate the ComboBox Controls

The ComboBox controls must also be populated with appropriate values. The following code populates each ComboBox control in the Form_Load event.

```
Private Sub Form_Load()
   ' Add colors to cmbFontColor.
   With cmbFontColor
   .AddItem "Black"
   .AddItem "Blue"
   .AddItem "Red"
   .AddItem "Green"
   .ListIndex = 0
   End With

   Dim i As Integer
   With cmbFontName
      For i = 0 to Screen.FontCount - 1
         .AddItem Screen.Fonts(i)
      Next i
      ' Set ListIndex to 0.
      .ListIndex = 0
   End With
```

```
   With cmbFontSize
      ' Populate the combo with sizes in
      ' increments of 2.
      For i = 8 To 72 Step 2
         .AddItem i
      Next i
      ' Set ListIndex to 0
      .ListIndex = 1 ' size 10.
   End With
End Sub
```

In the ComboBox Controls' Click event: Set the SelFontName, SelColor, or SelFontSize Property

To set the font, color, and font size for a RichTextBox control, use the SelFontName, SelColor, and SelFontSize properties. For each of the ComboBox controls, set the appropriate property in the Click event. After setting the property, you may want to set the focus back to the RichTextBox control:

```
Private Sub cmbFontName_Click()
   rtfData.SelFontName = cmbFont
   rtfData.SetFocus
End Sub

Private Sub cmbFontSize_Click()
   rtfData.SelFontSize = cmbFontSize.Text
   rtfData.SetFocus
End Sub

Private Sub cmbFontColor_Click()
   ' Change font colors of text using the
   ' Select Case statement with the ListIndex of the
   ' ComboBox control. Set the colors with
   ' the intrinsic constants for color.
   Me.Show
      With rtfData
   Select Case cmbFontColor.ListIndex
   Case 0
      .SelColor = vbBlack
   Case 1
      .SelColor = vbBlue
   Case 2
      .SelColor = vbRed
   Case 3
      .SelColor = vbGreen
   End Select
   End With
   ' Return focus to the RichTextbox control.
   rtfData.SetFocus
End Sub
```

In the SelChange Event: Use the SelFontName, SelColor, or SelFontSize Property to Change the Appropriate ComboBox Control's List Property

The ComboBox control can also be used to notify the user of text attributes as the insertion point is moved in the RichTextBox control. The SelChange event occurs either when the insertion point is moved, or when selected text is changed. Thus, in the SelChange event, check the SelFontName, SelFontColor, and SelFontSize properties and reset the appropriate ComboBox control.

```
Private Sub rtfData_SelChange()
   ' SelFontSize returns the font size, or Null if
   ' it's mixed.
   If Not IsNull(rtfData.SelFontSize) Then
      cmbFontSize.Text = rtfData.SelFontSize
   End If

   ' Show Font name in the ComboBox.
   cmbFont.Text = rtfData.SelFontName

' Show color of text in the ComboBox. Use the
' intrinsic constants for color to determine
' the color of the text.
   Select Case rtfData.SelColor
      Case vbBlack
         cmbFontColor.ListIndex = 0
      Case vbBlue
         cmbFontColor.ListIndex = 1
      Case vbRed
         cmbFontColor.ListIndex = 2
      Case vbGreen
         cmbFontColor.ListIndex = 3
   End Select
End Sub
```

Using the Slider Control

A Slider control consists of a scale, defined by the Min and Max properties, and a "thumb," which the end user can manipulate using the mouse or arrow keys. At run time, the Min and Max properties can be dynamically reset to reflect a new range of values. The Value property returns the current position of the thumb. Using events such as the MouseDown and MouseUp events, the Slider control can be used to graphically select a range of values.

Possible Uses

- To set the value of a point on a graph.
- To select a range of numbers to be passed into an array.
- To resize a form, field, or other graphic object.

TickStyle and TickFrequency Properties

The Slider control consists of two parts: the thumb and the ticks, as shown below:

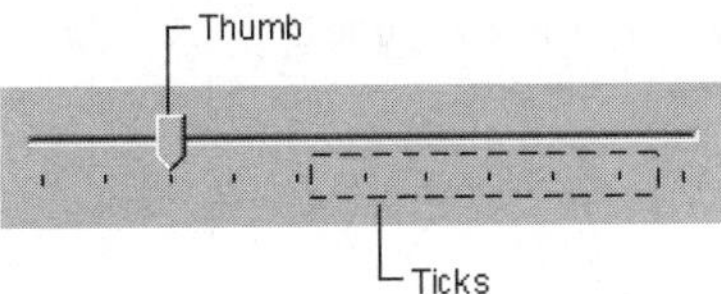

The appearance of the control depends on the TickStyle property. In brief, the ticks can appear along the bottom of the control, as shown above (the default style), along the top, along both top and bottom, or not at all.

In addition to the placement of the ticks, you can also program how many ticks appear on the control by setting the TickFrequency property. This property, in combination with the Min and Max properties, determines how many ticks will appear on the control. For example, if the Min property is set to 0, the Max to 100, and the TickFrequency to 5, there will be one tick for every five increments, for a total of 21. If you reset the Min and Max properties at run time, the number of ticks can be determined by using the GetNumTicks method, which returns the number of ticks on the control.

Set the Min, Max Properties at Design Time or Run Time

The Min and Max properties determine the upper and lower limits of a Slider control, and you can set these properties at either design time or run time. At design time, right-click on the control and click Properties to display the Property Pages dialog box, as shown on the following figure:

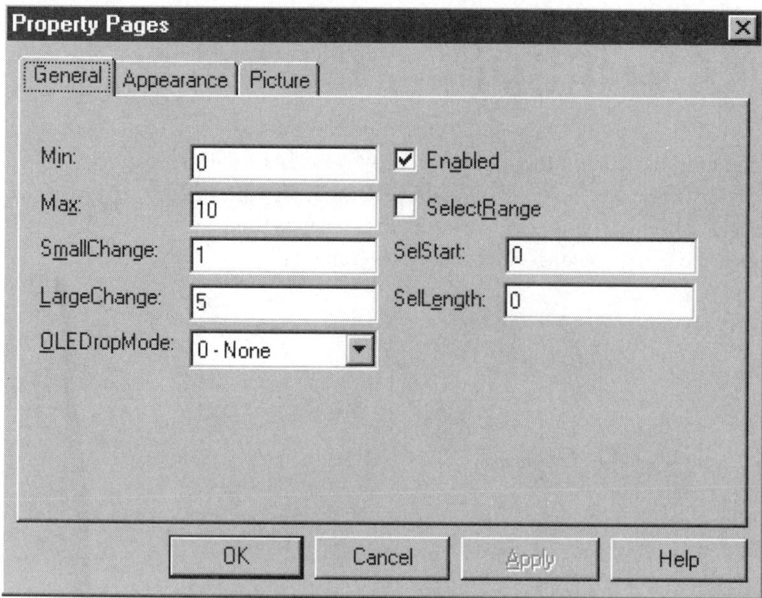

At run time, you can reset the Min and Max settings to accommodate different ranges. For example, if you are using the Slider to change values in a database, you can use the same control and bind it to different fields depending on what table the user is editing.

SmallChange and LargeChange Properties

The SmallChange and LargeChange properties determine how the Slider control will increment or decrement when the user clicks it. The SmallChange property specifies how many ticks the thumb will move when the user presses the LEFT ARROW or RIGHT ARROW keys. The LargeChange property specifies how many ticks the thumb will move when the user clicks the control or when the user presses the PAGEUP or PAGEDOWN keys.

Selecting Ranges

If the SelectRange property is set to True, the Slider control changes its appearance, as shown below:

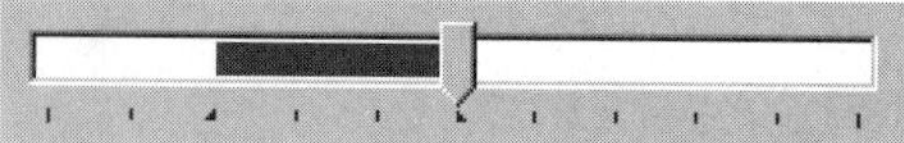

To select a range of values, you must use the SelStart and SelLength properties. For a detailed example of this, see "Slider Scenario 2: Select a Range of Values with the Slider" in this chapter.

Slider Scenario 1: Resize a Graph Control Proportionally

One possible use of the Slider is to resize a PictureBox control on a form while keeping its proportions.

The code below uses the following objects:

- Form named "frmPictureBox"
- Slider control named "sldResize"
- PictureBox control named "picPhoto"

To resize a PictureBox control with a Slider control

1. Create two global variables for the Height and Width properties.
2. Use the Form's Load event to set global variables and the Max property.
3. Resize the height and width of the PictureBox through the Scroll event.

Create Two Global Variables for Height and Width

One simple formula for retaining proportions would be:

```
picPhoto.Height = sldResize.Value * _
OriginalHeight / 100
picPhoto.Width = sldResize.Value * OriginalWidth / 100
```

This formula depends on two constant values: the original height and width of the PictureBox control. These values should be set when the form is loaded, and should be available as global variables, as shown below:

```
Option Explicit
Private gHeight As Long
Private gWidth As Long
```

Use the Form Load Event to Set Global Values and the Max Property

To set the values for the global variables, use the Form object's Load event. It's also more efficient to calculate the values of `OriginalHeight/100` and `OriginalWidth/100` once, and store those values in global variables, as shown below:

```
gHeight = picPhoto.Height / 100
gWidth = picPhoto.Width / 100
```

The Load event can also be used to set the Max property of the Slider control. The Max property specifies the maximum value the Slider will accommodate. To keep the math simple, set the value of the Max property to 100:

```
sldResize.Max = 100
```

The complete code below, then, sets the global variables and the Max property in the Form object's Load event:

```
Private Sub Form_Load()
   gHeight = picPhoto.Height/100
   gWidth = picPhoto.Width/100
   sldResize.Max = 100
End Sub
```

Resize the Height and Width of the PictureBox Through the Scroll Event

The Slider control has a Scroll event that occurs whenever the Slider's thumb is moved by the user. Use this event when you wish to continually process the Value property of the Slider control. In the present scenario, this means the size of the PictureBox will be dynamically changed as the thumb is moved. (If you don't want the user to be distracted by the dynamically changing control, you should use the Click event. The Click event updates the size of the control after the thumb has been released.) The code below shows the formula within the Scroll event:

```
Private Sub sldResize_Scroll()
   picPhoto.Height = sldResize.Value * gHeight
   picPhoto.Width = sldResize.Value * gWidth
End Sub
```

The Complete Code

The complete code is shown below:

```
Private gHeight As Long
Private gWidth As Long

Private Sub Form_Load()
   gHeight = picPhoto.Height / 100
   gWidth = picPhoto.Width / 100
   sldResize.Max = 100
End Sub

Private Sub sldResize_Scroll()
   picPhoto.Height = sldResize.Value * gHeight
   picPhoto.Width = sldResize.Value * gWidth
End Sub
```

Slider Scenario 2: Select a Range of Values with the Slider

Another feature of the Slider control is the ability to select a range of values. In this implementation, when the user presses the SHIFT key while clicking on the Slider control, the MouseDown event occurs. Code in that event sets the SelectRange and SelStart properties. When the user releases the mouse button, the MouseUp event occurs, and in that code the SelLength property is set, from which a range of values can be extracted.

The code below uses the following objects:

- Form named "frmSlider"
- Slider control named "sldSelect"

To select a range of values with the Slider control

1. Set the Slider control's **SelectRange** property to **True**.
2. In the MouseDown event, test to see if the SHIFT key is down.
3. In the MouseUp event, set the **SelLength** property to **Value – SelStart**.

Set the Slider Control's SelectRange Property to True

To enable the selection of a range of values, the SelectRange property must be set to True. One place to do this is the Form object's Load event, as shown below:

```
Private Sub Form_Load()
   sldSelect.SelectRange = True
End Sub
```

Alternatively, you can set the property to True at design time by right-clicking on the control, and clicking on Properties to display the Property Pages dialog box.

MouseDown Event: Test to See If the Shift Key is Down

In order to select a range, the user must hold down the SHIFT key while moving the slider's thumb. The MouseDown event has a *shift* argument, which allows you to determine if the SHIFT key is being held down. The If statement can be used to test for this possibility, as shown below:

```
Private Sub sldSelect_MouseDown _
(Button As Integer, Shift As Integer, _
x As Single, y As Single)

   If Shift = 1 Then
      ' If the user has the Shift key down,
      ' handle it here.
   End If
End Sub
```

MouseDown Event: Set the SelStart and SelLength Properties

If the SHIFT key is being held down by the user, the code then sets the SelStart and SelLength properties to appropriate values. The SelStart property specifies where a selection of values will begin. In the present context, the SelStart property would be set to where the thumb is placed — the Slider control's Value property.

The SelLength property specifies a range of values to select; this property begins at the SelStart value. In the MouseDown event, a new range is being selected, so any previous range must be deselected by setting the SelLength property to 0. This is shown in the code below:

```
sldSelect.SelStart = SldResize.Value
' Set previous SelLength (if any) to 0.
sldSelect.SelLength = 0
```

MouseUp Event: Set the SelLength to the Value-SelStart Property

To select a range, the user must hold the SHIFT key down while dragging the mouse. The code to set the new range is therefore found in the MouseUp event, which occurs when the end user releases the slider thumb. The code below sets the SelLength property with a simple formula, the value of the thumb minus the SelStart property:

```
sldSelect.Value - sldSelect.SelStart
```

However, it is possible for the user to release the SHIFT key while selecting a range. In that case no selection should occur. Therefore the above code will only execute if the SHIFT key is still down. As with the MouseDown event, an If statement can test for this possibility:

```
Private Sub sldSelect_MouseUp _
(Button As Integer, Shift As Integer, _
x As Single, y As Single)

   If Shift = 1 Then
   ' If user selects backwards from a point,
   ' an error will occur.
   On Error Resume Next
   ' Else set SelLength using SelStart and
   ' current value.
      sldSelect.SelLength = _
      sldSelect.Value - sldSelect.SelStart
   Else
      'If user lifts SHIFT key, set SelLength
      ' to 0 (to deselect the SelRange) and exit.
      sldSelect.SelLength = 0
   End If
End Sub
```

The Complete Code

The complete code is shown below:

```
Private Sub Form_Load()
   sldSelect.SelectRange = True
End Sub

Private Sub sldSelect_MouseDown _
(Button As Integer, Shift As Integer, _
x As Single, y As Single)

   If Shift = 1 Then
      sldSelect.SelStart = sldSelect.Value
      ' Set previous SelLength (if any) to 0.
      sldSelect.SelLength = 0
   End If
End Sub

Private Sub sldSelect_MouseUp _
(Button As Integer, Shift As Integer, _
x As Single, y As Single)

   If Shift = 1 Then
   ' If user selects backwards from a point,
   ' an error will occur.
   On Error Resume Next
   ' Else set SelLength using SelStart and
   ' current value.
      sldSelect.SelLength = _
      sldSelect.Value - sldSelect.SelStart
   Else
      'If user lifts SHIFT key, set SelLength
      ' to 0 (to deselect the SelRange) and exit.
      sldSelect.SelLength = 0
   End If
End Sub
```

Using the StatusBar Control

A StatusBar control is a frame that can consist of several panels which inform the user of the status of an application. The control can hold up to sixteen frames. Additionally, the control has a “simple” style (set with the Style property), which switches from multi-panels to a single panel for special messages.

The StatusBar control can be placed at the top, bottom, or sides of an application. Optionally, the control can “float” within the application’s client area.

Possible Uses

- To inform the user of a database table's metrics, such as number of records, and the present position in the database.
- To give the user information about a RichTextBox control's text and font status.
- To give status about key states (such as the Caps Lock or the Number Lock).

The Panel Object and the Panels Collection

The StatusBar control is built around the Panels collection. Up to sixteen Panel objects can be contained in the collection. Each object can display an image and text, as shown below:

At run time, you can dynamically change the text, images, or widths of any Panel object, using the Text, Picture and Width properties. To add Panel objects at design time, right-click on the control, and click on Properties to display the Property Pages dialog box, as shown in Figure 2.26 below:

Figure 2.26 StatusBar panels page

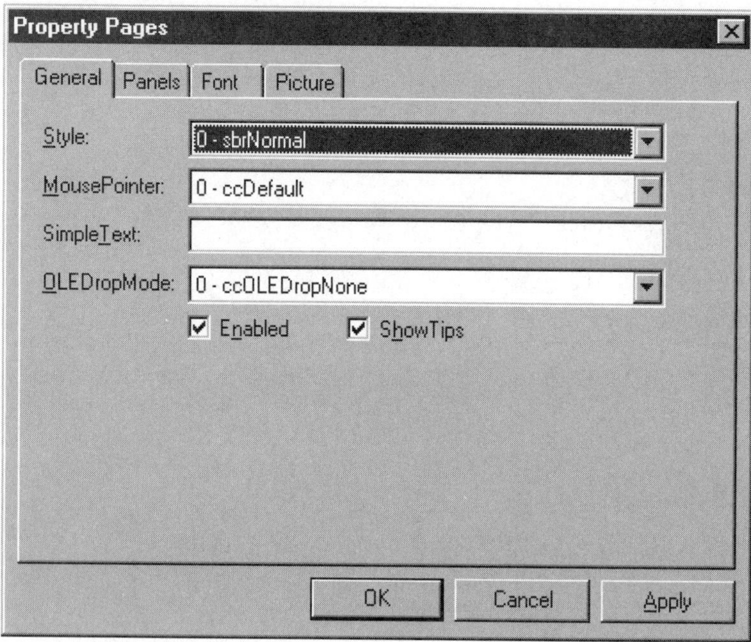

Using this dialog box, you can add individual Panel objects and set the various properties for each panel.

Use the Set Statement with the Add Method to Create Panels at Run Time

To add Panel objects at run time, use the Set statement with the Add method. First declare an object variable of type Panel, then set the object variable to a Panel created with the Add method, as shown in the code below:

```
' The StatusBar control is named "sbrDB."
Dim pnlX As Panel
Set pnlX = sbrDB.Panels.Add()
```

Once you have created a Panel object and set the object variable to reference the new object, you can set the various properties of the Panel:

```
pnlX.Text = Drivel.Drive
pnlX.Picture = LoadPicture("mapnet.bmp")
pnlX.Key = "drive"
```

If you plan to have the control respond when the user clicks on a particular Panel object, be sure to set the Key property. Because the Key property must be unique, you can use it to identify particular panels.

Use the Select Case Statement in the PanelClick Event to Determine the Clicked Panel

To program the StatusBar control to respond to user clicks, use the Select Case statement within the PanelClick event. The event contains an argument (the *panel* argument) which passes a reference to the clicked Panel object. Using this reference, you can determine the Key property of the clicked panel, and program accordingly, as shown in the code below:

```
Private Sub sbrDB_PanelClick(ByVal Panel As Panel)
   Select Case Panel.Key
   Case "drive"
      Panel.Text = Drivel.Drive
   Case "openDB"
      Panel.Text = rsOpenDB.Name
   Case Else
   ' Handle other cases.
   End Select
End Sub
```

The Style Property: Automatic Status Functions

One feature of the StatusBar control is its ability to display key states, time, and date with a minimum of code. By simply setting the Style property, any Panel object can display one of the following:

Constant	Value	Description
sbrText	0	(Default). Text and/or a bitmap. Set text with the Text property.
sbrCaps	1	Caps Lock key. Displays the letters CAPS in bold when Caps Lock is enabled, and dimmed when disabled.
sbrNum	2	Number Lock. Displays the letters NUM in bold when the number lock key is enabled, and dimmed when disabled.
sbrIns	3	Insert key. Displays the letters INS in bold when the insert key is enabled, and dimmed when disabled.
sbrScrl	4	Scroll Lock key. Displays the letters SCRL in bold when scroll lock is enabled, and dimmed when disabled.
sbrTime	5	Time. Displays the current time in the system format.
sbrDate	6	Date. Displays the current date in the system format.
sbrKana	7	Kana. displays the letters KANA in bold when kana lock is enabled, and dimmed when disabled. (enabled on Japanese operating systems only)

The code below creates eight Panel objects, and assigns one of the eight styles to each:

```
Private Sub MakeEight()
   ' Delete the first Panel object, which is
   ' created automatically.
   StatusBar1.Panels.Remove 1
   Dim i As Integer

   ' The fourth argument of the Add method
   ' sets the Style property.
   For i = 0 To 7
      StatusBar1.Panels.Add , , , i
   Next i

   ' Put some text into the first panel.
   StatusBar1.Panels(1).Text = "Text Style"
End Sub
```

Bevel, AutoSize, and Alignment Properties Program Appearance

Using the Bevel, AutoSize, and Alignment properties, you can precisely control the appearance of each Panel object. The Bevel property specifies whether the Panel object will have an inset bevel (the default), raised, or none at all. All three bevels are shown in the following figure:

Inset Bevel | No Bevel | Raised Bevel

Settings for the Bevel property are:

Constant	Value	Description
sbrNoBevel	0	The Panel displays no bevel, and text looks like it is displayed right on the status bar.
sbrInset	1	The Panel appears to be sunk into the status bar.
sbrRaised	2	The Panel appears to be raised above the status bar.

The AutoSize property determines how a Panel object will size itself when the parent container (either a Form or a container control) is resized by the user. The figure below shows a StatusBar control before being resized:

When the *container* (the Form on which the StatusBar control is placed) of the control is resized, notice that the first panel retains its width, the second "springs" to fill the extra space, and the third sizes according to its contents (and therefore retains its width):

No Autosize | Spring | This panel sizes to content

Settings for the AutoSize property are:

Constant	Value	Description
sbrNoAutoSize	0	None. No autosizing occurs. The width of the panel is always and exactly that specified by the Width property.
sbrSpring	1	Spring. When the parent form resizes and there is extra space available, all panels with this setting divide the space and grow accordingly. However, the panels' width never falls below that specified by the MinWidth property.
sbrContents	2	Content. The panel is resized to fit its contents.

Tip Set the AutoSize property to Content (2) when you want to assure that the contents of a particular panel are always visible.

The Alignment property specifies how the text in a panel will align relative to the panel itself as well as any image in the panel. As with a word processor, the text can be aligned left, center, or right, as shown below:

Settings for the Alignment property are:

Constant	Value	Description
sbrLeft	0	Text appears left-justified and to right of bitmap.
sbrCenter	1	Text appears centered and to right of bitmap.
sbrRight	2	Text appears right-justified but to the left of any bitmap.

Style Property and the SimpleText Property

The StatusBar control features a secondary mode in which the multiple panels are replaced by a single panel that spans the width of the control. This single panel has one property, the SimpleText property which specifies what text is displayed on the panel. To display this single panel, set the Style property of the StatusBar to sbrSimple (1).

One reason for switching to the Simple style and displaying a single panel is to notify the user that a lengthy transaction is occurring. For example, if you are performing a database operation, the Simple style may be used to notify the user of the current state of the transaction, as seen in the code below:

```
Private Sub GetRecords(State)
   ' The query finds all records which match
   ' the parameter State. While the query
   ' is creating the recordset, show the
   ' SimpleText on the StatusBar control.
   sbrDB.SimpleText = "Getting records ..."
   sbrDB.Style = sbrSimple ' Simple style.
   sbrDB.Refresh   ' You must refresh to see the
                   ' Simple text.

   Set rsNames = mDbBiblio.OpenRecordset _
   ("select * from Names Where State= " & _
   State)
End Sub
```

StatusBar Scenario: Show Various Properties of a Database

When editing records of a database, a possible application of the StatusBar control would be to inform the user of various properties such as the name of the table being edited, its creation date, and the date of the last update.

The code below uses the following objects:

- Form named "frmDataviewer"
- StatusBar Control named "sbrData"
- Data control named "datData"

To add a StatusBar that shows database properties

1. Use the Add method to create a collection of Panel objects.
2. Configure each Panel object with the AutoSize property.
3. Use the Panel object's Text property to display database properties.
4. Reset the properties using the Select Case statement in the PanelClick event.

Use the Add Method to Create a Collection of Panel Objects

To create a collection of Panel objects at run time, use the Add method. First, declare a variable as type Panel. As you add each Panel object, the variable will contain the reference to the newly created object. The code below uses the Form object's Load event to create three Panel objects.

```
Private Sub Form_Load()
   Dim pnlX As Panel
   Dim i As Integer
   For i = 1 to 3 ' First panel already exists.
      Set pnlX = sbrData.Panels.Add()
   Next i
End Sub
```

Note that after adding three Panel objects to the collection, there are really four panels on the control because the control creates one by default.

Configure Each Panel Object with the AutoSize Property

One of the features of the StatusBar control is the ability of panels to automatically resize according to their contents. The example iterates through all the Panel objects, and sets the AutoSize property for each to sbrSpring (1). With this setting, each panel "springs" to share the total width of the control.

```
Private Sub Form_Load()
   Dim pnlX As Panel
   Dim i As Integer
   For i = 1 to 3 ' First panel already exists.
      Set pnlX = sbrData.Panels.Add()
   Next i

   ' Change the AutoSize of all panels.
   For i = 1 to 4               ' < -- New code
      sbrData.Panels(i).AutoSize = sbrSpring ' New
   Next i                                ' New
End Sub
```

Use the Panel Object's Text Property to Display Database Properties

To change the information displayed in any panel, set the Text property of the Panel object. The code below displays information about a database that has been opened with Data Access Objects.

In the Form object's Load event, database variables are first created and assigned to an open database ("Biblio.mdb") and a recordset ("Authors"). The code then assigns the Name, DateCreated, LastUpdated, and LockEdit properties to each Panel object's Text property.

```
' Declare database variables.
Dim myDB As Database, myRs As Recordset
' Set the Database to the BIBLIO.MDB database.
Set myDB = DBEngine.Workspaces(0). _
OpenDatabase("BIBLIO.MDB")
' Set the recordset variable to the Authors table.
Set myRs = _
myDB.OpenRecordset("Publishers", dbOpenTable)
' Set Text properties with recordset properties.
sbrData.Panels(1).Text = "name: " & myRs.Name
sbrData.Panels(2).Text = "Date Created: " & _
myRs.DateCreated
sbrData.Panels(3).Text = "Last Updated " & _
myRs.LastUpdated
sbrData.Panels(4).Text = "Lockedits: " & myRs.LockEdits
```

Reset Properties Using the Select Case Statement in the PanelClick Event

The StatusBar control can also be used to reset the properties that are being displayed. In the present scenario, a DataGrid control is bound to the Data control. For more information on how to data-bind controls, see "Using the ADO Data Control" in Chapter 7, "Using Visual Basic's Standard Controls," of the *Microsoft Visual Basic 6.0 Programmer's Guide*. Among the properties displayed in the StatusBar, only the LockEdits property can be reset. To accomplish this, use a Select Case statement within the PanelClick event to determine which Panel object was clicked. The PanelClick event contains a reference to the Panel that the user clicked. Using this reference, you can reset the Text property of the clicked Panel object.

The code below first creates a variable of type Recordset and sets it to the recordset opened with the Data control. The Select Case statement is then used to test the Panel object's Index property. If the Index is 4, the LockEdits property is toggled between –1 (True) and 0 (False). Finally, the Panel object's Text property is updated with the new information.

```
Private Sub sbrData_PanelClick(ByVal Panel As Panel)
   Dim myRs As Recordset ' Declare Recordset variable.
   ' The Data control is named "datData"
   Set myRs = datData.Recordset ' Set variable.

   Select Case Panel.Index
   Case 1 to 3
      ' Can't set these panels.
   Case 4 ' Updateable Property is settable.
      ' Toggle the property.
      myRs.LockEdits = Abs(myRs.LockEdits) - 1
      ' Update the Panel object's Text property.
      sbrData.Panels(4).Text = "LockEdits: " _
      & myRs.LockEdits
   End Select
End Sub
```

Using the SysInfo Control

The SysInfo control can be used to detect system events such as desktop resizing, resolution changes, time changes, or to provide operating system platform and version information. You can also use it to manage changes to AC and battery power or changes in hardware configuration.

In Windows 95, whenever a new device is added to the system it is automatically detected. Your applications can benefit from this "plug and play" technology by using the properties and events of the SysInfo control. Applications written specifically for notebook computers, for instance, can respond when a PC card is inserted or removed from the PC card slot.

The SysInfo control is invisible at run time.

The SysInfo control

Possible Uses

- To determine operating system platform and version
- To detect desktop and monitor size and resolution changes
- To detect and manage plug and play devices
- To monitor battery and power status

SysInfo Control Features

Using the SysInfo control, you can monitor information provided by the operating system as well as respond to system-generated events. The features of this control fall into one of the following groups:

- Operating system properties (OSVersion and WorkAreaHeight properties, for example).
- Events tied to changes in the system (DisplayChanged, TimeChanged, and SettingChanged events, for example).
- Plug and Play events (DeviceArrival, DeviceRemoveComplete events, for example).
- Power status events and properties (PowerSuspend and PowerResume events and ACStatus and BatteryStatus properties, for example).

The following sections describe the uses of these events and properties in the contexts described above.

Operating System Properties and Events

The operating system properties and events of the SysInfo control can be used to detect the current operating system and version, some global setting changes, or changes to desktop size and resolution.

Operating System Platform and Version Properties

The following table lists the properties which can be used to determine the current operating system platform and version:

Category	Item	Description
Properties	OSPlatform	Returns a value that identifies the operating system under which the application is currently running.
	OSVersion	Returns a value that identifies the version of the operating system under which the application is currently running.
	OSBuild	Returns a value that provides the build number of the operating system under which the application is currently running.

For More Information "SysInfo Scenario 1: Detect the Current Operating System and Version," later in this chapter, provides examples of how these properties are used.

Desktop Size and Screen Resolution Properties and Events

The following table lists the operating system properties and events that specifically apply to managing desktop and screen resolution changes:

Category	Item	Description
Properties	ScrollBarSize	Returns the system metric for the width of a scroll bar in twips.
	WorkAreaHeight	Returns the height of the visible desktop adjusted for the Windows 95 and Windows NT 4.0 taskbar.
	WorkAreaLeft	Returns the coordinate for the left edge of the visible desktop adjusted for the Windows 95 and Windows NT 4.0 taskbar.
	WorkAreaTop	Returns the coordinate for the top edge of the visible desktop adjusted for the Windows 95 and Windows NT 4.0 taskbar.
	WorkAreaWidth	Returns the width of the visible desktop adjusted for the Windows 95 and Windows NT 4.0 taskbar.
Events	DisplayChanged	Occurs when system screen resolution changes.
	SysColorsChanged	Occurs when a system color setting changes, either by an application or through the Control Panel.

The DisplayChanged event is triggered when the user changes the screen resolution. Using the WorkAreaHeight, WorkAreaWidth, WorkAreaRight, and WorkAreaLeft properties with the DisplayChanged event you can determine the current system metrics (the usable screen area) and adjust accordingly. If the taskbar is visible in Windows 95 or Windows NT 4.0, it will be excluded from the calculation of usable screen area.

If the user changes the scroll bar size using the Display settings in the Windows 95 or Windows NT 4.0 Control Panel, is it possible that the display area will need to be updated so that the new scroll bars will be positioned correctly. You can use the ScrollBarSize property with the DisplayChanged event to adjust to this change.

For More Information The section "SysInfo Scenario 2: Adjust to Changes in Screen Size and Resolution," later in this chapter, provides examples of how these properties and events are used.

Managing Hardware Configuration and Plug and Play Events

If the operating system supports this feature, the plug and play events provide you with a way to manage changes in a system's hardware configuration. For instance, if the hardware profile has changed, if the system is docked or undocked, or if a PC card has been added to or removed from a PC slot.

The following table lists the SysInfo control events that specifically apply to managing hardware configuration and Plug and Play devices.

Events	Description
ConfigChanged	Occurs when the hardware profile on the system has changed.
ConfigChangeCancelled	Occurs when the operating system sends a message that a change to the hardware profile was canceled.
DeviceArrival	Occurs when a new device is added to the system.
DeviceEventOther	A notification event that does not map onto the general events.
DevModeChange	Occurs when the user changes device mode settings.
DeviceQueryRemove	Occurs just before a device is removed from the system.
DeviceQueryRemoveFailed	Occurs if code in the DeviceQueryRemove event canceled the removal of a device.
DeviceRemoveComplete	Occurs after a device is removed.
DeviceRemovePending	Occurs after all applications have given approval to remove a device and the device is about to be removed.
QueryChangeConfig	Occurs on a request to change the current hardware profile.

The ConfigChanged event notifies you when the hardware profile in Windows 95 has changed. Notebook computers often have separate hardware profiles for their docked and undocked configurations. When docked, the notebook may include a network connection, an external monitor, or access to a compact disc drive, for example.

The device-specific events of the SysInfo control give you feedback on changes to devices within a hardware configuration. You can write your application to dynamically make use of hardware when it's added to the system.

Using Power Status Properties and Events

The power status events and properties can be used to monitor AC and battery power states on a desktop or notebook computer. Features like power suspend, power resume, and battery status are more likely to be implemented on a notebook computer, however, they have application across all types of computers.

The following table lists the events and properties of the SysInfo control which pertain to battery and power states:

Category	Item	Description
Properties	ACStatus	Returns a value that indicates whether the system is using AC or battery power.
	BatteryFullTime	Returns a value that indicates the full charge life of the battery.

(continued)

Category	Item	Description
	BatteryLifePercent	Returns the percentage of full battery power remaining.
	BatteryLifeTime	Returns a value that indicates the remaining life of the battery.
	BatteryStatus	Returns a value that indicates the status of the battery's charge.
Events	PowerQuerySuspend	Occurs when system power is about to be suspended.
	PowerResume	Occurs when the system comes out of suspend mode.
	PowerStatusChanged	Occurs when there is a change in the power status of the system.
	PowerSuspend	Occurs immediately before the system goes into suspend mode.

The power events are especially useful in providing your application with a safety net should power be suspended. The PowerSuspend event notifies your application that power is about to be suspended. You can then store the application state or any unsaved files before this occurs.

The PowerStatusChanged event informs you of changes in the AC and battery power status. If battery power is running dangerously low you can still save your data.

For More Information The section "SysInfo Scenario 3: Monitor Battery Power Status" provides examples of how some of these properties and events are used to monitor and manage changes in battery and AC power.

SysInfo Scenario 1: Detect the Current Operating System and Version

You can detect and display the current operating system platform, version, and build number by using a CommandButton control and the OSPlatform, OSVersion, and OSBuild properties. You can test this by adding a CommandButton control to a form and then adding the following code the cmdDetectOS_Click event procedure:

```
Private Sub cmdDetectOS_Click()
   Dim MsgEnd As String
   Select Case sysDetectOS.OSPlatform
      Case 0
         MsgEnd = "Unidentified"
      Case 1
         MsgEnd = "Windows 95, ver. "& _
CStr(sysDetectOS.OSVersion) & "(" & _
CStr(sysDetectOS.OSBuild) & ")"
      Case 2
         MsgEnd = "Windows NT, ver. " & _
CStr(sysDetectOS.OSVersion) & "(" & _
CStr(sysDetectOS.OSBuild) & ")"
   End Select
   MsgBox "System: " & MsgEnd
End Sub
```

For More Information See OSPlatform, OSVersion, and OSBuild properties in the *Microsoft Visual Basic 6.0 Controls Reference.*

SysInfo Scenario 2: Adjust to Changes in Screen Size and Resolution

Using a few of the operating system properties and events provided by the SysInfo control, you can detect and respond to changes in screen size and resolution.

The following example tests the size of the active form after a change in screen resolution and adjusts the size of the form if it exceeds the visible screen area.

To resize a form after screen resolution changes, use the DisplayChanged event with the WorkAreaWidth, WorkAreaLeft, and WorkAreaTop properties.

To resize a form after screen resolution changes

1. Create a new project in Visual Basic.
2. Add a SysInfo control to the form.
3. Add the following code to the SysInfo control's DisplayChanged event procedure:

```
Private Sub sysDetectOS_DisplayChanged()
   If Screen.ActiveForm.Width > _
sysDetectOS.WorkAreaWidth Then
      Screen.ActiveForm.Left = _
sysDetectOS.WorkAreaLeft
      Screen.ActiveForm.Width = _
sysDetectOS.WorkAreaWidth
   End If
   If Screen.ActiveForm.Height > _
sysDetectOS.WorkAreaHeight Then
      Screen.ActiveForm.Top = _
```

```
sysDetectOS.WorkAreaTop
      Screen.ActiveForm.Height = _
sysDetectOS.WorkAreaHeight
   End If
End Sub
```

SysInfo Scenario 3: Monitor Battery Power Status

Using just one of the power status properties, you can monitor the charge status of a battery. The BatteryLifePercent property is used to provide a percentage value for a ProgressBar control. A Timer control sets the interval at which the power status is tested.

To create a simple battery meter using the BatteryLifePercent property

1. Create a new project in Visual Basic.
2. Add a SysInfo, a Timer, and a ProgressBar control to the form.
3. Set the Interval property of the Timer control to 5000.
4. Add the following code to the Timer control's Timer event:

```
Private Sub tmrBattery_Timer()
   If sysBattery.BatteryLifePercent <> 255 Then
      prgBattery.Value =  _ sysBattery.BatteryLifePercent
      prgBattery.Enabled = True
   Else
      prgBattery.Value = 0
      prgBattery.Enabled = False
   End If
End Sub
```

When the application is run, the SysInfo control queries the operating system for the existence of a battery and then displays its current charge level using the BatteryLifePercent property.

A simple battery meter

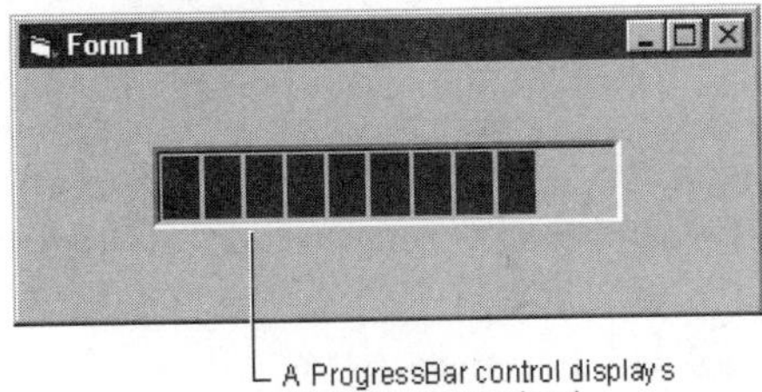
Form1
A ProgressBar control displays the battery charge level.

This example can be enhanced by using one of the power status events to detect when a change occurs to the system's power status. The following example adds a Label control to the form and uses the PowerStatusChanged event to notify the user when the power status changes.

To update changes to battery power status

1. Add a Label control to the form.
2. Add the following code to the Sysinfo control's PowerStatusChanged event:

```
Private Sub sysBattery_PowerStatusChanged()
   Select Case sysBattery.BatteryStatus
      Case 1
         lblStatus.Caption = "Battery OK"
      Case 2
         lblStatus.Caption = "Battery Low"
      Case 4
         lblStatus.Caption = "Battery Critical"
      Case 8
         lblStatus.Caption = "Battery Charging"
      Case 128, 255
         lblStatus.Caption = "No Battery Status"
   End Select
End Sub
```

The battery meter, enhanced with the PowerStatusChanged event

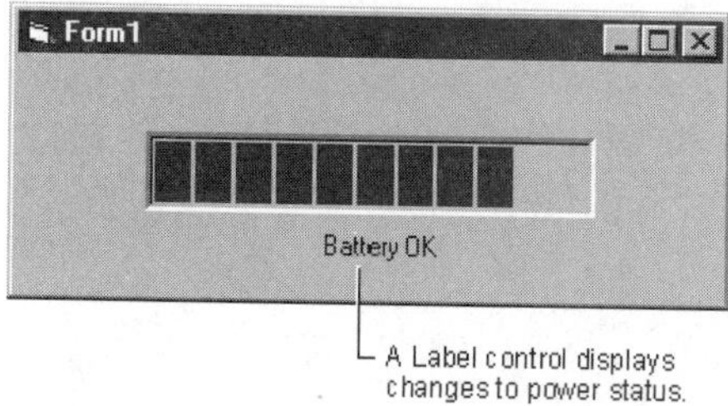

A Label control displays changes to power status.

The BatteryStatus property is used in a Select Case statement to return a value that indicates the current battery status setting. Whenever the PowerStatusChange event is fired, the Label control is updated with the current status. For example, if the battery runs down or is removed from the computer.

Using the Tabbed Dialog Control

The Microsoft Tabbed Dialog control provides an easy way of presenting several dialogs or screens of information on a single form using the same interface seen in many commercial Microsoft Windows applications.

The Tabbed Dialog control provides a group of tabs, each of which acts as a container for other controls. Only one tab is active in the control at a time, displaying the controls it contains to the user while hiding the controls in the other tabs.

The Tabbed Dialog control

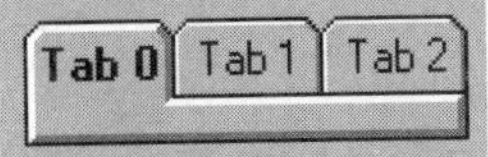

Possible Uses

- To create a Microsoft Office or Windows 95 style tabbed dialog box.
- To create a custom tabbed dialog box.

Setting Tabs and Tab Rows

Before setting the number of tabs you want to add to the Tabbed Dialog control, you should first decide what your dialog box will contain and how it will be organized.

While you can set the numbers of tabs at both design time and run time, you will more than likely find that creating your tabbed dialog at design time is much quicker and easier. You can set properties at design time using the Tabbed Dialog Property Pages which is available by right-clicking the control and then selecting Properties.

Setting properties at design time

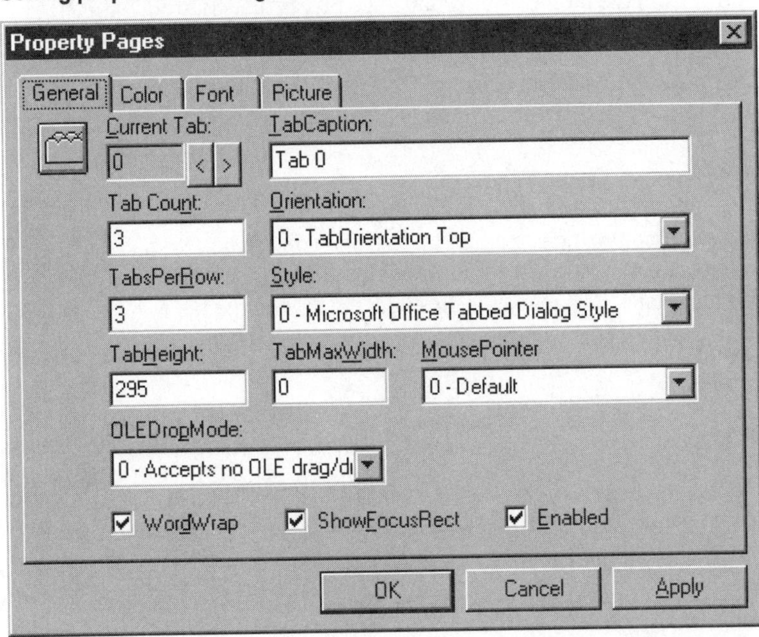

You set the Tab and TabsPerRow properties to define the number of tabs and rows in your dialog box. For example, if you want to a create a tabbed dialog that contains twelve tabs you set the Tab Count option to "12" and the TabsPerRow option to "4" — this creates a tabbed dialog containing three rows of four tabs each. By default, the number of tabs is set at 3.

When the number of tabs and rows has been set, each tab is indexed and can then be selected individually. For example, you can select individual tabs in the Current Tab option to change the TabCaption property. Tabs are indexed beginning at zero (0).

At run time, the user can navigate through the tabs by either clicking on them, by pressing CTRL+TAB, or by using mnemonics defined in the caption of each tab. For example, if you wanted to create a tab called "Print" and allow the user to access the tab with the keyboard combination ALT+P, you set the TabCaption property to "&Print."

Adding Controls to Tabs

Each tab in the Tabbed Dialog control is essentially a container for other controls. When you create a tabbed dialog box, you group controls together that perform similar functions, such as printing a document or setting display options for your application. Once you've determined how many tabs you need in your tabbed dialog box, you add whichever controls you need to perform those functions.

To add controls to individual tab pages at design time, first select the tab by clicking on it, then draw the controls on the tab page.

> **Note** You should not add controls to individual tab pages using the double-click method. Double-clicking a control from the toolbox onto a tab page places that control on every tab in the Tabbed Dialog control.

For More Information See "Containers for Controls" in Chapter 7, "Using Visual Basic's Standard Controls," in the *Microsoft Visual Basic 6.0 Programmer's Guide.*

Enabling and Disabling Tabs at Run Time

Depending upon the functionality of your application or a particular tabbed dialog box you create, you may want to disable some tabs in certain situations. You use the TabEnabled property to enable and disable individual tabs. When a tab is disabled, the text on the tab is grayed out and the user cannot select that tab. For example:

```
SSTab1.TabEnabled(2) = False
```

The TabEnabled property specifies the tab number, then disables it by setting the value to False.

> **Note** Use the Enabled property to enable or disable the entire Tabbed Dialog control.

Tab Customizing Properties

Using the Tabbed Dialog control properties, you can customize the look and functionality of your tabbed dialog box. You can set these properties at design time using the control's Property Pages or at run time in code.

The Style Property

The Style property gives you two options for setting the style of your tabbed dialog box. By default, the Style property is set to display as a Microsoft Office tabbed dialog. The tabs that appear when this option is selected look like those in Microsoft Office for Microsoft Windows 3.1 applications. By default, the selected tab caption text is displayed in bold.

The Microsoft Office tabbed dialog style

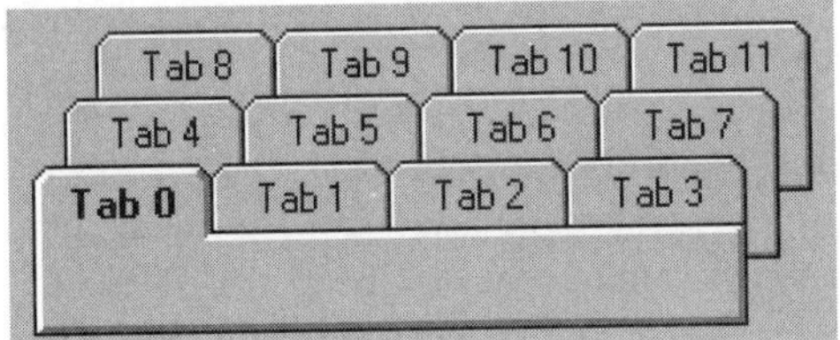

The second option available is the Windows 95 Property Pages tabbed dialog style. This tabbed dialog style conforms to the user interface standards developed for Windows 95. The selected tab caption text, unlike the Microsoft Office style, is not displayed as bold.

The Windows 95 Property Pages tabbed dialog style

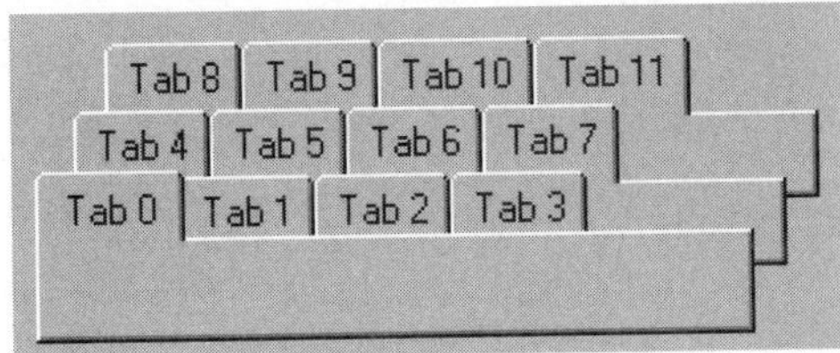

To set this property at run time use the Visual Basic constants ssStyleTabbedDialog or ssStylePropertyPage to specify either style.

The TabOrientation Property

The TabOrientation property allows you to locate the tabs of your tabbed dialog box on either of the four sides (top, bottom, left, right). For example:

Tab orientation set to left

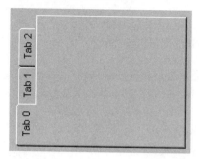

When you set the orientation of the tabs to something other than top or bottom, you must also change the font style of the tabs. Setting the tabs to left or right rotates the text vertically and only TrueType fonts display vertically in the Tabbed Dialog control. Change the font style using the Font property or by selecting the Font tab in the control's Property Pages. Arial is a common substitute for the Windows default sans serif font.

You can set this property at run time using the following Visual Basic constants: ssTabOrientationTop, ssTabOrientationBottom, ssTabOrientationLeft, and ssTabOrientationRight.

The Picture Property

You can add pictures (bitmaps, icons, or metafiles) to any or all of the tabs in the Tabbed Dialog control. For example:

Adding a picture to a tab

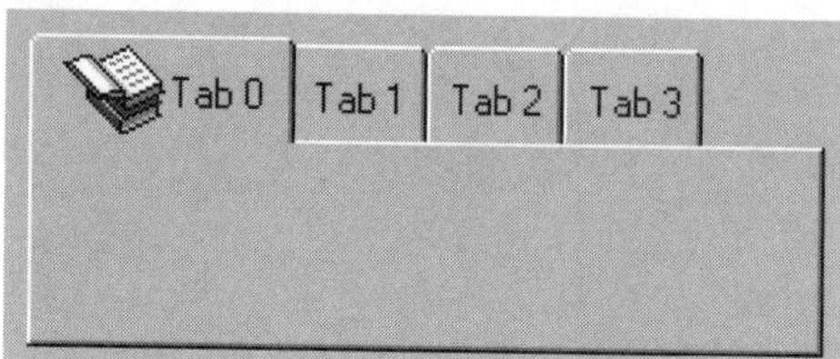

At design time, you set the Picture property for a tab by clicking that tab and then setting the property in the Properties window. At run time, you can set the Picture property using the LoadPicture function or the Picture property of another control or of a Form object.

> **Note** When setting the Picture property at design time, the graphic is saved and loaded with the Form object containing the Tabbed Dialog control. If you create an executable file, the file contains the image. When you load a graphic at run time, the graphic isn't saved with the application.

Setting the Picture property affects the value of the TabPicture property for the current tab as well as displays the picture in the active tab.

Adjusting Tab Height and Width

Depending upon its size, you may need to resize the tab height to accommodate the image. Use the TabMaxHeight property to adjust the height of the tabs. The TabMaxHeight property sets the height for every tab in the control — individual tabs cannot be adjusted separately.

If you're using the Microsoft Office style tabbed dialog, you may also need to set the TabMaxWidth property to allow both the image and the text to fit on the tab. If you're using the Windows 95-style tabbed dialog, the TabMaxWidth property is ignored and the width of each tab adjusts to the combined width of the image and the length of the text in its caption.

Setting the WordWrap Property

When using the Microsoft Office style tabbed dialog, you may specify the exact width of the tabs using the TabMaxWidth property. Having done so, you can then allow tab captions to wrap to the next line, if necessary, by setting the WordWrap property to True. Although caption text will wrap, you are still limited by the height and width of the tabs. In other words, you may still get clipped or hidden caption text if the height and width are insufficient.

The Windows 95-style tabbed dialog sets tab width based on the length of the caption text; the TabMaxWidth and WordWrap property settings are ignored.

Completing Your Custom Tabbed Dialog Box

Once you've completed adding controls to each tab, you can finish designing your custom tabbed dialog box to resemble a standard tabbed dialog box. For example, if you want it to display like a standard Windows 95 Property Pages dialog box, follow these steps:

- Resize the underlying form so that the Tabbed Dialog control is centered and equal amounts of space remain on the top, right and left edges. Leave a larger amount of space below the control.
- Add two command buttons — an OK and a Cancel button. Align them below the right edge of the Tabbed Dialog control.
- Set the form's BorderStyle property to Fixed Dialog.

Using the TabStrip Control

A TabStrip acts like the dividers in a notebook or the labels on a group of file folders. By using a TabStrip control, you can define multiple pages for the same area of a window or dialog box in your application.

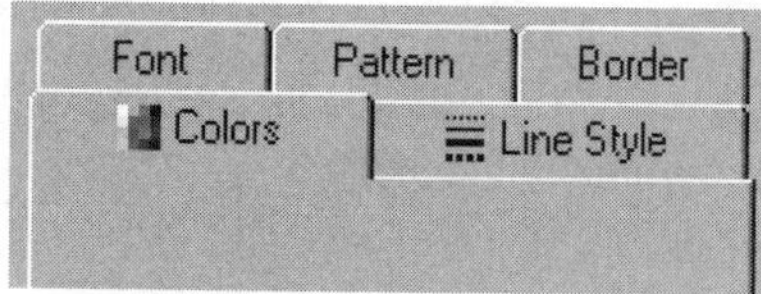

Possible Uses

- To create a tabbed dialog that sets various text attributes for a RichTextBox control.
- To create a tabbed dialog that sets preferences for an application.

The Tabs Collection

The control consists of one or more Tab objects in a Tabs collection. At both design time and run time, you can affect the Tab object's appearance by setting properties, and at run time, by invoking methods to add and remove Tab objects.

Associate the ImageList Control with the TabStrip Control

To identify a tab's function, you can assign an image from the ImageList control to the Tab object. You must first associate an ImageList control with the TabStrip control, and this can be accomplished at either design time or run time.

To associate an ImageList control with a TabStrip control at design time:

1. Populate the ImageList control with images for the tabs.
2. Right-click on the TabStrip control and click **Properties** to open the **TabStrip Property Page** dialog box.
3. On the **General** tab, click the **ImageList** box and select the ImageList control you have populated.
4. To associate an ImageList control with the control at run time, simply set the ImageList property to the name of the ImageList control, as shown in the example below:

```
Private Sub Form_Load()
   ' The TabStrip control is named "tabRTF," and the
   ' ImageList control is named "imlRTF."
   tabRTF.ImageList = imlRTF
End Sub
```

Create Tabs at Design Time or Run Time

You can create Tab objects at both design and run time. To create Tab objects at design time, use the Property Pages dialog box.

To create Tab objects at design time

1. Right-click the TabStrip control and click **Properties** to display the **Property Pages** dialog box.
2. Click **Tabs** to display the Tabs page, as shown in Figure 2.36, below:

TabStrip Property Pages

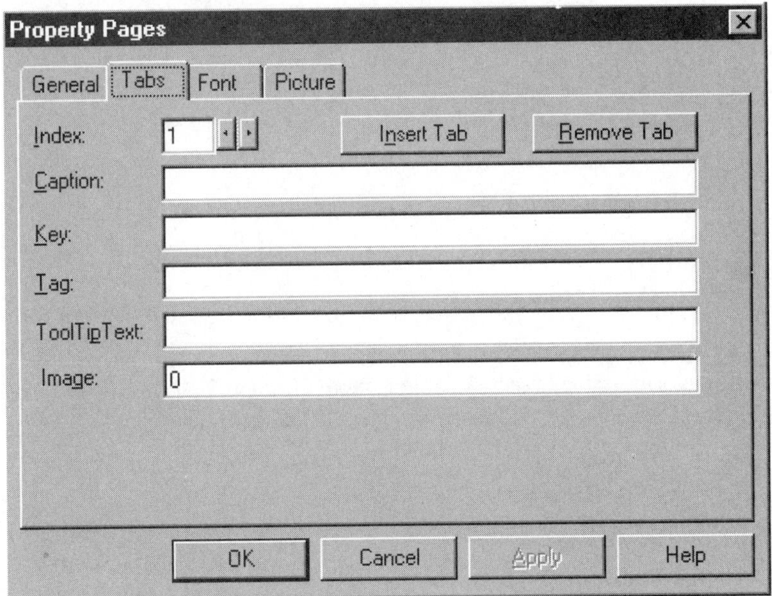

Create Tab Objects at Run Time Using the Add Method

To create Tab objects at run time, use the Add method for Tab objects.

> **Note** One Tab object is created for you by default.

To create a collection of Tab objects at run time

1. Declare a variable as type Tab. As you add each Tab object, the variable will contain the reference to the newly created object. Use this reference to set various properties of the new Tab object.
2. Using the Set statement with the Add method, set the object variable to the new Tab object.
3. Using the object variable, set the properties of the new Tab object.

The code below uses the Form object's Load event to create two Tab objects, then sets the Caption, Image, and Key properties of the new Tab object.

```
Private Sub Form_Load()
   ' The TabStrip control is named "tabData"
   ' Declare a variable, then use the Set
   ' statement with the Add method to create a new
   ' Tab object, while setting the object variable to
   ' the new Tab. Use the reference to set properties.
   Dim tabX As Tab
   ' Tab 1: Find text.
   Set tabX = tabData.Tabs.Add()
   tabX.Key = "find"
   tabX.Caption = "Find"
   tabX.Image = "Find" ' Assuming this image exists.

   ' Tab 2: Draw objects.
   Set tabX= tabData.Panels.Add()
   tabX.Key = "draw"
   tabX.Caption = "Draw"
   tabX.Image = "draw" ' Assuming this image exists.
End Sub
```

Tip Using the Add method without setting the object variable is more efficient than setting the properties with the object variable. In this case, the code above could be rewritten as:

```
tabData.Tabs.Add , "find", "Find", "find"
tabData.Tabs.Add , "draw", "Draw", "draw"
```

Use the Client Area to Position Container Controls

The TabStrip control is commonly used to create tabbed dialog boxes. Each page in the dialog box consists of a *tab* and a *client area*, as seen in the figure below:

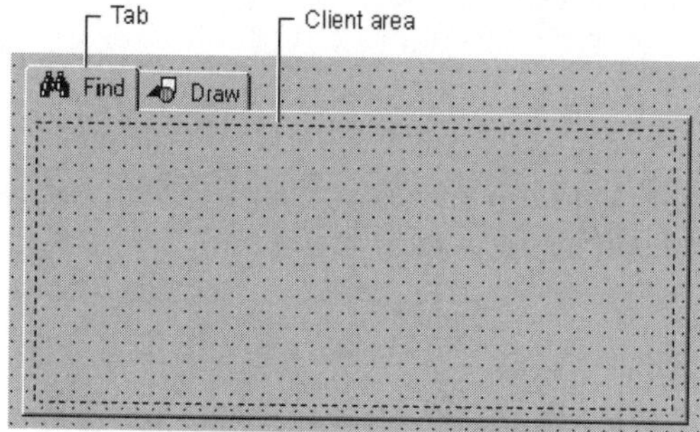

At run time, when the user clicks on a tab, you must program the client area to be reconfigured with a different set of container controls (discussed below in "Managing Tabs and Container Controls").

At design time, draw a container control, such as the PictureBox or Frame control, on the form. If you use a Frame control, you can set its BorderStyle property to be invisible at run time. Copy and paste the same control to create an array of controls; create one control for each Tab object you have created.

On each container control, draw the controls that should appear on a tab. Your form may appear something like Figure 2.37, below:

Figure 2.37 TabStrip at design time with two PictureBox controls

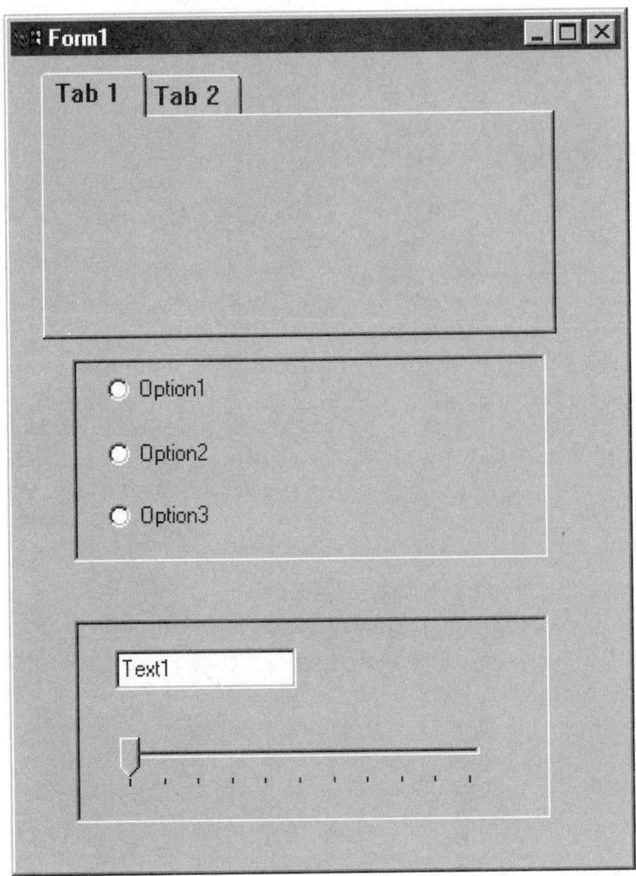

After you have created the container controls, there is one additional technique required to position them over the TabStrip control's client area: use the Move method with the ClientLeft, ClientTop, ClientWidth, and ClientHeight properties of the Tabstrip control, as shown in the code below:

```
Private Sub Form_Load()
   ' The name of the TabStrip is "tabRTF."
   ' The Frame control is named "fraTab."
   For i = 0 To fraTab.Count - 1
   With fraTab(i)
      .Move tabRTF.ClientLeft, _
      tabRTF.ClientTop, _
      tabRTF.ClientWidth, _
      tabRTF.ClientHeight
   End With
   Next i
End Sub
```

Managing Tabs and Container Controls

A tabbed dialog box contains more than one Tab object. As seen above, a Frame control (or other container control) should be associated with each Tab object. To efficiently manage the numerous Tab objects and container controls, the following strategy can be used:

1. At design time, create all the Tab objects you need.
2. Create a control array of container controls, one member for each Tab object.
3. On each container control, draw the controls that you want to have on a tab page.
4. At run time, use the control's SelectedItem property to determine the Index of the clicked Tab object.
5. Use the ZOrder method to bring the appropriate container control to the front.

The code to bring the proper container control to the front would then resemble the code below:

```
Private Sub tabRTF_Click()
   picRTF(tabRTF.SelectedItem.Index - 1).ZOrder 0
End Sub
```

Tip At design time, you can set the Index property of the control array to become a 1-based array. Because the Tabs collection is also a 1-based collection, the above code would then be rewritten:

```
picRTF(TabRTF.SelectedItem.Index).ZOrder 0
```

For More Information For an example of code implementing the strategy outlined above, see "TabStrip Scenario: Create a Tabbed Dialog Box."

Tab Style Property: Buttons or Tabs

The Style property determines whether the TabStrip control looks like notebook tabs (Tabs),

or push buttons (Buttons).

The advantages of each are outlined below:

Style	Possible Use
Tabs	Use the Tabs style to create Tabbed dialog boxes. With this style, the complete tabbed dialog, including the client area, is drawn for you. Your code must manage what appears in the client area.
Buttons	The Buttons style can be used to create a toolbar or task bar — in other words, when you do not need the client area, but prefer to have only the buttons as an interface element. Alternatively, you may wish to use the Buttons style when you do not need a well-defined client area drawn for you.

MultiRow Tabs

Another feature of the TabStrip control is the MultiRow property. When this property is set to True, a large number of Tab objects appear in rows, as seen in the figure below:

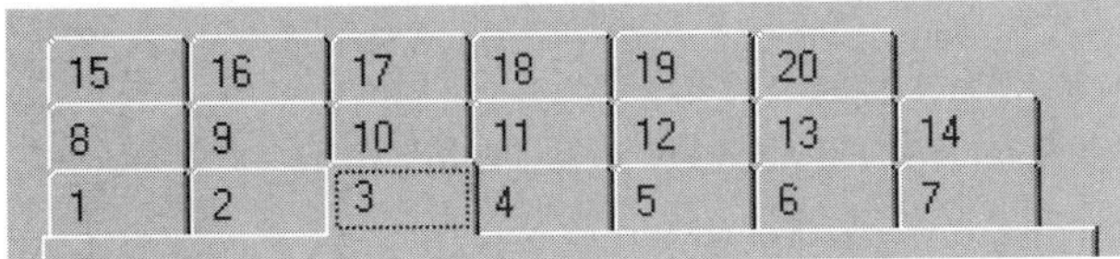

If the MultiRow property is set to False, the same set of tabs appears in a single row, with a pair of scroll buttons at the rightmost end:

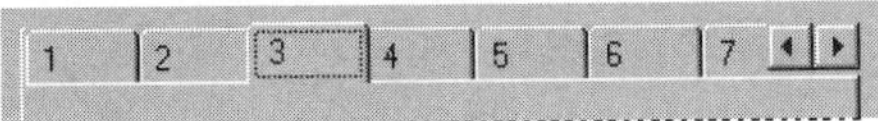

The TabWidthStyle property determines the appearance of each row, and, if TabWidthStyle is set to Fixed, you can use the TabFixedHeight and TabFixedWidth properties to set the same height and width for all tabs in the TabStrip control.

Tabstrip Scenario: Create a Tabbed Dialog Box

The TabStrip control is used to create dialog boxes which contain a number of tabs. Each tab usually has some relationship to a larger theme, and is therefore related to other tabs in the same dialog box. In this scenario, we create a tabbed dialog box which sets the fonts, and indents of a RichTextBox.

The following objects are used in the code below:

- Form object named "frmRTF"
- RichTextBox control named "rtfData"
- TabStrip control named "tabRTF"
- Form object named "frmTab"
- Frame control named "fraTab"
- ComboBox named "cmbFonts"
- OptionButton control named "optNormal"
- OptionButton control named "optBullet"

To create a Tabbed Dialog Box

1. Create two forms, one named "frmRTF" to contain the RichTextbox, and a second named "frmTab" to contain the TabStrip control.
2. At design time, create two Tab objects on the TabStrip control.
3. Create a Frame control array named "fraTab" on frmTab.
4. Draw the ComboBox on fraTab(0) and two OptionButton controls on fraTab(1).
5. Use the Move method in the Load event to position the Frame controls.
6. In the TabStrip control's Click event, use the SelectedItem property to determine the Index of the clicked Tab.
7. Use the Index with the ZOrder method to bring the right Frame to the front.

Create two Forms, One Named "frmRTF" to Contain the RichTextbox, and a Second Named "frmTab" to Contain the TabStrip Control

This scenario requires two forms: the first is named "frmRTF," and contains the RichTextBox control, the second, named "frmTab," contains the TabStrip control.

To create two Form objects

1. On the **File** menu, click **New Project** to display the **New Project** dialog box.
2. Double-click the Standard EXE Project icon, and a new form named Form1 will be created for you.
3. If the Properties window is not showing, press F4 to display it.
4. Click the **Name** box and type "frmRTF."
5. Draw a RichTextBox control on the form.

   Note You must have the RichTextBox (RichTx32.ocx) loaded into the Toolbox. See "Loading ActiveX Controls" for more information.

6. On the Properties page window, click the **Name** box and type "rtfData."
7. On the Project Explorer window, click **Add Form** to display the **Add Form** dialog box.
8. Double-click the Form icon to insert another form into the project.
9. On the Properties window, click the name box and type "frmTab."
10. Draw a TabStrip control on frmTab, and name it "tabRTF."

You must also have some code that shows the second form. A quick way to do this would be to place a Show method in the DblClick event of the first Form object (frmRTF), as shown below:

```
Private Sub Form_DblClick()
   frmTab.Show
End Sub
```

At Design time, Create Two Tab Objects on the TabStrip Control

You can create Tab objects at design time and at run time. In this scenario, you should create the two tabs at design time. Right-click on the TabStrip control and click Properties to display the Property Pages dialog box. Then click the Tabs tab and click Insert Tab twice. Be sure to give the tabs appropriate captions — "Fonts," and "Indents."

Create a Control Array Named "fraTab" on frmTab

A TabStrip control functions by managing Tab objects. Each Tab object is associated with a container control that appears in the tab's client area. It's most efficient to use a control array to create the container controls. In this scenario, draw a Frame control on the same form as the TabStrip control, and name it "fraTab."

To create a control array

1. Draw a Frame control on frmTab.
2. Click the **Name** box on the Properties window and type "fraTab."
3. Click the Frame control and copy it to the clipboard by either pressing CTRL+C or clicking **Copy** from the **Edit** menu.
4. Paste the same control back on the form by pressing CTRL+V. A dialog box will ask you if you want to create a control array. Click **Yes**.

Draw the ComboBox on fraTab(0) and Two OptionButton controls on fraTab(1)

On the control named fraTab(0), draw a ComboBox control, and name it "cmbFonts." To populate the ComboBox with all available fonts on your system, use the following code:

```
Private Sub Form_Load()
   Dim i   ' Declare variable.
   ' Determine number of fonts.
   For i = 0 To Printer.FontCount - 1
      ' Put each font into list box.
      cmbFonts.AddItem Printer.Fonts(I)
   Next i
   cmbFonts.ListIndex = 0
End Sub
```

To set the SelFontName property of the RichTextBox control, use the following code:

```
Private Sub cmbFonts_Click()
   frmRtf.rtfData.SelFontName = cmbFonts.Text
End Sub
```

Draw two OptionButton controls on the second Frame control named fraTab(0). Name the first OptionButton control "optNormal," and change its Caption property to "Normal." Name the second control "optBullet," and set its Caption property to "Bullet." The code for these controls sets the SelBullet property to True or False. The code for each is shown below:

```
Private Sub optBullet_Click()
   ' The Form object's ScaleMode is set to Twips.
   frmRTF.rtfData.BulletIndent = 500
   frmRTF.rtfData.SelBullet = True
End Sub

Private Sub optNormal_Click()
   frmRTF.rtfData.SelBullet = False
End Sub
```

Use the Move Method in the Load Event to Position the Frame Controls

To position the Frame controls over the client area, use the Move method in the Form object's Load event, as shown below:

```
Private Sub Form_Load()
   ' The name of the TabStrip is "tabRTF."
   ' The Frame control is named "fraTab."
   For i = 0 To   fraTab.Count - 1
   With fraTab(i)
      .Move tabRTF.ClientLeft, _
      tabRTF.ClientTop, _
      tabRTF.ClientWidth, _
      tabRTF.ClientHeight
   End With
   Next I

   ' Bring the first fraTab control to the front.
   fraTab(0).ZOrder 0
End Sub
```

In the TabStrip Control's Click Event, Use the SelectedItem Property to Determine the Index of the Clicked Tab

To determine which Tab object, use the SelectedItem property. This property returns a reference to the clicked tab. However, the Tabs collection is a 1-based collection (the collection index begins with 1), and the fraTab array is a 0-based collection. To make sure the two are synchronized, subtract 1 from the Index, as shown below.

```
Private Sub tabRTF_Click()
fraTab(tabRTF.SelectedItem.Index - 1).ZOrder 0
End Sub
```

Tip At design time, you can set the Index property of the Frame control array to become a 1-based array. Thus the code above would read:

```
fraTab(tabRTF.SelectedItem.Index).ZOrder 0
```

The Complete Code

The complete code is shown below:

```
Private Sub Form_Load()
   Dim i As Integer' Declare variable.
   ' Determine number of fonts.
   For i = 0 To Printer.FontCount - 1
```

```
      ' Put each font into list box.
      cmbFonts.AddItem Printer.Fonts(i)
   Next i

   cmbFonts.ListIndex = 0

   ' The name of the TabStrip is "tabRTF."
   ' The Frame control is named "fraTab."
   For i = 0 To fraTab.Count - 1
   With fraTab(i)
      .Move tabRTF.ClientLeft, _
      tabRTF.ClientTop, _
      tabRTF.ClientWidth, _
      tabRTF.ClientHeight
   End With
   Next i

   ' Bring the first fraTab control to the front.
   fraTab(0).ZOrder 0
End Sub

Private Sub cmbFonts_Click()
   frmRTF.rtfData.SelFontName = cmbFonts.Text
End Sub

Private Sub optBullet_Click()
   frmRTF.rtfData.BulletIndent = 500
   frmRTF.rtfData.SelBullet = True
End Sub

Private Sub optNormal_Click()
   frmRTF.rtfData.SelBullet = False

End Sub

Private Sub tabRTF_Click()
   fraTab(tabRTF.SelectedItem.Index - 1).ZOrder 0
End Sub
```

This following code goes into the form named “frmRTF.”

```
Private Sub Form_DblClick()
   frmTab.Show
End Sub
```

Using the Toolbar Control

A Toolbar control contains a collection of Button objects used to create a toolbar you can associate with an application.

Typically, a toolbar contains buttons that correspond to items in an application's menu, providing a graphic interface for the user to access an application's most frequently used functions and commands. The Toolbar control can also contain other controls, such as ComboBox or TextBox controls.

To create a toolbar, you must add Button objects to a Buttons collection; each Button object can have optional text and/or an image, supplied by an associated ImageList control. Set text with the Caption property, and an image with the Image property for each Button object. At design time, you can add Button objects to the control with the Toolbar Property Pages dialog box. At run time, you can add or remove buttons from the Buttons collection using Add and Remove methods.

To add other controls at design time, simply draw the desired controls on the toolbar. Alternatively, you can create a Button object with a Placeholder style and position the desired control over the button in a Resize event.

Double-clicking a toolbar at run time invokes the Customize Toolbar dialog box, which allows the user to hide, display, or rearrange toolbar buttons. To enable or disable the dialog box, set the AllowCustomize property. You can also invoke the Customize Toolbar dialog box by invoking the Customize method. If you wish to save and restore the state of a toolbar, or allow the end user to do so, use the SaveToolbar and RestoreToolbar methods.

Possible Uses

- Provide a consistent interface between applications with matching toolbars.
- Place commonly used functions, such as File operations, in an easy to access place.
- Provide a graphical, intuitive interface for your application.

The Buttons Collection

The Toolbar control consists of one or more Button objects in a Buttons collection. At both design time and run time, you create Button objects. Each button can have an image, a caption, a ToolTip, or all three, as shown below:

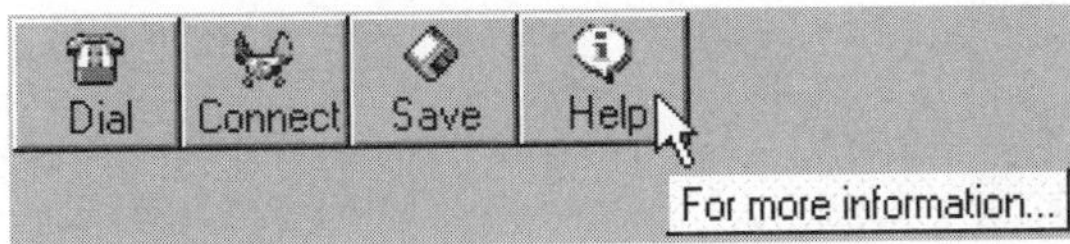

Each button object also has a Style property (discussed below) that determines how the button will behave.

Associate the ImageList Control with the Toolbar Control

Toolbars usually feature icons that represent a function of the application. For example, an icon of a floppy disk is generally understood to represent a "Save File" function. To get your toolbar to display such images, you must first associate an ImageList control with the Toolbar control, and this can be accomplished at either design time or run time.

To associate an ImageList control with a Toolbar control at design time

1. Populate the ImageList control with images for the Toolbar.
2. Right-click on the Toolbar control and click **Properties** to open the **Property Pages** dialog box.
3. On the **General** tab, click the **ImageList** box and select the ImageList control you have populated.

To associate an ImageList control with the Toolbar control at run time, simply set the ImageList property to the name of the **ImageList** control, as shown in the example below:

```
Private Sub Form_Load()
   ' The Toolbar control is named "tlbTools," and the
   ' ImageList control is named "imlTools."
   tlbTools.ImageList = imlTools
End Sub
```

Create Buttons at Design Time or Run Time

To create Button objects at design time

1. Right-click on the Toolbar control and click **Properties** to display the Toolbar **Property Pages**.
2. Click the **Buttons** tab to display the dialog box shown below:

Toolbar control property pages

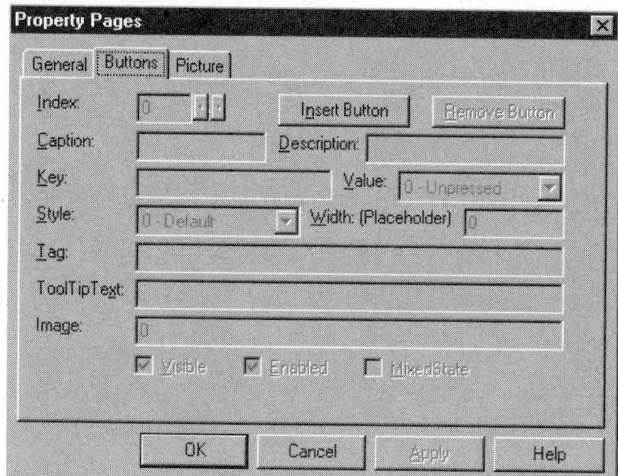

3. Click **Insert Button** to insert a new Button object.
4. Set appropriate properties, such as Key, Caption, Image, and ToolTipText.
5. Set the Button object's Style property by clicking the **Style** box and selecting a style.

To create a collection of Button objects at run time

1. Declare an object variable of type Button. As you add each Button object, the variable will contain the reference to the newly created object. Use this reference to set various properties of the new Button object.
2. Using the Set statement with the Add method, set the object variable to the new Button object.
3. Using the object variable, set the properties of the new Button object.

The code below uses the Form object's Load event to create one Button object, then sets the Key, Caption, ToolTipText, and Style properties of the new Button object.

```
Private Sub Form_Load()
   ' Declare a variable, then set using the Set
   ' statement with the Add method, create a new
   ' Button object, and set the object variable to
   ' the new Button. Use the reference to set
   ' properties.
   Dim myButton As Button
   Set myButton = tlbTools.Buttons.Add()
   myButton.Key = "left"
   myButton.Caption = "Align Left"
   myButton.ToolTipText = "Align Left"
   myButton.Style = tbrSeparator
End Sub
```

Tip Using the arguments of the Button collection's Add method is more efficient than setting the properties with the object variable. In this case, the code above could be rewritten as:

```
tlbTools.Buttons.Add , "left", "Align Left", _
tbrSeparator
```

Button Style Property Determines Button Behavior

An important property of the Button object is the Style property. The Style property determines how a button behaves — and the function assigned to the button can have a bearing on which style is applied to it. The five button styles are listed below, with their possible uses:

Constant	Value	Possible Use
tbrDefault	0	Use the Default button style when the function it represents has no dependence on other functions. For example, a Save File operation can be performed at any time. Further, when the button is depressed, it springs back again when the function is finished.
tbrCheck	1	The Check style should be used when the function it represents is a toggle of some kind. For example, when using a RichTextBox control, selected text can be either bold or not. Thus, when the button is depressed, it stays depressed until it is pressed again.
tbrButtonGroup	2	Use the ButtonGroup style when a group of functions are mutually exclusive. That is, only one of the functions represented by the group of buttons can be on at a time. For example, text in a RichTextBox control can only be left-aligned, center-aligned, or right-aligned — it cannot be more than one style at a time. Note: although only one button at a time can be depressed, all buttons in the group can be unpressed.
tbrSeparator	3	The separator style has no function except to create a button that is eight pixels wide. Use the separator style to create a button that separates one button from another. Or use it to enclose the group of buttons with the ButtonGroup style.
tbrPlaceholder	4	The placeholder style functions as a "dummy" button: use this button to create a space on the Toolbar control where you want to have another control (such as a ComboBox or ListBox control) appear.

Placing Controls on the Toolbar

You can easily place other controls, such as the ComboBox, TextBox, or OptionButton control, on the Toolbar control at design time.

To place other controls on the Toolbar control at design time

1. Create Button objects and assign appropriate properties.
2. Create a space on the toolbar where you want the other control to appear, then add a button with the Placeholder style, and set the Width property to an appropriate value.
3. Draw the other control in the space occupied by the placeholder button.

Reposition Other Controls in the Resize Event

If the Wrappable property is set to True, the Toolbar control wraps automatically when the end user resizes the form. While Button objects wrap automatically, controls placed on them do not. To enable controls to wrap, first create a Button object with the Placeholder style, and draw the control in the space created by the button (as shown in the above topic). Then reposition the control over the button using the Move method in the Form object's Resize event, as shown below:

```
Private Sub Form_Resize()
   ' The Toolbar is named "tlbRTF"
   ' The Button object's Key is "btnFonts"
   ' The Combobox is named "cmbFonts"

   ' The ComboBox is placed over the position of the
   ' Button object using the Move method.
   With tlbRTF.Buttons("btnFonts")
      cmbFonts.Move .Left, .Top, .Width
      cmbFonts.ZOrder 0
   End With
End Sub
```

Use the Select Case Statement in the ButtonClick Event to Program Button Functionality

The ButtonClick event occurs whenever a button (except buttons with the placeholder or separator style) is clicked. You can identify the button that was clicked by its Index property or its Key property. Using either of these properties, use the Select Case statement to program the button's function, as shown in the example code below:

```
Private Sub tlbRTF_Click(ByVal Button As Button)
   Select Case Button.Key
   Case "OpenFile"
      ' Call a user-defined function to open a file.
      OpenFile
   Case "Bold"
      ' Call a user-defined function to bold text.
      BoldText
   Case Else
      ' Handle other cases.
   End Select
End Sub
```

Use the MixedState Property to Signify Indeterminate States

In some cases, a function of your application may return an indeterminate state — a state that is a combination of two or more states. For example, if the user selects text in a RichTextBox, and some of the text is italicized, the button that represents italicized text cannot be either checked or unchecked; the text in the selection is both. To signify this indeterminate state, set the MixedState property to True. This dithers the image on the button to create a third state of the button's image.

Set ToolTip Text with the ToolTipText Property

A *ToolTip* is the text that appears above a button whenever the cursor hovers (without clicking) over a Button object.

You can add a ToolTip to any button at design time by typing the text you want to appear in the ToolTipText box of the Toolbar control's Property Pages.

At run time, you can dynamically change the ToolTip by setting the ToolTipText property for the Button object. The following code occurs in a CommandButton control that changes the Key and ToolTipText property of one button:

```
Private Sub cmdChangeButton_Click()
   ' The name of the toolbar is "tlbFunctions"
   ' Reset the Key and ToolTipText properties of
   ' a button with Key property value "1 funct"
   tlbfuncts.Buttons("1 funct"). _
   ToolTipText = "Function 7"

   tlbfuncts.Buttons("1 funct").Key = "7 funct"
End Sub
```

Allowing End Users to Customize the Toolbar

If you set the AllowCustomize property to True, the end user can customize the toolbar by double-clicking it. Double-clicking the toolbar displays the Customize Toolbar dialog box, shown below:

Customize Toolbar dialog box

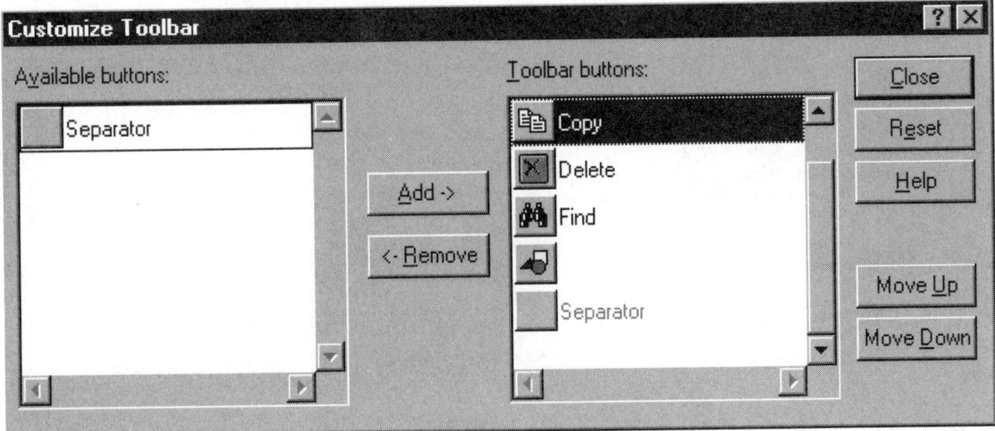

Alternatively, you can display the dialog box by invoking the Customize method.

Using the SaveToolbar and RestoreToolbar Methods

If you allow your end user to reconfigure the Toolbar control, you can save and restore the toolbar by using the SaveToolbar and RestoreToolbar methods. For example, if several users use the same application but have different toolbar preferences, use the SaveToolbar method to allow each person to create a customized toolbar. Then create a login procedure that identifies each user, and uses that information to restore the user's personalized toolbar with the RestoreToolbar method.

The SaveToolbar method saves the current state of the Toolbar control to the system registry. The method requires three arguments. The first argument, *key*, must be an integer. The second and third arguments, *subkey* and *value*, must be strings. To store different versions of the same toolbar in the same *subkey*, set the *value* argument to a different string.

The code below uses two constants to define the first two arguments. In the Form object's Load event, the code invokes a procedure named "Login" that returns the password of the user. The code then uses that value to restore a previously stored toolbar. The command button named "cmdSaveToolbar" saves the current state using the same three values.

```
' Declarations: SaveToolbar method constants.
Const SaveKey = 1
Const SaveSubKey = "MyToolbar"
Dim mSaveVal As String ' Module variable that
                       ' identifies user.


Private Sub Form_Load()
   ' Run a login procedure that identifies the
   ' user. Use the user's password to identifiy the
   ' user's toolbar.
   mSaveVal = LogIn()
```

```
    ' Restore state of Toolbar1 using Constants.
    Toolbar1.RestoreToolbar SaveKey, SaveSubKey, _
    mSaveVal
End Sub

Public Function LogIn()
    ' Ask the user for a password.
    LogIn = InputBox("Password")
End Function

Private Sub cmdSaveToolbar_Click()
    ' Save the toolbar using the same constants.
    Toolbar1.SaveToolbar SaveKey, SaveSubKey, mSaveVal
End Sub
```

Toolbar Scenario 1: Provide an RTF Text Editor with an OpenFile Button

With the RichTextBox control, you can create applications that incorporate an RTF text editor to allow end users to edit documents without starting up a second application. When you incorporate such a text editor into the application, you can provide a toolbar that gives the end user access to common operations such as opening a file and changing font characteristics. This simple scenario populates the Toolbar control with only one Button object. When the user clicks the button, the Open File dialog box is opened.

The following objects are used in this scenario:

- Form object named "frmRTF"
- Toolbar control named "tlbRTF"
- RichTextBox control named "rtfData"
- ImageList control named "imlToolbar"
- CommonDialog control named "dlgOpenFile"

To incorporate a toolbar into your application

1. At design time, populate an ImageList control with appropriate images.
2. Associate the ImageList control with the Toolbar control.
3. Create buttons for the toolbar at design time.
4. Create a File menu with an Open menu item named "mnuOpen."

5. In the Form_Load event, configure a CommonDialog control to open Rich Text Format (RTF) files.
6. In the mnuOpen_Click event, use the CommonDialog control to open a file.
7. In the Toolbar control's Button_Click event, use the Select Case statement with the Key property to identify the clicked Button object and invoke the mnuOpen_Click event.

Populate an ImageList Control with Appropriate Images

At design time, populate the ImageList control with the images you will need to populate your Toolbar control. This is easily accomplished.

To populate an ImageList at design time

1. Right-click on the ImageList control, then click **Properties** to open the **Property Pages** dialog box.

   – or –

   Click the ImageList control, then press F4 to get the Properties Window, and double-click the **Custom** property.
2. Click the **Images** tab.
3. Click **Insert Picture**. In the **Select Picture** dialog box, find the image you wish to have appear in the Toolbar control. Repeat this until you have all the images you require. (The sample application uses the bitmap named "open.bmp.")

Associate the ImageList Control with the Toolbar Control

Also at design time, after you have populated the ImageList control, you must associate it with the Toolbar control.

To associate the ImageList control with the Toolbar control at design time

1. Right-click on the ImageList control, then click **Properties** to open the **Property Pages** dialog box.

   – or –

   Click the ImageList control, then press F4 to get the Properties Window, and double-click the **Custom** property.
2. On the **General** tab, click the **ImageList** box and select the ImageList control that you have just populated.

Create Buttons for the Toolbar at Design Time

Once you have populated the ImageList control and associated it with the Toolbar control, you can begin to create the Button objects themselves. In this scenario, we will create two buttons, one with the Placeholder style, and a second with the Default style.

To add buttons to the Toolbar Control at design time

1. Right-click on the Toolbar control, then click **Properties.**
2. In the **Property Pages** dialog box, click the **Buttons** tab.
3. Click **Insert Button**.
4. Click the **Style** box and select Separator.
5. Click **Insert Button** again — the style is set to Default automatically.
6. In the **Key** box, type **openFile**.
7. In the **Description** box, type **Open File**.
8. In the **Image** box, type **1**.
9. Click **OK**.

Create a File Menu with an Open Menu Item Named "mnuOpen"

Because the Open File operation is commonly invoked from a menu bar, we must create a menu first.

To create a menu

1. Select the form "frmRTF."
2. Press CTRL+E to display the **Menu Editor** dialog box.
3. In the **Caption** box, type **File**.
4. In the **Name** box, type **mnuFile**.
5. Click the **Next** button.
6. In the **Caption** box, type **Open**.
7. In the **Name** box, type **mnuOpen**.
8. Click the right-pointing arrow to indent the menu item.

Configure a CommonDialog Control to Open Rich Text Format (RTF) Files

Use the CommonDialog control to create an Open File dialog box. This can be done in the Form object's Load event, as shown below:

```
Private Sub Form_Load()
   ' Configure dlgOpenFile for opening and
   ' saving files.
```

```
    With dlgOpenFile
        .DefaultExt = ".rtf"
        .Filter = "RTF file (*.RTF) | *.RTF"
    End With
End Sub
```

Use the CommonDialog Control to Open a File

In the present scenario, the Toolbar control's single button simply represents a common operation, an Open File function, that is also found on the menu bar. Thus, the code for the Open File operation should be placed in the mnuOpen object's Click event, as shown below:

```
Private Sub mnuOpen_Click()
    ' Declare a string variable to hold the file name.
    ' Then invoke the ShowOpen method to show
    ' the dialog box. Set the variable to the Filename
    ' property. Finally, load the RichTextBox control.
    Dim strOpen As String
    dlgOpenFile.ShowOpen
    strOpen = dlgOpenFile.Filename
    rtfData.LoadFile strOpen, rtfRTF
End Sub
```

Use the Select Case Statement with the Key Property to Identify the Clicked Button Object and Invoke the mnuOpen_Click Event

When any Button object on the Toolbar control is clicked, the ButtonClick event occurs. To determine which Button object was clicked, use the Select Case statement with either the Key property or the Index property.

The example below uses the Key property of the Button object.

```
Private Sub tlbRTF_ButtonClick _
(ByVal Button As Button)
    Select Case Button.Key
    ' User clicked "open file" button.
    Case "openFile"
        mnuOpen_Click ' Invoke the mnuOpen Click event
    End Select
End Sub
```

You can now run the project and open an RTF file by clicking the button on the toolbar.

Toolbar Scenario 2: Set the Text Alignment of a RichTextBox Control Using Grouped Buttons

This scenario builds upon the previous scenario, where a Toolbar control is used to open a file loaded into a RichTextBox control. In this scenario, you will add three buttons to the Toolbar control with icons for left-aligned, center-aligned, and right-aligned.

The three buttons are all a part the ButtonGroup (tbrButtonGroup) style which allows only one of the three to be pressed at any time.

> **Important** To specify which buttons are part of a button group, you must "enclose" the group with two other buttons which have the Separator (tbrSeparator) style. For example, if there are three buttons in a group, and they are the fourth through the sixth buttons, then the third and seventh buttons must have the Separator style to enclose the group.

When the user clicks in the RichTextBox control, the SelChange event occurs. In that event, the code checks the SelAlignment property which returns the alignment of the current selection. That value is used to depress the appropriate button in the Toolbar control.

For More Information See "Style Property (Button Object)" in the *Microsoft Visual Basic 6.0 Controls Reference* for more information about the ButtonGroup style .

The following objects are used in this scenario:

- Form object named "frmRTF"
- Toolbar control named "tlbRTF"
- RichTextBox control named "rtfData"
- ImageList control named "imlToolbar"

To create a toolbar that sets text alignment

(The following operations are described at a high-level. For more specific information, see "Using the Toolbar Control.")

1. At design time, insert the appropriate images into an ImageList control associated with the Toolbar control.
2. Create the Button objects using the **Property Pages** dialog box.
3. In the ButtonClick event, use the Select Case statement to determine which button was pressed, and set the alignment appropriate to the button.
4. In the RichTextBox control's SelChange event, use the Select Case statement to reflect alignment.

Insert the Appropriate Images into an ImageList Control Associated with the Toolbar Control

As in the previous Toolbar Control Scenario, you must first insert the appropriate images for the button group into an ImageList control.

To add to the ImageList control at design time

1. Right-click on the ImageList control and click **Properties**.
2. In the **Property Pages** dialog box, click the **Images** tab.
3. Click **Insert Picture** to display the **Select Picture** dialog box which allows you to find the images you need. This scenario uses images found in the Tools\Bitmaps\Tlbr_W95 directory. The images used are named: Lft.bmp, Cnt.bmp, and Rt.bmp.
4. For each image you insert, type an appropriate key for the image in the **Key** box. In this scenario, the images and their keys are as follows:

Image	Key
Lft.bmp	"left"
Cnt.bmp	"center"
Rt.bmp	"right"

5. Associate the ImageList with the Toolbar control by right-clicking the Toolbar control and clicking **Properties**, then selecting the ImageList control from the drop-down box **ImageList**.

Create the Button Objects Using the Property Pages Dialog Box

You can create Button objects at design time by using the Toolbar control's Property Pages dialog box. For specific information on how to do this, see "Toolbar Scenario 1: Provide an RTF Text Editor an OpenFile Button."

To create a group of three buttons, you must actually create five buttons, three of which are enclosed by two Button objects with the Separator style. The Style, Key, ToolTipText, and Image properties for the five buttons should be set as shown in the table below:

Button	Style	Key	ToolTipText	Image
1	tbrSeparator	[none]	[none]	[none]
2	tbrButtonGroup	left	Align Left	1
3	tbrButtonGroup	center	Center	2
4	tbrButtonGroup	right	Align Right	3
5	tbrSeparator	[none]	[none]	[none]

Use the Select Case Statement to Determine Which Button was Pressed, and Set the Alignment Appropriate to the Button

The ButtonClick event occurs when the user clicks on any Button object (except buttons with the Separator or Placeholder styles). Use the Select Case statement with the Key property to determine which button was clicked, and set the alignment of the RichTextBox using the SelAlignment property of the RichTextBox control. After setting the alignment, return the focus to the control by using a SetFocus method, as shown in the code below:

```
Private Sub tlbRTF_ButtonClick(ByVal Button _
As Button)
   ' Use the Select Case statement with the Key
   ' property to determine which button was clicked.
   Select Case Button.Key
   Case "left"
      rtfData.SelAlignment = rtfLeft
      rtfData.SetFocus ' Return focus to RichTextBox.
   Case "center"
      rtfData.SelAlignment = rtfCenter
      rtfData.SetFocus
```

Use the Select Case Statement to Reflect Alignment

When the user clicks on a line in the RichTextBox control, the Toolbar buttons will reflect the alignment of the line. This can be accomplished using the RichTextBox control's SelChange event, as shown in the code below.

```
Private Sub rtfData_SelChange()
   ' When the insertion point changes, set the Toolbar
   ' buttons to reflect the attributes of the line
   ' where the cursor is located.
   Select Case rtfData.SelAlignment
   Case rtfLeft ' 0
      tlbRTF.Buttons("left").Value = tbrPressed
   Case rtfRight ' 1
      tlbRTF.Buttons("right").Value = tbrPressed
   case Else ' Null—no buttons are shown pressed.
      tlbRTF.Buttons("left").Value = tbrUnpressed
      tlbRTF.Buttons("center").Value = tbrUnpressed
      tlbRTF.Buttons("right").Value = tbrUnpressed
   End Select
End Sub
```

Running the Code

You can now run the project. Use the Open File button (created in "Toolbar Scenario 1: Provide an RTF Text Editor with an OpenFile Button") to open a file. You can also click the three grouped buttons to change the alignment of the text.

Using the TreeView Control

The TreeView control is designed to display data that is hierarchical in nature, such as organization trees, the entries in an index, the files and directories on a disk.

Typical TreeView

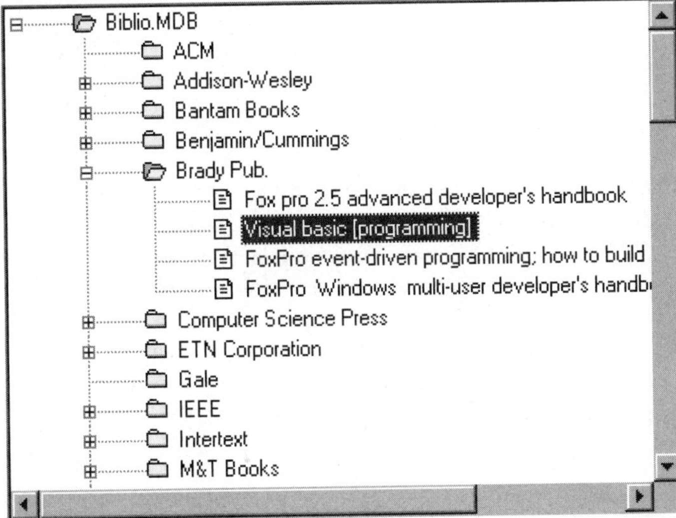

Possible Uses

- To create an organization tree that can be manipulated by the user.
- To create a tree that shows at least two or more levels of a database.

Setting Node Object Properties

A "tree" is comprised of cascading branches of "nodes," and each node typically consists of an image (set with the Image property) and a label (set with the Text property). Images for the nodes are supplied by an ImageList control associated with the TreeView control. For more information on using the ImageList control with other controls, see "Using the ImageList Control" earlier in this chapter.

A node can be expanded or collapsed, depending on whether or not the node has child nodes — nodes which descend from it. At the topmost level are "root" nodes, and each root node can have any number of child nodes. The total number of nodes is not limited (except by machine constraints). The figure below shows a tree with two root nodes; "Root 1" has three child nodes, and "Child 3" has a child node itself. "Root 2" has child nodes, as indicated by the "+" sign, but is unexpanded.

Root and child nodes

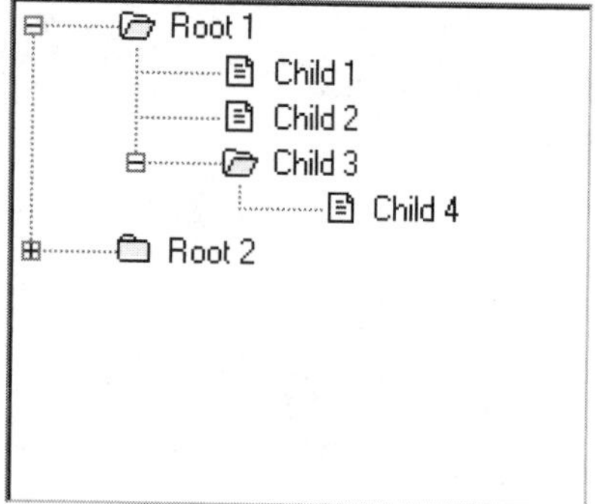

Each node in a tree is actually a programmable Node object, which belongs to the Nodes collection. As in other collections, each member of the collection has a unique Index and Key property which allows you to access the properties of the node. For example, the code below uses the Index of a particular node ("7") to set the Image and Text properties:

```
tvwMyTree.Nodes(7).Image = "closed"
tvwMyTree.Nodes(7).Text = "IEEE"
```

However, if a unique key, for example "7 ID" had been assigned to the node, the same code could be written as follows:

```
tvwMyTree.Nodes("7 ID").Image = "closed"
tvwMyTree.Nodes("7 ID").Text = "IEEE"
```

Node Relationships and References to Relative Nodes

Each node can be either a child or a parent, depending on its relationship to other nodes. The Node object features several properties which return various kinds of information about children or parent nodes. For example, the following code uses the Children property to return the number of children — if any — a node has:

```
MsgBox tvwMyTree.Nodes(10).Children
```

However, some of the properties do not return information, as the Children property does, but instead return a *reference* to another node object. For example, the Parent property returns a reference to the parent of any particular node (as long as the node is not a root node). With this reference, you can manipulate the parent node by invoking any methods, or setting properties, that apply to Node objects. For example, the code below returns the Text and Index properties of a parent node:

```
MsgBox tvwMyTree.Nodes(10).Parent.Text
MsgBox tvwMyTree.Nodes(10).Parent.Index
```

Tip Use the Set statement with an object variable of type Node to manipulate references to other Node objects. For example, the code below sets a Node object variable to the reference returned by the Parent property. The code then uses the object variable to return properties of the relative node:

```
Dim tempNode As Node ' Declare object variable.
' Set object variable to returned reference.
Set tempNode = tvwMyTree.Nodes(10).Parent
MsgBox tempNode.Text ' Returns parent's Text.
MsgBox tempNode.Index ' Returns parent's Index.
```

Adding Node Objects to the Nodes Collection

To add a Node to the tree, use the Add method (Nodes collection). This method includes two arguments, *relative* and *relationship*, which can determine where the node will be added. The first argument *relative* names a node; the second argument *relationship* specifies the relationship between the new node and the node named in *relative*.

For example, the following code adds a node named "11 node" as a child of another node named "7 node." The intrinsic constant tvwChild specifies that the new node is a child of the node named in the previous argument. The third argument assigns the Key property to the new node.

```
tvwMyTree.Nodes.Add "7 node", tvwChild, "11 node"
```

Other possible relationships include:

Constant	Value	Description
tvwLast	1	The Node is placed after all other nodes at the same level of the node named in *relative*.
tvwNext	2	The Node is placed after the node named in *relative*.
tvwPrevious	3	The Node is placed before the node named in *relative*.
tvwChild	4	The Node becomes a child node of the node named in *relative*.

For example, suppose there were three existing nodes, and you wished to place a fourth node between the second and the third nodes, the code would be:

```
' Assuming the second node's Key value is "2 node".
tvwMyTree.Nodes.Add "2 node", tvwNext
```

Other arguments of the Add method are *key*, *text*, and *image*. Using these arguments, you can assign the Key, Text, and Image properties as the Node object is created.

For More Information For more information about the Nodes collection's Add method, see "Add Method" by typing "Add Method" in the Index search and clicking "Add Method (Nodes Collection)." Or see the *Microsoft Visual Basic 6.0 Controls Reference.*

A second way of adding nodes is to declare an object variable of type Node, and then use the Set statement with the Add method. The Set statement sets the object variable to the new node. You can then use the object variable to set the node's properties, as shown below:

```
Dim nodX As Node
Set nodX = tvwMyTree.Nodes.Add("10 node", tvwChild)
nodX.Key = "11 node"
nodX.Text = "IEEE"
nodX.Image = "closed"
```

Tip Using the Set statement with the Add method makes reading and debugging your code easier. However, using the Add method and its arguments to add nodes creates faster code.

TreeView Control Scenario: Bind the TreeView to the Biblio.mdb Database

Sample Application: DataTree.vbp

The code examples in this chapter are taken from the DataTree.vbp sample application which is listed in the Samples!Alink("vbsamples") directory.

It is possible to bind the data from a database to a TreeView control. The following example binds a TreeView control to the Biblio database which is found on the Visual Basic CD. The scenario uses the Publishers table as the first level of tree nodes. If a publisher has one or more book titles, those titles are added to the tree as child nodes of the specific publisher.

Data-bound TreeView control

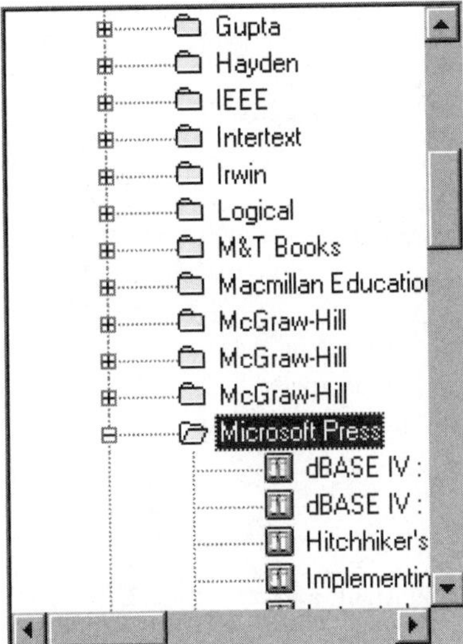

The following objects are used in the code below:

- Data Access Object Library (3.5)
- Form object named "frmDataTree"
- TreeView control named "tvwDB"
- CommandButton control named "cmdLoad"

To bind the Biblio.mdb Database to the TreeView control

1. Add a reference to the Data Access Objects (DAO 3.0) to your project.
2. Create module-level variables for the Database and Node objects.
3. In the Form Load event, set the Database object variable to the Biblio database using the OpenDatabase statement.
4. Create the top level node object using the Nodes collection's Add method.
5. In a CommandButton's Click event, create two Recordset variables and set them to the Publishers and Titles tables.
6. Use the "Do Until" statement to create a Node object for each publisher in the table.
7. For each publisher, check the PubID field in the Titles recordset for matches; add a child node for each match.

Add a Reference to the Data Access Objects (DAO 3.5) to Your Project

To bind a database to the TreeView control, you must first add a reference to the current version of Data Access Objects (DAO).

Create Module-Level Variables for the Database Object and Node Object

Because you will want to access the Biblio.mdb database several times during a single session, it's more efficient to keep a single copy of the database open by creating a module-level Database object. Thereafter, you can access the database without reopening it. In the Declarations section of the form, write:

```
Private mDbBiblio As Database
```

If you want the database to be used by other modules, use the Public statement, and rename the variable to reflect its global status, i.e., `gDbBiblio`.

When creating Node objects, use the Set statement (shown below) with a variable of type Node.

```
Dim TempNode As Node
Set TempNode = tvwDB.Nodes.Add()
```

While you can create the variable whenever you add Node objects, it is more efficient to declare a single module-level Node object variable once and use it to create all Node objects. Again in the Declarations section, write:

```
Private mNode As Node
```

Set the Database object variable to the Biblio database using the OpenDatabase statement

The Form object's Load event can be used to initialize the Database variable. The code for this would be:

```
Set mDbBiblio = DBEngine.OpenDatabase("BIBLIO.MDB")
```

After you have successfully initialized the Database object variable, you can freely access it from anywhere within the code module.

Form Load Event: Create the Top Level Node Object Using the Nodes Collection's Add Method

Now that the Database object variable has been initialized with the Biblio database, you may want to create the first node in the tree and assign it the name of the open database. You must first use the Node collection's Add method to create the first Node object. You should also use the Set statement with the mNode object variable, as shown below:

```
Set mNode = tvwDB.Nodes.Add() ' Create the first node.
mNode.Text = mDbBiblio.Name
```

Notice that in the code above, using the Set statement simultaneously created the Node while assigning it to the mNode object variable. Since the mNode variable now contains the newly created Node object, you can assign various properties to the new Node. In the above case, the name of the Database (i.e. the Database object's Name property) has been assigned to the new node's Text property.

CommandButton Click Event: Create Two Recordset Variables and Set Them to the Publishers and Titles Tables

The present scenario assumes that a button called "cmdLoad" exists, and that when the user clicks it, the TreeView control is populated with two tables from the Biblio database. To accomplish this task, you must first declare two DAO object variables in the button's Click event. The first variable, rsPublishers, will contain the Publishers table. The second, rsTitles, will contain the Titles table. The code below declares the two variables then uses the OpenRecordSet method to assign the tables to the variables:

```
Dim rsPublishers As Recordset
Dim rsTitles As Recordset

Set rsPublishers = mDbBiblio. _
OpenRecordset("Publishers", dbOpenDynaset)
Set rsTitles = mDbBiblio. _
OpenRecordset("titles", dbOpenDynaset)
```

Use the Do Until Statement to Create a Node Object for Each Publisher in the Table

Now that you have two open recordsets, you can iterate through each recordset, create a Node object, and assign an appropriate value to the object's Text property. First, you must iterate through the Publishers table and create a Node object for each Publisher in the table.

The simplified code below can be stated as, "Do until the End of the Recordset: create a Node object and assign its Text property the value of the Title field; move to the next record and repeat":

```
Do Until rsPublishers.EOF
   Set mNode = tvwDB.Nodes.Add(1, tvwChild)
   mNode.Text = rsPublishers!Name
   rsPublishers.MoveNext
Loop
```

Note that in the Add method above, we used two arguments. The first argument (1) is the Index property of the Node to which we want to add a Child node. That is, we want all the Publisher nodes to be children of the first (root) node (which was created in the Form's Load event). The second argument uses a constant (tvwChild) that specifies the new Node will be a child node of the Node with index "1."

For Each Publisher, Check the PubID Field in the Titles Recordset for Matches; Add a Child Node for each Match

The code above will populate the first level of the TreeView with the contents of the Publishers table. However, we wish to go one level deeper and add child nodes to each Publisher node. Each child node will then represent a book that the Publisher prints.

To accomplish this, while we have the reference to the newly created Publisher node (mNode), we need to iterate through the Titles recordset and check every record's PubID field. If that field corresponds to the PubID field in the Publishers recordset, the book is published by our present publisher. But before we can add a node to mNode, we must first assign a variable (intIndex) the value of mNode's Index property, as shown below:

```
intIndex = mNode.Index
```

We can now use this variable in the Add method, which requires the Index property of the Node object to which a child node is being added:

```
Set mNode = tvwDB.Nodes.Add(intIndex, tvwChild)
```

The simplified code below can be stated as, "Do until the End of the Recordset: create a child Node object and assign its Text property the value of the Title field; move to the next record and repeat":

```
Do Until rsTitles.EOF
   If rsPublishers!PubID = rsTitles!PubID Then
      Set mNode = tvwDB.Nodes.Add(intIndex, tvwChild)
      mNode.Text = rsTitles!Title ' Text property.
   End If
Loop
```

Completing the Code

The code above shows the basic strategy for populating a table with two related tables. The complete code is shown below:

```
' Be sure to set References to DAO 3.5
' In the Declarations section, declare module-level
' object variables:
Private mDbBiblio As Database
Private mNode As Node

Private Sub Form_Load()
   ' In Form_Load event, set object variable and
   ' create first Node object of TreeView control.

   Set mDbBiblio = DBEngine.Workspaces(0). _
   OpenDatabase("BIBLIO.MDB")

   tvwDB.Sorted = True
   Set mNode = tvwDB.Nodes.Add()
   mNode.Text = "Publishers"
   mNode.Tag = mDbBiblio.Name   ' Set Tag property.
   mNode.Image = "closed"       ' Set Image
                                ' property.
End Sub

Private Sub cmdLoad_Click()
   ' Declare DAO object variables and assign
   ' recordsets to them.
   Dim rsPublishers As Recordset
   Dim rsTitles As Recordset
   Set rsPublishers = mDbBiblio. _
   OpenRecordset("Publishers", dbOpenDynaset)
   Set rsTitles = mDbBiblio. _
   OpenRecordset("titles", dbOpenDynaset)

   ' Go to the first record.
   rsPublishers.MoveFirst

   Dim intIndex As Integer ' Variable for index.

   ' Do until the last record (EOF): add a Node
   ' object and use the Name field as the
   ' new Node object's text.
   Do Until rsPublishers.EOF
      Set mNode = tvwDB.Nodes.Add(1, tvwChild)
      mNode.Text = rsPublishers!Name
      mNode.Tag = "Publisher"  ' Tag identifies the
```

```
                                ' table.
        ' Assign a unique ID to the Key
        mNode.Key = CInt(rsPublishers!PubID) & " ID"
        ' Set the variable intIndex to the Index
        ' property of the newly created Node. Use this
        ' variable to add child Node objects to the
        ' present Node.
        intIndex = mNode.Index
        ' While on this record, search the Title table
        ' for any occurence of the same PubID in the
        ' Titles recordset. If one is found, add a Node
        ' object to the TreeView control, and set the
        ' new Node object properties with the found
        ' record's Title, ISBN and Author fields.
        Do Until rsTitles.EOF
           If rsPublishers!PubID = rsTitles!PubID Then
              Set mNode = tvwDB.Nodes. _
              Add(intIndex, tvwChild)
              mNode.Text = rsTitles!Title  ' Text.
              mNode.Key = rsTitles!ISBN ' Unique ID.
              mNode.Tag = "Authors"     ' Table name.
              mNode.Image = "leaf"      ' Image.
           End If
        rsTitles.MoveNext ' Next record in Titles.
        Loop
        ' Reset rsTitles to first Titles record.
        rsTitles.MoveFirst
        ' Move to next Publisher record.
        rsPublishers.MoveNext
    Loop
End Sub
```

Enhancing the Code

The example can be improved by using a SQL statement to create a smaller "Titles" recordset. The code below creates a recordset of only the records which have the same PubID value:

```
Set rsTitles = mDbBiblio.OpenRecordset _
("select * from Titles Where PubID = " & _
rsPublishers!PubID)
```

The code can then iterate through this smaller recordset more efficiently. The modified code is shown below:

```
Private Sub cmdLoad_Click()
   Dim rsPublishers As Recordset
   Dim rsTitles As Recordset
   Set rsPublishers = mDbBiblio. _
```

```
    OpenRecordset("Publishers", dbOpenDynaset)
    Dim intIndex
    Do Until rsPublishers.EOF
       Set mNode = tvwDB.Nodes.Add(1, tvwChild)
       mNode.Text = rsPublishers!Name
       mNode.Tag = "Publisher" ' Identifies the table.
       mNode.Key = rsPublishers!PubID & " ID"
       mNode.Image = "closed"
       intIndex = mNode.Index
       ' While on this record, create a recordset
       ' using a query that finds only titles that have
       ' the same PubID. For each record in the
       ' resulting recordset, add a Node object to the
       ' TreeView control, and set the new Node object
       ' properties with the record's Title, ISBN and
       ' Author fields.
       Set rsTitles = mDbBiblio.OpenRecordset _
       ("select * from Titles Where PubID = " & _
       rsPublishers!PubID)
       Do Until rsTitles.EOF
          Set mNode = tvwDB.Nodes. _
          Add(intIndex, tvwChild)
          mNode.Text = rsTitles!TITLE  ' Text.
          mNode.Key = rsTitles!ISBN    ' Unique ID.
          mNode.Tag = "Authors"      ' Table name.
          mNode.Image = "smlBook"      ' Image.
          ' Move to next record in rsTitles.
          rsTitles.MoveNext
       Loop
       ' Move to next Publishers record.
       rsPublishers.MoveNext
    Loop
End Sub
```

Using the UpDown Control

An UpDown control is a pair of arrow buttons that the user can click to increment or decrement a value, such as a scroll position or a number displayed in a *buddy* control. The buddy control can be any other kind of control, as long as it has a property that can be updated by the UpDown control.

To the user, an UpDown control and its buddy control often look like a single control. You can specify that an UpDown control automatically position itself next to its buddy control and that it automatically set the value of the buddy control to its current value. For example, you can use an UpDown control with a Textbox control to prompt the user for numeric input. The illustration below shows an UpDown control with a Textbox control as its buddy control, a combination that is sometimes referred to as a spinner control.

Possible Uses

- To increment or decrement the value of a field in an application.

Basic Operation

To use the UpDown control, you must first set the BuddyControl property to another control, and the BuddyProperty to a scrollable property on the other control. The Min and Max properties determine the limits of the control, and the Wrap property determines if the value will wrap when the end user scrolls past the Min or Max values. The Increment property specifies the amount by which the Value property will be changed when either the up or down arrow is clicked.

Use the AutoBuddy Property to Set a Buddy Control Automatically

At design time, setting the AutoBuddy property to True causes the UpDown control to automatically "buddy" with the previous control in the TabOrder.

To automatically set a buddy control

1. Draw the buddy control on the form.
2. Draw the UpDown control on the form.
3. Right-click the UpDown control and click **Properties** to display the **Property Pages** dialog box.
4. Click **Buddy** to display the Buddy tab, as seen in Figure 2.43 below.
5. Click the **AutoBuddy** check box to set the AutoBuddy property to True.
6. Click the **SyncBuddy** check box to set the SyncBuddy property to True.

Figure 2.43 Buddy Tab on the UpDown control property pages

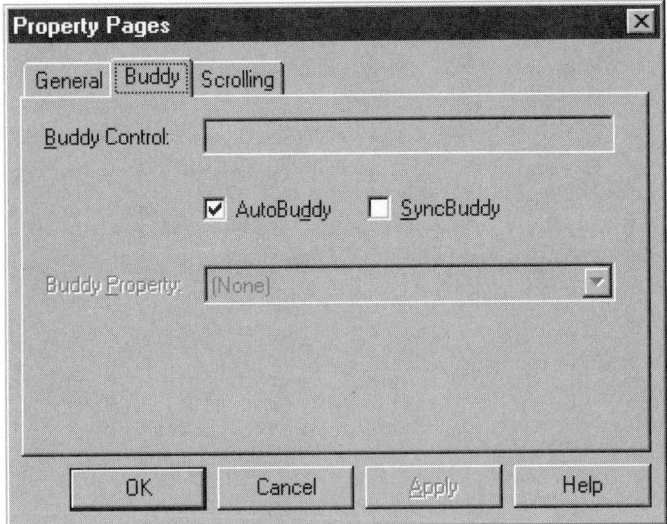

Determining the Scroll Behavior

The UpDown control includes several events and properties that allow you to determine how the control scrolls.

The Increment and Wrap Properties

The Wrap property determines how the control will behave when the end user holds down either the up or down button. If set to False, when the Max or Min value is reached, the controls ceases to scroll, and stops at the Max or Min value. When set to True, the control will return to either the Min or Max value and continue to increment (or decrement) through the values as determined by the Min and Max properties.

The Increment property specifies the amount by which the Value property will be changed when either the up or down arrow is clicked. This value cannot be a negative number. One use of this is to toggle a field or OptionButton between True (–1) and False (0), as shown in the code below:

```
Private Sub Form_Load()
   ' The UpDown control is named "updToggle."
   ' An OptionButton control is named "optToggle."
   With updToggle
      .BuddyControl = optToggle
      .Min = -1
      .Max = 0
      .Increment = 1
      .Wrap = True
   End With
End Sub
```

```
' Change the Value of the OptionButton with
' the UpDown control's Value property.
Private Sub updToggle_Change()
   optToggle.Value = updToggle.Value
End Sub
```

The UpClick and DownClick Events

Using the UpClick and DownClick events, you can control exactly how the UpDown control scrolls through a series of values. For example, if you want to allow the end user to scroll rapidly upward through the values, but slower going down through the values, you can set reset the Increment property to different values, as shown below:

```
Private Sub updScroll_UpClick()
   ' The name of the UpDown controls is "updScroll"
   updScroll.Increment = 5
End Sub

Private Sub updScroll_DownClick()
   ' When the user clicks the down button, the
   ' Increment switches to 1 for finer resolution.
   updScroll.Increment = 1
End Sub
```

Using the Winsock Control

A WinSock control allows you to connect to a remote machine and exchange data using either the User Datagram Protocol (UDP) or the Transmission Control Protocol (TCP). Both protocols can be used to create client and server applications. Like the Timer control, the WinSock control doesn't have a visible interface at run time.

Possible Uses

- Create a client application that collects user information before sending it to a central server.
- Create a server application that functions as a central collection point for data from several users.
- Create a "chat" application.

Selecting a Protocol

When using the WinSock control, the first consideration is whether to use the TCP or the UDP protocol. The major difference between the two lies in their connection state:

- The TCP protocol control is a connection-based protocol, and is analogous to a telephone — the user must establish a connection before proceeding.
- The UDP protocol is a connectionless protocol, and the transaction between two computers is like passing a note: a message is sent from one computer to another, but there is no explicit connection between the two. Additionally, the maximum data size of individual sends is determined by the network.

The nature of the application you are creating will generally determine which protocol you select. Here are a few questions that may help you select the appropriate protocol:

1. Will the application require acknowledgment from the server or client when data is sent or received? If so, the TCP protocol requires an explicit connection before sending or receiving data.
2. Will the data be extremely large (such as image or sound files)? Once a connection has been made, the TCP protocol maintains the connection and ensures the integrity of the data. This connection, however, uses more computing resources, making it more "expensive."
3. Will the data be sent intermittently, or in one session? For example, if you are creating an application that notifies specific computers when certain tasks have completed, the UDP protocol may be more appropriate. The UDP protocol is also more suited for sending small amounts of data.

Setting the Protocol

To set the protocol that your application will use: at design-time, on the Properties window, click Protocol and select either sckTCPProtocol, or sckUDPProtocol. You can also set the Protocol property in code, as shown below:

```
Winsock1.Protocol = sckTCPProtocol
```

Determining the Name of Your Computer

To connect to a remote computer, you must know either its IP address or its "friendly name." The IP address is a series of three digit numbers separated by periods (xxx.xxx.xxx.xxx). In general, it's much easier to remember the friendly name of a computer.

To find your computer's name

1. On the Taskbar of your computer, click **Start**.
2. On the **Settings** item, click the **Control Panel**.
3. Double-click the Network icon.
4. Click the **Identification** tab.
5. The name of your computer will be found in the **Computer name** box.

Once you have found your computer's name, it can be used as a value for the RemoteHost property.

TCP Connection Basics

When creating an application that uses the TCP protocol, you must first decide if your application will be a server or a client. Creating a server means that your application will "listen," on a designated port. When the client makes a connection request, the server can then accept the request and thereby complete the connection. Once the connection is complete, the client and server can freely communicate with each other.

The following steps create a rudimentary server:

To create a TCP server

1. Create a new Standard EXE project.
2. Change the name of the default form to frmServer.
3. Change the caption of the form to "TCP Server."
4. Draw a Winsock control on the form and change its name to tcpServer.
5. Add two TextBox controls to the form. Name the first txtSendData, and the second txtOutput.
6. Add the code below to the form.

```
Private Sub Form_Load()
    ' Set the LocalPort property to an integer.
    ' Then invoke the Listen method.
    tcpServer.LocalPort = 1001
    tcpServer.Listen
    frmClient.Show ' Show the client form.
End Sub

Private Sub tcpServer_ConnectionRequest _
(ByVal requestID As Long)
    ' Check if the control's State is closed. If not,
    ' close the connection before accepting the new
    ' connection.
    If tcpServer.State <> sckClosed Then _
    tcpServer.Close
    ' Accept the request with the requestID
    ' parameter.
    tcpServer.Accept requestID
End Sub

Private Sub txtSendData_Change()
    ' The TextBox control named txtSendData
    ' contains the data to be sent. Whenever the user
    ' types into the  textbox, the  string is sent
    ' using the SendData method.
    tcpServer.SendData txtSendData.Text
End Sub

Private Sub tcpServer_DataArrival _
(ByVal bytesTotal As Long)
    ' Declare a variable for the incoming data.
    ' Invoke the GetData method and set the Text
    ' property of a TextBox named txtOutput to
    ' the data.
    Dim strData As String
    tcpServer.GetData strData
    txtOutput.Text = strData
End Sub
```

The procedures above create a simple server application. However, to complete the scenario, you must also create a client application.

To create a TCP client

1. Add a new form to the project, and name it frmClient.
2. Change the caption of the form to TCP Client.
3. Add a Winsock control to the form and name it tcpClient.

4. Add two TextBox controls to frmClient. Name the first txtSend, and the second txtOutput.
5. Draw a CommandButton control on the form and name it cmdConnect.
6. Change the caption of the CommandButton control to Connect.
7. Add the code below to the form.

   Important Be sure to change the value of the RemoteHost property to the friendly name of your computer.

```
Private Sub Form_Load()
   ' The name of the Winsock control is tcpClient.
   ' Note: to specify a remote host, you can use
   ' either the IP address (ex: "121.111.1.1") or
   ' the computer's "friendly" name, as shown here.
   tcpClient.RemoteHost = "RemoteComputerName"
   tcpClient.RemotePort = 1001
End Sub

Private Sub cmdConnect_Click()
   ' Invoke the Connect method to initiate a
   ' connection.
   tcpClient.Connect
End Sub

Private Sub txtSendData_Change()
   tcpClient.SendData txtSend.Text
End Sub

Private Sub tcpClient_DataArrival _
(ByVal bytesTotal As Long)
   Dim strData As String
   tcpClient.GetData strData
   txtOutput.Text = strData
End Sub
```

The code above creates a simple client-server application. To try the two together, run the project, and click Connect. Then type text into the txtSendData TextBox on either form, and the same text will appear in the txtOutput TextBox on the other form.

Accepting More Than One Connection Request

The basic server outlined above accepts only one connection request. However, it is possible to accept several connection requests using the same control by creating a control array. In that case, you do not need to close the connection, but simply create a new instance of the control (by setting its Index property), and invoking the Accept method on the new instance.

The code below assumes there is a Winsock control on a form named sckServer, and that its Index property has been set to 0; thus the control is part of a control array. In the Declarations section, a module-level variable intMax is declared. In the form's Load event, intMax is set to 0, and the LocalPort property for the first control in the array is set to 1001. Then the Listen method is invoked on the control, making it the "listening" control. As each connection request arrives, the code tests to see if the Index is 0 (the value of the "listening" control). If so, the listening control increments intMax, and uses that number to create a new control instance. The new control instance is then used to accept the connection request.

```
Private intMax As Long

Private Sub Form_Load()
   intMax = 0
   sckServer(0).LocalPort = 1001
   sckServer(0).Listen
End Sub

Private Sub sckServer_ConnectionRequest _
(Index As Integer, ByVal requestID As Long)
   If Index = 0 Then
      intMax = intMax + 1
      Load sckServer(intMax)
      sckServer(intMax).LocalPort = 0
      sckServer(intMax).Accept requestID
      Load txtData(intMax)
   End If
End Sub
```

UDP Basics

Creating a UDP application is even simpler than creating a TCP application because the UDP protocol doesn't require an explicit connection. In the TCP application above, one Winsock control must explicitly be set to "listen," while the other must initiate a connection with the Connect method.

In contrast, the UDP protocol doesn't require an explicit connection. To send data between two controls, three steps must be completed (on both sides of the connection):

1. Set the RemoteHost property to the name of the other computer.
2. Set the RemotePort property to the LocalPort property of the second control.
3. Invoke the Bind method specifying the LocalPort to be used. (This method is discussed in greater detail below.)

Because both computers can be considered "equal" in the relationship, it could be called a peer-to-peer application. To demonstrate this, the code below creates a "chat" application that allows two people to "talk" in real time to each other:

To create a UDP Peer

1. Create a new Standard EXE project.
2. Change the name of the default form to frmPeerA.
3. Change the caption of the form to "Peer A."
4. Draw a Winsock control on the form and name it udpPeerA.
5. On the **Properties** page, click **Protocol** and change the protocol to UDPProtocol.
6. Add two TextBox controls to the form. Name the first txtSend, and the second txtOutput.
7. Add the code below to the form.

```
Private Sub Form_Load()
   ' The control's name is udpPeerA
   With udpPeerA
      ' IMPORTANT: be sure to change the RemoteHost
      ' value to the name of your computer.
      .RemoteHost= "PeerB"
      .RemotePort = 1001     ' Port to connect to.
      .Bind 1002             ' Bind to the local port.
   End With
   frmPeerB.Show             ' Show the second form.
End Sub

Private Sub txtSend_Change()
   ' Send text as soon as it's typed.
   udpPeerA.SendData txtSend.Text
End Sub

Private Sub udpPeerA_DataArrival _
(ByVal bytesTotal As Long)
   Dim strData As String
   udpPeerA.GetData strData
   txtOutput.Text = strData
End Sub
```

To create a second UDP Peer

1. Add a standard form to the project.
2. Change the name of the form to frmPeerB.
3. Change the caption of the form to "Peer B."
4. Draw a Winsock control on the form and name it udpPeerB.
5. On the **Properties** page, click **Protocol** and change the protocol to UDPProtocol.

6. Add two TextBox controls to the form. Name the TextBox txtSend, and the second txtOutput.

7. Add the code below to the form.

```
Private Sub Form_Load()
   ' The control's name is udpPeerB.
   With udpPeerB
      ' IMPORTANT: be sure to change the RemoteHost
      ' value to the name of your computer.
      .RemoteHost= "PeerA"
      .RemotePort = 1002' Port to connect to.
      .Bind 1001             ' Bind to the local port.
   End With
End Sub

Private Sub txtSend_Change()
   ' Send text as soon as it's typed.
   udpPeerB.SendData txtSend.Text
End Sub

Private Sub udpPeerB_DataArrival _
(ByVal bytesTotal As Long)
   Dim strData As String
   udpPeerB.GetData strData
   txtOutput.Text = strData
End Sub
```

To try the example, press F5 to run the project, and type into the txtSend TextBox on either form. The text you type will appear in the txtOutput TextBox on the other form.

About the Bind Method

As shown in the code above, you must invoke the Bind method when creating a UDP application. The Bind method "reserves" a local port for use by the control. For example, when you bind the control to port number 1001, no other application can use that port to "listen" on. This may come in useful if you wish to prevent another application from using that port.

The Bind method also features an optional second argument. If there is more than one network adapter present on the machine, the *LocalIP* argument allows you to specify which adapter to use. If you omit the argument, the control uses the first network adapter listed in the Network control panel dialog box of the computer's Control Panel Settings.

When using the UDP protocol, you can freely switch the RemoteHost and RemotePort properties while remaining bound to the same LocalPort. However, with the TCP protocol, you must close the connection before changing the RemoteHost and RemotePort properties.

PART 2

Creating ActiveX Components

Component software development cuts programming time and produces more robust applications, by allowing developers to assemble applications from tested, standardized components. The move to component software, sparked by the success of products like Microsoft Visual Basic, is one of the most prominent trends in the software industry.

Microsoft has led the effort to define an open, extensible standard for software interoperability. The Component Object Model (COM), including Automation and the ActiveX specification, makes it possible for software components you create to work smoothly with software components you buy off the shelf.

Visual Basic makes ActiveX component creation happen. ActiveX controls, ActiveX Documents, code components, and applications that provide objects — Visual Basic gives you the tools to rapidly create, debug, and deploy software components.

Getting Started

Before you begin, you should know how to use class modules to define new classes, how to create objects from classes, and how to use ActiveX components. These subjects are discussed in Chapter 9, "Programming with Objects," and Chapter 10, "Programming with ActiveX Components," in the *Microsoft Visual Basic 6.0 Programmer's Guide.*

Chapter 1 ActiveX Components

Outlines what you can do with Visual Basic's component software features.

Chapter 2 Creating an ActiveX DLL

Provides step-by-step procedures that get you off to a running start with in-process debugging, multiple projects, global objects, object lifetime concepts, and circular references.

Chapter 3 Creating an ActiveX EXE Component

Provides step-by-step procedures that introduce threads, events in class modules, call-backs, and out-of-process debugging.

Chapter 4 Creating an ActiveX Control

Provides a series of step-by-step procedures that create a simple control. Introduces ActiveX control concepts, raising events, debugging design-time behavior, and property pages.

Chapter 5 Creating an ActiveX Document

Provides a series of step-by-step procedures that create a simple ActiveX document and demonstrate ActiveX document concepts, navigation, properties and methods, menus, and debugging techniques.

Chapter 6 General Principles of Component Design

Contains information of importance to all component designers, including terminology, concepts, instancing for class modules, polymorphism, and object models.

Chapter 7 Debugging, Testing, and Deploying Components

Contains more general information, such as setting up test projects, debugging features, adding Help, version compatibility, and localization.

Chapter 8 Building Code Components

Takes OLE servers into a new world, providing in-depth discussions of in-process and out-of-process components, threading, instancing, call-backs, and events.

Chapter 9 Building ActiveX Controls

Contains in-depth explanations of how Visual Basic ActiveX controls work, what features you can implement, subtleties of debugging, discussions of implementation techniques, and all the other things you expect of a cool new feature.

Chapter 10 Creating Property Pages for ActiveX Controls

Provides in-depth discussion of property pages, including implementation techniques and design guidelines.

Chapter 11 Building ActiveX Documents

Provides in-depth discussions of terminology, concepts, Internet features, navigation, debugging, migrating from forms, and in-process vs. out-of-process implementation.

Chapter 12 Creating Data Sources

Provides in-depth discussion and step-by-step procedures for creating ActiveX components that can act as data sources.

Appendix A ActiveX Component Standards and Guidelines

Contains updated guidelines for object naming, component shutdown, implementing collections and Application objects, and other object model issues.

CHAPTER 1

ActiveX Components

An *ActiveX component* is a unit of executable code, such as an .exe, .dll, or .ocx file, that follows the ActiveX specification for providing objects. ActiveX technology allows programmers to assemble these reusable software components into applications and services.

You can buy ActiveX components that provide generic services, such as numerical analysis or user interface elements. You can create components that encapsulate your own business transactions, and combine these with generic components. Reusing tested, standardized code in this fashion is called *component software development.*

Component software development using ActiveX technology should not be confused with object-oriented programming (OOP). OOP is a way to build object-based software components; ActiveX is a technology that allows you to combine object-based components created using many different tools. To put it another way, OOP is concerned with creating objects, while ActiveX is concerned with making objects work together.

For example, you can use an OOP tool such as Microsoft Visual C++ to construct a set of useful objects. These objects can be used and further extended by other C++ developers. If you package your objects in an ActiveX component, however, they can be used and further extended with any programming tool that supports ActiveX technology.

This chapter introduces the components you can build with Microsoft Visual Basic, and lists the portions of "Creating ActiveX Components" that apply to each.

Contents

Readers of this book should be familiar with the material in Chapter 9, "Programming with Objects," and Chapter 10, "Programming with ActiveX Components," in the *Microsoft Visual Basic 6.0 Programmer's Guide.*

They're Not Just OLE Servers Anymore

Thread-safe DLLs. ActiveX controls. Scalable components for operation on remote computers. ActiveX documents. Native code. If you've created OLE servers with Visual Basic in the past, get ready for some surprises.

In addition to developing new kinds of software components, Visual Basic now supports the Component Object Model (COM) vision of component software evolution, by allowing you to implement multiple interfaces on class modules.

In keeping with the broad set of new features outlined in this chapter, Visual Basic terminology is shifting as well. They're components now, not just OLE servers.

The new terminology may seem disconcerting at first, but in the long run it will make a lot more sense, as Visual Basic becomes the fastest, easiest way to develop robust, interoperable software components. You'll also find it a lot easier to discuss interactions between components without the overworked word "server."

And if you really want to, you can continue to use the old terminology. Just pronounce "ActiveX component" as *oh-lay* ser-*ver*.

Features of Visual Basic ActiveX Components

With Visual Basic you can create components ranging from code libraries to Automation-enabled applications. You can create and distribute ActiveX control packages, with full licensing capability, or Internet applications with ActiveX documents that can display themselves in Internet browsers. With the Enterprise Edition of Visual Basic, you can run code components — such as business rule servers — on remote computers.

Figure 1.1 shows a Visual Basic application that uses several components, all of them built with Visual Basic.

Figure 1.1 Visual Basic application using components

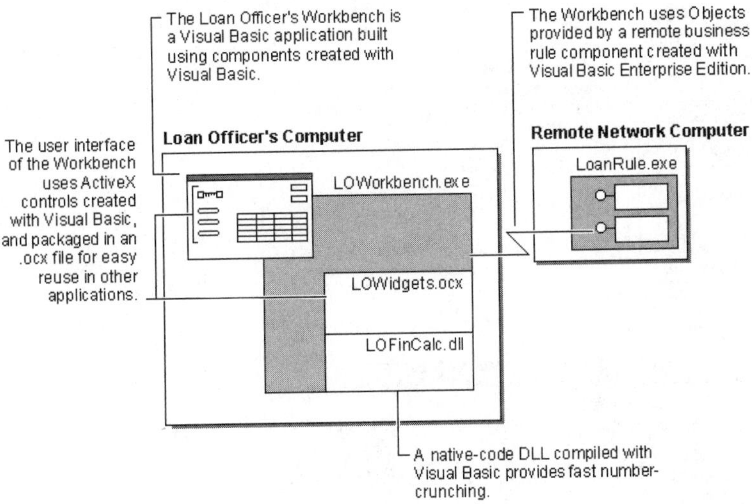
The Loan Officer's Workbench is a Visual Basic application built using components created with Visual Basic.
The Workbench uses Objects provided by a remote business rule component created with Visual Basic Enterprise Edition.
The user interface of the Workbench uses ActiveX controls created with Visual Basic, and packaged in an .ocx file for easy reuse in other applications.
Loan Officer's Computer
LOWorkbench.exe
LOWidgets.ocx
LOFinCalc.dll
Remote Network Computer
LoanRule.exe
A native-code DLL compiled with Visual Basic provides fast number-crunching.

Visual Basic ActiveX components are Internet- and intranet-enabled. Figure 1.2 shows a business analyst viewing a form on his desktop computer at the home office, while a sales representative views the same information through a Web page, using a Visual Basic ActiveX document.

Figure 1.2 Visual Basic activates the Internet

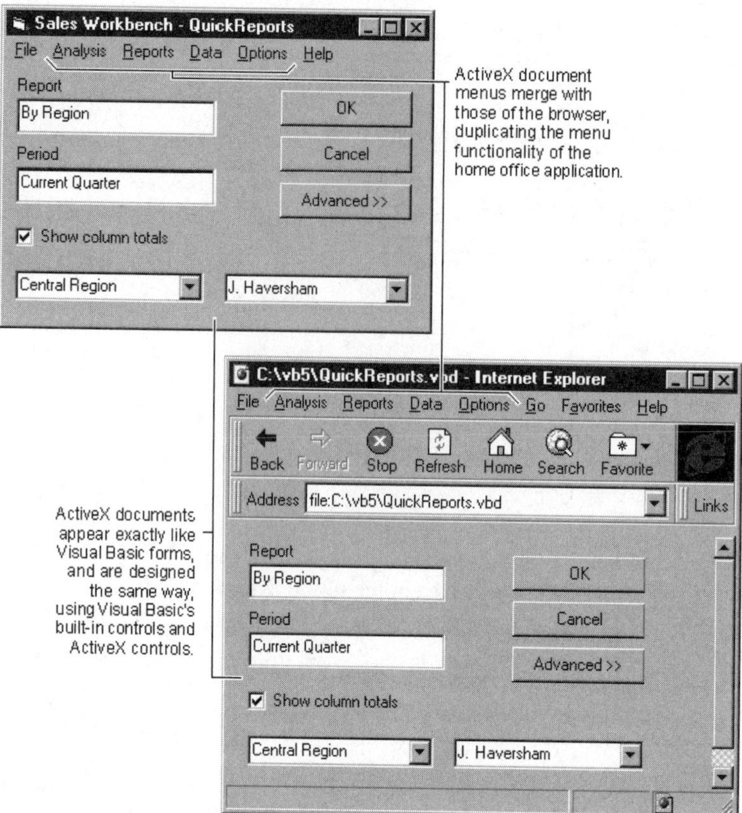

Which Type of Component Should I Build?

With all the different types of ActiveX components to choose from, how do you decide which type of component is best for a given situation? It may help to think of them in terms of functionality:

- If you need an invisible component that provides a service, you'll want to build a code component — either an ActiveX EXE or an ActiveX DLL.
  - If you need a component that can run in the same process with your application, you'll want an ActiveX DLL. An example of this would be a component that performs complex calculations.
  - If you need a component that can serve multiple applications and can run on a remote computer, you'll want an ActiveX EXE. For example, a business rules server that enforces tax rules would best be implemented as an ActiveX EXE.

- If you need a visible component that can be dropped into an application at design time, you'll want to build an ActiveX control. An example of this might be a phone number control that properly formats and validates phone numbers; such a control would undoubtedly be useful in many applications.
- If you need a visible component that can take over an application window at run time, choose an ActiveX document. The above example shows a sales application that can be viewed in a Web browser, duplicating the functionality of a desktop application.

No matter which type of ActiveX component you choose to build, Visual Basic makes reusability a reality.

Features for Building Components

The following are some of the features Visual Basic provides for creating software components.

- Components can provide several types of objects, as described in the related topics "ActiveX Controls," "ActiveX Documents," and "Code Components," later in this chapter.
- Objects provided by components can raise events. You can handle these events in a host process or in another application — with the Enterprise Edition, such an application can even be running on a remote computer.
- Components can be *data-aware*, binding directly to any source of data without the need for a data control. You can also create an ActiveX component that acts as a data source to which other objects can bind. For example, you could create your own data control (similar to the ADO Data control or the Remote Data control), but instead of binding via ADO or RDO you could bind to a flat file or a proprietary binary data format.
- *Friend functions* allow the objects provided by a component to communicate with each other internally, without exposing that communication to applications that use those objects.
- The *Implements* keyword lets you add standard interfaces to your objects. These common interfaces enable polymorphic behavior for objects provided by a component, or for objects provided by many different components.
- You can use *enumerations* to provide named constants for all component types.
- You can choose a default property or method for each class of object your component provides.
- You can allow users of your component to access the properties and methods of a global object without explicitly creating an instance of the object.

These features are discussed in detail in Chapter 6, "General Principles of Component Design," along with other subjects relevant to all component types.

For More Information Components that perform computation-intensive tasks may benefit from compilation to native code. This subject is covered in Chapter 8, "More About Programming," in the *Microsoft Visual Basic 6.0 Programmer's Guide.*

ActiveX Controls

ActiveX controls, formerly called OLE controls, are standard user interface elements that allow you to assemble forms and dialog boxes rapidly. ActiveX controls also bring the Internet alive, adding compelling new functionality to World Wide Web pages.

Visual Basic has always featured a variety of controls that you could use in your applications. Now you can create your own controls, for use with Visual Basic and other development tools. With ActiveX controls, your investment in Visual Basic carries forward to the Internet.

Designing an ActiveX control can be as easy as designing a Visual Basic form — you can use familiar Visual Basic graphics commands to paint your control, or create a control group using existing controls.

ActiveX controls can be debugged in process, so you can step directly from the code for your test form into the code for your ActiveX control project.

You can add data-binding to your Visual Basic ActiveX control, so that a user can easily bind the individual fields within the control to the appropriate fields in a database or other source of data. You can also use data-binding to create an ActiveX control that other controls can bind to, similar to the Visual Basic Data control.

Visual Basic makes it easy to create polished ActiveX control packages by adding property pages, named constants, and events to your controls.

You can compile your ActiveX controls directly into your application's executable, or into .ocx files that can be used with development tools such as Visual Basic and Microsoft Visual C++, with end-user products such as Microsoft Office, and on the Internet.

Chapter 4, "Creating an ActiveX Control," offers a quick step-by-step introduction to control creation — including the radical idea of running code at design time to debug your control's design-time behavior.

For More Information Chapter 9, "Building ActiveX Controls," and Chapter 10, "Creating Property Pages for ActiveX Controls," discuss control creation issues in depth. Chapter 6, "General Principles of Component Design," and Chapter 7, "Debugging, Testing, and Deploying Components," also contain many topics of interest to control designers.

ActiveX Documents

One of the most exciting features of Visual Basic is the ability to create *ActiveX documents,* forms that can appear within Internet browser windows. Visual Basic ActiveX documents offer built-in viewport scrolling, Hyperlinks, and menu negotiation.

ActiveX documents are designed the same way you design Visual Basic forms. They can contain insertable objects, such as Microsoft Excel pivot tables. They can also show message boxes and secondary forms.

Visual Basic ActiveX documents can also appear in the Microsoft Office Binder, and you can write code to save your document's data in Binder data files.

With Internet Explorer 3.0 or later, you can also save properties of your ActiveX document by writing to and reading from the document's data file.

You can package ActiveX documents in either in-process or out-of-process components.

Chapter 5, "Creating an ActiveX Document," is a step-by-step introduction to document creation.

For More Information ActiveX document design is covered in detail in Chapter 11, "Building ActiveX Documents." You can find out more about how to use documents in your Internet applications in Part 5, "Building Internet Applications," in this book. Topics of general interest to component designers can be found in Chapter 6, "General Principles of Component Design," and Chapter 7, "Debugging, Testing, and Deploying Components."

Code Components

Code components are like libraries of objects. A client application uses a code component by creating an object from one of the classes the component provides, and invoking the object's properties, methods, and events.

> **Note** In earlier documentation, code components were referred to as OLE Automation servers.

You might create a code component that provides extended financial functions for spreadsheet users, or you might encapsulate business rules used by your organization, so that all applications process the same data consistently.

With Visual Basic, you can build code components to run in process, allowing faster access to their objects, or out of process, so that they have separate threads of execution from their clients.

You can use code components to provide standard libraries of modal and modeless dialogs — although frequently a code component will have no user interface.

Visual Basic allows you to suppress all forms of user interaction, even system alert messages, and to record such events in the system log. This unattended execution capability is extremely useful for code components designed to run on remote computers.

In an out-of-process code component that has been designed for unattended execution, you can mark a class as multithreaded. Each object created from such a class can be on a separate thread of execution within the out-of-process component.

To simplify the creation of reusable code libraries that can also be used with desktop tools (such as the Microsoft Office suite), Visual Basic allows you to mark objects in a code component as global, so that their methods can be invoked without explicitly creating an instance of the global object.

Whatever you used to call them, it's a whole new ball game.

For More Information A step-by-step introduction to in-process code components, including in-process debugging, can be found in Chapter 2, "Creating an ActiveX DLL." Chapter 3, "Creating an ActiveX EXE Component," gives a similar introduction to the creation and debugging of out-of-process code components. Advanced topics are covered in Chapter 8, "Building Code Components." Topics of general interest to component designers can be found in Chapter 6, "General Principles of Component Design," and Chapter 7, "Debugging, Testing, and Deploying Components."

CHAPTER 2

Creating an ActiveX DLL

Components provide reusable code in the form of objects. An application that uses a component's code, by creating objects and calling their properties and methods, is referred to as a *client*.

Components can run either in-process or out-of-process with respect to the clients that use their objects. An in-process component, or ActiveX DLL, runs in another application's process. The client may be the application itself, or another in-process component that the application is using.

Figure 2.1 In-process components are used by applications or other in-process components

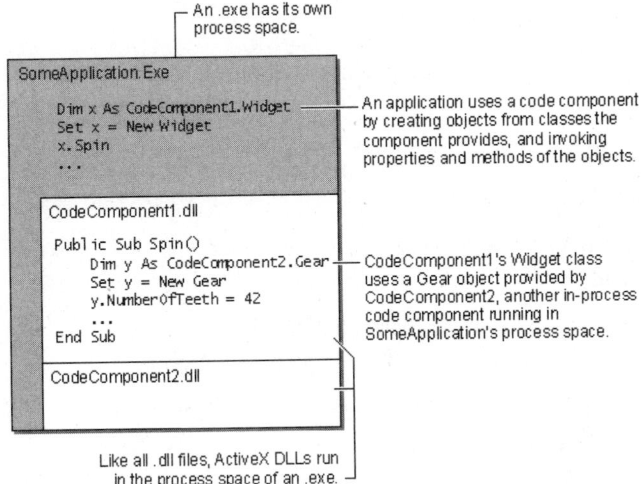

The series of step-by-step procedures in this chapter builds an in-process component called ThingDemo, with class modules that demonstrate object lifetime, global objects, and objects that control modal and modeless dialog boxes.

You'll also see how to debug an ActiveX DLL in process, by running the DLL and a test project together in the Microsoft Visual Basic development environment.

The procedures for creating the ThingDemo component build on each other. The sequence in which you perform the procedures is therefore important.

Contents

- Creating the ThingDemo DLL Project
- Creating Properties and Methods for the Thing Class
- Adding Code for Initialize and Terminate Events
- Creating the TestThing Test Project
- Creating and Testing Thing Objects
- Running the TestThing Test Application
- Circular References and Object Lifetime
- Adding a Form to the ThingDemo Project
- Using the Global Object in TestThing
- Compiling and Testing the ThingDemo DLL
- Circular References and Component Shutdown
- ActiveX DLL Creation Summary

These procedures will be easier to follow if you set up your development environment as described below.

Before You Begin

1. On the **View** menu, click **Toolbox** to open the Toolbox.
2. On the **View** menu, click **Project Explorer** to open the Project Explorer window. The Project Explorer window will be used extensively to switch between project files.
3. If the Project Explorer window is in Folder view, as shown below, click the **Toggle Folders** button on the Project Explorer window toolbar to turn the folders off.

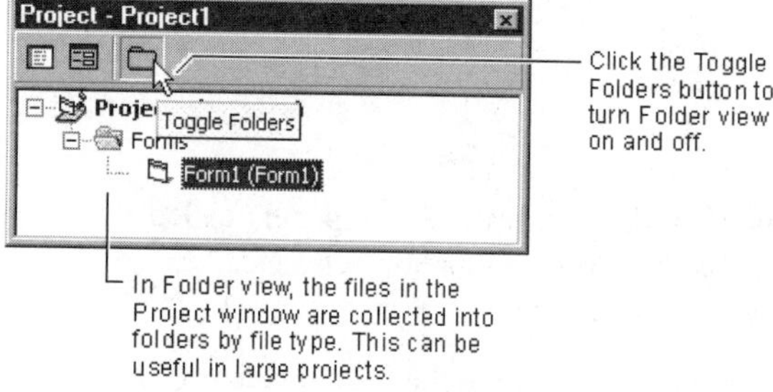
Project - Project1
Toggle Folders
Form1 (Form1)
Click the Toggle Folders button to turn Folder view on and off.
In Folder view, the files in the Project window are collected into folders by file type. This can be useful in large projects.

4. On the **View** menu, click **Properties Window** to open the Properties window.
5. On the **Tools** menu, click **Options** to open the **Options** dialog box.

   Select the **Editor** tab, and make sure **Require Variable Declaration** is checked. This makes it much easier to catch typing errors.

   Select the **Environment** tab. Make sure **Prompt To Save Changes** is checked, then click **OK**. This will make it easy to save changes to the project as you go along.

Creating the ThingDemo DLL Project

How easy is it to create an ActiveX DLL with Visual Basic? If you can declare variables and write procedures, you can create an in-process component.

This section provides step-by-step instructions on how to define a simple class, and demonstrates the life cycle of objects provided by components. You can use objects created from this class with any application that can use Automation to control objects.

To create the ThingDemo project

1. On the **File** menu, click **New Project**.
2. In the **New Project** dialog box, double-click the ActiveX DLL icon. Visual Basic automatically adds a class module, Class1, to the new project.
3. Press F4 to open the Properties window. Double-click the **Name** property and change it to **Thing**. This is the name you'll use to create objects from the class.

   The default value for the Instancing property is MultiUse. This allows clients to create multiple instances of the Thing class. For a full discussion of the Instancing property, see "Instancing for Classes Provided by ActiveX Components," in Chapter 6, "General Principles of Component Design."

4. On the **Project** menu, click **Project1 Properties** to open the **Project Properties** dialog box. Select the **General** tab, fill out the information shown below, then click **OK**.

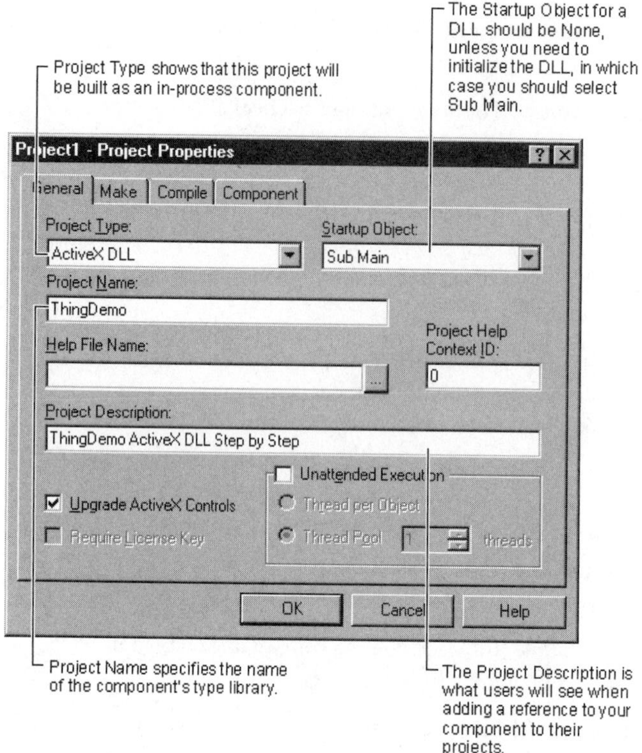

The Startup Object for a DLL should be None, unless you need to initialize the DLL, in which case you should select Sub Main.
Project Type shows that this project will be built as an in-process component.
Project1 - Project Properties
General
Make
Compile
Component
Project Type:
ActiveX DLL
Startup Object:
Sub Main
Project Name:
ThingDemo
Help File Name:
Project Help Context ID:
0
Project Description:
ThingDemo ActiveX DLL Step by Step
Unattended Execution
Upgrade ActiveX Controls
Require License Key
Thread per Object
Thread Pool
1
threads
OK
Cancel
Help
Project Name specifies the name of the component's type library.
The Project Description is what users will see when adding a reference to your component to their projects.

The project name, ThingDemo, is also used as the name of the component's type library. It can be combined with the name of each class the component provides, to produce unique class names.

If two components each provide a Thing class, the fully qualified class name lets you specify which component's Thing class you want to use, for example, `ThingDemo.Thing`.

5. On the **Project** menu, click **Add Module** to open the **Add Module** dialog box. Double click the **Module** icon to add a module to the project.

   Note If you've used the **Options** dialog box (accessed from the **Tools** menu) to disable the **Add Module** dialog box, you'll just get the module. This is okay.

6. In the Code window for the module, add the following code:

```
Option Explicit
Public gdatServerStarted As Date
```

```
Sub Main()
   ' Code to be executed when the component starts,
   '   in response to the first object request.
   gdatServerStarted = Now
   Debug.Print "Executing Sub Main"
End Sub

' Function to provide unique identifiers for objects.
Public Function GetDebugID() As Long
   Static lngDebugID As Long
   lngDebugID = lngDebugID + 1
   GetDebugID = lngDebugID
End Function
```

7. On the **File** menu, click **Save Project** to save the project files, using the following names. Visual Basic will provide the extensions automatically.

File	File name	Extension
Module	ThingDemo_Module1	.bas
Class module	ThingDemo_Thing	.cls
Project	ThingDemo	.vbp

For More Information See "Choosing a Project Type and Setting Project Properties," in Chapter 6, "General Principles of Component Design."

Creating Properties and Methods for the Thing Class

You create properties for a class by adding public variables and property procedures to the class module. You create methods for a class by adding Public Sub and Public Function procedures to the class module. The following step-by-step procedures create two properties and one method for the Thing class.

- The Name property is a string that can be retrieved and set by client applications.
- The read-only DebugID property returns a sequence number that shows the order in which Thing objects were created. This is useful for debugging.
- The ReverseName method reverses the order of the letters in the Name property.

To create the Name property

- Add the following code to the Declarations section of the Thing class module:

```
Option Explicit
Public Name As String
```

The variable `Name` becomes a property of the Thing class because it's declared Public.

Important Don't confuse the Name property you're creating here with the Name property of the class module. The Name property of the class module allows you to specify the class name (Thing) at design time; it's not available at run time.

To create the read-only DebugID property

1. Add the following code to the Declarations section of the Thing class module:

   ```
   ' To store the value of the DebugID property.
   Private mlngDebugID As Long
   ```

2. From the **Tools** menu, choose **Add Procedure** to open the **AddProcedure** dialog box. In the **Name** box, type **DebugID**. Click **Property** and **Public**, then click **OK**.
3. In the Code window, delete the Property Let procedure and change the Property Get procedure as follows:

   ```
   Public Property Get DebugID() As Long
      DebugID = mlngDebugID
   End Property
   ```

   The purpose of a Property Let procedure is to allow users to assign a new value to the DebugID property. Deleting it makes the property read-only.

   Tip Because property procedures come in two parts, you may find it easier to work with them in Full Module View. You can toggle between Procedure View and Full Module View using the buttons in the bottom left corner of the Code window.

   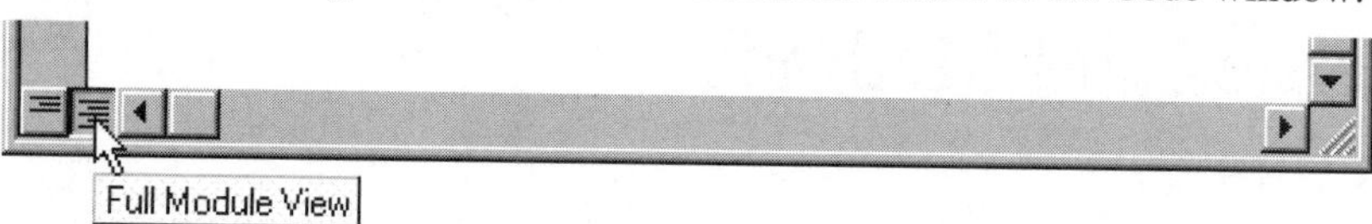

The variable `mlngDebugID` is a private data member which is used to store the value of the DebugID property. Because it's declared Private, it's not visible to client applications, and thus cannot be changed by clients. This is an example of *encapsulation*, discussed in detail in "Classes: Putting User-Defined Types and Procedures Together," in the *Microsoft Visual Basic 6.0 Programmer's Guide.*

The Property Get procedure returns the value of the private variable, allowing clients to read the property value using code like the following:

```
Private Sub Command1_Click()
   Dim t As ThingDemo.Thing
   Set t = New ThingDemo.Thing
   MsgBox t.DebugID
End Sub
```

To create the ReverseName method

1. On the **Tools** menu, click **Add Procedure** to get the **Add Procedure** dialog box. In the **Name** box, type **ReverseName**. Click **Sub** and **Public**, then click **OK**.
2. Enter the following code in the new Sub procedure of the Thing class module:

```
Public Sub ReverseName()
   Dim intCt As Integer
   Dim strNew As String
   For intCt = 1 To Len(Name)
      strNew = Mid$(Name, intCt, 1) & strNew
   Next
   Name = strNew
End Sub
```

   Note Remember that the Name property you've just created — and used in the ReverseName method — is not the same as the Name property of the class module. Unlike the Name property you created, the class module's Name property is not available at run time.

Adding Code for Initialize and Terminate Events

Class modules have two built-in events: Initialize and Terminate. The code you place in the Initialize event procedure is the first code executed when the object is created, before any properties are set or any methods are executed.

The code you place in the Terminate event is executed when all references to the object have been released, and the object is about to be destroyed.

The following procedure adds code to support the DebugID property, and Debug.Print methods that will display the object's properties when it's being created and destroyed.

To add code to the Initialize and Terminate events of the Thing class

1. In the **Object** box of the Thing class module, select **Class**. The **Initialize** event appears in the **Procedure** box, and the Code window displays the code template for the event procedure. Add the following code to the event procedure:

```
Private Sub Class_Initialize()
   ' Get a debug ID number that can be returned by
   '   the read-only DebugID property.
   mlngDebugID = GetDebugID
   Debug.Print "Initialize Thing " & DebugID _
      & ", Name=" & Name
End Sub
```

2. In the **Procedure** box of the class module, select **Terminate**. Add the following code to the event procedure:

```
Private Sub Class_Terminate()
   On Error Resume Next
   Debug.Print "Terminate Thing " & DebugID _
      & ", Name=" & Name
End Sub
```

   Important You should always handle errors in the Class_Terminate event procedure. Errors in Class_Terminate cannot be handled by applications that use your component, and will therefore be fatal to the application.

   By contrast, unhandled errors in the Initialize event are raised at the point where the application created the object, and thus can be handled by the application.

Normally, the Initialize event procedure contains any code that needs to be executed at the moment the object is created, such as providing the time stamp for the DebugID property. The Terminate event contains any clean-up code you need to execute when the object is being destroyed.

Important The Initialize and Terminate events should never interact with the user. For demonstration purposes, this example uses the two events to give you a visual indication that a Thing object is being created or destroyed.

For More Information See "Coding Robust Initialize and Terminate Events," in Chapter 6, "General Principles of Component Design."

Creating the TestThing Test Project

In order to test the ThingDemo component, you need a test project. The test project creates instances of the classes a component provides, and exercises their properties, methods, and events.

To enable debugging of in-process components, Visual Basic allows you to load two or more projects into a *project group*. In addition to enabling in-process debugging, the project group makes it easier to load your component project and test project.

To add a test project to the project group

1. On the **File** menu, click **Add Project** to open the **Add Project** dialog box.

   Important Do not click **Open Project** or **New Project**, as these will close your ActiveX DLL project.

2. Double-click the Standard EXE icon to add an ordinary EXE project. You can now see both projects in the Project Explorer window, and the caption of the Project Explorer window shows the default project group name.

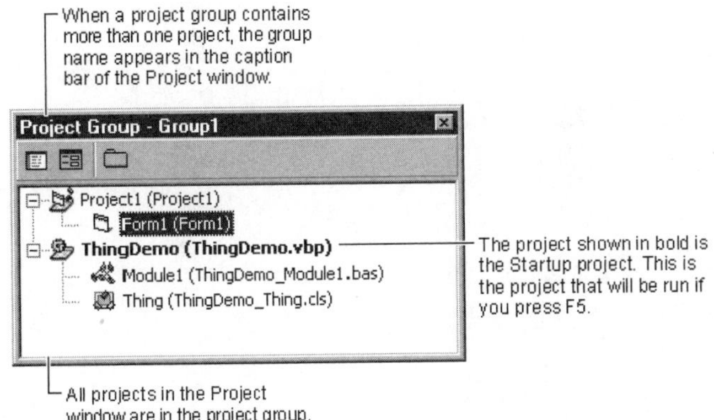
When a project group contains more than one project, the group name appears in the caption bar of the Project window.
Project Group - Group1
Project1 (Project1)
Form1 (Form1)
ThingDemo (ThingDemo.vbp)
Module1 (ThingDemo_Module1.bas)
Thing (ThingDemo_Thing.cls)
The project shown in bold is the Startup project. This is the project that will be run if you press F5.
All projects in the Project window are in the project group.

Notice that ThingDemo appears in bold-face type in the Project Explorer window. This means ThingDemo is the *Startup project* — that is, the project that will be run when you press F5.

3. In the Project Explorer window, right-click on **Project1** to open the context menu. Click **Set as Start Up** to make the EXE project the Startup project for the project group.

   Important The test project must be the Startup project for the group. If the DLL project is the Startup project for the group, the test project will never be run.

4. On the **Project** menu, click **References** to open the **References** dialog box. Check **ThingDemo**, then click **OK**.

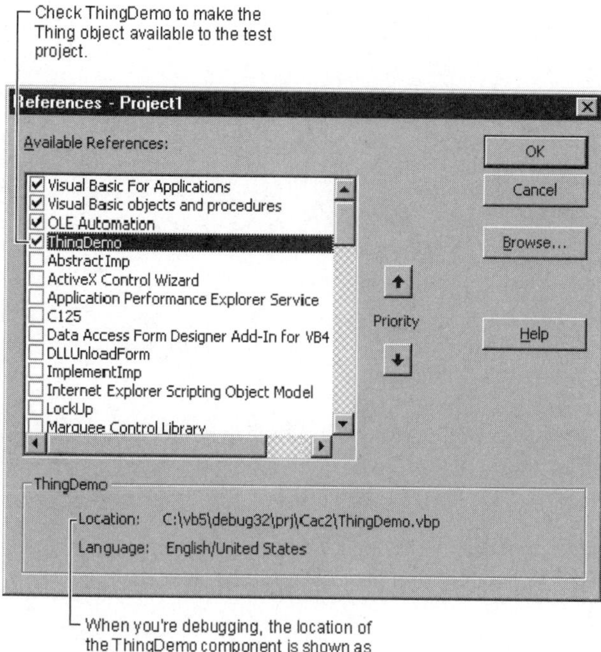

If **ThingDemo** doesn't appear in the list of available references, click **Cancel** to close the dialog box. In the Project Explorer window click **Project1** to make it the active project, and then repeat Step 3.

When working with project groups, make sure you have the right project active before clicking the **Project** menu.

5. Press F2 to open the **Object Browser**. In the **Project/Library** list, select **ThingDemo** to show its modules and classes. You can use the Object Browser to examine the Thing object and its properties and methods.

   Click **Close** to close the **Object Browser** when you're done.

6. On the **File** menu, click **Save Project Group** to save the test project and the project group. Name the files as shown below. Name the test project ThingTest. Name the project group ThingDemo. Visual Basic will give the project group file a .vbg extension.

File	File name	Extension
Form	ThingTest_Form1	.frm
Project	ThingTest	.vbp
Project group	ThingDemo	.vbg

For More Information Test projects for DLLs are discussed in more detail in "Creating a Test Project for an In-Process Component," in Chapter 7, "Debugging, Testing, and Deploying Components."

Creating and Testing Thing Objects

To test a class — in this case, the Thing class — your test project must request that the component create an object from the class.

Resize Form1 in the test project and place five command buttons and a check box on it, as shown in Figure 2.2. If you have never created a form in Visual Basic, see Chapter 2, "Developing an Application in Visual Basic," in the *Microsoft Visual Basic 6.0 Programmer's Guide.*

Figure 2.2 The test form for the Thing class

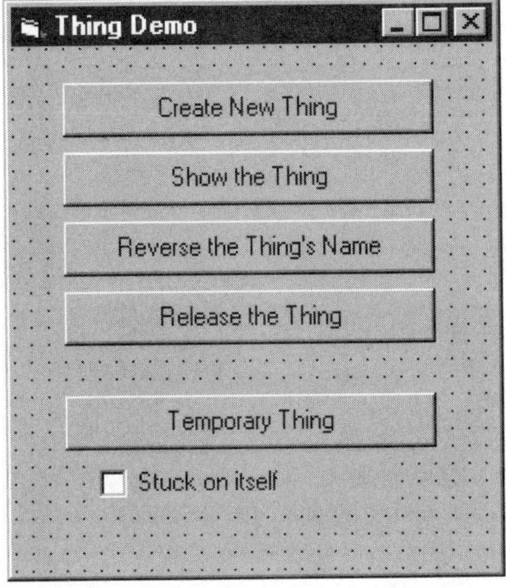

The following table lists the property values you need to set.

Object	Property	Setting
Form	Caption	Thing Demo
Command1	Caption	Create New Thing
Command2	Caption	Show the Thing
Command3	Caption	Reverse the Thing's Name
Command4	Caption	Release the Thing
Command5	Caption	Temporary Thing
Check1	Caption	Stuck on itself

To add code to create a Thing and call its properties and methods

1. Place the following code in the Declarations section of the test application's form module:

   ```
   Option Explicit
   ' Reference to a Thing object.
   Private mthTest As Thing
   ```

2. In the **Object** box, select **Command1**. Add the following code to the Click event procedure:

   ```
   ' Button "Create New Thing".
   Private Sub Command1_Click()
      Set mthTest = New Thing
      mthTest.Name = _
      InputBox("Enter a name for the Thing", _
      "Test Thing")
   End Sub
   ```

3. In similar fashion, add the following code to the Click event procedures of Command2, Command3, and Command4:

   ```
   ' Button "Show the Thing".
   Private Sub Command2_Click()
      MsgBox "Name: " & mthTest.Name, , _
         "Thing " & mthTest.DebugID
   End Sub

   ' Button "Reverse the Thing's Name".
   Private Sub Command3_Click()
      mthTest.ReverseName
      ' Click "Show the Thing" by setting its Value.
      Command2.Value = True
   End Sub

   ' Button "Release the Thing".
   Private Sub Command4_Click()
      Set mthTest = Nothing
   End Sub
   ```

You don't need to add code for Command5 or the check box yet.

Running the TestThing Test Application

The procedures in this topic illustrate the key events in the lifetime of an object provided by an in-process component, including what happens when the DLL is unloaded forcefully by clicking the End button.

To run the TestThing test application

1. Press CTRL+F5 to run the project group. Notice that no messages have appeared in the Immediate window yet.

   Note By default the **Compile On Demand** option is checked on the **General** tab of the **Options** dialog box (accessed from the **Tools** menu). When you're debugging a component with **Compile On Demand** checked, you may find it useful to use CTRL+F5 (or **Start with Full Compile**, on the **Run** menu) to compile all the projects in the group before entering run mode. Compile errors usually require resetting the project, which means returning to design mode.

2. On the **Thing Demo** dialog box, click **Create New Thing**. Before you respond to the InputBox requesting a name for the Thing, notice that the Immediate window now contains two debug messages:

   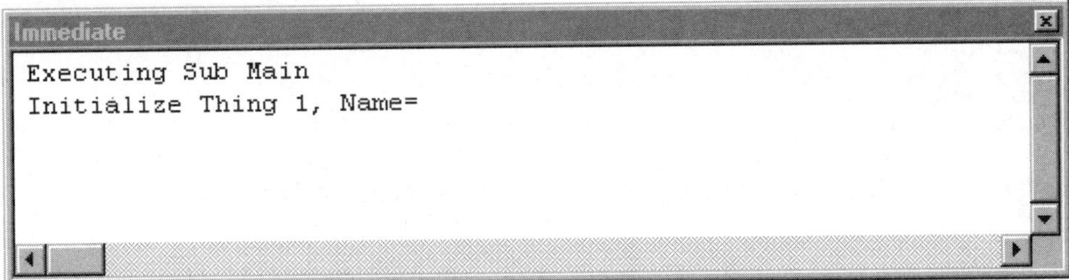

   When the Command1_Click event procedure creates the test Thing object, two things happen. First, before the object is created, the code in `Sub Main` is executed. Only *after* `Sub Main` executes is the Thing object created.

   Notice that the Name property has no value yet.

   Important The Sub Main procedure of an ActiveX component is executed when the component receives the first request for one of the objects it provides, *before* the component creates the object. You should not put lengthy tasks in the Sub Main procedure, because a request to create an object may time out while waiting for `Sub Main` to execute. This is discussed in "Starting and Ending a Component," in Chapter 6, "General Principles of Component Design."

3. Type **First Thing** in the **InputBox** and click **OK**. The code you put in the Command1_Click event procedure assigns the value to the Name property of the Thing object.

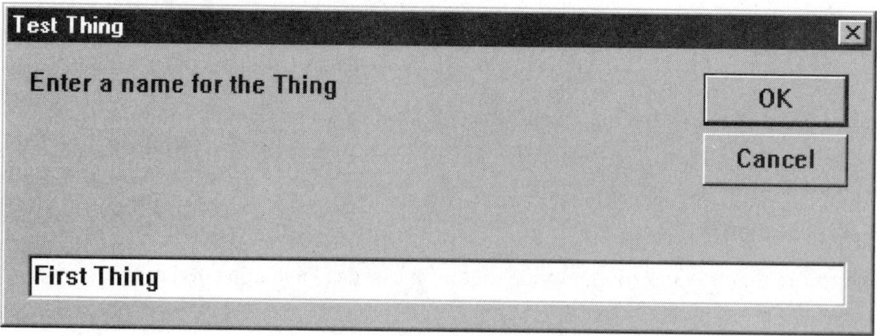

4. Click **Show the Thing** to display the Thing object's properties. Notice that the Name property now has a value. Click **OK** to dismiss the message box.
5. Click **Reverse the Thing's Name** to call the ReverseName method of the Thing object. After the method returns, **Show the Thing** (Command2) is clicked by setting its Value property to True, and the MsgBox statement in Command2_Click() displays the updated property values. Click **OK** to dismiss the message box.

6. Click **Create New Thing** again, to destroy the existing Thing object and create a new one.

   In the Immediate window, you will see a debug message from the Initialize event of the new Thing, as the New operator causes the object to be created. This is followed by the Terminate message from the original Thing, the one you named First Thing.

   The original Thing object is destroyed when the reference to the new Thing object is placed in the variable `mthTest`. At that point, there are no variables holding references to the original Thing, so it must be destroyed.
7. Type **Second Thing** in the **InputBox**, then click **OK**.
8. Click the **Close** box on **Thing Demo** to return to design mode. *Do not use the* **End** *button on the Visual Basic toolbar.*

   Before the program closes, the Terminate message for the Thing object you named Second Thing is displayed in the Immediate window.

   When you close a program, Visual Basic cleans up all the variables that still contain object references. As each variable is set to Nothing, the object it referred to is destroyed.

When a program is ended abruptly, with the End button or by an End statement in code, Visual Basic reclaims any memory and resources the program was using. However, the cleanup is done as if the program had suffered a fatal error. Objects will not get their Terminate events.

To observe the effects of the End button

1. Run the program again. Create a new Thing, and name it anything you like.
2. This time, end the program using the **End** button on the toolbar. The Terminate message for the form's Thing object is *not* displayed in the Immediate window.

   Important Remember that ending your program with the **End** button, or with an End statement in your code, halts the program *immediately,* without executing the Terminate events of any objects. It's always better to shut your program down by unloading all the forms.

For More Information The rules of object lifetime are introduced in Chapter 9, "Programming with Objects," in the *Microsoft Visual Basic 6.0 Programmer's Guide.*

Circular References and Object Lifetime

In normal program operation, an object is not destroyed until all references to it have been released. This has implications for object lifetime. The procedures in this topic illustrate this by allowing Thing objects to indulge in a little Narcissism.

To add the StuckOnMyself property to the Thing class

1. In the Project Explorer window, double-click **Thing** to bring the code window for the class module to the front.
2. Add the following code to the Declarations section:

   ```
   ' Private data for the StuckOnMyself property.
   Private mthStuckOnMyself As Thing
   Private mblnStuckOnMyself As Boolean
   ```

3. On the **Tools** menu, click **Add Procedure** to open the **Add Procedure** dialog box. In the **Name** box, type **StuckOnMyself**. Click **Property** and **Public**, then click **OK**.

   Modify the property procedures as follows:

   ```
   Public Property Get StuckOnMyself() As Boolean
      StuckOnMyself = mblnStuckOnMyself
   End Property

   Public Property Let StuckOnMyself(ByVal NewValue _
         As Boolean)
      mblnStuckOnMyself = NewValue
      If mblnStuckOnMyself Then
         Set mthStuckOnMyself = Me
   ```

```
    Else
        Set mthStuckOnMyself = Nothing
    End If
End Property
```

This code illustrates the power of property procedures. When a user requests the value of the StuckOnMyself property, the Property Get procedure is called, and simply returns the value of the module-level Boolean variable `mblnStuckOnMyself`.

When the user sets the value of the StuckOnMyself property, the Property Let procedure is called. After assigning the new value to the module-level Boolean variable `mblnStuckOnMyself`, the Property Let either places a reference to the Thing object (Me) in the module-level variable `mthStuckOnMyself`, or sets the variable to Nothing.

For More Information Property procedures are the best way to implement properties for objects provided by components. See "Implementing Properties in Components," in Chapter 6, "General Principles of Component Design."

What Are Circular References?

A *circular reference* occurs when two objects hold references to each other — or when an object holds a reference to itself, as in the StuckOnMyself property. You can read more about circular references in "Dealing with Circular References," in Chapter 6, "General Principles of Component Design."

The next procedure adds code to TestThing to demonstrate circular references by selectively exercising the StuckOnMyself property. It also illustrates another way to create an object.

To exercise the StuckOnMyself property from TestThing

1. In the Project Explorer window, double-click **Form1** to bring the form to the front.
2. Double-click the **Temporary Thing** button to open the code window, and add the following code to the Command5_Click event procedure:

```
' Button "Temporary Thing".
Private Sub Command5_Click()
    Dim thTemp As New Thing
    thTemp.Name = InputBox( _
        "Enter a name for the temporary Thing", _
        "Temporary Thing")
    ' Create a circular reference if the check box
    '    captioned "Stuck on itself" is checked.
    If Check1.Value = vbChecked Then
        thTemp.StuckOnMyself = True
    End If
End Sub
```

No code is needed for the check box. If Check1 is checked, the Command5_Click event procedure sets the StuckOnMyself property of the new Thing object.

Notice that instead of explicitly creating a new Thing with the New operator, the Temporary Thing button uses a variable declared As New, allowing *implicit creation* of the object. The next procedure demonstrates this. It also shows how object lifetime is affected by variable scope, and illustrates the effects of circular references on object lifetime.

To demonstrate circular references in TestThing

1. Press CTRL+F5 to run the project group.
2. Click **Create New Thing**. In the **InputBox**, type the name **Long Term Thing**, and then click **OK**. In the Immediate window, notice the messages from Sub Main and the Thing's Initialize event.
3. Click **Temporary Thing** to create a very short-lived Thing. Because the object variable `thTemp` that holds the reference to this Thing is a procedure-level variable, its lifetime — and hence the lifetime of the object — is limited to the execution of the procedure.

   You will first see an **InputBox**, because Visual Basic must evaluate the code to the right of the equal sign before assigning the result to the new Thing object's Name property.

   Before you enter a name in the input box, look in the Immediate window. There hasn't been an Initialize message from the new Thing object, because it has not yet been created. Because the variable `thTemp` was declared As New, a Thing object will be created the moment one of its properties or methods is invoked — and not a moment sooner.
4. Type any name you like in the InputBox and then click **OK**.

   You'll see two messages in the Immediate window, an Initialize message and a Terminate message. The Initialize event occurs the moment the name from the **InputBox** is assigned to `thTemp.Name`. Visual Basic finds that `thTemp` contains Nothing, creates a Thing object, and places a reference to the object in `thTemp`.

   Although the value of the DebugID property has already been set — it's what happens first in the Initialize event — the Name property is still blank. This underscores the fact that the Initialize event occurs before any other code is executed, or any properties are set.

   Only after all this has happened can Visual Basic assign the value from the InputBox function to the Thing's Name property. That's a lot of activity for one line of code.

But wait, there's more. As soon as the Thing is created, the Command5_Click event procedure ends. The variable `thTemp` goes out of scope, which is exactly the same as if it had been set to Nothing. There are no more references to the temporary Thing, so it is destroyed. Its Terminate event displays its properties, including the name you assigned to it.

5. Press CTRL+BREAK to enter Break mode, then press F8 to enter Single Step mode. Click **Temporary Thing** to enter the Command5_Click event procedure.

   Press F8 once more, to move to the line of code that sets the Thing's name:

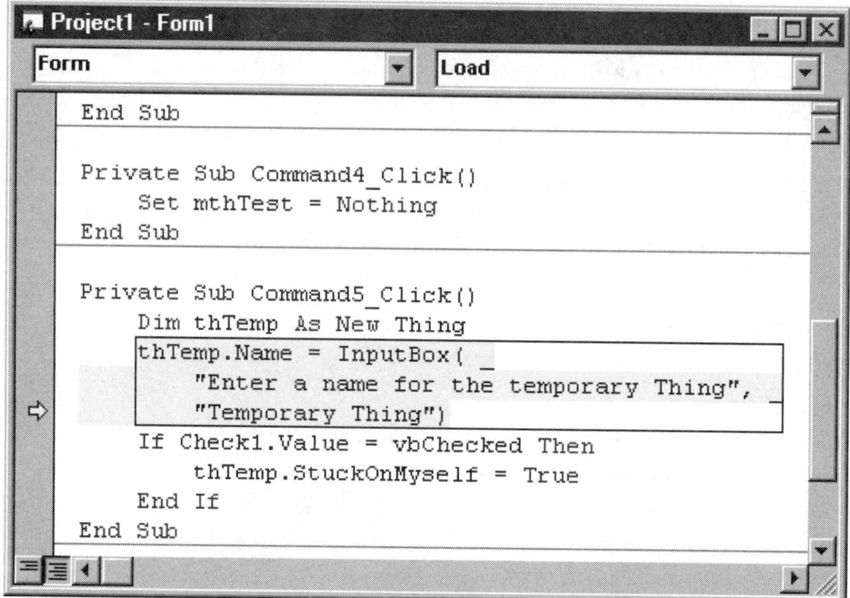

   Before you go on to the next step, you might take a guess at what the next line of code will be.

6. Press F8 to execute the InputBox statement. Type any name you like in the InputBox, and then click **OK**.

   Because you're debugging the ThingDemo component in the same environment as the test program, Visual Basic can step directly into the component's code from the test program.

   Continue pressing F8 through the code for the Initialize event, the DebugID property, and the Terminate event. When you reach the last line of Class_Terminate(), press F5 to return to Run mode.

   In-process debugging is a powerful tool for learning about the order in which events occur in a component.

7. Check **Stuck on itself**, and then click **Temporary Thing** again, to create a Thing with a reference to itself. Type the name **Renegade** in the InputBox, and then click **OK**.

   In the Immediate window you will see an Initialize message for the Thing, but no Terminate message. The object was not destroyed when the variable `thTemp` went out of scope, because there was still a reference to the object — in the `mthStuckOnMyself` variable belonging to the StuckOnMyself property.

   When will this erstwhile temporary Thing be destroyed? If you could set the Renegade Thing's StuckOnMyself property to False, there would be no more references — but TestThing can't do this, because the program no longer has a reference to use to call StuckOnMyself!

   The object is orphaned, and will go on taking up memory until the DLL is unloaded. As you'll see in a later procedure, the circular reference in the Renegade Thing's StuckOnMyself property will keep the entire DLL in memory.

8. Click **Release the Thing** to destroy the Thing you named Long Term Thing, observing its Terminate message in the Immediate window, and then click **Temporary Thing** several times. Enter a new name for each "temporary" object.

   As with the first Renegade object, you won't see any Terminate messages for these objects in the Immediate window, because the circular references will keep them from being destroyed.

9. On the **Thing Demo** dialog box, click the **Close** box to return to design mode. Presto! Like magic, a whole series of Terminate messages appear in the Immediate window.

   When Visual Basic shuts down TestThing, it also shuts down ThingDemo. Being the tidy sort, it clears all of ThingDemo's object variables — including the self-references being held by the Renegade Thing and its cohorts.

As you can see, it's important to avoid keeping extra object references in an in-process component. A client may create and release hundreds of objects while using a component. If they all persist in memory the way the renegade Things did, performance will eventually degrade.

For More Information Circular references are discussed in "Dealing with Circular References," in Chapter 6, "General Principles of Component Design," and in Appendix A, "ActiveX Component Standards and Guidelines."

Adding a Form to the ThingDemo Project

In-process components can serve as libraries of procedures and dialog boxes, saving you programming time and giving your applications a consistent look and feel.

The procedures in this topic demonstrate the way objects can be used to control modal or modeless dialog boxes. The same form is used for both cases, as shown in Figure 2.3.

Figure 2.3 The dlgDemo dialog box

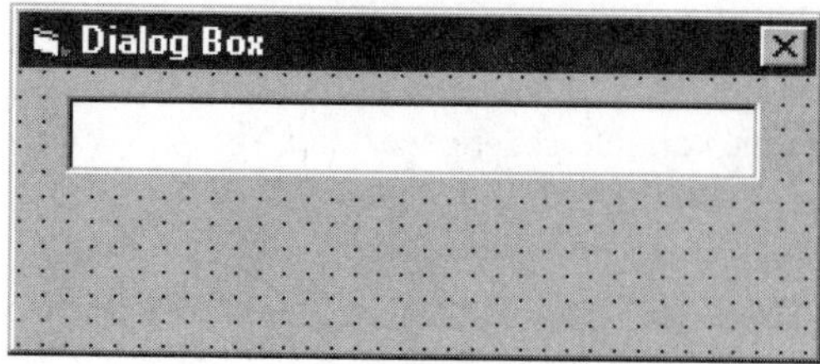

To add a form to the ThingDemo project

1. In the Project Explorer window, click **ThingDemo** to make it the active project.

   Important Whenever you're working with a project group, make sure the right project is active before adding a new module.

2. On the **Project** menu, click **Add Form** to open the **Add Form** dialog box. Double-click the Form icon to add a form.

Design the form as you would any Visual Basic form, and save it as ThingDemo_dlgDemo.frm. The following table lists property settings for the objects in the form.

Object	Property	Setting
Form	Name	dlgDemo
	BorderStyle	Fixed Dialog
	Caption	Dialog Box
TextBox	Name	txtDemo
	Text	(Empty)

The dialog box is not invoked directly from the client, because forms are private classes. Clients cannot create instances of private classes, and you should never pass instances of private classes to client applications. This is discussed in "Data Types Allowed in Properties and Methods," in Chapter 6, "General Principles of Component Design."

To display the dialog box, clients will call the ShowDialog method of a global Dialogs object, which will create and show the dlgDemo form.

To add code to the dlgDemo form

1. Double-click on dlgDemo to open its code window, and add the following code.

   ```
   ' Declare an event.
   Event NotifyClients(ByVal Data As String)
   ```

2. Add the following code to the Change event of the text box. When the contents of the text box change, the NotifyClients event is raised with the new contents as its argument.

```
Private Sub txtDemo_Change()
   RaiseEvent NotifyClients(txtDemo.Text)
End Sub
```

3. To prevent the dialog box from being closed without the knowledge of the Dialogs object, place the following code in the QueryUnload event procedure.

```
Private Sub Form_QueryUnload(Cancel As Integer, _
      UnloadMode As Integer)
   ' If the Close button was pressed, hide the
   '   dialog box instead of unloading it.
   If UnloadMode = vbFormControlMenu Then
      Cancel = True
      Me.Visible = False
   End If
End Sub
```

If dlgDemo is shown as a modal dialog, hiding the dialog rather than unloading it allows the ShowDialog method of the Dialogs class to retrieve the value in the text box.

To create the Dialogs class

1. From the **Project** menu, choose **Add Class Module** to open the **Add Class Module** dialog box. Double-click the Blank Class Module icon to add a class module to the project.
2. In the Properties window, change the Name property of the class to `Dialogs`.
3. In the Properties window, change the Instancing property to GlobalMultiUse, so that you can call the ShowDialog method without explicitly creating a Dialogs object.
4. To create a WithEvents variable that can handle the NotifyClients event of dlgDemo, and to create an event that Dialogs object can raise for its own clients, add the following code to the Declarations section:

```
Private WithEvents mdlg As dlgDemo
Event NotifyClients(ByVal Data As String)
```

5. In the **Object** box, select **mdlg** to show the event procedure for the NotifyClients event raised by dlgDemo. Add the following code:

```
Private Sub mdlg_NotifyClients(ByVal Data As String)
   RaiseEvent NotifyClients(Data)
End Sub
```

The Dialogs object receives the NotifyClients event from its dlgDemo form whenever the contents of the dialog's text box changes. The Dialogs object immediately raises its own NotifyClients event, passing along the data to its own client.

6. In the code window, select **Class** from the **Object** box. In the **Procedure** box, select **Initialize** and add the following code to the Class_Initialize event procedure:

```
Private Sub Class_Initialize()
   Debug.Print "Dialogs object created"
   Set mdlg = New dlgDemo
End Sub
```

7. In the **Procedure** box, select **Terminate** and add the following code to the Class_Terminate event procedure:

```
Private Sub Class_Terminate()
   Debug.Print "Dialogs object terminated"
   Unload mdlg
   Set mdlg = Nothing
End Sub
```

   When terminating, an object that controls a form should always unload the form and set its reference to the form to Nothing, to avoid tying up resources with orphaned forms.

8. On the **Tools** menu, click **Add Procedure** to open the **Add Procedures** dialog box. In the **Name** box, type **ShowDialog**. Click **Function** and **Public**, then click **OK**.

   In the code window, change the newly created Function procedure to appear as follows:

```
Public Function ShowDialog( _
      Optional ByVal Text As String = "", _
      Optional ByVal Modal As Boolean = True) _
      As String
   With mdlg
      .txtDemo.Text = Text
      If Modal Then
         .Caption = "Modal Dialog Box"
         .Show vbModal
         ShowDialog = .txtDemo.Text
      Else
         .Caption = "Modeless Dialog Box"
         .Show vbModeless
      End If
   End With
End Function
```

   Typed optional arguments let the compiler catch type mismatch errors, instead of waiting until run-time errors occur. Typed optional arguments are discussed in Chapter 5, "Programming Fundamentals," in the *Microsoft Visual Basic 6.0 Programmer's Guide.*

9. Save the class module as ThingDemo_Dialogs.cls.

The ShowDialog method that displays the dialog has two optional arguments:

- The initial text it's going to display
- A Boolean argument that determines whether the dialog is modal

The Text argument is assigned to the text box on dlgDemo before the dialog box is shown. The default value of the Modal argument is True, so omitting it causes the dialog to be modal.

If the dialog is shown Modal, the ShowDialog method returns the contents of the `txtDemo` text box after the dialog has been dismissed by the user.

If the dialog is shown Modeless nothing is returned, because the client received a NotifyClients event whenever the contents of the text box changed.

For More Information Events are discussed in "Adding Events to Classes," in Chapter 6, "General Principles of Component Design."

Using the Global Object in TestThing

TestThing will call the ShowDialog method to display a modal dialog in its Form_Load event procedure, as the application is starting. It will also show a modeless dialog when the main form is clicked.

To add code to call the ShowDialog method

1. In the Project Explorer window, click **Form1** to select it, then press F7 — or click the **Code** button on the Project Explorer window toolbar — to open the code window for the form. Place the following code in the Form_Load event.

```
Sub Form_Load()
   Me.Caption = ShowDialog(Me.Caption)
End Sub
```

   Notice that no object variable is declared, and that the ShowDialog method is called as if it were an ordinary function procedure. This is possible because the Dialogs object's Instancing property is set to GlobalMultiUse.

2. In the Declarations section, add the following code:

```
Private WithEvents mdgs As Dialogs
```

   The variable is declared WithEvents, so that Form1 can handle the NotifyClients events raised by the Dialogs object.

3. In the **Object** box, select **mdgs** to show the event procedure. Add the following code:

```
Private Sub mdgs_NotifyClients(Byval Data As String)
   Me.Caption = Data
End Sub
```

   Whenever the NotifyClients event is received, Form1 assigns the data to its caption property. The modeless dialog box thus controls the form's caption.

4. To show the modeless dialog and start event handling, add the following code to the Form_Click event procedure:

```
Private Sub Form_Click()
   If mdgs Is Nothing Then
      Set mdgs = New Dialogs
   End If
   mdgs.ShowDialog Me.Caption, False
End Sub
```

    Important The Dialogs object created here is not the global instance used to show the modal dialog in the Load event. The global instance will be created automatically when the ShowDialog method is invoked in Form_Load, and will be used for any subsequent method invocations that omit the object variable. The instance used to show the modeless dialog box is explicitly created and assigned to the WithEvents variable, so its NotifyClients event can be handled.

Okay! The Dialogs object creates and manipulates a dlgForm object, and receives its NotifyClients event. Form1 creates two different Dialogs objects, one implicitly (the global instance used to show the modal dialog) and one explicitly (used to show the modeless dialog).

The modeless dialog communicates with the Dialogs object by raising a NotifyClients event. The Dialogs object responds by raising its own NotifyClients event, which Form1 handles by assigning the data to its Caption property. Time to see if it all works!

To see if it all works

1. Press CTRL+F5 to run the project group. The first thing you'll see is the dialog box, containing the caption of Form1:

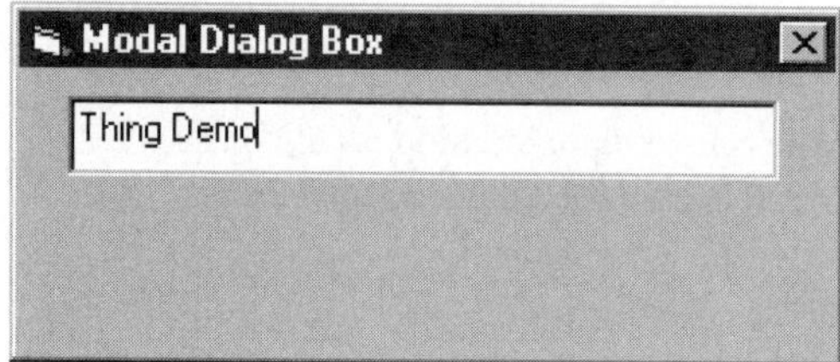

2. Enter a new caption, and close the dialog box. The main form appears, showing its new caption.

3. Click on the main form to create another Dialogs object, which will show a modeless dialog box containing the current caption of the main form. Enter another caption, and observe that with each keystroke the main form's caption changes:

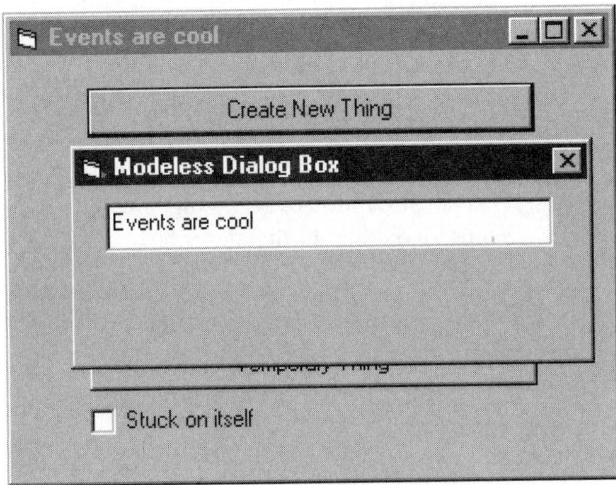

Each change to the contents of the text box raises a NotifyClients event from dlgDemo to the Dialogs object. The Dialogs object then raises its own NotifyClients event, which the main form receives.

You may find it instructive to run the project again, pressing F8 this time to step through the code one line at a time. You can clearly see that two different Dialogs objects are involved, because you'll step through their separate Initialize events.

Among the interesting things you'll notice is that the *modal* dialog box raises NotifyClients events, just as the modeless dialog box does. Form1 doesn't have a WithEvents variable containing a reference to the global Dialogs object, so it's unable to handle these events.

Important The "global" in "global object" simply means that the methods and properties of the object added to the global name space of your project, so that they can be used without first declaring an object variable. It *does not* mean that there is only one such object, or that multiple client applications can share a single object. An instance of the class will be created for each client that uses methods of the class without qualifying them. Only one such global object will be created for each client.

Client Support for Modeless Forms

The display of modeless forms from in-process components requires communication with the client's message loop. Not all clients support this. For an explanation of this limitation, see "Displaying Forms from Code Components," in Chapter 8, "Building Code Components."

For More Information Global objects are discussed in "Instancing for Classes Provided by ActiveX Components," in Chapter 6, "General Principles of Component Design," and in Chapter 8, "Building Code Components."

Compiling and Testing the ThingDemo DLL

Once an in-process component project is tested and debugged in the development environment, you can compile and test the .dll file.

An ActiveX component is compiled the same way any Visual Basic project is compiled — by choosing Make from the File menu. The .dll file includes a type library that describes your objects and allows them to be browsed.

Visual Basic makes it easy to add the necessary lines to the Windows Registry. You don't have to write any code, and you don't have to understand the format of registry entries. When you make the executable file, Visual Basic automatically registers it on your computer.

> **Note** When you distribute your application as part of an integrated solution, registration is done during setup. If you use the Visual Basic Package and Deployment Wizard, registration of your component will be included in the setup process automatically. This is discussed in "Deploying ActiveX Components" in Chapter 7, "Debugging, Testing, and Deploying Components."

For More Information The Package and Deployment Wizard is described in Chapter 17, "Distributing Your Applications," in the *Microsoft Visual Basic 6.0 Programmer's Guide.*

To compile and test the OLE DLL executable

1. If the TestThing project is still in run mode, click the **Close** button on Form1 to return to design mode.
2. In the Project Explorer window, click **ThingDemo** to select the project.
3. On the **File** menu, click **Make ThingDemo.dll** to open the **Make Project** dialog box. Click **OK** to build the .dll file.
4. On the **File** menu, click **Remove Project** to remove ThingDemo from the project group, so that Visual Basic will use the compiled binary component (.dll file) instead of the project.

   Visual Basic displays a warning message, because the TestThing project contains a reference to ThingDemo. Click **Yes** to remove ThingDemo anyway.

   When you remove ThingDemo from the project group, Visual Basic looks for ThingDemo.dll in the Windows Registry. If the .dll file exists, Visual Basic automatically updates the reference you set in "Creating the TestThing Project."

   To switch back to using the project instead of the binary component, you can click **Add Project** on the **File** menu, and add the ThingDemo project back to the project group.
5. Press F5 to run TestThing using the .dll file.

You can compile TestThing.exe, and run it with the .dll. You can also test the compiled ThingDemo.dll from other applications.

To use ThingDemo.dll in another copy of Visual Basic

1. Open a new instance of Visual Basic. In the **New Project** dialog box, double-click the EXE Project icon to open a new EXE project.
2. On the **Project** menu, click **References** to open the **References** dialog box. Check **ThingDemo ActiveX DLL**, and then click **OK**.

   You can now add code to create Thing and Dialogs objects and invoke their properties and methods.
3. Press F5 to run the project.

For More Information You can read more about test projects and debugging techniques in Chapter 7, "Debugging, Testing, and Deploying Components."

Circular References and Component Shutdown

The following procedure shows how Visual Basic unloads an in-process component after the client has released all references to its objects. It also shows how circular references can prevent this unloading, and highlights an important difference between public and private objects.

The procedure can only be run using the compiled component and compiled test project, because Visual Basic never unloads an in-process component project running in the development environment.

To observe DLL unloading

1. Add a new class module to ThingDemo. Name it **TellTale**, and set its Instancing property to Private. Add the following code to its Terminate event:

   ```
   Private Sub Class_Terminate()
      MsgBox "Private object destroyed"
   End Sub
   ```

   A private object cannot be created by clients, and should never be passed to them. As you'll see, private objects *do not* keep in-process components from unloading, and a client that uses a reference to a private object after its component has unloaded will suffer a catastrophic program failure.
2. Add the following code to Module1 in ThingDemo:

   ```
   Option Explicit
   Private mtt As TellTale     ' New code.

   Sub Main
      Debug.Print "Executing Sub Main"
      Set mtt = New TellTale    ' New code.
   End Sub
   ```

Once the projects are compiled, Debug statements can't be used to show what's happening internally. Like a canary in a coal mine, the TellTale object will give us an indication of what's happening in the compiled component.

3. On the **File** menu, click **Make Project Group** to compile both ThingDemo and ThingTest. On the **Start** menu, click **Run** to open the **Run** dialog box, and browse to find and run ThingTest — or use the Windows Explorer.
4. Close the modal dialog box, and click **Create Temporary Thing**. Enter any name you like in the input box, and click **OK**.

   As you saw earlier, the temporary Thing doesn't hang around long. The only reason to create it now is to load ThingDemo.dll and execute Sub Main. For this procedure, the interesting question is what happens when the Things are all gone.
5. Wait a few minutes. Go get a cup of coffee. You deserve it. When you come back, after a few minutes have elapsed, you'll see a message box with the message "Private object destroyed."

   What happened? There were no references to public objects, so after a decent interval (usually about two minutes, although this will vary depending on how frequently it gets idle time) Visual Basic will attempt to unload the in-process component.

   When the DLL is unloaded, Visual Basic frees the memory it was using — including variables containing private object references. As a result the TellTale object is destroyed, and you get a visual cue that the DLL has unloaded.

   If you create a new Thing object at this point, you'll notice a slight pause as the DLL is reloaded.
6. Now for the circular references. Check the **Stuck on itself** box, and then click **Create Temporary Thing** to create a Thing object with a reference to itself.
7. Wait a few minutes. Go get another cup of coffee. Drink it. Wait a few more minutes. Do some other work. However long you wait, the DLL will not unload, because the reference to the Thing object keeps Visual Basic from unloading it.

   Visual Basic can't tell the difference between an internal reference to a public object and an external (client) reference to a public object, so it has no choice but to keep the DLL loaded.
8. Close ThingTest's main form. The private object is again destroyed, because unloading the client application also unloads any in-process components it's using.

For More Information The rules for component shutdown are listed in "Starting and Ending a Component," in Chapter 6, "General Principles of Component Design," and discussed in more detail in Appendix A, "ActiveX Component Standards and Guidelines."

ActiveX DLL Creation Summary

In order to introduce new concepts in the most natural order, the procedures in this chapter have not followed the normal sequence of steps for creating an in-process component. When you create a new ActiveX DLL, the steps you'll generally follow are these:

- Determine the features your component will provide.
- Determine what objects are required to divide the functionality of the component in a logical fashion.
- Design any forms your component will display.
- Design the interface — that is, the properties, methods, and events — for each class provided by your component.
- Create a project group consisting of your component project and a test project.
- Implement the forms required by your component.
- Implement the interface of each class.
- As you add each interface element or feature, add features to your test project to exercise the new functionality.
- Compile your DLL and test it with all potential target applications.

For More Information General design issues for ActiveX components are discussed in Chapter 6, "General Principles of Component Design," and Chapter 7, "Debugging, Testing, and Deploying Components." Issues exclusive to DLLs, including testing, packaging, and deployment, are discussed in Chapter 8, "Building Code Components." The step-by-step procedures in Chapter 3, "Creating an ActiveX EXE Component," demonstrate other component features, including events, call-backs, unattended operation, and multithreading.

CHAPTER 3

Creating an ActiveX EXE Component

Components provide reusable code in the form of objects. An application that uses a component's code, by creating objects and calling their properties and methods, is referred to as a *client.*

Components can run either in-process or out-of-process with respect to the clients that use their objects. An out-of-process component, or ActiveX EXE, runs in its own address space. The client is usually an application running in another process.

Figure 3.1 Client and out-of-process component

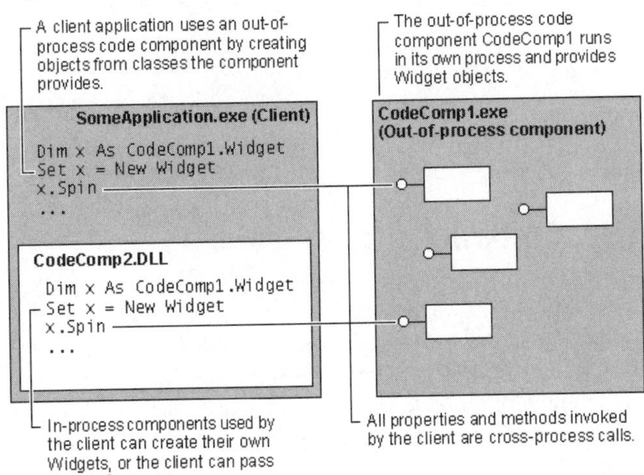

The fact that an out-of-process component runs in its own process means that a client can tell it to do something, and then go about its business while the component does the work. When such a system is properly set up, the component can tell the client when the task is done using an *asynchronous notification*, as explained in "Asynchronous Call-Backs and Events" in Chapter 8, "Building Code Components."

Note "In-Process and Out-of-Process Components," in Chapter 6, "General Principles of Component Design," discusses differences between in-process and out-of-process code components.

The step-by-step procedures in this chapter explore the creation and use of out-of-process components by building a simple component called CoffeeWatch. Coffeewatch demonstrates the behavior of modal and modeless dialog boxes, and shows one way to implement asynchronous notifications using events.

You'll also see how to debug an ActiveX EXE out of process, by running the component and a test project in two separate instances of the Visual Basic development environment.

The procedures for creating the Coffee component build on each other. The sequence in which you perform the procedures is therefore important:

Contents

Sample Applications: Coffee2.vbp, CoffWat2.vbp, MTCoffee.vbp

Coffee2.vbp and CoffWat2.vbp contain expanded source code for this chapter. In addition to asynchronous notifications using events, they include an alternate version using call-back methods on a secondary interface, and an example of all-code timers you can use instead of the Timer control. MTCoffee illustrates some features of multithreading. All three sample applications are listed in the Samples directory.

Before You Begin

These procedures will be easier to follow if you set up your development environment as described below.

Before You Begin

1. On the **View** menu, click **Toolbox** to open the Toolbox.
2. On the **View** menu, click **Project Explorer** to open the Project Explorer window. The Project Explorer window will be used extensively to switch between project files.

3. If the Project Explorer window is in Folder view, as shown below, click the **Toggle Folders** button on the Project Explorer window toolbar to turn the folders off.

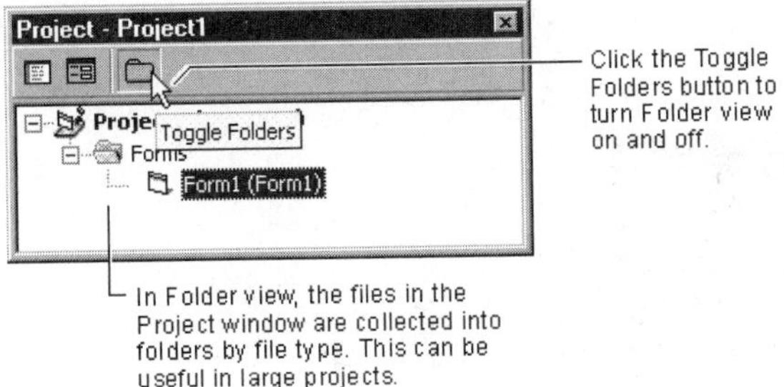
Project - Project1
Toggle Folders
Forms
Form1 (Form1)
Click the Toggle Folders button to turn Folder view on and off.
In Folder view, the files in the Project window are collected into folders by file type. This can be useful in large projects.

4. On the **View** menu, click **Properties Window** to open the Properties window.
5. On the **Tools** menu, click **Options** to open the **Options** dialog box.

   Select the **Editor** tab, and make sure **Require Variable Declaration** is checked. This makes it much easier to catch typing errors.

   Select the **Environment** tab. Make sure **Prompt To Save Changes** is selected, then click **OK**. This will make it easy to save changes to the project as you go along.

Creating the Coffee Project

This topic creates the Coffee project, with its CoffeeMonitor class and its TestForm form class.

To create the Coffee project

1. On the **File** menu, click **New Project**.
2. In the **New Project** dialog box, double-click the ActiveX EXE icon. Visual Basic automatically adds a class module, Class1, to the new project.
3. Press F4 to switch to the Properties window. Double-click the **Name** property and change it to **CoffeeMonitor**. This is the name you'll use to create objects from the class.

   The default value for the Instancing property is MultiUse. This allows clients to create multiple instances of the CoffeeMonitor class. For a full discussion of the Instancing property, see "Instancing for Classes Provided by ActiveX Components," in Chapter 6, "General Principles of Component Design."

4. On the **Project** menu, click **Project1 Properties** to open the **Project Properties** dialog box. Select the **General** tab, fill out the information shown below, then click **OK**.

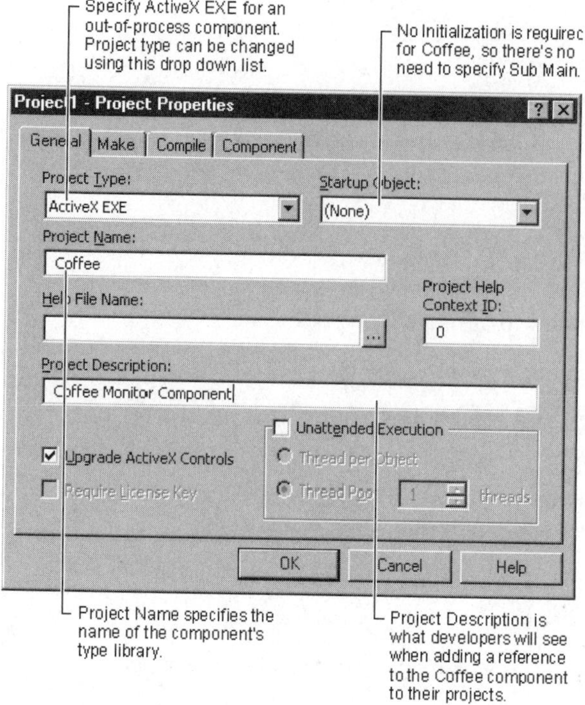
Specify ActiveX EXE for an out-of-process component. Project type can be changed using this drop down list.
No Initialization is requirec for Coffee, so there's no need to specify Sub Main.
Project1 - Project Properties
General
Make
Compile
Component
Project Type:
ActiveX EXE
Startup Object:
(None)
Project Name:
Coffee
Help File Name:
Project Help Context ID:
0
Project Description:
Coffee Monitor Component
Unattended Execution
Upgrade ActiveX Controls
Require License Key
Thread per Object
Thread Pool
1
threads
OK
Cancel
Help
Project Name specifies the name of the component's type library.
Project Description is what developers will see when adding a reference to the Coffee component to their projects.

The project name, Coffee, is also used as the name of the component's type library. It can be combined with the name of each class the component provides, to produce unique class names.

If two components each provide a CoffeeMonitor class, the fully qualified class name lets you specify which component's CoffeeMonitor class you want to use, for example, `Coffee.CoffeeMonitor`.

5. On the **Project** menu, click **Add Form** to open the **Add Form** dialog box. Double click the Form icon to add a form to the project.

   Note If you've used the **Options** dialog box (accessed from the **Tools** menu) to disable the **Add Form** dialog box, you'll just get the form. This is okay.

6. Press F4 to open the Properties window. Change the following property settings:

Object	Property	Setting
Form	(Name) Caption	TestForm TestForm – Modal

7. On the **File** menu, click **Save Project** to save the project files, using the following names. Visual Basic will provide the extensions automatically.

File	File name	Extension
Form	Coffee_TestForm	.frm
Class module	Coffee_CoffeeMonitor	.cls
Project	Coffee	.vbp

For More Information See "Choosing a Project Type and Setting Project Options," in Chapter 6, "General Principles of Component Design."

Showing Forms from the CoffeeMonitor Class

Out-of-process components can show both modal and modeless forms. The first use for the CoffeeMonitor will be to demonstrate this, because the results may not be quite what you expect.

The procedure in this topic adds a ShowForm method to the CoffeeMonitor class, plus public constants for use with the method.

To show forms from the CoffeeMonitor class

1. In the Project Explorer window, double-click **CoffeeMonitor** (or select it and then click the Code button on the Project Explorer window toolbar), to open its code window.
2. In the Declarations section, add the following Public Enum:

```
Option Explicit
Public Enum cfeModality
   cfeModal = vbModal
   cfeModeless = vbModeless
End Enum
```

An enumeration declared Public in a class module is added to your component's type library. It will not be associated with the class in which it was defined, but will become part of the global name space.

Why would you provide your own constants, when Visual Basic includes vbModal and vbModeless? Your component may be used with a development tool that doesn't provide these constants. Providing constants compatible with Visual Basic is a flexible solution.

Note Putting the prefix "cfe" in front of the constant names identifies the constants as belonging to the Coffee component, and reduces the chance of name collisions with other components. Some component authors follow the prefix with two or three uppercase letters identifying the Enum; this seems superfluous here. See "Providing Named Constants for Your Component" in Chapter 6, "General Principles of Component Design."

3. On the **Tools** menu, click **Add Procedure** to open the **Add Procedure** dialog box. Type **ShowForm** in the **Name** box, click **Sub** and **Public**, and then click **OK**.

   A public Sub or Function procedure in a class module defines a method of the class, while a public property procedure defines a property. See "Adding Properties and Methods to Classes," in Chapter 6, "General Principles of Component Design."

4. Add the following code to the Sub procedure:

```
Public Sub ShowForm(Optional Modality As _
      cfeModality = cfeModal)
   Dim frm As New TestForm
   If Modality = cfeModeless Then
      frm.Caption = "TestForm - Modeless"
   Else
      frm.Caption = "TestForm - Modal"
   End If
   frm.Show Modality
End Sub
```

   The typed optional argument Modality specifies a Modal form if the argument is omitted. Typed optional arguments are discussed in "Passing Arguments to Procedures" in Chapter 5, "Programming Fundamentals," in the *Microsoft Visual Basic 6.0 Programmer's Guide.*

   Because the constants in cfeModality are compatible with the vbModal and vbModeless constants supplied by Visual Basic, you can simply pass the Modality argument to the form's Show method. The Show method will automatically raise an error if an invalid value is supplied.

5. On the **File** menu, click **Make Coffee.exe** to create a reference executable.

   The reference executable, which you only need to create once, will help your test application keep its connection to this project. See "Creating a Test Project for an Out-of-Process Component" in Chapter 7, "Debugging, Testing, and Deploying Components."

6. Press CTRL+F5 to run the project.

   Note If **Compile On Demand** is checked (on the **General** tab of the **Options** dialog box, accessible from the **Tools** menu), you should use CTRL+F5 (or select **Start with Full Compile** from the **Run** menu) to ensure that your component is fully compiled before you begin testing. A compilation error that occurs after the component is providing objects to the test program can be very awkward. **Compile On Demand** is checked by default.

   Important You must put your project in run mode before editing or running the test program, as explained in "Creating a Test Project for an Out-of-Process Component" in Chapter 7, "Debugging, Testing, and Deploying Components."

Creating the CoffeeWatch Test Project

"Out of process" means the component is running in a separate process from the client application. Therefore you need a separate process for your test program — which means starting another instance of the Visual Basic development environment.

The following procedure creates the test program and adds a reference to the out-of-process Coffee component.

To create the CoffeeWatch test project

1. Use the Windows **Start** menu or the Explorer to open another instance of Visual Basic. On the **New Project** dialog box, double-click the Standard EXE icon to open a new Standard EXE project.
2. On the **Project** menu, click **Project1 Properties** to open the **Project Properties** dialog box. Select the **General** tab, type **CoffeeWatch** in the **Project Name** box, then click **OK**.
3. On the **Project** menu, click **References** to open the **References** dialog box. Check the entry for Coffee.vbp, as shown below, then click **OK**.

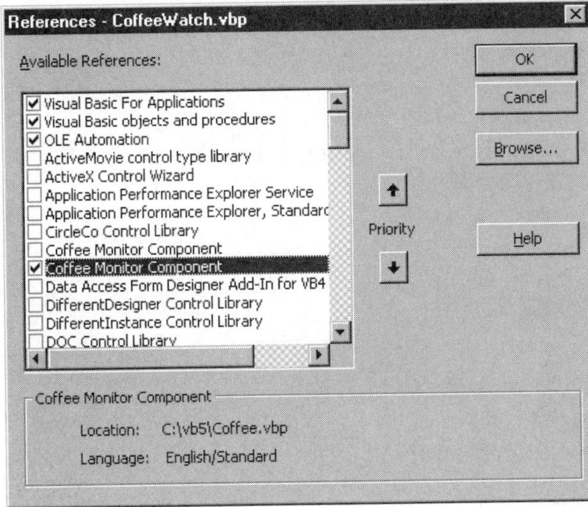

You can tell the entries apart by observing the Location in the information panel at the bottom of the dialog box.

> **Important** You must check the entry for the project file (.vbp) in order to debug the project in the development environment. If you set a reference to the .exe file, visible just above the .vbp entry in the figure above, CoffeeWatch will obtain objects from an instance of the executable instead.

4. Add two command buttons to Form1, and set their properties as shown in the following table:

Object	Property	Setting
Command button	(Name) Caption	cmdModal Show Modal Form
Command button	(Name) Caption	cmdModeless Show Modeless Form
Form	Caption	CoffeeWatch

5. In the Declarations section of the code window for Form1, add the following declaration:

```
Option Explicit
Private mcmnTest As CoffeeMonitor
```

   The prefix for the variable begins with the letter "m" to indicate that this is a module-level variable. The letters "cmn" were chosen to represent the CoffeeMonitor class type.

6. Add the following code to the Load event for Form1:

```
Private Sub Form_Load()
   Set mcmnTest = New CoffeeMonitor
End Sub
```

7. Add the following code to the Click event procedures for the command buttons:

```
Private Sub cmdModal_Click()
   mcmnTest.ShowForm cfeModal
End Sub

Private Sub cmdModeless_Click()
   mcmnTest.ShowForm cfeModeless
End Sub
```

8. On the **File** menu, click **Save Project** to save the project files, using the following names. Visual Basic will provide the extensions automatically.

File	File name	Extension
Form	CoffeeWatch_Form1	.frm
Project	CoffeeWatch	.vbp

If you have the Auto List Members option enabled, you've noticed that the methods of the CoffeeMonitor class appeared in the list of available classes. This is because the reference you established in step 3 made the Coffee component's type library information available.

Note The Auto List Members option can be set on the Editor tab of the Options dialog box, available from the Tools menu.

How Modal and Modeless Forms Behave Out of Process

As mentioned in "Showing Forms from the CoffeeManager Class," modal and modeless forms displayed by an out-of-process component have a different relationship to a client application's forms than they would if displayed by an in-process component. Running CoffeeWatch will demonstrate this.

To demonstrate modal and modeless form behavior with the out-of-process Coffee component

1. Press F5 to run the CoffeeWatch test program.
2. Click **Show Modal Form** to display a modal form from the Coffee component.

   Depending on your system configuration, the order programs were started, and so on, the modal form may come up in front of CoffeeWatch — or you may see something like this:

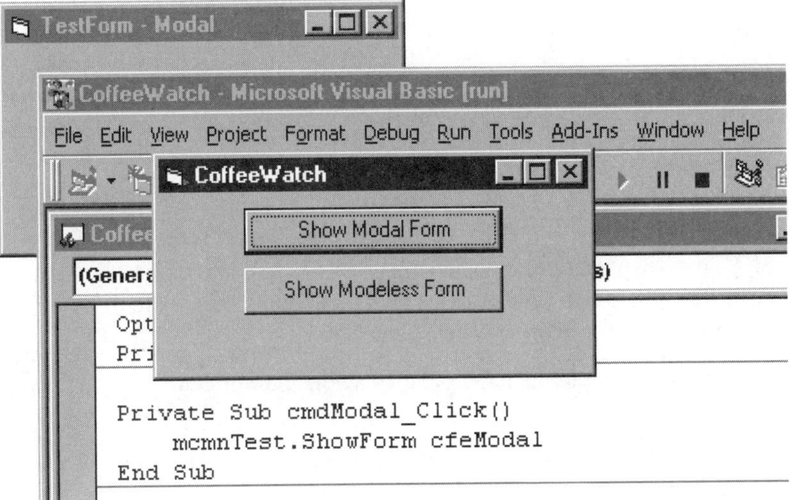

3. TestForm is not really modal with respect to the CoffeeWatch form. To see this, click anywhere on the **CoffeeWatch** form. The **Component Request Pending** dialog box appears, as shown here:

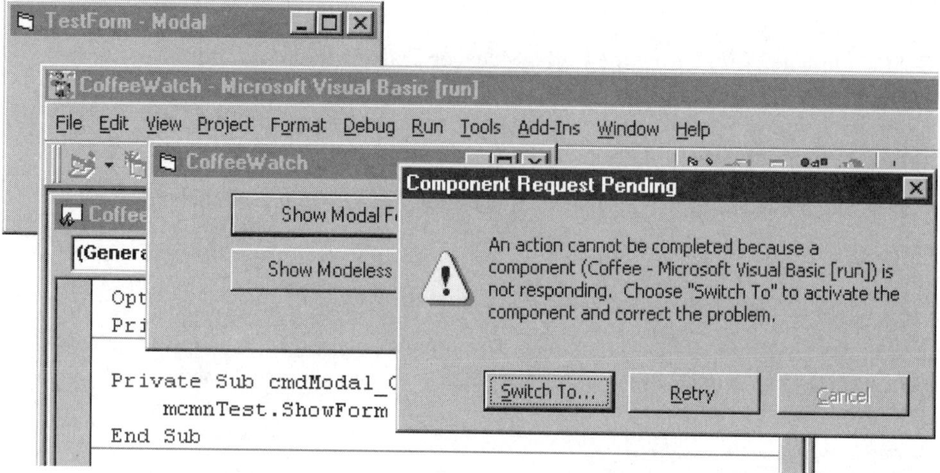

The dialog box appears because CoffeeWatch is waiting on its call to `CoffeeMonitor.ShowForm`, which is waiting on the modal TestForm. However, if TestForm were truly modal with respect to Form1, clicking on Form1 would generate a system sound indicating that Form1 was disabled.

4. Click **Switch To**, to bring **TestForm** to the front.

   Note Depending on your system configuration and the order in which programs are loaded, the copy of Visual Basic in which Coffee is running may come to the front along with TestForm, obscuring CoffeeWatch.

5. Click on **CoffeeWatch** again, to bring it to the front and display the **Component Request Pending** dialog box again.

   Note If you can't see **CoffeeWatch** (the form, not the project), use the taskbar (or press ALT+TAB) to bring it to the front.

   In the strict sense of the word, TestForm is modal to CoffeeWatch. That is, you can't do anything with CoffeeWatch until TestForm is dismissed. However, because the two forms are in different processes, CoffeeWatch can appear on top of TestForm.

6. Click **Switch To**, to bring **TestForm** to the front, and then click TestForm's close box to dismiss the modal form.

7. Click **Show Modeless Form** to show **TestForm** as a modeless form.

   TestForm behaves like a modeless form that's not owned by CoffeeWatch. That is, it doesn't stay on top of CoffeeWatch. You can verify this by clicking on each of the two forms, to bring them alternately to the front.

Important Because TestForm is in a different process from CoffeeWatch, you cannot make CoffeeWatch the owner of TestForm as you would if the forms were in the same process — that is, by passing a reference to CoffeeWatch in the OwnerForm argument of TestForm. For details see "Displaying Forms from Code Components," in Chapter 8, "Building Code Components."

8. DO NOT dismiss the modeless **TestForm**. Instead, close **CoffeeWatch** by clicking its close box.

   TestForm doesn't close. (It may be hidden behind the instance of Visual Basic containing the CoffeeWatch project — use the taskbar or ALT+TAB to bring it to the front.)

   This illustrates two important points: First, a form displayed by an out-of-process component is not dependent on the client application. Nor is its lifetime limited by the client's lifetime.

   Second, a loaded form can keep an out-of-process component's executable from unloading. For details, see "Starting and Ending a Component" in Chapter 6, "General Principles of Component Design."

   In its Terminate event, CoffeeMonitor should unload any forms it has shown.

9. Dismiss **TestForm** by clicking its close box. The Coffee component remains in run mode. To return Coffee to design mode, click the **End** button, or select **End** from the **Run** menu.

   Once you put an ActiveX EXE project in run mode, it remains in run mode. This is convenient for testing, but it's different from the behavior of the made .exe. The executable for an out-of-process component unloads when the last client releases its last reference to an object provided by the component, as discussed in "Starting and Ending a Component."

   Note The only way to test the shutdown behavior of an out-of-process component is to test with the made executable.

The lesson to take away from all this is that out-of-process code components are generally not the best way to show forms.

Providing an Asynchronous Notification Event

One of the most interesting uses for out-of-process components is to provide asynchronous notifications to the client. That is, the client doesn't remain blocked while the component executes a method — instead, it goes about its business while the component works on a task or watches for an occurrence of interest. The component's notification arrives out of the blue, without any specific action on the part of the client.

The procedure in this topic sets up a simple asynchronous notification based on a common data processing problem: How do you know when the coffee is ready?

The demonstration assumes that you have a coffee maker with a serial interface (however, the demonstration will work even if you don't). The Coffee component tests the serial port periodically to see if the coffee maker's High bit is set, indicating that the coffee is ready.

Before you begin this procedure, make sure you've returned the Coffee project to design mode, as described at the end of "How Modal and Modeless Forms Behave Out of Process."

To set up an asynchronous notification event in the CoffeeMonitor class

1. In the Project Explorer window, right-click **TestForm** to open the context menu, and select **View Object** to open the form designer. Add a Timer control, and set its properties as follows:

Object	Property	Setting
Timer control	(Name)	TmrCoffee
	Enabled	True
	Interval	10000

   There's no need to put code in the tmrControl_Timer event procedure. As you'll see, CoffeeMonitor will handle the control's Timer event, test the serial port, and raise the CoffeeReady event to notify CoffeeWatch.

2. In the Project Explorer window, double-click **CoffeeMonitor** (or select it and then click the **Code** button on the Project Explorer window toolbar), to open its code window. Highlight all of the code except Option Explicit, and comment it out using the **Comment Block** button on the Edit toolbar, as shown here:

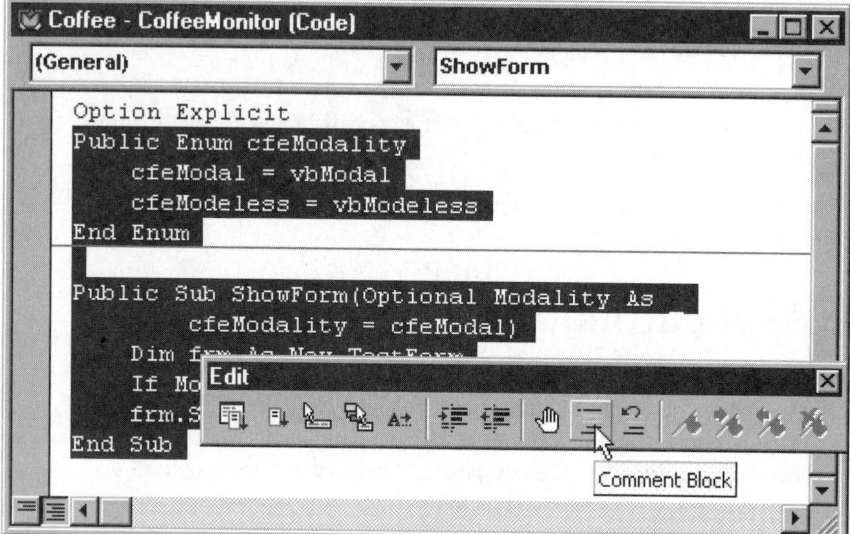

In order to view all the code at once, make sure you've selected Full Module View, as shown by the buttons in the lower left-hand corner of the code window.

You can show the Edit toolbar using the context menu accessed by right-clicking the menu or standard toolbar, as shown here:

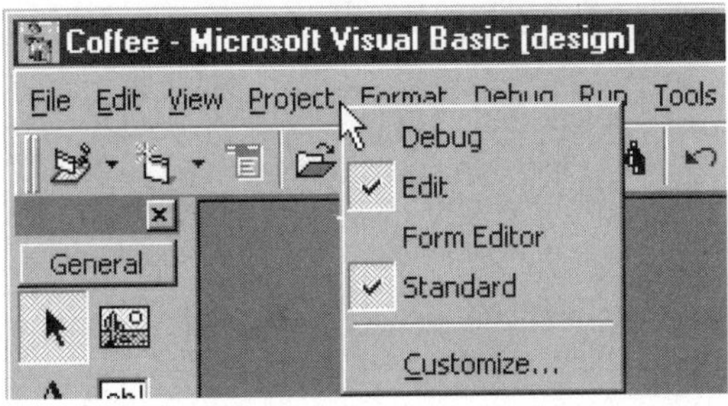

3. In the Declarations section, add the following variables and event declaration:

```
Option Explicit
Private mTestForm As TestForm
Private WithEvents mwtmrCoffee As Timer
Event CoffeeReady()
```

- CoffeeMonitor will raise the CoffeeReady event to notify the CoffeeWatch program when the coffee's ready.
- The variable `mTestForm` will hold a reference to an instance of TestForm, whose only purpose is to hold the Timer control.
- The variable `mwtmrCoffee` will hold a reference to the Timer control on the TestForm. The variable is declared WithEvents so that the CoffeeMonitor object can handle the timer's events.

4. In the left (**Object**) drop-down menu, select **Class** to make the event procedure templates for the class module available in the right (Procedure) drop-down menu, and to open the template for the default event (Initialize). Add the following code to create and load an instance of TestForm when the CoffeeMonitor object is created:

```
Private Sub Class_Initialize()
   Set mTestForm = New TestForm
   Load mTestForm
   Set mwtmrCoffee = mTestForm.tmrCoffee
End Sub
```

After the instance of TestForm is created and loaded, a reference to `tmrCoffee` is placed in the variable `mwtmrCoffee`. When the reference is placed in the WithEvents variable, Visual Basic connects the timer's events to the associated event procedures in CoffeeMonitor.

5. In the **Procedure** drop-down menu, select the Terminate event for the class. Add the following code to the event procedure template:

```
Private Sub Class_Terminate()
   Set mwtmrCoffee = Nothing
   Unload mTestForm
   Set mTestForm = Nothing
End Sub
```

As we saw in "How Modal and Modeless Forms Behave Out of Process," earlier in this chapter, objects that use forms in out-of-process components need to dispose of the forms when they're done with them. The first step is to set the WithEvents variable to Nothing, so that CoffeeMonitor will stop handling the Timer control's events. Then TestForm can be unloaded, and the variable containing the reference to it can be set to Nothing.

> **Note** Strictly speaking, there's no need to set `mTestForm` to Nothing here. Visual Basic will set the variable to Nothing when it destroys the CoffeeMonitor object.

6. In the **Object** drop-down menu, select **mwtmrCoffee**. The Timer control's only event, Timer, appears in the **Procedure** drop-down menu, and the event procedure template is added to the code window. Add the following code:

```
Private Sub mwtmrCoffee_Timer()
   ' (Code to test serial port omitted.)
   RaiseEvent CoffeeReady
End Sub
```

Event procedures associated with a WithEvents variable always begin with the variable name, as discussed in "Adding Events to Classes" in Chapter 6, "General Principles of Component Design."

When the CoffeeMonitor object receives the Timer event, it raises its own CoffeeReady event to notify any clients (CoffeeWatch, in this case) that the coffee's ready.

(This code simply raises the CoffeeReady event every ten seconds. If you actually have a coffee pot with a serial port, you can add code to test coffee maker's status, and conditionally raise the event.)

> **Note** One of the advantages of using events to provide notifications is that only one reference is needed. That is, TestForm doesn't need a reference to the CoffeeMonitor object in order for the Timer control to send CoffeeMonitor an event. This avoids the circular reference problem described in "Dealing with Circular References" in Chapter 6, "General Principles of Component Design."

7. Press CTRL+F5 to run the project. Remember, when working with out-of-process components, the component project must be in run mode before you can edit or run the client project.

Component projects should be run with CTRL+F5 (or **Start with Full Compile** on the **Run** menu) if **Compile On Demand** is checked, as discussed in "Showing Forms from the CoffeeMonitor Class."

For More Information Events are introduced in "Adding an Event to a Class" and "Adding Events to Forms," in Chapter 9, "Programming with Objects," in the *Microsoft Visual Basic 6.0 Programmer's Guide.*

Receiving an Asynchronous Notification Event

When you use events for asynchronous notifications, most of the work is done by the component author. Setting up a client to receive the events is pretty easy.

To receive the CoffeeReady event in CoffeeWatch

1. Switch to the instance of Visual Basic that has the CoffeeWatch project loaded.
2. In the Project Explorer window of the CoffeeWatch project, right-click **Form1** to open the context menu, and select **View Code** to open the code window. Comment out the code in the Click events of the two buttons.
3. Modify the code in the Declarations section as follows:

   ```
   Option Explicit
   Private WithEvents mwcmnTest As CoffeeMonitor
   ```

   Notice the letter "w" added to the variable `mwcmnTest`, to remind the author that this is a WithEvents variable. This is one author's private convention. The letters "cmn" have been chosen to indicate a variable of type CoffeeMonitor.
4. Add the following code to the Load event of Form1, to create a new CoffeeMonitor object and assign it to the WithEvents variable. At run time, Visual Basic connects the object's events to their event procedures when this assignment takes place.

   ```
   Private Sub Form_Load()
      Set mwcmnTest = New CoffeeMonitor
   End Sub
   ```

5. In the **Object** drop-down menu, select **mwcmnTest** to obtain access to its event procedures. Add the following code to the CoffeeReady event.

   ```
   Private Sub mwcmnTest_CoffeeReady()
      MsgBox "COFFEE!"
   End Sub
   ```

6. That's it. Press F5 to run the project.

   Every ten seconds you'll get a notification from Coffee. CoffeeWatch is not blocked in the meantime — you can move and resize it, and click the buttons.
7. Close the CoffeeWatch form to return to design mode.

Sharing the CoffeeMonitor

Of course, a thorough programmer would want to be sure of getting coffee notifications regardless of which application she was using. You could create separate CoffeeMonitor objects for each program in which you wanted to be notified, but that could cause problems if your computer doesn't have multiple serial ports.

One way to allow multiple clients to hook up to a single CoffeeMonitor object is to provide a connector object, as shown in the following procedure.

To create the Connector object

1. Switch to the instance of Visual Basic containing the Coffee project, and click the **End** button to return to design mode.

2. On the **Project** menu, select **Add Module** to add a standard module to the Coffee project. (If you have the **Add Module** dialog box enabled, double-click the Module icon when the dialog box appears.) Add the following variable declarations to the Declarations section:

   ```
   Option Explicit
   Public gCoffeeMonitor As CoffeeMonitor
   Public glngUseCount As Long
   ```

   The variable `gCoffeeMonitor` is used to keep a reference to the single shared CoffeeMonitor. The `glngUseCount` variable keeps track of the number of Connector objects using the CoffeeMonitor.

3. On the **Project** menu, select **Add Class Module** to add a class module to the Coffee project. (If you have the **Add Class Module** dialog box enabled, double-click the Class Module icon when the dialog box appears.) In the Properties window, set **(Name)** to **Connector**.

4. Add the following code to the Connector class's code window:

   ```
   Public Property Get CoffeeMonitor() As CoffeeMonitor
      Set CoffeeMonitor = gCoffeeMonitor
   End Property
   ```

   The Connector's read-only CoffeeMonitor property returns a reference to the single global instance of CoffeeMonitor.

5. In the **Object** drop-down menu, select **Class** to open the template for the default event (Initialize). Add the following code to create the global instance of CoffeeMonitor:

   ```
   Private Sub Class_Initialize()
      If gCoffeeMonitor Is Nothing Then
         Set gCoffeeMonitor = New CoffeeMonitor
      End If
      glngUseCount = glngUseCount + 1
   End Sub
   ```

The first time a client requests a Connector object, it will create the global CoffeeMonitor. Each Connector object increases the use count of the CoffeeMonitor.

Tip The Initialize event of the first object a component creates is a good place to initialize the component. You'll be much less likely to encounter object creation time-out problems and deadlocks that may occur if Sub Main is used to initialize the component.

6. In the **Procedure** drop-down menu, select the Terminate event for the class. Add the following code to the event procedure template:

```
Private Sub Class_Terminate()
   glngUseCount = glngUseCount - 1
   If glngUseCount = 0 Then
      Set gCoffeeMonitor = Nothing
   End If
End Sub
```

Just as objects should dispose of any forms they create, so they should release any objects they use. Because the reference to the global CoffeeMonitor is in a global variable, the last Connector object must release it.

Note A compiled out-of-process component shuts down when all clients release their references to its objects, unless it has a loaded form. When compiled, the Coffee component would be kept running by the TestForm that CoffeeMonitor keeps a reference to. Since the CoffeeMonitor object is kept from terminating by the global variable, the component would never shut down. This is discussed in "Starting and Ending a Component," in Chapter 6, "General Principles of Component Design."

7. In the Project Explorer window, double-click **CoffeeMonitor** to activate it. In the Properties window, set the **Instancing** property of the class to **PublicNotCreatable**.

Important Make sure you have the CoffeeMonitor class active before you set the Instancing property. If you set the Instancing property of the wrong class, you'll get an error later when you run CoffeeWatch.

Any client can create an instance of the Connector class, because its Instancing property is set to MultiUse (the default). Clients can use a Connector object's CoffeeMonitor property to get a reference to the single shared CoffeeMonitor object. By making CoffeeMonitor a PublicNotCreatable class, you allow clients to use the shared global instance — while preventing them from creating their own CoffeeMonitors.

8. Press CTRL+F5 to run the project. Remember, when working with out-of-process components, the component project must be in run mode before you can edit or run the client project.

When prompted to save the new files, use the following names. Visual Basic supplies the extensions.

File	File name	Extension
Class module	Coffee_Connector	.cls
Module	Coffee_Module1	.bas

Using the Shared CoffeeMonitor

This procedure shows how to use the Connector object to get a reference to a single shared CoffeeMonitor object.

To receive the CoffeeReady event in CoffeeWatch

1. Switch to the instance of Visual Basic that has the CoffeeWatch project loaded.
2. In the Project Explorer window of the CoffeeWatch project, right-click **Form1** to open the context menu, and select **View Code** to open the code window. Modify the code in the Declarations section as follows:

   ```
   Option Explicit
   Private WithEvents mwcmnTest As CoffeeMonitor
   Private mcctTest As Connector
   ```

   The new variable, `mcctTest`, will hold a reference to the Connector object. The letters 'cct' have been chosen to indicate a variable of type Connector.
3. Change the code in the Load event of Form1, so that it first creates a Connector object, and then obtains a reference to the shared CoffeeMonitor object using the Connector's CoffeeMonitor property.

   ```
   Private Sub Form_Load()
      Set mcctTest = New Connector
      Set mwcmnTest = mcctTest.CoffeeMonitor
   End Sub
   ```
4. Press F5 to run the project.

   Once again, you'll get a notification from Coffee every ten seconds.
5. Close the CoffeeWatch form to return to design mode.
6. Switch to the Coffee project, and click the **Break** button (or select **Break** from the **Run** menu) to enter break mode. In the Immediate window, type:

   ```
   ?TypeName(gCoffeeWatch)
   ```

   The result is Nothing, showing that the shared CoffeeMonitor object was released.
7. Click the **End** button to return to design mode.

You may find it interesting to run the Coffee project again, then make CoffeeWatch.exe and run multiple instances of it. (You must run the Coffee project first, so that its type library information is available.) You can set break points in Coffee, to observe the workings of the events and properties of its objects while it provides objects to several clients.

A Bug in Connector

There's a bug in the Connector class. If all clients release their Connector objects (but keep their references to the shared CoffeeMonitor), the last Connector will release the global reference. At that point, any client that creates a Connector will cause a second CoffeeMonitor to be created — because the new Connector will find that the global variable `gCoffeeWatch` contains Nothing. If CoffeeMonitor really used the serial port, this could cause a conflict.

The sample applications Coffee2.Vbp and CoffWat2.Vbp explore a possible solution to this bug.

Asynchronous Call-Back Methods

An alternate technique for notifying clients is the asynchronous call-back method, discussed in "Asynchronous Notifications Using Call-Back Methods" in Chapter 8, "Building Code Components." Call-backs are somewhat more complicated to implement, but they allow the component to receive return values and errors raised by the client, and they have a slight performance advantage.

The sample applications Coffee2.Vbp and CoffWat2.Vbp include an alternate implementation of CoffeeReady using call-backs.

Multithreading

Code components with no user interface can be marked for unattended execution, which is to say they can have no user interaction. For out-of-process components this option also enables multithreading, as explained in "Scalability and Multithreading," in Chapter 8, "Building Code Components."

The sample application MTCoffee.vbp demonstrates a simple multithreading scenario.

For More Information The basics of raising and handling events are introduced in "Adding Events to a Class," in Chapter 9, "Programming with Objects," in the *Microsoft Visual Basic 6.0 Programmer's Guide*. Events in components are discussed in "Adding Events to Classes" in Chapter 6, "General Principles of Component Design."

Creating and Testing the Coffee Executable

Once an out-of-process component project is tested and debugged in the development environment, you can compile and test the .exe file.

An ActiveX component is compiled the same way any Visual Basic project is compiled — by choosing Make from the File menu. The .exe file includes a type library that describes your objects and allows them to be browsed. Visual Basic automatically registers the component in your Windows registry when you make the executable file.

> **Note** When you distribute your application as part of an integrated solution, registration is done during setup. If you use the Visual Basic Package and Deployment Wizard, registration of your component will be included in the setup process automatically. This is discussed in "Deploying ActiveX Components" in Chapter 7, "Debugging, Testing, and Deploying Components."

For More Information The Package and Deployment Wizard is described in Chapter 17, "Distributing Your Applications," in the *Microsoft Visual Basic 6.0 Programmer's Guide.*

To compile and test the Coffee executable

1. If the Coffee project is still in run mode, click the **End** button to return to design mode.
2. On the **File** menu, click **Make Coffee.exe** to open the **Make Project** dialog box. Click **OK** to build the .exe file.
3. Switch to the **CoffeeWatch** project. On the **Project** menu, click **References** to open the **References** dialog box. Remove the check mark from the Coffee Monitor Component entry for the .vbp file, and check the entry for the .exe file.

   You can tell the entries apart by observing the Location in the information panel at the bottom of the dialog box.
4. On the **File** menu, click **Make CoffeeWatch.exe** to open the **Make Project** dialog box. Click **OK** to build the .exe file.
5. (Optional) Press F5 to run CoffeeWatch using the compiled Coffee executable.
6. Use the Explorer (or the **Run** box, on the **Start** menu) to start one or more instances of CoffeeWatch.exe.

   Notice that all the instances of CoffeeWatch appear to get their CoffeeReady events at the same time. In reality, the clients get their events one after the other — a single thread of execution traces through all of the event handlers. You can see this demonstrated in the sample applications for this chapter.

   > **Important** When multiple objects are handling events from one event source — a scenario referred to as *multicasting* — the order in which they get events is undefined, and implementation dependent. You should never write code that depends on any particular order of event arrival among the multicasting clients.

   Events are anonymous — that is, the object that raises the event doesn't know how many objects (if any) are handling the event.

To switch back to using Coffee.vbp, you can use the References dialog box to clear the entry for the .exe file and check the entry for the .vbp file instead.

Note You can compile CoffeeWatch.exe using either the compiled Coffee.exe, or Coffee.vbp. The latter is useful for debugging with multiple clients. The CoffeeWatch executable will be compiled using whichever entry is currently checked in the References dialog box.

For More Information You can read more about test projects and debugging techniques in Chapter 7, "Debugging, Testing, and Deploying Components."

ActiveX EXE Component Creation Summary

In order to introduce new concepts in the most natural order, the procedures in this chapter have not followed the normal sequence of steps for creating an out-of-process component. When you create a new ActiveX EXE component, the steps you'll generally follow are these:

1. Determine the features your component will provide.
2. Determine what objects are required to divide the functionality of the component in a logical fashion.
3. Design any forms your component will display.
4. Design the interface — that is, the properties, methods, and events — for each class provided by your component.
5. Create a separate test project, usually a Standard EXE project.
6. Implement the forms required by your component.
7. Implement the interface of each class.
8. As you add each interface element or feature, add features to your test project to exercise the new functionality.
9. Compile your EXE and test it with all potential target applications.

For More Information General design issues for ActiveX components are discussed in Chapter 6, "General Principles of Component Design," and Chapter 7, "Debugging, Testing, and Deploying Components." Issues exclusive to code components are discussed in Chapter 8, "Building Code Components." The step-by-step procedures in Chapter 2, "Creating an ActiveX DLL," demonstrate other component features, including global objects, modal and modeless forms in in-process components, and other uses of events.

CHAPTER 4

Creating an ActiveX Control

The series of step-by-step procedures in this chapter builds a simple ActiveX control called ShapeLabel. Although the control itself is not very interesting, building it will quickly demonstrate the major events in the life of an ActiveX control, introduce you to the intricacies of running code at design time, and show the basic steps for creating and hooking up a property page.

All of the subjects introduced in these procedures are covered in greater depth in later chapters. References to in-depth material will be found in each procedure. In addition, Chapter 9, "Building ActiveX Controls," shows how you can use the ActiveX Control Interface Wizard to make building controls even easier.

The procedures for creating the ShapeLabel control build on each other, so the sequence in which you perform the procedures is important.

Contents

Sample Application: CtlPlus.vbg

Fills in all the properties, methods, and events required to make ShapeLabel a functional control. Expands on the material in this chapter, showing additional control creation features, at the expense of some of the basic material covered in the step-by-step procedures. The sample applications are listed in the Samples directory.

These procedures will be easier to follow if you set up your Visual Basic development environment to show the necessary windows.

Before You Begin

1. On the **View** menu, click **Toolbox** to open the Toolbox.
2. On the **View** menu, click **Project explorer** to open the Project Explorer window. The Project Explorer window will be used extensively to switch between project files.
3. If the Project Explorer window is in Folder view, as shown below, click the **Toggle Folders** button on the Project Explorer window toolbar to turn the folders off.

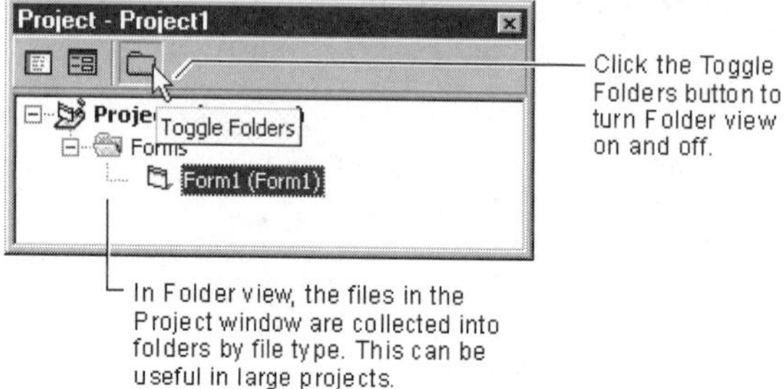

Project - Project1
Toggle Folders
Form1 (Form1)
Click the Toggle Folders button to turn Folder view on and off.
In Folder view, the files in the Project window are collected into folders by file type. This can be useful in large projects.

4. On the **View** menu, click **Properties window** to open the Properties window.
5. On the **View** menu, click Immediate window to open the Immediate window. You will need this window open at design time, in order to demonstrate the control's code running at design time.
6. On the **Tools** menu, click **Options** to open the **Options** dialog box.

   Select the **Editor** tab, and make sure the **Require Variable Declaration** check box is selected. This makes it much easier to catch typing errors.

   Select the **Environment** tab. Make sure **Prompt To Save Changes** is checked, then click **OK**. This will make it easy to save the changes to the project as you go along.

Creating the ControlDemo Project

ActiveX controls can be added to any project type. When a control is compiled as part of an .exe file, however, it cannot be shared with other applications. The ShapeLabel control will be compiled into an .ocx file in a later procedure in this chapter, so it can be shared. Thus the ControlDemo project will be created as an ActiveX control project.

An ActiveX control project can contain as many controls as you like. When you build the project, the resulting .ocx file contains all the controls you've added.

To create the ControlDemo project

1. On the **File** menu, click **New Project** to open the **New Project** dialog box. (This will close your current project or project group; you will be prompted to save any changes you have made.) Double-click the ActiveX Control icon to create a new project.

   Visual Basic automatically adds a UserControl designer to the project. The default name, UserControl1, appears as the caption of the designer.

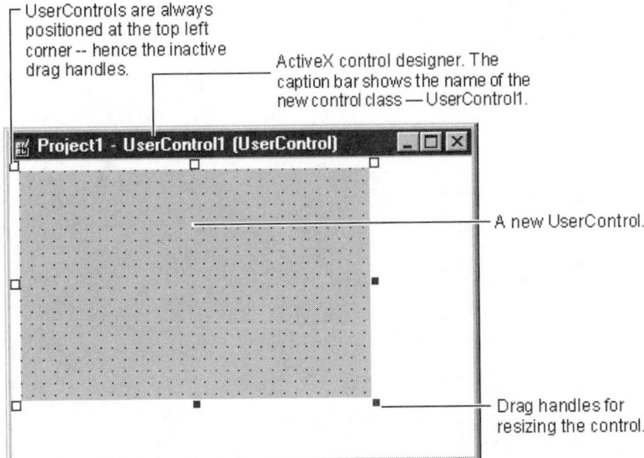
UserControls are always positioned at the top left corner -- hence the inactive drag handles.
ActiveX control designer. The caption bar shows the name of the new control class — UserControl1.
Project1 - UserControl1 (UserControl)
A new UserControl.
Drag handles for resizing the control.

2. On the **Project** menu, click **Project1 Properties** to open the **Project Properties** dialog box. Select the **General** tab, fill out the information shown below, and then click **OK**.

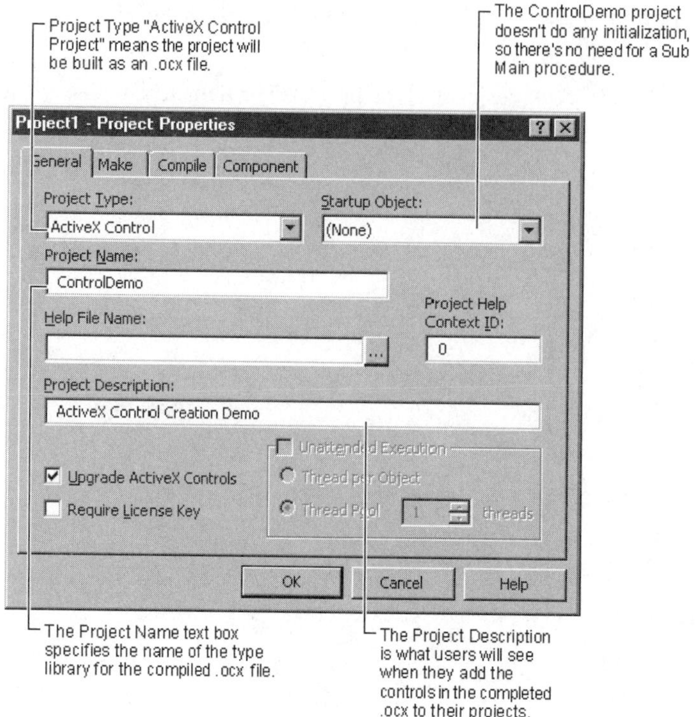

3. Double-click **UserControl1** in the Project Explorer window to bring the designer to the front.

4. In the Properties window, double-click the **Name** property and change the name of the user control to ShapeLabel. The new name appears in the caption of the designer and in the Project Explorer window.

   The name you specify becomes the class name of your control, just as CommandButton is the class name for a command button. Chapter 9, "Building ActiveX Controls," provides guidelines for choosing class names for controls.

   Notice that the Properties window looks much as it would for a Visual Basic form. Some properties you're used to seeing are missing, however, and there are properties not found on ordinary Visual Basic forms. These properties are discussed in Chapter 9, "Building ActiveX Controls."

5. Within the control designer, resize the control using the drag handle at the lower right corner of the control, dragging up and left to make the control smaller.

   This sets the default size of the control. For convenience in later procedures, the ShapeLabel control should be of modest size.

6. On the **File** menu, click **Save Project** to save the project files. Name them as shown in the following table. Visual Basic will provide the indicated extensions automatically.

File	Filename	Extension
User control	ControlDemo_ShapeLabel	.ctl
Project	ControlDemo	.vbp

   Binary information in a control — such as bitmaps — will be saved in a binary file with the same name and an extension of .ctx.

For More Information See "Setting Up a New Control Project and Test Project" and "Debugging Controls," in Chapter 9, "Building ActiveX Controls."

Adding the TestCtlDemo Project

In order to test the ShapeLabel control, you need a test project.

To allow debugging of in-process components, Visual Basic allows you to load two or more projects into a *project group*. In addition to enabling in-process debugging, the project group makes it easier to load your .ocx project and test project.

To add a test project to the project group

1. On the **File** menu, click **Add Project** to open the **Add Project** dialog box.

   Important Do not click **Open Project** or **New Project**, as these will close your control project.

2. Double-click the Standard EXE icon to add an ordinary .exe project. You can now see both projects in the Project Explorer window, and the caption of the Project Explorer window shows the default project group name.

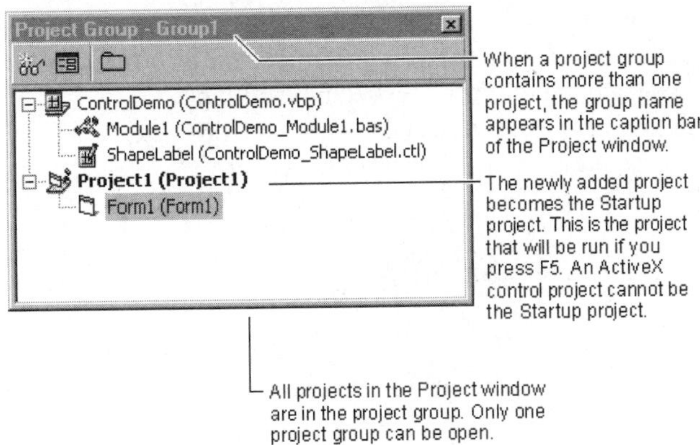
Project Group - Group1
ControlDemo (ControlDemo.vbp)
Module1 (ControlDemo_Module1.bas)
ShapeLabel (ControlDemo_ShapeLabel.ctl)
Project1 (Project1)
Form1 (Form1)
When a project group contains more than one project, the group name appears in the caption bar of the Project window.
The newly added project becomes the Startup project. This is the project that will be run if you press F5. An ActiveX control project cannot be the Startup project.
All projects in the Project window are in the project group. Only one project group can be open.

The new project immediately becomes the Startup project for the project group. The Project Explorer window identifies the Startup project by displaying its name in bold type. An ActiveX control project, like ControlDemo, cannot be the Startup project.

3. On the **File** menu, click **Save Project Group** to save the test project and the project group. Name the files as shown below. Visual Basic will provide the indicated extensions automatically.

File	Filename	Extension
Form	TestCtlDemo_Form1	.frm
Project	TestCtlDemo	.vbp
Project group	ControlDemo	.vbg

For More Information Test projects for ActiveX controls are discussed in more detail in "Debugging Controls," in Chapter 9, "Building ActiveX Controls."

Running the ShapeLabel Control at Design Time

Unlike other programmable objects, controls have both design-time and run-time behavior. That is, some of the code in your control will execute when a developer places an instance of the control on a form at design time.

For example, the code you place in the UserControl_Resize event procedure will be executed both at design time and at run time.

In order to debug the design-time behavior of your control, you must be able to execute code in the control while the test form on which you place the control remains in design mode.

The following two procedures demonstrate this neat trick. In the first procedure, you'll add code to the Resize event of the ShapeLabel control. In the second procedure, you'll put part of ControlDemo into run mode — while the test project remains in design mode — and then add an instance of the ShapeLabel control to a form in the test project.

To add code to the Resize event

1. In the Project Explorer window, double-click **ShapeLabel** to make it the active designer.
2. Double-click the **ShapeLabel** control to open the code window.

3. In the **Procedure** box, click the Resize event to go to its event procedure. Add the following code:

```
Private Sub UserControl_Resize()
   Static intCt As Integer
   intCt = intCt + 1
   Debug.Print "Resize " & intCt
End Sub
```

> **Note** The name of the event procedure has the prefix "UserControl," just as the Form_Resize event procedure for an ordinary form has the prefix "Form."

In developing an ordinary Visual Basic application, you would now click the Start button on the toolbar, or press F5, to run your application. In order to put a ShapeLabel control on Form1, however, you have to run just the code for the control, leaving everything else in design mode.

To run the ShapeLabel control at design time

1. In the Project window, double-click **ShapeLabel** to bring its designer to the front, then press CTRL+F4 to close the window. Closing the designer's window puts the ShapeLabel control in run mode. As soon as the control is in run mode, its icon (the default toolbox icon for a user control) is enabled in the toolbox.

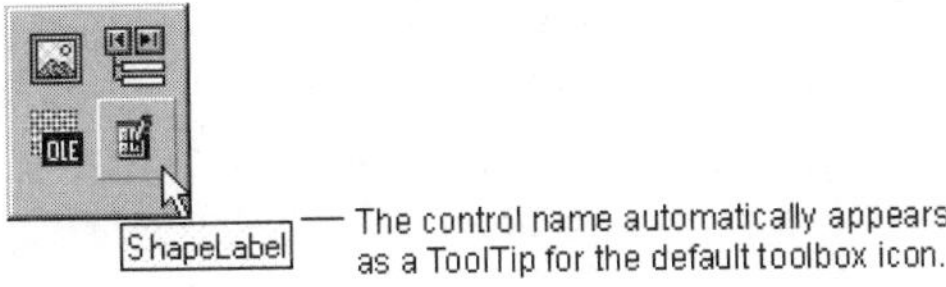

The control name automatically appears as a ToolTip for the default toolbox icon.

> **Important** Don't click the **Start** button on the toolbar, or press F5, because this would put the entire project group into run mode, and you would be unable to add the new control to a form.
>
> When you put a control in run mode, it doesn't matter how you close the designer's window. (You always can tell if the designer is open, because the control's toolbox icon will be grayed.)

2. In the Project Explorer window, double-click **Form1** to bring it to the front.

3. Double-click the ShapeLabel icon to add a ShapeLabel control to Form1. The control appears as a flat gray rectangle with grab handles:

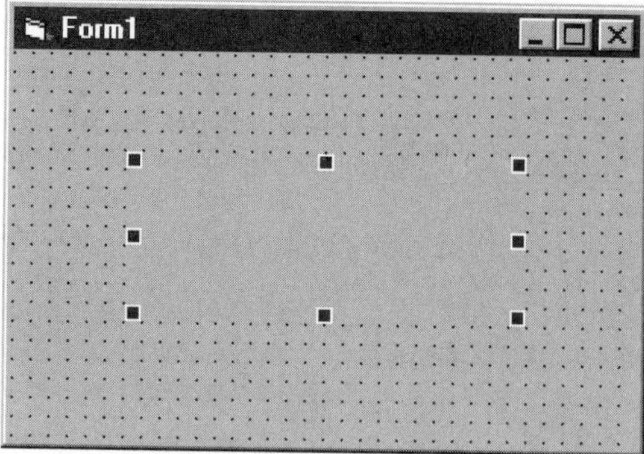

In the Properties window you can see the default properties for a new control. The ShapeLabel control you just added to the form has been given a default name, ShapeLabel1.

> **Note** Naming your control when you begin designing it avoids confusion. Suppose you place a control with a default name, such as UserControl1, on a form. Automatic numbering of new controls would append a number to the control name, resulting in a confusing name like UserControl11.

4. The ShapeLabel control's Resize event occurred when it was placed on the form, as you can see by looking at the Immediate window. Use the grab handles to resize the control several times. Each time you resize it, the Resize event occurs again.

   If you simply move the control around the form, the Resize event does not occur.

5. On Form1, double-click the **ShapeLabel** control to open the code window for Form1. The cursor will be on the default event procedure, ShapeLabel1_GotFocus. You can use the **Procedure** box to view the other three events Visual Basic automatically provides for your control. Close the code window when you are done.

6. In the Project Explorer window, double-click **ShapeLabel** to open the ShapeLabel designer. Notice that the ShapeLabel control you placed on Form1 is shaded with hatch marks to indicate that it is inactive.

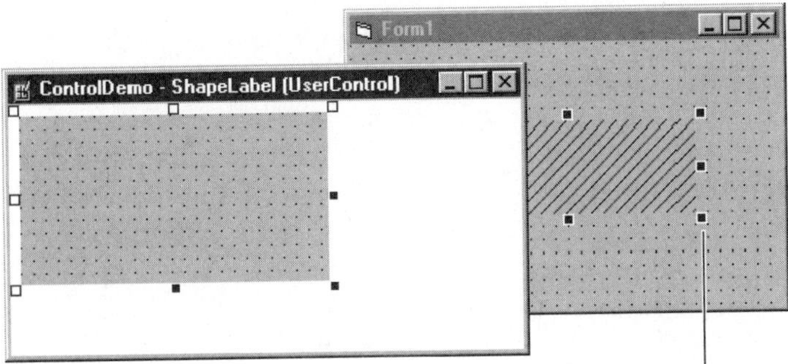

The control instance can still be resized using the grab handles, but it cannot repaint itself until you activate it by closing the ShapeLabel designer.

Opening a control's designer makes all instances of the control inactive. Changing the code in the control's code window may also make control instances inactive.

7. Code in ShapeLabel's code module cannot be executed while the designer is open. Use the grab handles to resize the shaded ShapeLabel control on Form1. The Resize event doesn't fire, so no new messages appear in the Immediate window.

8. Be sure the **ShapeLabel** designer is in front, then press CTRL+F4 to close the window, reactivating the control instance. The shading disappears from the control on Form1, indicating that the instance is active again.

   If the control has become inactive because of changes to its code, you can right-click the test form to bring up its context menu, and click **Update UserControls** to reactivate control instances.

   Note Due to the number of windows required by these procedures, you may frequently find that ShapeLabel's designer has disappeared behind another form. You can double-click **ShapeLabel** in the Project Explorer window to bring the designer to the front.

For More Information More information about running code at design time can be found in "Debugging Controls," in Chapter 9, "Building ActiveX Controls."

Life and Times of a UserControl Object

The life of an ordinary Visual Basic form is marked by certain key events, such as Initialize, Load, QueryUnload, and Unload. In order to create well-behaved applications, it's important to know when these events occur in the life cycle of a form.

The same is true for controls. The key events in the life cycle of a UserControl are Initialize, InitProperties, ReadProperties, WriteProperties, and Terminate. The following procedure explores these events.

To observe key events for ShapeLabel

1. In the Project Explorer window, double-click **ShapeLabel** to open its designer.
2. Double-click the designer to open a code window for ShapeLabel, and enter code in the following event procedures:

```
Private Sub UserControl_Initialize()
   Debug.Print "Initialize"
End Sub

Private Sub UserControl_InitProperties()
   Debug.Print "InitProperties"
End Sub

Private Sub UserControl_ReadProperties(PropBag As _
      PropertyBag)
   Debug.Print "ReadProperties"
End Sub

Private Sub UserControl_WriteProperties(PropBag _
      As PropertyBag)
   Debug.Print "WriteProperties"
End Sub

Private Sub UserControl_Terminate()
   Debug.Print "Terminate"
End Sub
```

   Note For UserControl objects, Load and Unload are superseded by the ReadProperties and WriteProperties events. This is discussed in more detail in "Understanding Control Lifetime and Key Events," in Chapter 9, "Building ActiveX Controls."

3. Be sure the **ShapeLabel** designer is in front, then press CTRL+F4 to close the window, putting the control in run mode. Debug messages will appear in the Immediate window:

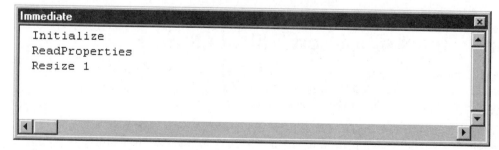

What's going on here? You haven't put another instance of the ShapeLabel control on Form1. Where did all these events come from?

This illustrates an important point about controls. A user puts a control on a form, and thereafter thinks of the control as a permanent fixture of the form. From the control author's perspective, however, controls are getting destroyed and re-created all the time.

When you put ShapeLabel in run mode by closing its designer, the instance of ShapeLabel on Form1 was destroyed and re-created, at which point it received an Initialize event. Why didn't you see a Terminate event first? Because the original instance of ShapeLabel you placed on Form1 was created before you added the code in the UserControl_Terminate event procedure! Welcome to the wild and woolly world of control creation.

> **Note** Control instances are also destroyed and recreated when you click **Update UserControls** on the form's context menu.

4. Press CTRL+F5, or click the **Start** button on the toolbar, to run TestCtlDemo. When the project is running, the grid on Form1 is gone, so you can't see the ShapeLabel, but you can see its life flash before your eyes in the Immediate window:

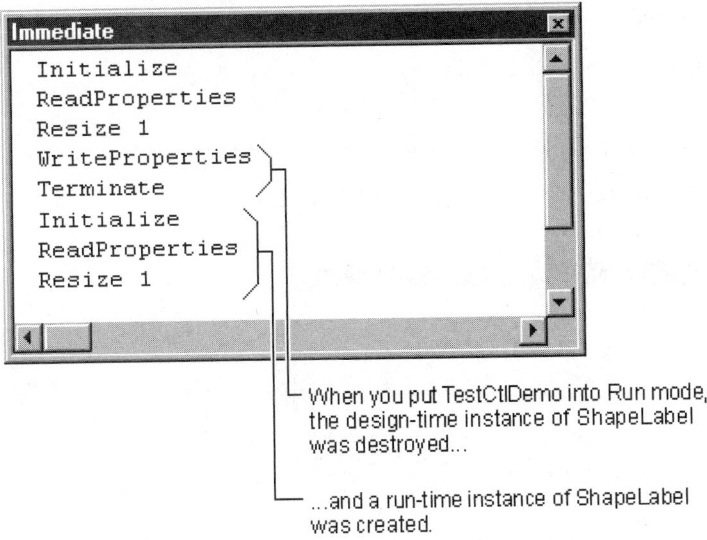
Immediate
Initialize
ReadProperties
Resize 1
WriteProperties
Terminate
Initialize
ReadProperties
Resize 1
When you put TestCtlDemo into Run mode, the design-time instance of ShapeLabel was destroyed...
...and a run-time instance of ShapeLabel was created.

After a control instance is created, the ReadProperties event gives you a chance to obtain the control's saved property values from the .frm file belonging to the form that contains the control instance.

When the design-time instance of the control is destroyed, the WriteProperties event gives you a chance to save the property values set at design time by the developer who's using your control. Property values are saved in the containing form's .frm file, as you'll see in "Saving the ShapeLabel Control's Property Values," later in this chapter.

The Terminate event occurs when the control is being destroyed.

Note By default, the **Compile On Demand** option is checked on the **General** tab of the **Options** dialog box (accessed from the **Tools** menu). Using CTRL+F5 (or **Start with Full Compile**, on the **Run** menu) overrides **Compile On Demand**, and fully compiles all the projects in the group before entering run mode. This is useful because compile errors usually require resetting the project, which means returning to design mode. When you're debugging controls, you may prefer to turn **Compile On Demand** off rather than remembering to use CTRL+F5.

5. Close Form1, to return the project to design mode. In the Immediate window, you'll see a Terminate event (but not WriteProperties — why not?) as the run-time instance of ShapeLabel is torn down. Then you'll see the Initialize, ReadProperties, and Resize events, as the design-time instance of the control is created.

   The run-time instance of a control never gets a WriteProperties event, because it doesn't need to save its property values. To see why not, consider ShapeLabel's future. When it's compiled into an .ocx file, you'll add it to another project, put an instance on a form, compile the project into an .exe, and run it. When you close that .exe, the only place the ShapeLabel instance could save its property values would be in the .exe file. This sort of behavior is not tolerated by well-behaved operating systems.

6. Scroll to the top of the Immediate window, click in the top left corner, and drag to select all the text in the window. Press the DELETE key to clear the window.

7. In the Project Explorer window, double-click **Form1** to bring Form1 to the front.

8. On the Toolbox, double-click the ShapeLabel icon to add another instance of the control to Form1. You'll see a new event this time.

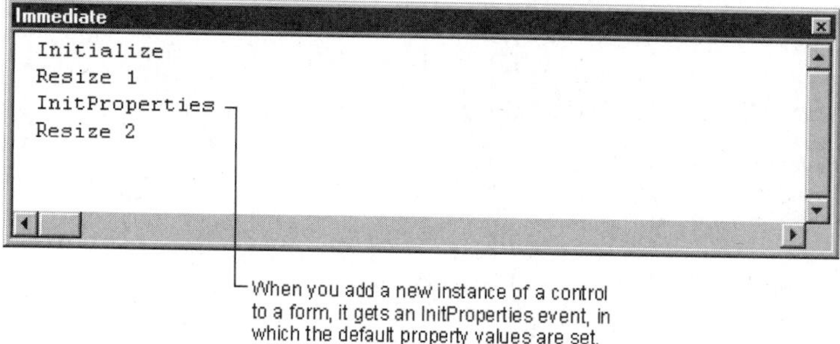

When you add a new instance of a control to a form, it gets an InitProperties event, in which the default property values are set.

   When a new instance of your control is placed on a container, it gets an InitProperties event. In the UserControl_InitProperties event procedure you can place code to:

   - Set the default values for each of the control's properties values.
   - Perform tasks whenever a user creates an instance of your control.

9. Close the Form1 designer by clicking its **Close** button or pressing CTRL+F4 while the designer is in front. In the Immediate window, you will see two sets of WriteProperties and Terminate events, one for each instance of ShapeLabel.

10. In the Project Explorer window, double-click **Form1** to open its designer again. When the designer opens, all the controls on Form1 are created, and their Initialize events are fired. All controls then receive ReadProperties events, which allow them to retrieve their saved property values. The InitProperties event does not occur, because both instances of the ShapeLabel control already exist.

For More Information Control lifetime, and key events therein, are discussed in "Understanding Control Lifetime and Key Events," in Chapter 9, "Building ActiveX Controls." "Exposing Properties of Constituent Controls," in the same chapter, explains how the ActiveX Control Interface Wizard simplifies the creation of code to save and retrieve property values.

Drawing the ShapeLabel Control

You can use graphics methods, such as Circle and Line, to draw your control, or you can create your control's appearance using existing ActiveX controls and Visual Basic intrinsic controls. Controls you add to the UserControl to create its appearance are called *constituent controls.*

As its name suggests, ShapeLabel's appearance is created using a Shape control and a Label control.

To add constituent controls to the ShapeLabel control

1. In the Project Explorer window, double-click **ShapeLabel** to open its designer.
2. In the **Toolbox**, double-click the **Visual Basic Shape** control to place a Shape control on the ShapeLabel designer. If you haven't used the Shape control before, hold the mouse over the Toolbox buttons until you find the one whose ToolTip is "Shape."
3. In the Properties window, set the following property values for the Shape control:

Property	Value
BorderStyle	0 – Transparent
FillColor	&H000000FF (Red)
FillStyle	0 – Solid
Name	shpBack
Shape	2 – Oval

Note To set color properties such as FillColor and ForeColor to specific colors, select the **Palette** tab of the color selection dialog.

4. In the **Toolbox**, double-click the **Label** control to add a label on top of the Shape control. In the Properties window, set the following property values for the Label control:

Property	Value
Alignment	2 – Center
BackStyle	0 – Transparent
ForeColor	&H00FFFFFF (White)
Name	lblCaption

5. Use the bottom grab handle to change the height of the label so that it is slightly taller than the text it contains. ShapeLabel should look something like this:

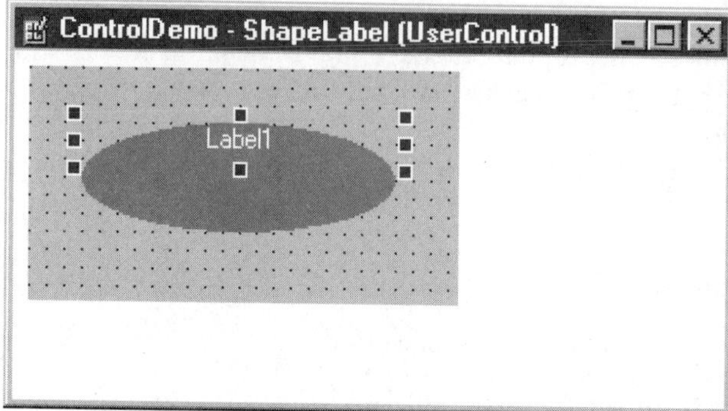

6. Double-click the **ShapeLabel** designer to bring the code window to the front, and replace the code in the UserControl_Resize event procedure with the following:

```
Private Sub UserControl_Resize()
   ' Size the Shape control to fill ShapeLabel's
   '   visible surface area.
   shpBack.Move 0, 0, ScaleWidth, ScaleHeight
   ' Center the Label control vertically, and
   '   make it the same width as ShapeLabel.
   lblCaption.Move 0, (ScaleHeight _
   lblCaption.Height) / 2, ScaleWidth
End Sub
```

7. When you're designing a user control, remember that the area you have to work with is bounded by the ScaleWidth and ScaleHeight of the control. Nothing outside this is visible to the user of your control. Furthermore, the size of the client area will change at the whim of the user. The Resize event is thus one of the most important events in control design.

8. Be sure the **ShapeLabel** designer is in front, then press CTRL+F4 to close the window, putting the control in run mode. In the Project window, double-click Form1 to bring it to the front.
9. The two ShapeLabel controls should now appear as red ovals, with centered white captions that read, "Label1." Resize the ShapeLabels to test the Resize event code.

For More Information See "Drawing Your Control," in Chapter 9, "Building ActiveX Controls."

Saving the ShapeLabel Control's Property Values

You can add properties and methods to an ActiveX control in the same way you add them to class modules: by creating Public procedures. Since ShapeLabel is going to be an enhanced label control, it makes sense for it to have a Caption property.

The following procedure adds a Caption property, and the support code to save and retrieve the property value. A control's property values are saved along with the other data that describes the container — in this case, Form1.

To add a Caption property to the ShapeLabel control

1. In the Project Explorer window, double-click **ShapeLabel** to open its designer, then double-click on **ShapeLabel** to bring its code window to the front.
2. On the **Tools** menu, click **Add Procedure** to open the **Add Procedure** dialog box. In the **Name** box, enter the name **Caption**. Click **Property** and **Public**, then click **OK**.
3. In the Code window, change the newly created property procedures to appear as follows:

```
Public Property Get Caption() As String
   Caption = lblCaption.Caption
End Property

Public Property Let Caption( _
      ByVal NewCaption As String)
   lblCaption.Caption = NewCaption
   PropertyChanged "Caption"
End Property
```

Note Be careful to change both property declaration lines by adding **As String**, as shown above. Property Get and Property Let declarations must match. Using specific type names speeds up execution, and provides type checking for the developer who uses your control.

The Property Let procedure is executed whenever a new value is assigned to the Caption property. It stores the new value directly in the Caption property of the lblCaption label on ShapeLabel.

The Property Get procedure is executed whenever the property value is retrieved. It reads the value stored in the Caption property of the lblCaption label.

Property Let procedures in controls must call PropertyChanged, as explained in "Adding Properties to Controls" in Chapter 9, "Building ActiveX Controls." This tells the Properties window to refresh its display, and informs Visual Basic that the form has changed.

Property procedures are discussed in "Adding Properties to a Class," in Chapter 9, "Programming with Objects," in the *Microsoft Visual Basic 6.0 Programmer's Guide.*

4. To initialize the Caption property, add the following code to the UserControl_InitProperties event procedure:

```
Private Sub UserControl_InitProperties()
   ' Let the starting value for the Caption
   '   property be the Name given to this
   '   instance of ShapeLabel.
   Caption = Extender.Name
   Debug.Print "InitProperties"
End Sub
```

What is this Extender object? To the user of a control, *extender properties* — such as Name, Top, and Left — appear to be part of your control. However, extender properties are really provided by the container your control is placed on. The Extender object of the UserControl gives you, the control designer, access to these properties from within your control.

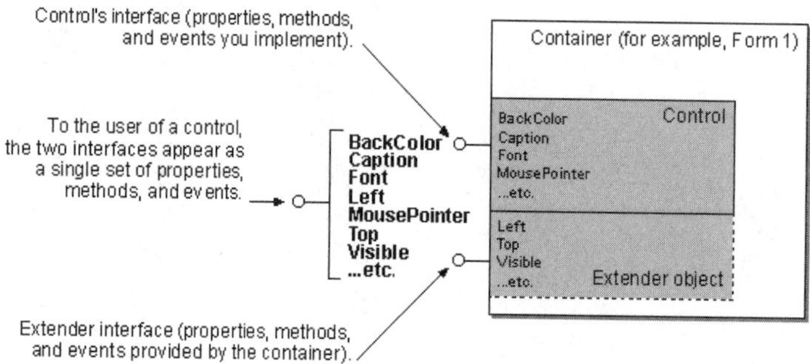

The read-only Name property of the Extender object returns the name the container (or the user) gives to a specific instance of your control. Using this name (for example, ShapeLabel1) as the initial value of the Caption property mimics the behavior of the Label control.

Tip If your control imitates the behavior of controls that provide similar functionality, using it will be more intuitive.

What would happen if you created a Name property for your control? You would be able to access it from within your control, but the only Name property your user would see would be the Name property of the Extender object.

This introduces a recurrent theme for controls: The container determines a large portion of your control's behavior and appearance. It's the container that determines your control's Name, and your Top and Left properties are maintained relative to the container's coordinates. This theme will be taken up again in Chapter 9, "Building ActiveX Controls."

One last item of business: Why put this code in the InitProperties event? Why not use the Initialize event? As you have seen, Initialize is called every time the control instance is created, which happens often. InitProperties happens only when the user places the control on the container. This makes it the appropriate place to set initial values for a control instance.

In addition, the UserControl object's Extender and AmbientProperties objects are not yet available when the Initialize event occurs. "Understanding Control Lifetime and Key Events," in Chapter 9, "Building ActiveX Controls," discusses appropriate uses of the Initialize event.

5. To save the value of your Caption property, add the following code to the UserControl_WriteProperties event procedure:

```
Private Sub UserControl_WriteProperties(PropBag As _
      PropertyBag)
   Debug.Print "WriteProperties"
   PropBag.WriteProperty "Caption", Caption, _
      Extender.Name
End Sub
```

The PropertyBag is just what its name implies, a "bag" in which property values are saved. The bag is provided by the container. You can't see into it, and you have no idea where or how the data is saved. All you can do is put values in and take them out.

The first argument of the WriteProperty method is the name of the property, which will be used as the retrieval key. You should use the name of the property for this argument, because it will appear in the .frm text file (in Visual Basic — other containers may use other file names to save project data), and may be seen by the user of the control.

The second argument is the value. A property value is saved as a Variant.

The third argument, oddly enough, is a default value. Why provide a default when saving the property value? Before saving the value, the WriteProperty method compares the property value with this default. If they are the same, the property value doesn't have to be saved, because default values will be set automatically when the control is reloaded. This keeps the .frm file from being cluttered with hundreds of default entries, a great favor to your users!

6. Place the following code in the ReadProperties event, to retrieve the persisted property value for the Caption property:

```
Private Sub UserControl_ReadProperties(PropBag As _
      PropertyBag)
   Debug.Print "ReadProperties"
   Caption = PropBag.ReadProperty("Caption", _
      Extender.Name)
End Sub
```

   The second argument of the ReadProperty method is a default value to be used if no value has been saved, if the user has deleted the property from the text file, or if the value has never been changed from the default, and therefore never saved by WriteProperty.

7. Be sure the **ShapeLabel** designer is in front, then click the **Close** button or press CTRL+F4 to close the window, putting the control into run mode. Like magic, the captions of the ShapeLabel controls change to match the default names of the two instances, ShapeLabel1 and ShapeLabel2.

   Use the Properties window to change the Caption properties of the two ShapeLabel controls on Form1, then click the **Close** button on the Form1 designer. In the Project Explorer window, double-click **Form1** to re-open the Form1 designer.

   From the messages in the Immediate window, you can see that the controls have been destroyed and re-created, but the values of the Caption properties have been saved and retrieved.

8. Press CTRL+F5 to run TestCtlDemo, the Startup project of the project group, and observe the run-time behavior of the ShapeLabel control.

9. Click the **Close** button on Form1 to return to design mode.

For More Information Details of saving and retrieving property values can be found in "Adding Properties to Controls," in Chapter 9, "Building ActiveX Controls." "Exposing Properties of Constituent Controls," in the same chapter, explains how the ActiveX Control Interface Wizard simplifies the creation of code to save and retrieve property values.

Giving the ShapeLabel Control a Property Page

Simple properties that you create using property procedures will be shown automatically in the Visual Basic Properties window. You can also connect your control to *property pages,* which display your control's properties in an alternate format.

Each property page you connect to your control becomes one tab on the tabbed Properties dialog box. Visual Basic handles all the details of presenting the pages as a tabbed dialog, and manages the OK, Cancel, and Apply buttons. All you have to do is lay out the controls that will be used to set the property values.

Property pages are useful when a group of properties interact in a complex fashion, as with the Toolbar control included with Visual Basic. They're also useful for controls that will be distributed internationally, because the captions can be localized for different languages. Property pages also allow your controls to be used with development tools that don't have a Properties window.

To add a property page to the project

1. In the Project Explorer window, click **ControlDemo** to select the control project. On the **Project** menu, click **Add Property Page** to open the **Add PropertyPage** dialog box. Double-click the Property Page icon to add a property page to the project.
2. In the Properties window, double-click the **Name** property, and change the name of the property page to **SLGeneral**. Double-click the **Caption** property, and change the caption to **General**.

   The caption is what will appear on the property page's tab when it's in use.

   Why name the page SLGeneral instead of General? You may have several controls in a project, and each one may have a General page. This is the ShapeLabel control's General page.
3. On the **File** menu, click **Save Project Group** to save the project group. Name the property page as shown in the following table. Visual Basic will provide the indicated extension automatically.

File	Filename	Extension
Property page	ControlDemo_SLGeneral	.pag

   Binary information in a property page — such as bitmaps — will be saved in a binary file with the same name and an extension of .pgx.

The designer for a property page looks much like the designer for a control, except that the caption bar of the designer shows the Caption property of the property page, instead of the Name property.

To design the General property page for the ShapeLabel control

1. Place a Label control on the property page, and set the Caption property of the label to the word **Caption**.
2. Underneath the label, place a TextBox control, and assign it the following property values:

Property	Value
Name	txtCaption
Text	<empty>

The property page should appear as shown below.

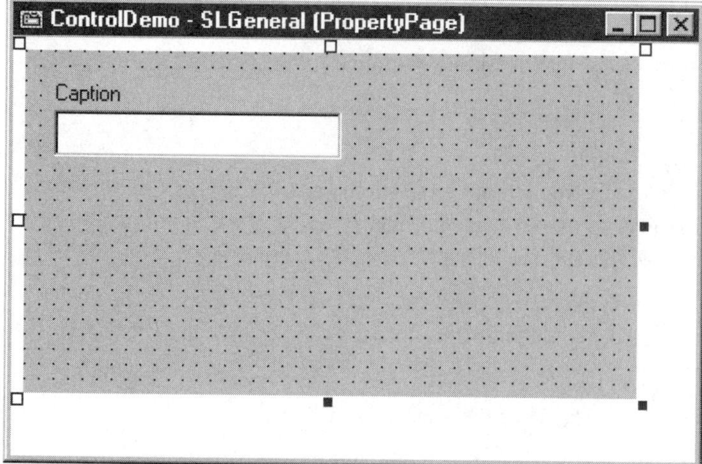

Placing the property description label above the text box in this fashion makes it easier to localize your control component for other languages, in which the word for "Caption" may be longer or shorter. Localization of controls is discussed in detail in Chapter 9, "Building ActiveX Controls."

3. Double-click the **property page**, to open a code window. In the **Events** drop-down menu, select the SelectionChanged event, and add the following code:

```
Private Sub PropertyPage_SelectionChanged()
   ' Display the caption of the first control in
   '    the list of currently selected controls.
   txtCaption.Text = SelectedControls(0).Caption
End Sub
```

The purpose of this event is to get the existing property values from the ShapeLabel control or *controls* that are currently selected. That's right, there may be more than one ShapeLabel control selected. Multiple selection is a wonderful thing for the user of your control, but it means more work for you.

A property page receives a SelectionChanged event whenever it is opened. It also receives this event when the list of selected controls changes. This is necessary because the **Property Pages** dialog box is modeless, so a user may select additional controls while the dialog box is open.

You have to decide how to handle multiple selection on a property-by-property basis. For example, if your property page displays the Width property of the first control in the SelectedControls collection — that is, `SelectedControls(0)`, as shown in the code above — it will be easy for the user to change the widths of all the selected controls to that value.

On the other hand, there is very little use in setting the captions of all the ShapeLabel controls on a form to the same value, so the logical thing to do with the Caption property is to disable txtCaption if the Count property of the SelectedControls collection is greater than one.

However, this procedure doesn't do the logical thing. For illustration purposes, the property page will be allowed to set multiple captions. Later, if you want to enable the behavior described above, you can add the following lines of code to the PropertyPage_SelectionChanged event procedure:

```
' Please don't do this yet!
If SelectedControls.Count > 1 Then
   txtCaption.Enabled = False
Else
   txtCaption.Enabled = True
End If
```

4. To set the property values for all currently selected controls, add the following code to the ApplyChanges event:

```
Private Sub PropertyPage_ApplyChanges()
   ' Use a generic Object variable, in case more
   '   than one kind of control is selected.
   Dim objControl As Variant
   For Each objControl In SelectedControls
      objControl.Caption = txtCaption.Text
   Next
End Sub
```

Your property page receives the ApplyChanges event when the user clicks the **Apply** or **OK** buttons of the **Property Pages** dialog box, or switches to another tab.

How do you know that every control in SelectedControls has a Caption property? As the designer of the control component, you determine which property pages are connected to any given control. A property page will only appear if *all* the currently selected controls have that page in their Property Pages list. The easiest thing to do is to make sure that the pages assigned to each control don't show properties the control doesn't have.

If you wish to use a general-purpose property page for a number of controls, and some of those controls don't have all the properties displayed on the page, you can add code to the ApplyChanges event to test the type of the control, and apply the property value as appropriate. Alternatively, you can use an On Error statement to trap and ignore errors from controls that don't have the property.

You only need to be concerned with the controls in your component, because controls that are not part of your component will never use your component's property pages.

Chapter 10, "Creating Property Pages for ActiveX Controls," discusses property page layout and assignment in greater detail.

5. To enable the **Apply** button of the **Property Page** dialog box when the Caption property is changed, add the following code to the Change event of the txtCaption text box:

```
Private Sub txtCaption_Change()
   ' The Changed property of the property page
   '   controls the Apply button of the Property
   '   Pages dialog box.
   Changed = True
End Sub
```

6. In the Project window, double-click **SLGeneral** to bring the property page designer to the front. Click the designer's **Close** button or press CTRL+F4 to close the designer and put the page in run mode. Like UserControl objects, PropertyPage objects must run while the rest of the project group is in design mode.

To connect the property page to the ShapeLabel control

1. In the Project Explorer window, double-click **ShapeLabel** to open the designer.
2. In the Properties window, double-click the **PropertyPages** property to display the **Connect Property Pages** dialog box.

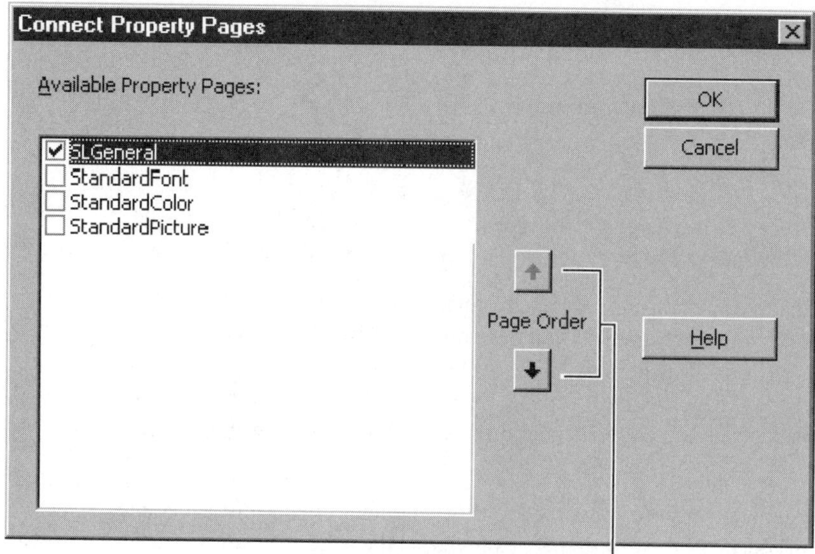

The Page Order buttons allow you to change the order in which the selected property pages will appear in the Property Pages tabbed dialog.

The **Connect Property Pages** dialog box can be used to connect multiple pages to a user control, and to control the display order of the tabs in the Property Pages dialog box for your control.

Property pages can also be connected at run time. This is discussed in Chapter 10, "Creating Property Pages for ActiveX Controls."

3. Check **SLGeneral**, and then click **OK**.
4. Bring the **ShapeLabel** designer to the front, then click its **Close** button or press CTRL+F4 to put the ShapeLabel control in run mode.
5. In the Project Explorer window, double-click **Form1** to open its designer.
6. Right-click on one of the ShapeLabel controls on Form1, to show the context menu, and click **Properties** to show the **Property Pages** dialog box.

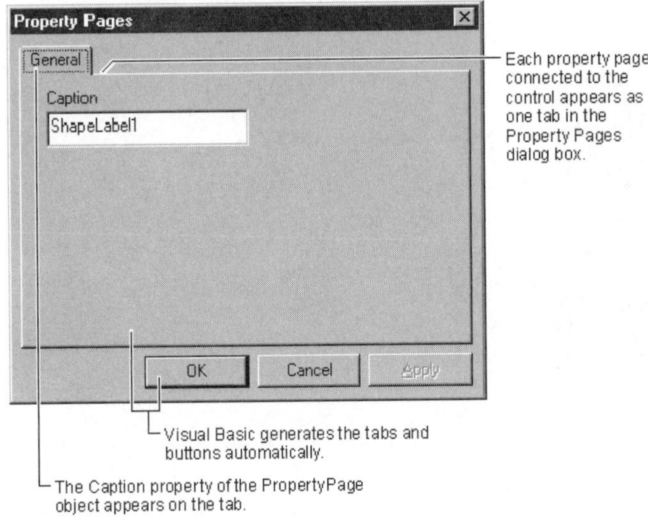

7. In the **Caption** box on the **General** tab, replace the current caption with a new value. When you do this, the **Apply** button is enabled. Click the **Apply** button to change the caption of the control.

   Note You could also change the caption by pressing **OK**, but this would close the **Property Pages** dialog box. The dialog box should stay open for the next step.

8. Hold down the CTRL key and click the second **ShapeLabel** control on Form1, so that both ShapeLabels are selected. Change the caption and click the **Apply** button to set both captions to the same value.

   You may want to try adding other controls, such as command buttons, to Form1, and observing the effects of different multiple selections on the **Property Pages** dialog box.

9. When you're done experimenting, click **OK** to close the **Property Pages** dialog box.

For More Information Property pages are discussed in detail in Chapter 10, "Creating Property Pages for ActiveX Controls."

Adding an Event to the ShapeLabel Control

It's important to distinguish between the events received by your UserControl object (or by the controls it contains) and the events your control raises. Events your control *receives* are opportunities for you to do something interesting; events your control *raises* provide opportunities for the developer who uses your control to do something interesting.

Figure 4.1 shows what happens when a control author simply uses the events received by the UserControl object, and doesn't raise any events for the developer who buys the control.

Figure 4.1 An ActiveX control that simply uses events

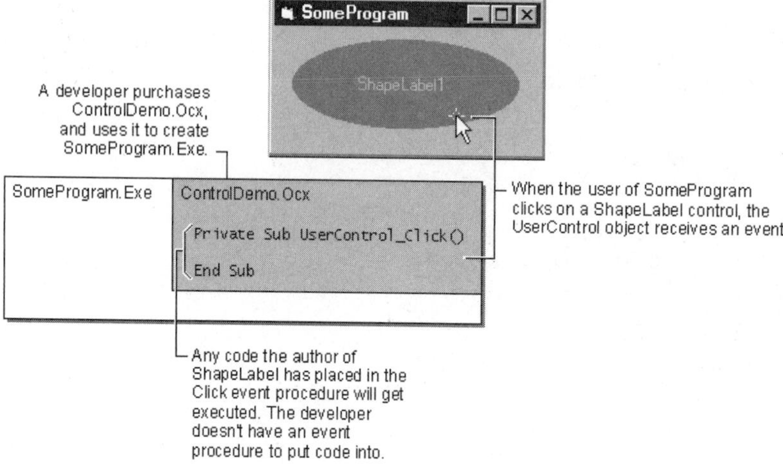

Figure 4.2 shows what happens when the author of ControlDemo.ocx — no doubt tired of developer complaints — improves the ShapeLabel control by raising a Click event for the developer to respond to.

Figure 4.2 A control that raises events for the developer to use

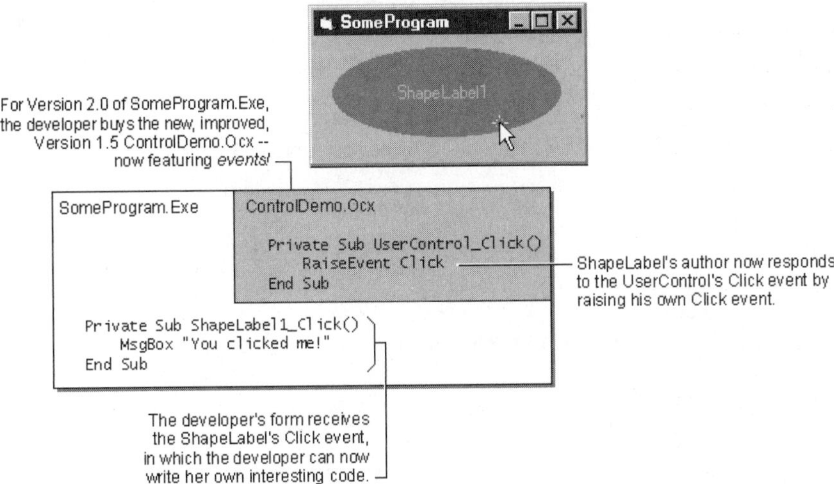
SomeProgram
ShapeLabel1
For Version 2.0 of SomeProgram.Exe, the developer buys the new, improved, Version 1.5 ControlDemo.Ocx -- now featuring *events!*
SomeProgram.Exe
ControlDemo.Ocx
Private Sub UserControl_Click()
RaiseEvent Click
End Sub
ShapeLabel's author now responds to the UserControl's Click event by raising his own Click event.
Private Sub ShapeLabel1_Click()
MsgBox "You clicked me!"
End Sub
The developer's form receives the ShapeLabel's Click event, in which the developer can now write her own interesting code.

There are many events that might be of interest to the user of the ShapeLabel control. The Visual Basic Label control raises a Click event, and ShapeLabel is just a fancy label, so the following procedure will add a Click event. To make the event more interesting, it will be raised only if the user clicks on the oval background.

Being compatible with other controls of the same type is an important reason to add a particular event to your control. Other criteria for choosing what events to raise can be found in "Raising Events from Controls," in Chapter 9, "Building ActiveX Controls."

To add a Click event to the ShapeLabel control

1. In the Project Explorer window, click **ShapeLabel** to select it, then press F7 or click the **Code** button on the Project Explorer window toolbar, to open the **Code** window.
2. In the **Object** box, select (**General**). In the **Procedure** box, select (**Declarations**) to position yourself at the top of the code module. Add the following code:

   ```
   Option Explicit
   ' Declare a public Click event with no arguments.
   Public Event Click()
   ```

3. In the **Object** box, select **lblCaption**. In the **Procedure** box, select the Click event for the label control. Add the following code to the lblCaption_Click event procedure:

   ```
   Private Sub lblCaption_Click()
      ' Raise a Click event whenever the user clicks
      '   on the label.
      RaiseEvent Click
   End Sub
   ```

The code above raises a Click event only if the user clicks on the constituent control lblCaption. It will seem more natural to users to be able to click anywhere on ShapeLabel's oval background, so the next step shows how to raise the click event if the user clicks on the colored oval.

4. In the **Object** box, select **UserControl**. In the **Procedure** box, select the **UserControl's MouseUp** event. Add the following code to the UserControl_MouseUp event procedure:

```
Private Sub UserControl_MouseUp(Button As Integer, _
   Shift As Integer, X As Single, Y As Single)
   ' Raise a Click event only if the color of the
   '   point that was clicked on matches the color
   '   of the Shape control.  Ignore clicks that are
   '   outside the oval.
   If Point(X, Y) = shpBack.FillColor Then
      RaiseEvent Click
   End If
End Sub
```

Determining whether an event occurred in a particular location is called *hit testing.*

You might expect to put the hit test code in the shpBack_Click event procedure, because shpBack is always resized to cover the entire surface of the ShapeLabel control. However, Shape controls don't receive Click events. Instead, the Click event is received by the object that contains the Shape — in this case, the UserControl object.

"Drawing Your Control," in Chapter 9, "Building ActiveX Controls," discusses the use of transparent backgrounds to create irregularly shaped controls.

5. In the Project Explorer window, click **Form1** to select it, then press F7 or click the **Code** button on the Project Explorer window toolbar, to open the Code window.

6. In the **Object** box, select one of the **ShapeLabel** controls you added to Form1. In the **Procedure** box, select the **Click** event.

   Note If the Click event does not appear, make sure the ShapeLabel designer is closed.

   Add the following code to the ShapeLabel1_Click event procedure:

```
Private Sub ShapeLabel1_Click()
   MsgBox "Thanks for clicking! My caption is: " _
      & ShapeLabel1.Caption
End Sub
```

   Note If the ShapeLabel you selected is not named ShapeLabel1, use the appropriate name when entering the code above.

You can click the arrow on the Procedure box to view all of the events for the ShapeLabel control. In addition to your Click event, there are four events — DragDrop, DragOver, GotFocus, and LostFocus — that are automatically provided for you by the container, Form1.

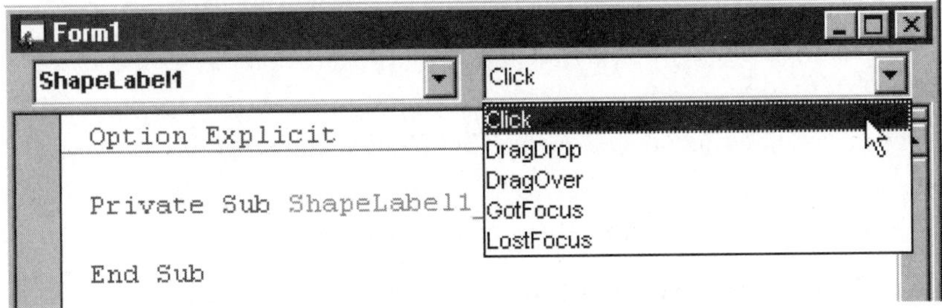

7. On the toolbar, click the **Start** button, or press CTRL+F5 to run TestCtlDemo. Try clicking various places on the form and on the ShapeLabel control, to verify that the Click event is being raised only when you click inside the oval background.
8. There's a subtle bug in the hit testing for ShapeLabel's click event. To see this, press the mouse button while the mouse pointer is in the lower half of the red oval. Holding the mouse button down, carefully move the mouse pointer until the tip of the arrow is on the white text of ShapeLabel's caption, then release the mouse button. The message box doesn't appear!

   The lblCaption_Click event procedure doesn't get executed, because the MouseDown event occurred over the UserControl. Therefore, when the MouseUp event occurs, it is received by the UserControl — even if the mouse has been moved completely off Form1.

   The hit test code in the MouseUp event works if the mouse button is released over the red background that shows through lblCaption's transparent background, but not if the button is released over the white foreground color of the text. (If the button is released outside ShapeLabel, the Point function returns –1, so releasing the mouse button over some random red spot will not raise the Click event.)

   Fixing this bug is left as an exercise for the reader. (Hint: Moving the hit test to the Click event of the UserControl won't help, because the Click event doesn't occur when the MouseUp event is over a different object from the MouseDown.)

Compiling the ControlDemo Component

Once you have created an ActiveX control project containing one or more UserControl objects, you can compile it into an .ocx file and use the controls in other applications. The following procedures demonstrate this.

Compiling the ControlDemo project

1. If the TestCtlDemo project is still in run mode, click the **Close** button on Form1 to return to design mode.

2. In the Project Explorer window, click **ControlDemo** to select the project.

3. On the **File** menu, click **Make ControlDemo.ocx** to open the **Make Project** dialog box. Click **OK** to build the .ocx file.

4. On the **File** menu, click **Remove Project** to remove **ControlDemo** from the project group, so that Visual Basic will use the compiled binary component (.ocx file) instead of the project.

   Visual Basic displays a warning message, because the TestCtlDemo project contains a reference to ControlDemo. Click **Yes** to remove ControlDemo anyway.

   When you remove ControlDemo from the project group, Visual Basic looks for ControlDemo.ocx in the Windows Registry. If the .ocx file exists, Visual Basic automatically updates the reference you set in the procedure "Adding the TestCtlDemo Project."

   To switch back to using the project instead of the binary component, you can click **Add Project**, on the **File** menu, and add the ControlDemo project back to the project group.

5. Press F5 to run TestCtlDemo using the .ocx file.

When ControlDemo is running from source code, you cannot access the ShapeLabel control from other applications, or from another copy of Visual Basic. This is because ActiveX control components must run in process. Once you have compiled a .ocx component, you can test it from other applications.

To use ControlDemo.ocx in another copy of Visual Basic

1. Open a new instance of Visual Basic. In the **New Project** dialog box, double-click the Standard EXE icon to open an .exe project.

2. On the **Project** menu, click **Components** to open the **Components** dialog box. On the **Controls** tab, check **ActiveX Control Creation Demo,** and then click **OK**.

   The icon for ShapeLabel appears on the Toolbox. You can now add ShapeLabel controls to the default form, and use the Properties window to set their properties. You can also right-click on an instance of ShapeLabel, and choose **Properties** from the Context menu to edit the control's properties with the property page.

3. Press F5 to run the project.

   You can also compile the project and run the .exe.

For More Information An .ocx file can contain multiple controls and property pages. "Distributing Controls," in Chapter 9, "Building ActiveX Controls," discusses control packaging and distribution.

Control Creation Recap

In order to introduce new concepts in the most natural order, the procedures in this chapter have not followed the normal sequence of steps for creating a new control.

When you create a new control, the steps you'll generally follow are these:

1. Determine the features your control will provide.
2. Design the appearance of your control.
3. Design the interface for your control — that is, the properties, methods, and events your control will expose.
4. Create a project group consisting of your control project and a test project.
5. Implement the appearance of your control by adding controls and/or code to the UserControl object.
6. Implement the interface and features of your control.
7. As you add each interface element or feature, add features to your test project to exercise the new functionality.
8. Design and implement property pages for your control.
9. Compile your control component (.ocx file) and test it with all potential target applications.

If your control component will provide more than one control, you should begin by deciding what controls the package will include. Your test project should have separate test forms for the individual controls, and at least one form that tests the controls together.

For More Information General design issues for ActiveX components are discussed in Chapter 6, "General Principles of Component Design," and Chapter 7, "Debugging, Testing, and Deploying Components." Issues exclusive to ActiveX control creation, testing, packaging, and deployment are discussed in Chapter 9, "Building ActiveX Controls," and Chapter 10, "Creating Property Pages for ActiveX Controls."

CHAPTER 5

Creating an ActiveX Document

The series of step-by-step procedures in this chapter builds a simple combination of two ActiveX documents and two forms. The project is not intended to be a functioning application, but building it will quickly demonstrate object lifetime, global objects, and a set of components working together in Internet Explorer. You will also see how to debug an ActiveX document using Visual Basic's debugging tools.

All of the subjects introduced in these procedures are covered in greater depth in later chapters. References to in-depth material will be found in each procedure. In addition, Chapter 11, "Building ActiveX Documents," shows how you can use the ActiveX Document Wizard to convert existing applications into ActiveX documents.

> **Note** To complete the step-by-step procedures in this chapter, you must have Microsoft Internet Explorer and access to the Internet or an intranet. You can install Internet Explorer from the Tools directory of your Visual Basic CD-ROM.
>
> The procedures for creating the ActXDoc project build on each other, so the sequence in which you perform the procedures is important.

Contents

Sample Application: ActXDoc.vbp

This application fills in all the properties, methods, and events required to create an ActiveX document. It shows additional ActiveX document creation features, at the expense of some of the basic material covered in the step-by-step procedures. The sample applications are listed in the Samples directory.

Creating the ActXDoc Project

The first step in authoring the ActXDoc project is to add a single UserDocument object to an ActiveX EXE project. A CommandButton and a TextBox control are then added to the form. Finally, using the Hyperlink object, you add code that navigates to another URL.

The step-by-step procedures in this chapter build a document object and test it in Internet Explorer, which is included with Visual Basic.

To create an ActiveX document

1. On the **File** menu, click **New Project** to open the **New Project** dialog box. (This will close your current project or project group; you will be prompted to save any changes you have made.) Double-click the ActiveX Document EXE icon.

   Visual Basic automatically adds a UserDocument designer to the project. If the designer is not immediately visible, right-click over its default name, **UserDocument1**, in the Project Explorer window, then click **View Object**. When the designer appears, its default name is visible in the title bar.

2. In the Properties window, double-click the **Name** property and change the name of UserDocument1 to FirstDoc. The new name appears in the title bar of the designer, and in the Project Explorer window.

3. In the Project Explorer window, click the Project1 icon. In the Properties window, double-click **Name**, and change the name of the project to ActXDoc. The title bar of the designer now reads "ActXDoc – FirstDoc (UserDocument)."

4. In the Project Explorer window, double-click the FirstDoc icon to bring it to the front.

5. On the Toolbox, double-click the CommandButton icon to put a CommandButton control on the designer.

6. On the Toolbox, double-click the TextBox icon to put a Textbox control on the designer.

7. Place the two controls as shown in the following illustration:

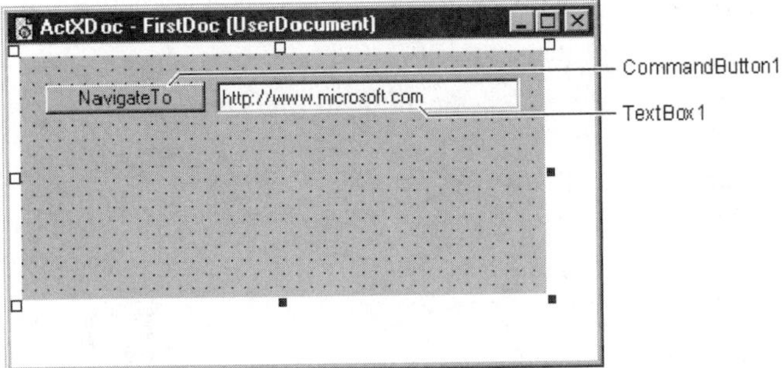

8. Change the appropriate properties of the two controls according to the following table:

Command1 property	Value
Name	cmdNavigateTo
Caption	Navigate To

Text1 property	Value
Name	txtURL
Text	http://www.microsoft.com

9. On the FirstDoc designer, double-click the Navigate To CommandButton control to add the following code to its Click event:

```
Private Sub cmdNavigateTo_Click()
   ' Use the Hyperlink object method NavigateTo
   ' to go to the URL in txtURL.
   Hyperlink.NavigateTo txtURL.Text
End Sub
```

Important When using the NavigateTo method, you must include the protocol portion of the URL. For example, by default, the above code will navigate to the value of the Text property of the txtURL TextBox control — "http://www.microsoft.com."

10. On the **File** menu, click **Save Project** to save the project files. Name them as shown in the following table. Visual Basic will provide the indicated extensions automatically.

File	File name	Extension
User document	FirstDoc	.dob
Project	ActXDoc	.vbp

Running and Debugging the ActXDoc Project

In order to view the FirstDoc document, you must first run the ActXDoc project, then run another container application in which to view the FirstDoc document. In this procedure, you will run Internet Explorer (included with Visual Basic), and navigate to a .vbd file to open the ActiveX document (a .vbd file is automatically generated for every ActiveX document in a project whenever the project is run).

To view the FirstDoc ActiveX document

1. Run the project by pressing F5.

   The project is now running. If you use Windows Explorer to view the directory where Visual Basic resides, you will find a FirstDoc.vbd file.

2. If this is the first time you've run the project, the **Project Properties** dialog box will appear. Click **Start Browser with URL**, and type the path of the FirstDoc.vbd file, which should be in the directory where you installed Visual Basic. Internet Explorer will open and display your ActiveX document.

3. Note in the text box that the default URL is http://www.microsoft.com. You can replace this URL with another of your choice.

4. Click the **Navigate To** button. The Web page at the URL in the text box will appear in the browser.

Debugging the FirstDoc ActiveX Document

Debugging an ActiveX document is similar to debugging other ActiveX components. You can use all the tools available in Visual Basic — setting breakpoints, watching variables, using debug statements, and so on.

It's also important to remember that the container hosting the ActiveX document is its client — using objects the ActiveX document provides. While the host container is accessing the ActiveX document, stopping the project will cause an error in the host container. To avoid this, at the end of each of these procedures you will quit Internet Explorer to release the reference.

For More Information For alternatives that cause Internet Explorer to release your ActiveX document, see "Debugging ActiveX Documents in Internet Explorer" in Chapter 11, "Building ActiveX Documents."

Putting Your Project into Break Mode

If you are running a project and are viewing it in Internet Explorer, you can put it into break mode (by pressing CTRL+BREAK) without causing any errors in the host application. However, be aware that modifying any code that causes Visual Basic to reset the project should be avoided.

To add a Stop statement to an ActiveX document

1. In Internet Explorer, click the **Back** button to return to the FirstDoc ActiveX document.
2. Press ALT+TAB to switch back to Visual Basic.
3. Press CTRL+BREAK to pause the program.
4. In the Code window, find the Click event for the cmdNavigateTo button, and place a Stop statement before the existing line of code, as shown:

```
Private Sub cmdNavigateTo_Click()
   Stop ' <--- Add this to the procedure.
   Hyperlink.NavigateTo txtURL.Text
End Sub
```

5. Press F5 to continue.
6. Press ALT+TAB to return to Internet Explorer.
7. Click **Navigate To**. Visual Basic will return to the front of your desktop with the Code window visible, and the Stop statement highlighted.
8. Press F5 to continue. Note that the Web page has been revisited.

Adding a Second ActiveX Document to the ActXDoc Project

Having one ActiveX document in a project is equivalent to having a single form in a project — somewhat limiting. To increase your capabilities, add a second ActiveX document to the ActXDoc project.

Unlike standard Visual Basic forms, you cannot use the Show method to show ActiveX documents. This is because the container application (in this case, Internet Explorer) determines when to show or hide the ActiveX document. Instead, you must navigate from one ActiveX document to another. To navigate between the two ActiveX documents, use the HyperLink object and its NavigateTo method.

To add a second ActiveX document to the ActXDoc project

1. Before adding a second ActiveX document to the project, add a CommandButton control to the FirstDoc designer. On the Toolbox, double-click the CommandButton icon to add a CommandButton control to the FirstDoc designer.
2. Set the appropriate properties for the control using the following table:

Command1 property	Value
Name	cmdGoNext
Caption	Go Next

3. Position the control on the FirstDoc designer as shown.

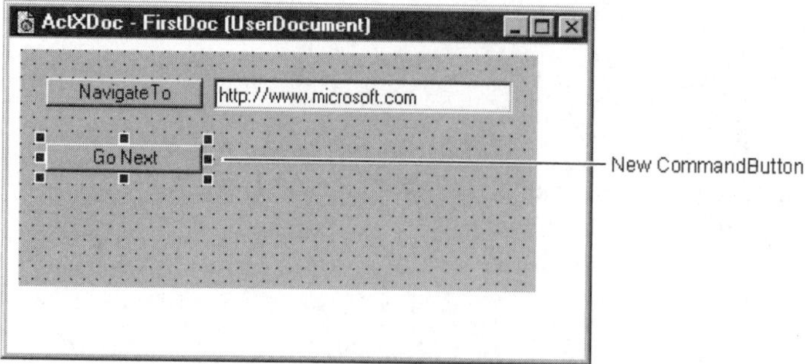

4. Double-click the **Go Next** button and add the following code to the button's Click event:

```
Private Sub cmdGoNext_Click()
   ' Note: the following path may not correspond to  ' the actual path to the
SecndDoc.vbd file on
   ' your machine.
   HyperLink.NavigateTo _
   App.Path & "\SecndDoc.vbd"
End Sub
```

   Note The App.Path code only works if you keep ActXDoc project in the same directory where you installed the Visual Basic application. If you save the project to another directory, replace `App.Path & "\SecndDoc.vbd"` with the hard-coded path of the SecndDoc.vbd file.

   When you are running the project, Visual Basic always creates a temporary .vbd file for each ActiveX document in your project, and the .vbd files will always be found in the same directory where Visual Basic has been installed. However, if you are compiling an .exe or .dll, Visual Basic will create the .vbd file in the same directory as the .exe or .dll file.

5. This next step will insert a second ActiveX document into the project. On the **Project** menu, click **Add UserDocument** to open the **Add User Document** dialog box.
6. Double-click the User Document icon to add an ActiveX document to the project.
7. On the Properties window, double-click **Name** and change the name of the new UserDocument object to SecndDoc. The caption should now read "ActXDoc – SecndDoc (UserDocument)."
8. Add **Label** and **CommandButton** controls to the SecndDoc User document, and use the following tables to set their properties.

Label1 property	Value
Name	lblCaption
Caption	SecndDoc

Command1 property	Value
Name	cmdGoBack
Caption	Go Back

9. Position the controls on the SecndDoc User document as shown:

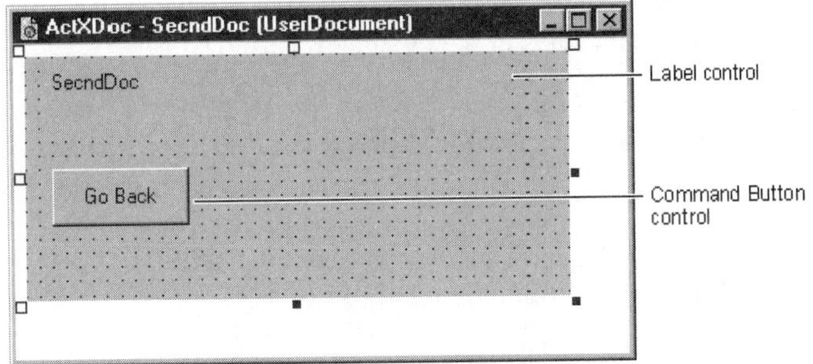

10. Add the following code to the Click event of the cmdGoBack button:

```
Private Sub cmdGoBack_Click()
   UserDocument.HyperLink.GoBack
End Sub
```

The HyperLink object features the GoBack method, which will navigate back to the previous document in the browser.

11. On the **File** menu, click **Save Project** to save the project files. Name them as shown in the following table. Visual Basic will provide the indicated extensions automatically.

File	File name	Extension
User document	SecndDoc	.dob

Running the Project

Now that you have added a second ActiveX document, you can run the project and navigate between the two.

1. Run the project by pressing F5. Internet Explorer will be launched.
2. In Internet Explorer, type the path of the FirstDoc.vbd file in the **Address** box.

Tip If you previously opened the FirstDoc ActiveX document in Internet Explorer, click the arrow next to the **Address** box to see a list of recent URLs. The FirstDoc document should be available from the drop-down list.

3. Click **Go Next**. You will now be on the SecndDoc document.
4. On the SecndDoc document, click **Go Back** to return to the FirstDoc ActiveX document.

Adding a Form to the ActXDoc Project

As with other Visual Basic projects, it's a simple matter to add a form to the FirstDoc ActiveX project. Adding controls to the form is exactly the same as in a standard Visual Basic project. The primary difference, of course, lies in the fact that forms must be called by the ActiveX document.

In this step-by-step procedure, you add a single form to the ActXDoc project.

To add a form to the ActXDoc project

1. On the **Project** menu, click **Add Form**, then double-click the Form icon in the **Add Form** dialog box. Set the form's properties using the following table:

Form1 property	Value
Name	frmAux
Caption	Auxiliary Form

2. On the Toolbox, double-click the TextBox icon to add a TextBox control to the form, and set its properties using the following table.

Text1 property	Value
Name	txtAux
MultiLine	True
Text	(nothing)

3. Resize the form, and place the control on the form so it resembles the following figure:

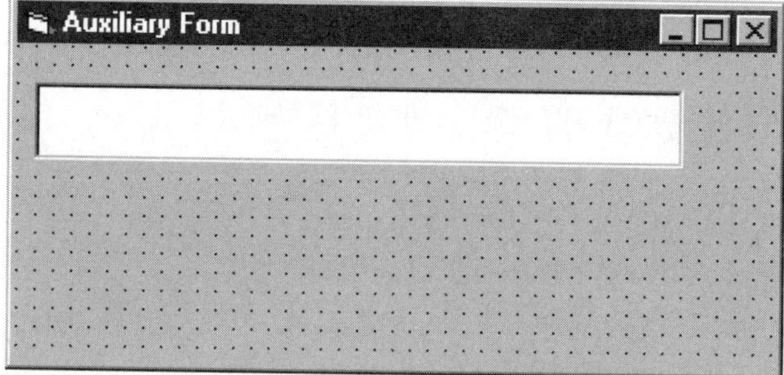

4. In the Project Explorer window, double-click the FirstDoc icon to bring its designer forward.
5. On the Toolbox, click the CommandButton icon and draw a new button on the FirstDoc designer, and set its properties according to the following table:

Command1 property	Value
Name	cmdShowForm
Caption	Show Form

6. Place the control just below the **Go Next** button as shown:

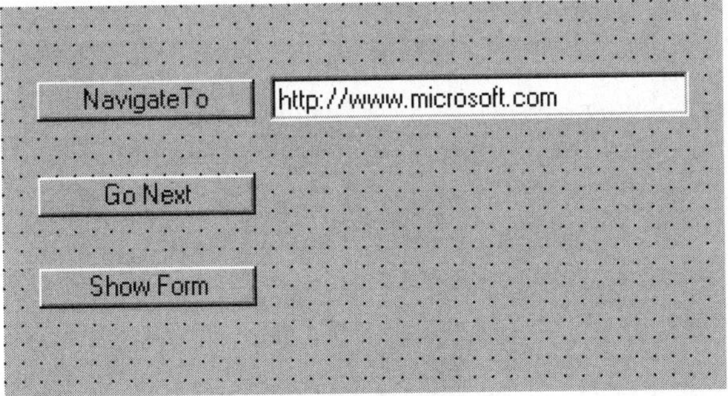

7. Double-click the Show Form CommandButton control, and add the following code to its Click event:

```
Private Sub cmdShowForm_Click()
   ' Show the auxiliary form, and set the Text
   ' property of txtAux to the URL of FirstDoc.
   frmAux.txtAux.Text = txtURL.Text
   frmAux.Show vbModal
End Sub
```

Important Some containers, such as Internet Explorer, don't support the showing of modeless forms called from within a DLL. If you want to show modeless forms, compile your ActiveX document as an .exe file. This will allow your applications to show both modeless and modal forms.

8. On the **File** menu, click **Save Project** to save the project files. Visual Basic will prompt you to name the form as its default (frmAux). Click **OK** to save the form with the default name.

Running the Project

You can now run the project and observe the interaction of the form with the ActiveX document.

To view the new form interacting with the ActiveX document

1. Press F5 to run the project.
2. Click the **Address** box and type the path of the FirstDoc.vbd.
3. Click the **Show Form** button to see the form.

Adding a Property to the UserDocument

As with the UserControl object, you can create public properties for UserDocument objects. When you create a public property, you expose the property so other applications can set or get its value. In the ActXDoc project, you'll create a single property that can be accessed by either another ActiveX document or by a form. In this procedure, you will also add a code module to the project to contain a single global module.

To add a property to FirstDoc

1. First add a code module to the project. On the **Project** menu, click **Add Module** to open the **Add Module** dialog box. Then double-click the Module icon to add a new code module to the ActXDoc project.
2. In the Properties window, double-click **Name** and change the name of the module to mGlobal.
3. In the Project Explorer window, double-click the module icon and add the following code to the Declarations section:

   ```
   ' Object variable for FirstDoc
   Public gFirstDoc As FirstDoc
   ```

   This global variable will contain the object reference that links the FirstDoc and SecndDoc ActiveX documents.
4. In the Project Explorer window, double-click the FirstDoc icon.
5. On the **Toolbox**, double-click the TextBox icon to add a new TextBox control to FirstDoc. Set its properties according to the following table.

Text1 property	Value
Name	txtFirstDoc
Text	(nothing)

6. Position the TextBox control below the first TextBox already present on the UserDocument, as shown:

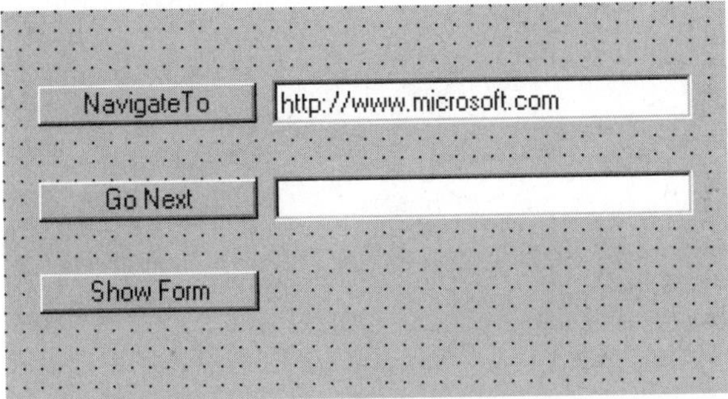

7. Double-click the FirstDoc designer to open its Code window.
8. On the **Tools** menu, click **Add Procedure**.
9. In the **Add Procedure** dialog box, type "strDocProp" into the **Name** box, and click the **Property** option to create a public property; then click **OK**.
10. Visual Basic will add code for Property Get and Property Let procedures to the module. However, modify the code as shown:

```
Public Property Get strDocProp() As String
   ' Note: in the line above, change the return type
   ' of the property from "As Variant" to
   ' "As String."
   strDocProp = txtFirstDoc.Text
End Property

Public Property Let strDocProp(ByVal _
NewStrDocProp As String)
   ' Note: in the line above, change the argument
   ' type from Variant to String.
   txtFirstDoc.Text = NewStrDocProp
End Property
```

    The code above exposes the strDocProp property as a public property of the FirstDoc ActiveX document. In other words, it delegates to the Text property of the TextBox control the work of displaying and storing the string. Now that the property is public, you can pass its value to the SecndDoc object. You will do this by modifying the code for the Go Next command button.

11. In the Code window, modify the Click event of the cmdGoNext button to include a Set statement with the global object gFirstDoc. When you set the object variable to Me, you create a reference to the FirstDoc ActiveX document. This reference can then be used to access the public properties and methods of the document.

```
Private Sub cmdGoNext_Click()
   ' Note: the following path may not correspond to
   ' the actual path to the SecndDoc.vbd file on
   ' your machine.
   Set gFirstDoc = Me ' <-- Add this line.
   HyperLink.NavigateTo _
   App.Path & "\SecndDoc.vbd"
End Sub
```

12. In the Project Explorer window, double-click the SecndDoc icon to bring its designer forward.

13. Double-click the SecndDoc designer to open its Code window and add the following code to the UserDocument object's Show event.

```
Private Sub UserDocument_Show()
   If Not gFirstDoc Is Nothing Then
      lblCaption.Caption = gFirstDoc.strDocProp
      Set gFirstDoc = Nothing
   End If
End Sub
```

In the code in step 11, you set the global object variable to the FirstDoc document. The code in step 13 tests to see if the global variable is set to an object. If it is, then the public properties of the ActiveX document are available, and the caption of the label is set to the strDocProp property from the FirstDoc document. Immediately after setting the Caption property, the global variable is destroyed (set to Nothing).

> **Note** It is bad practice to allow the global variable to retain a reference to the FirstDoc UserDocument; the reasons for this are covered in Chapter 11, "Building ActiveX Documents."

14. On the **File** menu, click **Save Project**, and save the code module as mGlobal.bas.

Running the Project

1. Press F5 to run the project.
2. Type the path of the FirstDoc.vbd. in the **Address** box of Internet Explorer.
3. Type something distinctive into the new TextBox control such as "HTML was never this easy."
4. Click **Go Next**. The text that was in the TextBox control will appear in the label of the SecndDoc document.

Saving Properties to the PropertyBag

When the end user of an ActiveX document views a document, there may be several text boxes that she or he will fill out as part of your application. If it's possible that the user will return repeatedly to the document, you may wish to save some time by saving the data to the PropertyBag.

In the following example, the PropertyChanged statement is inserted into the Change event of the TextBox (txtFirstDoc) control. This causes Internet Explorer to prompt the user to save changes. If the user responds positively, the code writes the property value to the PropertyBag.

For More Information To learn more about the PropertyBag, see "Saving the Properties of Your Control," in Chapter 9, "Building ActiveX Controls."

To write and read a property to the PropertyBag

1. In the Project Explorer window, double-click the FirstDoc icon to bring its designer forward.
2. Double-click the TextBox (txtFirstDoc) control to view its code.
3. In the Code window, from the drop-down list of events for txtFirstDoc, click **Change**. Add the PropertyChanged statement, as shown:

```
Private Sub txtFirstDoc_Change()
   PropertyChanged
End Sub
```

4. Add the following code to the UserDocument object's WriteProperties event:

```
Private Sub UserDocument_WriteProperties _
(PropBag As VB.PropertyBag)
   PropBag.WriteProperty "StrDocProp", _
   txtFirstDoc.Text, "Hello"
   Debug.Print "WriteProperties"
End Sub
```

5. The code in step 4 saves the value of the Text property of the TextBox control to the PropertyBag. To retrieve the value, add the following code to the ReadProperties event:

```
Private Sub UserDocument_ReadProperties _
(PropBag As VB.PropertyBag)
   txtFirstDoc.Text = _
   PropBag.ReadProperty("StrDocProp", _
   "Hello")
   Debug.Print "ReadProperties"
End Sub
```

Running the Project

Now that the property can be written to and read from the PropertyBag, run the project to test it.

1. Press F5 to run the project.
2. Click the **Address** box and type the path of the FirstDoc.vbd.
3. Type some distinctive text, such as your name, into the blank TextBox control.
4. On the **File** menu, click **Close**. Internet Explorer will present a dialog box asking if you would like to save the your changes. Click **Yes**.
5. Run Internet Explorer again.
6. Click the **Address** box and type the path of the FirstDoc.vbd. The text you typed will be present in the TextBox control.

Using the PropBag in conjunction with the WriteProperties and ReadProperties events, you can easily persist data for your object.

Adding a Menu to the ActXDoc Project

You can add menus to your ActiveX document using the Menu Editor. Because an ActiveX document alone cannot have a menu, the menu you create will be merged with the application you used to view the ActiveX document. Thus, you must consider menu negotiation when adding a menu to an ActiveX document.

When users navigate to your ActiveX document, they may not have any indication of its origin (or that it is an ActiveX document). To remedy this, you should always include an "About" form with your ActiveX document.

To add a menu and About box to the FirstDoc ActiveX document

1. On the **Project** menu, click **Add Form**.
2. In the **Add Form** dialog box, double-click the **About Dialog** icon to add an About Box form to the project.
3. Set the Caption property of the form and controls according to the following table.

Object	Caption value
FrmAbout	About FirstDoc
LblTitle	FirstDoc ActiveX Document
LblVersion	Version 1.0
LblDescription	ActiveX document

4. Delete the Label control named lblDisclaimer.
5. In the Project Explorer window, double-click **FirstDoc** to bring its designer forward.

6. Click the FirstDoc designer to select it, and on the **Tools** menu, click **Menu Editor** to display the menu editor dialog box.
7. Click the **Caption** box and type **&Help**.
8. Click the **Name** box and type **mnuHelp**.
9. Click the **NegotiatePosition** box, and click **Right**.
10. Click the **Next** button to create a new menu item.
11. In the **Caption** box, type **About FirstDoc**.
12. In the **Name** box, type **mnuAbout**.
13. Click the right-facing arrow button to indent the menu item.
14. Click **OK**.
15. Double-click the FirstDoc designer to bring its Code window to the front.
16. Add the following code to the mnuAbout Click event:

```
Private Sub mnuAbout_Click()
   frmAbout.Show vbModal
End Sub
```

Running the Project

Once you have added a menu to the UserDocument, you can run the project, view the ActiveX document in Internet Explorer, and see the how the menu has been negotiated.

1. Run the project by pressing F5.
2. In Internet Explorer, type the path of the FirstDoc.vbd file in the **Address** box or select it from the drop-down list of previously typed addresses.
3. On Internet Explorer's command bar, click the **Help** menu, and among the menu items will be the **FirstDoc Help** menu item.
4. Click **About FirstDoc** to see the new **About** box.

Life Cycle of a UserDocument

The life of an ordinary Visual Basic form is marked by certain key events, such as Initialize, Load, QueryUnload, and Unload. In order to create well-behaved applications, it's important to know when these events occur in the life cycle of a form.

Although ActiveX documents look like forms, they behave differently, primarily because they are contained by another application. When programming an ActiveX document, some attention must be given to the ephemeral nature of an ActiveX document. This is especially true when the container application is a Web browser, such as Internet Explorer.

Key events in the life cycle of a UserDocument object include Initialize, InitProperties, Show, Hide, and Terminate. The following procedure demonstrates these events.

To observe the key events of the FirstDoc UserDocument

1. In the Project Explorer window, double-click **FirstDoc** to bring its designer forward.
2. Double-click the designer to open a Code window for the UserDocument object, and enter code in the following event procedures:

```
Private Sub UserDocument_Initialize()
   Debug.Print "Initialize"
End Sub

Private Sub UserDocument_InitProperties()
   Debug.Print "InitProperties"
End Sub

Private Sub UserDocument_Show()
   Static intCount As Integer
   intCount = intCount + 1
   Debug.Print "Show " & intCount
End Sub

Private Sub UserDocument_Hide()
   Static intCount As Integer
   intCount = intCount + 1
   Debug.Print "Hide " & intCount
End Sub

Private Sub UserDocument_Terminate()
   Debug.Print "Terminate"
End Sub
```

3. Run the project by pressing F5.
4. In Internet Explorer, view the ActiveX document by navigating to the URL of the FirstDoc.vbd file, or by clicking the arrow next to the **Address** box and selecting FirstDoc.vbd from the list.
5. Press ALT+TAB to bring Visual Basic back to the front of your window. Notice in the Immediate window that three events — Initialize, InitProperties, and Show — have been printed to the window. As with the UserControl object, the Intialize event precedes InitProperties.

   Note You will notice that Show is followed by a 1, indicating that the ActiveX document has been shown once by Internet Explorer. As long as a reference to the ActiveX document exists in the Internet Explorer cache, this number will increment once each time you navigate to the ActiveX document from another URL.

6. Press ALT+TAB to return to Internet Explorer. Navigate another URL, either by typing a valid URL into the **Address** box of Internet Explorer, or using your list of Favorites. It does not matter which HTML page you navigate to.

7. After navigating to the new URL, press ALT+TAB to switch back to Visual Basic. In the Immediate window you will notice that the Hide and Terminate events have occurred.

8. Press ALT+TAB to return to Internet Explorer. Click **Back** until the FirstDoc ActiveX document is once again in view.

9. Press ALT+TAB again to switch back to Visual Basic. Notice in the Immediate window that the Initialize, InitProperties, and Show events have been fired.

The Initialize and InitProperties Events

The Initialize and InitProperties events have some similarities, but you should be aware of how they differ. In brief, the Initialize event always occurs when the ActiveX document is loaded, while InitProperties will only occur every time until the document is saved. After that event has fired, the ReadProperties and WriteProperties events will fire. To see an example of this:

1. If Internet Explorer is still running, close it.

2. If the ActXDoc project is still running, stop it. This is necessary in order to see the InitProperties event occur.

3. Restart the ActXDoc project.

4. In Internet Explorer, type the path of the FirstDoc.vbd file in the **Address** box, or select it from the drop-down URL history list.

5. Type something distinctive into the TextBox (txtFirstDoc) control.

6. Close Internet Explorer. You will be prompted to save your changes. Click **Yes**.

7. Restart Internet Explorer. (Do not stop the ActXDoc project.)

8. Press ALT+TAB to return to Visual Basic.

9. Note in the Immediate window that InitProperties occurred only once: the first time that the FirstDoc document was viewed in Internet Explorer. The second time you viewed the FirstDoc document the Initialize event occurred, but not the InitProperties; instead, the ReadProperties event occurred.

   You should note this behavior, as it impacts where you place your code. Needless to say, if you always want a procedure to run on startup, you should put it into the Initialize event. If you want a procedure to run only the first time a user views your ActiveX document, place it in the InitProperties event.

   You should be cautious, however, about the limitations of using the Initialize event. In brief, any procedures that require knowledge of the container (such as the Parent property) are unavailable when the Initialize event occurs. An alternate event that occurs after the ActiveX document has been sited in the container is the Show event.

ActiveX Document Creation Recap

When you create a new ActiveX document, the steps you'll generally follow are:

1. Determine the features your document will provide.
2. Design the appearance of your document.
3. Design the interface for your document; that is, the properties, methods, and events your document will expose.
4. Create a project consisting of your user document and any auxiliary forms.
5. Add controls and/or code to the UserDocument object.
6. Implement the interface and features of your document.
7. Compile your document to create a .vbd file and test it with all potential target applications.

CHAPTER 6

General Principles of Component Design

This chapter and Chapter 7, "Debugging, Testing, and Deploying Components," contain those topics that apply to all types of ActiveX components. These chapters provide necessary background for the in-depth treatment of component types in subsequent chapters.

This chapter begins with "Component Basics," a group of topics that explain key terminology and concepts of component design.

The rest of the topics in Chapter 6 and Chapter 7 are organized according to the general sequence of development tasks for components:

1. Determine the features your component will provide.
2. Determine what objects are required to divide the functionality of the component in a logical fashion.

   See "Adding Classes to Components."
3. Design any forms your component will display.
4. Design the interface — that is, the properties, methods, and events — for each class provided by your component.

   See "Adding Properties and Methods to Classes," "Adding Events to Classes," "Providing Named Constants for Your Component," "Providing Polymorphism by Implementing Interfaces," and "Organizing Objects: The Object Model" later in this chapter.

   The remainder of the task-oriented topics are contained in Chapter 7, "Debugging, Testing, and Deploying Components." In addition to the following development tasks, they cover distribution, version compatibility, and creating international versions of your component.
5. Create the component project and test project.
6. Implement the forms required by your component.

7. Implement the interface of each class, provide browser strings for interface members, and add links to Help topics.
8. As you add each interface element or feature, add code to your test project to exercise the new functionality.
9. Compile your component and test it with all potential target applications.

Contents

Component Basics

A software component created with Microsoft Visual Basic is a file containing executable code — an .exe, .dll, or .ocx file — that provides objects other applications and components can use.

An application or component that uses objects provided by other software components is referred to as a *client*. A client uses the services of a software component by creating instances of classes the component provides, and calling their properties and methods.

In earlier versions of Visual Basic, you could create components called *OLE servers*. The features of components created with Visual Basic are greatly expanded, including the ability to raise events, improved support for asynchronous callbacks, and the ability to provide ActiveX controls and documents.

For More Information The core information on creating OLE servers, referred to as code components, includes Chapter 2, "Creating an ActiveX DLL"; Chapter 3, "Creating an ActiveX EXE Component"; Chapter 6, "General Principles of Component Design"; Chapter 7, "Debugging, Testing, and Deploying Components"; Chapter 8, "Building Code Components"; and Appendix A, "ActiveX Component Standards and Guidelines."

In-Process and Out-of-Process Components

An application or component that uses objects provided by another component is called a *client.*

Components are characterized by their location relative to clients. An *out-of-process* component is an .exe file that runs in its own process, with its own thread of execution. Communication between a client and an out-of-process component is therefore called *cross-process* or *out-of-process* communication.

An *in-process* component, such as a .dll or .ocx file, runs in the same process as the client. It provides the fastest way of accessing objects, because property and method calls don't have to be marshaled across process boundaries. However, an in-process component must use the client's thread of execution.

For More Information Chapter 8, "Building Code Components," discusses in-process and out-of-process components in depth, including thread-safe DLLs and multithreaded EXE components. Control components (.ocx files) are always in-process, as discussed in depth in Chapter 9, "Building ActiveX Controls." Components that provide active documents can run in process or out of process, as discussed in Chapter 11, "Building ActiveX Documents."

What's in a Name?

The names you select for your class modules and for their properties, methods, and events make up the interface(s) by which your component will be accessed. When naming these elements, and their named parameters, you can help the user of your component by following a few simple rules.

- Use complete words whenever possible, as for example "SpellCheck." Abbreviations can take many forms, and hence can be confusing. If whole words are too long, use complete first syllables.
- Use mixed case for your identifiers, capitalizing each word or syllable, as for example ShortcutMenus, or AsyncReadComplete.
- Use the same word your users would use to describe a concept. For example, use Name rather than Lbl.
- Use the correct plural for collection class names, as for example Worksheets, Forms, or Widgets. If the collection holds objects with a name that ends in "s," append the word Collection, as for example SeriesCollection.
- Use a prefix for the named constants in Enums, as discussed in "Providing Named Constants for Your Component," later in this chapter.
- Use either the verb/object or object/verb order consistently for your method names. That is, use InsertWidget, InsertSprocket, and so on, or always place the object first, as in WidgetInsert and SprocketInsert.

Important The following names cannot be used as property or method names, because they belong to the underlying IUnknown and IDispatch interfaces: QueryInterface, AddRef, Release, GetTypeInfoCount, GetTypeInfo, GetIDsOfNames, and Invoke. These names will cause a compilation error.

For More Information An expanded version of this list can be found in "Object Naming Guidelines," in Appendix A, "ActiveX Component Standards and Guidelines."

Choosing a Project Type and Setting Project Properties

When you open a new project, you have three choices for project type: ActiveX EXE, ActiveX DLL, and ActiveX Control. The type you choose determines what kinds of objects your component can provide.

The following list may assist you in selecting the correct project type for your component.

1. If your component is going to provide ActiveX controls, open a new ActiveX control project. Controls can only be provided by control components (.ocx files), which must be compiled from ActiveX control projects. Control components always run in process.

   Note Control components are limited in their ability to provide other kinds of objects because class modules in ActiveX control projects can only have two Instancing settings, PublicNotCreatable or Private. Objects in control components are best used to enhance the features of controls; put objects with other uses in a separate ActiveX DLL project.

2. If your component is going to provide ActiveX documents, you can open either an ActiveX EXE project or an ActiveX DLL project. (The New Project dialog box provides templates for new projects that will provide ActiveX documents.)

   See Chapter 11, "Building ActiveX Documents," for a discussion of the reasons to choose an in-process or out-of-process component to provide active documents.

3. If you're creating an out-of-process component, open a new ActiveX EXE project. Reasons to create an out-of-process component include:

   - The component can run as a standalone desktop application, like Microsoft Excel or Microsoft Word, in addition to providing objects.
   - The component can process requests on an independent thread of execution, notifying the client of task completion using events or asynchronous call-backs. This frees the client to respond to the user.
   - If you're using COM or Remote Automation to run components on remote computers (Enterprise Edition only), some components may need to be .exe files.

4. If you're creating an in-process component, open a new ActiveX DLL project. Reasons to create an in-process component include:
   - An in-process component shares its client's address space, so property and method calls don't have to be marshaled. This results in much faster performance.
   - An in-process component designed for unattended execution (that is, no user interaction) can be marked thread-safe. When used by a multithreaded client, it can provide objects on any of the client's threads of execution, while retaining the performance benefits of in-process method and property calls.

Once you've opened a project for your new component, there are some project properties you should always set.

To set properties for a new component project

1. On the **Project** menu, click **Project1 Properties** to open the **Project Properties** dialog box.
2. On the **General** tab, set the **Project Name**.

   This is the most important property of any new component. It identifies your component in the Windows registry and the Object Browser; its uniqueness is therefore important.

   It's also the default name of the compiled component, and the name of the *type library* that contains descriptions of the objects and interfaces provided by your component. See "Polymorphism, Interfaces, Type Libraries, and GUIDs," later in this chapter.
3. On the **General** tab, set the **Project Description**.

   Project description is the text string a developer or user will see when setting a reference to your component, or when selecting your control component in the **Components** dialog box.
4. On the **General** tab, set the **Startup Object**.

   Click **None** if there is no code you need to execute to initialize your component. If your component requires initialization, click **Sub Main**, add a module to your project, and in that module declare a Public Sub named Main. Place your initialization code in this Sub procedure.

   > **Important** See "Starting and Ending a Component" later in this chapter for an explanation of the need to keep the processing in Sub Main to a minimum.

   > **Note** Do not place Sub Main in a class module. Placing Sub Main in a class module turns it into a method named Main, rather than a startup procedure.

Setting Other Properties

Depending on the type of component you're creating, other project properties may be of interest to you.

Unattended Execution

Located on the General tab, this property can be set for code components that have no user interaction. In an ActiveX DLL project, this makes the DLL thread-safe (via Apartment-model threading).

In an ActiveX EXE project, it allows the component to be multithreaded. The implications and limitations of this property are discussed in Chapter 8, "Building Code Components."

> **Note** Components that contain UserDocuments, UserControls, and forms cannot be marked for Unattended Execution.

Help File Name and Project Help Context ID

Providing a Help file for your component is highly recommended. See "Providing User Assistance for ActiveX Components," in Chapter 7, "Debugging, Testing, and Deploying Components," for information on linking help topics to the properties and methods of the classes your component provides.

Start Mode

For out-of-process components that will double as standalone desktop applications, the Start Mode property on the Components tab allows you to debug both startup modes, as discussed in "Debugging Out-of-Process Components," in Chapter 7, "Debugging, Testing, and Deploying Components."

Make Tab Properties

Properties on the Make tab allow you to control file version numbers and version information about your component. Use of this tab to provide such information is highly recommended.

> **Important** Incrementing file version numbers is extremely important for components, as it helps ensure that Setup for your component will never overwrite a newer version with an older one.

Version Compatibility

On the Component tab, you can select a Version Compatibility mode. For new projects, this option is automatically set to Project Compatibility the first time you compile your component, as discussed in "How to Test ActiveX Components," in Chapter 7, "Debugging, Testing, and Deploying Components."

For successive versions of your component, you can select Binary Compatibility to ensure that programs compiled with old versions continue to work with the new version. See "Version Compatibility in ActiveX Components," in Chapter 7, "Debugging, Testing, and Deploying Components."

Compile Tab Properties

Properties on the compile tab allow you to select p-code or native code for your compiled component, as discussed in Chapter 8, "More About Programming," in the *Microsoft Visual Basic 6.0 Programmer's Guide.*

Remote Server

In the Enterprise Edition of Visual Basic, setting this Component tab property generates the support files required to run your component on a remote computer.

Polymorphism, Interfaces, Type Libraries, and GUIDs

Components deliver services by providing classes from which clients can create objects. Clients use services by creating objects and calling their properties and methods.

Information about the classes provided by your component is contained in a type library. In Visual Basic, the type library is included as a resource in the compiled component. Clients access the type library by setting references to it.

Setting the Type Library Name

Project Name, on the General tab of the Project Properties dialog box, sets the name of your component's type library, and is used to qualify the names of classes. For example, the following code fragment declares a variable that will hold a reference to an object of the Widget class, provided by a component whose project name is SmallMechanicals:

```
Public gwdgDriveLink As SmallMechanicals.Widget
```

Some applications can manipulate objects, but cannot declare variables of a specific object type. Such applications declare generic object variables As Object, and use the project name in the *projectname* argument of the CreateObject function to get a new object reference, as shown in the following syntax:

Set *objectvariable* = **CreateObject(**"*projectname.class*"**)**

The combination of project name and class name is sometimes referred to as a *fully qualified class name*, or as a *programmatic ID*. The fully qualified class name may be required to correctly identify an object as belonging to your component. For example, you might implement a Window class in your component. Microsoft Excel also provides a Window object, which could lead to the following confusion for client applications:

```
' A variable of the Microsoft Excel Window class.
Dim xlWindow As Excel.Window
' A variable of the ProgramX component's Window class.
Dim pxWindow As ProgramX.Window
' A variable of the Window class that belongs to the
```

```
'   component - Microsoft Excel or ProgramX - that
'   appears first in the client application's
'   References dialog box!
Dim xWindow As Window
```

Default Interfaces

An interface is a set of properties and methods, or events. Every class provided by your component has at least one interface, called the *default interface*, which is composed of all the properties and methods you declare in the class module.

The default interface is usually referred to by the same name as the class, though its actual name is the class name preceded by an underscore. The underscore prefix is a convention, signifying that the name is hidden in the type library.

If the class raises events, it also has an IConnectionPointContainer interface that enumerates those events. Events are outgoing interfaces, as opposed to the incoming interfaces composed of properties and methods. In other words, clients make requests by calling *into* your class's properties and methods, while the events raised by your class call *out* to event handlers in clients.

Incoming and outgoing interfaces are symbolized differently in interface diagrams, as shown in Figure 6.1.

Figure 6.1 Incoming and outgoing interfaces

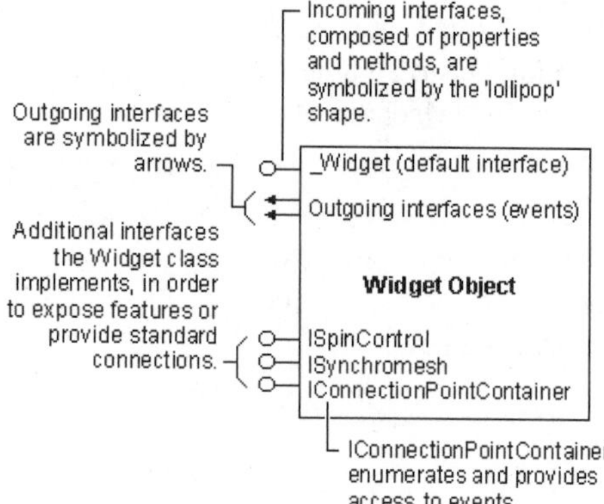

> **Important** You should consider interfaces as contracts between you and the user of your component, because changing an interface may cause applications compiled against your component to fail.

Visual Basic provides two mechanisms for enhancing components without affecting compiled applications: version compatibility for interfaces, and multiple interfaces. In order to discuss these mechanisms, however, you have to learn to dig GUIDs.

Type Libraries, Interfaces, and GUIDs

GUID (pronounced *goo*-id) stands for Globally Unique IDentifier, a 128-bit (16-byte) number generated by an algorithm designed to ensure its uniqueness. This algorithm is part of the Open Software Foundation (OSF) Distributed Computing Environment (DCE), a set of standards for distributed computing.

GUIDs are used to uniquely identify entries in the Windows registry. For example, Visual Basic automatically generates a GUID that identifies your type library in the Windows registry.

Visual Basic also automatically generates a GUID for each public class and interface in your component. These are usually referred to as *class IDs* (CLSID) and *interface IDs* (IID). Class IDs and interface IDs are the keys to version compatibility for components authored using Visual Basic.

> **Note** You may also see GUIDs referred to as UUIDs, or Universally Unique IDentifiers.

What If Visual Basic Runs Out of GUIDs?

This is not a problem we need to worry about in our lifetimes. The algorithm that generates GUIDs would allow you to compile several new versions of your component every second for centuries — without repeating or colliding with GUIDs generated by other developers.

Version Compatibility for Interfaces

When a developer compiles a program that uses your component, the class IDs and interface IDs of any objects the program creates are included in the executable.

The program uses the class ID to request that your component create an object, and then queries the object for the interface ID. An error occurs if the interface ID no longer exists.

During development of a new component Visual Basic generates new CLSIDs and IIDs every time you compile, as long as either Project Compatibility or No Compatibility is selected on the Component tab of the Project Properties dialog box. Once you've released a component, however, and begin working on an enhanced version of it, you can use the Binary Version Compatibility feature of Visual Basic to change this behavior.

As described in detail in "Version Compatibility in ActiveX Components," in Chapter 7, "Debugging, Testing, and Deploying Components," binary version compatibility preserves the class IDs and interface IDs from previous versions of your component. This allows applications compiled using previous versions to work with the new version.

To ensure compatibility, Visual Basic places certain restrictions on changes you make to default interfaces. Visual Basic allows you to add new classes, and to enhance the default interface of any existing class by adding properties and methods. Removing classes, properties, or methods, or changing the arguments of existing properties or methods, will cause Visual Basic to issue incompatibility warnings.

If you decide to ship an incompatible interface, Visual Basic changes the major version number of the type library and suggests that you change the executable name and Project Name, so that the new version of your component will not over-write the old on your users' hard disks.

Multiple Interfaces: Polymorphism and Compatibility

The Implements statement, discussed in "Polymorphism," in Chapter 9, "Programming with Objects," in the *Microsoft Visual Basic 6.0 Programmer's Guide,* allows your classes to implement additional interfaces.

When two classes implement the same secondary interface, they are said to be *polymorphic* with respect to that interface. That is, a client can make early-bound calls to the properties and methods of the interface without having to know the class of the object it's using.

By creating standard interfaces and implementing them in multiple classes, provided by one or more components, you can take advantage of polymorphism in your applications, or across your entire organization.

For More Information "Creating Standard Interfaces with Visual Basic," later in this chapter, explains how to create interfaces by defining class modules that have no implementation code.

Interfaces and Compatibility

Multiple interfaces provide an alternate means of enhancing and evolving your components while maintaining compatibility with older applications compiled against earlier versions.

The ActiveX rule you must follow to ensure compatibility with multiple interfaces is simple: *once an interface is in use, it can never be changed.* The interface ID of a standard interface is fixed by the type library that defines the interface.

The way to enhance standard interfaces is to create a new standard interface, embodying the enhancements. Future components, or future versions of existing components, can implement the old interface, the new interface, or both, as shown in Figure 6.2.

Figure 6.2 Providing compatibility with multiple interfaces

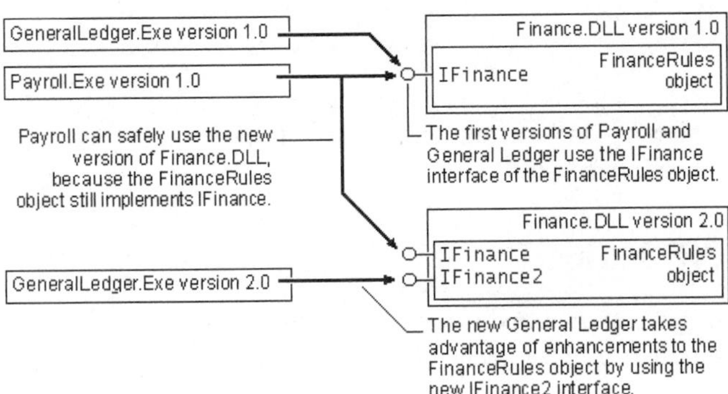

The IFinance and IFinance2 interfaces are defined in separate type libraries, which are referenced by the components that implement the interfaces (in this case, versions 1.0 and 2.0 of Finance.dll), and by the applications that use the interfaces (Payroll and GeneralLedger).

System evolution is possible because future applications can take advantage of new interfaces. Existing applications will continue to work with new versions of components, as long as the components continue to implement the old interfaces as well as the new.

Applications That Work with Multiple Versions of Components

You can write applications that can use any of several versions of a component. For example, version 2.0 of GeneralLedger.exe could be written to use IFinance2 if that interface was available, and to use IFinance otherwise.

Obviously, GeneralLedger would be able to provide only a limited set of features in the latter case. This ability to provide limited functionality in the absence of the preferred interface is often referred to as *degrading gracefully*.

To work with either interface, GeneralLedger might contain code like the following:

```
Dim fnr As FinanceRules
Dim ifin As IFinance
Dim ifin2 As IFinance2

On Error Resume Next
Set fnr = New FinanceRules
' (Error handling code omitted.)
' Attempt to access the preferred interface.
Set ifin2 = fnr
If Err.Number <> 0 Then
   ' Access the more limited interface.
   Set ifin = fnr
   ' (Code to provide limited functionality,
   '   using the object variable ifin.)
```

```
Else
    ' (Code to provide full functionality,
    '    using the object variable ifin2.)
End If
```

For More Information "Providing Polymorphism by Implementing Interfaces," later in this chapter, discusses the use and naming of standard interfaces.

Starting and Ending a Component

Your component starts the first time a client application requests an object from one of your classes. A new instance of the class is created, and the client receives a reference to the newly created object.

If your component has a Sub Main procedure, it will execute when the first object is requested. The object will not be created until Sub Main has finished.

> **Important** Don't execute lengthy initialization activities in Sub Main, as this may cause object creation to time out and fail.

You should not show forms or user messages from your Sub Main, because they can cause the same problems as lengthy initialization tasks. Visual Basic does not allow forms as start up objects in ActiveX EXE and ActiveX DLL projects, for precisely this reason.

A desktop application that provides objects should test App.StartMode, and show its main form only if it was started standalone. In this case, Sub Main may happen long before the first object is requested.

> **Note** If you have selected ActiveX Component for the Start Mode option, on the Component tab of the Project Properties dialog box, Sub Main will not execute immediately when you put your component into run mode. Visual Basic does this to allow accurate debugging of your startup code. Once your component is compiled, Sub Main will not execute until the first time a client requests an object, so the development environment exactly duplicates this behavior.

Handling Lengthy Initialization Tasks

You can perform initialization in the Class_Initialize event of the first object created. When initialization is complete, set a global flag so that subsequent instances of the class don't execute the initialization task.

Alternatively, you can defer some initialization tasks until the service is actually needed. In this case, each object must test before using the service, to ensure it has been initialized — and to initialize it if it has not. This technique works best when initialization consists of many small, independent tasks.

A very large initialization task that cannot be broken up can be performed in the background, using a call-back timer. You can start the timer at the end of Sub Main, as discussed in Chapter 8, "Building Code Components." In the timer's Tick event, disable the timer and run the lengthy task. At the end of the Tick event, set a global flag to indicate that the component is initialized. You can then notify any objects that have been created while initialization was in progress.

> **Important** Don't use a Timer control for this purpose, because the Timer control requires a form to be loaded.

When you use this technique, make sure each object tests the global flag during its own Initialize event. If the component is not initialized, each object should insert itself into a global collection, so it can be notified when background initialization is complete.

You can add a notification method — for example NotifyInitComplete — to each class. Make this a Friend method, so it's only visible within your component.

For More Information Friend methods are discussed in "Private Communications Between Your Objects," later in this chapter.

Component Shutdown

Your component should shut down when all clients have released all references to the objects the component provides. (A desktop application that provides objects is an exception to this rule.)

Visual Basic does a number of things to make it easy for your component to shut down properly. The most important of these is keeping track of references to your public objects, because your component should never close while clients still hold references to objects.

> **Important** Only references to *public* objects will keep a component running. References to private objects — objects provided by Visual Basic, or objects from classes marked Private — will not prevent component shutdown and subsequent catastrophic failure of the client. References to private objects should never be passed to clients.

The rules Visual Basic uses to determine when to shut down are different for in-process and out-of-process components.

Out-of-Process Component Shut Down

An out-of-process component written with Visual Basic will shut down when:

- The component has no forms loaded.

  A loaded form will keep your component running past the point at which all references have been released. Forms should be unloaded when the object that created them terminates.

- No out-of-process client applications are holding references to the component's public objects.

Internal references to public objects *will not* keep a component running if clients have released all their references. Neither will references held by an in-process component the out-of-process component is using.

- No code in the component's modules is currently executing, or in the calls list waiting to be executed.
- The component is not in the process of being started in response to a client application's request for an object.

In-Process Component Shut Down

In the long run, the lifetime of an in-process component is controlled by its client, because the component runs in the client's process. When the client closes, the component is unloaded regardless of any outstanding object references, open forms, and so on.

A client may ask an in-process component to unload when the client is no longer using objects the component provides. The following rules describe the way a Visual Basic in-process component determines whether it should unload in response to a client request.

- The component has no forms visible.

  A visible form will keep your component in memory, even if there are no object references; an invisible form will not.

- There are no references to the component's public objects.

  If your in-process component is holding a reference to one of its own public objects, Visual Basic will not unload it. Visual Basic cannot tell whether the reference is internal or external.

- No code in the component's modules is currently executing, or in the calls list waiting to be executed.
- The component is not in the process of being started in response to a client application's request for an object.

  Note A client application written in Visual Basic may not attempt to unload an in-process component immediately after the last reference is released. The frequency of attempts depends on how frequently idle time becomes available; in general it will be around two minutes.

For More Information A more complete discussion of the rules for component shutdown can be found in "ActiveX Component Shutdown," in Appendix A, "ActiveX Component Standards and Guidelines."

Adding Classes to Components

Only one thing distinguishes a component from other applications you author using Visual Basic: A component project has at least one public class from which client applications can create objects.

Like any other Visual Basic application, your component may have numerous class modules that encapsulate its internal functionality. When you allow clients to create instances of a class, objects created from that class can be manipulated by clients, and your application becomes a component.

Creating New Classes

From the Project menu, you can choose Add Class Module, Add User Control, or Add User Document to define a new public class. Other choices on the Project menu allow you to add objects that can be used within your application, but only UserControls, UserDocuments, and class modules can define public classes.

Each public class you add will be the blueprint for one kind of public object in your object model. You can provide a class name, define interfaces for the class, and set the Instancing property (or the Public property, in some cases) to determine how objects will be created from the class.

Name Property

Choose class names carefully. They should be short but descriptive, and formed from whole words with individual words capitalized — for example, BusinessRule.

The class name is combined with the name of the component to produce a fully qualified class name, also referred to as a *programmatic ID* or *ProgID*. For example, the fully qualified class name of a BusinessRule class provided by the Finance component, is `Finance.BusinessRule`.

The topic "What's in a Name?" earlier in this chapter, outlines the rules for naming classes, properties, and methods.

Defining Interfaces

The default interface for a class is composed of the properties and methods you define for it, as discussed in "Adding Properties and Methods to Classes," later in this chapter.

The default interface of a class is an *incoming interface*, as explained in "Polymorphism, Interfaces, Type Libraries, and GUIDs" earlier in this chapter. You can also add *outgoing interfaces*, or events, as described in "Adding Events to Classes" later in this chapter.

Visual Basic includes information about the class module's default interface and outgoing interfaces in the type library it creates when your component is compiled.

For More Information You can implement additional incoming interfaces on a class, as described in "Providing Polymorphism by Implementing Interfaces" later in this chapter.

Public or Instancing Property

UserControl classes have a Public property that determines whether the class is public or private. UserDocument classes are always public. This is discussed in the in-depth chapters on ActiveX controls and documents, Chapter 9, "Building ActiveX Controls," and Chapter 11, "Building ActiveX Documents."

Class modules have a more complex public life, controlled by the Instancing property. For each class your component will provide to other applications, set the Instancing property of the class module to any value *except* Private, as discussed in the related section "Instancing for Classes Provided by ActiveX Components."

You don't have to make all your classes public; if there are objects you want to use only within your component, set the Instancing properties of the class modules that define them to Private. (For a UserControl, set the Public property to False.)

For More Information Class modules in Visual Basic are introduced in Chapter 9, "Programming with Objects," in the *Microsoft Visual Basic 6.0 Programmer's Guide*. Topics specific to classes defined in class modules, ActiveX controls, and ActiveX documents are discussed in depth in Chapter 8, "Building Code Components"; Chapter 9, "Building ActiveX Controls"; and Chapter 11, "Building ActiveX Documents." Object models are discussed in "Organizing Objects: The Object Model," later in this chapter.

Instancing for Classes Provided by ActiveX Components

The value of the Instancing property determines whether your class is private — that is, for use only within your component — or available for other applications to use.

As its name suggests, the Instancing property also determines how other applications create instances of the class. The property values have the following meanings.

- *Private* means that other applications aren't allowed access to type library information about the class, and cannot create instances of it. Private objects are only for use within your component.
- *PublicNotCreatable* means that other applications can use objects of this class only if your component creates the objects first. Other applications cannot use the CreateObject function or the New operator to create objects from the class.
- *MultiUse* allows other applications to create objects from the class. One instance of your component can provide any number of objects created in this fashion.

  An out-of-process component can supply multiple objects to multiple clients; an in-process component can supply multiple objects to the client and to any other components in its process.

- *GlobalMultiUse* is like MultiUse, with one addition: properties and methods of the class can be invoked as if they were simply global functions. It's not necessary to explicitly create an instance of the class first, because one will automatically be created.
- *SingleUse* allows other applications to create objects from the class, but every object of this class that a client creates starts a new instance of your component. Not allowed in ActiveX DLL projects.
- *GlobalSingleUse* is like SingleUse, except that properties and methods of the class can be invoked as if they were simply global functions. Not allowed in ActiveX DLL projects.

Class Modules and Project Types

The value of the Instancing property is restricted in certain project types. Allowed values are shown in the following table:

Instancing Value	ActiveX EXE	ActiveX DLL	ActiveX Control
Private	Yes	Yes	Yes
PublicNotCreatable	Yes	Yes	Yes
MultiUse	Yes	Yes	
GlobalMultiUse	Yes	Yes	
SingleUse	Yes		
GlobalSingleUse	Yes		

Dependent Objects (PublicNotCreatable)

The value of the Instancing property determines the part an object plays in your component's object model, as discussed in "Organizing Objects: The Object Model."

If the Instancing property of a class is PublicNotCreatable, objects of that class are called *dependent objects*. Dependent objects are typically parts of more complex objects.

For example, you might allow a client application to create multiple Library objects, but you might want Book objects to exist only as parts of a Library. You can make the Book class PublicNotCreatable, and let the user add new books to a Library object by giving the Library class a Books collection with an Add method that creates new books only within the collection.

Your component can support as many dependent objects as necessary. You can write code in the Add method of a collection class to limit the number of objects in the collection, or you can allow the number to be limited by available memory.

For More Information Dependent objects are discussed in detail in "Dependent Objects," later in this chapter.

Externally Creatable Objects

All values of the Instancing property besides PublicNotCreatable and Private define externally creatable objects — that is, objects that clients can create using the New operator or the CreateObject function.

MultiUse vs. SingleUse

In ActiveX DLLs, Instancing for an externally creatable class will most commonly be MultiUse. This setting allows an in-process component to supply any number of instances of the class to the client executable, and to any other in-process component.

For ActiveX EXEs, the Instancing values SingleUse and MultiUse define very different behaviors for a class. MultiUse makes the most efficient use of memory, because it allows one instance of your component to provide multiple objects to multiple client applications without duplication of resources or global data.

For example, suppose the SmallMechanicals component provides a Widget class, and the Instancing property of the class is set to MultiUse. If one client application creates two Widget objects, or if two client applications each create a Widget object, all the Widgets will be supplied from one instance of your component.

If the Instancing property of the Widget class is set to SingleUse, the result of both scenarios above is that a separate copy of your component will be loaded into memory for each Widget created. The uses and limitations of this behavior are discussed in Chapter 8, "Building Code Components," and in Appendix A, "ActiveX Component Standards and Guidelines."

MultiUse and Multithreading

If your component is an ActiveX EXE marked for unattended execution (that is, it has no user interaction whatever), and the Instancing property of the Widget class is set to MultiUse, the result of both scenarios above is that two Widget objects are created in same copy of SmallMechanicals, each on its own thread of execution.

Apartment Model threading is used, meaning that each thread is like an apartment, and objects in different apartments are unaware of each other's existence. This is accomplished by giving each Widget its own copy of the SmallMechanicals component's global data.

For More Information The use of multithreading or SingleUse instancing to avoid blocked execution is discussed in Chapter 8, "Building Code Components."

Global Objects

Frequently it's useful to have utility functions that users of your component can employ without first creating an instance of one of your objects. In out-of-process components, such functions are frequently implemented as properties or methods of the Application object.

If the Instancing property for a class is marked GlobalMultiUse or GlobalSingleUse, then properties and methods of the class can be invoked without explicitly creating an instance of the object.

For example, suppose you want your SmallMechanicals component to provide a GlobalUtility object whose methods are general-purpose functions. You can add a class module to the SmallMechanicals project, set the Name property to GlobalUtility, and set the Instancing property to GlobalMultiUse.

Now you can add properties and methods to the class module. For example, you might implement a ReversePolarity method and a read-only WidgetCount property:

```
Public Sub ReversePolarity()
   ' (Code to reverse polarity on all Widgets.)
End Sub
```

In the client application, the ReversePolarity method can be invoked without first creating a GlobalUtility object:

```
Private Sub Command1_Click()
   ' No object variable is required.
   ReversePolarity
End Sub
```

> **Note** The properties and methods of a GlobalMultiUse object are not part of the global name space of the component that provides the object. For example, within a project that contains the GlobalUtility class, you must explicitly create an instance of GlobalUtility in order to use the object's properties and methods. Other limitations of global objects are listed in "Global Objects and Code Libraries," in Chapter 8, "Building Code Components."

Be careful when choosing names for the properties and methods of global objects. Using common or obvious names may result in name collisions with other components. Name conflicts must be resolved by qualifying the property or method with the type library name:

```
Private Sub Command1_Click()
   SmallMechanicals.ReversePolarity
   Esalen.ReversePolarity
End Sub
```

> **Important** The "global" in global objects refers to the fact that all of the object's properties and methods are available in the global name space of your project. It does *not* mean that one object is automatically shared by all clients. Each client that uses your component gets its own global object.

For More Information "Providing Named Constants for Your Component," later in this chapter, discusses the use of global objects to provide string constants and non-integer constants. Code components are discussed in depth in Chapter 8, "Building Code Components."

Coding Robust Initialize and Terminate Events

Classes you define in Visual Basic, whether class modules, UserControls, or UserDocuments, have built-in Initialize and Terminate events. The code you place in the Initialize event will be the first code executed when an object is created.

For example, in the first part of the following code fragment the Widget class of the SmallMechanicals component sets the value of its read-only Created property at the moment an object is created.

```
' Code for the component's Widget class module.
' Storage for the read-only Created property.
Private mdatCreated As Date

' Implementation of the read-only Created property.
Public Property Get Created() As Date
   Created = mdatCreated
End Property
' Set the value for the read-only Created property when ' the object is created.  Private
Sub Class_Initialize()
   mdatCreated = Now
End Sub
' Code for the client application.
Private Sub cmdOK_Click()
   Dim wdgX As New SmallMechanicals.Widget
   ' Display date/time object was created.
   MsgBox wdgX.Created
End Sub
```

In the last part of the code fragment, the client creates a Widget object. The variable `wdgX` will contain the reference to the Widget object; it is declared As New, so the Widget is created at the first use of `wdgX` in code. When the MsgBox function is executed, the Widget is created, and the very first code it executes is its Class_Initialize event procedure. When the read-only Created property of the newly created Widget is evaluated, its value has already been set, and therefore MsgBox correctly displays the time the Widget was created.

Errors that occur in the Class_Initialize event procedure are returned to the point in the client at which the object was requested. Thus, adding the following line to the Widget's Class_Initialize event procedure will cause error 31013 to occur on the client's MsgBox statement.

```
   Err.Raise Number:=31013
```

Handling Errors in the Terminate Event

The Terminate event is the last event in an object's life. You can place cleanup code in the Class_Terminate event procedure, and this code will be executed when the last reference to the object has been released, and the object is about to be destroyed. Complex objects that contain dependent objects should release references to their dependent objects in the Terminate event.

Errors in the Terminate event require careful handling. Because the Terminate event is not called by the client application, there is no procedure above it on the call stack. *This means that an unhandled error in a Terminate event will cause a fatal error in the component.*

> **Important** For in-process components, your fatal error is your client's fatal error. Because the component is running in the client's process, the client application will be terminated by a component's fatal error.

Standard Modules vs. Class Modules

Classes differ from standard modules in the way their data is stored. There is never more than one copy of a standard module's data. This means that when one part of your program changes a public variable in a standard module, and another part of your program subsequently reads that variable, it will get the same value.

Class module data, on the other hand, exists separately for each instance of the class.

Avoid making the code in your classes dependent on global data — that is, public variables in standard modules. Many instances of a class can exist simultaneously, and all of these objects share the global data in your component.

Static Class Data

Using global variables in class module code violates the object-oriented programming concept of encapsulation, because objects created from such a class do not contain all their data. However, there may be occasions when you want a data member to be shared among all objects created from a class module. For example, you might want all objects created from a class to share a property value, such as the name or version number of your component.

This deliberate violation of encapsulation is sometimes referred to as *static class data*. You can implement static class data in a Visual Basic class module by using Property procedures to set and return the value of a Public data member in a standard module, as in the following code fragment:

```
' Read-only property returning application name.
Property Get ComponentName() As String
   ' The variable gstrComponentName is stored in a
   '   standard module, and declared Public.
   ComponentName = gstrComponentName
End Property
```

You can implement static class data that is not read-only by providing a corresponding Property Let procedure — or Property Set for a property that contains an object reference — to assign a new value to the standard module data member.

Important When designing a class that uses static data, remember that your component may be providing objects simultaneously to several client applications (if it's an out-of-process component) or to a client and several in-process components (if it's an in-process component). All the objects created from the class will share the static data, even if they're being used by different clients.

Adding Properties and Methods to Classes

The default interface of a class in your component is simply the set of all public properties, methods, and events in the class module, UserControl, or UserDocument that defines the class.

Adding properties and methods is easy — a method is any Public Sub or Public Function procedure you declare in the module that defines your class; a property is any public property procedure or public variable you declare.

Important The following names cannot be used as property or method names, because they belong to the underlying IUnknown and IDispatch interfaces: QueryInterface, AddRef, Release, GetTypeInfoCount, GetTypeInfo, GetIDsOfNames, and Invoke. These names will cause a compilation error.

For More Information The mechanics of property and method declaration are discussed in "Adding Properties to a Class" and "Adding Methods to a Class," in Chapter 9, "Programming with Objects," in the *Microsoft Visual Basic 6.0 Programmer's Guide*.

Implementing Properties in Components

"Adding Properties to a Class," in Chapter 9, "Programming with Objects," in the *Microsoft Visual Basic 6.0 Programmer's Guide* discusses in detail the many kinds of properties you can add to your classes, including simple data values, read-only properties, and property arrays.

"Adding Properties to a Class" also describes the two ways you can declare properties: as public variables, or as property procedures.

In general, properties of objects provided by components should be implemented as property procedures. Property procedures are more robust than data members. A property whose type is an enumeration, for example, cannot be validated unless implemented as a Property Get and Property Let.

The only exception to this rule is a simple numeric or string property which requires no validation and which, when changed, does not immediately affect other properties of the object.

An object property — that is, any property that contains an object reference instead of an ordinary data type — should almost always be implemented with property procedures. An object property implemented as a public object variable can be set to Nothing accidentally, possibly destroying the object. This is discussed in "Organizing Objects: The Object Model," later in this chapter.

> **Note** Internally, Visual Basic generates a pair of property procedures for every public variable you declare. For this reason, declaring public variables doesn't provide any size or performance benefits.

For More Information See "Adding Properties to a Class," in Chapter 9, "Programming with Objects," in the *Microsoft Visual Basic 6.0 Programmer's Guide.*

Persisting a Component's Data

Most components have properties; in most cases you'll want to establish default values for those properties in the Initialize event of the class. Those default values are frozen when you compile the component, so how do you allow a developer to change the default values to meet their own special conditions? Classes have a special property, Persistable, that allows you to store a component's values between instances.

Suppose that you had an ActiveX DLL that calculates loans, with an InterestRate property used in the calculations. You could initialize the InterestRate to some arbitrary value, but since interest rates periodically go up or down, the InterestRate property would need to be modified each time the component is run. With class persistence, you can store the InterestRate value and modify it only when the interest rate changes. Each time your component is run it can retrieve the InterestRate from storage, so the component will always provide the latest rate.

While ActiveX controls have always been able to persist their data, persistence for ActiveX components is slightly different. A control stores property settings inside its .cls file, but a component can't do that. Instead, it uses a PropertyBag object that can be saved just about anywhere — in a file, a database, a cell in a spreadsheet, or even in the registry.

For More Information To learn more about persisting ActiveX controls, see "Saving the Properties of Your Control," in Chapter 9, "Building an ActiveX Control."

Setting Up Class Persistence

In order to be persistable, a class must meet two conditions: it must be public and creatable. If you think about it, this makes sense — after all, persistence wouldn't be useful in a private component. If a class meets both conditions, the Persistable property appears in the Properties window.

By default, the Persistable property is set to 0 (NotPersistable). By changing this value to 1 (Persistable), three new events are added to the class: ReadProperties, WriteProperties, and InitProperties. As you might guess, these events are use to read, write, and initialize the class's properties.

Persisting a Property

You can mark a property as persistable by implementing the PropertyChanged method in a Property Let or Property Set procedure, as in the following example:

```
Private mInterestRate As Single
Public Property Let InterestRate(newRate As Single)
   mInterestRate = newRate
   PropertyChanged "InterestRate"
End Sub
```

Calling the PropertyChanged method marks the InterestRate property as dirty. The WriteProperties event will fire when the class is terminated if any property in the class has called PropertyChanged.

The ReadProperties, WriteProperties, and InitProperties Events

The WriteProperties event procedure is used when a class is terminating to write the current property values to a private storage known as a PropertyBag object. The following code is used to save a property to the built-in PropertyBag:

```
Private Sub Class_WriteProperties(PropBag As PropertyBag)
   PropBag.WriteProperty "InterestRate", mInterestRate, conDefaultRate
End Sub
```

The PropertyBag's WriteProperty method in the above code takes three arguments: the name of the property to save ("InterestRate"), the value to save (mInterestRate), and a default value (DefaultRate). If the new value matches the constant conDefaultRate, the WriteProperty method doesn't have to write out the value.

The ReadProperties event is fired when a class is initialized — but only if the PropertyBag has something in it. If the PropertyBag is empty, the InitProperties event will be fired instead. Code in the ReadProperties and InitProperties events is used to set the initial property values:

```
Private Sub Class_ReadProperties(PropBag As PropertyBag)
   mInterestRate = PropBag.ReadProperty("InterestRate", conDefaultRate)
End Sub
Private Sub Class_InitProperties ()
   mInterestRate = conDefaultRate
End Sub
```

Note that the constant conDefaultRate is used in both procedures to provide a default value. By using a constant to define the default values you eliminate the risk of accidentally defining different default values in different procedures.

When you first create an instance of the Loan class using the New keyword, the InitProperties event will be fired; once the class has been persisted and is then recreated, the ReadProperties event will be fired instead.

Using the PropertyBag Object to Persist an Object

In order to persist an ActiveX component, you need to create an instance of a PropertyBag object. This may seem redundant — after all, the class already has it's own PropertyBag. Why can't you just use that? Simple. When the object goes away, so does its PropertyBag. It only exists in memory; for persistence you need to store a copy of the object somewhere so you can retrieve it later.

Think of a PropertyBag as a sack that you can fill up with stuff and stash away somewhere for safekeeping. Where you stash it is entirely up to you. The following form code demonstrates how you can persist an object to a text file:

```
Private pb As PropertyBag      ' Declare a PropertyBag object.
Private LoanObject As Loan     ' Declare a Loan object.

Private Sub Form_Unload(Cancel As Integer)
   Dim varTemp as Variant

   ' Instantiate the PropertyBag object.
   Set pb = New PropertyBag
   ' Save the object to the PropertyBag using WriteProperty.
   pb.WriteProperty "MyLoanObject", LoanObject
   ' Assign the Contents of the PropertyBag to a Variant.
   varTemp = pb.Contents
   ' Save to a text file.
   Open "C:\Loandata.txt" For Binary As #1
   Put #1, , varTemp
   Close #1
End Sub
```

The Contents property of the PropertyBag object contains the Loan object stored as an array of bytes. In order to save it to a text file, you first must convert it to a data type that a text file understands — in this case, a Variant.

Depersisting an Object

Once the object is contained inside a text file (or any other type of storage), it can easily be transported to another location. Imagine that our Loan object contains not only the InterestRate, but also property values, to represent all of the fields in a loan application. You could take the Loandata.txt file and send it to the central office for approval. The code for a form that would reuse the Loan object would look something like this:

```
Private pb As PropertyBag      ' Declare a PropertyBag object.
Private LoanObject As Loan     ' Declare a Loan object.

Private Sub Form_Load()
   Dim varTemp As Variant
   Dim byteArr() as Byte
```

```
    ' Instantiate the PropertyBag object.
    Set pb = New PropertyBag
    ' Read the file contents into a Variant.
    Open "C:\Loandata.txt" For Binary As #1
    Get #1, , varTemp
    Close #1
    ' Assign the Variant to a Byte array.
    ByteArr = varTemp
    ' Assign to the PropertyBag Contents property.
    Pb.Contents  = ByteArr
    ' Instantiate the object from the PropertyBag
    Set LoanObject = pb.ReadProperty("MyLoanObject")
End If
```

You may have noticed that the object had to be assigned three times: first from the text file to a Variant, then from a Variant to a Byte array, then to the Contents property. That's because the Contents property will only accept a Byte array — if you tried to assign any other data type you would get an error.

So what's going on here? Can you actually take an object created in one place and reuse it in another, complete with its data? Well, not exactly. The original object is long gone. What you are passing in a PropertyBag is an exact copy of the object, not the object itself. This ability to "clone" an object for reuse is a powerful concept, especially when it comes to designing workflow applications.

Implementing Methods in Components

When you declare a method, declare all of its arguments as explicit data types whenever possible. Arguments that take object references should be declared as specific class types — for example, As Widget instead of As Object or As Variant.

Strongly typed arguments allow many user errors to be caught by the compiler, rather than occurring only under run-time conditions. The compiler always catches errors, while run-time testing is only as good as the test suite coverage.

This is as true of optional parameters as it is of the method's fixed parameters. For example, the Spin method of a hypothetical Widget object might allow either direct specification of spin direction and speed, or specification of another Widget object from which angular momentum is to be absorbed:

```
Public Sub Spin( _
   Optional ByVal SpinDirection As Boolean = True, _
   Optional ByVal Torque As Double = 0, _
   Optional ByVal ReactingWidget As Widget = Nothing)
   ' (Code to ensure that a valid combination of
   '  arguments was supplied.)
   ' (Implementation code.)
End Sub
```

For More Information See "Adding Methods to a Class," in Chapter 9, "Programming with Objects," in the *Microsoft Visual Basic 6.0 Programmer's Guide.* The choice of ByVal or ByRef arguments may affect the performance of your component, as discussed in "How Marshaling Affects ActiveX Component Performance," in Chapter 8, "Building Code Components."

Data Types Allowed in Properties and Methods

Classes can have properties and methods of any public data type supported by Automation. This includes all arguments of properties and methods, as well their return values. The allowed data types include:

- Public objects provided by another component, such as DAO or a component authored using Visual Basic.
- Public objects provided by Visual Basic for applications, such as the Error and Collection objects.
- Objects defined in public classes in the component.
- Public enumerations declared in public class modules.
- Standard system data types defined by Automation, such as OLE_COLOR and OLE_TRISTATE.
- The intrinsic data types provided by Visual Basic.
- User-defined types.

On the Evils of Returning Private Objects

The following data types are not allowed, and references to them should never be returned to client applications:

- All of the objects provided in the Visual Basic (VB) object library — for example, controls. Use the Object Browser to view the entire list.
- All forms.
- All class modules whose Instancing property is set to Private.
- References to ActiveX controls.

Visual Basic prevents you from passing nonvisual private objects to or from out-of-process components. Attempting to do so causes error 98, "A property or method call cannot include a reference to a private object, either as an argument or as a return value." This error is always received by the client.

In other cases, it is possible to trick Visual Basic and pass private objects to client programs. Don't do this. *References to private objects will not keep a component running.*

If your component shuts down, because all references to your public objects have been released, any remaining private objects will be destroyed, *even if clients still hold references to them.*

Subsequent calls to the properties and methods of these objects will cause errors, in the case of out-of-process components. In the case of in-process components, a fatal program fault may occur in the client.

> **Important** Private objects are private for a reason, usually because they were not designed to be used outside your project. Passing them to a client may decrease program stability and cause incompatibility with future versions of Visual Basic. If you need to pass a private class of your own to a client, set the Instancing property to a value other than Private.

For More Information Chapter 8, "Building Code Components," shows how events can eliminate the need for public call-back classes, allowing Standard EXE projects to use call-backs without providing public objects or passing out references to private objects.

Choosing a Default Property or Method for a Class

You can mark the most commonly used public property or method of a class as the default method. This allows the user of a class to invoke the member without naming it.

To set a property or method as the default

1. On the **Tools** menu, click **Procedure Attributes** to open the **Procedure Attributes** dialog box.
2. Click **Advanced** to expand the **Procedure Attributes** dialog box.
3. In the **Name** box, select the property or method that is currently the default for the class. If the class does not currently have a default member, skip to step 5.

   > **Note** You can use the Object Browser to find out what the current default member of a class is. When you select the class in the Class list, you can scroll through the members in the Members list; the default member will be marked with a small blue circle beside its icon.

4. In the **Procedure ID** box, select **None** to remove the default status of the property or method.
5. In the **Name** box, select the property or method you want to be the new default.
6. In the **Procedure ID** box, select **(Default)**, then click **OK**.

> **Important** A class can have only one default member. If a property or method is already marked as the default, you must reset its procedure ID to None before making another property or method the default. No compile errors will occur if two members are marked as default, but there is no way to predict which one Visual Basic will pick as the default.

Fixing Defaults You Have Accidentally Made Private or Friend

The Procedure Attributes dialog box only allows you to select public properties and methods as the default for a class. If you make a public property or method the default for a class, and later change the declaration to Private or Friend, the property or method may continue to behave as if it were still declared Public.

To correct this problem, you must make the property or method Public again, because the Procedure Attributes dialog box will not show procedures declared Private and Friend. Once you have changed the declaration to Public, you can use the Procedure Attributes dialog to remove the Default attribute. You can then change the declaration back to Friend or Private.

Adding Events to Classes

You can add events to any class in your component. Events declared in classes provided by your component can be handled by clients regardless of whether your component is running in process or out of process. All events are public.

You declare an event using the Event keyword:

```
Event SomethingHappened(ByVal HowMuch As Double, _
      ByVal When As Date)
```

Note You can declare event arguments just as you do arguments of procedures, with the following exceptions: Events cannot have named arguments, optional arguments, or ParamArray arguments. Events do not have return values.

You raise the event from within your class module's code, whenever the circumstances that define the event occur.

```
If blnSomethingHappened Then
   RaiseEvent SomethingHappened(dblPriceIncrease, _
      Now)
End If
```

When the event is raised in an instance of the class, code in the SomethingHappened event procedures of any clients that are handling the event *for that particular object* will be executed. Events must be handled on an object-by-object basis; a client cannot elect to handle an event for all currently existing objects of a particular class.

If multiple clients have references to the same object, and are handling an event it raises, control will not return to your component until all clients have processed the event.

You can allow clients to respond to events by declaring a parameter ByRef instead of ByVal. This allows any client to change the value of the argument. When execution resumes, on the line after RaiseEvent, you can examine the value of this argument and take appropriate action.

This capability is frequently used for Cancel arguments, as with the QueryUnload event of Visual Basic forms.

> **Note** Visual Basic raises a separate QueryUnload event for each form; if one form cancels the event, events for subsequent forms are not raised.

Events can be used instead of call-back functions, as discussed in Chapter 8, "Building Code Components." The capabilities of the two approaches are identical, but implementation of events is much simpler, for you and for the user of your component.

Events cannot be handled within the class that declared them.

For More Information Raising events in controls is discussed in detail in Chapter 9, "Building ActiveX Controls." The syntax for raising and handling events is covered in "Adding Events to a Class," in Chapter 9, "Programming with Objects," in the *Microsoft Visual Basic 6.0 Programmer's Guide.*

Providing Named Constants for Your Component

Enumerations provide an easy way to define a set of related named constants. For example, the built-in enumeration VbDayOfWeek contains numeric constants with the names vbMonday, vbTuesday, and so on.

You can use an enumeration as the data type of a property or method argument, as in the following example:

```
Private mdowDayOfWeek As VbDayOfWeek
Property Get DayOfWeek() As VbDayOfWeek
   DayOfWeek = mdowDayOfWeek
End Property
Property Let DayOfWeek(ByVal NewDay As VbDayOfWeek)
   If (NewDay < vbUseSystemDayOfWeek) _
         Or (NewDay < vbSaturday) Then
      Err.Raise Number:=31013, _
         Description:="Invalid day of week"
   Else
      DayOfWeek = mdowDayOfWeek
   End If
End Property
```

When users of your component enter code that assigns a value to this property, the Auto List Members feature will offer a drop down containing the members of the enumeration, as shown in Figure 6.3.

Figure 6.3 Auto List Members displays enumerations

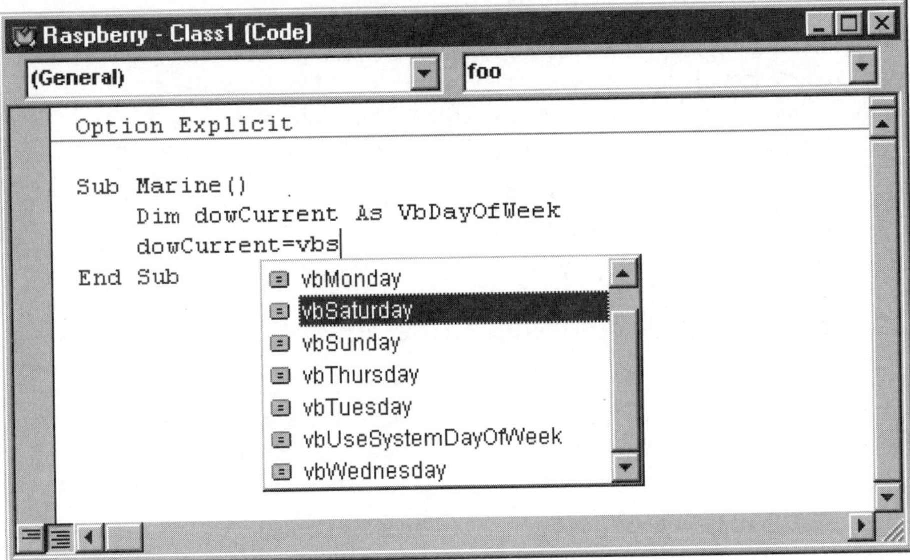

> **Tip** You might think that you could save space by declaring the internal variable `mdowDayOfWeek` As Byte instead of As VbDayOfWeek — since the latter effectively makes the variable a Long. However, on 32-bit operating systems the code to load a Long is faster and more compact than the code to load shorter data types. Not only could the extra code exceed the space saved, but there might not be any space saved to begin with — because of alignment requirements for modules and data.

You can make the members of an enumeration available to users of your component by marking the enumeration Public and including it in any public module that defines a class — that is, a class module, UserControl, or UserDocument.

When you compile your component, the enumeration will be added to the type library. Object browsers will show both the enumeration and its individual members.

> **Note** Although an enumeration must appear in a module that defines a class, it always has global scope in the type library. It is not limited to, or associated in any other way with the class in which you declared it.

General Purpose Enumerations

The members of an enumeration need not be sequential or contiguous. Thus, if you have some general-purpose numeric constants you wish to define for your component, you can put them into a catch-all Enum.

```
Public Enum General
   levsFeetInAMile = 5280
   levsIgnitionTemp = 451
   levsAnswer = 42
End Enum
```

Avoiding Enumeration Name Conflicts

In the preceding code example, both the Enum and its members were prefixed with four lowercase characters chosen to identify the component they belong to, and to reduce the chance that users of the component will encounter name conflicts. This is one of the general naming rules discussed in "What's in a Name?" earlier in this chapter.

For More Information Enumerations are discussed in detail in Chapter 8, "More About Programming," and Chapter 9, "Programming with Objects," in the *Microsoft Visual Basic 6.0 Programmer's Guide.*

Providing Non-Numeric and Non-Integer Constants

The members of an Enum can have any value that fits in a Long. That is, they can assume any integer value from –2,147,483,648 to 2,147,483,647. When you declare a variable using the name of an Enum as the data type, you're effectively declaring the variable As Long.

Occasionally you may need to provide a string constant, or a constant that isn't an integer value. Visual Basic doesn't provide a mechanism for adding such values to your type library as public constants, but you can get a similar effect using a global object with read-only properties.

If your component doesn't contain a global object, such as Application, add a public class module named GlobalConstants to your project. Set the Instancing property to GlobalMultiUse.

For each constant you want to provide, add to the GlobalConstants class module a Property Get procedure that returns the desired value. For example, the following code provides Avogadro's Number as a constant, and mimics the vbCrLf constant in Visual Basic.

```
Public Property Get Avogadro() As Double
   Avogadro = 6.02E+23
End Property
Public Property Get vbCrLf() As String
   vbCrLf = Chr$(13) & Chr$(10)
End Property
```

Because the Instancing property is GlobalMultiUse, a user of the component doesn't have to explicitly create an instance of the GlobalConstants class in order to use the constants. The constants can be used as if they were part of Visual Basic:

```
strNewText = "Line1" & vbCrLf & "Line2"
```

Note A user of Visual Basic, Microsoft Excel, or any other application that hosts Visual Basic for Applications would never see this version of the vbCrLf constant, because the VBA type library is always higher in the References dialog than the type library of any component.

For More Information Global objects are discussed in "Instancing for Classes Provided by ActiveX Components," earlier in this chapter, and in Chapter 8, "Building Code Components."

Private Communications between Your Objects

There may be circumstances in which you want your component's objects to be able to communicate with each other, without interference from users of your component. For example, you might want your Widgets collection class to set the Parent property of a newly created Widget, and thereafter to have Parent be read-only.

Public methods on a class can be called by other objects, but they can also be called by clients. Private methods cannot be called from outside the component, but neither are they visible to other objects within your component.

The solution is to use Friend methods. In the following code fragment, the hypothetical Widget object exposes a public read-only Parent property, and a Friend method (called SetParent) that the Widgets collection can use to set the value of the Parent property after creating a new Widget.

```
' A Widget is always part of a mechanism.
Private mmchParent As Mechanism

Public Property Get Parent() As Mechanism
   Set Parent = mmchParent
End Property
Friend Sub SetParent(ByVal NewParent As Mechanism)
   Set mmchParent = NewParent
End Sub
```

When a method is declared with the Friend keyword, it's visible to other objects in your component, but is not added to the type library or the public interface. This is illustrated in Figure 6.4.

Figure 6.4 Friend methods have project scope

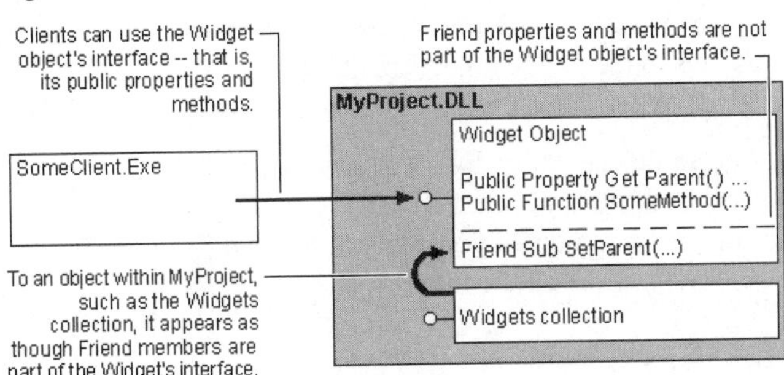
Clients can use the Widget object's interface -- that is, its public properties and methods.
Friend properties and methods are not part of the Widget object's interface.
MyProject.DLL
Widget Object
SomeClient.Exe
Public Property Get Parent() ...
Public Function SomeMethod(...)
Friend Sub SetParent(...)
To an object within MyProject, such as the Widgets collection, it appears as though Friend members are part of the Widget's interface.
Widgets collection

At run time, the Widgets collection class (within the project) sees a different interface from that seen by clients. The view of the Widget's interface within the project (and the compiled DLL) includes the Friend method SetParent, which the Widgets collection calls.

The client only sees the public properties and methods of the Widget's interface, because Friend methods are not added to the type library.

Using the Friend Keyword with Properties

You can also declare property procedures with the Friend keyword. In fact, the different property procedures that make up a property can have different scope. Thus the earlier code example can be rewritten as a pair of property procedures:

```
' A Widget is always part of a mechanism.
Private mmchParent As Mechanism

Public Property Get Parent() As Mechanism
   Set Parent = mmchParent
End Property
Friend Property Set Parent(ByVal NewParent As _
      Mechanism)
   Set mmchParent = NewParent
End Sub
```

From within the component, Parent is a read/write property. To clients, it's a read-only property, because only the Property Get appears in the component's type library.

You can think of Friend as a different scope, halfway between Public and Private.

> **Important** In order to invoke Friend methods and properties, you must use strongly typed object variables. In the example above, the Widgets collection must use a variable declared As Widget in order to access the SetParent method or the Property Set Parent. You cannot invoke Friend methods from variables declared As Object.

Hiding Object Properties that Return Private Objects

"Using Properties and Collections to Create Object Models" describes the use of private objects in object models. When linking such objects to the public objects in the object model, you can declare all parts of the property procedure using the Friend keyword.

For example, each Widget object might have Socket object, which for some reason you don't want to expose to users of your component. You could add the following object property to the Widget object, so that from inside your component you could access the Socket, without adding the property to the type library or the public interface:

```
' Create the Socket object on demand (As New).
Private msoc As New Socket
Friend Property Get Socket() As Socket
   Set Socket = msoc
End Property
```

For More Information Friend methods are introduced in Chapter 9, "Programming with Objects," in the *Microsoft Visual Basic 6.0 Programmer's Guide.*

Providing Polymorphism by Implementing Interfaces

One of the most striking features of the Component Object Model (COM) is the ability of an object to implement multiple interfaces. In addition to enabling polymorphism, multiple interfaces provide a mechanism for incremental or evolutionary development, without the need to recompile all the components in the system when changes occur.

By defining features in terms of interfaces, composed of small groups of closely-related functions, you can implement component features as needed, knowing that you can expand them later by implementing additional interfaces.

Maintaining compatibility is simplified, because new versions of a component can continue to provide existing interfaces, while adding new or enhanced interfaces. Succeeding versions of client applications can take advantage of these when it makes sense for them to do so.

Inheritance and Polymorphism

As explained in "Polymorphism," in Chapter 9, "Programming with Objects," in the *Microsoft Visual Basic 6.0 Programmer's Guide,* most object-oriented programming tools provide polymorphism through inheritance. This is a powerful mechanism for small-scale development tasks, but has generally proven to be problematic for large-scale systems.

In part, these difficulties arise as a result of necessary changes to classes deep in the inheritance tree. Recompilation is required in order to take advantage of such changes, and failure to recompile may lead to unpleasant surprises when the time finally arrives for a new version.

More seriously, an over-emphasis on inheritance-driven polymorphism typically results in a massive shift of resources from development tasks to up-front design tasks, doing nothing to address development backlogs or to shorten the time before the end user can discover — through hands-on experience — whether the system actually fulfills the intended purpose.

As a consequence, tools for rapid prototyping and Rapid Application Development (RAD) have gained wider acceptance than OOP tools.

Visual Basic and COM

Visual Basic follows the COM example, emphasizing multiple interfaces as a more flexible way to provide polymorphism. Software can evolve interface by interface, rather than having to be derived from all necessary antecedents during a lengthy design process.

Objects can begin small, with minimal functionality, and over time acquire additional features, as it becomes clear from actual use what those features should be. Legacy code is protected by continuing to support old interfaces while implementing new ones.

The Implements Feature

Visual Basic provides the Implements keyword as the means for incorporating a secondary interface. For example, if your project had a reference to a type library that described the IFinance interface, you could place the following code in a class module:

```
Implements IFinance
```

Because type libraries contain only interfaces, and no implementation, you would then add code for each of the properties and methods of the IFinance interface, as described in "Implementing and Using Standard Interfaces."

An Interface Is a Contract

When you create an interface for use with Implements, you're casting it in concrete for all time. This *interface invariance* is an important principle of component design, because it protects existing systems that have been written to an interface.

When an interface is clearly in need of enhancement, a new interface should be created. This interface might be called Interface2, to show its relationship to the existing interface.

While generating new interfaces too frequently can bulk up your components with unused interfaces, well-designed interfaces tend to be small and independent of each other, reducing the potential for performance problems.

Factoring Interfaces

The process of determining what properties and methods belong on an interface is called *factoring*.

In general, you should group a few closely-related functions on an interface. Too many functions make the interface unwieldy, while dividing the parts of a feature too finely results in extra overhead. For example, the following code calls methods on three different interfaces of the Velociraptor class:

```
Public Sub CretaceousToDoList(ByVal vcr1 As _
      Velociraptor, ByVal vcr2 As Velociraptor)
   Dim dnr As IDinosaur
   Dim prd As IPredator
   vcr1.Mate vcr2
   Set dnr = vcr1
   dnr.LayEggs
   Set prd = vcr1
   prd.KillSomethingAndEatIt
End Sub
```

In order to use methods on the IDinosaur and IPredator interfaces, you must assign the object to a variable of the correct interface type.

Where possible, interfaces designed to use flexible data structures will outlast interfaces based on fixed data types.

As noted above, it's much harder to go wrong in designing interfaces than in creating large inheritance trees. If you start small, you can have parts of a system running relatively quickly. The ability to evolve the system by adding interfaces allows you to gain the advantages object-oriented programming was intended to provide.

For More Information The Implements feature is discussed in detail in "Polymorphism" in Chapter 9, "Programming with Objects," in the *Microsoft Visual Basic 6.0 Programmer's Guide.*

Creating Standard Interfaces with Visual Basic

You can create standard interfaces for your organization by compiling abstract classes in Visual Basic ActiveX DLLs or EXEs, or with the MkTypLib utility, included in the Tools directory.

The MkTypLib utility may be more comfortable for you if you're an experienced user of Microsoft Visual C++.

Basic programmers may find it easier to create an interface using a Visual Basic class module. Open a new ActiveX DLL or EXE project, and add the desired properties and methods to a class module. Don't put any code in the procedures. Give the class the name you want the interface to have, for example `IFinance`, and make the project.

> **Note** The capital "I" in front of interface names is an ActiveX convention. It is not strictly necessary to follow this convention. However, it provides an easy way to distinguish between abstract interfaces you've implemented and the default interfaces of classes. The latter are usually referred to by the class name in Visual Basic.

The type library in the resulting .dll or .exe file will contain the information required by the Implements statement. To use it in another project, use the Browse button on the References dialog box to locate the .dll or .exe file and set a reference. You can use the Object Browser to see what interfaces a type library contains.

> **Important** The Implements feature does not support outgoing interfaces. Thus, any events you declare in the class module will be ignored.

As explained in "Providing Polymorphism by Implementing Interfaces," earlier in this chapter, an interface once defined and accepted must remain invariant, to protect applications written to use it. *DO NOT* use the Version Compatibility feature of Visual Basic to alter standard interfaces.

For More Information "Providing Polymorphism by Implementing Interfaces," earlier in this chapter, discusses such important concepts as interface invariance and factoring. The next section, "Implementing and Using Standard Interfaces," explains how interfaces are implemented and used in components.

Implementing and Using Standard Interfaces

Once you've defined a standard interface, either by creating a type library with the MkTypLib utility or by compiling a Visual Basic project containing abstract classes (that is, class modules with properties and methods that don't contain any code), you can implement that interface in classes your components provide.

Suppose you had a LateCretaceous system that included a number of components, each of which provided objects representing flora, fauna, and business rules of that era. For example, one component might provide a Velociraptor class, while another provided a Tyrannosaur class.

You might create a standard interface named IPredator, which included Hunt and Attack methods:

```
' Code for the abstract IPredator class module.
Public Sub Hunt()
End Sub
Public Sub Attack(ByVal Victim As IDinosaur)
End Sub
```

Notice that the argument of the Attack method uses another interface, IDinosaur. One would expect this interface to contain methods describing general dinosaur behavior, such as laying eggs, and that it would be implemented by many classes — Velociraptor, Tyrannosaur, Brontosaur, Triceratops, and so on.

Notice also that there's no code in these methods. IPredator is an *abstract class* that simply defines the interface (referred to as an *abstract interface*). Implementation details will vary according to the object that implements the interface.

For example, the Tyrannosaur class might implement IPredator as follows:

```
Implements IPredator
Private Sub IPredator_Hunt()
   ' Code to stalk around the landscape roaring, until
   '    you encounter a dinosaur large enough to
   '    qualify as a meal.
End Sub
Private Sub IPredator_Attack(ByVal Victim As IDinosaur)
   ' Code to charge, roaring and taking huge bites.
End Sub
```

Important As noted in "Providing Polymorphism by Implementing Interfaces," earlier in this chapter, an interface is a contract. You must implement *all* of the properties and methods in the interface.

By contrast, the Velociraptor class might implement IPredator as shown here:

```
Implements IPredator
Private Sub IPredator_Hunt()
   ' Fan out and hunt with a pack, running down
   '   small dinosaurs or surrounding large ones.
End Sub
Private Sub IPredator_Attack(ByVal Victim As IDinosaur)
   ' Code to dart in from all sides, slashing the
   '   victim and wearing it down.
End Sub
```

Using Implemented Interfaces

Once you have classes that implement IPredator, you can upgrade your existing applications one by one to use the new, more competitive interface. You can access the Hunt and Attack methods by assigning a Velociraptor or Tyrannosaur object to a variable of type IPredator, as shown here:

```
Dim tyr As New Tyrannosaur
Dim prd As IPredator
Set prd = tyr
prd.Hunt
```

You can also declare procedure arguments `As IPredator`, and pass the procedure any object that implements the IPredator interface, as here:

```
Public Sub DevourTheCompetition(ByVal Agent As _
      IPredator, ByVal Target As IDinosaur)
   Agent.Hunt
   Agent.Attack Target
End Sub
```

The Sub procedure shown above could be called with any predatory dinosaur as the first argument, and any dinosaur at all as the second. The caller of the procedure can use whatever predatory dinosaur is most appropriate for the occasion. This kind of flexibility is important in maintaining a business advantage.

Setting References to Type Libraries

A type library containing abstract interfaces provides a reference point for both implementing and using interfaces.

In order to implement an interface, you must use the References dialog box to set a reference to the type library. This is because the type library contains the information required to specify the arguments and return types of the interface's members.

In similar fashion, any application that uses objects which have implemented an abstract interface must also have a reference to the type library that describes the interface. Information about implemented interfaces cannot be included in the type libraries of components, because there is no way to resolve naming conflicts.

> **Important** In order to marshal data between processes or between remote computers, out-of-process components must include in their Setup programs any type libraries that describe abstract interfaces. In-process components should also include these type libraries, because a developer may want to pass its objects to other applications, either on the local computer or on a remote computer. See "Deploying ActiveX Components," in Chapter 7, "Debugging, Testing, and Deploying Components."

Summary

The following list provides an outline for implementing multiple interfaces:

1. Define a set of interfaces, each containing a small group of related properties and methods that describe a service or feature your system requires. This *factoring* process is discussed in "Providing Polymorphism by Implementing Interfaces," earlier in this chapter.

2. Create a type library containing abstract interfaces — abstract classes, if you create the type library by compiling a Visual Basic project — that specify the arguments and return types of the properties and methods. Use the MkTypLib utility or Visual Basic to generate the type library, as described in "Creating Standard Interfaces with Visual Basic."

3. Develop a component that uses the interfaces, by adding a reference to the type library and then using the Implements statement to give classes secondary interfaces as appropriate.

4. For every interface you've added to a class, select each property or method in turn, and add code to implement the functionality in a manner appropriate for that class. See "Polymorphism" in Chapter 9, "Programming with Objects," in the *Microsoft Visual Basic 6.0 Programmer's Guide.*

5. Compile the component and create a Setup program, making sure you include the type library that describes the abstract interfaces.

6. Develop an application that uses the component by adding references to the component and to the type library that describes the abstract interfaces.

7. Compile the application and create a Setup program, including the component (and the abstract type library, if the component runs out of process or — with the Enterprise Edition — on a remote computer).

The next section discusses how the process outlined here can be used to gradually enhance a system.

Systems That Evolve Over Time

The observant reader will no doubt have noticed a bug in the code given earlier in this topic. If predatory dinosaurs only ate other dinosaurs, how did they keep the Mammals down? A more general IPredator interface might accept as a victim any object that implemented IAnimal.

This illustrates a key advantage of component software development using multiple interfaces: As the LateCretaceous system evolves into, say, the Pleistocene system, components that provide predatory dinosaur objects can be replaced by components that provide SaberTooth and DireWolf objects.

A legacy application compiled to use dinosaurs may be still be able to function quite nicely using the new predator classes, as long as it doesn't include code specific to dinosaurs.

The key points to remember when using multiple interfaces in this fashion are:

- Once an interface is defined and in use, it must never change. This concept of *interface invariance* is discussed in "Providing Polymorphism by Implementing Interfaces," earlier in this chapter, and in "Polymorphism" in Chapter 9, "Programming with Objects," in the *Microsoft Visual Basic 6.0 Programmer's Guide*.
- If an interface needs to be expanded, create a new interface. This is discussed in "Polymorphism, Interfaces, Type Libraries, and GUIDs," earlier in this chapter.
- New versions of components can provide new features by implementing new and expanded interfaces.
- New versions of components can support legacy code by continuing to provide old interfaces.
- New versions of applications can take advantage of new features (that is, new and expanded interfaces), and if necessary can be written so as to degrade gracefully when only older interfaces are available. (See "Polymorphism, Interfaces, Type Libraries, and GUIDs," earlier in this chapter.)

Implements and Code Reuse

The Implements statement also allows you to reuse code in existing objects. In this form of code reuse, the new object (referred to as an *outer object*) creates an instance of the existing object (or *inner object*) during its Initialize event.

In addition to any abstract interfaces it implements, the outer object implements the default interface of the inner object. (To do this, use the References dialog box to add a reference to the component that provides the inner object.)

When adding code to the outer object's implementations of the properties and methods of the inner object, you can delegate to the inner object whenever the functionality it provides meets the needs of the outer object.

For example, the Tyrannosaur class might implement the interface of a Dinosaur object (instead of an abstract IDinosaur interface). The Dinosaur object might have a LayEggs method, which the Tyrannosaur class could implement by simple delegation:

```
Private dnoInner As Dinosaur
Private Sub Class_Initialize()
   Set dnoInner = New Dinosaur
End Sub
Private Sub Dinosaur_LayEggs()
   ' Delegate to the inner object.
   dnoInner.LayEggs
End Sub
```

This is an extremely powerful and flexible way to reuse code, because the outer object can choose to execute its own code before, after, or instead of delegating to the inner object.

For More Information Code reuse with the Implements statement is discussed in more detail in "Polymorphism," in Chapter 9, "Programming with Objects," in the *Microsoft Visual Basic 6.0 Programmer's Guide.*

Organizing Objects: The Object Model

An *object model* defines a hierarchy of objects that gives structure to an object-based program. By defining the relationships between objects that are part of the program, an object model organizes the objects in a way that makes programming easier.

The public object model of a component is especially important because it's used by all the programmers who employ the component as part of their applications.

> **Note** Users of C++ or other object-oriented programming languages are used to seeing *class hierarchies.* A class hierarchy describes *inheritance.* That is, it shows how objects are derived from simpler objects, inheriting their behavior. By contrast, object models are hierarchies that describe *containment.* That is, they show how complex objects like Worksheets contain collections of other objects, such as Button, Picture, and PivotTable objects. Object models can be created with Visual Basic, Visual C++, and other tools that support COM and ActiveX.

Chapter 9, "Programming with Objects," in the *Microsoft Visual Basic 6.0 Programmer's Guide,* includes an introduction to object models and a discussion of design considerations for collection classes.

For More Information Further information on object models can be found in Appendix A, "ActiveX Component Standards and Guidelines."

Do I Need an Object Model?

You don't have to create an elaborate object model for your component. A control component (.ocx file) might contain three UserControl objects, and no class modules at all. A code component meant to be used as a simple library of functions might have one global object with a zillion methods.

Again, you might create a code component named Finance with three classes in it, each class representing a self-contained business rule. If the rules are independent of each other, there's no reason to link them into a hierarchy. A client application that uses these rules simply creates one or more objects of each class, as needed.

Each class module in such a component would have its Instancing property set to MultiUse, so that client applications could create objects from the class, and so that the component could handle multiple objects from each class. Figure 6.5 shows such an object model.

Figure 6.5 A flat object model with several externally creatable objects

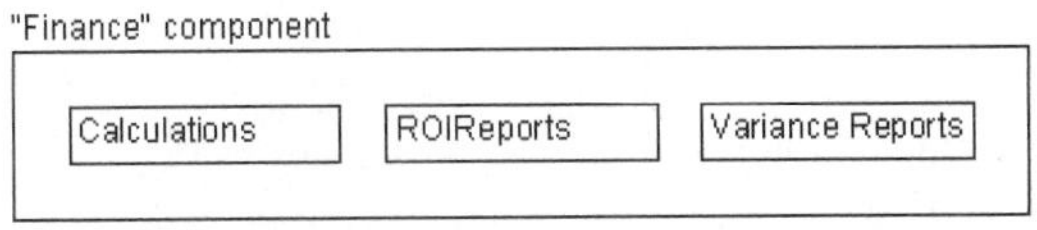

"Finance" component

Calculations | ROIReports | Variance Reports

Object Models and Interfaces

As the functionality of an object increases, so does the complexity of its interface. This can make the object hard to use.

You can reduce the complexity of an object's default interface by factoring out groups of related functions, and defining an interface for each group. A client can work with only those interfaces that provide needed features.

By defining standard interfaces in this fashion, you can implement interfaces on other objects, gaining the benefits of polymorphism. This approach to software design in discussed in "Providing Polymorphism by Implementing Interfaces," earlier in this chapter.

Sometimes an object is too large even when its features are factored into separate interfaces. When an object becomes very complex, as for example the TreeView and Toolbar controls, breaking pieces of it off as separate objects may make sense.

Once the whole is divided, you need a way of organizing its constituent parts. Splitting the Node object off from the TreeView control gains you nothing if you can't show the relationship between them. Object models make it easy to provide this organization to the user of your component.

For More Information The use of multiple interfaces is covered in "Providing Polymorphism by Implementing Interfaces."

Externally Creatable Objects

Part of the additional importance of object models in components comes from the fact that components can provide objects in two different ways — as externally creatable objects or as dependent objects.

In an ordinary program that uses private objects, you can create objects from any class the program defines. A client application, however, can only create objects from some of the classes a component provides. *Externally creatable objects* are those that a client application can create using the New operator with the Set statement, by declaring a variable As New, or by calling the CreateObject function.

When a client uses one of these mechanisms to request an externally creatable object, the component returns a reference the client can use to manipulate the object. When the client sets the last variable containing this reference to Nothing, or allows it to go out of scope, the component destroys the object.

You can make a public object externally creatable by setting the Instancing property of the class module to any value *except* Private or PublicNotCreatable.

For More Information A discussion of the Instancing property can be found in "Instancing for Classes Provided by ActiveX Components," earlier in this chapter.

Dependent Objects

Sometimes there is a clear relationship between two objects, such that one object is a part of the other. In Microsoft Excel, for example, a Button object is always part of another object, such as a Worksheet.

An object that's contained in another object is called a *dependent object.* Client applications can manipulate dependent objects, just as they can manipulate externally creatable objects, but they cannot create dependent objects using CreateObject or New.

Set the Instancing property of a class module to PublicNotCreatable to make the objects created from that class dependent objects.

> **Note** Dependent objects are also referred to as *nested objects.*

Getting References to Dependent Objects

If a client application can use dependent objects but can't create them, how are they created?

A component can provide dependent objects in several ways. Most commonly an externally creatable object will have a collection with an Add method which the client can invoke. The component creates the dependent object in the code for the Add method, and returns a reference to the new object, which the client can then use.

For example, a Microsoft Excel Worksheet object has a collection of Button objects. A client application can add a new button to the worksheet by calling the Add method of the Buttons collection, as shown in the following code fragment:

```
' Note: The variable wsBudget contains a reference to
'   a Worksheet object.
Dim btnOK As Excel.Button
' Parameters of the Add method specify the top, left,
' width, and height of the new button. The return value
' is a reference to the new Button object.
Set btnOK = wsBudget.Buttons.Add(100, 100, 150, 125)
' Set the caption of the new Button object.
btnOK.Caption = "OK"
```

It's important to remember that the variable btnOK contains a reference to the object, not the object itself.

> **Note** The distinction between externally creatable objects and dependent objects is made for the benefit of the client applications that manipulate a component's objects. From *within* a component, you can always create objects from any of the component's classes, regardless of the value of the Instancing property.

For More Information The next section, "Combining Externally Creatable and Dependent Objects," discusses the process of identifying the types of objects needed for each part of an object model.

Combining Externally Creatable and Dependent Objects

The relationships between the externally creatable objects a component provides and the dependent objects they contain are expressed in the component's object model. Once you've analyzed the functionality your component will provide, you can:

1. Determine what objects you need to implement that functionality.
2. List the properties and methods each object will require.
3. Determine the relationships between the objects.
4. Identify the top-level objects that need to be created by client applications.

Visual Basic gives you the flexibility to implement many possible object models. A component can provide several unrelated creatable objects, each containing one or more dependent objects; it can also provide a single hierarchy containing a number of objects, only one or two of which are externally creatable.

One characteristic common to all of these implementations is that they require more design time. It's important to spend adequate time and effort determining how your objects will interact and how they will be used designing your object model to avoid having to redefine objects, or split one object into two, in a future version of your component.

Such changes make it much more difficult for applications that use your component to migrate to newer versions. Adding new objects, or exposing objects that were formerly private, does not cause such problems.

For More Information The next section, "Using Properties and Collections to Create Object Models," discusses techniques for linking dependent and externally creatable objects in an object model.

Using Properties and Collections to Create Object Models

Objects in a hierarchy are linked together by *object properties*, that is, properties that return references to objects. An object that contains other objects will have properties that return either references to the objects themselves, or references to collections of objects.

For example, consider a Bicycle object that contains two Wheel objects; each Wheel object might in turn contain a Rim object and a collection of Spoke objects.

Figure 6.6 shows a possible object model for the externally creatable Bicycle object and its dependent objects.

Figure 6.6 An externally creatable object with a hierarchy of dependent objects

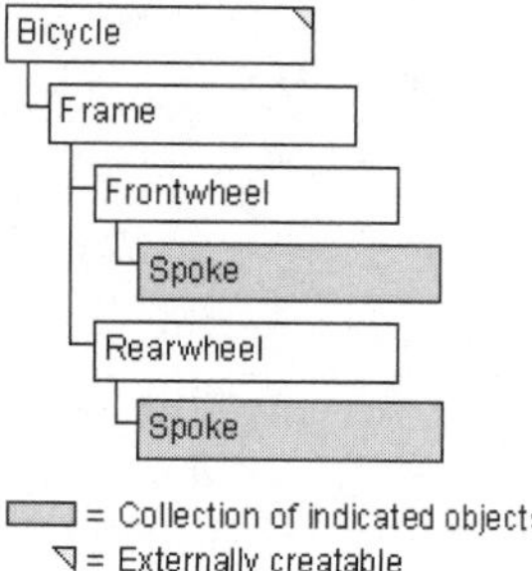

The Bicycle object would have a Frame property that returned a reference to its Frame object. The Frame object would have a FrontWheel and BackWheel property, each of which would return a Wheel object. The Wheel object would have a Spokes property that would return a Spokes collection object. The Spokes collection would contain the Spoke objects.

You may also have dependent objects that are used internally by classes in your component, and which you do not want to provide to users of your component. You can set the Instancing properties of the class modules that define these objects to Private, so they won't appear when users browse your type library.

For example, both the Frame and Wheel objects might have collections of Bearing objects, but there may be no reason to expose the Bearings object, or the collections containing it, for manipulation by client applications.

> **Important** In order to keep the Bearings property from appearing in the type library, you must declare it using the Friend keyword, as described in "Private Communications Between Your Objects," earlier in this chapter.

The Simple Way to Link Dependent Objects

Frequently it makes sense for a complex object to have only one instance of a dependent object. For example, a Bicycle object only needs one Frame object. In this case, you can implement the linkage as a simple property of the complex object:

```
Private mFrame As Frame
Public Property Get Frame() As Frame
   Set Frame = mFrame
End Property
Private Sub Class_Initialize()
   ' Create the Frame when the Bicycle is initialized.
   Set mFrame = New Frame
End Sub
```

It's important to implement such properties as shown above, using a read-only property procedure, rather than simply declaring a public module-level variable, as shown below.

```
Public Frame As Frame   'Bad idea.
```

With the second implementation, a user of your component might set the Frame property to Nothing. If there are no other references to the Frame object, it will be destroyed. The effect of this on the Bicycle object is left to the reader's imagination.

Linking a Fixed Number of Objects

Even when a complex object contains more than one instance of a dependent object, it may make more sense to implement the linkage with properties instead of with a collection. For example, a Bicycle object always has two wheels:

```
' Create the Wheel objects on demand (As New), instead
'   of in the Bicycle object's Initialize event.
Private mwhlFront As New Wheel
Private mwhlRear As New Wheel

Public Property Get FrontWheel() As Wheel
   Set FrontWheel = mwhlFront
End Property
Public Property Get RearWheel() As Wheel
   Set RearWheel = mwhlRear
End Property
```

Using Collections in Your Object Model

When the relationship between two objects in a hierarchy is such that the first object contains an indeterminate number of the second, the easiest way to implement the link is with a collection. A *collection* is an object that contains a set of related objects.

For example, the linkage between the FrontWheel object and its Spoke objects in Figure 6.6 is a *collection class*. A collection class is a class module that exists solely to group all the objects of another class. In this case, the collection class is named Spokes, the plural of the name of the class of objects it contains. (See "What's In a Name?," earlier in this chapter, for more information on naming classes.)

Implementing this part of the object model example requires three class modules. From the bottom up, these are:

- The Spoke class module, which defines the properties and methods of a single spoke.
- The Spokes class module, which defines a collection object to contain Spoke objects.
- The Wheel class module, which defines an entire wheel, with a collection of spokes.

Dependent Class: Spoke

The Spoke class module is the simplest of the three. It could consist of as little as two Public variables, as in the following code fragment:

```
' Properties for Spoke
Public PartNumber As Integer
Public Alloy As Integer
```

The Instancing property of the Spoke class is set to PublicNotCreatable. The *only* way for a client application to create a Spoke object is with the Add method of the Spokes collection, as discussed in the next section.

> **Note** This is not a very robust implementation. In practice you would probably implement both of these properties as Property procedures, with code to validate the values that are assigned to them.

For More Information For details on using Property procedures, see Chapter 9, "Programming with Objects," in the *Microsoft Visual Basic 6.0 Programmer's Guide*.

Dependent Collection Class: Spokes

The Spokes class module is the template for a collection Spoke objects. It contains a Private variable declared as a Collection object:

```
Private mcolSpokes As Collection
```

The collection object is created in the Initialize method for the class:

```
Private Sub Class_Initialize()
   Set mcolSpokes = New Collection
End Sub
```

The methods of the Spokes class module *delegate* to the default methods of the Visual Basic Collection object. That is, the actual work is done by the methods of the Collection object. The Spokes class might include the following properties and methods:

```
' Read-only Count property.
Public Property Get Count() As Integer
   Count = mcolSpokes.Count
End Property
' Add method for creating new Spoke objects.
Public Function Add(ByVal PartNumber As Integer, _
               ByVal Alloy As Integer)
   Dim spkNew As New Spoke
   spkNew.PartNumber = PartNumber
   spkNew.Alloy = Alloy
   mcolSpokes.Add spkNew
   Set Add = spkNew
End Function
```

As with the Spoke class, the Instancing property of the Spokes class is set to PublicNotCreatable. The only way to get a Spokes collection object is as part of a Wheel object, as shown in the following section describing the Wheel class.

For More Information See "Object Models" in Chapter 9, "Programming with Objects," in the *Microsoft Visual Basic 6.0 Programmer's Guide,* for a discussion of collections, including a more detailed explanation of delegation, a list of methods you need to implement, and instructions for creating a collection that works with For Each.

Externally Creatable Class: Wheel

The Wheel class module has Instancing set to MultiUse, so that any client application can create a Wheel object. The Wheel class module contains a Private variable of the Spokes class:

```
' Create the Spokes collection object on demand.
Private mSpokes As New Spokes
Public Property Get Spokes() As Spokes
   Set Spokes = mSpokes
End Property
```

Every Wheel object a client creates will have its own Spokes collection. The collection is protected against accidentally being set to Nothing by making it a read-only property (Property Get). A developer can access the methods and properties of the Spokes collection as shown in the following code fragment:

```
Dim whl As Wheel
Dim spk As Spoke
Set whl = New Wheel
Set spk = whl.Spokes.Add PartNumber:=3222223, Alloy:=7
 Call a method of the Spoke object.
spk.Adjust
MsgBox whl.Spokes.Count    ' Displays 1 (one item).
```

The Add method is used to create a new spoke in the Spokes collection of the Wheel object. The Add method returns a reference to the new Spoke object, so that its properties and methods can be called. A spoke can only be created as a member of the Spokes collection.

The difference between the Wheel object, which can be created by any client, and its dependent objects is the value of the Instancing properties of the classes.

For More Information The Spokes object is created on demand, while the Collection object `mcolSpokes` was explicitly created. Chapter 9, "Programming with Objects," in the *Microsoft Visual Basic 6.0 Programmer's Guide,* discusses the use of As New for creating variables on demand, including performance implications.

Considerations for Linking Objects in an Object Model

Generally speaking, a simpler implementation will be faster. Accessing an item in a collection involves a series of nested references and function calls. Whenever you know that there will always be a fixed number of a dependent object type, you can implement the linkage as a property.

Regardless of how the object model is linked, the key difference between externally creatable objects and dependent objects is the value of the Instancing property of the class module. An object that can be created by other applications will have its Instancing property set to any value except Private or PublicNotCreatable.

All dependent objects, whether they are contained in other dependent objects or in objects that can be created by other applications, will have their Instancing properties set to PublicNotCreatable.

Using Externally Creatable Objects as Dependent Objects

At times you may want to use objects in both ways. That is, you may want the user to be able to create a Widget object independent of the object model, while at the same time providing a Widgets collection as a property of the Mechanism object.

In fact, you may even want to allow the user to create independent instances of the Widgets collection, to move independent Widgets into and out of any Widgets collection, and to copy or move Widgets between collections.

You can make the objects externally creatable by setting the Instancing property of the Widget class and the Widgets collection class to MultiUse.

Important If the Widget object can be created directly by client applications, you cannot depend on all Widget objects getting initialized by the code in the Add method of the Widgets collection. Objects that will be both creatable and dependent should be designed to require no initialization beyond their Initialize events.

Allowing free movement of Widgets requires implementation of Insert, Copy, and Move methods for your collection. Insert and Move are fairly straightforward, because moving or inserting a reference to an object is as good as moving the object. Implementing Copy, however, requires more work.

This is because client application never actually has the object in its possession. All the client application has is a reference to an object the component has created on its behalf. Thus, when you implement Copy, you must create a duplicate object, including duplicates of any dependent objects it contains.

For More Information See the next section, "Dealing with Circular References," for a discussion of problems that may arise when linking objects together. See Appendix A, "ActiveX Component Standards and Guidelines," for more information on object models.

Dealing with Circular References

Containment relationships allow you to navigate through a hierarchy from a high-level object to any of the objects it contains.

Object models that strictly express containment are like trees. Any given branch (object) may divide into smaller branches (dependent objects), but the smaller branches do not loop around and rejoin the trunk or lower branches.

Object models with loops, or *circular references,* result when a dependent object has a property or variable that holds a reference to one of the objects that contains it.

For example, an Order object might have a Contact property that contains a reference to a Contact object, representing the individual who placed the order. The Contact object might in turn have a Company property that contains a reference to a Company object.

Up to this point, the hierarchy is a tree. However, if the Company object has a MostRecentOrder property that contains a reference to the Order object, a circular reference has been created.

Note You could avoid the circular reference in this case by making the MostRecentOrder property a text key that could be used to retrieve the Order object from the component's Orders collection.

Circular References in Visual Basic Components

Consider the simplest form of circular reference, a Parent property. The Parent property of a dependent object contains a reference to the object that contains it.

For example, in the Microsoft Excel object model, a Button object is contained by a Worksheet object. If you have a reference to a Button object, you can print the name of the Worksheet that contains it using code like the following:

```
' If the variable btnCurrent contains a reference to a
' Microsoft Excel Button object, the following line of
' code displays the Name property of the Worksheet
' object that contains the button.
MsgBox btnCurrent.Parent.Name
```

Microsoft Excel is written using C++ and low level COM interfaces, and it maintains the Parent properties of its objects without creating circular references. If you implement such a relationship in Visual Basic, you have to take into account the way Visual Basic handles the creation and destruction of objects.

Visual Basic destroys an object when there are no longer any references to it. If an object's parent has a collection that contains a reference to the object, that's enough to keep the object from being destroyed. In the same way, an object continues to exist if the parent has an object property that contains a reference to the object.

When a parent object is destroyed, the variables that implement its properties go out of scope, and the object references are released. This allows the dependent objects to terminate. If a dependent object has a Parent property, however, Visual Basic cannot destroy the parent object in the first place, because the dependent object has a reference to it.

The dependent object cannot be destroyed, either, because the parent has a reference to it. This situation is illustrated for an out-of-process component in Figure 6.7.

Figure 6.7 Circular reference prevents objects from being destroyed

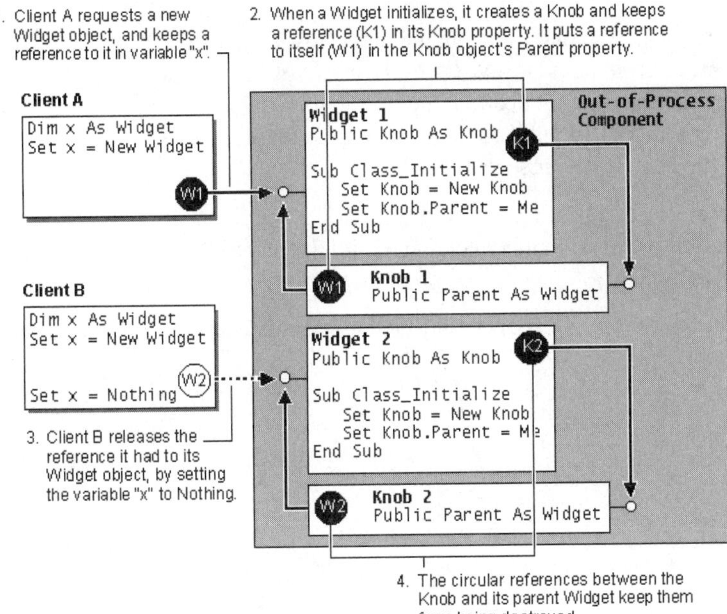
1. Client A requests a new Widget object, and keeps a reference to it in variable "x".
2. When a Widget initializes, it creates a Knob and keeps a reference (K1) in its Knob property. It puts a reference to itself (W1) in the Knob object's Parent property.
Client A
Dim x As Widget
Set x = New Widget
W1
Out-of-Process Component
Widget 1
Public Knob As Knob
K1
Sub Class_Initialize
Set Knob = New Knob
Set Knob.Parent = Me
End Sub
Knob 1
Public Parent As Widget
Client B
Dim x As Widget
Set x = New Widget
W2
Set x = Nothing
Widget 2
Public Knob As Knob
K2
Sub Class_Initialize
Set Knob = New Knob
Set Knob.Parent = Me
End Sub
3. Client B releases the reference it had to its Widget object, by setting the variable "x" to Nothing.
Knob 2
Public Parent As Widget
4. The circular references between the Knob and its parent Widget keep them from being destroyed.

Client application B has released its reference to its Widget object. The Widget object has a reference to a Knob object, whose Parent property refers back to the Widget object, keeping both objects from terminating.

A similar problem occurs if the Widget object contains a collection of Knob objects, instead of a single Knob. The Widget object keeps a reference to the Knobs collection object, which contains a reference to each Knob. The Parent property of each Knob contains a reference to the Widget, forming a loop that keeps the Widget object, Knobs collection, and Knob object alive.

The objects client B was using will not be destroyed until the component closes. For example, if client A releases its Widget object, there will be no external references to the component. If the component does not have any forms loaded, and there is no code executing in any procedure, then the component will unload, and the Terminate events for all the objects will be executed. However, in the meantime, large numbers of orphaned objects may continue to exist, taking up memory.

> **Note** If a circular reference exists between objects in two out-of-process components, the components will never terminate.

Circular References and In-Process Components

If you implement your component as a DLL, so that it runs in the process of the client application, it's even more important to avoid circular references. Because an in-process component shares the process space of the client application, there is no distinction between "external" and "internal" references to a public object. As long as there's a reference to an object provided by the component, it stays loaded.

This means that a circular reference keeps an in-process component loaded indefinitely, and the memory taken up by orphaned objects cannot be reclaimed until the client application closes.

For More Information See Appendix A, "ActiveX Component Standards and Guidelines," for more information on object models.

CHAPTER 7

Debugging, Testing, and Deploying Components

This chapter describes the procedures you'll use to debug, register, and distribute your component, and the version compatibility features that allow you to enhance your component without breaking existing applications that use it.

In addition, you'll find topics related to distributing components, including Help files, browser strings, and creating versions of your component for use internationally.

Chapter 6, "General Principles of Component Design," contains a road map relating the topics covered in these two chapters to the general sequence of development tasks for components.

Contents

For More Information See Chapter 13, "Debugging Your Code and Handling Errors"; Chapter 16, "International Issues"; and Chapter 17, "Distributing Your Applications," in the *Microsoft Visual Basic 6.0 Programmer's Guide.*

Testing and Debugging ActiveX Components

Visual Basic provides two different component debugging scenarios. For in-process components, you can load a test project (Standard EXE or ActiveX EXE) and one or more component projects into the development environment as a *project group*. You can run all the projects in the group together, and step directly from test project code into in-process component code.

Out-of-process components can be debugged using two instances of the development environment. One instance of Visual Basic runs the test project, while the second runs the component project. You can step directly from test project code into component code, and each instance of Visual Basic has its own set of breakpoints and watches.

Combinations of these scenarios are possible. You can debug an application that uses both in-process and out-of-process components, as shown in Figure 7.1.

Figure 7.1 Debugging in-process and out-of-process components

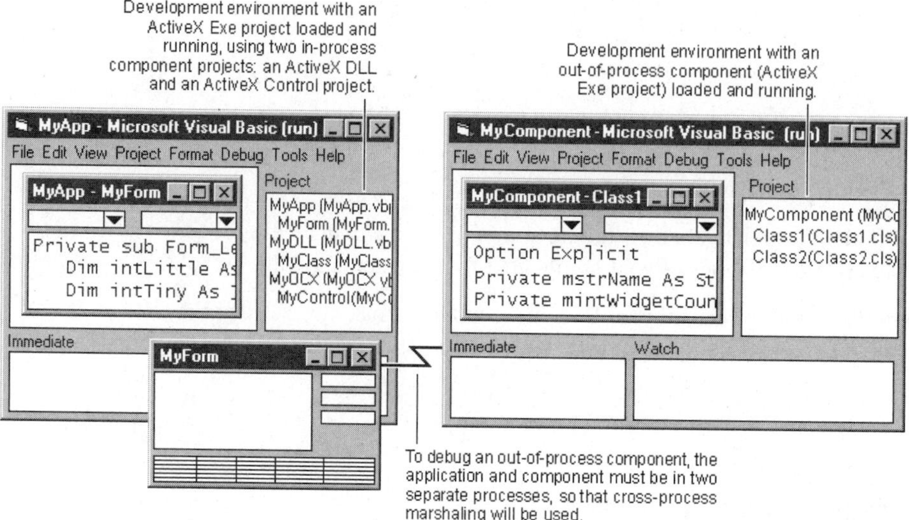

When an ActiveX EXE project is in run mode, like MyComponent in Figure 7.1, the client application (MyApp) can create objects and access their properties and methods. Each out-of-process component a client uses must be in its own instance of the development environment. The client application and all of its in-process components — DLLs and OCXs — can run together in a single instance of the development environment.

For More Information There are special considerations for debugging and testing ActiveX control projects, and other project types that include private controls. See "Setting Up a New Control Project and Test Project" and "Debugging Controls," in Chapter 9, "Building ActiveX Controls." Information specific to debugging and testing ActiveX Documents can be found in Chapter 11, "Building ActiveX Documents." The fundamentals of debugging are covered in Chapter 13, "Debugging Your Code and Handling Errors," in the *Microsoft Visual Basic 6.0 Programmer's Guide.*

How to Test ActiveX Components

To test a component, you need to create a client application. Components exist to provide objects for clients, which makes it hard to test them by themselves.

Your test project should invoke all the properties, methods, and events of each object provided by your component, testing both valid and invalid values of all arguments.

For example, rather than simply making one call to the Spin method of the Widget object, make a series of calls that try valid and invalid values of all arguments. Pay particular attention to the highest and lowest valid values, as these *boundary conditions* are a frequent source of problems.

Test for both functionality and error cases. Make sure your component behaves well in case of errors, such as unexpected input. It's especially important to make sure you've covered all error conditions in event procedures of in-process components, because such errors can be fatal to client applications that use the component.

> **Tip** Your test project can also be used to test the compiled component, as described in "How to Test Compiled Components," later in this chapter.

Make the Test Program Generic for Better Coverage

You can improve your testing process by making the test program more generic. For example, if you create a text box for each argument of the Spin method, and a button to invoke the method, you can use an automated test tool to maintain and run comprehensive test suites. This makes it easier to test combinations of properties and methods.

Testing Components as Part of an Application

If you're creating components as part of an application, you can use the application itself as the test program. In theory, thorough testing of the application will discover any problems with its components.

In practice, however, this is rarely true. An application may not exercise all the interfaces of the components it uses, even under stress testing.

It's also a lot more work to set up test cases when you have to figure out what application behavior must be tested in order to test a particular feature of the component. You'll be better served by a comprehensive test program that directly tests each element of each object's interface.

If each component has been tested separately, testing your application with the components provides an extra level of quality assurance.

Creating a Test Project

The test project must be an EXE project. Unless you're testing call-backs, your test project can be a Standard EXE project. To test call-backs, use an ActiveX EXE project, so it can include public classes that implement the call-back methods. Call-backs are discussed in "Asynchronous Call-Backs and Events," in Chapter 8, "Building Code Components."

The way you set the test project up depends on whether you're testing an in-process or out of process component. The reason for this is explained in "Testing and Debugging ActiveX Components."

> **Note** ActiveX Documents cannot be debugged without a browser or other active document container. See Chapter 11, "Building ActiveX Documents," for details.

For More Information See "Testing and Debugging ActiveX Components," earlier in this chapter, for a list of topics related to testing and debugging.

Creating a Test Project for an In-Process Component

This section explains how to set up test projects to exercise most of the objects in-process components can provide. ActiveX documents, however, cannot be tested as described here. For more information, see Chapter 11, "Building ActiveX Documents."

To create a test project for an in-process component

1. The test project is loaded in the same copy of the development environment where your component project is loaded. On the **File** menu, click **Add Project** to open the **Add Project** dialog box, click the Standard EXE icon to select it, then click **OK** to add a Standard EXE project to the project group.

   The caption of the Project window changes to **Project Group**, with a default name, to indicate that multiple projects are loaded.

   As described in "How to Test ActiveX Components," use an ActiveX EXE project as your test project if your component implements call-backs.

2. On the **File** menu, click **Save Project Group** to save the group containing the component and test project. From now on, you can open both projects simply by opening the project group.

3. (ActiveX control components skip this step.) Make sure the test project is active — that is, that one of its files is highlighted in the Project window. On the **Project** menu, click **References** to open the **References** dialog box. Locate your component in the list, and check it.

Note When setting up a test program for ActiveX control projects, don't set a reference. A control project automatically adds itself to the **Components** dialog box the first time you place a control on a test project form. For additional information, see "Debugging Controls," in Chapter 9, "Building ActiveX Controls."

If your component still does not appear in the **References** dialog box of your test project, make sure at least one class module in the component has its Instancing property set to a value *other than* Private and PublicNotCreatable.

4. In the Project window, right-click the test project, and click **Set As Start Up** on the context menu to make the test project the one that runs when you press F5.

   Note Because ActiveX control projects cannot be startup projects, a test project added to an ActiveX control project will automatically assume the startup role. If the test project entry in the Project window is in bold-face type, the test project is already the startup project.

5. Add code to test the properties and methods of each public class provided by your component.

With the test project selected in the Project window, you can use the Object Browser to verify that the public classes, methods, and properties of your component are available. You can also use the Object Browser to examine and add description strings, and to verify that Help topics are correctly linked.

The view you get in the Object Browser differs depending on which project is currently active — that is, which one is selected in the Project window. When your component project is active, the Object Browser will show both public members and Friend functions. When the test project is active, only the public members are visible.

For More Information Friend functions are discussed in "Private Communications Between Your Objects," in Chapter 6, "General Principles of Component Design." Special considerations for debugging ActiveX control projects, including running code at design time, are covered in "Debugging Controls," in Chapter 9, "Building ActiveX Controls." ActiveX Documents cannot be debugged without a browser or other active document container; see Chapter 11, "Building ActiveX Documents."

Creating a Test Project for an Out-of-Process Component

This section explains how to set up test projects to exercise most of the objects out-of-process components can provide. ActiveX documents, however, cannot be tested as described here; see Chapter 11, "Building ActiveX Documents."

To create a test project for an out-of-process component

1. On the **File** menu of your out-of-process component (ActiveX EXE project), click **Make <project name>** to create an executable file.

   Important The reason you create this executable is to help your test project keep its reference to the component project. The executable is not required for debugging.

2. On the Project menu, click **<project> Properties** to open the **Project Properties** dialog box. Select the **Components** tab, click **ActiveX Component** in the **Start Mode** box, and then click **OK**.

   Use the ActiveX Component setting when testing your component with a client test program. If your component can also function as a stand-alone desktop application, use the Stand-alone setting to test that mode of operation, as described in "Debugging Out-of-Process Components."

3. Press CTRL+F5 to run your component project.

   Important Your component project *must* be in run mode! When you run your component in the development environment, Visual Basic switches its Windows registry entries from the executable (created in step 1) to the project, and switches them back when you return to design mode. You cannot add a reference to the component *project* unless it's in run mode; a reference to the executable will not allow you to debug the component project in the development environment.

   Always start your component project by pressing CTRL+F5, or by clicking **Start With Full Compile** on the **Run** menu, so that all compilation errors are resolved before your component begins supplying objects to your test application. Compiling component code on demand (the default) can lead to situations in which you have to shut down the component, leaving the test program holding invalid object references. (To disable demand compilation, select **Options** from the **Tools** menu, select the **General** tab of the **Options** dialog box, and clear **Compile On Demand**. This affects the current session as well as future instances of Visual Basic.)

4. Open a second instance of the Visual Basic development environment. In the **New Project** dialog box, click the Standard EXE icon to select it, and then click **OK** to open a new Standard EXE project.

   Note As described in "How to Test ActiveX Components," you must use an ActiveX EXE project as your test project if your component implements asynchronous call-backs.

5. On the **Project** menu, click **References** to open the **References** dialog box. Locate your component in the list, and check it.

   If your component does not appear in the **References** dialog box, switch back to the component project and make sure it's running. If the component project does not stay in run mode when you press CTRL+F5, click **<Project> Properties** on the **Project** menu, to open the **Project Properties** dialog box. Select the **Component** tab, and make sure that **ActiveX Component** is selected in the **Start Mode** box.

   If your component is running, but does not appear in the **References** dialog of your test project, stop the component and make sure at least one of its class modules has its Instancing property set to a value *other than* Private or PublicNotCreatable.

6. Add code to test the properties and methods of each public class provided by your component.

   See Chapter 10, "Programming with Components," in the *Microsoft Visual Basic 6.0 Programmer's Guide*, for more information on referencing other applications' objects from within a client application.

   > **Important** Unless you recompile the executable in step 1 each time you make changes to code in your component project, you can only make changes to the test project while the component project is in run mode.
   >
   > When the component project is not in run mode, the test project doesn't have access to its type library, and will fall back on the type library in the compiled executable you created in Step 1.
   >
   > The executable created in step 1 prevents the test project from losing its reference to the component project, but does not provide access to the features you've added since creating the executable.

You can use the Object Browser in the test project to verify that the public classes, methods, and properties of your component are available. In the test project, the Object Browser will show only the public members.

For More Information "Debugging Out-of-Process Components," later in this chapter, describes debugging techniques. ActiveX Documents cannot be debugged without a browser or other active document container. See Chapter 11, "Building ActiveX Documents."

Project Compatibility: Avoiding MISSING References

In the course of building, testing, and debugging components, you may occasionally see the following error message when you attempt to run your test project: "Connection to type library or object library for remote process has been lost. Press OK for dialog to remove reference."

There are two reasons for this error: Either the type library for your component project is not available, or the GUID of your component's type library has changed, and therefore your test project can no longer locate it. See "Polymorphism, Interfaces, Type Libraries, and GUIDs," in Chapter 6, "General Principles of Component Design," for information about GUIDs and type libraries.

The solution varies, depending on the setting of the Version Compatibility option in your *component* project. You can find the Version Compatibility option on the Component tab of the Project Properties dialog box, available from the Project menu.

If Your Component Is Using Project Compatibility

When you make your component project into an executable (.exe, .dll, or .ocx file) for the first time, as described in "Creating a Test Project for an Out-of-Process Component," Visual Basic automatically sets the Version Compatibility option to Project Compatibility and inserts the path to your made executable. This ensures that your test project and component project remain connected from one development session to the next.

If you're using Project Compatibility for your component project, the solution to the error depends on whether you're debugging the component in the development environment, or attempting to test the made executable.

If You're Debugging the Component Project Out of Process

When you're debugging an out-of-process component (ActiveX EXE projects) in a second instance of the development environment, the test project loses its connection when the component project is in design mode, because the component project's type library is not available.

Run your component project. Switch back to the test project and press Esc to dismiss the error message. You can then run the test project.

> **Note** You may encounter this situation with an ActiveX DLL project if you're debugging an in-process component in a separate instance of the development environment, for example when debugging an in-process component that provides ActiveX documents.

If the Component Project Is Running

If you've just made your component executable for the first time, or manually switched from No Compatibility to Project Compatibility — as described later in this topic — the GUID of your component's type library will have changed, and the test project will be unable to locate it.

Click OK on the error message to open the References dialog box. You'll see the word MISSING next to your component. Remove the check mark and click OK, to clear the missing reference. On the Project menu, click References to open the References dialog box again. Check your component and click OK.

If You're Testing the Made Executable Component

In order to switch between the component project and the made executable component, you must make an up-to-date version of the executable, as described in "How to Test Compiled Components," later in this chapter. If you haven't done this, the type library GUIDs of the executable and the component project will not match, and the test project will not be able to find the executable.

Make the component executable. Switch back to the test project and press ESC to dismiss the error message. You can then run the test project.

If Your Component Project Is Using No Compatibility

If you for some reason you want to use the No Compatibility option for your project, you will have to refresh the reference each time you close your project group (in-process components) or projects (out-of-process components) and reopen them.

To refresh a test application's reference to your component

1. On the **Project** menu of your test project, click **References** to open the **References** dialog box.
2. Locate the entry for your component, which will be marked MISSING. Clear the selection, and click **OK**.

   If there is no entry marked MISSING, locate the component project (the file name and path shown in the **References** dialog box must have the extension .vbp) and check it, then click **OK**. Skip to step 4.

   If your component project does not appear, click **OK** to close the dialog.
3. Make sure your out-of-process component is running. If your component isn't in run mode, there's no type library for the test application to get a reference to.
4. Open the **References** dialog box again. Locate the entry for your component project (.vbp file), and verify that it's no longer marked MISSING. Check it and click the **OK** button.
5. Press F5 to run the test application.

Setting the Project Compatibility Option

The easiest way to set Project Compatibility is to make your component executable (.exe, .dll, or .ocx) for the first time. As described earlier, Visual Basic automatically sets Project Compatibility the first time you make the executable.

If for some reason your project has been set to No Compatibility, you can manually change it to one of the other two Version Compatibility options. Binary Compatibility, described in "Version Compatibility," later in this chapter, is the option to use if you're developing an enhanced version of an existing component.

The option you should use for all new development is Project Compatibility.

To set the Project Compatibility option

1. On the **File** menu of your component project, click **Make <project name>** to create an executable file. If there's an existing executable, overwrite it.

   The only reason to make an executable at this point is to help your test project keep its reference to the component project.

2. On the **Project** menu of your component project, click **<project> Properties** to open the **Project Properties** dialog box.

3. On the **Components** tab, click **Project Compatibility** in the **Version Compatibility** box.

4. Type the name of your executable in the box at the bottom of the **Version Compatibility** box, or use the ellipsis button to browse for it, and then click **OK**.

   Note The Project Compatibility option actually has nothing whatever to do with the Binary Compatibility option (described in "Version Compatibility").

For More Information Type libraries and GUIDs are discussed in "Polymorphism, Interfaces, Type Libraries, and GUIDs," in Chapter 6, "General Principles of Component Design."

Debugging Out-of-Process Components

This topic describes debugging procedures for most objects provided by out-of-process components. ActiveX documents, however, cannot be debugged as described here. See Chapter 11, "Building ActiveX Documents."

To debug an out-of-process component

1. Set breakpoints and watch expressions as needed in your class module code.

2. Run the component project by pressing CTRL+F5 or clicking **Start With Full Compile** on the **Run** menu.

   The component will compile, but Sub Main will not run until the first object is created in response to a client request.

3. Start a second instance of Visual Basic, and open your test project. Set breakpoints and watch expressions as needed.

4. Run the test project. When a breakpoint is encountered in the component code, the component project receives focus.

   Note When an out-of-process component enters break mode, focus may not immediately switch to the component project. If you click anywhere on the client, the **Component Busy** dialog box will be displayed. Click the **Switch To** button to give the focus to the component project.

5. When you're finished with the debugging session, close your test project before stopping the component.

   Important If you stop the component project before closing your test project, all of the objects the component was providing will be destroyed. Your test project may get errors when you try to close it.

Start with Full Compile

Always start your out-of-process component project by pressing CTRL+F5, or by clicking Start With Full Compile on the Run menu, so that all compilation errors are resolved before your component begins supplying objects to your test application.

The default in Visual Basic is to compile code on demand. This means that there may be code in your component which is not compiled until the client calls it. Some compile errors cannot be fixed without returning to design mode, which means shutting down the component. In that case, the test program is left holding invalid object references.

> **Note** To disable demand compilation, select Options from the Tools menu, select the General tab of the Options dialog box, and clear Compile On Demand. This affects the current session as well as future instances of Visual Basic.

Editing the Test Project

As you develop your component, you'll frequently add new functionality between debugging sessions. Before editing your test project to add code to exercise the new features, be sure to put your component project in run mode.

When the component project is not in run mode, the test project doesn't have access to its type library. If you're using Project Compatibility, the test project will fall back on the type library in the compiled executable. If it's been a while since you made the executable, the type library won't contain information on the features you've added.

If you're using the No Compatibility option of Version Compatibility, there will be no type library information at all.

Your component project should always be in run mode when you're editing the test project.

Shutting Down an Out-of-Process Component

When you're debugging objects that have Terminate event code, remember that the Terminate event is not executed if you stop your component project using the End button on the toolbar, or if you choose End or Restart from the Run menu.

Shutting down test projects will release all the objects your component is providing to those projects. As those objects close down, they should release all references to private objects within your component.

This allows your component to meet the four rules for component shutdown, as listed in "Starting and Ending a Component," in Chapter 6, "General Principles of Component Design."

Unfortunately, even when all objects have been released by your test projects, and all four shutdown conditions have been met, an out-of-process component will not return to design mode. To return to design mode, you will have to use the End button.

If your component maintains internal references to objects, you can simulate normal shutdown by creating a Sub procedure that releases all such references. You can call this procedure from the Immediate window before stopping your component — or place an End statement in the Sub. However, there is no guarantee that the order in which private objects are terminated will be the same under actual shutdown conditions.

The only way to accurately test shutdown behavior is with the compiled component.

> **Tip** Debugging causes artificial changes in focus that may prevent your code from behaving as you expect. For debugging situations that are sensitive to focus or activation, such as mouse and key events, use `Debug.Print` to log debugging information.

Debugging Components as Stand-alone Desktop Applications

If your out-of-process component can double as a stand-alone desktop application, like Microsoft Excel, you have two startup and shutdown modes to test.

Such applications typically have code like the following, to allow them to start up with or without a main window:

```
Sub Main
   If App.StartMode = vbSModeAutomation Then
      ' ...code to start invisibly...
   Else      ' (App.StartMode = vbSModeStandalone)
      ' ...code to show main form...
   End If
End Sub
```

StartMode is a read-only property of the App object which can be used at run time to determine whether your application was started in response to a request from a client application, or by the user, through the Start button on the Taskbar.

> **Note** Do not place Sub Main in a class module. Placing Sub Main in a class module turns it into a method named Main, rather than a startup procedure. Your Sub Main procedure must be in a standard module.

While debugging, you can control the mode your component starts in using the settings in the Start Mode box, on the Component tab of the Project Properties dialog box. Use the Standalone setting to start your component as if the user had opened it using the Start button on Taskbar; use the ActiveX Component setting to compile your component so that Sub Main will run when the client (your test project) first creates an object.

Debugging with Multiple Clients

If you need to debug a problem that only occurs when multiple client applications are using objects from your component, you can start additional instances of Visual Basic, or compile your test project and run the .exe file to provide the extra instances. You can run as many client applications as you need.

Components can be debugged whether they're being called from a different Visual Basic project or from a client written in another language. For example, if you're designing a component specifically for Microsoft Excel users, you may want to use Microsoft Excel as the client when you're debugging.

For More Information "Using Break on Error in Components," later in this chapter, explains how to use the Error Trapping options with component projects. See "Testing and Debugging ActiveX Components," earlier in this chapter, for a list of topics related to testing and debugging.

Debugging In-Process Components

This topic describes debugging procedures for most objects provided by in-process components. ActiveX documents, however, cannot be debugged as described here. See Chapter 11, "Building ActiveX Documents."

To debug an in-process component

1. Set breakpoints and watch expressions as needed in your class module or UserControl code.
2. Run the project group by pressing CTRL+F5 or clicking **Start With Full Compile** on the **Run** menu.

   The in-process component will compile, but Sub Main will not run until the first object is created in response to a client request.

   While debugging, you can step from the test project directly into code in the component project.
3. When you're finished with the debugging session, click the **Close** button on test project's main window to return to design mode.

   > **Important** Closing the test project by clicking the **End** button will cause all projects to close. Objects in the component will not receive Terminate events. Shutting down in this fashion will not correctly test the shutdown behavior of your component.

Start with Full Compile

You may find it more convenient to start the project group by pressing CTRL+F5, or by clicking Start With Full Compile on the Run menu, so that all compilation errors are resolved before your component begins supplying objects to your test application.

The default in Visual Basic is to compile code on demand. This means that there may be code in your component which is not compiled until the client calls it. Some compile errors cannot be fixed without returning to design mode, which means returning the whole project group to design mode.

> **Note** To disable demand compilation, select Options from the Tools menu, select the General tab of the Options dialog box, and clear Compile On Demand. This affects the current session as well as future instances of Visual Basic.

Shutting Down an In-Process Component

In-process components will not unload while running in the development environment, even if all references to objects are released by the test project, and all other component shutdown conditions are met. The only way to test DLL unloading behavior is with the compiled component.

For More Information The next section, "Using Break on Error in Components," explains how to use the Error Trapping options with component projects. ActiveX control projects must be debugged while the client is in design mode, as well as run mode. See "Debugging Controls," in Chapter 9, "Building ActiveX Controls." ActiveX Documents cannot be debugged without a browser or other active document container. See Chapter 11, "Building ActiveX Documents." See "Testing and Debugging ActiveX Components," earlier in this chapter, for a list of topics related to testing and debugging.

Using Break on Error in Components

You can change the way Visual Basic enters break mode when an error occurs in your component by setting the Error Trapping option in your component project.

In your component project, choose Options from the Tools menu to open the Options dialog box, and select the General tab. There are three options in the Default Error Trapping State box, as described below.

> **Note** The setting in the Default Error Trapping State box controls the default setting of the option when you start Visual Basic; it also toggles the option in the current session. If you wish to change the setting for the current session only, without affecting the default, select Toggle from the code window context menu.

Suppose you have a component that provides a Widget object that has a Spin method. The following descriptions assume that the test application has called the Spin method of the Widget object, and that an error has occurred in the Spin method's code.

- Break on All Errors: The component project is activated, and the Spin method's code window receives the focus. The line of code that caused the error is highlighted. Visual Basic always enters break mode on such an error, even if error handling is enabled in the Spin method.

  Note You can press ALT+F8 or ALT+F5 to step or run past the error.

- Break in Class Module: If error handling is not enabled in the Spin method, or if you are deliberately raising an error for the client by calling the Raise method of the Err object in the Spin method's error handler, the component project is activated, and the Spin method's code window receives the focus. The line of code that caused the error is highlighted.

  Note You can press ALT+F8 or ALT+F5 to step or run past the error.

  If error handling is enabled in Spin, then the error handler is invoked. As long as you don't raise an error in the error handler, Visual Basic does not enter break mode.

- Break on Unhandled Errors: Visual Basic never enters break mode in properties or methods of the component. If error handling is not enabled in the client procedure that called the Spin method, execution stops on the line of code that made the call.

  To understand the behavior of Break on Unhandled Errors in a component project, remember that the component's properties and methods are always called by somebody else. An error in a property or method can always be handled by passing it up the call tree into the client procedure that called the property or method.

  Note When an out-of-process component enters break mode, focus may not immediately switch to the component project. If you click anywhere on the client, the Component Busy dialog box will be displayed. Click the Switch To button to give the focus to the component project.

For More Information See Chapter 13, "Debugging Your Code and Handling Errors," in the *Microsoft Visual Basic 6.0 Programmer's Guide*.

How to Test Compiled Components

When you choose Make from the File menu, your component will be registered automatically in the Windows Registry. You can switch your test application between the component project and the compiled component using the procedures in this topic.

In-Process Components

The following procedures perform the switch for an in-process component (ActiveX DLL project or ActiveX control project).

To switch from an in-process component project to the compiled .dll or .ocx file

1. On the **File** menu, click **Make <projectname>** to create the compiled in-process component.
2. In the Project window, select the component project.
3. On the **File** menu, click **Remove <projectname>** to remove the component project from the project group.

   A warning message will appear: "The project is referenced from another project. Are you sure you want to remove it?" Click **OK** to remove the project.
4. Press F5 to run the test project.

   Visual Basic automatically switches references to the compiled .ocx or .dll file.

To switch back to testing your in-process component project

1. On the **File** menu, click **Add Project** to open the **Add Project** dialog box.
2. Use the **Recent** or **Existing** tab to open your component project.
3. Press F5 to run the test project.

   Visual Basic automatically switches references back to the component project.

Out-of-Process Components

Remember that an out-of-process component must be tested using two instances of the development environment. The following procedures perform the switch for an out-of-process component (ActiveX EXE project).

To switch from an out-of-process component project to the compiled executable

1. On the **File** menu of the component project, click **Make <projectname>** to create an up-to-date version of the executable.

   Important If you neglect to make the executable, you'll get the following error message when you attempt to run your test project: "Connection to type library or object library for remote process has been lost. Press **OK** for dialog to remove reference."
2. In the test project, press F5 to run the project.

   When the component project is not running, Visual Basic automatically switches registry entries to point to the compiled executable.

To switch back to testing your out-of-process component project

1. In the component project, press Ctrl+F5 to run the project.
2. In the test project, press F5 to run the project.

   When the component project is running, Visual Basic automatically switches registry entries back to it.

You may also want to create an executable file from your test application, and run several instances of it to test your component with multiple client applications.

Testing Your Component with Other Applications

You can test your component from any application that can make Automation calls. For example, you can open a Microsoft Excel module, add a reference to your component by choosing References from the Project menu, and write procedures to create and use objects provided by your component.

Even if you do not expect your component to be used as an extension of end user software tools like Microsoft Excel and Microsoft Access, it's a good idea to test it with such tools. The more programming tools your component works with, the more value it will have for your company or for your customers.

For More Information See "Testing and Debugging ActiveX Components," earlier in this chapter, for a list of topics related to testing and debugging.

Generating and Handling Errors in ActiveX Components

There's no such thing as an unhandled error in a component. Untrapped errors in a method of your component, or errors you generate using the Raise method of the Err object, will be raised in the client application that called the method.

Raising errors or returning error codes to the client is the appropriate behavior for components. A well behaved component does not intrude on the client application's user interface by displaying message boxes containing error text.

Users of an application may be blissfully unaware that your component is part of the application they're using. Seeing error messages from a program unknown to them will not improve their day, or help them solve the problem.

For More Information The basics of error handling are discussed in Chapter 13, "Debugging Your Code and Handling Errors," in the *Microsoft Visual Basic 6.0 Programmer's Guide.*

Deciding How to Generate Error Messages

When an application calls a method of an object your component provides, there are two general ways in which the method can provide error information.

- Basic-style: The method can raise an error. The client application can implement an error handler to trap errors that may be raised by the method.
- Windows API-style: The value returned by the method can be an error code. The client application can examine the return value to determine whether an error has occurred.

There are a number of programming tradeoffs to consider when you select an error generation strategy for your component, but the most important consideration should be the convenience of the developer who will use your component.

For example, if your methods always return an error value, the developer using your component must use *in-line error handling,* that is, the developer must always test the return value after calling a method. This is the way Windows API calls work.

If you raise errors, on the other hand, the developer has the choice of implementing in-line error handling (On Error Resume Next) or writing error-handling routines (On Error GoTo). This flexibility is a hallmark of the coding style familiar to Basic developers.

Be Consistent

Whichever error generation strategy you adopt, be consistent. Developers will not appreciate having to test return values from some methods, and trap errors from others.The more difficult it is to use a component, the less benefit there is from re-using the code.

If you decide to return error values instead of raising them, it's better for all return values to be error codes. This means that if a method also returns a data value, you must use a ByRef parameter for the data. While this is an inconvenience for the user of the method, it's less of an inconvenience than having to test the data type of a return value, to see whether it's an error, before using it as a data value.

> **Note** Client applications that use out-of-process components should always employ some form of error handling, because failures in the underlying cross-process communication layer will be raised as errors in the client application.

For More Information The next section, "Guidelines for Raising Errors from Your Component," discusses standards and techniques for raising errors from ActiveX components.

Guidelines for Raising Errors from Your Component

Use the Raise method of the Err object to raise errors that can be trapped by client applications. When you call the Raise method in the error handler of one of your methods or Property procedures, or when error handling is turned off (On Error GoTo 0), the error will be raised in the client application, in the procedure that directly called your method.

If the procedure that called your method has no error handler, the error condition moves up the call tree of the client until it reaches a procedure that has an error handler, just as any other error would.

When raising an error condition from your component, you don't need to worry about whether the client is written in Visual Basic, Microsoft Visual C++, or another programming language. Any client application can receive the errors your component raises.

Here are a few guidelines you should follow when raising errors from a component.

- The error number you return to client applications is generated by adding an intrinsic constant (vbObjectError) to your internal error number. The resulting value is the one you should document for your users.
- The internal error numbers you add to vbObjectError should be in the range 512 to 65535 (&H200 to &HFFFF). Numbers below 512 may conflict with values reserved for use by the system.
- Establish a "fatal error" or "general failure" code and message for conditions from which your component can't recover.
- When calling Err.Raise, supply both an error number and a text string describing the error.
- Document your errors in the Help file for your component. For the convenience of your users, you may want to show error numbers in both decimal and hexadecimal format.

For example, you might implement the SpinDirection property of the Widget object as a Property procedure, to ensure that it accepts only certain values, as in the following code fragment from the Widget class module of the hypothetical SmallMechanicals component.

```
' Enumeration for SpinDirection property values.
'   (The prefix "sm" identifies it as belonging to the
'   SmallMechanicals component.)
Public Enum smSpinDirection
   smSDClockwise
   smSDCounterClockwise
End Enum
```

```
' Module-level storage for SpinDirection property.
Private msdSpinDirection As smSpinDirection

' Implementation of the SpinDirection property.
Property Get SpinDirection() As smSpinDirection
   SpinDirection = msdSpinDirection
End Property

Property Let SpinDirection(ByVal sdNew As _
      smSpinDirection)
   ' The Select Case does nothing if sdNew contains
   ' a valid value.
   Select Case sdNew
      Case smSDClockwise
      Case smSDCounterClockwise
      Case Else
         Err.Raise _
            (ERR_SPN_INVALID + vbObjectError), _
            CMP_SOURCENAME, _
            LoadResString(ERR_SPN_INVALID)
   End Select
   ' If no error, assign the new property value.
   msdSpinDirection = sdNew
End Property
```

The code above assumes that `ERR_SPN_INVALID` and `CMP_SOURCENAME` are public constants declared in a standard module, and that error text strings are stored in a resource file.

Because there is no error handler in the Property Let procedure used to set the value of the SpinDirection property, the error is raised in the client application, in the procedure that attempted to set the invalid value.

The text string for the error message is loaded from the component project's resource file, using the internal error number as an index. This technique reduces the amount of memory required to run the component. By concentrating all the text strings in one place, it also simplifies the creation of international versions of the component.

> **Note** Programmers who have used the C++ language will recognize vbObjectError as *facility interface* (FACILITY_ITF), the base constant for the range of errors reserved for a component's interface.

For More Information The next section, "Handling Errors in a Component," discusses the handling of internal errors, particularly those raised by components your component is using. For more on the Err object and resource files, see "Err object" in the *Microsoft Visual Basic 6.0 Language Reference* volume of the *Microsoft Visual Basic 6.0 Reference Library*and "resource files" in the index.

Providing error messages in multiple languages is discussed in "Localizing Components," later in this chapter, and Chapter 16, "International Issues," in the *Microsoft Visual Basic 6.0 Programmer's Guide.*

Handling Errors in a Component

When authoring a component, you should be prepared to handle three types of errors:

- Errors generated in your component code that you handle internally.
- Errors generated in your component code that you want to pass back to the client application.
- Errors generated by another component from which your component has obtained object references.

Handling Errors Internally

Handling the first of these three error types is no different for a component than for any other application developed using Visual Basic. This type of error handling is covered in Chapter 13, "Debugging Your Code and Handling Errors," in the *Microsoft Visual Basic 6.0 Programmer's Guide.*

Passing Errors Back to the Client

As outlined in "Raising Errors from Your Component," you can use the Raise method of the Err object to raise errors in a client application that calls methods provided by your component. For the error to be raised in the client, you must call Raise from your method's error-handling routine, or with error handling disabled, as in the following fragment of code from the Run method of a hypothetical Widget object.

```
Public Sub Run()
   ' Use in-line error handling.
   On Error Resume Next
   ' (Many lines of Run method code omitted.)
   ' If the following test fails, raise an error in
   ' the client that called the method.
   If intWidgetState <> STATE_RUNNING Then
      ' Disable in-line error handling.
      On Error Goto 0
      Err.Raise _
         Number:=(ERR_WDG_HALTED + vbObjectError), _
         Source:=CMP_SOURCENAME, _
         Description:=LoadResString(ERR_WDG_HALTED)
   End If
   ' (Run method code continues.)
End Sub
```

When you raise errors for invalid parameter values, you can simply place the Err.Raise statements at the beginning of the method, before the first On Error statement. The same is true of code to validate property values; place it at the beginning of the Property Let or Property Set.

Raising Errors from Error Handlers

Frequently your properties and methods will include code to handle internal errors. Such code may from time to time contain cases in which no sensible internal response is possible. In such cases, it's reasonable for the property or method to fail and return an error to the client:

```
   On Error Goto ErrHandler
   ' (Code omitted.)
   Exit Sub

ErrHandler:
   Select Case Err.Number
      ' Errors that can be handled (not shown).
      Case 11
         ' Division by zero cannot be handled in any
         ' sensible fashion.
         Err.Raise ERR_INTERNAL + vbObjectError, _
            CMP_SOURCENAME, _
            LoadResString(ERR_INTERNAL)
      ' Other errors (not shown).
   End Select
```

In most cases it doesn't make sense to return the original "Divide by zero" error to the client. The client has no way of knowing why such an error occurred within your property or method, so the message is of no use in finding a solution.

If the developer of the client was aware of the possibility of this internal error, because of the excellent documentation you provided, he may have included code to handle it, and shown the end user of the application a useful error message.

If the developer didn't handle it, `ERR_INTERNAL` might at least serve a diagnostic purpose by including the method parameters in the error message text, as information to pass on to the author of the component.

Handling Errors from Another Component

If your component uses objects provided by another component, you must handle errors that may result when you call methods of those objects. You should be able to obtain a list of these errors from the second component's documentation.

It's important to handle such errors within your component, and not return them to the client application that called your component. The client was written to use your component, and to respond to your component's error codes. The user or programmer who wrote it may have no knowledge of secondary components you're using.

Encapsulation of Errors

The idea that a client application should receive errors only from the components it calls directly reflects the object-oriented concept of *encapsulation*. In the case of errors, encapsulation means that an object is self-contained. Although the object in your component may use other objects supplied by other components, the client application is ignorant of those objects.

For this reason, you should always specify the *source* argument of the Raise method when you handle an error from another component. Otherwise, the Source property of the client application's Err object will contain the name of the component your component called.

> **Note** You should not use the value of the Source property of the Err object for program flow decisions. The Source property may provide useful context information when you're debugging your component, but the text it contains may be version dependent.

The following code fragment shows the error handler for a method that uses objects in another component. When it encounters an error it cannot handle, or an unanticipated error, the error handler raises an error for the client, using its own error numbers and descriptions.

```
' Code from the Spin method of a hypothetical Widget
' object.
Public Sub Spin(ByVal Speed As Double)
   On Error Goto ErrHandler
   ' Code containing calls to objects in the Gears
   ' component (omitted).
   Exit Sub

ErrHandler:
   Select Case Err.Number
      ' Other errors (not shown).
      ' --- Errors from the Gears component. ---
      Case vbObjectError + 2000
         ' Error 2000 is handled by shifting to
         ' another gear (code not shown).
      Case vbObjectError + 3000
         ' Error 3000 causes spin-down; error must be
         ' returned to caller.
         Err.Raise ERR_SPN_SPINDOWN + vbObjectError, _
            CMP_SOURCENAME, _
            LoadResString(ERR_SPN_SPINDOWN)
      ' --- Unanticipated errors from components. ---
```

```
      Case vbObjectError To (vbObjectError + 65536)
         Err.Raise ERR_SPN_FAILURE + vbObjectError, _
            CMP_SOURCENAME, _
            LoadResString(ERR_SPN_FAILURE)
      ' Other errors (not shown).
   End Select
End Sub
```

Note Some components use older error return mechanisms. Such components may return error numbers in the range 0–65535.

When the Gears component raises Error 3000, the Spin method must return an error to the application that called it. The error returned is an error of the Spin method. The application using the Spin method doesn't know that Spin is implemented using the Gears component, and could not be expected to deal with Error 3000. All it needs to know is that a spin-down condition has occurred.

In the preceding example a global constant, `CMP_SOURCENAME`, is used for the *source* argument of the Raise method. If you raise errors outside an error handler, and do not specify the *source* argument, Visual Basic uses the name you entered in the Project Name field of the General tab in the Project Properties dialog box, combined with the Name property of the class module.

While this may be useful for you to know while debugging your component, it's better for the compiled component to specify a consistent value for the *source* argument in all errors it raises.

Note It's frequently easier to use in-line error handling when making calls to components, because the same error may require a different response depending on the method that was called, or the circumstances in which it was called. If you're calling two different components, they may use the same number for different errors.

Bending Encapsulation Rules

There may be cases in which some of the error messages returned by a secondary component may contain information of use to the end user of the client application. For example, an error message might contain the name of a file.

In such cases, you may want to bend encapsulation rules to pass along this information. The safest way to do this is to include the text of the Description property of the Err object in your own error message text, as in the following fragment of error-handling code:

```
' Error 3033 is returned from a call to another
' component; the message text contains a file name that
' will be useful in resolving the problem.
Case vbObjectError + 3033
   ' Raise a Print Run Failure error to the client,
   ' and append the message text from Error 3033.
   Err.Raise _
      ERR_PRINTRUNFAILURE + vbObjectError, _
      CMP_SOURCENAME, _
      LoadResString(ERR_PRINTRUNFAILURE) _
         & Err.Description
```

In some cases, it may be useful to the end user to know what component originated the error, and the original error number and message text. You can include all of this information in the description of the error you raise.

For More Information See Chapter 13, "Debugging Your Code and Handling Errors," in the *Microsoft Visual Basic 6.0 Programmer's Guide,* or see "Error" or "Err" in the *Microsoft Visual Basic 6.0 Language Reference*.

Providing User Assistance for ActiveX Components

Creating a Help file for your component is highly recommended. One of the most important benefits of components is enabling code reuse, a goal you will be much more likely to achieve if developers and end users can easily get Help for the objects you've authored. ActiveX components support both Windows Help and HTML Help files.

You can also provide browser strings that briefly describe your objects and their properties, methods, and events. Users of your component can view these description strings using the Object Browsers in their programming tools, and jump to the Help topics you've provided.

For More Information See Appendix D, "Adding Help to Your Application," in the *Microsoft Visual Basic 6.0 Programmer's Guide*.

When it comes to user assistance, don't underestimate the importance of choosing good names for your objects and their interfaces. See "What's in a Name?" in Chapter 6, "General Principles of Component Design," and "Object Naming Guidelines" in Appendix A, "ActiveX Component Standards and Guidelines."

How to Specify a Help File for Your Component

To specify a Help file for your component

1. On the **Project** menu, click **Project Properties** to open the **Project Properties** dialog box, then click the **General** tab.
2. In the **Help File Name** box, enter the path and name of the Help file you've created for your component.
3. In the **Project Help Context ID** box, enter the context ID for the specific Help topic to be called when the user clicks the "**?**" button while your component's type library is selected in the **Object Browser**.

For More Information The next section, "Providing Help and Browser Strings for Objects," gives the procedure for linking objects and their interface members to Help topics. User assistance features available for components are listed earlier in this section.

Providing Help and Browser Strings for Objects

Objects are created from classes. The Object Browser displays information about the classes from which objects are created.

The following procedure can be used to link Help topics and provide browser strings for classes, and for their properties, methods, and events. When Visual Basic creates the type library for your component, it includes this information. Users of your component can view the description strings using the Object Browsers in their programming tools, and jump to your Help topics.

For an alternate method of supplying Help and browser strings for properties, methods, and events, see "Providing Help and Browser Strings for Properties, Methods, and Events," later in this chapter.

To enter description strings and link your classes and their members to Help topics

1. Press F2 to open the **Object Browser**. In the **Project/Library** box, select your project.

   If you're not sure which is the **Project/Library** box, hover the mouse pointer over the boxes until you see the tool tip.

2. In the **Classes** list, right click the name of a class to bring up the context menu, and click **Properties** to open the **Member Options** dialog box.

   Alternatively, in the **Members** list, right click the name of a property, method, or event to bring up the context menu, and click **Properties** to open the **Member Options** dialog box.

3. In the **Help Context ID** box, type the context ID of the Help topic to be shown if the user clicks the "**?**" button when this class or member is selected in the **Object Browser**.

   The path and name of the Help file for the project should appear in the **Help File** box. If it does not, see "How to Specify a Help File for Your Component" for instructions on setting it.

4. In the **Description** box, type a brief description of the class or member.

5. Click **OK** to return to the **Object Browser**. The description string you entered should appear on the panel at the bottom of the browser.

6. Repeat steps 2 through 5 for each class and for each member of each class.

Figure 7.2 shows the Object Browser and Member Options dialog box as they would appear when setting the description and Help context ID for a class in a hypothetical test application.

Figure 7.2 Setting the description and Help context ID

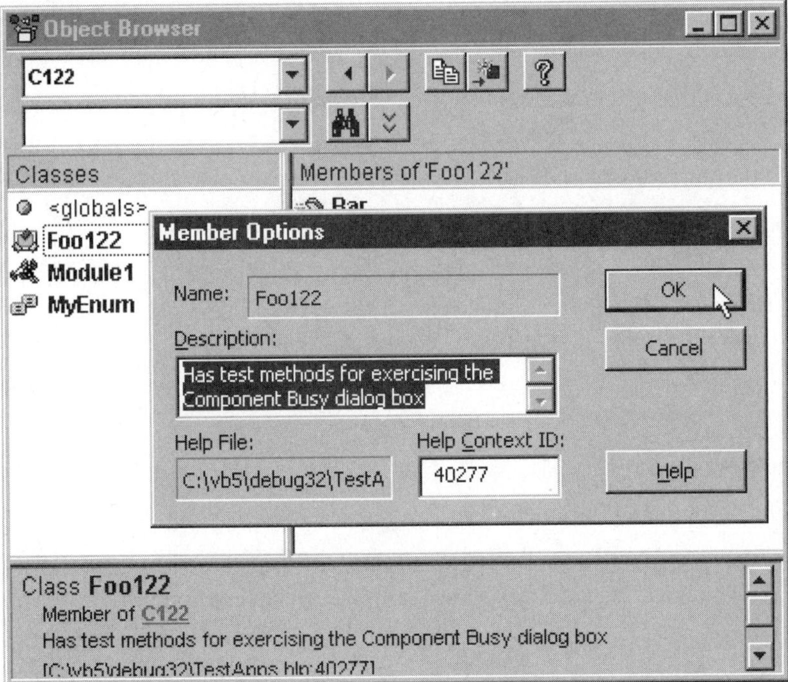

Note You can enter Help context IDs and descriptions for private classes in your component, but this information will only be available to you when you're actually working on your component project. It will not appear in the type library for your component.

You cannot supply browser strings or Help topics for enumerations.

For More Information Creating Help files is discussed in the *Microsoft Windows Help Authoring Kit*, available from Microsoft Press. User assistance features available for components are listed earlier in this section.

Providing Help and Browser Strings for Properties, Methods, and Events

You can use the Procedure Attributes dialog box to enter description strings for your properties, methods, and events, and to provide links to topics in your Help file. When Visual Basic creates the type library for your component, it includes this information. Users of your component can view the description strings using the Object Browsers in their programming tools, and jump to the Help topics.

You can use the Visual Basic Object Browser to enter description strings for your classes, as described in "Providing Help and Browser Strings for Objects," earlier in this chapter. The Object Browser can also be used to enter this information for properties, methods, and events.

To enter description strings and link Help topics to your properties, methods, and events

1. In the Project window, select a module and press F7 (or click **View Code** on the Project window toolbar) to open its code window.
2. On the **Tools** menu, click **Procedure Attributes** to open the **Procedure Attributes** dialog box.
3. Select a property, method, or event in the **Name** box.
4. In the **Help Context ID** box, type the context ID of the Help topic to be shown if the user clicks the "?" button when this member is selected in the **Object Browser**.

   The path and name of the Help file for the project should appear in the **Help File** box. If it does not, see "How to Specify a Help File for Your Component" for instructions on setting it.
5. In the **Description** box, type a brief description of the member.
6. Click the **Apply** button to save the information.
7. Repeat steps 3 through 6 for each property and method in the module.

Figure 7.3 shows the Procedure Attributes dialog box as it would appear when setting the description and Help context ID for a member of a class in a hypothetical test application.

Figure 7.3 Setting the description and Help context ID

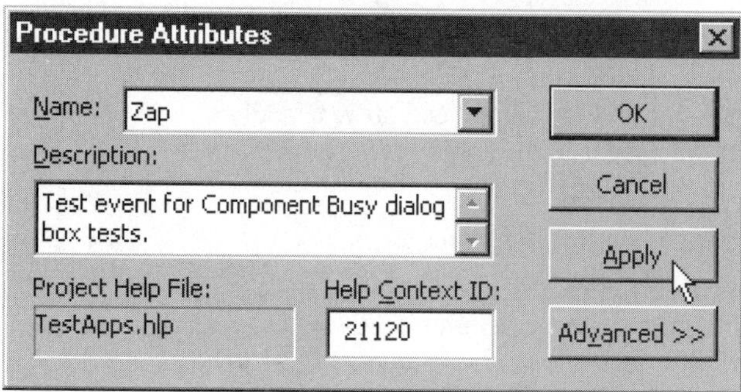

> **Note** You can enter Help context IDs and descriptions for members of private classes in your component, but this information will only be available to you when you're actually working on your component project. It will not appear in the type library for your component. You cannot supply browser strings or Help topics for enumerations.

For More Information Creating Help files is discussed in the *Microsoft Windows Help Authoring Kit*, available from Microsoft Press. User assistance features available for components are listed in "Providing User Assistance for ActiveX Components," earlier in this chapter.

Deploying ActiveX Components

In addition to providing objects for use by client applications, some components can function as standalone desktop applications, in the way Microsoft Excel does. If your component is in this category, you can distribute it as you would any Visual Basic application.

Chapter 17, "Distributing Your Applications," in the *Microsoft Visual Basic 6.0 Programmer's Guide,* contains all the information you need to use the Package and Deployment Wizard, or to create a custom Setup for your application.

This section and "Setting Base Addresses for In-Process Components," later in this chapter, discuss the distribution of components that are not stand-alone applications.

Ways to Distribute Components

There are several ways to distribute a component. For example:

- As part of your own Visual Basic applications.
- As a tool users can access from Automation-enabled desktop applications such as Microsoft Excel and Microsoft Access.
- As a component other developers can include in their applications, or use with the Internet.
- As part of an enterprise application, running on a remote computer (requires the Enterprise Edition of Visual Basic).

For all of these distribution scenarios except the first, you can create a stand-alone Setup for your component.

Distributing a Component as Part of a Visual Basic Application

To distribute your component as part of a Visual Basic application, you can use Package and Deployment Wizard to create a setup program for the application. If your application has a reference to the component, Package and Deployment Wizard will locate the component using its registry entries, and include it — along with its support files — in the list of files needed to create distribution media.

As with components that are also stand-alone desktop applications, this scenario is largely covered by ordinary application setup. The only additional consideration is the use of implemented interfaces.

Including Type Libraries for Implemented Interfaces

If you've used the Implements keyword to add additional interfaces to your classes, as described in "Providing Polymorphism by Implementing Interfaces" in Chapter 6, "General Principles of Component Design," you may need to include the type libraries for those interfaces in Setup for your component.

You need to include the type library that includes a particular interface if:

- Any classes the interface has been added to are provided by out-of-process components.
- The application will provide objects to other applications, and some of those objects implement the interface.

The reason type libraries need to be included with your application in these two situations is that invoking an object's properties and methods cross-process requires marshaling their arguments. In order to marshal the arguments, type library information must be available.

Stand-alone Setup for a Component

To distribute your component for use by other developers, by Internet providers, or as part of an Enterprise application, use Package and Deployment Wizard to create a stand-alone setup program. The Package and Deployment Wizard will automatically include necessary support files. Be sure to include your Help file.

> **Important** For in-process components, see the related topic "Setting Base Addresses for In-Process Components," later in this chapter , which contains important information regarding base addresses and their effect on the performance of your component.

Developers who use your component can install it on their computers, and then use the Package and Deployment Wizard or the Setup Toolkit to include it in the distribution media for their applications.

The steps required to produce Setup for your component will also give you the file dependency information you need to provide to developers who want to use your component with Microsoft Excel, Microsoft Visual C++, or other Automation-enabled development tools.

Distributing Type Libraries for Implemented Interfaces

If you've used the Implements keyword to add additional interfaces to your classes, as described in "Providing Polymorphism by Implementing Interfaces" in Chapter 6, "General Principles of Component Design," you need to include the type libraries for those interfaces in Setup for your component.

Special Considerations

Distribution issues particular to ActiveX controls — such as licensing — and to ActiveX documents can be found in Chapter 9, "Building ActiveX Controls," and Chapter 11, "Building ActiveX Documents."

If you plan to use your component for Internet development, the Package and Deployment Wizard can create CAB files for you. You can obtain the most up-to-date information on Internet setup options from the Microsoft Visual Basic Web site.

For More Information See Chapter 17, "Distributing Your Applications," in the *Microsoft Visual Basic 6.0 Programmer's Guide*.

Setting Base Addresses for In-Process Components

In 32-bit operating systems, the code pages for an in-process component (.dll or .ocx file) are shared between processes that use the component, as long as the component can load at its *base address*. Thus three clients could be using the controls in your component, but the code would be loaded into memory only once.

By contrast, if the memory locations used by an in-process component conflict with memory locations used by other in-process components or by the executable, the component must be *rebased* to another logical memory location in the executable's process space.

Rebasing requires the operating system to dynamically recalculate the logical memory locations where code and data are loaded. This recalculation slows down the load process, and code that is dynamically relocated generally *cannot be shared between executables*.

You can greatly improve your component's memory use by choosing a good base address.

Setting the Base Address

To enter the base address for your component, open the Project Properties dialog box and select the Compile tab. The address is entered in the DLL Base Address box, as an unsigned decimal or hexadecimal integer.

The default value is &H11000000 (285,212,672). If you neglect to change this value, your component will conflict with every other in-process component compiled using the default. Staying well away from this address is recommended.

Choosing a Base Address

Choose a base address between 16 megabytes (16,777,216 or &H1000000) and 2 gigabytes (2,147,483,648 or &H80000000).

The base address must be a multiple of 64K. The memory used by your component begins at the initial base address and is the size of the compiled file, rounded up to the next multiple of 64K.

Your program cannot extend above two gigabytes, so the maximum base address is actually two gigabytes minus the memory used by your component.

> **Note** Executables will usually load at the 4 megabyte logical address. The region below 4 megabytes is reserved under Windows 95, and regions above two gigabytes are reserved by both Windows 95 and Windows NT.

Use a Good Random Number Generator

Because there is no way to know what base addresses might be chosen by other in-process components your users might employ, the best practice is to choose an address at random from the indicated range, and round it up to the next multiple of 64K.

If your company produces many in-process components, you may wish to randomly calculate the base address of the first, and then arrange the others above or below the first, thus guaranteeing at least that your company's components will not have memory conflicts.

Version Compatibility in ActiveX Components

A component can be part of another application because it provides Automation interfaces that the other application can manipulate. Each public class module has a default interface that includes all the properties and methods you added to the class module, plus any secondary interfaces implemented using the Implements feature.

Once your component has been used in an application — or, in the case of ActiveX controls, embedded in a document or on a Web page — you can change its interfaces only at the risk of breaking the client application.

Suppose, for example, that the Spin method of your Widget object has one argument, Speed. If you distribute a new version of your component, in which you redefine the Spin method so that it also requires a Direction argument, you could cause run-time errors in existing applications.

At the same time, a successful component will inevitably spark requests for enhancements. You will want to provide new objects, or add new properties and methods to existing objects. Occasionally you will even want to change the arguments of existing methods of existing objects.

For More Information See "Polymorphism, Interfaces, Type Libraries, and GUIDs," in Chapter 6, "General Principles of Component Design," for background information and concepts.

When Should I Use Version Compatibility?

Visual Basic provides two mechanisms for maintaining backward compatibility while enhancing software components — the Version Compatibility feature and the Implements feature.

Version Compatibility

Visual Basic's Version Compatibility feature is a way of enhancing your components while maintaining backward compatibility with programs that were compiled using earlier versions. The Version Compatibility box, located on the Component tab of the Project Properties dialog box, contains three options:

- No Compatibility: Each time you compile the component, new type library information is generated, including new class IDs and new interface IDs. There is no relation between versions of a component, and programs compiled to use one version cannot use subsequent versions.
- Project Compatibility: Each time you compile the component, the type library identifier is kept, so that your test projects can maintain their references to the component project. All class IDs from the previous version are maintained; interface IDs are changed only for classes that are no longer binary-compatible with their earlier counterparts.

  Note This is a change in Project Compatibility from Visual Basic 5.0, where all class IDs and interface IDs in the project changed if any one class was no longer binary-compatible.

  Important For the purpose of releasing compatible versions of a component, Project Compatibility is the same as No Compatibility.

- Binary Compatibility: When you compile the project, if any binary-incompatible changes are detected you will be presented with a warning dialog. If you choose to accept the warning, the component will retain the type library identifier and the class IDs. Interface IDs are changed only for classes that are no longer binary-compatible. This is the same behavior as Project Compatibility.

  If, however, you choose to ignore the warning, the component will also maintain the interface IDs. This option is only available when the compiler determines that the change was in the procedure ID or signature of a method.

Caution You should only choose the Ignore button if you are absolutely sure that the changes you have made won't break compatibility. If you aren't absolutely sure, take the safe alternative and choose the Accept button to allow the interface ID's to be changed.

Important The option to override the compiler's warning represents a change in behavior from Visual Basic 5.0. It is important that you fully understand the implications of incompatible changes before proceeding with this option.

Visual Basic also warns you when changes to your code would make the new version incompatible with previously compiled applications.

Note When people talk about Version Compatibility, they're usually referring to Binary Compatibility.

The appropriate use of these options is described below.

Using the Implements Statement for Compatibility

The Implements statement allows you to add multiple interfaces to class modules, as described in "Polymorphism, Interfaces, Type Libraries, and GUIDs" and "Providing Polymorphism by Implementing Interfaces," in Chapter 6, "General Principles of Component Design," and in "Polymorphism" in Chapter 9, "Programming with Objects," in the *Microsoft Visual Basic 6.0 Programmer's Guide.*

Multiple interfaces allow your systems to evolve over time, without breaking existing components or requiring massive re-compiles, because a released interface is never changed. Instead, new functionality is added to a system by creating new interfaces.

This approach is much more in keeping with the design philosophy of the Component Object Model (COM), on which the ActiveX specification is based.

Note The Binary Compatibility option of Version Compatibility is useful in conjunction with Implements and multiple interfaces, to prevent changes to the default interfaces of your classes.

When to Use Version Compatibility Options

If you decide to use the Version Compatibility feature, you may find the following rules helpful in determining when to use the different options:

Use No Compatibility to Make a Clean Break

When you begin working on a new version of an existing component, you may decide that the only way to make necessary enhancements is to break backward compatibility. In this case, set No Compatibility the first time you compile your project. This guarantees that you'll start with a clean slate of identifiers, and that existing programs won't mistakenly try to use the incompatible version.

Before compiling an existing project with No Compatibility, you must also:

- Change the file name of your component, so that the incompatible version won't overwrite earlier versions on your users' hard disks.
- Change the Project Name on the General tab of the Project Properties dialog box, so that the incompatible component will have a different type library name. This ensures that the objects the component provides will have unique programmatic IDs.

These items are discussed in more detail in "Levels of Binary Version Compatibility," later in this chapter.

After compiling once with No Compatibility, switch to Project Compatibility to simplify your development tasks.

Use Project Compatibility for New Development

Use the Project Compatibility setting when you're developing the first version of a component. Project Compatibility preserves the type library identifier, so that you're not continually setting references from your test projects to your component projects.

Using Project Compatibility also makes it easier to switch between the component project and the compiled component when you're testing.

Project Compatibility is discussed in "Project Compatibility: Avoiding MISSING Reference," earlier in this chapter.

Use Binary Compatibility for New Versions of Existing Components

Switch to Binary Compatibility mode when you begin work on the second version of any component, if you want applications compiled using the earlier version to continue to work using the new version.

Switching to Binary Compatibility is discussed in the related topic "Providing a Reference Point for Binary Version Compatibility," later in this chapter.

Don't Mix Binary Compatibility and Multiple Interfaces

If you use multiple interfaces and the Implements statement to provide backward compatibility, don't use Binary Compatibility to modify the abstract interfaces you've defined for use with Implements.

If you enhance any of the interfaces in a component, Visual Basic will change their interface IDs. The technique of evolving component software by adding interfaces depends on *interface invariance.* That is, an interface once defined is never changed — including the interface ID.

For More Information See "Providing Polymorphism by Implementing Interfaces," in Chapter 6, "General Principles of Component Design," for information about component software design using multiple interfaces.

Maintaining Binary Compatibility

Visual Basic maintains backward compatibility by preserving class ID and interface ID information from previous versions of your component, as described in "Polymorphism, Interfaces, Type Libraries, and GUIDs," in Chapter 6, "General Principles of Component Design." This information is not maintained in the type library, but is stored elsewhere in your component.

When a client application is compiled using a particular version of your component, the class ID and interface ID of each object it uses will be compiled in. When the client is run, the class ID is used to create an instance of the class, and the interface ID is used to verify that it's safe to make the property and method calls that were compiled into the client.

If you make a new version of your component, using the Binary Compatibility option, the new version will contain the class IDs and interface IDs the old client needs to create objects and use their properties and methods, as well as class IDs and interface IDs of the enhanced versions of the classes.

New client applications compiled using the new version of your component can make use of the enhancements, because they compile in the new class IDs and interface IDs.

For example, suppose that in version 1.0 of your component, your Widget object has a Spin method, and that you've compiled a client application that creates a Widget object and calls the Spin method.

Now suppose you set the Binary Compatibility option and compile a new version of your component, in which the Widget object also has an Oscillate method. Visual Basic creates a new interface ID for the enhanced Widget. Because adding a method doesn't break binary compatibility, Visual Basic also maintains the class ID and interface ID of the old Widget.

When your previously compiled application uses these old IDs, it gets an enhanced Widget — which is fine, because the new Widget still has the Spin method the old application needs to call.

> **Note** Binary Compatibility applies only to the default interface of a class — that is, the Public Sub, Function, and Property procedures you add to the class module. Interfaces you add using Implements are ignored.

Incompatible Interface Changes

Suppose that instead of adding an Oscillate method, you changed the arguments of the Spin method. For example, you might add a Direction argument.

If you could compile your component using the old class ID and interface ID for the Widget class, your old client application would be in trouble. It would be able to create the new Widget, but when it called the Spin method it would put the wrong arguments on the stack. At the very least, a program error would occur. Even worse, data could be corrupted.

Preventing Incompatibility

If you've selected the Binary Compatibility option, Visual Basic warns you when you're about to compile an incompatible version of your component. You can reverse the edits that would make your component incompatible, or change the file name and Project Name so that the new version will not replace the old when users run Setup.

If you choose to disregard the warnings, and compile an incompatible version of your component with the same file name and Project Name, Visual Basic may dump some of the interface IDs from previous versions of your component.

When the incompatible component is installed on a computer that has a client application compiled using an earlier version, it will overwrite the earlier version. Subsequently, when the client application attempts to create objects, it will receive error 429, "OLE Automation server cannot create object."

This averts more serious and subtle errors that might occur when the application attempts to invoke the properties and methods of the incompatible interface.

Limited Protection for Late-Bound Client Applications

Late binding is used when variables are declared As Object, because the compiler doesn't know the class ID of the objects and interfaces that may be assigned to the variable at run time. Applications that use late binding create instances of your classes using the CreateObject function and the programmatic ID, as shown here:

```
Dim obj As Object
Set obj = CreateObject("MyComponent.MyObject")
```

The CreateObject function looks up the class ID in the Windows Registry, and uses it to create the object. Thus it will always create the most recent version of the object.

As long as you preserve binary compatibility, late-bound clients will continue to work successfully with your component.

If you make an incompatible version of your component using the same programmatic IDs for your objects, late-bound clients can still create the objects, because they're looking up the class ID instead of having it compiled in. When they call methods whose arguments have changed, or methods you've deleted, program failure or data corruption may occur.

For More Information See "Polymorphism, Interfaces, Type Libraries, and GUIDs," in Chapter 6, "General Principles of Component Design," for background information and concepts.

Levels of Binary Version Compatibility

Visual Basic defines three levels of version compatibility for the interfaces you describe in your class modules.

- *Version identical* means that the interfaces are all the same, so the new version of the type library is exactly the same as the old one. The code inside methods or Property procedures may have been changed or enhanced, but this is transparent to client applications.
- *Version compatible* means that objects and/or methods have been added to the type library, but no changes were made to existing properties or methods. Both old and new client applications can use the component.
- *Version incompatible* means that at least one property or method that existed in the old type library has been changed or removed. Existing client applications that have references to the component cannot use the new version.

Version-Identical Interfaces

Once your component has been distributed as part of an application, there are several situations that might cause you to release an update. You might want to optimize the performance of a method that had turned out to be a bottleneck for users. You might also need to change the internal implementation of an object's method to reflect changes in the business rule on which the method was based.

You can change the code in existing Property procedures or methods, and still have a version-identical interface, as long as you do not change the names or data types of their parameters, the order of the parameters, the name of the property or method, or the data type of the return value.

When you create the executable for a version-identical upgrade, you can use the same file name for the executable. Visual Basic uses the same version number for the type library.

> **Important** When you release a new version of your component with a version-identical or version-compatible interface, and retain the same file name for the executable, you should always use the Make tab of the Project Properties dialog box to increment the file version number. This ensures that the setup programs for applications that use your component will replace old versions during setup.

Version-Compatible Interfaces

When you enhance your component by adding new classes, or new properties and methods to existing classes, you can continue to use the same name for your executable. As long as you make no changes to existing properties and methods, Visual Basic updates the version number of the type library but keeps it compatible with the old version number.

Client applications that are built using the new version of your component will compile with the new version number, and can make use of all the new features. They cannot be used with earlier versions of your component, however, because type library versions are only upward-compatible.

As with version-identical releases, remember to increment the file version number of the executable.

Version-Incompatible Interfaces

Sometimes design decisions made in an earlier version of a component fail to anticipate future needs. If you want the code in the component to be useful in new development projects, you have to change the interface.

For example, the CupsPerAnnum parameter of the Coffee method might be implemented as an Integer in the first version of a component. It may become apparent, after the component has been in use for some time, that some clients need to pass a larger value than can be contained in an Integer.

Changing the declaration of a method is only one of several actions that will cause Visual Basic to make the version number of the type library incompatible, rendering the new version unusable with client applications compiled with earlier versions. The following changes will cause a version incompatibility:

- Changing the Project Name field on the General tab of the Project Properties dialog box.
- Changing the Name property of any class module whose Public property is True (controls), or whose Instancing property is not Private (class modules).
- Deleting a public class module, or setting its Instancing property to Private.
- Deleting a public variable, procedure, or Property procedure from a public class module or control, or changing it to Private or Friend.
- Changing the name or data type of a public variable, procedure, or Property procedure in a public class module or control.
- Changing the names, data types, or order of the parameters of a public procedure or Property procedure in a public class module or control.
- Changing the Procedure ID (DispID) or other parameters in the Procedure Attributes dialog box.

Time to Take Stock

When you've identified a necessary change that will cause your component to be incompatible with earlier versions, it's a good idea to take the time to evaluate the entire set of interfaces, before plunging ahead and creating an incompatible version of your component.

Consider Multiple Interfaces

Remember that there are alternatives to using Version Compatibility. Consider enhancing your component by adding new interfaces with the Implements statement, as described in "Providing Polymorphism by Implementing Interfaces," in Chapter 6, "General Principles of Component Design."

Multiple interfaces, a key feature of the Component Object Model (COM) — on which the ActiveX specification is based — provide a more flexible way to enhance software components. They allow you to evolve your systems over time, without breaking existing components.

You don't have to tackle the daunting task factoring your existing class module interfaces into small interfaces more suitable for use with Implements — one of the benefits of using multiple interfaces is that you can start small, adding new interfaces to the system only where new functionality is required.

Going Ahead with Incompatibility

If you decide to go ahead with an incompatible version, you can minimize future problems for the users of your component by concentrating in one release all the changes you can anticipate that might break compatibility again if they have to be made in later releases.

In planning for an incompatible change, treat the project as a fresh start. Devote as much care to planning as you would if you were creating a brand new component.

Creating an incompatible version requires three steps: changing the project name, changing the file name, and compiling with No Compatibility selected.

Changing the Project Name

The key change you must make, when you need to distribute an incompatible version of your component, is the project name. The project name, which is set on the General tab of the Project Properties dialog box, is the first part of the programmatic ID of each class your component provides.

For example, the SmallMechanicals component might provide a Widgets class. A client application would create a variable to contain a reference to a Widget object as follows:

```
Private wdgDriver As SmallMechanicals.Widget
```

The programmatic ID is the combination of project name and class name, and it must be unique. If you create a new version of this component, you might give it the project name SmallMechanicals200. Both versions of the Widget object could then be registered in the same Windows Registry without confusion.

Changing the File Name

You must change the file name of an incompatible component. If you use the old file name without incrementing the file version number, the incompatible component may not install on computers where the old file exists. If you increment the file version, the new file will over-write the old, and applications that used the old version will fail.

Compiling with No Compatibility

Before you compile the incompatible component for the first time, open the Project Properties dialog box (accessible from the Project menu), select the Component tab, then select No Compatibility in the Version Compatibility box.

Do not omit this step. Compiling with No Compatibility ensures that the new executable will not contain any GUIDs (for example, class IDs or interface IDs) that belong to the previous version. This is necessary for applications that use the original version to continue working correctly.

> **Tip** After compiling once with No Compatibility, switch to Project Compatibility to simplify your development tasks.

Alternatives to Version-Incompatible Changes

If you prefer not to make the change to multiple interfaces, as described above, you can take a similar approach with classes.

That is, you can avoid changes that cause version incompatibility by adding new objects, properties, and methods, instead of changing existing ones. Existing applications continue using the old methods and objects, while developers of new applications can use the new objects.

For example, you might discover that to take advantage of enhancements to your General Ledger system, you need to add a SubAccount parameter to several business rules in your FinanceRules component.

If each rule is implemented as a method of the GL object, you could avoid creating an incompatible version of the component by adding a new object named GL97. This object would have the same methods as the GL object, but with a SubAccount parameter where appropriate.

If you need to add new versions of existing methods to an object, you can give the new methods the same name with a version or sequence number added — for example, "Execute2."

This approach is not as flexible or efficient as implementing multiple interfaces. You may end up replicating entire classes, and class interfaces may become large and unwieldy — for example, you might find yourself using a Query class with an Execute method, an Execute2 method, an Execute3 method, and so on. However, it's a step in the right direction.

For More Information Software evolution using multiple interfaces is discussed in "Providing Polymorphism by Implementing Interfaces," in Chapter 6, "General Principles of Component Design."

Providing a Reference Point for Binary Version Compatibility

To determine the degree of compatibility between two versions of a component, Visual Basic needs a reference point. You provide this reference point by entering the path to a previously compiled version of your component in the Version Compatibility box on the tab of the Project Properties dialog box.

You need to do this whenever you begin work on a new version of a component you have shipped, put into production, or used as part of an application.

To specify a reference version of the component type library

1. Open the project.
2. From the **Project** menu, choose **Project Properties** to open the **Project Properties** dialog box, and select the **Component** tab.
3. Click **Binary Compatibility** to lock down the class IDs in the project.

   Note As explained in "Project Compatibility: Avoiding MISSING References," the **Project Compatibility** setting actually has nothing to do with the Version Compatibility feature.

4. Update the box at the bottom of the **Version Compatibility** frame with the full path and name of the most recent version of your component.

Whenever you make a new executable from your component project, Visual Basic compares the new interfaces of your classes to the ones described in the file you have specified. Visual Basic updates the type library version number according to the level of compatibility between the interfaces.

Using Binary Version Compatibility

Whenever you begin work on a new version of an existing component, you need to specify a type library which Visual Basic can use as a reference point for determining compatibility. In most cases, this will be the type library included in executable (.exe, .dll, or .ocx file) for the last version of the component you distributed.

Each time you build an interim version of your updated component, Visual Basic extracts information about the old interfaces from this .exe file and compares it to the new interfaces of your class modules.

Keeping the Reference Version Separate from Interim Builds

> **Important** Keep the copy of the .exe file you specify as your reference version separate from the build copy of the new version.

Each time you make an interim build, Visual Basic adds a new set of interface identifiers to the executable, one identifier for each class module. If you specify your build copy as the reference version, it will accumulate a complete set of interface identifiers for every version-compatible interim build you have ever done. (Interface identifiers do not change for version-identical builds.)

In addition to the sixteen bytes taken up by each interface identifier, having unused interface identifiers in your executable — only your test applications ever use the interim versions — can slow down cross-process access to your component in some situations, and the Windows Registry of any computer your component is installed on will be cluttered with unused interface identifiers.

If your reference version is a copy of your last released executable, all your interim builds will have the same interface version number, and your final build will have only the interface identifiers it needs: all the sets from the reference version (to provide backward compatibility) plus the set of interface identifiers for all the classes in your new release.

> **Note** When you're developing the first version of a component, using Project Compatibility instead of Binary Compatibility, exactly the opposite is true: The reference version should be your interim build. This does not bulk up the type library, because Project Compatibility *never* saves the interface identifiers.

Avoiding Version Trees

Because Visual Basic produces the version number for the new type library by incrementing the type library version number it finds in the reference version, the released versions of your component form a chain, each link derived from its predecessor. As mentioned earlier, each new release contains all the interface identifiers for preceding versions, so that a client application compiled with any previous version will still work with the latest.

What's a Version Tree?

Version trees arise when your component's version history acquires branches — that is, when you produce two physically distinct components based on the same source code. It's important to keep the version history of your component straight, and avoid such branching.

Figure 7.4 shows some of the problems that can be caused by version trees. (The version numbers are for illustrative purposes only, and are not intended to represent actual type library version numbers.)

Figure 7.4 Problems with version trees

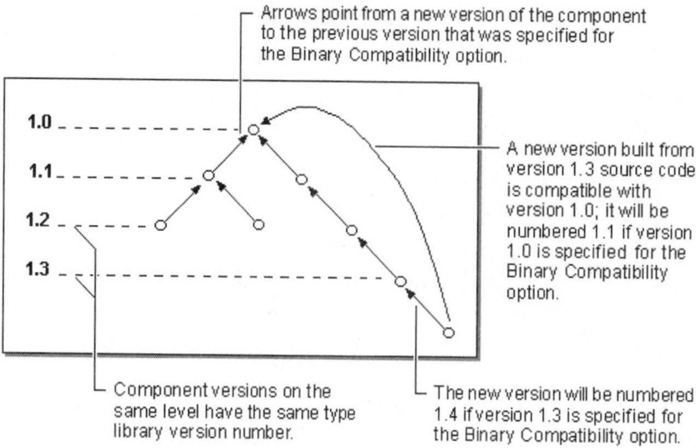

The long branch at the right shows four successive versions of a component executable, and a new executable that has been created by adding to the source code for the executable whose type library version is 1.3.

The correct continuation of this version history is for the latest executable to be compiled with the version 1.3 executable as its reference version. The new type library version number is 1.4. The .exe file maintains compatibility with client applications compiled using any of its predecessors.

Because it's at the end of a chain of compatible versions, the new executable could also be compiled with the version 1.0 executable as its reference version. In this case, its type library version number will be 1.1. This could cause problems for clients compiled to take advantage of features of the new version. If they're placed on a computer with the earlier version 1.1 executable, the new features will not be available, and the applications will fail.

A different problem arises when the new component is installed on computers that have client applications compiled with type library version numbers 1.1, 1.2, and 1.3. Standard practice is to increase the file version number of each new executable file, to ensure that Setup will replace earlier versions of the executable. (Remember that file version numbers are independent of type library version numbers.)

Thus the new executable, containing interface identifiers for type library versions 1.0 and 1.1, will replace older executables that contained interface identifiers for type library versions 1.0 through 1.3.

If the computer already has client applications compiled with type library versions 1.2 and 1.3, those clients will be unable to use the new version of the component.

Divergent Versions

The left side of the tree shows divergent versions. This can arise when the source code for an early version of your component is taken as the basis of a new component, and classes are added that do not exist in your main version history.

If the executable for your component is used as the reference version for the divergent version, the type library version numbers of the divergent version and its successors will overlap the version numbers of your components. The results for client applications will be disastrous.

> **Tip** You can easily avoid the creation of version trees by always setting aside a copy of the previous version of your component's executable file (.exe, .dll, or .ocx) as the reference version for the next release, as described earlier in this topic.
>
> If you decide to use the source code of an earlier version of your component as the basis of a new component, give the new component a different project name and executable name.

Version Trees with Project Compatibility

Version trees can also arise when you're using Project Compatibility, the difference being that it's the major version number of the type library that changes (instead of the minor version number, as shown in Figure 7.4). The consequences to client applications can be equally disastrous.

As with Binary Compatibility, the best way to avoid this is not to split your source tree. If you take a copy of your source code at a particular stage of the project as the basis for another component, use a different project name and executable name for this new project.

Version Compatibility Messages

For performance reasons, Visual Basic does not fully compare interfaces as you edit. When you run your component project, Visual Basic will always display a compatibility warning if the new version is incompatible with the old. (Version-identical and version-compatible interfaces will compile without compatibility warnings.)

> **Note** Version compatibility is judged on a project-wide basis. A change in the declaration of just one method in one class module causes the entire project to be marked as incompatible with the previous version. See "Levels of Version Compatibility," earlier in this chapter, for a listing of changes that will cause a version incompatibility.

Version Incompatibility Warnings

Suppose you add a new argument to the Spin method of the Widget object. When you run the project, you'll get a warning that binary compatibility has been broken. You can examine the old declaration by clicking the Declaration button on this message. If you made the change accidentally, you can click Edit to bring up the code and fix it.

If you choose to accept the warning, the component will retain the type library identifier and the class IDs. Interface IDs are changed only for classes that are no longer binary compatible. This is the same behavior as Project Compatibility.

If, however, you choose to ignore the warning, the component will also maintain the interface IDs. This option is only available when the compiler determines that the change was in procedure ID or signature of a method.

> **Caution** You should only choose the Ignore button if you are absolutely sure that the changes you have made won't break compatibility. If you aren't absolutely sure, take the safe alternative and choose the Accept button to allow the interface IDs to be changed.

> **Important** The option to override the compiler's warning represents a change in behavior from Visual Basic 5.0. It is important that you fully understand the implications of incompatible changes before proceeding with this option.

Incompatible EXE File

If you have not changed the project name, when you use the Make EXE File command, you will get a warning that your application is incompatible with the .exe file you specified as your reference version, as shown in Figure 7.5.

Figure 7.5 Warning for incompatible .exe file

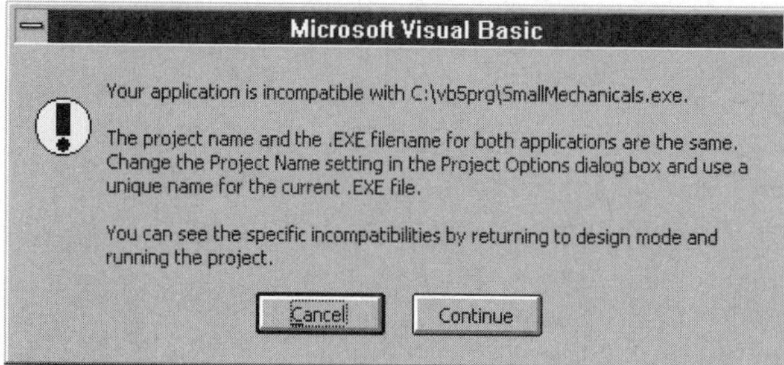

Clicking Continue at this point creates an executable file that could cause existing client applications to fail. In order for existing clients to continue working, you must take the following steps when you create an incompatible version of a component:

- Change the file name.
- Change the project name.
- Compile with Version Compatibility set to No Compatibility.

These steps are discussed in detail in "Levels of Binary Version Compatibility," earlier in this chapter.

Localizing ActiveX Components

You can localize components created using Visual Basic by first collecting all the text strings used in your component into a source file for the Windows Resource Compiler (.rc file). You can then create localized versions of this source file by translating the strings to each of your target locales.

Before you compile each localized version of your component, use the Resource Compiler to create a Windows resource (.res file) from the appropriate source file, and include the resource file in your project.

Components without a visible interface are extremely easy to localize in this fashion, because you only have to localize error messages. The code fragments in "Generating and Handling Errors" demonstrate this technique.

For components that display forms, the process is more complicated. You need to place the captions of forms and controls into the resource file, and retrieve them in the Form_Load event procedure for each form.

Satellite DLLs

In areas where multiple languages are in use, using resource files can be a problem. Not only do you have to compile separate versions of your component for each language, but they all share the same Project Name, and thus only one language can be installed on a user's computer at any given time.

"Localizing Controls," in Chapter 9, "Building ActiveX Controls," describes a technique for using a *satellite DLL* to provide the translated strings for each language. Satellite DLLs accompany your component, and can be swapped in and out without recompiling the component.

If you use a LocaleID-based naming convention, multiple satellite DLLs can coexist on one computer, allowing the user to switch from one language to another by changing the system LocaleID.

Limitations

Unfortunately, code components can only make limited use of this feature. Unlike control components, they don't receive a LocaleID from the client application. The best a code component can do is to use API calls to obtain the system LocaleID.

Out-of-process code components can never do any better than this, because they have to serve multiple clients. With in-process components, however, you can offer developers a better option by providing an object with a LocaleID property that can be set by client applications. When the property is set, your component can load text strings from the appropriate satellite DLL.

For More Information For information on writing code for applications that will be distributed world-wide, see Chapter 16, "International Issues," in the *Microsoft Visual Basic 6.0 Programmer's Guide*. To learn about the functions for retrieving text strings and other resources, see the LoadResString function in the *Microsoft Visual Basic 6.0 Language Reference*.

CHAPTER 8

Building Code Components

Code components, formerly called OLE servers, are libraries of objects that provide an easy way to package your code for reuse. For example, you can create libraries of procedures that can be used with Microsoft Visual Basic or with desktop applications that host Visual Basic for Applications, such as Microsoft Office.

With the Enterprise Edition of Visual Basic, code components can become parts of enterprise systems, running unattended on remote computers to provide data services and business rules. The information in "Scalability and Multithreading" and "Asynchronous Call-Backs and Events," later in this chapter, will be of particular interest in this context.

Code components can be wizards and add-ins for Visual Basic. Part 3, "Extending the Visual Basic Environment with Add-Ins," describes how to create wizards and add-ins. Many of the topics in this chapter provide useful background information for creating add-ins.

"Building Code Components" assumes familiarity with the material in Chapter 6, "General Principles of Component Design," and Chapter 7, "Debugging, Testing, and Deploying Components," as well as Chapter 9, "Programming with Objects," in the *Microsoft Visual Basic 6.0 Programmer's Guide.*

The following topics describe key features of code components created with Visual Basic.

Contents

Sample Applications: Coffee2.vbp, CoffWat2.vbp, MTCoffee.vbp

Coffee2.vbp and CoffWat2.vbp demonstrate two techniques for asynchronous notifications — events and call-back methods on a secondary interface — and provide an example of all-code timers you can use instead of the Timer control. MTCoffee.vbp illustrates some features of multithreading. The sample applications are listed in the Samples directory.

For More Information See Chapter 3, "Creating an ActiveX EXE Component," for step-by-step procedures that illustrate multithreading and asynchronous processing. Similar step-by-step procedures in Chapter 2, "Creating an ActiveX DLL," illustrate global objects and modeless forms. Visual Basic code components can also provide ActiveX documents, as discussed in Chapter 11, "Building ActiveX Documents."

Global Objects and Code Libraries

You can build libraries of general-purpose procedures in Visual Basic by making the procedures methods of a class module. Set the Instancing property of the class module to any value *except* Private or PublicNotCreatable, so that clients can create instances of the class.

When you choose the value GlobalMultiUse for the Instancing property of a class, and then make the project, you can subsequently use the properties and methods of the class without having to explicitly create an instance of the class.

Properties and methods of a GlobalMultiUse object (or *global object*) are added to the *global name space* of any project that uses the object. That is, in another project you can set a reference to the component, and the names of the global object's properties and methods will be recognized globally, just as if they were part of Visual Basic.

> **Important** The properties and methods of a global object only become part of the global name space when the component is referenced from *other projects*. Within the project where you created the GlobalMultiUse class module, objects created from the class are just ordinary objects.

The following code fragments show the difference between using MultiUse and GlobalMultiUse objects. Both assume that you've used the References dialog box to set a reference to a component that provides a Financials object whose methods are general-purpose financial functions.

Code required to use a MultiUse Financials object:

```
' This code goes in a standard module.
' Declare a global variable to contain the instance.
Public gfins As New Financials
```

```
' This code goes in a form that uses a method of the
'  Financials object.
Private Sub cmdCalculateResult_Click()
   txtResult.Text = gfins.LeastReasonableReturn( _
      CCur(txtBeginningBalance.Text))
End Sub
```

Note When you use the code above, the Financials object is created the first time the variable `gfins` is used in code. This incurs a slight increase in overhead on each function call. You can avoid this by explicitly creating the Financials object in Sub Main (for standalone executables) or on first object creation (for components).

By contrast, the code to use a GlobalMultiUse Financials object requires no global variable:

```
Private Sub cmdCalculateResult_Click()
   txtResult.Text = LeastReasonableReturn( _
      CCur(txtBeginningBalance.Text))
End Sub
```

Visual Basic creates a hidden instance of the Financials class the first time a line of code containing one of its methods is executed.

Note As explained later in this topic, the hidden instance incurs the same slight overhead per call as declaring `gfins` As New in the previous code example.

In the Object Browser, procedures that are part of a project's global name space are displayed in the <globals> entry in the Classes list. Figure 8.1 shows this for a project group that uses the Financials class.

Figure 8.1 Methods of a GlobalMultiUse class appear in <globals>

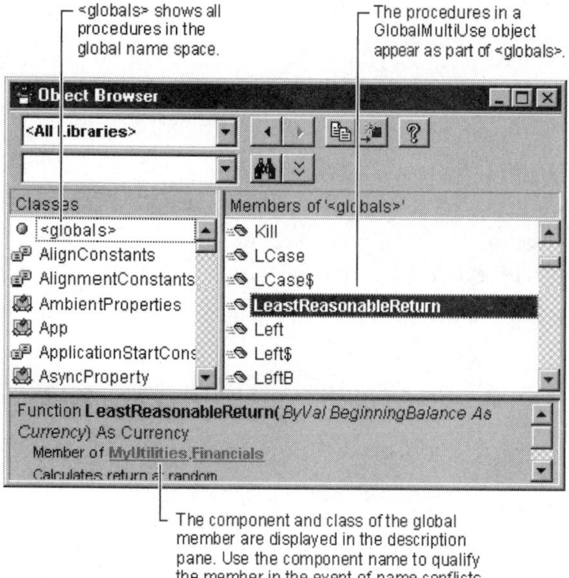

The Object Browser displays the names of classes and members defined in your projects in bold type.

> **Tip** You can move directly to the code that defines classes and members by double-clicking names displayed in bold type.

Components That Use Global Objects Internally

Setting the Instancing property of a class to GlobalMultiUse or GlobalSingleUse allows *client* programs to use the properties and methods of the class as if they were global functions, but within the project where you defined the GlobalMultiUse class module, objects created from the class are *not* global.

For example, suppose your MyUtilities project contains a Utilities class whose Instancing property is set to GlobalMultiUse, and that the class has an InvertMatrix method. Any client project that has a reference to MyUtilities can call InvertMatix as if it were a global function. However, *within* the MyUtilities project, you cannot use InvertMatrix as if it were a global function.

If you want to use a global instance of the Utilities class within the MyUtilities project, you can add the following declaration to a standard module in MyUtilities:

```
Public Utilities As New Utilities
```

Thereafter, whenever you need to use InvertMatrix (or any other procedure supplied by the Utilities class), you can qualify it with the class name:

```
Utilities.InvertMatrix aintMyLargeMatrix
```

The first time you use a method of the Utilities class in this fashion, an instance of the class is created automatically, because the global variable is declared As New. Using the class name as the name of the variable makes it clear which of the modules within your component is supplying the procedure.

Note You must declare the global variable in a standard module, not a class module, in order for this technique to work.

Creating Object Properties for Global Objects

Visual Basic has properties of its <globals> that are themselves objects — for example, the App object and the Printers collection. You can create similar object properties for your own global classes.

Suppose you've created a Registry class for accessing the Windows registry, and that you have a Globals class whose Instancing property is GlobalMultiUse. The following code fragment shows how you can add a Registry property to your Globals class:

```
Private mRegistry As Registry

Private Sub Class_Initialize()
   Set mRegistry = New Registry
End Sub

Public Property Get Registry() As Registry
   Set Registry = mRegistry
End Sub
```

Once you've compiled your component, you can reference it from other projects. If the Registry class includes a FindKeyContaining method, you might write code like this to use it:

```
Private Sub Command1_Click()
   lblResult.Caption = _
      Registry.FindKeyContaining(txtInput.Text)
End Sub
```

This code assumes that the form contains a text box in which the user enters a string to be located (`txtInput`), and a label in which the registry key is displayed (`lblResult`). Notice that you didn't have to create an instance of Globals before using the Registry object.

Tip Always use Property Get when you add an object property to your global object. If you use a public variable instead, you can accidentally destroy the object the property provides by setting the property to Nothing.

Guidelines for Using Global Objects

You may find the following useful in getting the most out of global objects:

- Constants you provide using Enums are Long integers; you can use global objects to provide string and floating point constants, as described in "Providing Named Constants for Your Component," in Chapter 6, "General Principles of Component Design."

- When you encounter name conflicts, use the *type library name* of the component to resolve the conflict.

  For example, suppose you were using both MyUtilities and YourUtilities, and that YourUtilities had a GlobalMultiUse class named General that also included a method named LeastReasonableReturn. You would code the following to ensure that the method in YourUtilities was used:

  ```
  Private Sub cmdCalculateResult_Click()
     txtResult.Text = _
        YourUtilities.LeastReasonableReturn( _
           CCur(txtBeginningBalance.Text))
  End Sub
  ```

  > **Important** If conflicting names are not qualified, Visual Basic uses the library that appears highest in the References dialog box. Unless the procedures have different arguments, no compile-time errors occur.

- Choose procedure names carefully. While it may seem convenient to use common words or phrases, this increases the likelihood that other libraries will contain functions with the same name. Qualifying procedures with the type library name may be even less convenient than explicitly declaring a global object variable.

  > **Important** Global name space pollution is a serious issue. For an example and discussion, see "Creating a Reference to an Object," in Chapter 10, "Programming with Components," in the *Microsoft Visual Basic 6.0 Programmer's Guide.*

- Implicit creation isn't the only way to use global objects. You can declare variables of a GlobalMultiUse class, and explicitly create instances. If you have two libraries with a lot of name conflicts, short global variable names may be easier to type than long, user-friendly type library names.

  > **Important** Each client that uses the properties and methods of a GlobalMultiUse class gets *its own instance of the class*. In other words, the "Global" in GlobalMultiUse does *not* mean "one global instance that all clients share."

Limitations of GlobalMultiUse Objects

When you're deciding whether to use a global object or explicitly declare a variable to hold an instance of an object, the following may be of use:

- You can't set the hidden reference to a global object to Nothing when you're done using it. Visual Basic does not provide any way to access the hidden global object directly.
- GlobalMultiUse is a convenience for programmers; you incur the same slight overhead on each procedure call as you would if you used a global variable declared As New (for example, As New Financials).
- As explained earlier in this topic, when you are authoring a component that provides a GlobalMultiUse class, you cannot use the properties and methods of the class if they were global procedures.
- You can't use global objects to replace global procedures in the VB and VBA libraries. These libraries always appear at the top of the References dialog box, before any other libraries. Procedures with the same name in a global object can only be accessed by qualifying the procedure name with the type library name.

GlobalSingleUse Objects

For out-of-process components only, you can set the Instancing property of a class module to GlobalSingleUse. If you do this, a separate instance of your component will be loaded into memory for each client. This requires a lot more memory than providing GlobalMultiUse objects.

If you simply want each client to have a separate thread of execution for your global procedures, consider using GlobalMultiUse for your global objects and making your out-of-process component multithreaded, as described in the next section, "Scalability and Multithreading."

> **Note** GlobalSingleUse is not allowed in ActiveX DLL projects, because multiple instances of a DLL cannot be loaded into a client's process space.

For More Information See "Scalability through Multiple Processes: SingleUse Objects," later in this chapter.

Scalability and Multithreading

When a component has one thread of execution, code for only one object can execute at any given time. The Automation feature of the Component Object Model (COM) deals with this situation by *serializing* requests. That is, the requests are queued and processed one at a time until all have been completed.

In a multithreading operating environment, serialization protects single-threaded objects from overlapping client requests — that is, from code in a property or method being executed while one or more previous client requests are still being executed. Overlapping requests can cause internal data errors if objects aren't designed for reentrancy, as discussed in "Apartment-Model Threading in Visual Basic."

Serialization is thus an extremely important feature of Automation. However, serialization of single-threaded components means that requests are sometimes blocked. For example, suppose you're using a Widget object that has two methods:

- The Spin method takes anywhere from several seconds to half an hour.
- The Flip method is almost instantaneous.

Because 32-bit applications are preemptively multitasked, a second application could call the Flip method while the Spin method is already running. As shown in Figure 8.2, the short Flip method is blocked until the long Spin method is complete.

Figure 8.2 Blocking in a component with MultiUse objects

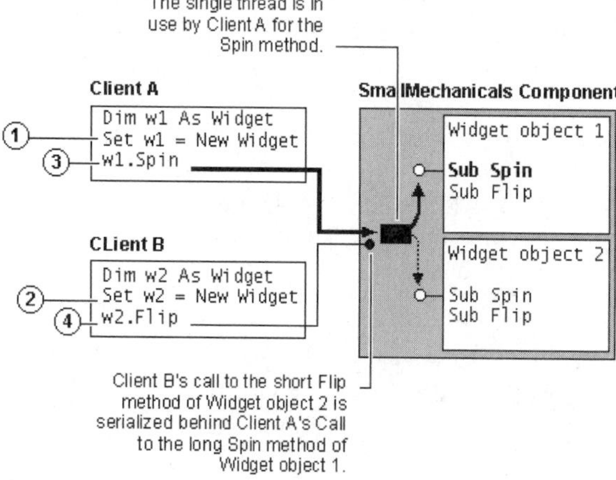

When short operations are blocked by long ones, productivity suffers and user frustration rises. Components that behave in this fashion are said to *scale poorly*. That is, they work poorly if many requests of mixed length are made.

Apartment-Model Threading in Visual Basic

In Visual Basic, *apartment-model* threading is used to provide thread safety. In apartment-model threading, each thread is like an apartment — all objects created on the thread live in this apartment, and are unaware of objects in other apartments.

Visual Basic's implementation of apartment-model threading eliminates conflicts in accessing global data from multiple threads by giving each apartment its own copy of global data, as shown in Figure 8.3.

Figure 8.3 Each thread has its own copy of global data

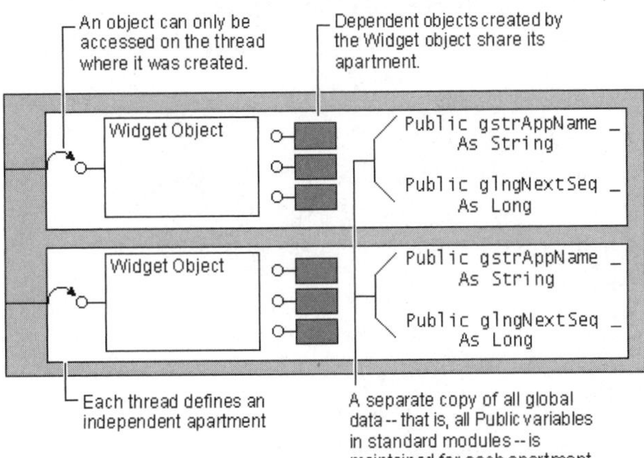

This means that you cannot use global data to communicate between objects on different threads.

Note Objects in different apartments can only communicate with each other if a client passes them references to each other. In this case, *cross-thread marshaling* is used to provide synchronization. Cross-thread marshaling is almost as slow as cross-process marshaling.

In addition to maintaining a separate copy of global data, a Sub Main procedure is executed for each new apartment (that is, for each new thread). Otherwise, there would be no way to initialize global data for the thread. This is discussed further in "Designing Thread-Safe DLLs" and "Designing Multithreaded Out-of-Process Components," later in this chapter.

Single-Threaded Components and the Apartment Model

All components created with Visual Basic use the apartment model, whether they're single-threaded or multithreaded. A single-threaded component has only one apartment, which contains all the objects the component provides.

This means that a single-threaded DLL created with Visual Basic is safe to use with a multithreaded client. However, there's a performance trade-off for this safety. Calls from all client threads except one are marshaled, just as if they were out-of-process calls. This is discussed in "Designing Thread-Safe DLLs," later in this chapter.

Ownership of Threads

A multithreaded in-process component has no threads of its own. The threads that define each apartment belong to the client, as explained in "Designing Thread-Safe DLLs," later in this chapter.

By contrast, a multithreaded out-of-process component may have a thread pool with a fixed number of threads, or a separate thread for each externally created object. This is discussed in "Designing Multithreaded Out-of-Process Components," later in this chapter.

Obtaining the Win32 Thread ID

In addition to maintaining a separate copy of your global data for each thread, Visual Basic maintains separate copies of the data supplied by global objects such as the App object. Thus the ThreadID property of the App object will always return the Win32 thread ID of the thread on which the property call was handled.

Where You Can Use Threading

Unlike earlier versions of Visual Basic, projects authored with Visual Basic 6 can take advantage of apartment-model threading without having to suppress visual elements such as forms and controls. Forms, UserControls, UserDocuments, and ActiveX designers are all thread-safe. You can select a setting for the Threading Model option without marking your project for Unattended Execution.

To set the threading model for an ActiveX DLL, ActiveX EXE, or ActiveX Control project

1. On the **Project** menu, select **<project> Properties** to open the **Project Properties** dialog box.
2. On the **General** tab, select the desired options in the **Threading Model** box.
   - For ActiveX DLL and ActiveX Control projects, you can select either Apartment Threaded or Single Threaded.
   - For ActiveX EXE projects, you can either specify that each new object is created on a new thread (Thread per Object), or limit your component to a fixed pool of threads. A thread pool size of one makes the project single-threaded; a larger thread pool makes the project apartment-threaded.

Note When you change the threading model for an existing project, an error will occur if the project uses single-threaded ActiveX controls. Visual Basic prevents the use of single-threaded controls in apartment-threaded projects, as described in "Converting Existing Projects to Apartment-Model Threading," later in this chapter.

When you specify Thread per Object (or a thread pool greater than one) for an ActiveX EXE project, only *externally created objects* are created on new threads. (See "Designing Multithreaded Out-of-Process Components," later in this chapter.) Thread per Object and Thread Pool are not available for ActiveX DLL and ActiveX Control projects, because thread creation is controlled by the client application.

Important For Professional and Enterprise Edition users, the consequences of selecting Thread per Object or Thread Pool are discussed in detail in "Designing Multithreaded Out-of-Process Components," later in this chapter.

Setting Unattended Execution

Unattended Execution allows you to create components that can run without operator intervention on network servers. Selecting Unattended Execution doesn't affect the threading model of your component.

To mark your ActiveX DLL or EXE project for unattended execution

1. On the **Project** menu, click **<project> Properties** to open the **Project Properties** dialog box.
2. On the **General** tab, check **Unattended Execution**, then click **OK**.

   Important Selecting the Unattended Execution option suppresses all forms of user interaction — including message boxes and system error dialogs. This is discussed in "Event Logging for Multithreaded Components," later in this chapter.

Limitations of Apartment-Model Threading

The following limitations apply to apartment-model threading in Visual Basic.

- The development environment doesn't support multithreaded debugging. If you have Microsoft Visual Studio, you can debug an apartment-threaded component with the Visual Studio debugger after compiling it to native code with debug information. You will also need a multithreaded client application to test and debug in-process components (.dll and .ocx files).
- MDI parent and child forms must share data in ways that are difficult to make thread-safe. MDI forms, therefore, are not allowed in apartment-threaded projects. On the Project menu, Add MDIForm is unavailable in apartment-threaded ActiveX DLL projects, and in ActiveX EXE projects with Thread per Object selected (or with a thread pool larger than one). If you change the threading model to Apartment-Threaded in a project that contains MDI forms, an error occurs.
- In addition to performing poorly, single-threaded ActiveX controls can cause numerous problems in multithreaded clients. Visual Basic therefore prevents the use of single-threaded controls in projects where Threading Model has been set to Apartment-Threaded. For details, see "Converting Existing Projects to Apartment-Model Threading," in the next section.
- Friend properties and methods can only be called by objects on the same thread. Because they are not part of an object's public interface, they cannot be marshaled between threads.
- ActiveX Documents in ActiveX EXE projects will not be apartment-model thread-safe unless you select Thread per Object or Thread Pool with a pool size greater than one.
- When a thread shows a form with vbModal, the form will be modal only to code and forms on that thread. Code running in other threads will not be blocked, and forms shown by other threads will remain active.

- Drag and drop between forms and controls will work only if the drag source and the drag target are on the same thread. (OLE drag and drop, however, will work universally.)
- DDE between forms will only work if the forms are on the same thread.

Converting Existing Projects to Apartment-Model Threading

You can add apartment threading to your existing projects by changing the Threading Model option, as described in Selecting a Threading Model for Your Project, and recompiling the project. For many projects, this is all you need to do.

If an existing ActiveX DLL, ActiveX EXE, or ActiveX Control project uses single-threaded constituent controls, attempting to change Threading Model to Apartment-Threaded will cause an error. Because of the number and severity of problems that single-threaded ActiveX controls cause for multithreaded clients, Visual Basic does not permit them to be used in ActiveX component projects.

If you have an existing project that employs a single-threaded control, contact the vendor to see whether an apartment-threaded version is available.

Forcing the Use of Single-Threaded Controls

It is possible to trick Visual Basic into using a single-threaded control in an apartment-threaded project, by manually editing the .vbp file. Do not do this. The problems that single-threaded ActiveX controls can cause include:

- If a user tabs to a single-threaded control on a form that's running on a different thread, she will not be able to tab off the control. This occurs because the single-threaded control's thread has no context for the focus on the form's thread. The only way for the user to change the focus in this situation is to use the mouse. Using a single-threaded control as a constituent of an apartment-threaded control causes similar problems.
- In a multithreaded application, activating a form by clicking on a single-threaded control will fail if the form is on a different thread. This also occurs when clicking on a single-threaded constituent of an apartment-threaded control.
- Using a single-threaded OCX in a multithreaded application causes performance problems, because all of the controls the OCX provides must run on the same thread. This means that for controls on forms running in different threads, all communication requires expensive cross-thread calls. An apartment-threaded ActiveX control that uses single-threaded constituent controls will cause similar performance problems.
- In a multithreaded application, the TAB key and access keys (for example, ALT+A) will not work for single-threaded controls that are not on the application's main thread. An apartment-threaded ActiveX control that uses single-threaded constituent controls will experience similar problems.
- If your apartment-threaded control sets the Picture property of a single-threaded constituent control (or any other property that takes a Picture object), errors will occur in multithreading clients. This is because the Picture object cannot be marshaled between threads.

Important Single-threaded controls can cause these and other problems in any multithreaded component or application you build, using Visual Basic or any other development tool.

Reentrancy

In the apartment model, *reentrancy* refers to the following sequence of events:

1. An apartment's thread of execution enters an object's code, because a property or method has been invoked.
2. While the thread is in the property or method, another thread invokes a property or method of the object, and Automation serializes this request — that is, it queues the request until the thread that owns the object's apartment finishes the member it's currently executing.
3. Before the thread reaches the end of the member, it executes code that yields control of the processor.
4. Automation tells the thread to begin executing the serialized request, so that the thread *reenters* the object's code.

The new request may be for the member the thread was already executing — in which case the thread enters the member a second time — or it may be for another member. If the second member doesn't yield, it will finish processing before the first member. If it changes module-level data the first member was using, the result may be unfortunate.

By serializing property and method calls for each apartment, Automation protects you from reentrancy — unless your code yields control of the processor. Ways in which your code can yield control of the processor include:

- Calling DoEvents.
- Invoking the properties or methods of an object on another thread, or in another process.
- Raising an event that's handled by an object on another thread, or in another process.
- Invoking a cross-thread or cross-process method from within a method.
- Showing a form.

Unless you've carefully written all of an object's code so that it doesn't matter whether two members are executing at the same time, you should not include code that yields control of the processor.

Designing Thread-Safe DLLs

Visual Basic greatly simplifies the job of authoring in-process components that can be used safely and efficiently by multithreaded clients. All in-process components created with Visual Basic use apartment-model threading, to provide synchronous access to objects.

Figure 8.4 shows how a multithreaded client uses a single-threaded in-process component.

Figure 8.4 Multithreaded client using single-threaded DLL

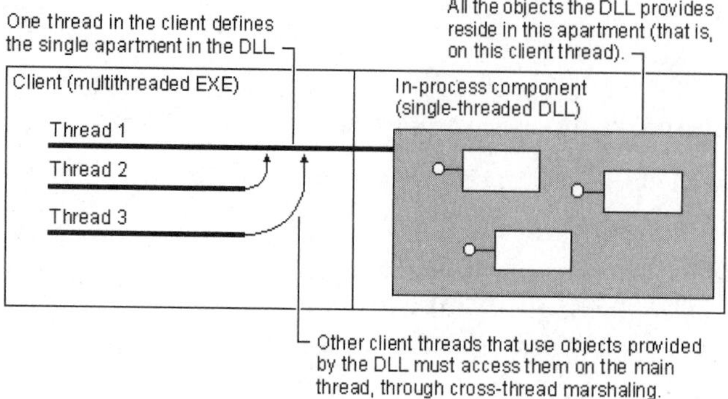

> **Note** For those who have done COM programming in C++, the client thread that handles all the calls to objects in the single-threaded in-process component will be the first thread that called OleInitialize().

Using a single-threaded DLL in this way is safe, but slow. Cross-thread marshaling is almost as slow as cross-process marshaling. You can improve the performance of an in-process component when it's used with multithreaded clients by making the component multithreaded.

To make an ActiveX DLL project multithreaded, select the desired threading options on the General tab of the Project Properties dialog box.

> **Note** In-process components can only use the threads on which their clients create objects and make method calls. You cannot create additional threads within an in-process component, so the other threading options are unavailable for DLL projects.

> **Important** Selecting the Unattended Execution option suppresses all forms of user interaction — including message boxes and system error dialogs. This is discussed in "Event Logging for Multithreaded Components," later in this chapter.

Marking an ActiveX DLL project for apartment-model threading provides the following benefits:

- All of the objects a client creates on a given thread will be created in the same apartment (thread) in the DLL. Calls to these objects do not require cross-thread marshaling, making them more efficient.
- Because an object is only accessed on the thread where it was created, calls are synchronized (serialized) so that a call is never interrupted by a call from another thread.
- Arguments for cross-thread calls are marshaled, and the calling thread is blocked. This synchronization of data protects the calling thread's state.

These points are illustrated in Figure 8.5.

Figure 8.5 Multithreaded client using multithreaded DLL

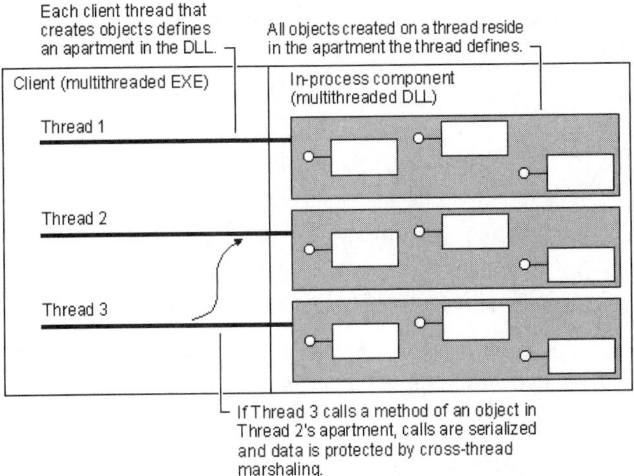

If Thread 2 is already making a call to one of the objects in its apartment in the DLL, a call from Thread 3 to one of Thread 2's objects will be serialized. When Thread 2 is free, it will process the call, using the arguments marshaled from Thread 3. Thread 3 is blocked while the request is serialized.

When the call requested by Thread 3 is complete, the return value and any ByRef arguments will be marshaled back to Thread 3. This synchronization ensures that Thread 3's data remains consistent.

> **Important** In an apartment-model DLL, a new apartment is created for each client thread that requests objects that the DLL provides. The first time a client thread requests such an object, Sub Main executes for the new apartment. A DLL cannot create threads of its own.

For More Information In coding the properties and methods of your objects, it's very important to observe reentrancy rules, as discussed in "Apartment-Model Threading in Visual Basic," earlier in this chapter.

Forms and Controls in Thread-Safe DLLs

When you create an instance of a form at run time, Visual Basic follows the same rules it uses for other private objects. That is, the new form is created on the thread where the New operator is executed. If you create a form implicitly (for example, by accessing a form property using a variable that was declared As New Form1), the form is created on the thread where the code was executed.

Apartment-threaded DLLs cannot create their own threads; the first time a client thread requests an object provided by your DLL, a new apartment is created, and Sub Main executes for that apartment. All public objects requested by that client will reside in the same apartment, and will share global data. Any private objects (including forms) that are created by the public objects will also reside in the apartment.

Visual Basic does not provide any way for apartments to become aware of each other. However, a multithreaded client could obtain a reference to an object on Thread A, and pass that reference to an object on Thread B. If your DLL allows this, you should read the information on reentrancy in "Apartment-Model Threading in Visual Basic."

> **Important** Modal forms shown by a thread do not block execution of code on other threads, and are not modal to forms on other threads. Showing a form yields control, just as calling DoEvents would, and therefore may cause the code in an object to be reentered.

Unlike forms, ActiveX controls are public objects that can be created and used by client forms. An instance of an ActiveX control always resides on the same thread as the client form that uses it.

> **Note** A special case of implicit form creation is the predeclared ID (for example, Form1), a hidden global form variable that Visual Basic maintains for every form class. Because Visual Basic duplicates global data for each apartment, there is a separate Form1 for every thread. To avoid confusion, you may find it helpful to avoid using predeclared IDs in apartment-threaded components, by explicitly declaring your own form variables.
>
> Duplicate global data means that a variable you declare Public in a standard module is global only to the thread; each thread has an instance of the variable. It also means that the properties of the App object, such as App.ThreadID, have separate instances for each thread.

Designing Multithreaded Out-of-Process Components

You can create a multithreaded out-of-process component that utilizes apartment-model threading. Objects the component provides can run on different threads of execution.

Visual Basic provides three models for assigning objects to threads in out-of-process components. You can select one of these models using the Unattended Execution box, on the General tab of the Project Properties dialog box.

Thread assignment model	Unattended Execution settings
One thread of execution	Select the Thread Pool option with one thread.
Thread pool with round-robin thread assignment	Select the Thread Pool option and specify the number of threads to allow.
Every externally created object is on its own thread	Select the Thread per Object option.

> **Note** The model you select cannot be changed at run time.

Like other private objects, forms reside on the thread where they were created. Private objects cannot be created with the CreateObject function, so they cannot be used to start new threads.

Important In a multithreaded executable, Sub Main executes independently for each new thread. Visual Basic provides no way to determine which thread was created first.

One Thread of Execution

This is the default setting, when you select Unattended Execution. This option allows you to compile components authored with earlier versions of Visual Basic, without having to modify them to take threading into account.

By recompiling a component with the Unattended Execution option, you remove any possibility that it will show message boxes that require operator intervention. Instead, such messages can be logged to the Windows NT event log (or to a file of your choice), as described in "Event Logging for Multithreaded Components," later in this chapter.

Round-Robin Thread Pool

As clients request objects, Visual Basic creates each object on the next thread in the pool, starting over with the first thread when it reaches the end of the pool.

For example, Figure 8.6 shows a component with three externally creatable classes (that is, classes whose Instancing property is set to any value *except* Private or PublicNotCreatable). The classes are named A, B, and C. To keep track of which object was requested by which client, the circle that represents each object contains the class name and the number of the client that created the instance.

Figure 8.6 Round-robin thread pool with five threads and four clients

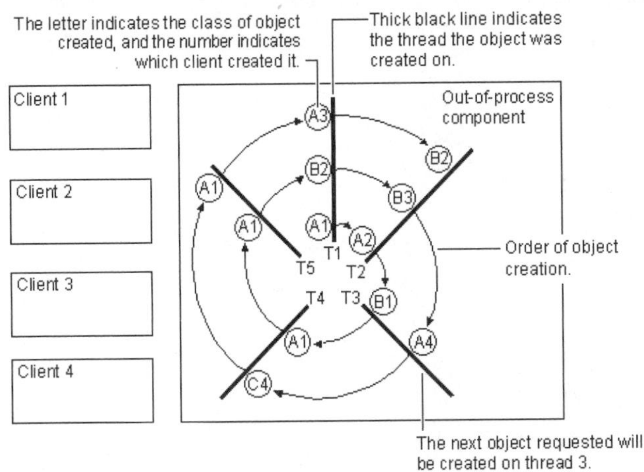

Four clients have created instances of these classes. Client 1 requested the first object, of class A, which was created on thread T1. Client 2 then requested an object of class A, which was created on thread T2, and so on. Some clients have created multiple instances of the same class — for example client 1, which is using a total of four instances of class A.

Figure 8.6 illustrates an important point about the round-robin threading model: You cannot predict which objects will be on the same thread — and therefore sharing global data. Objects used by different clients may share global data, while objects used by the same client may not.

For example, the objects on thread T1 are used by clients 1, 2, and 3, yet they share the thread's instance of global data. Objects used by client 1 can be found on threads T1, T3, T4, and T5. Of those objects, only the two on thread T5 share global data.

In addition, calls to the properties and methods of objects on the same thread will be serialized, and can therefore block each other — for example, if client 1 calls a method of its A object on thread T1 just before client 2 calls a method of its B object on thread T1, client 2 will have to wait until the call made by client 1 finishes.

The most serious aspect of this serialization of calls and sharing of global data is that the designer of a client application *cannot predict when objects will share global data, or when they will block each other.* The behavior of the round-robin thread pool algorithm is therefore referred to as *nondeterministic.*

Load Balancing

Another important point about round-robin threading is illustrated by Figure 8.7.

Figure 8.7 Round-robin threading lacks load balancing

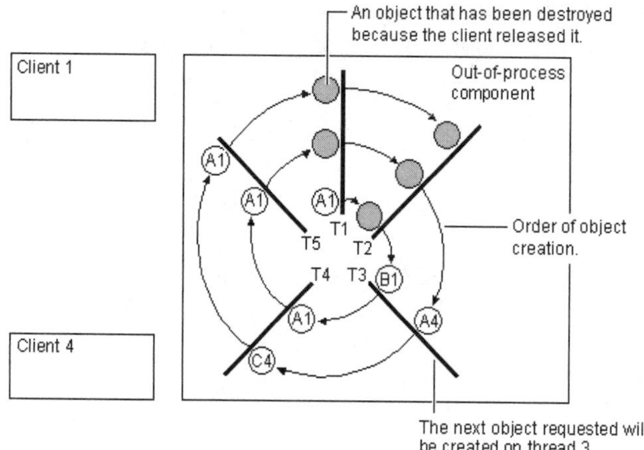

Clients 2 and 3 have released their objects and closed. Thread T1 has only one object on it, and thread T2 has none — yet the next object will still be created on thread T3. In fact, objects will be created on threads T3, T4, and T5 before an object is created on either of the under-utilized threads!

One Important Advantage

The advantage that the round-robin threading model offers in exchange for these drawbacks is that it puts a limit on the total number of threads. This is a significant advantage, because multiprocessing works best if the total number of active threads roughly matches the number of processors.

For More Information Externally creatable objects are discussed in "Externally Creatable Objects," in Chapter 6, "General Principles of Component Design."

Thread Per Object

As clients request objects, each object is created on a new thread. When the last client releases its last reference to objects on that thread, the thread is terminated.

Note that a client may have references to several objects on a thread. Suppose the client creates a Widget object, which in turn creates two dependent objects, a Sprocket and a Gear. If the client gets reference to the Sprocket object and then releases the Widget, the thread must continue to exist until the Sprocket is released.

Retaining unused threads in this fashion will eventually degrade system performance, so avoiding dangling object references is critical when you're using a multithreaded component.

No Control over Number of Threads

The big drawback to the thread-per-object model is that you have no control over the number of objects (and hence threads) that clients create. Creating too many threads will bog down the operating system in thread-maintenance overhead.

Too many *active threads* — that is, threads that are actively executing code — will bog down the operating system even more quickly. Generally speaking, you want about the same number of active threads as you have processors, to guarantee that there's never an idle processor. When you have just one processor, that's not very many active threads.

Internal and External Object Creation

If a client requests an instance of any externally creatable class, Visual Basic will create the object either on the next thread in the pool, or on a new thread. However, if that object turns around and requests an instance of an externally creatable class, what happens will depend on how the second instance is created:

- If the new object is created using the New operator, or with a variable declared As New, then the sibling object will not be on another thread. It will share the thread (and global data) of the object that created it, just like any dependent object.
- If the new object is created using the CreateObject function, it will be as if a client had requested the object. Visual Basic will create the object either on the next thread in the pool or on a new thread, depending on the thread assignment model.

  Note If an object uses CreateObject to create an object on another thread, any calls it makes to the properties and methods of that object will be subject to cross-thread marshaling.

For More Information Dependent objects are discussed in "Dependent Objects," in Chapter 6, "General Principles of Component Design."

Using Multiple Threads of Execution

Multithreading on a single-processor machine may not provide quite the results you expect. Consider, for example, the two methods shown in Figure 8.8.

Figure 8.8 Multithreaded method calls may appear to be slower

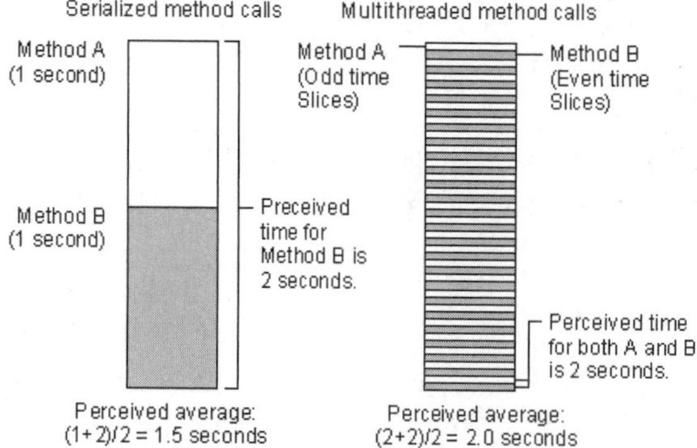

Method A and method B are called at the same time. In a single-threaded component, the requests are serialized, so that B doesn't begin until A has finished. With multithreading, the two active threads duel for the processor's attention.

Not only does the perceived average completion time increase, but more processor time is spent switching between threads.

The problem is that method A and method B take about the same amount of time. On a single-processor machine, multithreading results in a perceived performance improvement only with a mix of long and short tasks.

For example, if method B required only three time slices to complete, the user of the system would perceive a huge improvement in the responsiveness of method B — and only a slight degradation in the time required to execute method A.

The scenarios in which multithreading shows to best advantage are those in which most threads spend a substantial percentage of the time blocked — for example, waiting for file I/O — so that only one or two threads are actively executing code at any given time.

Event Logging for Multithreaded Components

Visual Basic only supports multithreading in components marked for unattended execution. In order to make it possible for a component to run unattended, the Unattended Execution option disables all user interaction, including message boxes and system error dialogs.

You can log such events to a file of your choice, or — on Windows NT — to the system event log. The LogMode property of the App object controls the way logging is done, and the LogPath property specifies the name of the log file.

Items entered in the log file include:

- Text from message boxes your component attempts to display.
- System errors, such as "Out of stack space."
- Text strings entered using the App.LogEvent method.

  Note When your component is running in the development environment, these entries go to the Immediate window instead of to the log file.

For More Information Search in the documentation index or the Object Browser for App Object, LogEvent, LogMode, LogPath, and StartLogging.

Debugging Limitations for Multithreaded Components

The Visual Basic development environment only supports one thread of execution. To debug the multithreaded behavior of your component, you must run your test application against the compiled component.

Out-of-Process Components

For out-of-process components, this means compiling both the component and the test program, and running multiple copies of the test program. (You can also run multiple copies of the test program using multiple instances of the development environment, but you cannot trace into the compiled component.)

In-Process Components

To test the multithreaded behavior of apartment-model DLLs, split your test program into two parts — a standard executable from which you control the tests, and a multithreaded out-of-process component. The standard executable is a client of the out-of-process component, which in turn is the test client for the DLL.

For example, the multithreaded out-of-process component might provide a TestMultiThreadDLL class. The standard executable might create varying numbers of TestMultiThreadDLL objects, passing each one a set of test parameters and then calling its BeginTest method.

The BeginTest method should enable a code-only timer, as demonstrated in Chapter 3, "Creating an ActiveX EXE Component," and then return immediately, in order to avoid tying up the single-threaded Standard EXE. The TestMultiThreadDLL object's timer would control creation and testing of the objects provided by the in-process component. Each TestMultiThreadDLL object would exercise one thread (apartment) in the in-process component.

> **Note** To use this testing technique, you must compile both the multithreaded out-of-process component and the DLL.

Using a Native Code Debugger

If you're compiling your component to native code, and you have Microsoft Visual C++, you can compile your component with symbolic debug information for the Visual Studio debugger, which supports multithreaded debugging.

Debug Messages

Because you can't debug multithreaded behavior in the development environment, you can't use Debug.Print and Debug.Assert to show debug message strings.

You can't use message boxes to show debug messages, either, because the Unattended Execution option completely suppresses user interaction.

Approaches to sending debug messages include:

- Create a single-threaded ActiveX DLL (that is, one that's *not* marked for unattended execution) with a public, creatable class that displays a modeless form with a list box. Give the class a DebugMsg method that takes a string argument and adds it to the top of the list box.

  You can call this single-threaded DLL from any thread in your multithreaded ActiveX EXE project. The calls will be slow, because of cross-thread marshaling (as described in "Designing Thread-Safe DLLs," earlier in this chapter), but this is not a big concern when you're debugging.

  > **Tip** Include the ThreadID in your debug message text.

- Create a single-threaded out-of-process component that works in the fashion described above.
- Create a program that handles Windows messages, using the AddressOf operator to subclass a Visual Basic form. Use the Windows API to create and register private messages which the component you're debugging can use to send debug strings.

For More Information Compiling to native code is discussed in "Compiling Your Project to Native Code," in Chapter 8, "More About Programming," in the *Microsoft Visual Basic 6.0 Programmer's Guide.* Subclassing windows with the AddressOf operator is discussed in Part 4, "Accessing DLLs and the Windows API."

Creating a Multithreaded Test Application

In order to test and debug in-process components (.dll and .ocx files), you will need a multithreaded client application. The steps to create a simple multithreaded application are as follows:

1. Open a new ActiveX EXE project, and name the default class module MainApp. Set the Instancing property for MainApp to PublicNotCreatable. A MainApp object will occupy the application's first thread, and display the main user interface.
2. On the **General** tab of the **Project Properties** dialog box, select **Sub Main** in the **Startup Object** box, select **Thread per Object** in the **Threading Model** box, and enter a unique value for the Project name. (Project Name determines the type library name; problems may arise if two applications have the same type library name.) "ThreadDemo" is the project name used in the example below. On the **Component** tab, select **Standalone** in the **Start Mode** box.
3. Add a form, name it frmProcess, and set the **Visible** and **ControlBox** properties to False. This form functions as a hidden window, which Sub Main will use to identify the main thread for the process. No code is needed for this form.
4. Add a standard module to the project. In this module, place the declarations, the Sub Main procedure, and the EnumThreadWndMain procedure shown below. As explained in the accompanying text and code comments, Sub Main will execute when your application starts, and every time you create a new thread. The Sub Main sample code demonstrates how to identify the first thread, so that you know when to create MainApp.
5. Add a form and name it frmMTMain. This form provides the main user interface for the test application. Add to it the single declaration and the Form_Unload event immediately above the heading "Multiple Instances of the Test Application."
6. In the Class_Initialize event procedure for MainApp, add code to show frmMTMain. Code to do this is provided below.

7. To create additional test threads, you must have at least one class in your project whose Instancing property is set to MultiUse. Add a class module and form and insert the code provided under the heading "Creating New Threads." Because you selected **Thread per Object** for this project, every public object that is externally created will start on a new thread. This means that you can create a new thread by using the CreateObject function to create an instance of your MultiUse class from its programmatic ID (ProgID), as discussed in the accompanying text.

8. Add code to frmMTMain to create new threads by creating instances of the MultiUse classes you defined. See the code in the example under the heading "Creating New Threads."

9. The development environment does not support multithreading. If you press F5 to run the project, all objects will be created on the same thread. In order to test multithreaded behavior, you must compile the ActiveX EXE project, and run the resulting executable.

   Important To ensure that each new MultiUse object starts a new thread, you must use Thread per Object rather than Thread Pool.

Determining the Main Thread During Sub Main

Sub Main executes for every new thread. The reason for this is that Visual Basic maintains a separate copy of your global data for each thread (each apartment). In order to initialize global data for the thread, Sub Main must execute. This means that if your Sub Main loads a hidden form, or displays your application's main user interface, new copies of those forms will be loaded for every new thread you create.

The following code determines whether or not Sub Main is executing in the first thread, so that you can load the hidden form only once and display the test application's main user interface only once.

```
' Root value for hidden window caption
Public Const PROC_CAPTION = "ApartmentDemoProcessWindow"

Public Const ERR_InternalStartup = &H600
Public Const ERR_NoAutomation = &H601

Public Const ENUM_STOP = 0
Public Const ENUM_CONTINUE = 1

Declare Function FindWindow Lib "user32" Alias "FindWindowA" _
   (ByVal lpClassName As String, ByVal lpWindowName As String) As Long
Declare Function GetWindowThreadProcessId Lib "user32"_
   (ByVal hwnd As Long, lpdwProcessId As Long) As Long
Declare Function EnumThreadWindows Lib "user32" _
   (ByVal dwThreadId As Long, ByVal lpfn As Long, ByVal lParam As Long) _
   As Long
```

```
' Window handle retrieved by EnumThreadWindows.
Private mhwndVB As Long
' Hidden form used to identify main thread.
Private mfrmProcess As New frmProcess
' Process ID.
Private mlngProcessID As Long

Sub Main()
   Dim ma As MainApp

   ' Borrow a window handle to use to obtain the process
   '  ID (see EnumThreadWndMain call-back, below).
   Call EnumThreadWindows(App.ThreadID, AddressOf EnumThreadWndMain, 0&)
   If mhwndVB = 0 Then
      Err.Raise ERR_InternalStartup + vbObjectError, , _
      "Internal error starting thread"
   Else
      Call GetWindowThreadProcessId(mhwndVB, mlngProcessID)
      ' The process ID makes the hidden window caption unique.
      If 0 = FindWindow(vbNullString, PROC_CAPTION & CStr(mlngProcessID)) Then
            ' The window wasn't found, so this is the first thread.
            If App.StartMode = vbSModeStandalone Then
               ' Create hidden form with unique caption.
               mfrmProcess.Caption = PROC_CAPTION & CStr(mlngProcessID)
               ' The Initialize event of MainApp (Instancing =
               '  PublicNotCreatable) shows the main user interface.
               Set ma = New MainApp
               ' (Application shutdown is simpler if there is no
               '  global reference to MainApp; instead, MainApp
               '  should pass Me to the main user form, so that
               '  the form keeps MainApp from terminating.)
            Else
               Err.Raise ERR_NoAutomation + vbObjectError, , _
                  "Application can't be started with Automation"
            End If
         End If
   End If
End Sub

' Call-back function used by EnumThreadWindows.
Public Function EnumThreadWndMain(ByVal hwnd As Long, ByVal _
   lParam As Long) As Long
   ' Save the window handle.
   mhwndVB = hwnd
   ' The first window is the only one required.
   ' Stop the iteration as soon as a window has been found.
   EnumThreadWndMain = ENUM_STOP
End Function
```

```
' MainApp calls this Sub in its Terminate event;
'  otherwise the hidden form will keep the
'  application from closing.
Public Sub FreeProcessWindow()
   Unload mfrmProcess
   Set mfrmProcess = Nothing
End Sub
```

Note This technique for identifying the first thread may not work in future versions of Visual Basic.

Notice that Sub Main takes no action for any thread after the first. When you add code that creates MultiUse objects (in order to start subsequent threads) be sure to include code to initialize those objects.

EnumThreadWindows is used with a call-back, EnumThreadWndMain, to locate one of the hidden windows Visual Basic creates for its internal use. The window handle of this hidden window is passed to GetWindowThreadProcessId, which returns the process ID. The process ID is then used to create a unique caption for the hidden window (frmProcess) that Sub Main loads. Subsequent threads detect this window, and thus can tell that they don't need to create the MainApp object. These gyrations are necessary because Visual Basic does not provide a way to identify the application's main thread.

The MainApp class, in its Initialize event, displays the test application's main form. MainApp should pass its Me reference to the main form, so that the form keeps MainApp from terminating. From the main user interface you can create all subsequent threads. Setting the Instancing property for MainApp to PublicNotCreatable helps you avoid displaying two main user interface forms.

A simple example of a MainApp class and its associated form (steps 5 and 6, above) might look like this:

```
' Code for a MainApp class.
Private mfrmMTMain As New frmMTMain

Private Sub Class_Initialize()
   Set mfrmMTMain.MainApp = Me
   mfrmMTMain.Caption = mfrmMTMain.Caption & " (" & App.ThreadID & ")"
   mfrmMTMain.Show
End Sub

Friend Sub Closing()
   Set mfrmMTMain = Nothing
End Sub

Private Sub Class_Terminate()
   ' Clean up the hidden window.
   Call FreeProcessWindow
End Sub
```

```
' Code for the form frmMTMain.
Public MainApp As MainApp

Private Sub Form_Unload(Cancel As Integer)
   Call MainApp.Closing
   Set MainApp = Nothing
End Sub
```

Multiple Instances of the Test Application

Including the process ID in the hidden window caption allows multiple instances of the test application to run without interfering with each other.

When you call CreateObject, the instance of the public class you create will be on a thread in the current application instance. This is because CreateObject always attempts to create an object in the current application before looking for other running EXE components that might supply the object.

Useful Properties for the Apartment

You may find it useful to expose the process ID as a read-only property of the module that contains Sub Main:

```
'This code not required for the test application
Public Property Get ProcessID() As Long
   ProcessID = mlngProcessID
End Property
```

This allows any object on the thread to get the process ID by calling the unqualified ProcessID property. You may also find it useful to expose a Boolean IsMainThread property in this fashion.

Creating New Threads

The Thread per Object option causes every public object that is externally created - that is, created using the CreateObject function - to start on a new thread. To create a new thread, simply use the programmatic ID (ProgID) of one of your MultiUse classes:

```
'This code not included in the test application
Dim tw As ThreadedWindow
Set tw = CreateObject("ThreadDemo.ThreadedWindow")
```

The variable tw now contains a reference to an object on a new thread. All calls to the properties and methods of this object that are made using tw will be subject to the extra overhead of cross-thread marshaling.

Note An object created with the New operator is not created on a new thread. It resides on the same thread where the New operator was executed. See "Designing Multithreaded Out-of-Process Components" and "How Object Creation Works in Visual Basic Components," both later in this chapter.

To ensure that MainApp doesn't terminate until all of the other threads are finished, you can give each public class a MainApp property. When an object creates a MultiUse object on a new thread, it can pass the new object a reference to the MainApp object as part of the initialization process. (You can also pass MainApp a reference to the new object, so that MainApp has a collection of references to all objects that control threads; however, remember that this will create circular references. See "Dealing with Circular References," in Chapter 6, "General Principles of Component Design.")

If you want a class that controls a thread to show a form, you should provide it with an Initialize method (not to be confused with the Initialize event) or a Show method that displays the form. Don't show the form in the Class_Initialize event procedure, as this could cause timing errors when you create instances of the class. In a very simple case, the code for a MultiUse ThreadedWindow class and its form, frmThreadedWindow, might look like this:

```
'Code for a MultiUse ThreadedWindow class.
Private mMainApp As MainApp
Private mfrm As New frmThreadedWindow

Public Sub Initialize(ByVal ma As MainApp)
   Set mMainApp = ma
   Set mfrm.ThreadedWindow = Me
   mfrm.Caption = mfrm.Caption & " (" & App.ThreadID & ")"
   mfrm.Show
End Sub

Friend Sub Closing()
   Set mfrm = Nothing
End Sub

'Code for the form frmThreadedWindow.
Public ThreadedWindow As ThreadedWindow

Private Sub Form_Unload(Cancel As Integer)
   Call ThreadedWindow.Closing
   Set ThreadedWindow = Nothing
End Sub
```

The following code snippet shows how you might initialize the ThreadedWindow object:

```
'Code for the test application's main form (frmMTMain).
Private Sub mnuFileNewTW_Click()
   Dim tw As ThreadedWindow
   Set tw = CreateObject("ThreadDemo.ThreadedWindow")
```

```
    ' Tell the new object to show its form, and
    '  pass it a reference to the main
    '  application object.
    Call tw.Initialize(Me.MainApp)
End Sub
```

If you have a number of classes that can control threads, you can make your code more generic by defining an IApartment interface to contain the Initialize method. When you implement IApartment in each class, you can provide the appropriate Initialize method code for that class. Your thread creation code might look like this:

```
'This code not required for the test application
Private Sub mnuFileNewObject_Click(Index As Integer)
   Dim iapt As IApartment
   Select Case Index
     Case otThreadedWindow
      Set iapt = CreateObject("ThreadDemo.ThreadedWindow")
     ' (other cases...)
   End Select
   ' Common code to initialize objects.
   Call iapt.Initialize(MainApp)
End Sub
```

Note You can make an IXxxxApartment interface that's known only to the multithreaded application by defining the interface in a separate type library. In the ActiveX EXE project, set a reference to the type library.

Keeping References to Threaded Objects

To ensure proper shutdown of a multithreaded application, you must keep careful track of all references to the MultiUse objects you use to create and control threads.

Define your object lifetime goals clearly. For example, consider the case of a MultiUse object that shows a form. The easiest way to manage object lifetime is to have the object pass the form a Me reference; the form then keeps the object alive. When the user closes the form, the form's Unload event must set all references to the MultiUse object to Nothing, so that the object can terminate and in turn clean up its reference to the form. (You may find it useful to give the MultiUse object a Friend method that cleans up the reference to the form, and all other internal object references; the form's Unload event can call this method.)

If the object that controls a thread creates additional objects on the thread, using the New operator, make sure you clean up references to those objects. The thread cannot close until all references to objects that were created on the thread have been released. Open threads consume system resources.

Friend Methods Cannot Be Used Cross-Thread

Because Friend properties and methods are not part of the public interface of a class, you cannot call them from another thread. Cross-thread calls between objects are limited to properties and methods that are declared Public.

Reentrancy

If a method of an object yields by calling DoEvents, showing a modal form, or making a secondary call to an object on another thread, then the code in the method can be entered by a second caller before the first call completes. If such a method uses or changes property values or module-level variables, this could result in an invalid internal state for the object. To protect against reentrancy, you can:

- Avoid yielding.
- Keep a module-level Boolean flag for each method. When a method begins, it tests this flag to determine whether a method call is in progress. If not, the method sets the flag to True and continues; otherwise it raises an error. You must be careful to turn this flag off when the method completes or exits for any reason.
- Write reentrant methods — that is, methods that don't depend on module-level data.

Asynchronous Tasks

Visual Basic doesn't provide a way to fork execution — that is, to have one thread initiate a method call on a new thread and immediately resume processing on the original thread. You can simulate this behavior in your test application by having the original method call turn on a timer and then return immediately. When the timer event occurs, you can turn the timer off and perform the asynchronous processing. This technique is discussed in "Asynchronous Call-Backs and Events," earlier in this chapter, and is demonstrated (see Chapter 3, "Creating an ActiveX EXE Component") in the Coffee sample application.

Using the Multithreaded Test Application

You must compile the multithreaded test application in order to test your apartment-threaded component, because the Visual Basic development environment does not currently support multiple threads of execution. If you have Visual Studio, you may find it useful to compile the test application with debugging information for native code debugging, so that you can use the Visual Studio debugger.

Scalability through Multiple Processes: SingleUse Objects

Visual Basic provides a second mechanism for using multiple threads of execution. By setting the Instancing property of a class to SingleUse, you cause each instance of the class to run in a separate instance of your component. This means that even though your component is single-threaded, each instance of the SingleUse class has its own thread of execution.

SingleUse objects require a lot more overhead than multiple objects in a multithreaded component. However, there are several reasons you might want to use SingleUse objects:

- If your component must show forms, active documents, or other user interface elements, you cannot mark it for unattended execution — and thus it cannot be multithreaded. Components that provide SingleUse objects can have forms and active documents.
- Your component can function as a standalone desktop application, and you want it to have an Application object that's not shared between clients.
- High-risk activities can be isolated in separate processes with SingleUse objects. If the object suffers a fatal error, other processes are not affected. By contrast, a fatal error in a multithreaded component terminates all threads.

Using Creatable SingleUse Objects to Avoid Blocking

Figure 8.9 shows how SingleUse objects have separate threads of execution, which can be preemptively multitasked.

Figure 8.9 A component with a SingleUse object

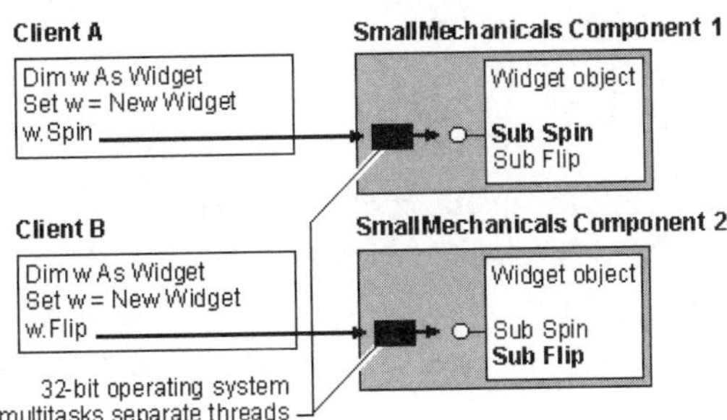

Components That Provide Multiple SingleUse Classes

The best way to provide exclusive use of an out-of-process component is to give it exactly one SingleUse class, with as many dependent objects as necessary.

If you set the Instancing property to SingleUse for more than one class module in your component, satisfying client requests for objects becomes somewhat complicated, and it becomes difficult to ensure that a client has objects from only one instance of the component.

You can think of each class as a hole, which will be filled when an object of that class is created. Figure 8.10 shows a component that provides three objects — Widget, Gear, and Sprocket. Each instance of the component can provide one object of each type.

Figure 8.10 Instancing with three classes marked SingleUse

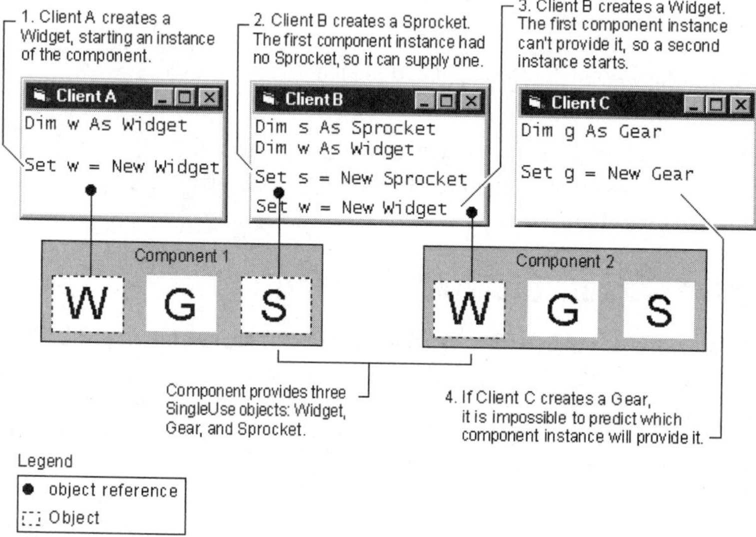

The lettered rectangles represent the potential to satisfy a request for an object of one of the three classes. A dotted outline indicates that the component has provided an object of that type, and so cannot provide another.

If Client A now creates a Sprocket object, that object will not be supplied by the same instance of the component that provided its Widget object. If the point of making the classes SingleUse was to make it possible for one client to have exclusive use of one component, this scheme will not guarantee it.

As noted above, a better way to accomplish exclusive use of an out-of-process component is to provide one SingleUse object as the only externally creatable object, and as many dependent objects as you need.

No Way to Predict Which Instance Provides an Object

It might appear from Figure 8.10 that Client B has one object from each of two instances of the component because of the order in which it created the objects. However, even if Client B had created its Widget object first, so that the second instance of the component was already running when Client B requested a Sprocket, there's no guarantee that the Sprocket would be provided by the second instance of the component.

As noted in the callout for Client C, when there are multiple instances of a component that could provide a particular object, the ActiveX specification does not guarantee which instance will provide the object. It's best to assume random selection.

Internal and External Instancing of SingleUse Classes

When a client creates two instances of a class marked SingleUse, two instances of the component executable are started. Within the component, however, it's possible to create multiple instances of such a class. Figure 8.11 shows the distinction between internal and external object creation.

Figure 8.11 Internal and external creation of SingleUse objects

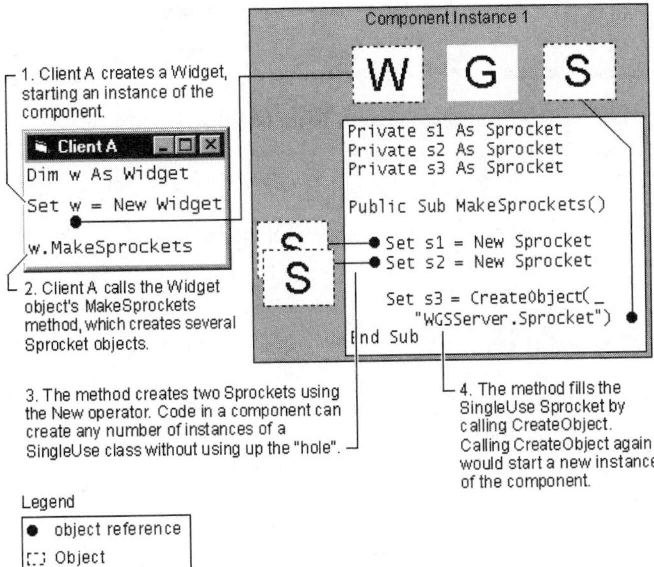
Component Instance 1
W
G
S
1. Client A creates a Widget, starting an instance of the component.
Client A
Dim w As Widget
Set w = New Widget
w.MakeSprockets
2. Client A calls the Widget object's MakeSprockets method, which creates several Sprocket objects.
S
Private s1 As Sprocket
Private s2 As Sprocket
Private s3 As Sprocket
Public Sub MakeSprockets()
Set s1 = New Sprocket
Set s2 = New Sprocket
Set s3 = CreateObject(_
"WGSServer.Sprocket")
End Sub
3. The method creates two Sprockets using the New operator. Code in a component can create any number of instances of a SingleUse class without using up the "hole".
4. The method fills the SingleUse Sprocket by calling CreateObject. Calling CreateObject again would start a new instance of the component.
Legend
object reference
Object

When code within the component creates an object from one of the component's own SingleUse classes using the Set statement with the New operator, or by declaring a variable As New, the object does not fill the "hole" that allows a client to create an instance of the class. Code within the component in Figure 8.11 could create any number of Sprocket objects in this fashion.

When the CreateObject function is used to create an object from a SingleUse class, however, it is as if the object had been created by a client. If the client in Figure 8.11 now attempts to create a Sprocket object, a second instance of the component will have to be started. Another instance of the component will also be started if the component instance in Figure 8.11 uses CreateObject to create another Sprocket.

SingleUse Really Means SingleUse

Once a client application creates an object from a SingleUse class, no client can ever create an object of that class from that instance of the component, even if the first client releases the object. That is, once the "hole" has been filled, it can never be empty — even if the object is destroyed.

In other words, marking a class module SingleUse means that during the lifetime of an instance of the component, only one instance of the class can be created externally — either by a client application, or by the component itself using the CreateObject function.

Debugging Limitations

When you run your component in the development environment, your client test programs can create only one instance of each SingleUse class during that debugging session. Once an instance of a class has been created, subsequent attempts to create an object from that class will cause Error 429, "OLE Automation server can't create object."

For debugging purposes, you can change SingleUse to MultiUse. However, to test the SingleUse behavior of your component, you must make the component executable.

For More Information To run your component alternately as an executable file and in the Visual Basic development environment, see "How to Test Compiled Components" in Chapter 7, "Debugging, Testing, and Deploying Components."

Asynchronous Call-Backs and Events

When a client makes a method call, it's blocked until the call returns. That is, the client can't execute any code while it's waiting. This is known as *synchronous processing*. By using *asynchronous processing*, you can free the client to do other things while it's waiting.

In asynchronous processing, the method call that starts a task returns instantly, without supplying a result. The client goes about its business, while the component works on the task. When the task is complete, the component notifies the client that the result is ready.

Asynchronous processing is also useful when clients need to be notified of interesting occurrences — for example, changes in database values, or the arrival of messages. A client tells a component it wants to be notified when certain things happen, and the component sends notifications when those things occur.

Both of these scenarios depend on *asynchronous notifications*. The client application is minding its own business, when out of the blue comes a notification that an asynchronous request is complete, or that something of interest has occurred.

For More Information Chapter 3, "Creating an ActiveX EXE Component," contains step-by-step procedures for implementing asynchronous notifications using both events and call-back methods.

Asynchronous Notifications Using Events

There are two parts to implementing asynchronous processing using events. The first part is the responsibility of the author of a component. The author must:

1. Define the tasks or notifications to be performed.
2. Provide one or more externally creatable classes to manage the tasks or notifications. This manager class may also do the work, or a worker class may be provided to do the actual processing.
3. Provide the manager class with methods that clients can call to initiate tasks or to request notifications.
4. Declare the events that clients must handle in order to receive notifications.
5. Write code to start the task, or the process of watching for interesting occurrences.
6. Write code to raise the event when the task is complete, or when the interesting occurrences are observed.

The second part is the responsibility of the developer who uses the component. The developer must:

1. Create a WithEvents variable to contain a reference to the object that will provide the notification events.
2. In the event procedures associated with the WithEvents variable, write code to handle the desired notification events.
3. Write code to request an instance of the component's manager class, and place the reference to it in the WithEvents variable.
4. Write code to call the methods that initiate tasks or that request notifications.

Figure 8.12 shows how the author's part and the developer's part interact to enable asynchronous processing for the CoffeeReady example from the step-by-step procedures in Chapter 3, "Creating an ActiveX EXE Component."

Figure 8.12 Asynchronous notifications using events

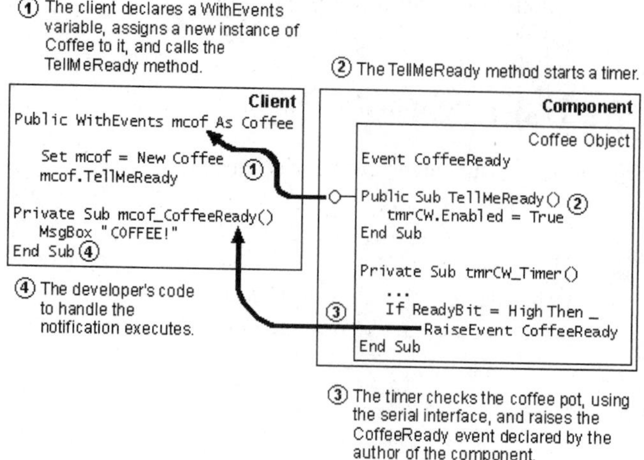

Note The numbers in Figure 8.12 indicate the order in which things happen in the finished application and component. They do not correspond to the numbers in the task lists.

A single event can be handled by multiple clients. One way to connect multiple clients to a single Coffee object would be to interpose a Connection object between the client and the Coffee object. In this way, each client would have its own Connection object, and each Connection object would supply its client with a reference to one central Coffee object.

The Coffee object's CoffeeReady event would be received by all clients that had a WithEvents variable containing a reference to the Coffee object.

Note Visual Basic's events can be thought of as *anonymous*. That is, the object that raises the event has no way of knowing whether a given event is handled by one, two, or two dozen objects — or by no objects at all. In addition, the object that raises an event has no way of knowing whether errors occur in the event-handling code of other objects.

Important When you're designing a system in which multiple clients receive the same event, *do not make assumptions about the order in which clients receive the event*. The order is undefined, and may differ depending on version number or platform.

For More Information You can see these tasks carried out in the step-by-step procedures in Chapter 3, "Creating an ActiveX EXE Component," which demonstrates asynchronous notifications using both events and call-back methods.

Asynchronous Notifications Using Call-Back Methods

There are two parts to implementing asynchronous processing using call-back methods. The first part is the responsibility of the author of a component. The author must:

1. Define the tasks or notifications to be performed.
2. Provide one or more externally creatable classes to manage the tasks or notifications. This manager class may also do the work, or a worker class may be provided to do the actual processing.
3. Create a type library containing the interface (or interfaces) that clients must implement in order to receive notifications. This interface must include all methods the component will call to notify the client.

   Note You can create type libraries with Visual Basic, as explained in "Creating Standard Interfaces with Visual Basic," in Chapter 6, "General Principles of Component Design."

4. Provide the manager class with methods that clients can call to initiate tasks or to request notifications.

   Note Each of these methods must have one argument declared as the interface type defined in step 3, so the client can pass the interface containing its implementation of the appropriate call-back method.

5. Write code to start the task, or the process of watching for interesting occurrences.
6. Write code to invoke the appropriate call-back method when the task is complete, or when the interesting occurrences are observed.

   Tip If a client provides a number of asynchronous services, you may want to group closely related call-backs on separate interfaces. This is because a client class must implement all the methods on an interface, whether it uses them or not. Having one big interface with all your call-back methods on it is thus inconvenient for clients.

The second part is the responsibility of the developer who uses the component. The developer must:

7. Create a public class that implements the interface defined by the component author.

   Note Use PublicNotCreatable for the Instancing property of this class. The class must be public so the component can invoke the call-back methods, but there's no reason to let other applications create instances of the class.

8. In the call-back methods the client will use, write code to handle the notifications.

   Tip All the methods of an interface must be implemented, but those you don't use can simply contain a comment.

9. Write code to request an instance of the component's manager class.
10. Write code to call the methods that initiate tasks or that request notifications.

Figure 8.13 shows how the author's part and the developer's part interact to enable asynchronous processing for the CoffeeReady example from the step-by-step procedures in Chapter 3, "Creating an ActiveX EXE Component."

Figure 8.13 Asynchronous notifications using call-back methods

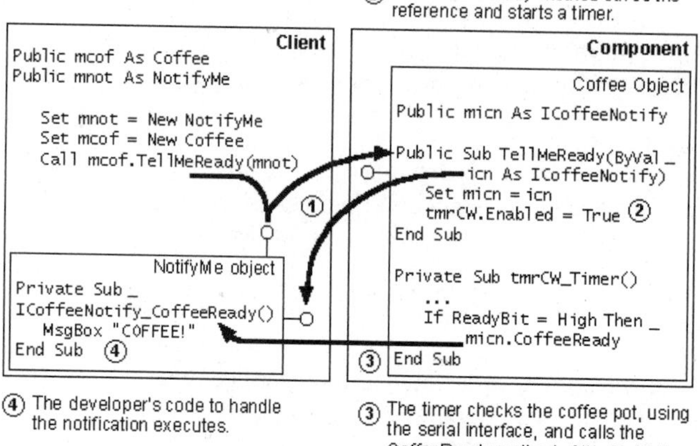
① The client creates an instance of its NotifyMe class, creates a Coffee object, and passes the TellMeReady method a reference to the NotifyMe object. Visual Basic queries for the ICoffeeNotify interface of the NotifyMe object.
② The TellMeReady method saves the reference and starts a timer.
Client
Public mcof As Coffee
Public mnot As NotifyMe
Set mnot = New NotifyMe
Set mcof = New Coffee
Call mcof.TellMeReady(mnot)
NotifyMe object
Private Sub _
ICoffeeNotify_CoffeeReady()
MsgBox "COFFEE!"
End Sub ④
Component
Coffee Object
Public micn As ICoffeeNotify
Public Sub TellMeReady(ByVal _
icn As ICoffeeNotify)
Set micn = icn
tmrCW.Enabled = True ②
End Sub
Private Sub tmrCW_Timer()
...
If ReadyBit = High Then _
micn.CoffeeReady
③ End Sub
④ The developer's code to handle the notification executes.
③ The timer checks the coffee pot, using the serial interface, and calls the CoffeeReady method of the NotifyMe object's ICoffeeNotify interface.

Note The numbers in Figure 8.13 indicate the order in which things happen in the finished application and component. They do not correspond to the numbers in the task lists.

Tip If the NotifyMe object is only going to be used once, the client doesn't have to keep a reference to it. In this case, the client code to call `TellMeReady` could be written as follows:

```
Call mcof.TellMeReady(New NotifyMe)
```

Call-Backs to Multiple Clients

One way for the Coffee object to handle multiple clients would be for the component to interpose a Connection object between the client and the Coffee object — so that each client would have its own Connection object, and each Connection object would supply its client with a reference to one central Coffee object.

The Coffee object's TellMeReady method would have to place the ICoffeeNotify references into a collection, so the timer could enumerate the collection and call each client's CoffeeReady method.

For More Information You can see these tasks carried out in the sample applications for Chapter 3, "Creating an ActiveX EXE Component," which demonstrate asynchronous notifications using both events and call-back methods. Implementing interfaces is discussed in "Providing Polymorphism by Implementing Interfaces," in Chapter 6, "General Principles of Component Design." Polymorphism is introduced in "Polymorphism," in Chapter 9, "Programming with Objects," in the *Microsoft Visual Basic 6.0 Programmer's Guide.*

When to Use Events or Call-Backs for Notifications

As you can see from the two preceding topics, call-backs are more work to implement than events. However, you should not base your decision about which to use on the amount of work involved. Call-backs and events represent different approaches to communication, and you should select the approach that best fits your needs.

You can characterize the difference between events and call-backs as follows: An event is like an anonymous broadcast, while a call-back is like a handshake.

The corollary of this is that a component that raises events knows nothing about its clients, while a component that makes call-backs knows a great deal.

Here's what these things mean to you as a developer:

- A client that has a reference to an object that raises events can handle those events by placing the reference into a WithEvents variable. The object that raises the events has no information about its clients. It's broadcasting to an unknown audience — perhaps to an empty theater.

  By contrast, a component that's making call-backs must have a reference to every object it's going to call. It has to know exactly how many of them there are.

- An object that raises events has no control over the order in which clients receive its events. (And you should take care to avoid creating dependencies on any ordering you may observe.)

  By contrast, a component making call-backs can control the order in which it calls clients back. It might give some clients higher priority, for example.

- When an object raises an event, all of its clients handle the event before the object that raised the event gets control again.

  By contrast, a component making call-backs gets control back after each call it makes to a client.

- If an event contains a ByRef argument, that argument can be altered by any client that handles the event. The last client's changes are the only ones visible to the object that raised the event, because (as noted above) the object that raised the event doesn't get control again until all of its clients have handled the event.

By contrast, a component making call-backs can examine changes to ByRef arguments after every call to a client, and can pass the next client fresh values for those arguments.

- If an unhandled error occurs in a client's event handler, the object that raised the event cannot receive the error. If the object is provided by an in-process component running in the client's address space, both client and component will terminate as a result of the unhandled error.

  By contrast, a component making call-backs will receive errors that occur in the call-back method, and must be prepared to handle them.

  Note An additional difference between events and call-back methods is that events cannot have optional arguments, named arguments, or ParamArray arguments.

A component can provide some notifications using call-backs, and some using events. The nature of the notification determines which mechanism should be used. You should use an event to provide a notification when all of the following statements are true:

1. The notification can be broadcast anonymously.
2. The order in which clients receive the notification is not important.
3. There's no need for the component to get control back until all clients have received the notification.
4. If the notification involves ByRef arguments, there's no need for the component to test the values of those arguments after each client receives the notification. The component only needs to know the last value assigned. (You can plan for clients to cooperate in their use of a ByRef argument — for example, once a Cancel argument is set to True, no client changes it — but there's no way to enforce this.)
5. The component doesn't need to know about errors that occur in the client.

If any one of the statements above is false, then you should do the extra work necessary to provide the notification using call-back methods.

You may also want to do the extra work to use call-backs when performance is critical. You can get vtable binding with call-back methods by using the Implements statement to add the call-back interface to the client's call-back object. Events are not vtable bound. (This will be much more noticeable with an in-process component that provides events or call-backs.)

Displaying Forms from Code Components

Code components can display modal or modeless forms, subject to certain restrictions.

In-Process Components That Show Modeless Forms

Modeless forms displayed by in-process components cannot function correctly unless they can communicate with the client's message loop. Therefore, in-process components created with Visual Basic can display modeless forms only in client processes that support such communication.

The following applications support the display of modeless forms by in-process components:

- Applications created with Visual Basic 5.0 or later.
- Microsoft Office 97 or later.
- Applications that have the Visual Basic Technology logo. (That is, that license Visual Basic for Applications version 5.0 or later.)

Applications that do not support the display of modeless forms by in-process components include:

- Applications created with earlier versions of Visual Basic.
- Earlier versions of Microsoft Office.
- Version 3.*x* of Microsoft Internet Explorer.

Determining Support for Modeless Forms at Run Time

To allow in-process components to detect at run time whether a client application supports the display of modeless forms, Visual Basic provides the Boolean NonModalAllowed property of the App object.

An in-process component should test this property before showing a modeless form. If the value is True, the form can be shown vbModeless. If the value is false, showing a modeless form will cause run-time error 369. The component should degrade gracefully by showing the form vbModal instead.

Important Debugging Limitation

When you're debugging an in-process component in the development environment, using a non-Visual Basic application as an out-of-process test program, modeless forms will appear to work even if the non-Visual Basic application doesn't support them.

Testing the NonModalAllowed property of the App object is of no use in this situation; the property will return True regardless of the client. The reason for this is that when debugging an in-process component with an out-of-process test application, Visual Basic cannot determine whether the test application supports modeless forms.

Before attempting to write an in-process component that will show modeless forms, for use with a specific non-Visual Basic application, you should compile a small test DLL with a method that displays the value of the NonModalAllowed property of the App object in a message box. Call this method from the non-Visual Basic application, to determine whether it supports modeless forms.

Forms Displayed by Out-Of-Process Components

Modal and modeless forms displayed as a result of method calls to out-of-process components will not necessarily appear in front of the client application's forms. The reason is that Automation does not define a z-order relationship between forms in different applications.

For More Information Chapter 3, "Creating an ActiveX EXE Component," provides a demonstration of the problems with showing forms from out-of-process components.

How Object Creation Works in Visual Basic Components

In certain circumstances, the mechanism you use to create objects — that is, CreateObject, the New operator, or a variable declared As New — can have subtle effects on object creation. These effects depend on whether or not Visual Basic uses the object creation services provided by the Component Object Model (COM).

When you create objects from classes that are provided by other components, Visual Basic always uses COM object creation services. As a result, when you're creating externally provided objects, there are no differences between the New operator, declaring a variable As New, and using the CreateObject function.

The CreateObject function always uses COM object creation services, whether you use it to create externally provided objects or to create instances of classes that are part of your project. So for CreateObject, there's no difference between external and internal object creation.

However, when you use the New operator (or a variable declared As New) to create an instance of a class that's *part of your project*, Visual Basic uses a very efficient private implementation of COM object creation.

In other words, Visual Basic uses the same mechanism for all object creation *except* creating objects with New or As New from classes in your project. This is summarized in the following table:

Object created from	Using CreateObject	Using New, As New
A class provided by another component	COM object creation services	COM object creation services
A class that's part of your project	COM object creation services	Visual Basic private object creation

Note The CreateObject function cannot be used on classes whose Instancing property is Private or PublicNotCreatable. The New operator can be used on any class.

The following are specific examples of the subtle differences that can arise depending on how you create objects from classes that are part of your project:

- If you use the New operator to create an instance of a SingleUse class, the object will be created in your current program instance — *as if its Instancing property were MultiUse.* Using CreateObject will start another instance of your component. (See "Scalability through Multiple Processes: SingleUse Objects," earlier in this chapter.)
- In a multithreaded out-of-process component with thread-per-object or round-robin threading, an instance of any of your project's externally creatable classes created with the New operator will *share the thread of the object that executed New* — while one created using CreateObject will be on another thread.
- In a component designed for use with Microsoft Transaction Server, an instance of any of your project's externally creatable classes created with the New operator will be *unknown to Microsoft Transaction Server.* Objects that will be used with Microsoft Transaction Server must be created using CreateObject.

How Binding Affects ActiveX Component Performance

Binding is the process of setting up a property or method call that's to be made using a particular object variable. It's part of the overhead of calling the property or method.

The time required to call a procedure depends on two factors:

- The time required to perform the task the procedure was designed to do, such as finding the determinant of a matrix.
- The overhead time required to place the arguments on the stack, invoke the procedure, and return.

As a component author, you'll do everything you can to minimize the first item. The second item, however, is not entirely under your control.

The overhead for a method call depends on the type of binding Visual Basic uses for the method call, which in turn depends on the way a client application declares object variables, which in turn depends on the developer of the client application.

To ensure that developers who use your component get the best possible performance, you may want to include the information in this topic in the Help file for your component.

> **Note** Binding affects all property and method calls, including those the objects in your component make to each other. Thus the binding issues discussed here can also affect the internal performance of your component.

Types of Binding

There are two main types of binding in Automation — late binding and early binding. Early binding is further divided into two types, referred to as DispID binding and vtable binding. Late binding is the slowest, and vtable binding is the fastest.

Late Binding

When you declare a variable As Object or As Variant, Visual Basic cannot determine at compile time what sort of object reference the variable will contain. Therefore, Visual Basic must use *late binding* to determine *at run time* whether the actual object has the properties and methods you call using the variable.

> **Note** Late binding is also used for variables declared As Form or As Control.

Each time you invoke a property or method with late binding, Visual Basic passes the member name to the GetIDsOfNames method of the object's IDispatch interface. GetIDsOfNames returns the *dispatch ID*, or DispID, of the member. Visual Basic invokes the member by passing the DispID to the Invoke method of the IDispatch interface.

For an out-of-process component, this means an extra cross-process method call, essentially doubling the call overhead.

> **Note** You cannot call the methods of the IDispatch interface yourself, because this interface is marked hidden and restricted in the Visual Basic type library.

Early Binding

If Visual Basic can tell at compile time what object a property or method belongs to, it can look up the DispID or vtable address of the member in the type library. There's no need to call GetIDsOfNames.

When you declare a variable of a specific class — for example, As Widget — the variable can only contain a reference to an object of that class. Visual Basic can use early binding for any property or method calls made using that variable.

This is the recommended way to declare object variables in Visual Basic components and applications.

> **Important** Whether early or late binding is used depends entirely on the way variables are declared. It has nothing to do with the way objects are created.

> **Tip** Early binding dramatically reduces the time required to set or retrieve a property value, because call overhead is a significant fraction of the total call time.

vTable Binding

In the fastest form of early binding, *vtable binding*, Visual Basic uses an offset into a virtual function table, or vtable. Visual Basic use vtable binding whenever possible.

Objects created from Visual Basic class modules support all three forms of binding, because they have *dual interfaces* — that is, vtable interfaces derived from IDispatch.

If client applications declare variables using explicit class names, Visual Basic objects will always be vtable bound. Using vtable binding to call a method of an in-process component created with Visual Basic requires no more overhead than calling a function in a DLL.

> **Note** For in-process components, vtable binding reduces call overhead to a tiny fraction of that required for DispID binding. For out-of-process components the change is not as great — vtable binding is faster by a small but significant fraction — because the bulk of the overhead comes from marshaling method arguments.

DispID Binding

For components that have type libraries but don't support vtable binding, Visual Basic uses DispID binding. At compile time, Visual Basic looks up the DispIDs of properties and methods, so at run time there's no need to call GetIDsOfNames before calling Invoke.

> **Note** While you can ensure that early binding is used (by declaring variables of specific class types), it's the component that determines whether DispID or vtable binding is used. Components you author with Visual Basic will always support vtable binding.

How Marshaling Affects ActiveX Component Performance

A client and an in-process component share the same address space, so calls to the methods of an in-process component can use the client's stack to pass arguments. This is not possible for an out-of-process component; instead, the method arguments must be moved across the boundary between the two processes. This is called *marshaling*.

A client and an out-of-process component communicate via a proxy/stub mechanism, as shown in Figure 8.14. The proxy and stub handle the marshaling and unmarshaling of arguments passed to methods of the component; they are completely transparent to the client.

Figure 8.14 A client and an out-of-process component

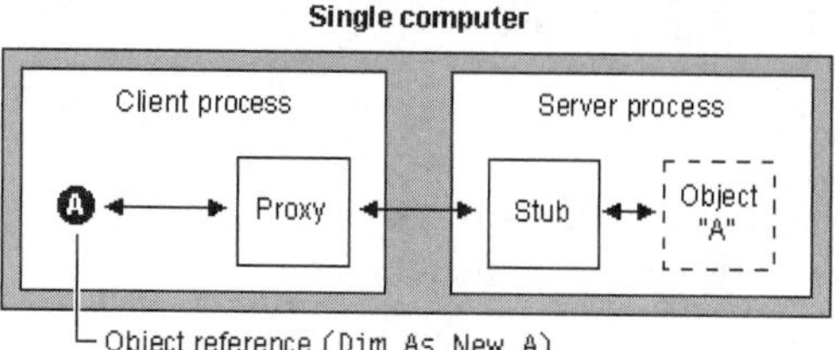

Marshaling is slower than passing parameters within a process, especially when parameters are passed by reference. It's not possible to pass a pointer to another address space, so a copy must be marshaled to the component's address space. When the method is finished, the data must be copied back.

Choosing Between ByVal and ByRef

Because of marshaling considerations, certain method arguments should be declared ByVal for out-of-process components and ByRef for in-process components, as described below.

Object References

When you're declaring methods for objects provided by an out-of-process component, always use ByVal to declare arguments that will contain object references.

The reason for this is that cross-process marshaling of object references requires significantly less overhead if it's one-way. Declaring an argument ByRef means that the object reference must be marshaled to your component, and then back to the client when the method is finished.

The only reason to use ByRef in the declaration of an argument that's going to contain an object reference is when the method will replace the client's object reference with a reference to another object.

Don't Pass Object References When Properties Will Do

If the method you're declaring requires a property value supplied by an object that belongs to the client, declare the argument with the data type of the *property* rather than the object's *class*. Marshaling an object reference requires significantly more overhead than marshaling a simple data type.

Other Data Types

It's common practice to declare parameters in Visual Basic procedures ByRef if they will be used to pass large strings and Variant arrays, even if the procedure doesn't make any changes to the parameter. It's much faster to pass a four-byte pointer to the data than to make a copy of the entire string or array and pass a pointer to the copy.

This practice works within the address space of your own process — that is, within your own program or with an in-process component — because the method to which you pass the parameter can use the pointer to access the data directly.

Cross-process marshaling reverses this practice. Data for a ByRef method argument is copied into the component's address space, and the method is passed a pointer to the local copy of the data.

The method uses the pointer to modify the copy. When the method ends, the data for any ByRef parameters is copied back into the client's address space. Thus a parameter declared ByRef will be passed cross-process *twice* per method call.

If you expect users to pass large strings or Variant arrays to a method of your component, *and the method does not modify the data,* declare the parameter ByVal for an out-of-process component and ByRef for an in-process component.

> **Important** If you declare a parameter of a method ByRef in an out-of-process component, developers using the component cannot avoid the effects of marshaling by putting parentheses around the parameter, or by using the ByVal keyword when they call the method. Visual Basic will create a copy of the data in this situation, but since Automation has no way of knowing the data is just a copy, it will marshal the copy back and forth between processes. The data is thus copied a total of three times.

Passing Parameters vs. Setting Properties

Properties make objects easy to use, but setting properties for an out-of-process component can be slow. When a client is using an out-of-process component, the extra overhead of cross-process marshaling makes it faster to call one method with five parameters than to set five properties and then call a method.

In cases where users of your component will frequently set a group of properties before calling a particular method, you can add a group of optional parameters to the method, one for each property. If one of these parameters is supplied, the method sets the corresponding property before proceeding.

If you give the optional parameters the names of the properties they are used to set, they can be used as named parameters (also known as *named arguments*), as in the following code fragments:

```
' Code fragment from a hypothetical Widget class.
Public Load As Double
Public Torque As Double
' ...other property declarations...
Public Sub Spin(ByVal Iterations As Long, _
      Optional Load As Variant, _
      Optional Torque As Variant)
   ' Before spinning the Widget, set any property
   '  values that were supplied. The object self-
   '  reference Me distinguishes between parameter
   '  and property.
   If Not IsMissing(Load) Then Me.Load = Load
   If Not IsMissing(Torque) Then Me.Torque = Torque
   ' ...code to spin the Widget...
End Sub

' Code fragment from a client, calling the Spin method
'  to spin the Widget 10000 times. Note the use of
'  the named parameter to set the Torque.
Dim wdgNew As New Widget
wdgNew.Spin 10000, Torque:=27.6
```

CHAPTER 9

Building ActiveX Controls

This chapter covers control creation in depth. The majority of the topics are organized according to the sequence of control development tasks outlined in "Control Creation Recap," at the end of Chapter 4, "Creating an ActiveX Control."

First and most important, however, is an introduction to the terminology and concepts of control creation, discussed in the sections "Control Creation Terminology," "Control Creation Basics," and "Interacting with the Container," later in this chapter.

These are followed by sections associated with the following development tasks:

1. Determine the features your control will provide.

   "Visual Basic ActiveX Control Features."

2. Design the appearance of your control.

   "Drawing Your Control."

3. Design the interface for your control — that is, the properties, methods, and events your control will expose.

   "Adding Properties to Controls," "Adding Methods to Controls," "Raising Events from Controls," and "Providing Named Constants for Your Control."

4. Create a project group consisting of your control project and a test project.

   "Setting Up a New Control Project and Test Project."

5. Implement the appearance of your control by adding controls and/or code to the UserControl object.

6. Implement the interface and features of your control.

   "Creating Robust Controls."

7. As you add each interface element or feature, add features to your test project to exercise the new functionality.

   "Debugging Controls."

8. Design and implement property pages for your control.

   This subject is covered in Chapter 10, "Creating Property Pages for ActiveX Controls."

9. Compile your control component (.ocx file) and test it with all potential target applications.

   "Distributing Controls."

The chapter ends with "Localizing Controls," which discusses localizing your control for other languages. The complete list of top-level subjects is:

Contents

Sample Application: CtlPlus.vbg

Includes a fully functional version of the ShapeLabel control created in the step-by-step procedures in Chapter 4, "Creating an ActiveX Control," and other controls that illustrate the control creation features in this chapter. The sample applications are listed in the Samples directory.

Control Creation Terminology

Controls are unlike other objects you create with Microsoft Visual Basic. They're not just code; they have visual parts, like forms — but unlike forms, they can't exist without some kind of container. In addition, controls are used — in different senses — by both developers and end users of applications.

These characteristics of controls require some additional terminology.

Control Class vs. Control Instance

The control you develop in Visual Basic is actually a *control class,* a description from which controls will be created. When you put a control on a form, you're creating an instance of this control class.

To avoid confusion, remember that the control class you're designing is distinct from the *control instances* you place on forms.

Control vs. Control Component

Controls are objects provided by *control components,* also known as .ocx files. A control component may provide more than one kind of control.

An ActiveX control project contains one or more .ctl files, each of which defines a control class. When you build the project, Visual Basic gives the control component an .ocx extension.

A developer who buys your control component and installs it can use any of the controls you defined (and made public).

Containers and Siting

A control instance cannot exist by itself. It must be placed on a container object, such as a Visual Basic form. The process of hooking a control instance up to its container is called *siting* — that is, assigning the control a *site* on the container.

When a control instance has been sited, its events are available as event procedures in the form's code window, and it has access to other services the container provides, such as Extender and AmbientProperties objects.

Interface vs. Appearance

A control consists of three parts, two public and one private. The control's *appearance* is public, because users see and interact with it. The control's *interface* — the set of all its properties, methods, and events — is also public, because it's used by any program that includes instances of the control.

The private part of a control is its *implementation,* the code that makes the control work. The effects of a control's implementation can be seen, but the code itself is invisible.

Author vs. Developer

The *author* of a control compiles her project as a control component, or .ocx file, which may contain one or more controls. A *developer* uses the control (or controls) to create an application, and includes the .ocx file in their setup program. The *user* installs and uses the application.

These terms avoid confusion between the developer of a control and the developer who uses the control in an application. The former will be referred to throughout as the author of the control.

For example, the author of the control is the only person who can place code in the event procedure for the UserControl object's Click event.

If she ends that code by raising her own Click event, the developer who adds an instance of the control to one of his forms will have an event procedure in which to place code he wants to execute when the user of his application clicks on that control instance.

When the user of the application clicks on the control, the author's code and the developer's code get executed.

> **Note** Developers are not the only direct consumers of ActiveX controls. You can design controls for users to place on documents in desktop applications such as Microsoft Office.

Design-Time Instance vs. Run-Time Instance

When a Visual Basic user puts a control on a form at design time, an actual instance of the control class is created. The user thinks of this control as a permanent fixture of the form. In fact, it's only a *design-time instance;* if the form is closed for any reason — clicking its Close button, closing the project, or pressing F5 to place the project in Run mode — this design-time instance is destroyed.

If the project is placed in Run mode, a *run-time instance* of the control is created when the form is loaded. This run-time instance is destroyed when the form is unloaded. When the form once again appears in design mode, a new design-time instance of the control is created.

A new design-time instance is also created the first time the form's .frm file is opened, after the project that contains the form is opened in the development environment. The .frm file contains all the values of the control instance's properties.

The property values in the in-memory copy of the .frm file are used by Visual Basic to re-create the control as modes change. When you make the project into an executable, the property values it contains are compiled in, so that a run-time instance of the control can be created when the compiled application is run.

Control lifetime is discussed in more detail in "Understanding Control Lifetime and Key Events," later in this chapter.

Control Creation Basics

If you're used to developing Visual Basic applications, the world of control creation may at first seem upside down and backward. Events flow in the opposite direction from what you're used to. Many properties you're used to setting as a consumer of controls are suddenly off limits. Focus is — well, we'll get to focus in due time.

In short, you're not the owner of an application any more — you're just a widget, a cog in somebody else's machine. Relax. Let things unfold naturally.

The topics in this section provide the basic facts and concepts you need to master this new way of thinking about controls.

The UserControl Object

An ActiveX control created with Visual Basic is always composed of a *UserControl object,* plus any controls — referred to as *constituent controls* — that you choose to place on the UserControl.

Like Visual Basic forms, UserControl objects have code modules and visual designers, as shown in Figure 9.1. You place constituent controls on the UserControl object's designer, just as you would place controls on a form.

Figure 9.1 UserControl designer and code window

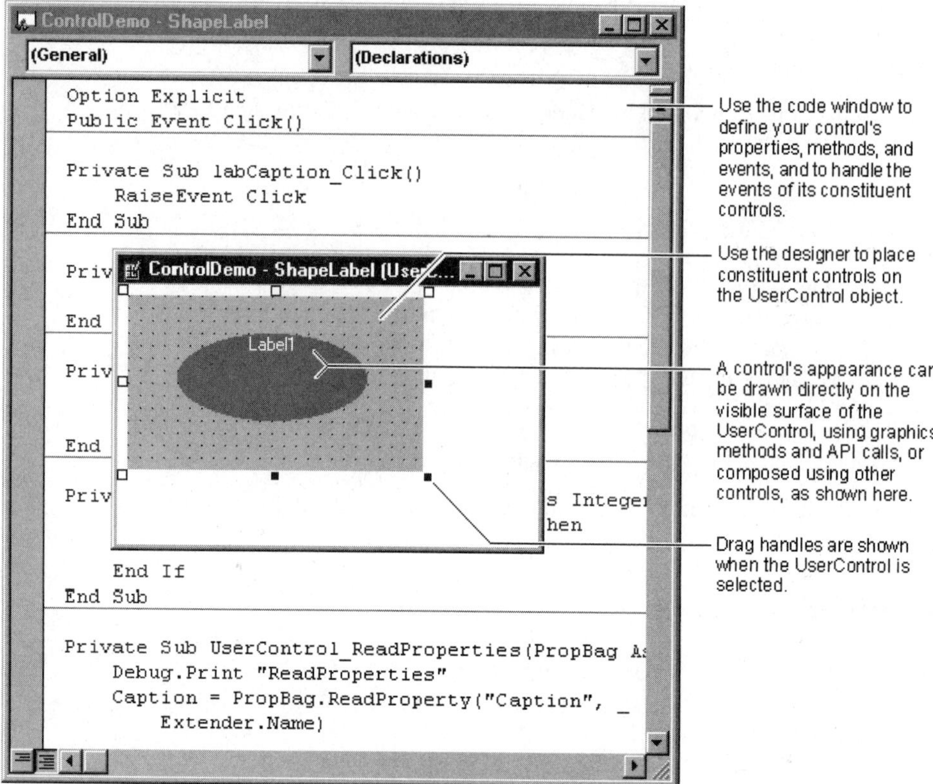

Like forms, user controls are stored in plain text files that contain the source code and property values of the UserControl and its constituent controls. Visual Basic uses the extension .ctl for these source files.

The relationship of .ctl files and ActiveX control projects to finished controls and .ocx files is shown in Figure 9.2.

Figure 9.2 ActiveX control projects are built into .ocx files

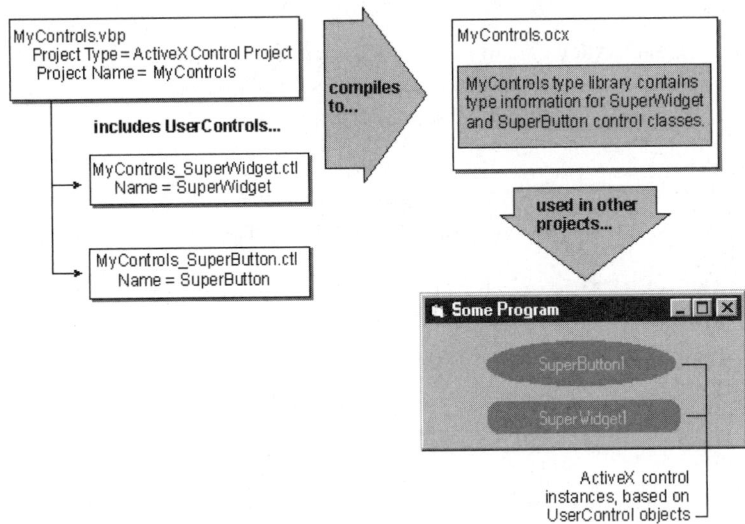

If a UserControl or its constituent controls use graphical elements which cannot be stored as plain text, such as bitmaps, Visual Basic stores those elements in a .ctx file with the same name you give to the .ctl file. This is analogous to the .frx files used to store graphical elements used in forms.

The .ctl and .ctx files completely define an ActiveX control's appearance and interface (properties, methods, and events). You can include .ctl files in any of the project types. "Two Ways to Package ActiveX Controls," later in this chapter, discusses this subject in depth.

Delegating to the UserControl and Constituent Controls That Compose Your ActiveX Control

Your ActiveX control is said to be *composed* of a UserControl and its constituent controls because each instance will actually contain those objects.

That is, whenever you place an instance of your ActiveX control on a form, a UserControl object is created, along with instances of any constituent controls you placed on the UserControl designer. These objects are *encapsulated* inside your control.

The UserControl object has an interface — that is, properties, methods, and events — of its own. The interface of your ActiveX control can *delegate* to the UserControl object's interface members, which are hidden from the user of your control by encapsulation.

That is, rather than writing your own code to implement a BackColor property, you can delegate to the UserControl object's BackColor property, and let it do all the work. In practice, this means that the BackColor property of your ActiveX control simply calls the BackColor property of the UserControl object.

In the same manner, you can piggy-back your control's Click event on the existing functionality of the UserControl object's Click event.

The interface for your ActiveX control can also delegate to the properties, methods, and events of the constituent controls you place on the UserControl designer, as discussed in "Exposing Properties of Constituent Controls," "Adding Methods to Controls," and "Exposing Events of Constituent Controls," later in this chapter.

For More Information For a discussion of what controls you can place on a UserControl designer, see "Controls You Can Use As Constituent Controls," later in this chapter.

Three Ways to Build ActiveX Controls

There are three models for control creation in Visual Basic. You can:

- Author your own control from scratch.
- Enhance a single existing control.
- Assemble a new control from several existing controls.

The second and third models are similar, because in both cases you put constituent controls on a UserControl object. However, each of these models has its own special requirements.

Authoring a User-Drawn Control

Writing a control from scratch allows you to do anything you want with your control's appearance and interface. You simply put code into the Paint event to draw your control. If your control's appearance changes when it's clicked, your code does the drawing.

This is the model you should select if you're creating a new visual widget, such as a button that crumbles to dust and disappears when clicked.

For More Information Creating a user-drawn control is discussed further in "Drawing Your Control," later in this chapter.

Enhancing an Existing Control

Enhancing an existing control means putting an instance of the control on a UserControl designer and adding your own properties, methods, and events.

You have complete freedom in specifying the interface for your enhanced control. The properties, methods, and events of the control you start with will only be included in your interface if you decide to expose them.

"Exposing Properties of Constituent Controls," later in this chapter, describes how to do this manually, and how to make it easier by using the ActiveX Control Interface Wizard.

Enhancing the appearance of an existing control is more difficult than enhancing the interface, because the control you're enhancing already contains code to paint itself, and its paint behavior may depend on Windows messages or other events.

It's easier to work with the control's built-in paint behavior, and instead enhance it by adding properties, methods, and events, or by intercepting and altering existing properties and methods. This is discussed further in "Drawing Your Control," later in this chapter.

Assembling a Control from Several Existing Controls

You can construct your control's appearance and interface quickly by assembling existing controls on a UserControl designer.

For example, the ShapeLabel control provided in the CtlPlus.vbg sample application, and discussed in the step-by-step procedures in Chapter 4, "Creating an ActiveX Control," uses a Shape control to provide its visual background and a Label control to display its caption.

Figures 9.3 and 9.4 show how multiple constituent controls can contribute to the appearance and interface of an ActiveX control.

Figure 9.3 Constituent controls provide ShapeLabel's appearance

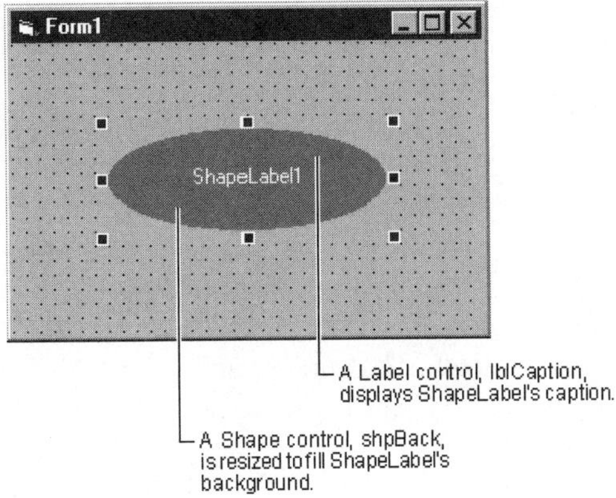
Form1
ShapeLabel1
A Label control, lblCaption, displays ShapeLabel's caption.
A Shape control, shpBack, is resized to fill ShapeLabel's background.

Constituent controls contribute to the appearance of an instance of your control by their mere presence on the UserControl designer. They contribute to your control's interface by *delegation,* as shown in Figure 9.4.

Figure 9.4 Constituent controls contribute to ShapeLabel's interface

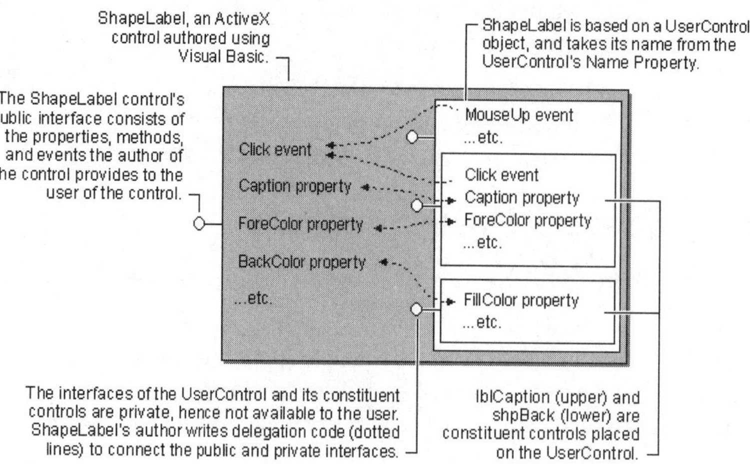

For example, ShapeLabel's Caption property delegates to the Caption property of the constituent control `lblCaption` as shown in the following code fragment.

```
Public Property Get Caption() As String
   Caption = lblCaption.Caption
End Property

Public Property Let Caption(NewCaption As String)
   lblCaption.Caption = NewCaption
   PropertyChanged "Caption"
End Property
```

For More Information "Drawing Your Control" and "Exposing Properties of Constituent Controls," later in this chapter, discuss control assemblies in more depth. The purpose and importance of PropertyChanged are discussed in "Adding Properties to Controls," later in this chapter.

Two Ways to Package ActiveX Controls

An ActiveX control created with Visual Basic is defined by a UserControl module. The source code you add to this module, to implement your ActiveX control, is stored in a .ctl file.

You can include UserControl modules in most Visual Basic project types, but only ActiveX control projects can provide controls to other applications. Controls in all other project types are private.

Thus there are two ways to package controls:

- *Public controls* can only exist in ActiveX control projects. You make a control public by setting the Public property of the UserControl object to True.

  Public controls can be used by other applications, once the ActiveX control project has been compiled into a control component (.ocx file).

- *Private controls* can exist in any project type. You make a control private by setting the Public property of the UserControl object to False.

  After the project is compiled, private controls cannot be used by other applications. They can be used only within the project in which they were compiled.

  If you attempt to set the Public property of a UserControl object to True, and the UserControl is not in an ActiveX control project, an error occurs.

If one of the controls in an ActiveX control project is meant to be used only as a constituent of other controls in the project, you can set the Public property of the UserControl to False. The control will then be available only to the controls of which it is a constituent part. Other applications will not be able to use it.

> **Note** You cannot include UserControl modules in a project marked for unattended execution. If the Unattended Execution box is checked on the General tab of the Project Properties dialog box, the project cannot contain any user interface elements.

> **Important** If you package your controls as a control component, be sure to set the description for each control. Some clients, such as Visual Basic, represent the entire .ocx file using the string you enter in the Project Description box of the Project Properties dialog box, but others display the browser strings for the individual controls. See "Providing Help and Browser Strings for Objects," in Chapter 7, "Debugging, Testing, and Deploying Components."

Including Controls as Compiled Code vs. Source Code

If you create your controls as public classes in an ActiveX control project, you can distribute the compiled control component (.ocx file) with any application you create. When you use SetupWizard to create a setup program for an application in which you've used such a control, the compiled .ocx file will be included automatically.

You can also create a setup program for the control component itself, and distribute it to other developers. "Licensing Issues for Controls," later in this chapter, discusses the licensing support available for control components authored using Visual Basic.

Changing the Packaging

Once you've authored a control, you can easily change the way the control is packaged.

For example, if you have some private controls that are part of a Standard EXE project, and you want to allow other applications to use them, you can add the .ctl files to an ActiveX control project, and compile it into a distributable control component (.ocx file).

Source Code

Instead of including the compiled control component in your applications, you can simply add the .ctl file to the project for the application. When the application is compiled, the control is compiled into the executable.

The primary advantages of including a control as source code are:

- There is no additional .ocx file to distribute.
- You don't have to debug your control for all possible test cases. You only have to debug the features used by your application.
- You don't have to worry about whether your application will work with future versions of the control, because the version your application uses is compiled in.

  Note Some developers may argue that avoiding the additional .ocx file is not really an advantage. All Visual Basic applications require support files, and SetupWizard automatically includes them in your setup program, so you're not avoiding any extra work.

Of course, there's no such thing as a free lunch. There are also disadvantages to including controls as source code:

- If you discover a bug in the control, you cannot simply distribute an updated .ocx file. You must recompile the entire application.
- Multiple applications will require more disk space, because instead of sharing one copy of an .ocx file, each application includes all the code for the control.
- Each time you use the source code in an application, there will be an opportunity to fix bugs or enhance the code. It may become difficult to keep track of which version of a control was used in which version of which application.
- Sharing source code with other developers may be problematic. At the very least, it's likely to require more support effort than distributing a compiled component. In addition, you give up control and confidentiality of your source code.

Understanding Control Lifetime and Key Events

Designing ActiveX controls involves a radical shift in perspective. The key events you must respond to are different — for example, your life will revolve around the Resize event — and there's no such thing as QueryUnload. But that's just the beginning.

"Control Creation Terminology," earlier in this chapter, introduced the idea that a control is not a permanent fixture of a form. Indeed, design-time and run-time instances of your control will be created and destroyed constantly — when forms are opened and closed, and when you run the project.

Each time an instance of your ActiveX control is created or destroyed, the UserControl object it's based on is created or destroyed, along with all of its constituent controls. ("The UserControl Object," earlier in this chapter, explains the basis of all ActiveX controls created with Visual Basic.)

Consider, for example, a day in the life of the ShapeLabel control used in the step-by-step procedures in Chapter 4, "Creating an ActiveX Control."

1. The user creates an instance of ShapeLabel — by double-clicking on the Toolbox, or by opening a form on which an instance of ShapeLabel was previously placed.
2. The constituent controls, a Shape and a Label, are created.
3. The UserControl object is created, and the Shape and Label controls are sited on it.
4. The UserControl_Initialize event procedure executes.
5. The ShapeLabel control is sited on the form.
6. If the user is placing a new ShapeLabel, the InitProperties event of the UserControl object occurs, and the control's default property values are set. If an existing form is being opened, the ReadProperties event occurs instead, and the control retrieves its saved property values.
7. The UserControl_Resize event procedure executes, and the constituent controls are resized according to the size the user made the new control instance, or the size they were before the form was closed.
8. The Show and Paint events occur. If there are no constituent controls, the UserControl object draws itself.
9. The user presses F5 to run the project. Visual Basic closes the form.
10. The UserControl object's WriteProperties event occurs, and the control's property values are saved to the in-memory copy of the .frm file.
11. The control is unsited.
12. The UserControl object's Terminate event occurs.
13. The UserControl object and its constituent controls are destroyed.

And that's not the half of it. The run-time instance of the form is now created, along with a run-time instance of the ShapeLabel control. When the user closes the form and returns to design mode, the ShapeLabel is destroyed and re-created once again.

The rest of this topic explains the key events in a UserControl object's life, and provides reference lists of the events you receive in several important scenarios.

Key UserControl Events

The meanings of the key events in the life of a UserControl object are as follows:

- The Initialize event occurs every time an instance of your control is created or re-created. It is always the first event in a control instance's lifetime.
- The InitProperties event occurs only in a control instance's first incarnation, when an instance of the control is placed on a form. In this event, you set the initial values of the control's properties.
- The ReadProperties event occurs the second time a control instance is created, and on all subsequent re-creations. In this event, you retrieve the control instance's property values from the in-memory copy of the .frm file belonging to the form the control was placed on.
- The Resize event occurs every time a control instance is re-created, and every time it is resized — whether in design mode, by the developer of a form, or at run time, in code. If your UserControl object contains constituent controls, you arrange them in the event procedure for this event, thus providing your control's appearance.
- The Paint event occurs whenever the container tells the control to draw itself. This can occur at any time, even before the control receives its Show event — for example, if a hidden form prints itself. For user-drawn controls, the Paint event is where you draw your control's appearance.
- The WriteProperties event occurs when a *design-time* instance of your control is being destroyed, if at least one property value has changed. In this event, you save all the property values a developer has set for the control instance. The values are written to the in-memory copy of the .frm file.
- The Terminate event occurs when the control is about to be destroyed.

In addition to the events listed above, the Show and Hide events may be important to your control. Show and Hide occur as indicated in Figure 9.5.

Figure 9.5 Show and Hide Events

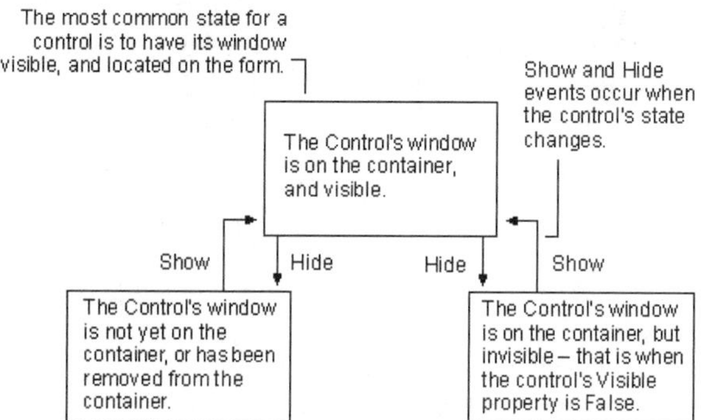

In order to draw to the screen in Windows, any control must have a window, temporarily or permanently. Visual Basic ActiveX controls have permanent windows. Before a control has been sited on a form, its window is not on the container. The UserControl object receives Show and Hide events when the window is added and removed.

While the control's window is on the form, the UserControl receives a Hide event when the control's Visible property changes to False, and a Show event when it changes to True.

The UserControl object does *not* receive Hide and Show events if the form is hidden and then shown again, or if the form is minimized and then restored. The control's window remains on the form during these operations, and its Visible property doesn't change.

If the control is being shown in an internet browser, a Hide event occurs when the page is moved to the history list, and a Show event occurs if the user returns to the page.

> **Note** If your control is used with earlier versions of Visual Basic, the UserControl object will not receive Show and Hide events at design time. This is because earlier versions of Visual Basic did not put any visible windows on a form at design time.

For More Information "Life and Times of a UserControl Object," one of the step-by-step procedures in Chapter 4, "Creating an ActiveX Control," demonstrates the key events in the life of a control and illustrates how often control instances are created and destroyed.

The Incarnation and Reincarnation of a Control Instance

Let's follow a control instance from its placement on a form, through subsequent development sessions, until it's compiled into an application. We'll assume the control was already developed and compiled into an .ocx file, before the curtain opens.

The scenarios that follow mention both Resize and Paint events. Which event you're interested in depends on the control creation model you're using, as discussed in "Three Ways to Build ActiveX Controls," earlier in this chapter.

If your control provides its appearance using constituent controls, you'll use the Resize event to size the constituent controls. If you're authoring a user-drawn control, on the other hand, you can ignore the Resize event and remarks about constituent controls. User-drawn controls draw their appearance in the Paint event. This is discussed in "Drawing Your Control," later in this chapter.

Note In all of these scenarios, the order and number of Resize and Paint events may vary.

The Control Instance Is Placed on a Form

When you double-click a control's icon in the Toolbox, a design-time instance of the control is placed on the form you're designing. The following events occur in the UserControl object at the heart of the control instance:

Event	What gets done
Initialize	Constituent controls have been created, but the control has not been sited on the form.
InitProperties	The control instance sets default values for its properties. The control has been sited, so the Extender and AmbientProperties objects are available. This is the only time the instance will ever get this event.
Resize, Paint	The control instance adjusts the size of its constituent controls, if any, according to its default property settings. A user-drawn control draws itself.

The developer of the form can now see the control, and set its properties in the Properties window. After the developer does this, she may press F5 to run the project.

From Design Mode to Run Mode

When F5 is pressed, the control's design-time instance on the form is destroyed. When the form is loaded at run time, the control is recreated as a run-time instance.

Event	What gets done
WriteProperties	Before the design-time instance is destroyed, it has a chance to save property values to the in-memory copy of the .frm file.
Terminate	Constituent controls still exist, but the design-time control instance is no longer sited on the form. It's about to be destroyed.
Initialize	Constituent controls have been created, but the run-time control instance has not been sited on the form.
ReadProperties	The control instance reads the property values that were saved in the in-memory .frm file. The control has been sited on the run-time instance of the form, so the Extender and AmbientProperties objects are available.
Resize, Paint	The control instance adjusts the size of its constituent controls, if any, according to its current property settings. A user-drawn control draws itself.

The developer tests the form by clicking the control, or taking other actions that cause the control's properties, methods, and events to be exercised.

From Run Mode to Design Mode

Finally the developer closes the form and returns to design mode. The run-time instance of the control is destroyed, and a design-time instance is created:

Event	What gets done
Terminate	The run-time instance never gets a chance to save property settings. Changes to property values while the program was running are discarded.
Initialize	Design-time instances of constituent controls have been created, but the design-time control instance has not been sited on the form.
ReadProperties	The control reads the property values that were saved in the in-memory copy of the .frm file. The control has been sited on the design-time instance of the form, so the Extender and AmbientProperties objects are available.
Resize, Paint	The control instance adjusts the size of its constituent controls, if any, according to its saved property settings. A user-drawn control draws itself.

Closing the Form

If the developer doesn't need to work on the form any more, she may close it. Or it may be quitting time, and she may close the whole project. In either case, the control instance on the form is destroyed.

Event	What gets done
WriteProperties	Before the design-time instance is destroyed, it has a chance to save property values to the in-memory copy of the .frm file.
Terminate	Constituent controls still exist, but the control instance is no longer sited on the form. It's about to be destroyed.

Note In all of the scenarios above, the control instance has been saving its property values to the in-memory copy of the .frm file. If the developer chooses not to save the project before closing it, those property settings will be discarded.

Additional Scenarios

When the developer re-opens the project, and opens the form to work on it again, the control is reincarnated as a design-time instance. It receives Initialize, ReadProperties, Resize, Paint, and WriteProperties events.

> **Note** A *WriteProperties* event? Yes, indeed. When the project is opened, Visual Basic creates an in-memory copy of the .frm file. As each control on the form is created, it gets a ReadProperties event to obtain its saved property values from the .frm file, and a WriteProperties event to write those property values to the in-memory copy of the .frm file.

Compiling the Project

When the project is compiled into an application or component, Visual Basic loads all the form files invisibly, one after another, in order to write the information they contain into the compiled file. A control instance gets the Initialize, ReadProperties, and WriteProperties events. The control's property settings are compiled into the finished executable.

Running the Compiled Program or Component

Whenever a user runs the installed application or component, and the form is loaded, the control receives Initialize, ReadProperties, and Resize events. When the form is unloaded, the control receives a Terminate event.

Controls on World Wide Web Pages

A control on an HTML page is specified using the HTML <OBJECT> and </OBJECT> tags. When the HTML is processed, the control is created and positioned. If the <OBJECT> tag includes any <PARAM NAME> attributes, the property values supplied with those attributes are passed to the control's ReadProperties event using the standard PropertyBag object, as discussed earlier in this topic.

Once the HTML page is active, the control's property values may also be set by scripts attached to events that occur on the page.

> **Note** If there are no <PARAM NAME> attributes other than those that set extender properties, the control may receive an InitProperties event rather than a ReadProperties event. This behavior is dependent on browser implementation, and should not be relied on.

Events You Won't Get in a UserControl object

Some events you're familiar with from working with forms don't exist in a UserControl object. For example, there is no Activate or Deactivate event, because controls are not activated and deactivated the way forms are.

More striking is the absence of the familiar Load, Unload, and QueryUnload events. Load and Unload simply don't fit the UserControl lifestyle; unlike a form, a control instance isn't loaded at some point after it's created — when a UserControl object's Initialize event occurs, constituent controls have already been created.

The UserControl object's Initialize and ReadProperties events provide the functionality of a form's Load event. The main difference between the two is that when the Initialize event occurs, the control has not been sited on its container, so the container's Extender and AmbientProperties objects are not available. The control has been sited when ReadProperties occurs.

> **Note** ReadProperties doesn't occur the first time a control instance is placed on a container — in that case the InitProperties occurs instead.

The UserControl event most like a form's Unload event is Terminate. The constituent controls still exist at this point, although you no longer have access to the container, because your control has been unsited.

The WriteProperties event cannot be used as an analog of Unload, because it occurs only at design time.

UserControl objects don't have QueryUnload events because controls are just parts of a form; it's not up to a control to decide whether or not the form that contains it should close. A control's duty is to destroy itself when it's told to.

Events Peculiar to UserControls

The GotFocus and LostFocus events of the UserControl object notify user-drawn controls when they should show or stop showing a focus rectangle. These events should not be forwarded to the user of your control, because the container is responsible for focus events.

If your UserControl has constituent controls that can receive focus, the EnterFocus event will occur when the first constituent control receives the focus, and the ExitFocus event will occur when focus leaves the last constituent control. See "How to Handle Focus in your Control," later in this chapter.

If you have allowed developers to set access keys for your control, the AccessKeyPress event occurs whenever a user presses an access key. See "Allowing Developers to Set Access Keys for Your Control," later in this chapter. The AccessKeyPress event can also occur if your control is a default button or cancel button. This is discussed in "Allowing Your Control to be a Default or Cancel Button," later in this chapter.

The AmbientChanged event occurs whenever an Ambient property changes on the container your control has been placed on. See "Using the AmbientProperties Object to Stay Consistent with the Container," later in this chapter.

Interacting with the Container

As explained in "Control Creation Terminology," earlier in this chapter, instances of your control never exist by themselves. They are always placed on container objects, such as Visual Basic forms.

Container objects supply additional properties, methods, and events that appear to the user to be part of your control. This is discussed in the related topic, "Understanding the Container's Extender Object." You can use the Parent property of the Extender object to access the properties and methods of the container your control has been placed on.

You can also obtain information about the container through the UserControl object's Ambient property. The object returned by this property offers hints for property settings, such as BackColor, that can make your control's appearance consistent with that of its container. The AmbientProperties object is discussed in "Using the AmbientProperties Object to Stay Consistent with the Container."

> **Note** The AmbientProperties and Extender objects are not available until your control has been sited on the container. Thus they are not available in the UserControl object's Initialize event. When the InitProperties or ReadProperties event occurs, the control instance has been sited.

All Containers Are Not Created Equal

A consequence of your control's dependence on container objects is that some features may not be available in all containers. Many ActiveX control features require support from the container a control is placed on, and will be disabled if the container doesn't provide the required support.

The following features are supported by Visual Basic forms, but may not be supported by all containers:

- Transparent control background, discussed in "Giving Your Control a Transparent Background," later in this chapter.
- The ControlContainer property, discussed in "Allowing Developers to Put Controls on Your Control," later in this chapter.
- Alignable controls, discussed in "Making Your Control Align to the Edges of Forms," later in this chapter.
- Modeless dialog boxes your control may show.

Understanding the Container's Extender Object

When you view an instance of your control in the Properties window, you'll see a number of properties you didn't author. These *extender properties* are provided by the container your control is placed on, but they appear to be a seamless extension of your control, as shown in Figure 9.6.

Figure 9.6 Extender properties, methods, and events are provided by the container

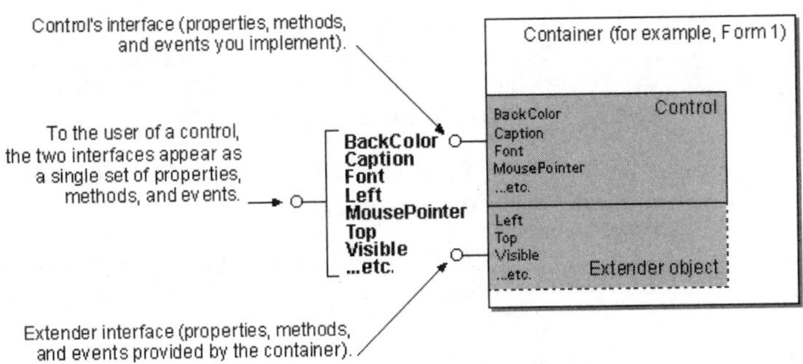

A UserControl object can access extender properties through its Extender object. For example, the ShapeLabel control in Chapter 4,"Creating an ActiveX Control" uses the following code to initialize its Caption property:

```
Private Sub UserControl_InitProperties()
   ' Let the starting value for the Caption
   '   property be the default Name of this
   '   instance of ShapeLabel.
   Caption = Extender.Name
End Sub
```

Extender properties are provided for the developer who uses your control. Generally speaking, the author of a control should not attempt to set them with code in the UserControl. For example, it's up to the developer to decide where a particular instance of your control should be located (Top and Left properties), or what icon it should use when dragged.

Extender Properties Are Late Bound

When you compile your control component, Visual Basic has no way of knowing what kind of container it may be placed on. Therefore references to Extender properties will always be late bound.

Standard Extender Properties

The ActiveX control specification lists the following properties that all containers should provide:

Property	Type	Access	Meaning
Name	String	R	The name the user assigns to the control instance.
Visible	Boolean	RW	Indicates whether the control is visible.

(continued)

(continued)

Property	Type	Access	Meaning
Parent	Object	R	Returns the object which contains the control, such as a Visual Basic form.
Cancel	Boolean	R	True if the control is the cancel button for the container.
Default	Boolean	R	True if the control is the default button for the container.

Although it is highly recommended that containers implement these properties, containers do not have to do so. Thus you should always use error trapping when referring to properties of the Extender object in your code, even standard properties.

Many containers provide additional extender properties, such as Left, Top, Width, and Height properties.

> **Note** If you wish your control to be invisible at run time, set the UserControl object's InvisibleAtRuntime property to True, as discussed in "Making Your Control Invisible at Run Time," later in this chapter. Do not use the Extender object's Visible property for this purpose.

Container-Specific Controls

If you design your control so that it requires certain Extender properties, your control will not work in containers that don't provide those properties. There is nothing wrong with building such *container-specific* controls, except that the potential market for them is smaller.

If you are creating a control designed to address a limitation of a particular container, such considerations may not matter to you. However, conscientious use of error trapping will prevent your control from causing unfortunate accidents if it is placed on containers it was not specifically designed for.

Working with Container Limitations

Visual Basic provides a rich set of extender properties and events, listed in the topic for the Extender object. Many containers provide only a limited subset of these.

In general, Extender properties, methods, and events are not the concern of the control author. Many Extender properties, such as Top and Left, or WhatsThisHelpID, cannot be implemented by a control, because the container must provide the underpinnings these properties require.

Collisions Between Control and Extender Properties

If an instance of your control is placed on a container that has an extender property with the same name as a property of your control, the user will see the extender property.

For example, suppose you gave your control a Tag property. When an instance of your control is placed on a Visual Basic form, a Tag property is supplied by the form's Extender object. If your control is called ShapeLabel, the user might write the following code:

```
ShapeLabel1.Tag = "Triceratops"
```

The code above stores the string "Triceratops" in the Tag property provided by the Visual Basic form's Extender object. If an instance of your control is placed on a container whose Extender object doesn't supply a Tag property, the same code will store the string in the Tag property you implemented.

In order to access the Tag property of your control on a Visual Basic form, the user could employ another Extender object property, as shown in the following code fragment:

```
ShapeLabel1.Object.Tag = "Triceratops"
```

The Object property returns a reference to your control's interface just as you defined it, without any extender properties.

Using the AmbientProperties Object to Stay Consistent with the Container

Containers provide *ambient properties* to give controls hints about how they can best display themselves in the container. For example, the ambient BackColor property tells a control what color to set its own BackColor property to in order to blend in with the container.

Visual Basic makes ambient properties available to your ActiveX control through an AmbientProperties object. The Ambient property of the UserControl object returns a reference to the AmbientProperties object.

The AmbientProperties object provided by Visual Basic contains all of the standard ambient properties defined by the ActiveX Controls Standard, whether or not they are actually provided by the container your control instance was placed on.

This means that you can safely access any of the properties of the AmbientProperties object visible in the Object Browser. If you access an ambient property not provided by the container, the AmbientProperties object returns a default value, as listed in the topics for the AmbientProperties object properties.

Containers That Provide Additional Ambient Properties

Control containers may define their own ambient properties. These container-specific ambient properties are not visible in the Object Browser, because they are not in Visual Basic's type library. You can learn about such properties in the documentation for a container, and access them as if they were properties of the AmbientProperties object.

Because these properties are not in the type library, Visual Basic cannot verify their existence at compile time. Therefore you should always use error handling when working with Ambient properties.

Another consequence of the lack of type library information is that calls to container-specific ambient properties are always late-bound. By contrast, calls to standard ambient properties are early-bound.

Important Ambient Properties

You can ignore many of the standard ambient properties. In a Visual Basic ActiveX control, you can ignore the MessageReflect, ScaleUnits, ShowGrabHandles, ShowHatching, SupportsMnemonics, and UIDead properties of the AmbientProperties object.

Ambient properties you should be aware of are listed below.

UserMode

The most important property of the AmbientProperties object is UserMode, which allows an instance of your control to determine whether it's executing at design time (UserMode = False) or at run time. Use of this property is discussed in "Creating Design-Time-Only or Run-Time-Only Properties," later in this chapter.

> **Tip** To remember the meaning of UserMode, recall that at design time the person working with your control is a *developer,* rather than an end user. Thus the control is not in "user" mode, so UserMode = False.

LocaleID

If you're developing a control for international consumption, you can use the LocaleID ambient property to determine the locale. Use of this property is discussed in "Localizing Your Control," later in this chapter.

DisplayName

Include the value of the DisplayName property in errors your control raises at design-time, so the developer using your control can identify the control instance that is the source of the error.

ForeColor, BackColor, Font, and TextAlign

These properties are hints your control can use to make its appearance match that of the container. For example, in the InitProperties event, which each instance of your UserControl receives when it is first placed on a container, you can set your control's ForeColor, BackColor, Font, and TextAlign to the values provided by the ambient properties. This is a highly recommended practice.

You could also give your control properties which the user could use to keep a control instance in sync with the container. For example, you might provide a MatchFormBackColor property; setting this property to True would cause your control's BackColor property always to match the value of the BackColor property of the AmbientProperties object. You can provide this kind of functionality using the AmbientChanged event, discussed below.

DisplayAsDefault

For user-drawn controls, this property tells you whether your control is the default button for the container, so you can supply the extra-heavy border that identifies the default button for the end user.

If you didn't set your control up to be a default button, you can ignore this property. See "Allowing Your Control to be a Default or Cancel Button," later in this chapter.

For More Information See "User-Drawn Controls," later in this chapter. Also, a full list of the properties of the AmbientProperties object is available in the *Microsoft Visual Basic 6.0 Language Reference* volume of the *Microsoft Visual Basic 6.0 Reference Library*.

The AmbientChanged Event

If your control's appearance or behavior is affected by changes to any of the properties of the AmbientProperties object, you can place code to handle the change in the UserControl_AmbientChanged event procedure.

The argument of the AmbientChanged event procedure is a string containing the name of the property that changed.

> **Important** If you're authoring controls for international use, you should always handle the AmbientChanged event for the LocaleID property. See "Localizing Controls," later in this chapter.

> **Note** If an instance of your control is placed on a Visual Basic form, and the FontTransparent property of the form is changed, the AmbientChanged event will not be raised.

Visual Basic ActiveX Control Features

Visual Basic allows you to author full-featured ActiveX controls. The topics included in this section explain many of the features of the UserControl object that enable ActiveX control capabilities.

You can read about other potential ActiveX control capabilities in "Adding Properties to Controls," "Adding Methods to Controls," and "Raising Events from Controls," later in this chapter.

You can also add property pages to your control, as discussed in Chapter 10, "Creating Property Pages for ActiveX Controls."

Many of the features described in this section are also demonstrated in the CtlPlus.vbg sample application which is listed in the Samples directory.

How to Handle Focus in Your Control

The way you handle focus for your control depends on which model you're using to develop your control. Models for building ActiveX controls are discussed in "Three Ways to Build ActiveX Controls," earlier in this chapter.

> **Important** If you're authoring a control that can be a container for other controls, as described in "Allowing Developers to Put Controls on Your Control," later in this chapter, note that the material in this topic *does not apply* to controls a developer places on an instance of your control. These *contained controls* will receive focus independent of your control and its constituent controls.

User-Drawn Controls

If you're authoring a user-drawn control, there won't be any constituent controls on your UserControl. If you don't want your control to be able to receive the focus, set the CanGetFocus property of the UserControl object to False. CanGetFocus is True by default.

If your user-drawn control can receive the focus, the UserControl object will receive GotFocus and LostFocus events when your control receives and loses the focus. A user-drawn control is responsible for drawing its own focus rectangle when it has the focus, as described in "User-Drawn Controls," later in this chapter.

This is the only function your UserControl's GotFocus and LostFocus events need to fulfill for a user-drawn control. You don't need to raise GotFocus or LostFocus events for the user of your control, because the container's extender provides these events if the CanGetFocus property is True.

> **Note** The UserControl object of a user-drawn control will also receive a EnterFocus event prior to GotFocus, and an ExitFocus event after LostFocus. You don't need to put any code in the event procedures of these event, and in fact it is recommended that you not do so.

User-drawn controls can respond to access keys, as described later in this topic.

Controls That Use Constituent Controls

If you're authoring a control that enhances a single constituent control, or is an assembly of constituent controls, your UserControl object will be unable to receive the focus, regardless of the setting of the CanGetFocus property, unless *none* of its constituent controls can receive the focus.

If no constituent controls can receive the focus, and CanGetFocus is True, then your UserControl object will receive the same events a user-drawn control receives. The only thing you need to do with these events is provide a visual indication that your control has the focus.

How Constituent Controls Are Affected by CanGetFocus

If your control contains at least one constituent control that can receive the focus, the CanGetFocus property of the UserControl object must be set to True. If you attempt to set CanGetFocus to False on a UserControl that has constituent controls that can receive focus, an error will occur.

Visual Basic will not allow a constituent control that can receive focus to be placed on a UserControl whose CanGetFocus property is False: Icons of controls that can receive focus are disabled in the Toolbox when the UserControl's design window is active.

EnterFocus and ExitFocus

When the focus moves from outside your control to any of your control's constituent controls, the UserControl object will receive an EnterFocus event. The GotFocus event for the constituent control that receives the focus will be raised *after* the UserControl_EnterFocus event procedure.

As long as the focus remains within your control, the UserControl object's focus-related events will not be raised. As the focus moves from one constituent control to another, however, the appropriate GotFocus and LostFocus events of the constituent controls will be raised.

When the focus moves back outside your control, the last constituent control that had the focus will receive its LostFocus event. When the event procedure returns, the UserControl object will receive its ExitFocus event.

You can use the EnterFocus event to change which constituent control receives the focus. You may wish to do this in order to restore the focus to the constituent control that last had it, rather than simply allowing the first constituent control in your UserControl's tab order to receive the focus, which is the default behavior.

> **Tip** If your control is complex — as for example an Address control with multiple constituent controls — you may be tempted to validate the data in the ExitFocus event. Don't. The user of your control can put code in the Validate event of the user control to handle data validation as they see fit. If it's absolutely necessary to validate data inside the control, use the Validate events in combination with the CausesValidation

properties of the constituent controls. Be aware that you can't always count on the Validate event for constituent controls, as is discussed in "Handling the Validate Event" below.

Generally speaking, it's not a good idea to use MsgBox when you're debugging focus-related events, because the message box immediately grabs the focus. It's a *very* bad idea to use MsgBox in EnterFocus and ExitFocus events. Use Debug.Print instead.

Receiving Focus via Access Keys

Avoid hard coding access keys for your control's constituent controls, because access keys permanently assigned to your control in this fashion will limit a user's freedom to choose access keys for her form. In addition, two instances of your control on the same form will have access key conflicts.

"Allowing Developers to Set Access Keys for Your Control," later in this chapter, discusses how you can give the user of your control the ability to set access keys on instances of your control.

Forwarding Focus to the Next Control in the Tab Order

If your control cannot receive the focus itself, and has no constituent controls that can receive the focus, you can give your control the same behavior displayed by Label controls. That is, when the access key for your control is pressed, the focus is forwarded to the next control in the tab order.

To enable this behavior, set the ForwardFocus property of the UserControl object to True.

Handling the Validate Event

The Validate event and CausesValidation property for a user control behave exactly like they do for any other control, but the behavior of Validate and CausesValidation for constituent controls may not yield the expected results. Let's review the standard behavior. When a control loses focus, its Validation event is fired before its LostFocus event — but only if the control about to receive the focus has its CausesValidation property set to True. This allows you to handle data validation before the control loses focus.

A user control exposes a Validate event and, via the Extender object, exposes a CausesValidation property. Code in the Validate event is executed when the focus is shifted from the user control to any control that had its CausesValidation property set to True; setting the CausesValidation property of the user control to True will enable the Validation event for any control passing focus to the user control.

The Validate event and CausesValidation property for constituent controls work as expected as long as the focus remains inside the user control. When the focus is shifted outside of the user control, the Validate event for the constituent control isn't fired. For that reason, it's best to avoid trying to handle validation within a user control.

Controls You Can Use As Constituent Controls

You can place any of the controls supplied with Visual Basic on a UserControl, with the exception of the OLE container control.

Any ActiveX control you've purchased, or any control written to the older OLE specification, can be placed on a UserControl.

As long as you're authoring a control for your own use, that's all you need to know. However, if you're going to distribute your control to others, even if you're giving it away, you need to consider distribution and licensing issues.

> **Note** Toolbox objects other than controls, such as insertable objects — for example, Microsoft Excel Charts — cannot be placed on UserControl objects.

The Easy Part — UserControl and Intrinsics

The UserControl object and the Visual Basic intrinsic controls are created by the Visual Basic run-time DLL. Anyone who installs your .ocx file will automatically get a copy of the run-time DLL and support files, so if you author your controls using just the UserControl and intrinsic controls, you have no further licensing or distribution issues to worry about.

The intrinsic controls include: PictureBox, Label, TextBox, Frame, CommandButton, CheckBox, OptionButton, ComboBox, ListBox, HScrollBar, VScrollBar, Timer, DriveListBox, DirListBox, FileListBox, Shape, Line, Image, and Data.

ActiveX controls included with the Professional Edition of Visual Basic are subject to licensing rules, as explained below.

> **Note** The Microsoft User Forms in Microsoft Office applications include a set of controls similar to the intrinsic controls. These controls may be used on a UserControl; however, you must distribute the support DLL for Microsoft User Forms in your Setup program.

Distributing Constituent Controls

An instance of your control is composed of a UserControl object and its constituent controls, as explained in "The UserControl Object," earlier in this chapter. In order to add an instance of your control to a form, a developer must be able to create these objects.

SetupWizard makes this task easy. When you create a Setup program for your .ocx file, SetupWizard includes all the .ocx files for the constituent controls, along with the Visual Basic run-time DLL and any necessary support files.

When a developer runs your Setup program, the .ocx files that provide the constituent controls are installed on his computer. The only other thing he needs to worry about is whether he has the legal right to use them.

If none of the constituent controls require a license, the developer is set. However, if you used controls you purchased, or any of the ActiveX controls included with Visual Basic, Professional Edition, there are licensing requirements to be met.

Licensing Constituent Controls

When you purchase a control, you generally acquire the right to distribute instances of that control royalty-free as part any application you create. However, such license agreements do *not* give you the right to sell or give away the control to other developers — which is what you're doing when you use it as a constituent control.

So the rule is: In order to use your control, a developer must have licenses for all the licensed controls you've used as constituent controls.

Most ActiveX Controls Included with Visual Basic Are Exempted

The licensing rule stated above applies to the DBGrid control. Any of the other ActiveX controls included with the Professional Edition of Visual Basic can be used as constituent controls of a control you intend to distribute to other developers.

For example, if you use the TreeView control as a constituent control, anyone who is licensed to use your control is licensed to use TreeView *as part of your control.* (If you didn't include licensing support when you made your .ocx, this means that anyone can use your control. See "Licensing Issues for Controls," later in this chapter.)

> **Important** Your license agreement for Visual Basic states that in order to distribute any redistributables included with Visual Basic, the software you author must add significant and primary functionality. This means that a control that uses TreeView as a constituent control must do significantly more than TreeView does by itself. Consult your Microsoft License Agreement for details.

For more information about how to use ActiveX controls included with the Professional and Enterprise Editions, see Part 1, "Using ActiveX Controls."

Distribution and Licensing Examples

Applying the rule yields the following examples.

ActiveX Controls Included with Visual Basic

Suppose you author some controls using some of the ActiveX controls included with Visual Basic, Professional Edition. SetupWizard adds the necessary .ocx files to your Setup program.

As long as you didn't use the DBGrid control, anyone who runs SetupWizard can use your controls. That's not always the case if you used DBGrid as a constituent control, as these scenarios show:

- A developer who has a copy of Visual Basic, Professional Edition buys your .ocx and installs it. She already has the supporting .ocx files for DBGrid, and the license for it, so she has everything she needs.
- A student who has a copy of Visual Basic, Learning Edition buys your control and installs it. He now has the supporting .ocx file for DBGrid, but doesn't have the license to use it.
- A stock market analyst who has a copy of Microsoft Excel buys your control and installs it. She now has the supporting .ocx files for DBGrid, but doesn't have the license to use it.

ActiveX Controls You've Purchased

Suppose you purchase MegaDino.ocx from Late Cretaceous Computing, and use the Tyrannosaur and Velociraptor controls from this .ocx to develop your own UltimatePredator control. You package this control in UPred.ocx, and you give it away.

Anyone to whom you give a copy of UPred.ocx must have purchased and installed MegaDino.ocx in order to use the UltimatePredator control legally. This is true regardless of the development software they're using.

In fact, if the creators of MegaDino.ocx and DinoRama.ocx used the standard registry key licensing scheme, people to whom you give UPred.ocx will be *unable* to use the UltimatePredator control unless they have MegaDino.ocx installed.

Shareware Controls

Suppose you author your control using a shareware control.

If you sell your control component (.ocx file), the purchaser must also pay the author of the shareware control the appropriate license fee.

If you distribute your control component as shareware, a person who wants to use it must pay the appropriate license fees to you and to the author of the shareware control you used.

Constituent Controls and the Internet

If you want people to be able to use your control on World Wide Web pages, remember that the rule for Web servers is exactly the same as the rule for developers. That is, in order to use your control, a Web server must have licenses for all the licensed controls you've used as constituent controls.

For More Information Licensing issues, including how to add licensing support for the controls you author, how licensing support works, and the mechanism for using licensed controls with the World Wide Web are discussed in "Licensing Issues for Controls," later in this chapter.

Object Models for Controls

Complex controls such as TreeView and Toolbar provide run-time access to their functionality through objects. For example, the TreeView control has a Nodes collection containing Node objects that represent the items in the hierarchy the TreeView control displays. Users can create new nodes using the Add method of the Nodes collection.

Objects like Node and Nodes are called *dependent objects.* Dependent objects exist only as a part of some other object, as Node objects are always part of a TreeView control. They cannot be created independently.

You can provide dependent objects like Node and Nodes by including class modules in your ActiveX control project and organizing them into an object model. Object models can be as simple as the Nodes collection with its Node objects, or arbitrarily complex.

> **Important** Control components can only provide dependent objects. They cannot provide objects that can be independently created, using the New operator or the CreateObject function.

For More Information Dependent objects are discussed in "Instancing for Classes Provided by ActiveX Components," in Chapter 6, "General Principles of Component Design." Also, you can read about object models in "Organizing Objects: The Object Model," which is also in Chapter 6, "General Principles of Component Design."

Some design considerations for collections in controls are discussed in "Creating Robust Controls," later in this chapter. More information on robust techniques for using objects can be found in "Private Communications Between Your Objects," in Chapter 6, "General Principles of Component Design."

Classes, class modules, and objects are discussed in Chapter 9, "Programming with Objects," in the *Microsoft Visual Basic 6.0 Programmer's Guide.*

Allowing Developers to Put Controls on Your Control

Some controls can act as containers for other controls. For example, if you place controls on a Visual Basic PictureBox control, all of the controls move when you move the PictureBox. Visual Basic users take advantage of this capability to group controls, produce scrollable pictures, and so on.

You can allow developers to place controls on your ActiveX control by setting the ControlContainer property of the UserControl object to True.

> **Note** Lightweight user controls cannot act as control containers. If the Windowless property of a UserControl object is set to True, the ControlContainer property will be ignored. Lightweight user controls are discussed in detail in "Creating Lightweight Controls" later in this chapter.

Controls a developer places on an instance of your ActiveX control can be accessed using the ContainedControls collection of the UserControl object. You can use this collection at either design time or run time.

The ContainedControls Collection vs. the Controls Collection

The ContainedControls collection is different from the Controls collection, which contains only the constituent controls you have used in designing your ActiveX control. This is illustrated in Figure 9.7, which supposes that the ShapeLabel control's ControlContainer property is True.

Figure 9.7 The Controls and ContainedControls collections

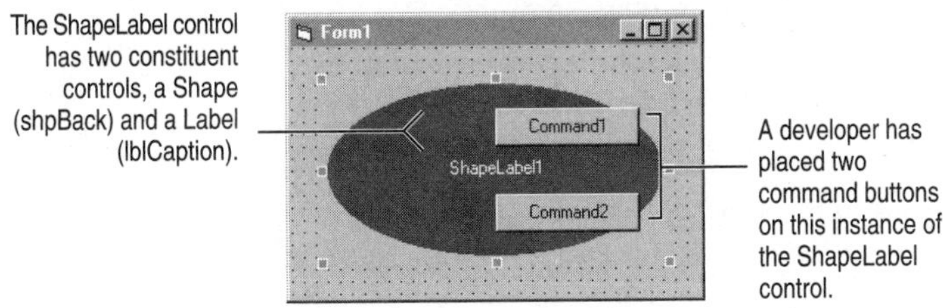
The ShapeLabel control has two constituent controls, a Shape (shpBack) and a Label (lblCaption).
Form1
Command1
ShapeLabel1
Command2
A developer has placed two command buttons on this instance of the ShapeLabel control.

If the control includes the code below, it will always display two names, shpBack and lblCaption.

```
Dim c As Object
For Each c In UserControl.Controls
   MsgBox c.Name
Next
```

If the control includes the code below, it will display Command1 and Command2 — for this instance only.

```
Dim c As Object
For Each c In _
         UserControl.ContainedControls
   MsgBox c.Name
Next
```

Availability of the ContainedControls Collection

You cannot access the ContainedControls collection in the Initialize event of your UserControl object. Support for the ControlContainer feature is provided by the object your control is placed on, so your control must be sited on the container object before ContainedControls is available. When the UserControl object receives its ReadProperties event, siting has occurred.

Once your control is sited, and support for the ControlContainer feature is present, the ContainedControls collection may not immediately contain references to the controls a developer has placed on your control. For example, if your control is on a Visual Basic form, the Count property of the ContainedControls collection will be zero until after the UserControl_ReadProperties event procedure has executed.

Performance Impact of ControlContainer

There is extra overhead required to allow a developer to place controls on instances of your ActiveX control. Clipping must be done for the contained controls, which must appear on top of all the constituent controls in your UserControl, and of course the ContainedControls collection must be maintained.

In other words, controls that serve as containers for other controls are heavyweight controls.

For best performance of your controls, you should set ContainedControls to True only if it makes sense for a particular control. For example, it doesn't make much sense for a control assembly like an Address Control to be a container for other controls.

Support for ControlContainer

ControlContainer support will not work for every container your control may be placed on. Visual Basic forms support the *ISimpleFrame* interface that enables the ControlContainer feature, so your control can always support this capability on a Visual Basic form.

If an instance of your control is placed on a container that is not aware of ISimpleFrame, ControlContainer support will be disabled. Your control will continue to work correctly in all other ways, but developers will be unable to place other controls on an instance of your control.

In order for the ContainedControls collection to be available, an ISimpleFrame-aware container must implement the IVBGetControls interface. Calls to the collection will cause errors if the container does not implement this interface, so it's a good idea to use error handling when you access the collection.

> **Note** Controls a developer places on a container with a transparent background are not visible. If you want your control to be used as a control container by developers, don't give it a transparent background.

Allowing Your Control to be Enabled and Disabled

The Enabled property is an odd beast. It's an extender property, but the Extender object doesn't provide it unless your control has an Enabled property of its own, with the correct procedure ID. If the extender's Enabled property isn't present, your control will not display the same enabled/disabled behavior as other controls.

Your property should delegate to the Enabled property of the UserControl object, as shown in the following code sample:

```
Public Property Get Enabled() As Boolean
   Enabled = UserControl.Enabled
End Property
```

```
Public Property Let Enabled(ByVal NewValue As Boolean)
   UserControl.Enabled = NewValue
   PropertyChanged "Enabled"
End Property
```

Add this code to the code window of the UserControl your ActiveX control is based on, as discussed in "Adding Properties to Controls," later in this chapter.

> **Note** You can easily add the Enabled property by using the ActiveX Control Interface Wizard to create the interface for your control. The wizard includes the Enabled property in its list of recommended properties.

Notice that the Enabled property of the UserControl object is qualified by the object's class name (UserControl). The class name can be used to distinguish properties and methods of the UserControl object from members of your ActiveX control which have the same names.

The Enabled property of the UserControl object acts much like the Enabled property of a form, enabling and disabling the UserControl and all of its constituent controls.

> **Note** The purpose and importance of PropertyChanged are discussed in "Adding Properties to Controls," later in this chapter.

Assigning the Procedure ID for the Enabled Property

In order for your Enabled property to work correctly, you need to assign it the Enabled procedure ID. Procedure IDs are discussed in "Properties You Should Provide," later in this chapter.

To assign the procedure ID for the Enabled property

1. On the **Tools** menu, click **Procedure Attributes** to open the **Procedure Attributes** dialog box.
2. In the **Name** box, select your **Enabled** procedure.
3. Click **Advanced** to expand the **Procedure Attributes** dialog box.
4. In the **Procedure ID** box, select **Enabled** to give the property the correct identifier.

When you give your Enabled property the correct procedure ID, the container's Extender object shadows it with its own Enabled property; when the user sets the extender property, the container sets your Enabled property.

The reason for this odd arrangement is to ensure consistent Windows behavior. When a form is disabled, it's supposed to disable all of its controls, but the controls are supposed to continue to paint themselves as if they were enabled.

A Visual Basic form conforms to this behavior by tricking its controls. It sets the Extender object's Enabled property to False for all of its controls, *without* calling the Enabled properties of the controls. The controls think they're enabled, and paint themselves so, but in code they appear to be disabled.

If your control has an Enabled property without the Enabled procedure ID, it will remain enabled in code while all the controls around it are disabled. You can see this by putting a command button and a control of your own on a form, and adding the following code:

```
Private Sub Command1_Click()
   Form1.Enabled = False
   Debug.Print Command1.Enabled
   Debug.Print MyControl1.Enabled
End Sub
```

Run the program before and after assigning the Enabled procedure ID to your control's Enabled property. In the first case, you'll see that the command button's Enabled property returns False, while your control's Enabled property returns True. After the procedure ID is assigned, both controls will return False.

Correct Behavior for the Enabled Property

You should avoid setting the UserControl's Enabled property, except in your control's Enabled property. The reason for this is that the container is responsible for enabling and disabling the controls it contains. It's rude for a control to tamper with properties the user is supposedly in control of.

Painting a User-Drawn Control's Disabled State

When you author a user-drawn control, you have to provide your own representation of your control's disabled state. If you have implemented an Enabled property as shown above, you can determine when you need to do this by testing the value of `UserControl.Enabled` in the UserControl_Paint event procedure.

For More Information See "User-Drawn Controls," later in this chapter.

Adding a Font Object to Your User Control

Although a UserControl object has a Font property, there are situations where you will need to implement a Font object of your own. For example, if you want to allow the end user of your control to select a font at run time, the standard Font property won't work.

Even though the Font property is exposed and can be set in the Properties window at design time or via code at run time, the font displayed on the user control doesn't change. This is because the control never receives notification that the property has changed; consequently, it never fires its Paint event.

To resolve this problem, you need to add your own StdFont object to the control. The StdFont object is exactly the same as the UserControl Font with one exception — it provides a FontChanged event. You need to declare it using the WithEvents keyword in order to expose the FontChanged event:

```
Private WithEvents mFont as StdFont
```

In the Initialize event of your user control, the following code creates an instance of the StdFont object and assigns it to the User Control's Font property:

```
Private Sub UserControl_Initialize()
   Set mFont = New StdFont
   Set UserControl.Font = mFont
End Sub
```

To expose your Font to the outside world, you'll need a Property Let / Property Set pair:

```
Public Property Get Font() as StdFont
   Set Font = mFont
End Property

Public Property Set Font (mnewFont as stdFont)
   With mFont
      .Bold = mnewFont.Bold
      .Italic = mnewFont.Italic
      .Name = mnewFont.Name
      .Size = mnewFont.Size
   End With
   PropertyChanged "Font"
End Property
```

Notice that this code uses With to set each property of the StdFont object individually: Simply assigning `mnewFont` to `mFont` would only change the default Name property.

You'll also need to add code in the FontChanged event to reassign the StdFont object and to force a Paint event:

```
Private Sub mFont_FontChanged(ByVal PropertyName As String)
   Set UserControl.Font = mFont
   Refresh
End Sub
```

Finally, in the Paint event you can add code to display text. The text will be displayed in the newly selected font.

```
Private Sub UserControl_Paint()
   Cls   ' Clear the display
   Print "Hello"
End Sub
```

Now the Font property of your user control can be set at either design time or at run time and the changes will immediately be visible.

Giving Your Control a Transparent Background

Setting the BackStyle property of the UserControl object to Transparent allows whatever is behind your control to be seen, in between the constituent controls on your UserControl's surface. When the BackStyle property is set to Transparent, the BackColor and Picture properties of the UserControl are ignored.

Bitmaps with Transparent Backgrounds

If you assign a bitmap to the UserControl's MaskPicture property, and set the MaskColor property of the UserControl equal to the background color of the bitmap, Visual Basic will clip around the parts of the bitmap that are not equal to the MaskColor — even if those parts are not contiguous.

You can draw on the visible surface of the Bitmap using the graphics methods of the UserControl object, such as Line, Circle, and PaintPicture. Visual Basic will clip your drawing to the visible parts of the bitmap.

> **Note** This feature is supported for image-type bitmaps, such as BMP, GIF, JPEG, and DIB. It is not supported for Windows metafiles, icons, or cursors.

Labels with Transparent BackStyle

If one of the constituent controls on the UserControl is a Label whose BackStyle property has also been set to Transparent, and whose Font property specifies a TrueType font, Visual Basic will clip around the font. In addition, mouse clicks that fall in the spaces between letters will be passed through to the container.

Performance Considerations

Setting BackStyle to Transparent may affect the performance of your control. Visual Basic must do a great deal of clipping to make the background show through correctly if your control uses:

- A large number of constituent controls.
- A complex bitmap.
- A Label control with a transparent background, a TrueType font, and a large amount of text.

To improve the performance of your control, you may be able to create a lightweight user control. The rules for creating controls that are both lightweight and transparent differ somewhat from regular controls. Lightweight user controls are discussed in depth in the next section, "Creating Lightweight Controls."

> **Note** Controls a developer places on a container with a transparent background are not visible. If you want your control to be used as a control container by developers, don't give it a transparent background.

Creating Lightweight Controls

Lightweight controls, sometimes referred to as windowless controls, differ from regular controls in one significant way: They don't have a window handle (hWnd property). Because of this they use fewer system resources, making them ideal for Internet applications, distributed applications, or any application where system resources may be a limiting factor. Examples of lightweight controls include the Label control and the Image control.

When designing a user control, you should consider creating a lightweight control unless your requirements meet one or more of the following criteria:

- Your control will contain constituent controls for which lightweight versions aren't available. A lightweight control can only contain other lightweight controls.
- Your control will act as a design-time container for other controls. Because you can't predict what kind of controls a developer may place on your control, it can't be a lightweight control.
- Your control needs to make calls to the Windows API that require a window handle (hWnd) as an argument. A lightweight control doesn't have an hWnd property; it returns the hWnd of its container, which may not produce the desired results.
- Your control needs to implement the BorderStyle property or the EditAtDesignTime property. These properties are disabled when the Windowless property is set to True.

You create a lightweight user control by setting the Windowless property to True at design time. Lightweight user controls can only contain other lightweight controls: If you attempt to place a windowed control on a lightweight user control, you will get a design-time error. The same is true if you attempt to set the Windowless property to True on a user control that already contains windowed controls.

Not all containers support lightweight controls. When your lightweight user control runs in a host that doesn't support it, it will automatically run in windowed mode. The system will assign it an hWnd on the fly. Hosts that are known to support lightweight controls include Visual Basic 4.0 or later, Internet Explorer 4.0 or later, and Visual Basic for Applications.

Creating Lightweight Controls with Transparent Backgrounds

Lightweight controls expose several new properties and a new event that are useful in creating controls with transparent backgrounds. With a windowed control, the MaskPicture and MaskColor properties are used to determine if a mouse click occurs within a valid area of the control's window; if not, the event is routed to the form. Because a lightweight control doesn't have a window, it's up to the control to determine what should receive the click event. The HitTest event provides notification when the cursor is over your control; you control the behavior of the HitTest event by setting a combination of several properties.

Control Regions

To understand how a lightweight control manages hit testing, you must first be familiar with the possible regions of a user control. A control has four possible regions:

- Mask region — the painted (nontransparent) area on the control, including the union of all contained controls or any areas on a user-drawn control that have been drawn upon.
- Outside region — the area outside of the mask area.
- Transparent region — the area inside a mask region that isn't painted — for example, the area inside a circle. This area is determined by the developer of the control.
- Close region — the area around the edges of the mask region. The width of the close region is determined by the control developer.

Figure 9.8

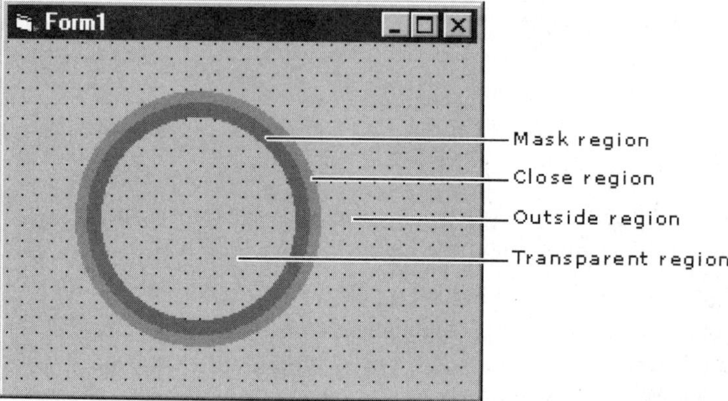

The actual composition of the mask region is dependent upon the setting of the BackStyle property:

- If the BackStyle is Transparent, the MaskPicture and MaskColor properties plus any constituent controls make up the mask region. The transparent region consists of any areas that match the MaskColor.
- If the BackStyle is Opaque, the entire surface of the control is the mask region; there is no transparent region.

Visual Basic doesn't know about the Transparent and Close regions: You have to define these regions yourself and test for them in the HitTest event.

The HitTest Event

The HitTest event is fired whenever the cursor is over a lightweight user control when the BackStyle is set to Transparent. You can add code to the HitTest event to determine whether mouse messages will be received by your control or passed on to the next object beneath it in the ZOrder. The HitTest event fires before any other mouse messages.

Because it's possible to layer several controls at design time, portions of other controls may be visible beneath the transparent areas of your control. In some cases, you might want to test for the existence of another control under your control. If one exists, you might allow it to receive the mouse events; if not, you might want to handle the mouse events yourself. The HitTest event gives you a second (and third) chance to handle the events if there is nothing underneath or if the controls underneath decline the events.

The HitTest event takes three arguments: the *x* and *y* coordinates specifying the location of the cursor, and a *HitResult* argument that corresponds to a control region. There are four possible settings for HitResult:

- 3 (constant vbHitResultHit) — the cursor is over the mask region of the control; the control receives all mouse messages.
- 2 (constant vbHitResultClose) — the cursor is over the close region of the control; mouse messages are ignored until the second pass.
- 1 (constant vbHitResultTransparent) — the cursor is over the transparent region of the control; mouse messages are ignored until the third pass.
- 0 (constant vbHitResultOutside) — the cursor is over the outside region the control; mouse messages are always ignored.

Hit testing is performed in the following order for layered controls:

- A first pass is made through the ZOrder; the topmost control returning a HitResult of 3 (Hit) receives mouse messages.
- If no control returns a HitResult of 3, a second pass is made; the topmost control returning a HitResult of 2 (Close) receives the mouse messages.
- If no control returns a HitResult of 2, a third pass is made; the topmost control returning a HitResult of 1 (Transparent) receives the mouse messages.
- If no control returns a HitResult of 1, the underlying container receives the mouse messages.

There's just one problem with this — the HitTest event will never return a HitResult of 1 or 2 because Visual Basic doesn't know about the close or transparent regions. You need to define these regions yourself in code; then if the X and Y coordinates fall within your defined region, you change the HitResult accordingly. The following code shows a HitTest event for a control with a square "hole" in its center:

```
Private Sub MyControl_HitTest(X As Single, _
   Y As Single, HitResult As Integer)

   ' Determine if the X,Y coordinates fall
   ' within the Close region.
   If (X > 200 And X < 210) Or (X > 390 And X < 400) Then
      If (Y > 200 And Y < 210) Or (Y > 390 And Y < 400) Then
         ' Coordinates are within the Close region.
         HitResult = vbHitResultClose
         ' We got a hit, so we can exit.
         Exit Sub
      End If
   End If

   ' Now check for the Transparent region.
   If (X > 210 And X < 390) Then
      If (Y > 210 And Y < 390) Then
         ' Coordinates are within the Transparent region.
         HitResult = vbHitResultTransparent
      End If
   End If
End Sub
```

In the above example, we first test to see if the coordinates fall within our Close region, in this case within 10 twips of the edge of our square hole. If so, we change the HitResult to 2 (vbHitResultClose) and exit. If not, we test to see if the coordinates are within the Transparent region, and if so we change the HitResult to 1 (vbHitResultTransparent). If neither test returns a hit, we go with the HitResult that was passed in.

Of course, in the case of a square region, it's fairly easy to determine the regions in code. As you might imagine, this procedure would be much more complex for a circular region, an irregularly shaped region, or for multiple regions within a control.

There's one more aspect to consider: With complex code being executed in the HitTest event, and with the HitTest event firing repeatedly as the cursor moves over your control, you might suspect that performance might be less than optimal. Your suspicion would be correct.

Performance Considerations for Hit Testing

Hit testing can be a pretty expensive operation in terms of performance. This isn't surprising when you consider what's going on behind the scenes. First of all, Visual Basic must perform calculations to clip your control to the mask defined by MaskPicture and MaskColor. Next, if your control contains other controls or user-drawn graphics, it must also clip around them. Finally, if you've defined Close and Transparent regions in your control, it needs to execute the code to check for those regions. With the HitTest event being fired repeatedly, this process could cause your control to perform very slowly.

Fortunately user controls have two additional properties, ClipBehavior and HitBehavior, that can be set in combination to improve performance. The following table shows the results of different pairs of settings:

	0 ClipBehavior None	**1 ClipBehavior Use Region**
0 HitBehavior None	Hit test always returns 0 – no clipping.	Hit test always returns 0 – clipped to mask region.
1 HitBehavior Use Region	Hit test returns 0 or 3 – no clipping.	(Default) Hit test returns 0 or 3 – clipped to mask region.
2 HitBehavior Use Paint	Hit test returns 0 or 3 – clipped to paint.	Hit test returns 0 or 3 – clipped to paint inside mask region.

When HitBehavior is set to 0 (vbHitBehaviorNone), the HitTest event will always return a HitResult of 0 (Outside). You can add code to determine where the hit occurred and change the HitResult accordingly. This may improve performance if there isn't a lot of code in the HitTest event procedure.

Setting ClipBehavior to 0 (vbClipBehaviorNone) can often improve performance because Visual Basic doesn't need to determine the boundaries between the Mask and Outside regions. This is especially true if the Mask region is complex — for instance, when it includes TrueType fonts or irregular shapes.

If your control will use hot spots (in other words, only portions of the visible area will accept clicks), setting ClipBehavior to 0 and HitBehavior to 1 (vbUseRegion) can improve performance.

Setting HitBehavior to 2 (vbUsePaint) may be necessary for user-drawn controls where the visible portion of the control isn't the same as the Mask region. This is the most expensive operation because the control needs to repaint each time the HitTest event is executed.

> **Important** When a lightweight user control is sited on a container that doesn't support the Windowless property, some HitBehavior and ClipBehavior settings may cause unpredictable results. If your control will be used in containers that don't support lightweight controls, you should use the default settings.

Allowing Developers to Set Access Keys for Your Control

Placing ampersand characters (&) in the captions of Label controls and CommandButton controls creates access keys with which the end user of an application can shift focus to the control. You can create a similar effect in your ActiveX controls.

For example, suppose you have created a user-drawn button. In the Property Let for your button's Caption property, you can examine the text of the caption the user has entered. If there's an ampersand in front of a letter, you can assign that letter to the AccessKeys property of the UserControl object.

When the end user presses one of the access keys enabled in this fashion, your UserControl object receives an AccessKeyPress event. The argument of this event contains the access key that was pressed, allowing you to support multiple access keys on a control.

Access Keys for Control Assemblies

Control assemblies may contain constituent controls that can get the focus, and that support access keys of their own. You can use this fact to provide access key functionality.

Suppose you've authored a general-purpose control that consists of a text box and a label; you want the user to be able to set an access key in the label's caption, and forward the focus to the text box. You can accomplish this by giving the label and text box TabIndex values of zero and one (the TabIndex values on the UserControl are not visible outside your control), and delegating the Caption property of your control to the label, thus:

```
Property Get Caption() As String
   Caption = Label1.Caption
End Property

Property Let Caption(NewCaption As String)
   Label1.Caption = NewCaption
   PropertyChanged "Caption"
End Property
```

When a developer assigns the text "&Marsupial" to your Caption property, the label control will do all the access key work for you.

> **Note** When the end user presses an access key on one of your constituent controls, the UserControl does *not* receive an AccessKeyPress event.

Control Assemblies with Fixed Text

For fixed-purpose control assemblies, such as an Address control, you can put ampersand characters (&) in the captions of constituent controls. Unfortunately, these hard-coded access keys may conflict with other access key choices the user wishes to make on a form.

In a more sophisticated variation of this scheme, you might add an AccessKeyXxxx property to your control for the appropriate constituent controls. That is, if the caption of the label next to the txtLastname control was "Last Name," you would add an AccessKeyLastName property. The developer using your control could assign any character from the label's caption to this property, and in the Property Let code you could change the caption to contain the ampersand.

Making Your Control Align to the Edges of Forms

When creating controls like toolbars and status bars, it's useful to be able to make the control align to one of the borders of the form it's placed on. You can give your ActiveX control this capability by setting the Alignable property of the UserControl object to True.

If the container your control is placed on supports aligned controls, it will add an Align property to the Extender object. When the user chooses an alignment, your control will automatically be aligned appropriately.

In the Resize event of your UserControl, you will have to redraw your user-drawn control or rearrange the constituent controls of your control assembly. You can use the Align property of the Extender object to determine which container edge the control instance has been aligned to.

> **Note** Not all containers support alignable controls. If you attempt to test the value of the Align property, make sure you use error trapping.

Making Your Control Invisible at Run Time

To author a control that's invisible at run time, like the Timer control, set the InvisibleAtRuntime property of the UserControl object to True.

> **Important** Don't use the Visible property of the Extender object to make your control invisible at run time. If you do, your control will still have all the overhead of a visible control at run time. Furthermore, the extender properties are available to the user, who may make your control visible.

Invisible Controls vs. Ordinary Objects

Before you create a control that's invisible at run time, consider creating an ordinary object provided by an in-process code component (ActiveX DLL) instead.

Objects provided by in-process code components require fewer resources than controls, even invisible controls. The only reason to implement an invisible control is to take advantage of a feature that's only available to ActiveX controls.

Setting a Fixed Size for Your Control

Controls that are invisible at run time typically maintain a fixed size. You can duplicate this behavior using the Size method of the UserControl object, as shown here:

```
Private Sub UserControl_Resize()
   Size 420, 420
End Sub
```

The Width and Height properties of a UserControl object are always given in Twips, regardless of ScaleMode.

Adding an AboutBox to Your Control

ActiveX controls typically have an About "property" at the top of the Properties window, with an ellipsis button. Clicking the button shows an About box identifying the control and the software vendor that created it.

Visual Basic makes it easy to provide such About boxes. You can have separate About boxes for each control in your control component (.ocx file), or one About box that all the controls in the component share.

To add an About box to a control component

1. Create an About box by adding a form to your ActiveX control project, and giving it appropriate text and controls. Name the form dlgAbout.
2. In the code window for any control in the project, add the following Sub procedure:

```
Public Sub ShowAboutBox()
   dlgAbout.Show vbModal
   Unload dlgAbout
   Set dlgAbout = Nothing
End Sub
```

   Important Unloading the About box and setting it to Nothing frees the memory it was using. This is a courtesy to the user of your controls.

3. On the **Tools** menu, click **Procedure Attributes** to open the **Procedure Attributes** dialog box. If the ShowAboutBox procedure is not selected in the **Name** box, click the drop down and select it.
4. Click **Advanced** to expand the **Procedure Attributes** dialog box.
5. In the **Procedure ID** box, select **AboutBox** to give the ShowAboutBox procedure the correct identifier.
6. Repeat steps 2 through 5 for each control in the project.

   Note The name of the About box form and the method that shows it can be anything you like. The procedure above used `dlgAbout` and `ShowAboutBox` for purposes of illustration only.

If you wish to have separate About boxes for each control, simply create additional forms, and show a different form in each control's ShowAboutBox method.

Of course, each form you add to the project increases its size. You can get the same effect with the single dlgAbout form by giving it a property named, let us say, ControlID. This property identifies which control dlgAbout is being shown for. In each control's ShowAboutBox method, set the ControlID property before showing dlgAbout. Place code in the Load event of dlgAbout to change the text and bitmaps on the About box appropriately.

For More Information Adding properties and methods to forms is discussed in Chapter 9, "Programming with Objects," in the *Microsoft Visual Basic 6.0 Programmer's Guide.*

Providing a Toolbox Bitmap for Your Control

The Toolbox bitmap size is 16 pixels wide by 15 pixels high, as specified by the ActiveX control specification. You can create a bitmap this size, and assign it to the ToolboxBitmap property of your UserControl object.

> **Important** Do not assign an icon to the ToolboxBitmap property. Icons do not scale very well to Toolbox bitmap size.

Visual Basic automatically uses the class name of your control as the tool tip text when users hover the mouse pointer over your icon in the Toolbox.

> **Tip** When creating bitmaps, remember that for many forms of color-blindness, colors with the same overall level of brightness will appear to be the same. You can avoid this by restricting your bitmap to white, black, and shades of gray, or by careful color selection.

Allowing Your Control to be a Default or Cancel Button

Default and cancel buttons are controlled by the container. To notify the container that your control is capable of being a default or cancel button, set the DefaultCancel property of the UserControl to True.

If you have set the Default or Cancel property to True for one of the constituent controls on your UserControl, you must set the DefaultCancel property of the UserControl to True or the constituent control property will be ignored.

User-drawn controls can examine the DisplayAsDefault property of the AmbientProperties object to determine whether they should draw the extra black border that visually identifies a default button.

If DefaultCancel is True, and the developer makes an instance of your control the default button, the UserControl's AccessKeyPressed event will occur when the user presses the Enter key. The argument of the event will contain the ASCII value 13.

If an instance of your control is the cancel button, the argument of the AccessKeyPress event will contain the ASCII value 27.

> **Important** The status of a default or cancel button can change at any time. You must place code in the UserControl's AmbientChanged event to detect changes in the DisplayAsDefault property, and adjust your control's appearance accordingly.

Adding Internet Features to Controls

ActiveX controls created with Visual Basic can support asynchronous downloading of property values, such as Picture properties that may contain bitmaps. Through the Hyperlink property of the UserControl object, they can also request that a browser jump to a URL, or navigate through the history list.

These features are available when the control is placed on a container that provides the necessary support functions, such as Microsoft Internet Explorer.

You may wish to design your control to support both normal loading of property values from a PropertyBag, which is not supported by browsers, and asynchronous downloading of property values.

> **Note** Asynchronous downloading of *local files* is available in any application. An absolute file path must be used (that is, a path starting from the root directory). Relative file locations will not work.

Asynchronous Downloading

A control requests asynchronous downloading of a property by calling the AsyncRead method of the UserControl object. This method can be called from any event, method, or property procedure of your control, as long as the control has already been sited on the container.

The call returns immediately, and downloading proceeds in the background, as shown in Figure 9.8a.

Figure 9.8a Starting asynchronous download of a bitmap property

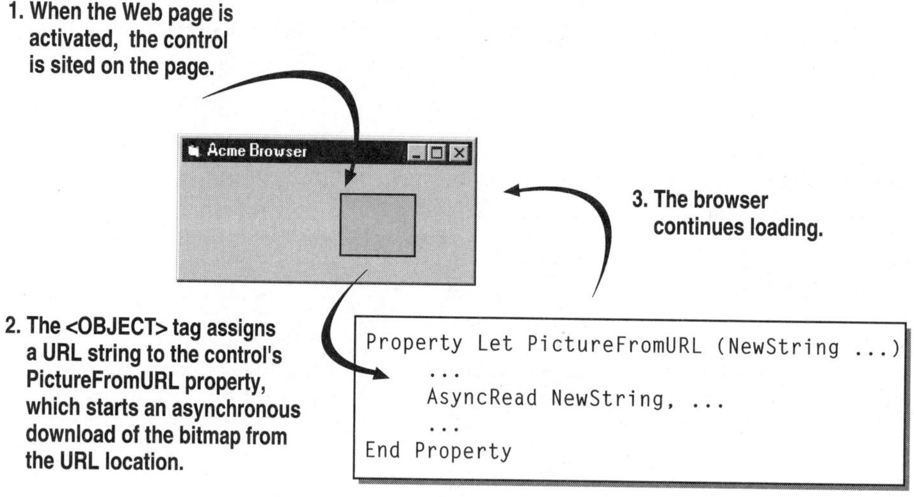
1. When the Web page is activated, the control is sited on the page.
Acme Browser
3. The browser continues loading.
2. The <OBJECT> tag assigns a URL string to the control's PictureFromURL property, which starts an asynchronous download of the bitmap from the URL location.
Property Let PictureFromURL (NewString ...)
...
AsyncRead NewString, ...
...
End Property

When the container has retrieved the entire property value, the control receives an AsyncReadComplete event that identifies the property whose value has been retrieved. The control can then access the retrieved data and set the property value, as shown in Figure 9.8b.

Figure 9.8b Asynchronous download completes

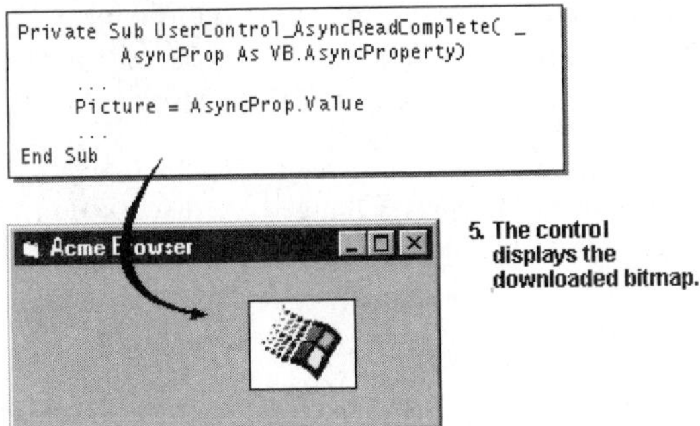
4. When downloading of the bitmap is complete, the control receives an AsyncReadComplete event, and assigns the downloaded bitmap to the control's Picture property.
Private Sub UserControl_AsyncReadComplete(_
AsyncProp As VB.AsyncProperty)
...
Picture = AsyncProp.Value
...
End Sub
5. The control displays the downloaded bitmap.

The example code in this topic follows this scheme to create a simple control that displays a bitmap.

To work through the example, open a new Standard EXE project. Use the Project menu to add a UserControl to the project. Place a PictureBox control on the UserControl, and set the properties as shown in the following table:

Object	Property	Setting
UserControl	Name	AsyncBitmap
PictureBox	Name	picBitmap
	AutoSize	True

The control will have two properties, an ordinary Picture property and a related PictureFromURL property. The Picture property is implemented with all three property procedures, because a Picture object can be assigned with or without the Set statement.

```
Public Property Get Picture() As Picture
   Set Picture = picBitmap.Picture
End Property

Public Property Let Picture(ByVal NewPicture _
      As Picture)
   Set picBitmap.Picture = NewPicture
   PropertyChanged "Picture"
End Property
```

```
Public Property Set Picture(ByVal NewPicture _
      As Picture)
   Set picBitmap.Picture = NewPicture
   PropertyChanged "Picture"
End Property
```

The Picture property of the ActiveX control simply delegates to the Picture property of the picture box, `picBitmap`. The picture box does all the work of displaying the bitmap.

The new property overrides the Picture property of the UserControl object. From now on, if you type Picture without qualifying it, you will get the ActiveX control's Picture property, as defined here. To access the Picture property of the UserControl, you must now qualify it by typing `UserControl.Picture`.

Note The purpose and importance of PropertyChanged are discussed in "Adding Properties to Controls," later in this chapter.

The PictureFromURL Property

When a URL string is assigned to the ActiveX control's PictureFromURL property, the Property Let begins a download of the bitmap. When the download is complete, the bitmap is assigned to the Picture property. PictureFromURL is thus an alternate way of assigning a value to the Picture property.

The PictureFromURL property stores the URL string in a private data member, in the Declarations section of the UserControl:

```
Option Explicit
Private mstrPictureFromURL As String
```

The Property Get simply returns this string, so the program can discover where the picture was downloaded from. The Property Let does all the work:

```
Public Property Get PictureFromURL() As String
   PictureFromURL = mstrPictureFromURL
End Property

Public Property Let PictureFromURL(ByVal NewString _
      As String)
   ' (Code to validate path or URL omitted.)
   mstrPictureFromURL = NewString
   If (Ambient.UserMode = True) _
         And (NewString <> "") Then
      ' If program is in run mode, and the URL string
      ' is not empty, begin the download.
      AsyncRead NewString, vbAsyncTypePicture, _
         "PictureFromURL"
   End If
   PropertyChanged "PictureFromURL"
End Property
```

When a URL string is assigned to the PictureFromURL property, the string is saved in the private variable. If the project the control has been added to is in run mode (which will always be true for a control on an HTML page) and if the URL string is not empty, the Property Let starts an asynchronous download, and then exits.

The asynchronous download is begun by calling the UserControl's AsyncRead method, which has the following syntax:

AsyncRead *Target*, *AsyncType* [, *Property*]

The *Target* argument specifies the location of the data. This can be a path or a URL. The host determines the correct method to retrieve the data.

The *AsyncType* argument specifies the form in which the retrieved data will be provided. It has the following possible values:

Constant	Description
vbAsyncTypePicture	The retrieved data is provided as a Picture object.
vbAsyncTypeFile	The retrieved data is placed in a file created by Visual Basic. A string containing the path to the file is provided. This is useful when the data contains a large AVI file to be played. The control author can assign the string to the file name property of the appropriate constituent control.
vbAsyncTypeByteArray	The retrieved data is provided as a byte array. It is assumed that the control author will know how to handle this data.

The *Property* argument is a string containing the name of the property whose value is to be downloaded. You can use this to enable multiple simultaneous downloads, because this same string is returned in the AsyncReadComplete event, and can be used in a Select statement.

The value of the Property argument can also be used as the argument of the CancelAsyncRead method, described below.

Completing the Download

As each requested download completes, the control receives an AsyncReadComplete event. The argument of the AsyncReadComplete event is a reference to an AsyncProperty object, which can be used to identify the downloaded property and retrieve the downloaded data.

```
Private Sub UserControl_AsyncReadComplete( _
      AsyncProp As VB.AsyncProperty)
   On Error Resume Next
   Select Case AsyncProp.PropertyName
      Case "PictureFromURL"
         Set Picture = AsyncProp.Value
         Debug.Print "Download complete"
   End Select
End Sub
```

You should place error handling code in this event procedure, because an error condition may have stopped the download. If this was the case, that error will be raised when you access the Value property of the AsyncProperty object.

When the downloaded bitmap is assigned to the Picture property, the control repaints.

> **Note** In addition to the Value property that contains the downloaded data and the PropertyName property that contains the name of the property being downloaded, the AsyncProperty object has an AsyncType property. This contains the same value as the AsyncType argument of the AsyncRead method that started the download.

A Bit More Code

So far, the example has no way to save a bitmap assigned at design time. That is, there is no code in the InitProperties, ReadProperties, and WriteProperties events. That code is omitted here, because the purpose of the example is to show asynchronous downloading of a local file.

One more bit of code will prove useful, however. The reason for using a picture box to display the bitmap, instead of simply using the Picture property of the UserControl, is to take advantage of the AutoSize property of the picture box. The following code resizes the entire control whenever the picture box is resized by the arrival of a new bitmap.

```
Private Sub picBitmap_Resize()
   ' If there's a Picture assigned, resize.
   If picBitmap.Picture <> 0 Then
      UserControl.Size picBitmap.Width, _
         picBitmap.Height
   End If
End Sub
```

The resizing only happens if the picture box actually contains a Picture object. This allows the user to specify the size of the empty picture box while the download is pending. The code is as follows:

```
Private Sub UserControl_Resize()
   If picBitmap.Picture = 0 Then
      picBitmap.Move 0, 0, ScaleWidth, ScaleHeight
   Else
      If (Width <> picBitmap.Width) _
            Or (Height <> picBitmap.Height) Then
         Size picBitmap.Width, picBitmap.Height
      End If
   End If
End Sub
```

If there is no Picture object, the picture box is sized to fill the visible area of the UserControl. If there is a Picture object, and the UserControl is resized, it will snap back to the size of the picture box.

Starting the Download

Close the UserControl designer. The control is now running, even though the rest of the project is in design mode. The default control icon on the Toolbox is enabled, so you can add an instance of the control to Form1.

Locate a large bitmap on your computer — the larger the better. Note the file name and path to the file. Add the following code to the Declarations section of Form1, substituting the name and path of your bitmap for the one shown here:

```
Option Explicit
Const DOWNLOADFILE = "file:\windows\forest.bmp"
```

Make sure the string begins with `file:\` so that it's a valid URL for a local file.

> **Note** The URL you pass to the AsyncRead method cannot be a relative URL. That is, you cannot specify relative pathnames for local files.

Place the following code in the form's Load event:

```
Private Sub Form_Load()
   AsyncBitmap1.PictureFromURL = DOWNLOADFILE
   DEBUG.PRINT "Load event complete"
End Sub
```

When the form loads, the URL for the local bitmap file will be assigned to the PictureFromURL property, starting the download.

Running the Sample

Press F5 to run the project. In the Immediate window, notice that the first message is "Load event complete," followed by the "Download complete" message from the AsyncReadComplete event.

If the bitmap was large enough, you may also have noticed that Form1 painted while the bitmap was still downloading. Close Form1, to return to design mode.

Run the project again, and this time click the Close button on Form1 as soon as you see it. Because the download is proceeding asynchronously in the background, the form becomes active and can respond to user input before the bitmap has been loaded.

Using the Control

Up to this point, the example only demonstrates downloading of a local file. It can't be used on a Web page, because controls in Standard EXE projects cannot be used by other applications. To use the control in other projects or on Web pages, add the source file to an ActiveX control project and compile it as an .ocx file. You'll need some additional code — for example, to save the Picture property, as shown here.

```
Private Sub UserControl_InitProperties()
   ' Use Nothing as the default when initializing,
   '   reading, and writing the Picture property,
   '   so than an .frx file won't be needed if
   '   there's no picture.
   Set Picture = Nothing
End Sub

Private Sub UserControl_ReadProperties( _
         PropBag As PropertyBag)
   Set Picture = _
      PropBag.ReadProperty("Picture", Nothing)
End Sub

Private Sub UserControl_WriteProperties( _
         PropBag As PropertyBag)
   PropBag.WriteProperty "Picture", Picture, Nothing
End Sub
```

You can use the ActiveX Control Interface Wizard to add standard properties, methods, and events — such as MouseMove — to the control.

Canceling Asynchronous Downloads

You can call the CancelAsyncRead method to cancel an asynchronous data load. CancelAsyncRead takes the property name as an argument; this must match the value of the PropertyName argument in a prior AsyncRead method call.

Only the specified data load is canceled. All others continue normally.

For More Information You can also use the AsyncReadProgress event to monitor the progress of an asynchronous download. The AsynchReadProgress event is discussed in "Downloading Data Asynchronously" in Chapter 11, "Building ActiveX Documents."

Navigating with the Hyperlink Object

The Hyperlink object gives your control access to ActiveX hyperlinking functionality. Using the properties and methods of the Hyperlink object, your control can request a hyperlink-aware container, such as Microsoft Internet Explorer, to jump to a given URL or to navigate through the history list.

You can access the Hyperlink object through the Hyperlink property of the UserControl object. The following code fragment assumes that the control's URLText property contains a URL string. Clicking on the control causes it to request that its container navigate to that URL.

```
Private Sub UserControl_Click()
   HyperLink.NavigateTo Target:=URLText
End Sub
```

If the target is not a valid URL or document, an error occurs. If the control is sited on a container that does not support hyperlinking, an application that is registered as supporting hyperlinking is started to handle the request.

The NavigateTo method accepts an optional *Location* argument, which specifies a location within the target URL. If a location is not specified, the server will jump to the top of the URL or document.

The NavigateTo method also accepts an optional *FrameName* argument, which specifies a frame within the target URL.

> **Note** If your control is placed on a container that does not support the IHLink interface, the Hyperlink property of the UserControl object will return Nothing. You should test the property for this value before attempting to use the Hyperlink object.

Moving Through the History List

You can call the GoForward and GoBack methods to navigate through the History list. For example:

```
Hyperlink.GoForward
```

If GoForward and GoBack are called when there are no entries in the History list to move forward to, an error occurs. GoForward and GoBack will also raise errors if the container is not hyperlink-aware.

For More Information Details of Internet support for ActiveX controls authored in Visual Basic can be found on the Microsoft Visual Basic Web site.

Information on designing Internet and intranet applications with Visual Basic can be found in Part 5, "Building Internet Applications."

Designing Controls for Use with HTML

A control on an HTML page is specified using the HTML <OBJECT> and </OBJECT> tags. When the HTML is processed, the control is created and positioned. If the <OBJECT> tag includes any <PARAM NAME> attributes, the property values supplied with those attributes are passed to the control's ReadProperties event using the standard PropertyBag object, as discussed in "Understanding Control Lifetime and Key Events."

Once the HTML page is active, the control's property values may also be set by scripts attached to events that occur on the page.

> **Note** If there are no <PARAM NAME> attributes other than those that set extender properties (such as Top and Left), the control may receive an InitProperties event rather than a ReadProperties event. This behavior is dependent on browser implementation, and should not be relied on.

The Package and Deployment Wizard makes it easy to create an Internet setup for your control, with cabinet (.cab) files that can be automatically downloaded when a user opens an HTML page containing an instance of your control. Support files, such as MSVBVM60.DLL, can be downloaded separately. P-code .ocx files are very compact, so if support files already exist on a user's computer, downloading can be very fast.

Visual Basic controls can support digital signatures, safe initialization, and safe scripting.

> **Important** In order to use a control that includes licensing support on an HTML page, a licensed copy of the control component must be installed on the Web server that provides the page. This is discussed in "Licensing Issues for Controls," later in this chapter.

Making Your Control Safe for Scripting and Initialization on HTML Pages

Code that's downloaded as a result of opening a page on the World Wide Web doesn't come shrink-wrapped, blazoned with a company name to vouch for its reliability. Users may be understandably skeptical when they're asked to okay the download. If you intend for your control to be used on HTML pages, there are several things you can do to reassure users.

- *Digital signatures* create a path to you (through the company that authorized your certificate), in the event that your control causes harm on a user's system. You can incorporate your signature when you use Package and Deployment Wizard to create an Internet setup for your control component.
- Marking your control *safe for scripting* tells users that there's no way a script on an HTML page can use your control to cause harm to their computers, or to obtain information they haven't supplied willingly.
- Marking your control *safe for initialization* lets users know there's no way an HTML author can harm their computers by feeding your control invalid data when the page initializes it.

This topic explains how to design your control so that when you create your Internet setup, you'll be able to mark your control as safe for scripting and safe for initialization.

> **Note** The default setting for Internet Explorer is to display a warning and to refuse to download a component that has not been marked safe for scripting and initialization.

For More Information The latest information on digital signatures, cabinet files, and Internet setup can be found on the Microsoft Visual Basic Web site.

Safe for Scripting

When a Web designer places your control on an HTML page, he uses a scripting language such as JavaScript or Visual Basic, Scripting Edition to access the control's properties, invoke its methods, and handle its events. By marking your control as safe for scripting, you're providing an implicit warrantee: "No matter what VBScript or JavaScript code is used, this control cannot be made to harm a user's computer, or to take information the user hasn't volunteered."

As the author of your control, you can be reasonably sure that in normal use it won't destroy data or compromise the security of a user's computer. Once your control is in the hands of a Web designer, however, you have no guarantee that it will be used in the ways you intended.

Keys to Scripting Safety

As an example of a control that's *not* safe for scripting, consider the rich text box. The RichTextBox control has a SaveFile method that can be used to write the contents of the control to a file. A malicious person could write a script that would cause this control to over-write an operating system file, so that the user's computer would malfunction.

What makes the control unsafe is not that it can save information to a file — it's the fact that *the script* can specify the filename. This observation provides the key to creating controls that are safe for scripting. As long as your control doesn't allow a script to specify the source or target for file or registry operations, or make API calls that can be directly controlled by a script, it is probably safe for scripting.

Thus, a control that permits a Web page designer to do any of the following is probably not safe for scripting:

- Create a file with a name supplied by a script.
- Read a file from the user's hard drive with a name supplied by a script.
- Insert information into the Windows Registry (or into an .ini file), using a key (or filename) supplied by a script.
- Retrieve information from the Windows Registry (or from an .ini file), using a key (or filename) supplied by a script.
- Execute a Windows API function using information supplied by a script.
- Create or manipulate external objects using programmatic IDs (for example, "Excel.Application") that the script supplies.

The line between safe and unsafe can be a fine one. For example, a control that uses the SaveSetting method to write information to its own registry key doesn't disqualify itself for safe scripting by doing so. On the other hand, a control that allows the registry key to be specified (by setting a property or invoking a method) is not safe.

A control that uses a temporary file may be safe for scripting. If the name of that temporary file can be controlled by a script, then the control is not safe for scripting. *Even allowing a script to control the amount of information that goes into the temporary file* will make the control unsafe for scripting, because a script could continue dumping information into the file until the user's hard disk was full.

As a final example, a control that uses API calls is not necessarily unsafe for scripting. Suppose, however, that the control allows a script to supply data that will be passed to an API, and doesn't guard against oversize data overwriting memory, or invalid data corrupting memory. Such a control is not safe for scripting.

As an indication of the seriousness of scripting safety, note that VBScript itself does not include methods to access the registry, save files, or create objects.

Choosing Constituent Controls

You might think that using a constituent control that's not safe for scripting would automatically make your ActiveX control unsafe for scripting. This is not necessarily true.

As explained in "Adding Properties to Controls," later in this chapter, the properties and methods of constituent controls do *not* automatically become part of your control's interface. As long as you avoid exposing the properties and methods that make a constituent control unsafe, you can use it without making your own control unsafe.

For example, if you use the RichTextBox as a constituent control, you should not expose its SaveFile method.

> **Important** Do not provide a property that returns a reference to an unsafe constituent control. A script could use this reference to access the properties and methods that make the control unsafe.

Documenting Scripting Safety

Determining whether a control is safe is not a trivial exercise. You may find it helpful to record your design decisions that affect safe scripting. A useful exercise is to construct tables containing the following:

- All of your control's public properties, methods, and events.
- All of the files and registry keys accessed, and all API calls used.

If there are any dependencies or data transfer between the elements of these two tables, then the control is probably not safe for scripting.

You may wish to have this documentation reviewed by an experienced programmer who understands both ActiveX controls and scripting.

Safe for Initialization

A control marked as safe for initialization carries an implicit guarantee that it will cause no harm no matter how its properties are initialized.

On an HTML page, your control's initial state is set using PARAM NAME attributes with the OBJECT tag that embeds your control on the page. If a malicious Web designer can make your control steal information or otherwise cause harm by placing invalid data in a PARAM NAME attribute, then your control is not safe for initialization.

The best defense against malicious data is to validate each property value that's obtained in your control's ReadProperties event. All the data a Web designer places in PARAM NAME attributes is supplied to your control through the PropertyBag object in the ReadProperties event. (A well-written control should perform this kind of validation anyway, to prevent problems caused by developers who manually edit .frm files.)

For More Information The most up-to-date information on authoring controls for the Internet can be found on the Microsoft Visual Basic Web site.

Using Show and Hide Events

The Show and Hide events can be very useful on Web pages. If your control is performing a resource-intensive task, such as showing a video clip or repeatedly downloading and displaying a stock value, you may want to pause this activity when the Hide event occurs.

The Hide event means that the user has moved on to another page, relegating the page your control is on to the History list. The Show event means that the user has returned to your page, and can thus be the signal for resuming resource-intensive display tasks.

For More Information The Show and Hide events are discussed in "Understanding Control Lifetime and Key Events," earlier in this chapter.

Using the Parent and ParentControls Properties

You can use the Parent property of the UserControl object to access the container. For example, in Internet Explorer, the following code will change the background color of the HTML page on which your control is located:

```
Parent.Script.get_document.bgColor = "Blue"
```

More information on the Internet Explorer Scripting Object Model can be found on Microsoft's Web site.

> **Important** Always use *late binding* for calls to the Internet Explorer Scripting Object Model. Using early binding will almost certainly cause compatibility problems in the future, while late binding will always work.

The ParentControls Collection

The ParentControls collection allows you to access the other controls on a container where your control has been sited. On some containers — Internet Explorer is one of them — ParentControls returns an extender object whose properties and methods are not merged with those of the controls. This prevents you from accessing the controls themselves.

To access the other controls on an HTML page, you can set the ParentControlsType property of the ParentControls collection to vbNoExtender. The ParentControls collection will thereafter return the interfaces of the controls themselves, without the extender.

```
ParentControls.ParentControlsType = vbNoExtender
```

> **Note** The Parent property and ParentControls collection can be used with many other containers. They are not limited to HTML browsers.

Binding a Control to a Data Source

Visual Basic allows you to mark properties of your control as *bindable*, allowing you to create data-aware controls. A developer can associate bindable properties with fields in any data source, making it easier to use your control in database applications.

Use the Procedure Attributes dialog box, accessed from the Tools menu, to mark properties of your control as bindable. Figure 9.9 shows the data binding options made available by clicking the dialog's Advanced button.

Figure 9.9 Data binding options for ActiveX control properties

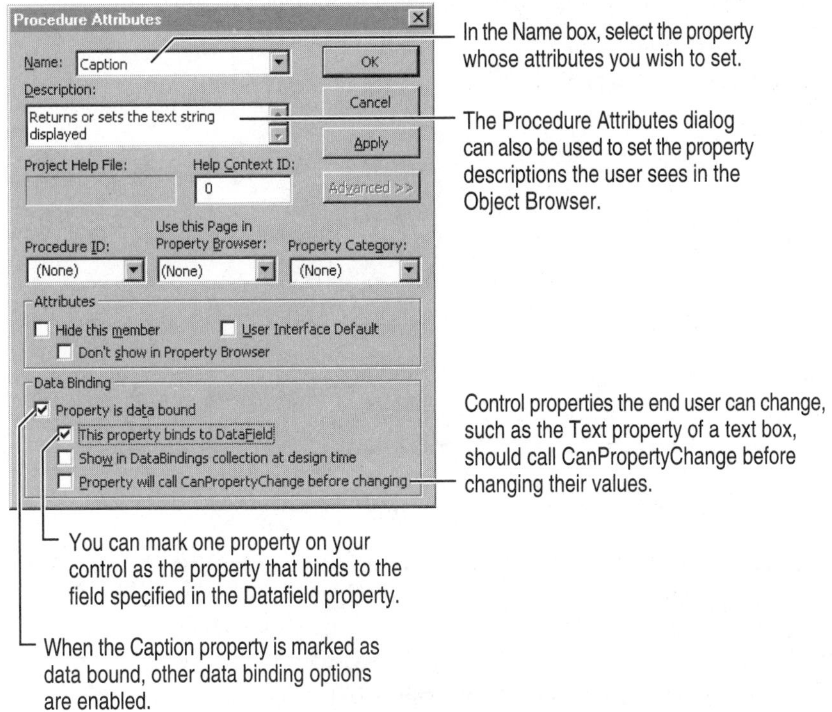
Procedure Attributes
Name: Caption
Description:
Returns or sets the text string displayed
OK
Cancel
Apply
Advanced >>
Project Help File:
Help Context ID:
0
Procedure ID:
Use this Page in Property Browser:
Property Category:
(None)
(None)
(None)
Attributes
Hide this member
User Interface Default
Don't show in Property Browser
Data Binding
Property is data bound
This property binds to DataField
Show in DataBindings collection at design time
Property will call CanPropertyChange before changing
In the Name box, select the property whose attributes you wish to set.
The Procedure Attributes dialog can also be used to set the property descriptions the user sees in the Object Browser.
Control properties the end user can change, such as the Text property of a text box, should call CanPropertyChange before changing their values.
You can mark one property on your control as the property that binds to the field specified in the Datafield property.
When the Caption property is marked as data bound, other data binding options are enabled.

The controls supplied with Visual Basic can be bound to data source fields using their DataSource and DataField properties. You can select one property of your control to be bound to the DataField property. Typically, this will be the most important piece of data your control holds.

Although you can mark only one field as bound to the field specified in the DataField property, you can mark additional properties of your ActiveX control as bindable. Developers can use the DataBindings collection to bind these additional bindable properties to data fields.

> **Note** Some development tools and control containers do not support data binding. This topic describes the support for data-bound controls provided by Visual Basic.

The DataBindings Collection

The DataBindings collection is an extender property that Visual Basic provides to users of your control. It allows the developer to access the list of bindable properties on your control.

> **Note** All bindable properties appear in the DataBindings collection at run time. At design time, only properties marked "Show in DataBindings collection at design time" will appear when the DataBindings property is accessed in the Properties window.

For example, you might create an Address control assembly, using labels and text boxes as constituent controls. The bindable properties of your control would correspond to the text boxes on your control, as shown in Figure 9.10.

Figure 9.10 An Address control assembly with multiple fields

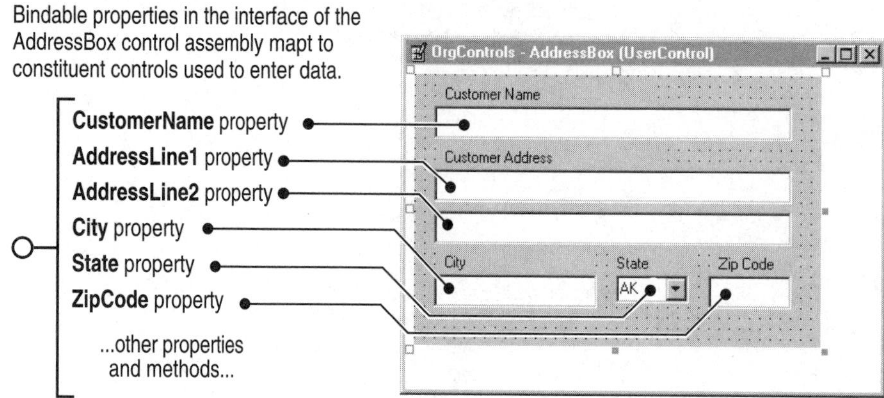

> **Note** If your control has multiple bindable properties, you must mark one as binding to the Extender object's DataField property. Otherwise, the Extender object will not provide a DataSource property for your control. You can mark a property as binding to DataField by selecting "This property binds to DataField" in the Procedure Attributes dialog box. The property you mark as binding to DataField can also be bound using the DataBindings collection.

The mapping between properties of the control and contents of the constituent controls is accomplished by delegation, as in this code fragment:

```
Public Property Get AddressLine1() As String
   AddressLine1 = txtAddressLine1.Text
End Property

Public Property Let AddressLine1(NewValue As String)
   If CanPropertyChange("AddressLine1")
      txtAddressLine1.Text = NewValue
      ' The following line tells Visual Basic the
      ' property has changed--if you omit this line,
      ' the data source will not be updated!
      PropertyChanged "AddressLine1"
   End If
End Property
```

Delegating to the text box control means that the text box does all the work of displaying the value and accepting user changes. Because the user can change the value of the property while the text box is displaying it, you must also mark the property as changed in the text box's Change event, as shown below.

```
Private Sub txtAddressLine1_Change()
   PropertyChanged "AddressLine1"
End Sub
```

Important In order for the new value to be written back to the data source, you must call PropertyChanged. If you don't call the PropertyChanged method, your control will not be bound for update.

For More Information The PropertyChanged method has another important purpose, as discussed in "Adding Properties to Controls," later in this chapter.

Calling CanPropertyChange

Your control should always call CanPropertyChange before changing the value of a property that can be data-bound. Do not set the property value if CanPropertyChange returns False. Doing so may cause errors in some control containers.

If your control always calls CanPropertyChange, you can check "Property will call CanPropertyChange before changing" on the Procedure Attributes dialog box.

Note At present, CanPropertyChange always returns True in Visual Basic, even if the bound field is read-only in the data source. This does not cause a problem with the code shown above, because Visual Basic doesn't raise an error when your program attempts to change a read-only field; it just doesn't update the data source.

Discovering and Setting Bindable Properties at Run Time

If a developer placed an instance of the AddressBox control on a form, she could execute the following code to list the bindable properties:

```
Dim dtb As DataBinding
For Each dtb In AddressBox1.DataBindings
   Debug.Print dtb.PropertyName
Next
```

At run time, the developer could use the following code to bind the AddressLine1 property to the AddrLine1 field, assuming that field was available on the data source specified by the DataSource extender property:

```
AddressBox1.DataBindings( _
   "AddressLine1").DataField = "AddrLine1"
```

Finding Out Whether a Field has Changed

You can test the DataChanged property of a DataBinding object to find out if the value of a field has changed. This property functions in the same way as the DataChanged extender property of bound controls.

Setting Multiple Data Bindings at Design Time

Bindable properties always appear in the DataBindings collection at run time. By default, they do not appear in the Data Bindings dialog box at design time.

If you want a bindable property to appear in the Data Bindings dialog box, select that property in the Procedure Attributes dialog box and check "Show This Property in the Bindings Collection."

Figure 9.11 Using the Data Bindings dialog box

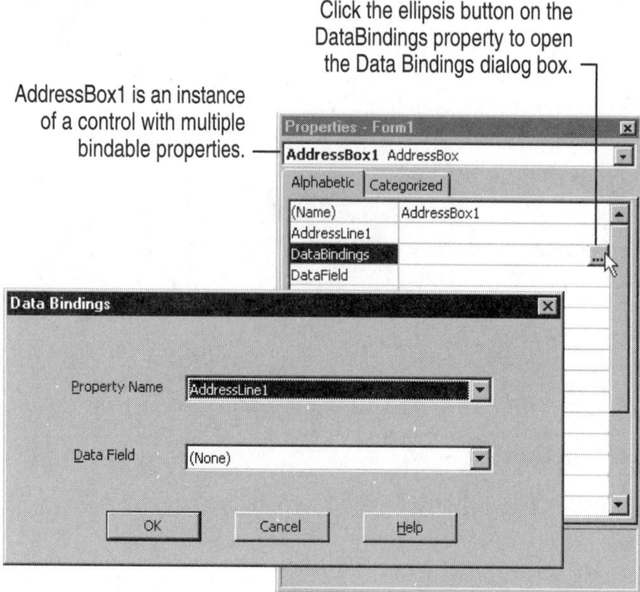

The Data Field box shows all fields available on the data source specified by the current value of the DataSource extender property on the control instance.

Attributes and Flags

If you have developed OLE controls in the past, you can use the following table to see what flags are set by the Procedure Attributes dialog box. The table also shows how these attributes are accessed through the Member object in the Visual Basic Extensibility Model.

Attribute	Flag	Member Object
Property is data bound.	BINDABLE	Bindable
This property binds to DataField.	DEFAULTBIND	DefaultBind
Show in DataBindings collection at design time.	DISPLAYBIND	DisplayBind
Property will call CanPropertyChange before changing.	REQUESTEDIT	RequestEdit

Allowing Developers to Edit Your Control at Design Time

Some controls, like the OLE control supplied with Visual Basic, allow you to edit the control's contents at design time. You can enable this behavior for your control by setting the EditAtDesignTime property of your UserControl object to True.

If a container supports this feature, it will add an Edit menu item to the context menu that appears when a developer right-clicks on an instance of your control at design-time.

The developer using the control can activate a control instance by right-clicking the control to get the Context menu, then clicking Edit. The control will be activated, and will behave as it does at run time.

This allows you to author controls with visual design features, such as letting the user size rows and columns, or set property values by typing directly into constituent controls. You can detect whether your control is running at design time by testing the UserMode property of the AmbientProperties object. This property is False at design time.

The control only remains active while it is selected. When the developer clicks on another control, the control will deactivate. To reactivate the control, the developer must select Edit from the context menu.

> **Note** When your control is activated in this fashion, the events of the UserControl object will occur, so that your control can operate normally, but your control will be unable to raise any events. The RaiseEvent method will simply be ignored; it will not cause an error.

Drawing Your Control

The way you draw your control's appearance depends on the control creation model you're using.

If you're creating a user-drawn control, you have to do all the drawing yourself. You have to know when to draw your control, what state it's in (for example, clicked or unclicked), and whether you should draw a focus rectangle.

If you're enhancing an existing control or creating a control assembly, on the other hand, your UserControl's constituent controls provide your control's appearance. The constituent controls draw themselves automatically, and all you have to worry about is whether they're positioned correctly on the UserControl.

For More Information Control creation models are discussed in "Control Creation Basics," earlier in this chapter.

User-Drawn Controls

When you're doing your own drawing, the only place you need to put drawing code is in the UserControl_Paint event procedure. When the container repaints the area your control is located on, the UserControl object will receive a Paint event.

If the built-in graphics methods of the UserControl object, such as Line and Circle, don't meet your drawing needs, you can use Windows API calls to draw your control. You can also "draw" text on your control using the Print method. Regardless of the drawing technique, the code goes in UserControl_Paint.

If your control has to change its appearance based on user actions, such as when the user clicks on the control, you can raise the Paint event by calling the UserControl's Refresh method.

> **Note** While you cannot draw on the transparent parts of a UserControl with BackStyle = Transparent, it is possible to create controls with transparent backgrounds that are mostly user-drawn. See "Giving Your Control a Transparent Background," earlier in this chapter.

> **Important** In Paint events, do not use DoEvents, or any other code that yields to other programs. Doing so will cause errors.

The following example demonstrates the basic principle of a three-state button, each of the three states being represented by a different bitmap. To work through the example, open a new Standard EXE project and use the Project menu to add a UserControl to the project. Place a PictureBox on the UserControl, and set object properties as follows:

Object	Property	Setting
UserControl	Name	TripleState
PictureBox	AutoRedraw	True
	Name	picStates
	Picture	(Any bitmap)
	Visible	False

> **Note** The example works best if the bitmap chosen for the Picture property changes color dramatically from left to right.

Add the following code to the Declarations section of the UserControl's code window.

```
Option Explicit
' Private variable keeps track of the current state.
Private mintState As Integer
```

A simple mechanism is used to provide the three states: Clicking on the control rotates through the states by incrementing the value of a private state variable each time the control is clicked. If the value becomes too large, it is reset to zero. Add this code to the UserControl's Click event.

```
Private Sub UserControl_Click()
   mintState = mintState + 1
   If mintState > 2 Then mintState = 0
   ' The following line causes Paint event to occur.
   Refresh
End Sub
```

Add the following code to the UserControl's Paint event. When the Paint event occurs, the code copies one-third of the bitmap in the invisible PictureBox to the UserControl. Which third is copied depends on the current value of the private state variable `mintState`.

```
Private Sub UserControl_Paint()
   PaintPicture picStates.Picture, 0, 0, ScaleWidth, _
      ScaleHeight, mintState * picStates.Width / 3, _
      0, picStates.Width / 3
End Sub
```

> **Note** Another way to provide a different appearance for the each of your control's states is to use the Select...Case statement.

When mintState is zero, its initial value, the first third of the hidden bitmap will be copied onto the UserControl, as shown in Figure 9.12.

Figure 9.12 Copying the first third of the hidden bitmap to the UserControl

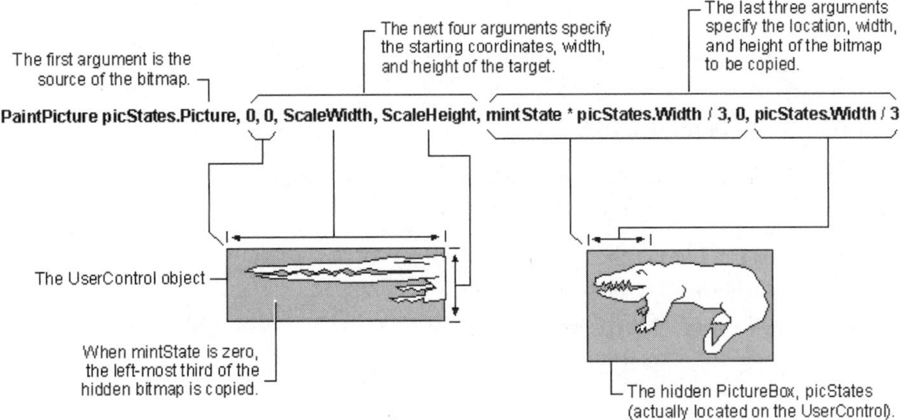

Click the Close box on the UserControl designer, to enable its icon in the Toolbox. Double-click the icon to place a copy of the control on a form, and press F5 to run the project. Click on the control to change the state.

You can hide the form behind another window, or minimize and restore the form, to verify that the control correctly retains its state, and repaints accordingly.

> **Tip** For better performance when drawing your own control, make sure the AutoRedraw property is set to False.

For More Information See "Drawing the ShapeLabel Control," in Chapter 4, "Creating an ActiveX Control."

Using Windows API calls is discussed in "Accessing the Microsoft Windows API," in Part 4, "Accessing DLLs and the Windows API." The PaintPicture method is discussed in Chapter 12, "Working with Text and Graphics," in the *Microsoft Visual Basic 6.0 Programmer's Guide.*

Working with Other Events

In similar fashion, you can simulate other event-driven appearance changes, such as button presses. To animate button presses, put state-changing code in the MouseUp and MouseDown events. Regardless of the events being used, the principle is the same: change the state, and call the Refresh method.

Showing That a User-Drawn Control Has the Focus

If your control can get the focus, you will need a second state variable to keep track of whether your control currently has the focus, so that each time your control redraws itself it will show (or not show) an appropriate indication that it has the focus.

The Windows API DrawFocusRect can be used to draw the type of single-pixel dotted line used to show focus in the CommandButton control. There is no comparable API for non-rectangular shapes.

For More Information See "How to Handle Focus in your Control," earlier in this chapter.

Showing a User-Drawn Control as Disabled

If you implement an Enabled property, you will need to keep track of whether your control is enabled, so you can provide a visual cue to the user when your control is disabled.

If you implement your control's Enabled property as discussed in "Allowing Your Control to be Enabled and Disabled," earlier in this chapter, you can simply test UserControl.Enabled to determine whether to draw your control as enabled or disabled.

The way you draw your control to indicate that it's disabled is entirely up to you.

User-Drawn Controls That Can Be Default Buttons

Setting the DefaultCancel property of your UserControl object to True tells the container your control can be a default or cancel button, so the Extender object can show Boolean Default and Cancel properties.

You can examine the value of the DisplayAsDefault property of the AmbientProperties object to determine whether your control should show the extra black border that tells the end user your control is the default button. Show the border only when the DisplayAsDefault property is True.

> **Important** Correct behavior for a button in Windows is to show the default border only if your control has been designated as the default button, *and* no other button has the focus. DisplayAsDefault is True only if both of these conditions are met. Other methods of determining when to display the border may result in incorrect behavior.

For More Information See "Understanding the Container's Extender Object," and "Using the AmbientProperties Object to Stay Consistent with the Container," earlier in this chapter.

Handling the FontChanged Event

If you want to display text on your user-drawn control, you can do so using the Print method in the UserControl_Paint event. For example, the following code would display "Push Me" on the TripleState control from the previous example:

```
Private Sub UserControl_Paint()
   Cls    ' Clear any previous text
   Print Spc(3); "Push Me"
End Sub
```

There is just one problem with the above example — the text will always be displayed in the default font, even if you have exposed the Font property for your control. Your control has no idea that the font has changed, so the Paint event isn't fired.

To circumvent this problem, you need to add a Font object to your user control and call the User Control's Refresh method in the FontChanged event of the Font object. The Font object must be declared using the WithEvents keyword in order to expose this event:

```
Option Explicit
Private WithEvents mFont as stdFont
```

For a complete example of using a Font object and the FontChanged event, see "Adding a Font Object to Your User Control," earlier in this chapter.

Providing Appearance Using Constituent Controls

If you're enhancing an existing control, that single constituent control will typically occupy the entire visible surface of your UserControl object. You can accomplish this by using the Move method of the constituent control in the Resize event of the UserControl, as shown below.

```
Private Sub UserControl_Resize()
   picBase.Move 0, 0, ScaleWidth, ScaleHeight
End Property
```

The code above assumes that an enhanced picture control is being authored. A PictureBox control has been placed on the UserControl, and named picBase.

If the control you're enhancing has a minimum size, or a dimension that increases in large increments — such as the height of a ListBox control, which changes by the height of a line of text — you will have to add code to determine whether the Move method has produced the desired result.

You can rely on the control you're enhancing to handle painting, including (where appropriate) default button highlighting.

> **Tip** You may also have to add code to resize your UserControl object, to accommodate a constituent control that can't be sized arbitrarily — such as a text box or list box. To avoid exhausting stack space with recursive calls to the Resize event, use static variables to determine when the UserControl_Resize event procedure is making recursive calls.

Resizing a Control Assembly

If you're authoring a control assembly, the Resize event will be more complex, because you have to adjust both size and relative location of multiple constituent controls.

Enforcing a Minimum Control Size

If you author a control with a large number of constituent controls, there may be a minimum size below which resizing the constituent controls is futile, because too little of each control is visible to be of any use, or because the enforced minimum sizes of some constituent controls has been reached.

There is no real harm in allowing the user to reduce the size of your control to absurdity. Most controls allow this, because preventing it is a lot of work, and because at some point you have to rely on your user's desire to produce an application that works and is usable.

In the event that resizing below some threshold causes your control to malfunction, you might make all of your constituent controls invisible, as an alternative to enforcing a minimum size.

The following code fragment provides a simple example of enforcing a minimum size.

```
Private Sub UserControl_Resize()
   Dim sngMinH As Single
   Dim sngMinW As Single

   ' Code to resize constituent controls. It is
   ' assumed that each of these will have some minimum
   ' size, which will go into the calculation of the
   ' UserControl's minimum size.

   sngMinW = <<Width calculation>>
   sngMinH = <<Height calculation>>
```

```
    If Width < sngMinW Then Width = sngMinW
    If Height < sngMinH Then Height = sngMinH
End Sub
```

Notice the <<pseudo-code placeholders>> for the calculation of your control's minimum width and height. These calculations will be in the ScaleMode units of your UserControl. They may be very complicated, involving the widths and heights of several of the constituent controls.

The Width and Height properties of the UserControl are then set, if necessary.

> **Important** The Width and Height properties of the UserControl include the thickness of the border, if any. If BorderStyle = 1 (Fixed Single), the area available for constituent controls will be reduced by two *pixels* (not Twips) in both width and height. If you have exposed the BorderStyle property for your user to set, include code to test the current value.

As an alternative, you could use the Size method:

```
If Width > sngMinW Then sngMinW = Width
If Height > sngMinH Then sngMinH = Height
If (sngMinW <> Width) Or (sngMinH <> Height) Then
   ' (Optionally, set recursion flag.)
   Size sngMinW, sngMinH
   ' (Clear recursion flag, if set.)
End If
```

This code is more slightly more complicated, but it simplifies things if you need to avoid recursion when resizing your control, as discussed below.

> **Important** The Width and Height properties of the UserControl are always expressed in Twips, regardless of the ScaleMode setting. If you have set ScaleMode to something other than Twips, use the ScaleX and ScaleY methods to convert your minimum size calculations to Twips.

Dealing with Recursion

No code for recursion is included in the example above, and recursion is virtually guaranteed. For example, if you attempt to resize the control so that both width and height are below the minimum values, the Resize event will reset the Width property, which will cause a second Resize to be raised immediately.

This second Resize event will test and reset the height, and then return — so that by the time the first Resize event tests the height, it will already have been reset to the minimum. Clearly, this can lead to confusing debugging situations.

Even if you use the Size method, a second Resize event will occur, repeating all your calculations. This can be avoided by setting a flag when you deliberately resize the control. The Resize event should check this flag, and skip all processing when it is True.

A recursion flag is not necessary for simple minimum size situations, but is virtually required for more complicated scenarios.

For example, if you use the code above in a control whose Align property is True, so that it aligns to the form it's placed on, as described in "Making Your Control Align to the Edges of Forms," earlier in this chapter, infinite recursion errors are guaranteed, until stack space is exhausted and an error occurs.

> **Important** Always use error handling in Resize event procedures. Errors here cannot be handled by the container, and your control component will therefore fail, causing the application using your control to fail, as well.

For More Information The models for creating controls are discussed in "Three Ways to Build ActiveX Controls," earlier in this chapter.

Adding Properties to Controls

You implement properties of your ActiveX control by adding property procedures to the code module of the UserControl that forms the basis of your control class.

By default, the only properties your control will have are the extender properties provided by the container. You must decide what additional properties your control needs, and add code to save and retrieve the settings of those properties.

Properties for controls differ in two main ways from properties of other objects you create with Visual Basic.

- Property values are displayed in the Properties window and Properties Pages dialog box at design time.
- Property values are saved to and retrieved from the container's source file, so that they persist from one programming session to the next.

As a result of these differences, implementing properties for controls has more requirements and options than for other kinds of objects.

Implement Control Properties Using Property Procedures

The most important consequence of the differences listed above is that control properties should always be implemented using property procedures instead of public data members. Otherwise, your control will not work correctly in Visual Basic.

Property procedures are required because you must notify Visual Basic whenever a property value changes. You do this by invoking the PropertyChanged method of the UserControl object at the end of every successful Property Let or Property Set, as shown in the following code fragment.

```
Private mblnMasked As Boolean

Public Property Get Masked() As Boolean
   Masked = mblnMasked
End Property
```

```
Public Property Let Masked(ByVal NewValue As Boolean)
   mblnMasked = NewValue
   PropertyChanged "Masked"
End Property
```

There are two reasons for notifying Visual Basic that a property value has changed:

- If you don't call PropertyChanged, Visual Basic cannot mark control instances as needing to be saved. They will not get WriteProperties events, and developers who use your control will lose any property values they set at design time.
- Because property values may be displayed in more than one place, the development environment must be informed when a property value changes, so it can synchronize the values shown in the Properties window, the Property Pages dialog box, and so forth.

Run-Time Properties

Properties that are available only at run time don't need to call the PropertyChanged method, unless they can be data-bound. However, they still need to be implemented using property procedures, as explained in the related topic "Creating Design-Time-Only or Run-Time-Only Properties."

For More Information Authoring controls that can be bound to data sources is discussed in "Binding Your Control to a Data Source," earlier in this chapter.

Showing Properties in the Properties Window

If you create both a Property Get and a Property Let, your property will automatically be displayed in the Properties window. In some cases, you may not want this.

For example, if displaying a property value requires a time-consuming calculation, the developer who uses your control may be annoyed at the length of time it takes to access the Properties window.

On the Property Attributes dialog, accessible from the Tools menu, select the property you wish to suppress. Click the Advanced button, check "Don't show in Property Browser," and then click Apply.

Properties You Don't Need to Implement

Right away, you can avoid a lot of work. The Extender object, which is provided by the container your control is placed on, will supply a number of properties for you. DragIcon, HelpContextID, TabIndex, Top, and Visible are a few of the extender properties supplied by Visual Basic forms.

For More Information To see all the properties Visual Basic's Extender object provides, search the Language Reference in the index for Extender Object. The Extender object is discussed in "Understanding the Container's Extender Object," earlier in this chapter. An odd exception is the Enabled property, which you must implement so that the Extender object can mask it. See "Allowing Your Control to be Enabled and Disabled," earlier in this chapter.

The UserControl object is discussed in "The UserControl Object," earlier in this chapter. General information on creating properties for objects, such as making a property the default for an object, is provided in "Adding Properties and Methods to Classes," in Chapter 6, "General Principles of Component Design."

Saving the Properties of Your Control

As discussed in "Understanding Control Lifetime and Key Events," earlier in this chapter, instances of controls are continually being created and destroyed — when form designers are opened and closed, when projects are opened and closed, when projects are put into run mode, and so on.

How does a property of a control instance — for example, the Caption property of a Label control — get preserved through all this destruction and re-creation? Visual Basic stores the property values of a control instance in the file belonging to the container the control instance is placed on; .frm/.frx files for forms, .dob/.dox files for UserDocument objects, .ctl/.ctx files for UserControls, and .pag/.pgx files for property pages. Figure 9.13 illustrates this.

Figure 9.13 An .frm file contains saved control properties

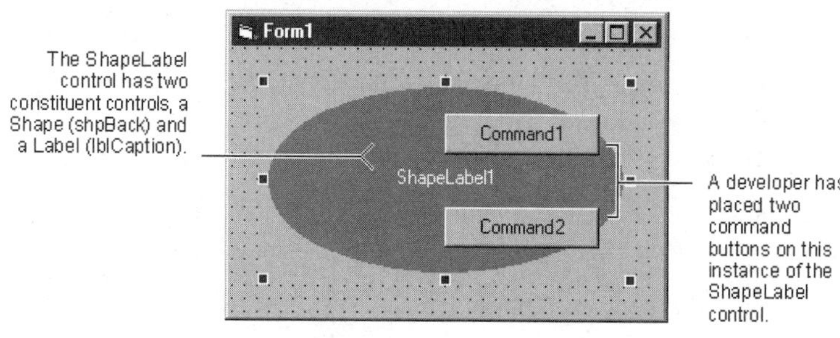

The ShapeLabel control has two constituent controls, a Shape (shpBack) and a Label (lblCaption).
Form1
Command1
ShapeLabel1
Command2
A developer has placed two command buttons on this instance of the ShapeLabel control.

If the control includes the code below, it will always display two names, shpBack and lblCaption.

```
Dim c As Object
For Each c In UserControl.Controls
   MsgBox c.Name
Next
```

If the control includes the code below, it will display Command1 and Command2 — for this instance only.

```
Dim c As Object
For Each c In _
      UserControl.ContainedControls
   MsgBox c.Name
Next
```

When you author a control, you must include code to save your property values before a control instance is destroyed, and read them back in when the control instance is re-created. This is illustrated in Figure 9.14.

Figure 9.14 Saving and retrieving property values

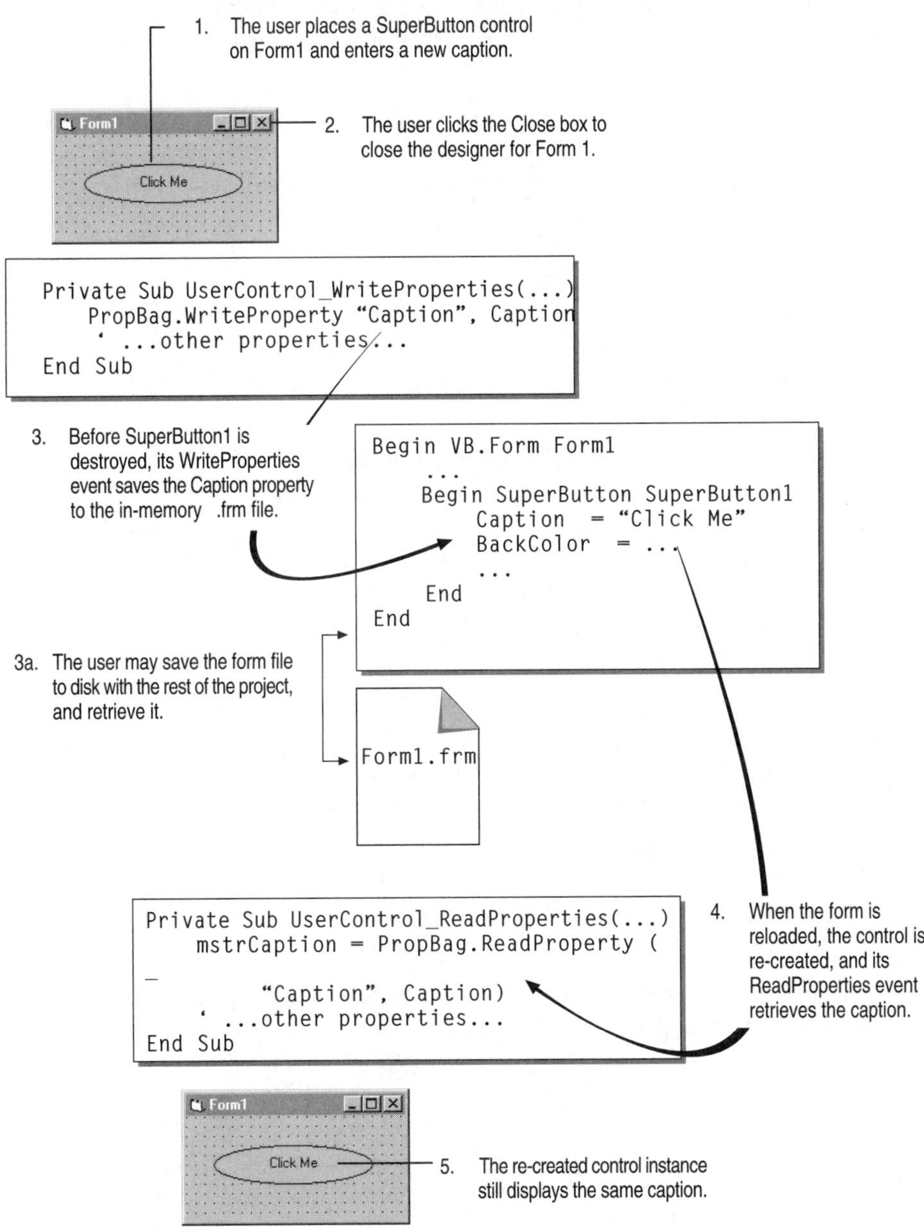
1. The user places a SuperButton control on Form1 and enters a new caption.
Form1
Click Me
2. The user clicks the Close box to close the designer for Form 1.
Private Sub UserControl_WriteProperties(...)
PropBag.WriteProperty "Caption", Caption
' ...other properties...
End Sub
3. Before SuperButton1 is destroyed, its WriteProperties event saves the Caption property to the in-memory .frm file.
Begin VB.Form Form1
...
Begin SuperButton SuperButton1
Caption = "Click Me"
BackColor = ...
...
End
End
3a. The user may save the form file to disk with the rest of the project, and retrieve it.
Form1.frm
Private Sub UserControl_ReadProperties(...)
mstrCaption = PropBag.ReadProperty (
_
"Caption", Caption)
' ...other properties...
End Sub
4. When the form is reloaded, the control is re-created, and its ReadProperties event retrieves the caption.
Form1
Click Me
5. The re-created control instance still displays the same caption.

Figure 9.14 is slightly oversimplified. You don't actually have to close a form to cause the WriteProperties event procedures of control instances to be executed. Saving a form file to disk causes WriteProperties events to be raised for all controls on the form.

> **Tip** This topic explains the mechanism for saving and retrieving property values in code, but you won't normally have to write all the code described here. The ActiveX Control Interface Wizard can generate most of the code to save and retrieve your property values.

> **Note** Internet Explorer also allows you to save and restore a control's data using the PutProperty and GetProperty methods. For more information, see "Saving State Across Pages With Get Property / Put Property" in "Adding Internet Features to ActiveX Documents" in "Building ActiveX Documents".

Saving Property Values

Use the PropertyBag object to save and retrieve property values. The PropertyBag is provided as a standard interface for saving property values, independent of the data format the container uses to save its source data.

The following code example uses the Masked property, a Boolean property described in the related topic "Adding Properties to Controls."

```
Private Sub UserControl_WriteProperties(PropBag As _
      PropertyBag)
   ' Save the value of the Boolean Masked property.
   PropBag.WriteProperty "Masked", Masked, False
   ' . . . more properties . . .
End Sub
```

The WriteProperty method of the PropertyBag object takes three arguments. First is a string that identifies the property being saved, followed by value to be saved — usually supplied by accessing the property, as shown above.

> **Note** If the value you're saving is contained in the default property of a constituent control, and that property is of type Variant — for example, the Text property of a text box — you must specify the property name. That is, you must use `Text1.Text` instead of just `Text1`.

The last parameter is the default value for the property. In this case, the keyword False is supplied. Typically, you would create a global constant, such as PROPDEFAULT_MASKED, to contain this value, because you need to supply it in three different places, in the WriteProperties, ReadProperties, and InitProperties event procedures.

The Importance of Supplying Defaults

It may seem strange, at first, to be supplying a default property value when you're *saving* the value of a property. This is a courtesy to the user of your control, because it reduces the size of the .frm, .dob, .pag, or .ctl file belonging to the container of the control.

Visual Basic achieves this economy by writing out a line for the property only if the value is *different* from the default. Assuming that the default value of the Masked property is False, the WriteProperty method will write a line for the property only if the user has set it to True.

You can easily see how this technique reduces the size of .frm files by opening a new Standard EXE project, adding a CommandButton to Form1, and saving Form1.frm. Use a text editor such as Notepad or Wordpad to open Form1.frm, and compare the number of properties that were written to the file for Command1 to the number of properties in the Properties window for Command1.

Wherever possible, you should specify default values for the properties of your control when initializing, saving, and retrieving property values.

Retrieving Property Values

Property values are retrieved in the ReadProperties event of the UserControl object, as shown below.

```
Private Sub UserControl_ReadProperties(PropBag As _
      PropertyBag)
   On Error Resume Next
   ' Retrieve the value of the Masked property.
   Masked = PropBag.ReadProperty("Masked", False)
   ' . . . more properties . . .
End Sub
```

The ReadProperty method of the PropertyBag object takes two arguments: a string containing the name of the property, and a default value.

The ReadProperty method returns the saved property value, if there is one, or the default value if there is not. Assign the return value of the ReadProperty method to the property, as shown above, so that validation code in the Property Let statement is executed.

If you bypass the Property Let by assigning the property value directly to the private data member or constituent control property that stores the property value while your control is running, you will have to duplicate that validation code in the ReadProperties event.

> **Tip** Always include error trapping in the UserControl_ReadProperties event procedure, to protect your control from invalid property values that may have been entered by users editing the .frm file with text editors.

Properties That Are Read-Only at Run Time

If you create a property the user can set at design time, but which is read-only at run-time, you have a small problem in the ReadProperties event. You have to set the property value *once* at run time, to the value the user selected at design time.

An obvious way to solve this is to bypass the Property Let, but then you have no protection against invalid property values loaded from source files at design time. The correct solution to this problem is discussed in "Creating Design-Time-Only, Run-Time-Only, or Read-Only Run-Time Properties," later in this chapter.

Initializing Property Values

You can assign the initial value of a property in the InitProperties event of the UserControl object. InitProperties occurs only once for each control instance, when the instance is first placed on a container.

Thereafter, as the control instance is destroyed and re-created for form closing and opening, project unloading and loading, running the project, and so on, the control instance will only receive ReadProperties events. This is discussed in "Understanding Control Lifetime and Key Events," earlier in this chapter.

Be sure to initialize each property with the same default value you use when you save and retrieve the property value. Otherwise you will lose the benefits that defaults provide to your user, described in "The Importance of Supplying Defaults," earlier in this chapter.

> **Tip** The easiest way to ensure consistent use of default property values is to create global constants for them.

Saving and Retrieving Binary Data

Except for standard objects, such as Picture, the ReadProperty and WriteProperty methods have only limited ability to store and retrieve binary data. Storing binary data in strings is problematic because of Unicode conversion and line length limitations in the .frm file, but the two methods will accept arrays of type Byte.

If you're already keeping the data for a property in a Byte array, you can save it by passing the Byte array to the Value argument of the WriteProperty method:

```
' Private storage for the Blob property.
Private mbytBlob(0 To 1023) As Byte

Private Sub UserControl_WriteProperties(PropBag As _
      PropertyBag)
   ' Save the binary data for the Blob property.
   PropBag.WriteProperty "Blob", mbytBlob
   ' . . . more properties . . .
End Sub
```

The data will be saved in the .frx file. When retrieving the data, assign the return value from the ReadProperty method to `mbytBlob`. If `mbytBlob` is of variable length, you must save its size as a separate entry, using a name such as "BlobSize," so that you can retrieve the size and ReDim the array before retrieving the data. (You do not need to have a BlobSize property in order to do this.)

You can also use this technique to store any binary property data that you can manage to copy to a Byte array.

Exposing Properties of Constituent Controls

By default, the properties of the UserControl object — and the constituent controls you add to it — are not visible to the end user of your control. This gives you total freedom to determine your control's interface.

Frequently, however, you will want to implement properties of your control by simply delegating to existing properties of the UserControl object, or of the constituent controls you've placed on it. This topic explains the manual technique of exposing properties of the UserControl object or its constituent controls.

Understanding delegation and property mapping will help you get the most out of the ActiveX Control Interface Wizard, which is designed to automate as much of the process as possible. It will also enable you to deal with cases that are too complicated for the wizard to handle.

Exposing Properties by Delegating

Suppose you want to create a control that allows the end user to edit a field with a special format, such as a Driver's License Number. You start by placing a single text box on a UserControl, and naming it something catchy like txtBase.

Because your new control is an enhancement of a single Visual Basic control, you also resize txtBase to fit the UserControl. You do this in the UserControl's Resize event, as discussed in "Providing Appearance Using Constituent Controls," earlier in this chapter.

To create the BackColor property of your control, you can simply expose the BackColor property of the text box, as shown in this code fragment from the UserControl's code module.

```
Public Property Get BackColor() As OLE_COLOR
   BackColor = txtBase.BackColor
End Property

Public Property Let BackColor(ByVal NewColor _
      As OLE_COLOR)
   ' . . . property validation code . . .
   txtBase.BackColor = NewColor
   PropertyChanged "BackColor"
End Property
```

The purpose and importance of PropertyChanged are discussed in "Adding Properties to Controls," earlier in this chapter.

The BackColor property you create for your control simply saves its value in the BackColor property of the text box control. Methods are exposed in similar fashion, by delegating the work to the corresponding method of the control you're enhancing. Delegation is discussed in "Composing Objects," in Chapter 9, "Programming with Objects," in the *Microsoft Visual Basic 6.0 Programmer's Guide.*

> **Tip** When you use the OLE_COLOR data type for color properties, the Properties window will automatically show the ellipsis button that brings up the standard color selection dialog box. Standard property types are discussed in the related topic "Using Standard Control Property Types."

> **Note** User controls don't support Dynamic Data Exchange (DDE). If you delegate DDE-related properties such as LinkMode or events such as LinkOpen, they will be displayed at design time but will cause an error at run time.

> **Important** Because properties of the UserControl object and constituent controls are exposed by delegation, you cannot expose design-time-only properties such as Appearance and ClipControls. The settings you choose for such properties will be fixed for your ActiveX control.

Mapping Properties to Multiple Controls

Frequently you will want to map more than one constituent control property to a property of your control. Delegation gives you the flexibility to handle this situation.

Suppose, for example, that you've created your control's appearance by placing several check boxes, option buttons, and labels on a UserControl. It makes sense for the BackColor of your UserControl to be the background color of your control. However, it also makes sense for the BackColor properties of the constituent controls to match this color.

The following code fragment illustrates such an implementation:

```
Public Property Get BackColor() As OLE_COLOR
   BackColor = UserControl.BackColor
End Property

Public Property Let BackColor(ByVal NewColor _
      As OLE_COLOR)
   Dim objCtl As Object
   ' . . . property validation code . . .
   UserControl.BackColor = NewColor
   For Each objCtl In Controls
      If (TypeOf objCtl Is OptionButton) _
            Or (TypeOf objCtl Is CheckBox) _
            Or (TypeOf objCtl Is Label) _
         Then objCtl.BackColor = NewColor
   Next
   PropertyChanged "BackColor"
End Property
```

When the property value is read, the value is always supplied from the BackColor property of the UserControl. Always choose a single source to be used for the Property Get.

> **Note** When you give your control a property which the underlying UserControl object already possesses, using that property name in your code will refer to the new property you have defined, unless you qualify the property name with UserControl, as shown above.

For More Information Using the Controls collection to iterate over all constituent controls is discussed in "Control Creation Terminology," earlier in this chapter. The purpose and importance of PropertyChanged are discussed in "Adding Properties to Controls," earlier in this chapter.

Multiple BackColor Properties

The implementation above raises an interesting question. What if you want to provide the user of your control with a way to set the background color of all the text boxes on your control? You've already mapped BackColor to its most natural use, but you can always get creative with property names.

For example, you might add a TextBackColor property, modeled on the example above, that would set the BackColor properties of all the text boxes on your control. Choose one text box as the source of the TextBackColor, for the Property Get, and you're in business. (It doesn't make much sense to use the UserControl's BackColor for this purpose.)

Mapping to Multiple Object Properties

As another example of multiple property mapping, you might implement TextFont and LabelFont properties for the control described above. One property would control the font for all the labels, and the other for all the text boxes.

When implementing multiple mapped object properties, you can take advantage of multiple object references. Thus you might implement the LabelFont property as shown in the following code fragment:

```
Public Property Get LabelFont() As Font
   Set LabelFont = UserControl.Font
End Property

' Use Property Set for object properties.
Public Property Set LabelFont(ByVal NewFont As Font)
   Set UserControl.Font = NewFont
   SyncLabelFonts
   PropertyChanged "LabelFont"
End Property
```

```
Private Sub SyncLabelFonts()
   Dim objCtl As Object
   For Each objCtl In Controls
      If TypeOf objCtl Is Label Then
         Set objCtl.Font = UserControl.Font
      End If
   Next
End Sub
```

The code in the `SyncLabelFonts` helper function assigns to each Label control's Font property a reference to the UserControl object's Font object. Because all of the controls have references to the same Font object, changes to that font will be reflected in all the labels.

A helper function is used because the same code must be executed when your control is initialized, and when saved properties are read.

> **Note** The purpose and importance of PropertyChanged are discussed in "Adding Properties to Controls," earlier in this chapter.

The code to initialize, save, and retrieve the LabelFont property is shown below. Optionally, you can set the characteristics of the UserControl's font to match those of the container's font, as discussed in "Using the AmbientProperties Object to Stay Consistent with the Container," earlier in this chapter.

```
Private Sub UserControl_InitProperties()
   SyncLabelFonts
End Sub

Private Sub UserControl_ReadProperties(PropBag As _
      VB.PropertyBag)
   On Error Resume Next
   Set LabelFont = PropBag.ReadProperty("LabelFont")
End Sub

Private Sub UserControl_WriteProperties(PropBag As _
      VB.PropertyBag)
   PropBag.WriteProperty "LabelFont", LabelFont
End Sub
```

Because the Font object is a standard object, it can be saved and retrieved using PropertyBags.

The developer using your control can now use the Property window to set a font for the LabelFont property. Supposing that the name you give your control is MultiEdit, she can also use code like the following at run time:

```
Private Sub Command1_Click()
   YourControl1.LabelFont.Bold = True
   YourControl1.LabelFont.Name = "Monotype Sorts"
End Sub
```

The beauty of this code is that it never calls the Property Let for the LabelFont property, as you can verify by adding the code above to a UserControl that has several constituent Label controls, and putting breakpoints in the Property Get and Property Let.

When Visual Basic executes the first line above, the Property Get is called, returning a reference to the UserControl's Font object. The Bold property of the Font object is set, using this reference. Because the constituent Label controls all have references to the UserControl's Font object, the change is reflected immediately.

Don't Expose Constituent Controls as Properties

You might wonder why you shouldn't simply expose constituent controls whole. For example, if your UserControl has a text box control named Text1 on it, you might try to write the following:

```
' Kids, don't try this at home.
Property Get Text1() As TextBox
   Set Text1 = Text1
End Property
```

The user of your control could then access all the properties and methods of Text1, and you've only written one line of code.

The code above will not compile, because TextBox is not a public data type. But that's not the real reason this is a bad idea.

It might simplify your life to expose all the properties and methods of a constituent control, rather than selectively exposing them, but consider the experience that awaits the user of your control. He now has direct access to the Text property of Text1, bypassing any validation code you might have written in a Property Let. He can also change the height and width of the text box, which may completely wreck the code you've written in your UserControl_Resize event procedure.

All in all, the developer is likely to conclude that your control is too buggy to be worth using. But wait, there's more. If the developer uses your control with other development tools, such as Microsoft Excel or Microsoft Access, type library information for the constituent controls will not be available. All references to Text1 will be late bound, so your control will be not only buggy, but slow.

Exposing constituent controls also limits your ability to change your control's implementation in the future. For example, you might want to base a future version of your control on a different constituent control than the intrinsic TextBox control. Unless the properties and methods of this SuperTextBox exactly matched those of the intrinsic TextBox, your users would be unable to upgrade without rewriting their code.

It's good programming practice to expose only those constituent control properties required for the operation of your control. For example, if the text box mentioned above holds a user name, you might expose the value of Text1.Text through a UserName property.

Using the ActiveX Control Interface Wizard

When you have a large number of constituent controls, or even one constituent control with many properties you wish to expose, the ActiveX Control Interface Wizard can significantly reduce the amount of work required to expose constituent control properties.

Using the ActiveX Control Interface Wizard is discussed in the related topic "Properties You Should Provide," later in this chapter.

Using Standard Control Property Types

The code examples in the related topic "Exposing Properties of Constituent Controls" show the use of the standard types Font and OLE_COLOR to create properties that use standard, system-supplied property pages, which the user can access with the ellipsis button in the Properties window.

Whenever possible, use the standard data types and enumerations provided by Visual Basic as data types of your control's properties. This makes life easy for your users, by presenting consistent property value choices in the Properties window.

Standard Enumerations

The following code uses the standard enumeration for the MousePointer property.

```
Public Property Get MousePointer() As _
      MousePointerConstants
   MousePointer = UserControl.MousePointer
End Property

Public Property Let MousePointer(ByVal NewPointer As _
      MousePointerConstants)
   UserControl.MousePointer = NewPointer
   PropertyChanged "MousePointer"
End Property
```

When the MousePointer property appears in the Properties window, it will have the same enumeration as the MousePointer properties of other controls.

You can use the Object Browser to determine what enumerations are available in the Visual Basic type libraries.

> **Note** The purpose and importance of PropertyChanged are discussed in "Adding Properties to Controls," earlier in this chapter.

Standard Data Types

Visual Basic provides four standard data types of special interest to control authors.

OLE_COLOR

The OLE_COLOR data type is used for properties that return colors. When a property is declared as OLE_COLOR, the Properties window will display a color-picker dialog that allows the user to select the color for the property visually, rather than having to remember the numeric equivalent.

An example of the use of OLE_COLOR can be found in "Exposing Properties of Constituent Controls," earlier in this chapter.

OLE_COLOR is treated internally as a Long.

OLE_TRISTATE

The OLE_TRISTATE data type is used for three-state check boxes. If you're authoring a control with check box functionality, declare its Value property as OLE_TRISTATE.

OLE_TRISTATE is an enumeration with the following values:

- 0 – Unchecked
- 1 – Checked
- 2 – Gray

OLE_OPTEXCLUSIVE

If you're developing a control with option-button functionality, use the OLE_OPTEXCLUSIVE data type for the Value property of your control. This will cause your control's Value property to behave like that of the intrinsic OptionButton control. That is, when instances of your control are grouped, and the user clicks an unselected control instance, the currently selected instance's Value is automatically set to 0 (thus unselecting the button), and the Value of the clicked instance is set to 1.

This behavior is handled by the container. The container checks the Value property for each control it contains, and groups those that are of type OLE_OPTEXCLUSIVE.

> **Note** You must use the Procedure Attributes dialog box to make the Value property the default property, in order for the control host to enable the behavior described.

OLE_OPTEXCLUSIVE is handled as a Boolean type internally.

OLE_CANCELBOOL

Use this data type for an event argument that allows the user to cancel the event. For example, the standard KeyPress event passes a Cancel parameter as its last parameter. If the user sets this parameter to False, the event is canceled.

OLE_CANCELBOOL is handled as a Boolean type internally.

Creating Design-Time-Only, Run-Time-Only, or Read-Only Run-Time Properties

To create a property that can be read at run time, but can be set only at design time, implement the property using property procedures. In the Property Let or Property Set procedure, test the UserMode property of the AmbientProperties object. If UserMode is True, raise an error, as shown in the following code fragment:

```
Private mdblSerendipity As Double

Property Get Serendipity() As Double
   Serendipity = mdblSerendipity
End Property

Property Let Serendipity() As Double
   ' (Code to validate property values omitted.)
   If Ambient.UserMode Then
      Err.Raise Number:=382 _
         Description:= _
         "Let/Set not supported at run time."
   End If
   Serendipity = mdblSerendipity
   PropertyChanged "Serendipity"
End Property
```

To suppress a property completely at run time, you can also raise a "Property is not available at run time" error in Property Get.

> **Note** Implementing properties of the Variant data type requires all three property procedures, Property Get, Property Let, and Property Set, because the user can assign any data type, including object references, to the property. In that case, the error raised in Property Let must also be raised in Property Set.

Error Values to Use for Property Errors

The following error values are provided by Visual Basic and should be used when raising errors for read-only or write-only properties:

Err.Number	Err.Description
382	Let/Set not supported at run time.
383	Let/Set not supported at design time.
393	Get not supported at run time.
394	Get not supported at design time.

If a property is read-only at run time and UserMode is True, raise error 382 in the Property Let or Property Set procedure. If a property is not available at run time, raise error 382 in the Let or Set procedure and error 383 in the Get procedure. Likewise, if a property is not available at design time, raise error 393 in the Let or Set procedure and error 394 in the Get procedure.

Handling Read-Only Run-Time Properties in the ReadProperties Event

The recommended practice for the ReadProperties event is to assign the retrieved value to the property, so that the Property Let is invoked. This allows the validation code in the Property Let to handle invalid values the user has manually entered into the container's source file, as described in "Saving the Properties of Your Control," earlier in this chapter.

Clearly, this is problematic for read-only run-time properties. The solution is to bypass the Property Let, and assign the retrieved value directly to the private member or constituent control property. If the property accepts only certain values, you can use a helper function that can be called from both Property Let and ReadProperties.

The following code fragment illustrates these two solutions:

```
Private Sub UserControl_ReadProperties(PropBag As _
      PropertyBag)
   ' Always use error trapping in ReadProperties!
   On Error Resume Next
   ' Retrieve the value of the HasWidgets property,
   ' which is read-only at run time.
   mblnHasWidgets = _
      PropBag.ReadProperty("HasWidgets", False)
   If Err.Number <> 0 Then
      ' If the .frm file contained a value that caused
      '   a type mismatch (error 13), substitute the
      '   default value for the property.
      mblnHasWidgets = False
      ' When using On Error Resume Next, always
      '   reset Err.Number after an error.
      Err.Number = 0
   End If

   ' Retrieve the value of the Appearance property,
   ' which can be set at design time
   ' and has two valid values, Appears3D
   ' and AppearsFlat.  (These constants should be
   ' defined in a Public Enum.)
   mintAppearance = _
      PropBag.ReadProperty("Appearance", Appears3D)
   ' Validate the value retrieved from the .frm
   '   file.
```

```
    Call ValidateAppearance(mintAppearance)
    If Err.Number <> 0 Then
       ' If the .frm file contained an invalid integer
       '   value (error 380) or a value that caused a
       '   type mismatch (error 13), substitute the
       '   default value for the property.
       mintAppearance = Appears3D
       ' When using On Error Resume Next, always
       '   reset Err.Number after an error.
       Err.Number = 0
    End If

    ' . . . more properties . . .
End Sub
```

The Property Let for the Appearance property would call the same ValidateAppearance helper function used in the example above, but would not trap errors — thus the error would be raised at the line of code that assigned the invalid value. The helper function might look something like this:

```
Private Sub ValidateAppearance(ByVal Test As Integer)
   Select Case Test
      Case Appears3D
      Case AppearsFlat
      Case Else
         ' Error 380 is the standard "Invalid property
         '   value" error.
         Err.Raise 380
   End Select
End Sub
```

Important If the wrong data type is entered in the source file, a type mismatch error will occur. Thus, errors can occur even for a Boolean or numeric property. (This is why you should *always* use error trapping in ReadProperties.) You can trap the error with On Error Resume Next, as above, and substitute the default value for the property.

Creating Run-Time-Only Properties

You can create a property that is available only at run time by causing property procedures to fail during design time (that is, when the UserMode property of the AmbientProperties object is False).

Visual Basic's Properties window does not display properties that fail during design-time.

Tip You can open the Procedure Attributes dialog box, select your run-time-only property, click the Advanced button, and check "Don't show in Property Browser" to prevent the Properties window from interrogating the property. This keeps the Properties window from putting you in break mode every time it queries the property, which is a nuisance when you're debugging design-time behavior.

Marking a Property as the Properties Window Default

When you first place a new control instance on a form or other container, Visual Basic chooses a property to highlight the Properties window. This will be the same as the last property that was highlighted, if the new control has that property. Otherwise, Visual Basic uses the property marked as the *user interface default.*

If you don't specify this user interface default, Visual Basic highlights a property according to various internal criteria, such as the order in which you added properties to the type library.

To specify the user interface default for your control

1. In the UserControl code window, place the cursor in one of the property procedures for the property.
2. On the **Tools** menu, click **Procedure Attributes** to open the **Procedure Attributes** dialog box.
3. The property should be shown in the **Name** box. If not, use the **Name** box to select it.
4. Click the **Advanced** button to show advanced features. Check **User Interface Default** in the **Attributes** box, then click **OK** or **Apply**.

   Tip The best candidate for the user interface default is the property users will most often set. For example, the Interval property is the user interface default for the Timer control.

Grouping Properties by Category

The Properties window has two tabs, one showing all of a control's properties in alphabetical order, and one which organizes the properties into categories.

You can assign each of your control's properties to one of the existing categories, or create new categories. Assigning categories is highly recommended, because Visual Basic places all unassigned properties in the Misc category.

To assign a property to a property category

1. In the UserControl code window, place the cursor in one of the property procedures for the property you want to assign to a category.
2. On the **Tools** menu, click **Procedure Attributes** to open the **Procedure Attributes** dialog box.
3. The property should be shown in the **Name** box. If not, use the **Name** box to select it.
4. Click the **Advanced** button to show advanced features. Select the desired category in the **Property Category** box, then click **OK** or **Apply**.

You can create a new category by typing a category name in the Property Category box. The category will be created only for this control. You can use the same category name for other controls, but it must be entered separately for each control.

> **Tip** To reduce user confusion, assign properties to the same categories they appear in for other controls. If possible, use existing categories. Create new categories only when you have a group of related properties that will clearly be easier to use if grouped in a new category.

Properties You Should Provide

Recommended properties include Appearance, BackColor, BackStyle, BorderStyle, Enabled, Font, and ForeColor. It's also a good idea to implement properties commonly found on controls that provide functionality similar to yours.

In addition, you may wish to selectively implement properties of any constituent controls on your UserControl object, as discussed in "Exposing Properties of Constituent Controls," earlier in this chapter.

All of the above properties should use the appropriate data types or enumerations, as discussed in the related topics "Using Standard Control Property Types" and "Exposing Properties of Constituent Controls," earlier in this chapter.

> **Note** If you're authoring a control that provides its appearance using constituent controls, implementing the Appearance property is problematic. For most controls, the Appearance property is available only at design time — but you can only delegate to run-time properties of constituent controls.

Procedure IDs for Standard Properties

Every property or method in your type library has an identification number, called a procedure ID or DISPID. The property or method can be accessed either by name (late binding) or by DISPID (early binding).

Some properties and methods are important enough to have special DISPIDs, defined by the ActiveX specification. These standard procedure IDs are used by some programs and system functions to access standard properties of your control.

For example, there's a procedure ID for the method that displays an About Box for a control. Rather than rummaging through your type library for a method named AboutBox, Visual Basic calls this procedure ID. Your method can have any name at all, as long as it has the right procedure ID.

To assign a standard procedure ID to a property

1. On the **Tools** menu, click **Procedure Attributes** to open the **Procedure Attributes** dialog box.

2. In the **Name** box, select the property.

3. Click **Advanced** to expand the **Procedure Attributes** dialog box.
4. In the **Procedure ID** box, select the procedure ID you want to assign to the property. If the procedure ID you need is not in the list, enter the number in the **Procedure ID** box.

   Important Selecting (None) in the procedure ID box does not mean that the property or method will not have a procedure ID. It only means that you have not selected a particular procedure ID. Visual Basic assigns procedure IDs automatically to members marked (None).

One Procedure ID to a Customer

A property or method of a control can have only one procedure ID, and no other property or method of the control can have the same procedure ID.

That is, every control in your control component can have a default property (procedure ID = 0), but only one property on each control can have that procedure ID.

If you assign the same procedure ID to two different members, the one that comes first in the type library is the only one that can be accessed. The other might as well not exist.

Procedure IDs of Interest

It's always a good idea to assign the standard procedure ID to a property, if there is one. The Procedure Attributes dialog box lists procedure IDs by the property name they are usually associated with. You may find the following IDs of particular interest.

AboutBox

Allows you to specify a method that shows an About Box for your control, as discussed in "Adding an About Box to Your Control," earlier in this chapter. There is no particular method name associated with this ID.

Caption, Text

Either of these procedure IDs will give a property the Properties window behavior demonstrated by the Caption and Text properties of Visual Basic intrinsic controls. That is, when a user types a value into the Properties window, the new value will be reflected immediately in the control.

This means that your Property Let procedure will be called for each keystroke the user enters, receiving a complete new value each time.

The property you assign these to need not be called Caption or Text, although those properties represent the kind of functionality these procedure IDs were designed to support.

(Default)

The default property of a control is the one that will be accessed when no property has been specified. For example, the following assigns the string "Struthiomimus" to the (default) Caption property of Label1:

```
Label1 = "Struthiomimus"
```

Enabled

This procedure ID must be assigned to the Enabled property of your control, in order for its enabled/disabled behavior to match that of other controls. This is discussed in "Allowing Your Control to be Enabled or Disabled," earlier in this chapter.

For More Information The procedure IDs of interest to control authors are listed in the Procedure ID box of the Procedure Attributes dialog box. For a complete list of DISPIDs, consult the ActiveX specification.

Providing Useful Defaults

Whenever you implement a property with the same name as one of the standard ambient properties, such as BackColor, Font, and ForeColor, you should consider whether the value of the corresponding property of the AmbientProperties object would be a useful default.

You can see an example of this behavior by changing the size of the font on a Visual Basic form, and then adding a label or command button. The new control uses the form's current font settings as its default font settings. Most of the intrinsic controls follow this example.

If you're authoring a check box, option button, or label, setting the control's default BackColor to match AmbientProperties.BackColor might be a useful service to your users.

Clearly, this requires some thought about how controls are used. For example, on a text box the Font property would be a good candidate for ambient matching, while the BackColor property would not.

For More Information See "Using the AmbientProperties Object to Stay Consistent with the Container," earlier in this chapter.

Using the ActiveX Control Interface Wizard

The ActiveX Control Interface Wizard can assist you in determining what properties to provide, and in delegating to the appropriate constituent controls.

After you have placed all the constituent controls you're going to use on your UserControl, start the wizard and select your control. The wizard will examine your constituent controls, and produce a list of all the properties, methods, and events that appear in all their interfaces, plus those in the UserControl object's interface, and the standard properties listed above. You can select from this list those properties, methods, and events you want in your control's interface.

The wizard will produce default mappings of your control's properties to properties of the UserControl object or of constituent controls. In subsequent steps, you can modify these mappings.

When you have finished determining your control's interface and delegating to existing properties, the wizard will generate property procedure code to implement the properties, using the correct data types for standard properties, and including delegation code for all your property mappings, enormously reducing the amount of work required to generate a full-featured control.

Adding Methods to Controls

You implement methods of your ActiveX control by adding Public Sub and Function procedures to the code module of the UserControl that forms the basis of your control class.

By default, the only methods your control will have are the extender methods provided by the container, such as the Move method. You can decide what additional methods your control needs, and add code to implement them.

Standard Methods

If your control is not invisible at run time, you should provide a Refresh method. This method should simply call UserControl.Refresh. For user-drawn controls, this will raise the Paint event; for controls built using constituent controls, it will force a refresh of the constituent controls.

It's also a good idea to implement methods commonly found on controls that provide functionality similar to yours. In addition, you may wish to selectively implement methods of the UserControl object, or of its constituent controls.

Using the ActiveX Control Interface Wizard

The ActiveX Control Interface Wizard can assist you in determining what methods to provide, and in delegating to the appropriate constituent controls.

After you have placed all the constituent controls you're going to use on your UserControl, start the wizard and select your control. The wizard will examine your constituent controls, and produce a list of all the properties, methods, and events that appear in all their interfaces, plus those in the UserControl object's interface. You can select from this list those properties, methods, and events you want in your control's interface.

The wizard will produce default mappings of your control's methods to methods of the UserControl object or of constituent controls. In subsequent steps, you can modify these mappings.

When you have finished with determining your control's interface, and delegating to existing methods, the wizard will generate Sub and Function procedures to implement the properties, including delegation code for all your mappings. This greatly reduces the amount of work required to generate a full-featured control.

Raising Events from Controls

It's important to distinguish between the events received by your UserControl object (or by the controls it contains) and the events your control raises. Events your control *receives* are opportunities for you to do something interesting; events your control *raises* provide opportunities for the developer who uses your control to do something interesting.

This principle is demonstrated, with illustrations, in the step-by-step procedure "Adding an Event to the ShapeLabel Control," in Chapter 4, "Creating an ActiveX Control."

For More Information General information on using events in components, including restrictions on arguments, can be found in "Adding Events to Classes" in Chapter 6, "General Principles of Component Design."

Exposing Events of Constituent Controls

The mechanism for exposing events is different from the delegation used to expose properties and methods. You expose an event in a constituent control by raising your own event, as in the following code fragment from a UserControl code module:

```
' Declaration of your control's Click event.
Public Event Click()

' When the txtBase text box control raises a Click,
'    your control forwards it by raising the Click
'    event you declared.
Private Sub txtBase_Click()
   RaiseEvent Click
End Sub

' You may also want to raise your control's Click event
'    when a user clicks on the UserControl object.
Private Sub UserControl_Click()
   RaiseEvent Click
End Sub
```

Notice that your Click event may be raised from multiple locations in your code. You can add your own code before and after raising the Click event.

The Difference Between Events and Properties or Methods

It may help to think of properties and methods as *incoming,* and events as *outgoing*. That is, methods are invoked from outside your control, by the developer who's using your control. Thus, the developer invokes a method of your UserControl object, and you respond by delegating to the method of your constituent control.

By contrast, events originate in your control and are propagated outward to the developer, so that she can execute code in her event procedures. Thus, your UserControl object responds to a click event from one of its constituent controls by raising its own Click event, thus forwarding the event outward to the developer.

Mouse Events and Translating Coordinates

The MouseDown, MouseMove, and MouseUp event procedures for the UserControl object have arguments giving the event location in the ScaleMode of the UserControl. Before raising your control's MouseDown, MouseMove, and MouseUp events, you must translate the event location to the coordinates of the container.

How do you know what the container's ScaleMode is? You don't. You don't even know if the container has a ScaleMode property. Fortunately, you don't have to worry about that, because Visual Basic provides the ScaleX and ScaleY methods for translating coordinates.

The following code fragment shows how to expose the MouseMove event from a UserControl whose ScaleMode is Twips. It assumes that the MouseMove event has been declared with the correct parameters (you can use the ActiveX Control Interface Wizard to generate event declarations).

```
Private Sub UserControl_MouseMove(Button As Integer, _
      Shift As Integer, X As Single, Y As Single)    RaiseEvent MouseMove(Button, Shift, _
      ScaleX(X, vbTwips, vbContainerPosition), _
      ScaleY(Y, vbTwips, vbContainerPosition))
End Sub
```

The ScaleX method translates from vbTwips to whatever the coordinate system of the container is; this information is obtained by Visual Basic using low-level ActiveX calls. The return value from ScaleX (the new X coordinate) is passed as the X argument of the MouseMove event.

If you change the ScaleMode of your UserControl at run time, you should use UserControl.ScaleMode instead of vbTwips in the code above, so that the correct translation is done regardless of current ScaleMode setting.

Importance of Testing

The code above, with its explicit vbTwips, will have to be changed if the ScaleMode of the UserControl is permanently changed at design time. It's important to test your control's response to mouse moves on forms with a variety of ScaleMode settings, to ensure that ScaleX and ScaleY have the correct arguments.

Constituent Controls

If your control includes constituent controls that have mouse events, you'll have to raise your control's mouse events there, too. Otherwise there will appear to be dead spots on your control, where the mouse events don't occur.

Constituent control mouse events are slightly more complicated, because they provide X and Y in the coordinates of the constituent control rather than the UserControl. The following code fragment shows how this is handled when the constituent control has the same ScaleMode as the UserControl:

```
Private Sub Label1_MouseMove(Button As Integer, _
      Shift As Integer, X As Single, Y As Single)
   RaiseEvent MouseMove(Button, Shift, _
      ScaleX(X + Label1.Left, _
         vbTwips, vbContainerPosition), _
      ScaleY(Y + Label1.Top, _
         vbTwips, vbContainerPosition))
End Sub
```

Adding the Left and Top properties of Label1 to the X and Y coordinates translates them to UserControl coordinates; ScaleX and ScaleY then transform the results to container coordinates.

If the UserControl's ScaleMode were set to Pixels, you would first have to call ScaleX and ScaleY to translate X and Y to pixels, before adding the results to Label1.Top and Label1.Left. The results of the addition would then be passed to ScaleX and ScaleY, as above.

Other Events That Provide Position

If you create events of your own that pass location information to the container, you must use the same technique to transform the locations into the container's coordinates. If you want to pass width and height information, use vbContainerSize instead of vbContainerPosition when calling ScaleX and ScaleY.

Using the ActiveX Control Interface Wizard

The ActiveX Control Interface Wizard can greatly simplify the task of forwarding events. This is discussed in the related topic "Events Your Control Should Raise."

Events the Container Provides for Your Control

The container's extender object may provide events for the benefit of developers using your control. If your control is used with Visual Basic, the user of your control gets four such events without any work on your part: GotFocus, LostFocus, DragOver, and DragDrop.

You don't need to be concerned with extender events. They are invisible to your control, and you cannot put code in their event procedures.

Specifying a Default Event for the Code Window

The first time you select a control instance in the Object box of the container's code window, Visual Basic selects an event to highlight in the Procedure box, and inserts into the code window an event procedure for that event.

If a control doesn't specify this *user interface default*, Visual Basic selects the first event alphabetically.

Note While you're working with a new control in the development environment, before you've specified the user interface default, Visual Basic may sometimes select the default event based on internal considerations, such as which event went into the type library first.

To specify the user interface default for your control's events

1. In the UserControl code window, place the cursor on the declaration of the event you want to specify as the user interface default.
2. On the **Tools** menu, click **Procedure Attributes** to open the **Procedure Attributes** dialog box.
3. The property should be shown in the **Name** box. If not, use the **Name** box to select it.
4. Click the **Advanced** button to show advanced features. Check **User Interface Default** in the **Attributes** box, then click **OK** or **Apply**.

   Tip You can only mark one event as the user interface default. Choose the event users will most frequently place code in.

Events Your Control Should Raise

Recommended events include Click, DblClick, KeyDown, KeyPress, KeyUp, MouseDown, MouseMove, and MouseUp. It's also a good idea to implement events commonly found on controls that provide functionality similar to yours.

In addition, you may wish to selectively implement events of the constituent controls on your UserControl object, or of the UserControl object itself.

It's important to use the same arguments, with the same data types, as these standard events, as discussed in "Exposing Events of Constituent Controls," earlier in this chapter. Data types are discussed in "Using Standard Control Property Types," earlier in this chapter.

Using the ActiveX Control Interface Wizard

The ActiveX Control Interface Wizard can assist you in determining what events to provide, and in forwarding the appropriate constituent control events.

After you have placed all the constituent controls you're going to use on your UserControl, start the wizard and select your control. The wizard will examine your constituent controls, and produce a list of all the properties, methods, and events that appear in all their interfaces, plus those in the UserControl object's interface, and the standard events listed above. You can select from this list those properties, methods, and events you want in your control's interface.

The wizard will produce default mappings of your control's events to events of the UserControl object or of constituent controls. In subsequent steps, you can modify these mappings.

When you have finished determining your control's interface, the wizard will generate code to raise the events you've selected, using the correct arguments and data types for standard events, and including event forwarding code for all your event mappings. This enormously reduces the amount of work required to generate a full-featured control.

Providing Named Constants for Your Control

As with other component types, public enumerations can be shared by all of the controls in a control component (.ocx file). Place public Enums for your component in any UserControl code module.

"Providing Named Constants for Your Component," in Chapter 6, "General Principles of Component Design," discusses techniques for providing constants, validating constants in properties, and so forth. See that topic for general information on the subject.

There are two additional factors specific to control components:

- Enum member names are used in the Properties window.
- Global objects cannot be used to simulate string constants.

Enum Member Names in the Properties Window

As an example of the first factor, consider the following Enum and property:

```
Public Enum DINOSAUR
   dnoTyrannosaur
   dnoVelociraptor
   dnoTriceratops
End Enum

Private mdnoFavoriteDinosaur As DINOSAUR

Public Property Get FavoriteDinosaur() As DINOSAUR
   FavoriteDinosaur = mdnoFavoriteDinosaur
End Property

Public Property Let FavoriteDinosaur(ByVal NewDino _
      As DINOSAUR
   mdnoFavoriteDinosaur = NewDino
   PropertyChanged "FavoriteDinosaur"
End Property
```

When you set the FavoriteDinosaur property in the Properties window, the drop down list will contain dnoTyrannosaur, dnoVelociraptor, and dnoTriceratops.

As you can see, there's a fine tradeoff here between names that will look good in the drop down, and names that will avoid collisions with names used in Enums for other components.

As a rule of thumb, don't abandon the prefix ("dno" in the example above) that groups constants in global lists. The prefix provides at least some protection from name conflicts. On the other hand, don't make your prefixes so long that they obscure the names.

Cannot Simulate String Constants Using Global Objects

Class modules in control components can have one of two values of the Instancing property, Private or PublicNotCreatable. The Instancing values that enable global objects are not available in control components, so it is not possible to simulate string constants using properties of global objects, as described in "Providing Named Constants for Your Component," in Chapter 6, "General Principles of Component Design."

Setting Up a New Control Project and Test Project

As discussed in "Two Ways to Package ActiveX Controls," earlier in this chapter, Visual Basic enables you to author shareable control components (.ocx files), or to include private controls as .ctl files in your component project. These two scenarios have different testing requirements.

Testing Private Controls

The only way to test a private control is to place it on a form within the project. Of course, there may be several forms in the project that use the control, but it is recommended that you create a separate form for testing your private controls.

The reason for this is that simply using the control is not likely to test it exhaustively. Once your application or component is compiled, user actions you have not anticipated may cause unexpected results in your control's code.

By including a test form that exercises all of your control's interface members, you can test your control more thoroughly.

Testing Controls in Control Components

When you're developing a control component, you need thorough test coverage of all aspects of your control. This coverage is best provided using a separate test project. Visual Basic allows you to run multiple projects, so you can load your test project and ActiveX control project and run them together for debugging purposes.

Once you have compiled your control component, the test project can be used as a test harness for quality assurance test suites.

If you use the ActiveX Control Interface Wizard to build the interface and generate code for your control, you can get a test project created by simply checking an option on the wizard's final screen.

Examples of creating a new ActiveX control project and a test project can be found in the step-by-step procedures "Creating the ControlDemo Project" and "Adding the TestCtlDemo Project," in Chapter 4, "Creating an ActiveX Control."

> **Tip** You may prefer to author your controls as private controls in a Standard EXE project, and to test them by placing them on forms within the project. When you're ready to compile an .ocx file, you can remove the .ctl files from the Standard EXE project and add them to an ActiveX control project.
>
> You can then set up the Standard EXE project as a test harness, using the Controls tab of the Components dialog box to add your controls to the Toolbox, as described in "Compiling the ControlDemo Component," in Chapter 4, "Creating an ActiveX Control."

For More Information "Two Ways to Package ActiveX Controls," earlier in this chapter, lists several reasons why you might want to create a control component, even if you're just distributing controls as part of your own applications.

Creating Robust Controls

For your user, the three most important things about an ActiveX control are robustness, robustness, and robustness. Because a control component runs in the process space of an application that uses it, fatal errors in your controls are also fatal errors for the application.

The following lists of DOs and DON'Ts are by no means all-inclusive. They only provide a starting point for producing robust controls.

Error Handling

DO	DON'T
Provide thorough error handling in every event procedure you put code in, whether the event belongs to the UserControl or to a constituent control. In particular, provide thorough error handling in the UserControl's Paint, Resize, and Terminate events.	Raise errors in any event procedures.

Unhandled errors in event procedures will be fatal to your control component, and the application using it, because there will never be a procedure on the call stack that can handle the errors.

It's perfectly safe to raise errors in property procedures and methods, because properties and methods are always invoked by other procedures, and errors you raise can be handled by the user in those procedures.

Object Models

If your control component includes dependent objects, such as a collection of ToolbarButton objects for a Toolbar control:

DO	DON'T
Create wrapper classes for collections of such objects, as described in "General Principles of Component Design" and "Standards and Guidelines."	Use the Collection object without a wrapper class. The Collection object accepts any variant, meaning your users could accidentally insert objects that might cause errors in your control's code.
Use property procedures for collection properties.	Implement such properties as simple data members.

For example, if you create a ToolbarButtons class as the wrapper class for a collection of ToolbarButton objects, add the property to your UserControl object as a read-only property procedure:

```
Private mToolbarButtons As ToolbarButtons

Property Get ToolbarButtons() As ToolbarButtons
   Set ToolbarButtons = mToolbarButtons
End Property

Private Sub UserControl_Initialize()
   Set mToolbarButtons = New ToolbarButtons
End Sub
```

By contrast, the following implementation allows your user to accidentally set ToolbarButtons to Nothing, destroying the collection:

```
Public ToolbarButtons As New ToolbarButtons
```

Implementing Properties

DO implement properties using property procedures, instead of public data members.

You can use Property Let to validate property values. If you use public data members, you'll have to check the data every time you use it; and if that happens in an event procedure, you won't be able to raise an error without bringing down the application that's using your control component.

In addition, your properties will not work correctly in the Properties window and Property Pages dialog box, as discussed in "Adding Properties to Your Control," earlier in this chapter.

Debugging Controls

The most important difference between debugging controls and debugging other objects is that some of the code in your control must execute while the form a control instance is placed on is in design mode.

For example, the code in the property procedures you use to implement your control's properties must execute when the developer using your control sets its properties using the Properties window.

Code that saves and retrieves your control's property values must also run at design time, whenever the user loads a form containing an instance of the control, puts the project in Run mode, or saves the project to disk.

Code in the Resize event (or the Paint event, for user-drawn controls) must run at design time to provide the design-time appearance of your control.

You can see this feature in action in the step-by-step procedure "Running the ShapeLabel Control at Design Time," in Chapter 4, "Creating an ActiveX Control."

For More Information General information on debugging components can be found in Chapter 7, "Debugging, Testing, and Deploying Components."

Running Code at Design Time

To put a control you're authoring into a state such that its code can execute at design time, you must close the control's visual designer, by clicking the Close box or pressing CTRL+F4.

When the designer is closed, Visual Basic enables the control's icon in the Toolbox, so that you can add instances of the control to forms for testing.

If code in your control hits a break point at design time, for example during a Property Let invoked by the Properties window, Visual Basic enters break mode, just as it would if your project were running. When you press F5 to continue execution, the code in your control resumes execution. Visual Basic remains in design mode.

You can see this by setting a break point in a property procedure, and then placing an instance of your control on a test form.

Making Changes to Existing Controls

When you open the UserControl designer for a control, Visual Basic disables all instances of the control and grays the control's icon in the Toolbox. If you have a test form open with instances of the control on it, Visual Basic covers the disabled control instances with cross-hatching.

You can also disable control instances by certain changes to code in the control's code window, such as adding a new property or method, or adding code to a previously unused event procedure.

Once a control instance has been disabled in this fashion, it cannot execute code. It will not even receive a Terminate event.

Refreshing Control Instances

When you close the UserControl designer, the disabled instances of the control are quietly destroyed (they get no more events) and replaced with fresh instances. You can see this by putting Debug.Print statements in the Initialize and Terminate events of a control.

You can also refresh the control instances by right-clicking the test form and selecting Update UserControls from the context menu. If there are any control designers open, they will be closed before the control instances are refreshed.

For More Information General information on debugging components can be found in Chapter 7, "Debugging, Testing, and Distributing Components."

Distributing Controls

As discussed in "Two Ways to Package ActiveX Controls," earlier in this chapter, Visual Basic lets you author shareable control components (.ocx files), or simply include private controls as .ctl files in the project for your application or component.

This topic and its related topics focus on distribution, versioning, and licensing issues for control components. Private controls are compiled directly into an executable or component, and are distributed along with it. Being private, they also have no versioning or licensing issues.

Distributing Control Components

When you distribute a control component, you're providing a tool other developers can use in their applications. Versioning issues address the question of how you update that tool without breaking your customers' code.

Because you're providing a tool, instead of a finished application, you have licensing issues to consider. You have to decide whether to include licensing support for your control. If you plan on building your controls using licensed controls from other authors, you need to consider how that affects your distribution plans.

Because the tool you're creating is an-process component ("ocx" is really just another way to spell DLL), you have to select a base address that will minimize memory conflicts, and thus avoid performance problems.

Finally, because the tool you're creating uses the Visual Basic run-time DLL, and possibly other support files, you have to create a Setup program.

Setup is covered in the remainder of this topic. The important subject of base addresses is discussed in "Setting Base Addresses for In-Process Components," in Chapter 7, "Debugging, Testing, and Deploying Components."

Important Be sure to set the description for each control in your control component. Some clients, such as Visual Basic, represent the entire .ocx file using the string you enter in the Project Description box of the Project Properties dialog box, but others display the browser strings for the individual controls. See "Providing Help and Browser Strings for Objects," in Chapter 7, "Debugging, Testing, and Deploying Components."

Creating Setup for ActiveX Control Components

ActiveX controls created with Visual Basic require the Visual Basic run-time DLL. Depending on what constituent controls you use, you may require additional support files. To ensure that you distribute all the necessary support files, using SetupWizard is recommended.

For the most part, using SetupWizard for control components is no different from using it for any other component created using Visual Basic. This subject is thoroughly covered in Chapter 7, "Debugging, Testing, and Deploying Components."

If you plan to use your control component for Internet or intranet development, you can obtain the most up-to-date information on setup options from the Microsoft Visual Basic Web site.

For More Information The SetupWizard is introduced in Chapter 17, "Distributing Your Applications," in the *Microsoft Visual Basic 6.0 Programmer's Guide.*

Licensing Issues for Controls

Licensing for controls is a sensitive issue. After you've spent hundreds of hours developing a control, what if somebody else puts an instance of it on a UserControl, exposes all the properties, methods, and events, adds one or two trivial properties, then compiles and sells it as a new control?

Visual Basic's licensing support protects your investment. When you add licensing support to your control component, a license key is compiled into it. This key covers all the controls in the component.

Running your Setup program transfers the license key to another computer's registry, allowing your controls to be used for development. Simply copying your .ocx file to another computer and registering it does not transfer the license key, so the controls cannot be used.

To add licensing support to your control project

- On the **Project** menu, click **<MyProject> Properties** to open the **Project Properties** dialog box. Select the **General** tab, check **Require License Key**, then click **OK**.

When you make the .ocx file, Visual Basic will create a .vbl file containing the registry key for licensing your control component. When you use the Package and Deployment wizard to create a setup for your .ocx, the .vbl file is automatically included in the setup procedure.

How Licensing Works

When a developer purchases your control component and runs your Setup program, the license key is added to the registry on her computer.

Thereafter, whenever the developer puts an instance of your control on a form, Visual Basic (or any other developer's tool) tells the control to create itself using the registry key.

If a developer has obtained a copy of your control component, but not the registry key, the control cannot create instances of itself in the development environment.

When a Developer Distributes Applications

When the developer compiles a program that uses one of your controls, the license key for your component is compiled in. When she creates a Setup for the program, your .ocx is included. Users can then purchase the compiled program and run Setup. Your control is installed on each user's machine — but your license key is not added to the registry.

Each time a user runs the program, the Visual Basic run-time DLL asks your control to create a run-time instance of itself, and passes it the key that was compiled into the program. Your control doesn't have to check the registry, because Visual Basic passed it the key.

Thus the user can run a compiled application without having to have the control component's license key in the registry.

Licensing and the User

Suppose the user later obtains a copy of Visual Basic. Noticing that your control component is installed on his computer, he adds your .ocx file to a project.

The first time he tries to put an instance of one of your controls on a form, Visual Basic tells the control to create itself using the registry key. The key is not there, so the control component can't be used in the development environment.

Licensing and General-Purpose User Applications

When desktop applications such as Microsoft Word and Microsoft Excel create control instances on documents or user forms, they tell the control to create an instance of itself using the license key in the registry. This means that a licensed control cannot be used by an end user unless the user has purchased your control component and installed it.

User documents cannot have the license key compiled into them. Suppose the user of a desktop application gives a coworker a copy of your control component along with a document that contains one of your controls. When the document is opened, the control will be asked to create its run-time instance — using the registry key.

In other words, the coworker must also have purchased and installed your control component. Otherwise, when the document is opened, the control instance cannot be created.

Corporate developers who author ActiveX controls for use by end users within their companies may find it more convenient to omit licensing support. This will make it easier for end users to distribute documents containing controls.

Licensing and the Control Author

Now suppose that someone who purchased your control component decides to use one of your controls to author a new control of her own. As with any other program, when she compiles her control component, your license key is compiled in. SetupWizard creates a license key for the new component, but does not add *your* license key to the setup program.

When a developer installs this new code component, its license key is placed in the registry. The developer then runs Visual Basic, and attempts to put an instance of the control on a form.

The control is asked to create itself using the registry key. In turn, it asks its *constituent controls* to create themselves using their registry keys. Your control doesn't find its license key in the registry, so control creation fails.

Distributing Controls That Use Licensed Controls

If the control author wishes to distribute a new control that uses a control you authored, she must inform purchasers that in order to use her control, they must have your control component installed on their computers.

Alternatively, the control author might negotiate with you for the right to distribute your license key along with her own, in the setup program for her control.

In either case, both license keys will be installed on a developer's machine, so the developer can create design-time instances of the second author's controls. When those controls are compiled into an executable program, both license keys are compiled in.

When the program is subsequently installed by a user and run, the second author's control is asked to create itself. Its constituent controls are also asked to create themselves, and passed their license keys. (And so on, if *your* control uses constituent controls with license keys.)

> **Note** Of the ActiveX controls included with the Professional Edition of Visual Basic, only the DBGrid control requires a license key on a developer's computer. For example, if you use the TreeView control as a constituent control, anyone who is licensed to use your control is licensed to use TreeView *as part of your control.* However, remember that your Microsoft License Agreement requires that you add significant and primary functionality to any redistributable, such as TreeView, in order to legally distribute it as part of software you develop.

For More Information Licensing and distribution of constituent controls, including those supplied with the Professional Edition of Visual Basic, is discussed in "Controls You Can Use As Constituent Controls," earlier in this chapter.

Licensing and the Internet

Licensed controls can be used on World Wide Web pages, in conjunction with browsers that support control licensing. Both the control component and the license key must be available to be downloaded to the computer of the person accessing a Web page.

The downloaded license key is not added to the registry. Instead, browser asks the control to create a run-time instance of itself, and passes it the downloaded license key.

The owner of the Web server that uses your control must have purchased and installed your control, just as a developer would, in order to supply both control and license.

If the license is not available, control creation will fail, and the browser will receive a standard control creation error. Whether the browser passes this message along to the person accessing the Web page, or simply ignores it, depends on the person who developed the browser.

> **Note** Of the ActiveX controls included with the Professional Edition of Visual Basic, only the DBGrid control requires a license key on a Web server. For example, if you use the TreeView control as a constituent control, anyone who is licensed to use your control is licensed to use TreeView *as part of your control.* However, remember that your Microsoft License Agreement requires that you add significant and primary functionality to any redistributable, such as TreeView, in order to legally distribute it as part of software you develop.

For More Information See "Controls You Can Use As Constituent Controls," earlier in this chapter.

Versioning Issues for Controls

When you create a new version of a control, there are several areas of backward compatibility you must address:

- Your controls interface; that is, its properties, methods, and events.
- UserControl properties that affect control behavior.
- Whether property values are saved and retrieved.
- Procedure attribute settings.

Interface Compatibility

You can add new properties, methods, and events without breaking applications compiled using earlier versions of your control component. However, you cannot remove members from the interface, or change the arguments of members.

You can use Visual Basic's Version Compatibility feature to avoid creating incompatible interfaces. On the Component tab of the Project Properties dialog box, click Binary Compatibility in the Version Compatibility box. This enables a text box in which you can enter the path and file name of the previous version of your component.

The default value in this text box is the last location where you built the component. If you are going to continue using that location to build the new version of your control component, it's a good idea to place a copy of your previous version in another location, and then enter that location in the text box.

For More Information Interface compatibility and the use of the Version Compatible Component box are discussed in "Version Compatibility in ActiveX Components," in Chapter 6, "General Principles of Component Design."

UserControl Properties

Be careful when changing properties of the UserControl object, such as ControlContainer. If a previous version of your control had this property set to True, so that developers could use the control to contain other controls, and you change the property to False in a subsequent version, existing applications may no longer work correctly if the new version is installed on the same computer.

Saving and Retrieving Property Values

You may retain a property for backward compatibility, but stop mentioning it in your Help file, and mark it as Hidden using the Procedure Attributes dialog box.

You can stop saving the value of such obsolete properties in the WriteProperties event, but you should continue to load their values in the ReadProperties event. If you stop loading a property value, you will break any previously compiled application that used the property.

Procedure Attribute Settings

Changing attributes of a procedure may break applications that were compiled using previous versions of your control. For example, it you use the Procedure Attributes dialog to change the default property or method of a control, code that relied on the default will no longer work.

Compiled Applications

In some cases, changing properties in a new version of your control will have no effect on applications that were compiled with an earlier version. This is because some services are provided by the container and are set when the application is compiled. Even though the settings have been changed in the new version of your control, the container won't initialize these properties.

Properties that are provided by the container may include Alignable, CanGetFocus, ControlContainer, DefaultCancel, ForwardFocus, Public, ToolboxBitmap, and Visible. If you change any of these properties in a later version of your control, you will need to recompile any applications that use the control.

Localizing Controls

You can increase the market for your control component by *localizing* it. A localized control displays text — captions, titles, and error messages — using the language of the locale in which the control is used for application development, rather than the language of the locale in which it was authored.

This topic examines localization issues specific to ActiveX controls. General localization issues are discussed in Chapter 16, "International Issues," in the *Microsoft Visual Basic 6.0 Programmer's Guide.*

Using the LocaleID

When you compile an executable with Visual Basic, the LocaleID (also referred to as the LCID) of the Visual Basic version is compiled in. Thus an application compiled with the German version of Visual Basic will contain &H0407, the LocaleID for Germany.

In the same way, the LocaleID is compiled into an ActiveX control component created with Visual Basic. This becomes the default LocaleID for your controls. If this were the end of the story, you would have to compile a new version of your component, using the correct version of Visual Basic, for every locale in which you wanted to distribute it.

Fortunately, control components are more flexible than compiled applications. Your component can be used with versions of Visual Basic for any locale, and even with development tools that support other locales, because they can determine the correct LocaleID at run time.

Discovering the LocaleID

The LocaleID property of the AmbientProperties object returns the LocaleID of the program your control was used in. The AmbientProperties object is available as a property of the UserControl object, as described in "Using the AmbientProperties Object to Stay Consistent with the Container," earlier in this chapter.

You can test the Ambient property as soon as an instance of your control is sited on the container; that is, in the InitProperties or ReadProperties events. Once you know the LocaleID, you can call code to load locale-specific captions, error message text, and so forth from a resource file or satellite DLL, as described later in this topic.

You need to call this code in both events, because the InitProperties event occurs only when a control instance is first placed on a container. Thereafter the control instance receives the ReadProperties event instead, as discussed in "Understanding Control Lifetime and Key Events," earlier in this chapter.

You should also call your locale code in the AmbientChanged event, because your control could be used in an application that resets its locale according to Windows Control Panel settings, which can be changed by the user at any time. Your control could also receive AmbientChanged events if it's used as a constituent control, as described later in this topic.

Avoid Accessing Constituent Controls in the Initialize Event

The constituent controls on your UserControl discover the LocaleID by checking the AmbientProperties object which the UserControl, like any good container, makes available to them. This happens automatically, with no effort on your part.

When the Initialize event occurs, your control has been created, and all the constituent controls have been created and sited on your control's UserControl object. However, your control has not yet been sited on the container, so the UserControl cannot supply the correct LocaleID to the constituent controls.

If code in the Initialize event accesses the properties and methods of the constituent controls, their responses will reflect the LocaleID of the version of Visual Basic you used to compile your component, rather than the LocaleID of the application in which your control is compiled. For example, a method call might return a string in the wrong language.

To avoid this, you should not access constituent controls in the Initialize event.

Responding to the AmbientChanged Event

The AmbientChanged event occurs whenever an Ambient property changes on the container your control has been placed on, as discussed in "Using the AmbientProperties Object to Stay Consistent with the Container," earlier in this chapter.

Applications compiled with Visual Basic use the LocaleID of the version of Visual Basic that compiled them. However, your control could be used in an application written using a development tool such as Microsoft Visual C++, in which it is possible to change an application's LocaleID in response to system messages.

For example, if a user opens the Control Panel and changes the locale, an application would receive a notification of the change, and reset itself accordingly. Your controls can handle this situation by including code to change locale dynamically, as in the following example.

```
Private Sub UserControl_AmbientChanged( _
      PropertyName As String)
   Select Case PropertyName
      Case "LocaleID"
         ' Code to load localized captions,
         ' messages, and so forth from a resource
         ' file or satellite DLL, as described below.

      ' Case statements for other properties.

   End Select
End Sub
```

A change in the locale can also occur if you use your control as a constituent of another control. As described above, constituent controls don't get the correct LocaleID when they're first sited on a UserControl object. When the outermost control has been sited on the application's form, all the constituent controls will receive AmbientChanged events with the correct LocaleID.

Base Language and Satellite DLLs

The most flexible localization technique is to compile your control component with the default text strings and error messages in the language of the locale you expect to be your largest market. Place text strings and error messages for other locales in satellite ActiveX DLLs, one for each locale.

This scheme makes your component very attractive to developers who create versions of their programs for multiple languages, because they can work with multiple locales on one development machine.

Satellite DLLs are also attractive to users in multilingual countries. Such users may have programs compiled by programmers in different locales; if two such programs use your control component, satellite DLLs allow both programs to coexist on a user's computer.

> **Important** Your control should not raise an error if the requested satellite DLL is not found, as this could cause the entire application to fail. In the event the satellite DLL is not available, simply use the default locale in which your control component was built.

Naming Satellite DLLs

If you use an open-ended naming convention for your satellite DLLs, you can supply additional DLLs later without recompiling your program. An example of such a naming convention would be to include the LocaleID in the DLL names. Using this convention, your satellite DLLs for the Belgian French, German, and US English locales might be named MyControls20C.dll, MyControls407.dll and MyControls409.dll.

If you use Windows API calls to load and extract resources from your satellite DLLs, you can create the name of the DLL to be loaded by converting the LocaleID to a string, and appending it to a base name. (Note that the examples above use the hexadecimal representation of the LocaleID.)

As an alternative to using API calls, you can build your satellite DLLs as Visual Basic ActiveX DLL projects. To do this, create a class module with methods for retrieving resources. Give the class a name such as Localizer. Add this class module to each DLL project.

Use your open-ended naming scheme for the Project Name, so that each DLL has a unique programmatic ID, or ProgID, in the Windows registry. Each time you compile a new satellite DLL, you create a new Localizer class, whose full programmatic ID includes the Project Name of the DLL.

In your ActiveX control project, you can then create an instance of the appropriate Localizer class using code such as the following:

```
Dim strProgID As String
Dim objLoc As Object
' Generate the ProgID of the Localizer object
' for the appropriate satellite DLL.
strProgID = "MyControls" & Hex$(AmbientProperties.LocaleID) _
   & ".Localizer"
Set objLoc = CreateObject(strProgID)
If objLoc Is Nothing Then
   ' Satellite DLL not found; use default locale.
Else
   ' Call methods of Localizer object to retrieve
   ' localized string and bitmap resources.
End If
```

The code above uses late binding (that is, the variable `objLoc` is declared As Object). You can get better performance with early binding, by using the Implements feature of Visual Basic. Instead of making the resource retrieval methods members of the Localizer class, you can define them in an abstract class named IResources.

In your Localizer class, use the Implements statement to implement IResources as a second interface. You can call the methods of this interface with early binding, as shown below.

```
' Early-bound variable for IResources interface.
Dim ires As IResources
' Get the IResources interface of the Localizer
' object obtained from the satellite DLL.
Set ires = objLoc
' Call the methods of your IResources interface
' to retrieve localized resources.
Set cmdOK.Caption = ires.GetString(ID_CMDOK)
```

As with the late-bound Localizer object, you can simply add the Localizer class module, with its second interface, to each satellite DLL project. The ability to add the same interface to several different classes is called *polymorphism.*

For More Information The Implements feature is discussed in "Providing Polymorphism by Implementing Interfaces," in Chapter 6, "General Principles of Component Design." Accessing satellite DLLs is discussed in Chapter 16, "International Issues," in the *Microsoft Visual Basic 6.0 Programmer's Guide.* Adding resource files to Visual Basic projects is discussed in Chapter 8, "More About Programming," in the *Microsoft Visual Basic 6.0 Programmer's Guide.*

Resource Files

An alternative to satellite DLLs is to place text strings and error messages in a resource file, and compile the file into your control component. There are disadvantages to this technique.

- If you use one resource file for each locale, you must compile a separate .ocx file for each locale. To avoid file name conflicts, you can put a locale indicator in the name of each .ocx file, as for example MyControlsDE.ocx for German, or MyControlsFR.ocx for French.
- Unfortunately, you cannot avoid type library name conflicts so easily. A developer can have only one locale version of your control installed at a time. This may be a drawback in multilingual markets.
- Although you can avoid the problem of compiling multiple .ocx files by putting the text and error message strings for all locales into a single resource file, the result will be a much larger .ocx file, and you will have to recompile the component to add support for new locales.

Localizing Interfaces

If you localize property, method, and event names, you must compile a separate version of your control for each locale. To allow multiple versions of your control to coexist on one computer, you must use a different name for your control in each version.

As a result of the different interface and control names, multilingual developers will have to rewrite their code for each language version of a program that uses your control. This will make your control component less attractive to such developers.

Microsoft applications, such as Visual Basic, do not localize interface member names.

Localizing Property Pages

Microsoft applications localize property pages, but not property names. If you use this scheme, the caption that shows up on a property page may not match the name of the property in the Properties window.

When localizing captions for properties on property pages, take care to select captions that make it obvious what the property is. Alternatively, you may wish to include the property name in parentheses.

For principles of form layout that simplify localization, see Chapter 16, "International Issues," in the *Microsoft Visual Basic 6.0 Programmer's Guide.*

Localizing Type Library Information

There is no way to retrieve a browser string from a localized DLL or resource file, so browser strings must be compiled into your type library. To produce localized type libraries, you must use the Procedure Attributes dialog box to change the browser strings for all your properties, methods, and events. You must then re-compile your executable.

Localizing type library information thus limits your ability to localize using satellite DLLs. You may wish to leave your browser strings in the default language of your control.

For More Information See Chapter 16, "International Issues," in the *Microsoft Visual Basic 6.0 Programmer's Guide.*

CHAPTER 10

Creating Property Pages for ActiveX Controls

Property pages offer an alternative to the Properties window for viewing ActiveX control properties. You can group several related properties on a page, or use a page to provide a dialog-like interface for a property that's too complex for the Properties window.

In Visual Basic, property pages are displayed in the Property Pages tabbed dialog box, as shown in Figure 10.1.

Figure 10.1 The Properties window and the Property Pages dialog box

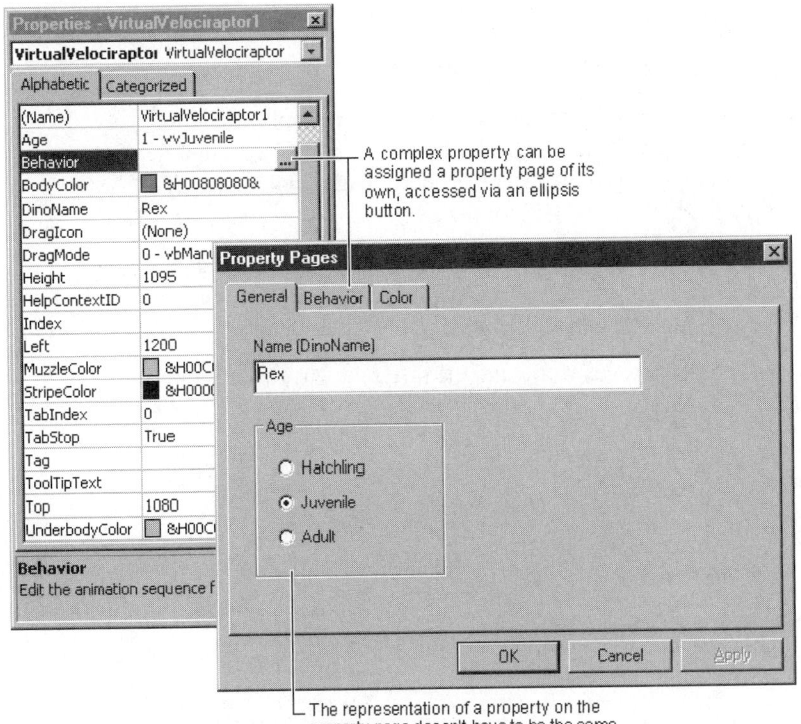

Each tab in the Property Pages dialog box represents one PropertyPage object. For example, the PropertyPage object that provides the General tab shown in Figure 10.1 was created using the PropertyPage designer shown in Figure 10.2.

Figure 10.2 The PropertyPage designer for the General tab

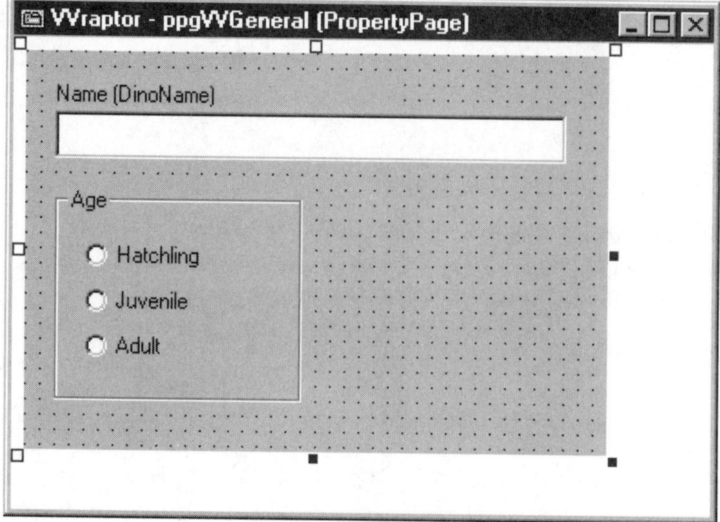

In the designer, the PropertyPage object doesn't display a tab. Nor does it display the OK, Cancel, and Apply buttons. These are provided automatically by the Property Pages dialog, and are not part of any individual PropertyPage object. The Property Pages dialog uses the Caption property of the PropertyPage object as the text for the tab.

In this example, the General page groups two properties, DinoName and Age. The page is laid out to simplify localization; the length of the captions can change without affecting the layout. This is discussed in "Property Page Design Guidelines," later in this chapter.

The following topics explain how property pages work, and the different ways you can use them in your ActiveX controls.

Contents

For More Information A simple property page example can be found in the step-by-step procedures in Chapter 4, "Creating an ActiveX Control." Control creation is covered in depth in Chapter 9, "Building ActiveX Controls." The Property Page Wizard can automate much of the work of creating property pages. Search for Property Page Wizard.

How Property Pages Work

Property pages look a lot like forms, and designing them is somewhat similar to designing forms. The way property pages work, however, is quite different from the way forms work.

For example, when the Property Pages dialog box creates an instance of a property page, the Initialize event is the first event the PropertyPage object gets — just as it would be for a form. However, unlike a form, the PropertyPage object doesn't get a Load event. The key event for PropertyPage objects is the SelectionChanged event.

This topic examines the three things your PropertyPage object must do:

- In the SelectionChanged event, obtain the property values to be edited.
- Set the PropertyPage object's Changed property whenever the user edits a property value.
- In the ApplyChanges event, copy the edited property values back to the selected control (or controls).

The SelectionChanged Event

The SelectionChanged event occurs when the property page is displayed, and when the list of currently selected controls changes.

For example, after selecting an instance of your control and opening the Property Pages dialog box, a developer might realize that she needed to change the properties of two instances of your control. By clicking the second instance while holding down the CTRL key, she could add the second instance to the list of selected controls. Each of your property pages would then receive a SelectionChanged event.

> **Important** You should always treat the SelectionChanged event as if your property page is being loaded for the first time. As you'll see, changing the selection fundamentally changes the state of the property page.

Coding the SelectionChanged Event for a Single Control

The most important thing you need to do in the SelectionChanged event is to set the values of the controls that display property values for editing. For example, consider the General page for the VirtualVelociraptor control (originally shown in Figure 10.1):

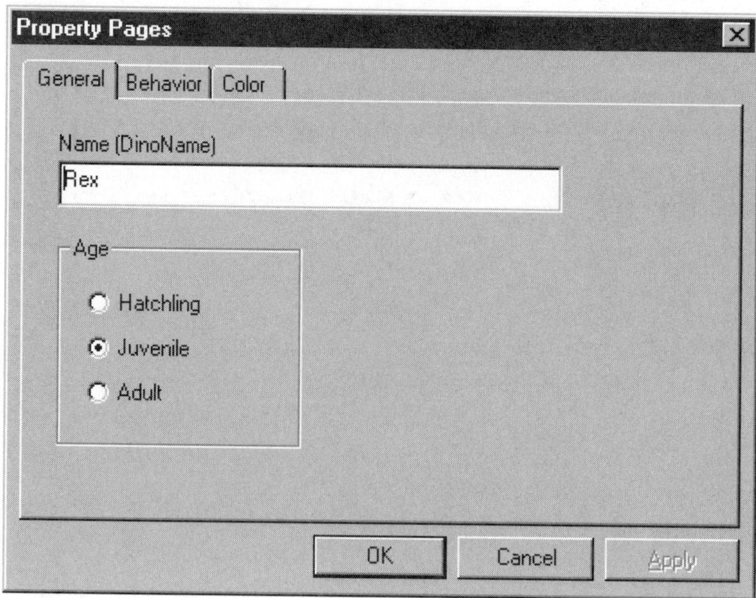

Suppose that the Age property of the VirtualVelociraptor control uses the following public Enum:

```
Public Enum DinoAge
   vvHatchling
   vvJuvenile
   vvAdult
End Enum
```

The SelectionChanged event of the property page might look like this:

```
Private Sub PropertyPage_SelectionChanged()
   ' Place the value of the DinoName property for the
   '   first selected control in the txtDinoName text
   '   box for display and editing.
   txtDinoName = SelectedControls(0).DinoName
   ' Use the value of the Age property of the first
   '   selected control to select the appropriate
   '   option button in the Age frame.
   optAge(SelectedControls(0).Age).Value = True
   ' (The code above depends on the fact that the
   '   elements of the DinoAge Enum have the values
   '   0, 1, and 2.)
End Sub
```

Tip The Property Page Wizard will populate your property page with text box controls and check boxes (for Boolean properties), and generate default code for the SelectionChanged event.

The SelectedControls Collection

The SelectedControls collection contains all the controls currently selected in the container the developer is working on. The collection may contain several instances of your control; if the property page is shared by more than one control in your control component, the collection may contain controls of multiple types.

> **Note** You don't need to worry about the collection containing controls other than your own — text boxes, for example — because the Property Pages dialog box only displays those pages that are used by *all* of the currently selected controls.

For the moment, ignore the possibility that multiple controls might be selected. What the code in the SelectionChanged event shown above is doing is taking the value of each property for the *first* control in the collection and assigning it to the appropriate control on the property page.

In the case of a single selected control, this places all of the control's property values in fields where the user can edit them.

Different Ways to Edit Properties

Instead of showing the property value of the Age property as a set of option buttons, you could use a drop-down list showing the elements of the enumeration:

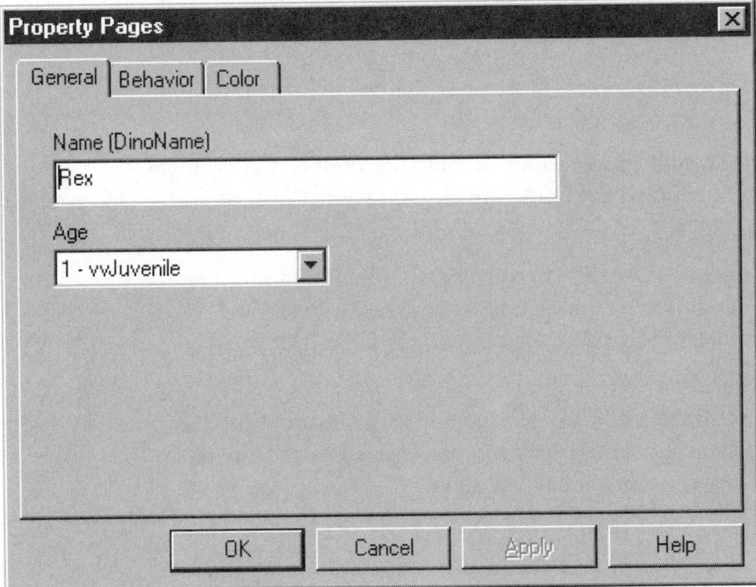

The drop-down list takes up less space than the option buttons did (an advantage that grows larger as the number of possible values increases), and it shows the names of the constants that would be used in code.

The following code fragment shows how you might set up such a list.

```
Private Sub PropertyPage_SelectionChanged()
   txtDinoName = SelectedControls(0).DinoName
   ' Create a drop-down list containing the values and
   '    names of the Enum elements for the Age
   '    property, and select the one that corresponds
   '    to the current value of the Age property.
   cboAge.AddItem vvHatchling & " - vvHatchling"
   cboAge.AddItem vvJuvenile & " - vvJuvenile"
   cboAge.AddItem vvAdult & " - vvAdult"
   cboAge.ListIndex = SelectedControls(0).Age
   ' (The index of each Enum element in the drop-down
   '    list is the same as the element's value.)
End Sub
```

Tip While you can choose any editable representation that makes sense for a property, remember that the more space each property takes up, the more tabs you'll need. Minimizing the number of tabs makes the property pages for your control easier to use. For most enumerations, a drop-down list will make the most efficient use of space.

Coding the SelectionChanged Event for Multiple Controls

To determine whether multiple controls are selected, you can test the Count property of the SelectedControls collection to see whether it's greater than one.

In order to deal with multiple selected control instances, it's useful to divide the properties of your control into two groups:

- Properties that can sensibly be set to the same value for multiple controls. For example, it's very convenient to be able to set the BackColor property of several Label controls to the same value.
- Properties that do not make sense to set to the same value for multiple controls. For example, it's not particularly helpful to set the Caption property of several Label controls to the same value. In fact, it might be quite annoying to the user to do so by accident.

One approach you might take in your SelectionChanged event is to disable the edit fields for properties of the second sort whenever multiple controls are selected. In the discussion of the ApplyChanges event, an alternate technique will be shown.

Shared Property Pages

If you have multiple controls in your project, and two such controls share a property page, make sure that you provide error trapping for the code that reads the property values. If the first control selected doesn't include all of the properties shown on the page, an error will occur when you try to read that property value.

Enabling the Apply Button by Setting Changed = True

In order to tell Visual Basic that the user has edited one or more properties on a property page, you must set the PropertyPage object's Changed property to True. Because there's no way to know which property a user might decide to change, you must do this for every property displayed on the page.

For example, to notify the PropertyPage of changes in the DinoName or Age properties from the previous example, you would use the following code:

```
Private Sub txtDinoName_Changed()
   Changed = True
End
Private Sub cboAge_Change()
   Changed = True
End
```

Note that this is exactly the same as coding `PropertyPage.Changed = True`.

Notifying the PropertyPage object that values have changed enables the Apply button on the Property Pages dialog box, and causes the ApplyChanges event to occur when the Apply button is pressed, when the user changes tabs, or when the dialog box is dismissed.

> **Note** You may wish to keep track of which properties have changed, so that you don't have to write them all out.

The ApplyChanges Event

The second most important event in a PropertyPage object is the ApplyChanges event. In this event you copy the edited property values back to the currently selected controls.

The ApplyChanges event occurs when the user:

- Clicks the OK button to dismiss the dialog.
- Clicks the Apply button.
- Selects another tab in the Property Pages dialog box.

The following code for the ApplyChanges event assumes that the SelectionChanged event was coded using a drop-down list for the Age property, as shown earlier.

```
Private Sub PropertyPage_ApplyChanges()
   Dim vv As VirtualVelociraptor
   ' Set the DinoName property of the FIRST selected
   '   control only.
   SelectedControls(0).DinoName = txtDinoName
```

```
    For Each vv In SelectedControls
        ' Transfer the value currently selected in the
        '    drop-down list for the DinoAge property to
        '    all of the selected controls.
        vv.DinoAge = cboAge.ListIndex
        ' (The code above works because the value of
        '    each of the three elements of the Enum is
        '    the same as its index number in cboAge.)
    Next
End Sub
```

Because it generally doesn't make sense to give all of the virtual velociraptors the same name, the DinoName property is applied only to the first selected control. The Age property, on the other hand, is applied to all the selected controls.

Note As the control author, it's up to you to decide which properties make sense to set for multiple selected controls.

Dealing with Errors in ApplyChanges

In the case shown above, there's no chance of error in the ApplyChanges event. The text property is a simple string, and the drop-down list limits user input for the Age property to only those values that are valid.

If your property page allows the user to enter values that may be rejected by the Property Let (or Property Set) procedure, you should use error trapping in the ApplyChanges event. The simplest scheme is to use On Error Resume Next, and test Err.Number after each property that may raise an error.

When an error occurs:

- Stop processing the ApplyChanges event.
- Display an error message, so the user understands what went wrong.
- Set the focus to the property that caused the error.
- Set the Changed property of the PropertyPage object to True.

  Important Setting `Changed = True` performs two functions. First, it re-enables the Apply button. Second, it prevents the Property Pages dialog box from being dismissed if the user clicked OK. *This is the only way to prevent the dialog box from closing.*

Connecting a Property Page to an ActiveX Control

Once you've added property pages to your ActiveX control project, you can use the Connect Property Pages dialog box to establish a connection between a control and the property pages you want it to use.

When a user shows the Property Pages dialog box for an instance of one of your controls, each of the pages you connected to the control will appear as one tab in the dialog box.

To connect property pages to a control

1. In the Project Explorer window, double-click the control to open its designer.
2. Press F4 to open the Properties window.
3. Double-click the **PropertyPages** property (or select the property and then click the ellipsis button) to open the **Connect Property Pages** dialog box.
4. Place a check mark beside each property page you want to appear when the developer who uses your control opens the **Property Pages** dialog box.
5. Use the **Page Order** buttons to put the pages in the order you want them to appear in the **Property Pages** dialog box, then click **OK**.

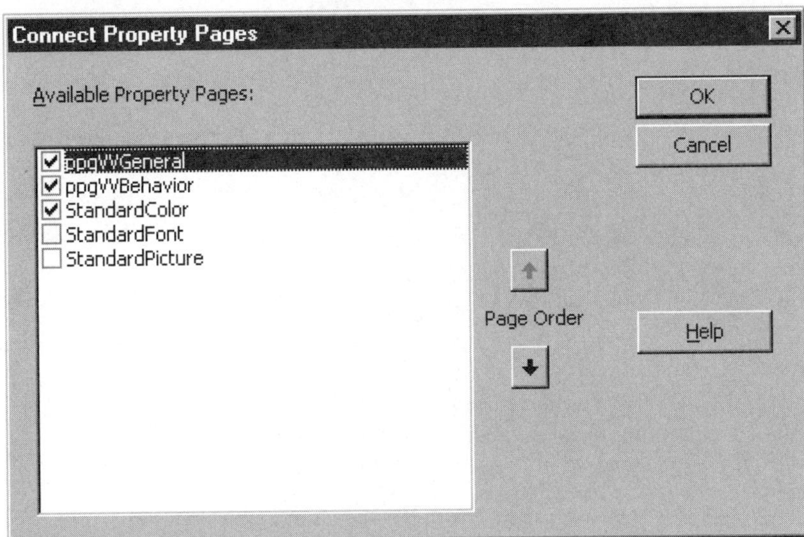

For More Information The standard property pages for fonts, colors, and pictures are discussed in "Using Standard Property Pages," later in this chapter.

Associating a Property Page with a Property

Sometimes a property is too complicated to set from the Properties window. A property might be an object, such as the Font object, with properties of its own. A property might consist of an array of values, or even a collection of objects — such as a collection of Toolbar buttons.

For example, Figure 10.3 shows how a property page might look for the Behavior property of a hypothetical VirtualVelociraptor control. This page allows cells to be added to and deleted from animation sequences for the control's various behaviors.

Figure 10.3 A property too complex for the Properties window

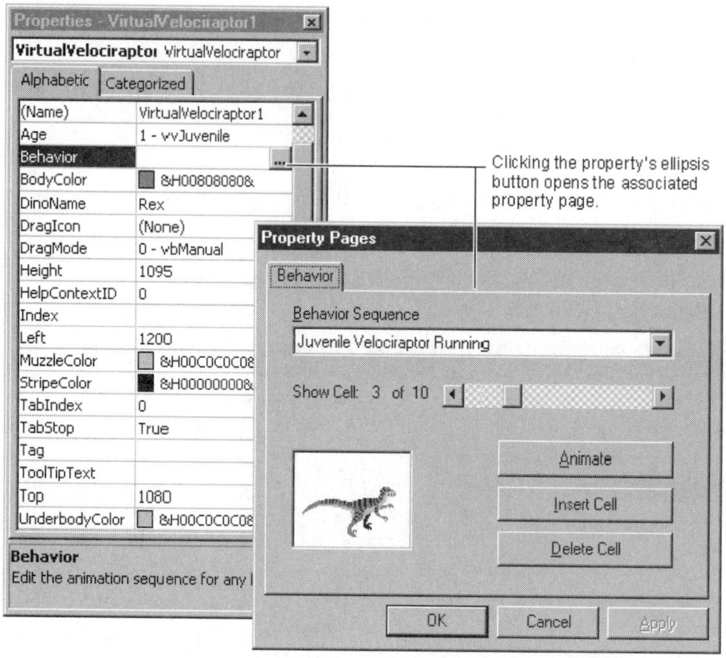

Clicking the property's ellipsis button opens the associated property page.

Notice that only the tab associated with the property is displayed. If you compare this picture with Figure 10.1, you'll notice that the page size used by the Property Pages dialog box is smaller in this picture. When multiple pages are displayed, the size of the largest page is used.

> **Note** If you declare a property of type Font, OLE_COLOR, or Picture, Visual Basic will automatically associate the property with a StandardFont, StandardColor, or StandardPicture page, as described in "Using Standard Property Pages," later in this chapter.

To associate a property page with an individual property

1. In the Project Explorer window, right-click the UserControl to open the context menu, and select **View Code** to open the code window.
2. On the **Tools** menu, select **Procedure Attributes** to open the **Procedure Attributes** dialog box, and click **Advanced** to expand the dialog box.
3. In the **Name** box, select the property you wish to associate with a property page.
4. Select the desired property page in the **Use this Page in Property Browser** list, as shown below, then click **Apply** or **OK**.

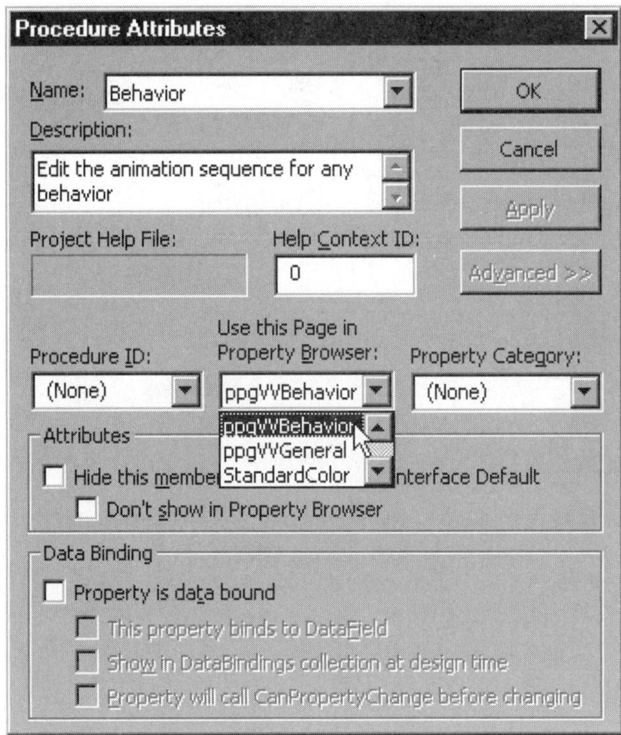

The EditProperty Event

Visual Basic allows you to associate multiple properties with the same property page. You might want to do this if your control has more than one property that uses the same property page layout, or if one property uses part of another property's layout. In the latter case, you can use the EditProperty event to enable only the necessary parts of the property page.

When the user clicks the ellipsis button for a property that's associated with a property page, the page receives the EditProperties event in addition to the events it normally receives. You can use the PropertyName argument of the EditProperties event to identify the property whose ellipsis button was clicked.

The EditProperties event gives you the opportunity to do a number of things to the property page, depending on the nature of your control and the complexity of the property being edited. For example, you might:

- If the property being edited is displayed in a single control on the PropertyPage, set the focus to that control.
- Enable and disable controls on the property page so that only those fields applicable to the specified property are enabled.

Not Showing Properties in the Properties Window

In some cases, you may not want a property displayed in the Properties window. For example, if displaying a property value requires a time-consuming calculation, the developer who uses your control may be annoyed at the length of time it takes to access the Properties window.

On the Property Attributes dialog, accessible from the Tools menu, select the property you wish to suppress. Click the Advanced button, check "Don't show in Property Browser," and then click Apply.

Using Standard Property Pages

Visual Basic provides three standard property pages: StandardFont, StandardColor, and StandardPicture. If you declare properties of type Font, OLE_COLOR, or Picture, Visual Basic's Properties window will automatically associate these properties with the appropriate standard property page.

Visual Basic will not automatically add these pages to the Property Pages dialog box, however. Use the procedure shown in "Connecting a Property Page to an ActiveX Control" to add standard property pages to the list of pages that will be displayed in the Property Pages dialog box.

> **Note** The format used to display standard property pages in the Property Pages dialog box differs from the format used by the Properties window. For example, the Color page is in an entirely different format, and the Font page does not display all Font object properties.

> **Tip** If you use the Property Page Wizard to create property pages for a control with properties declared Font, OLE_COLOR, or Picture, the wizard will automatically add the appropriate standard property pages to the list of pages to be displayed.

Standard Property Pages and Multiple Properties

If your control has more than one property that uses a standard property page, and you add the page to your control's PropertyPages property, the standard page will include a list of properties the user can select from.

For example, Figure 10.4 shows the Properties window and Property Pages dialog box for the hypothetical VirtualVelociraptor control, which has several properties of type OLE_COLOR:

Figure 10.4 The Properties window for a control with multiple color properties

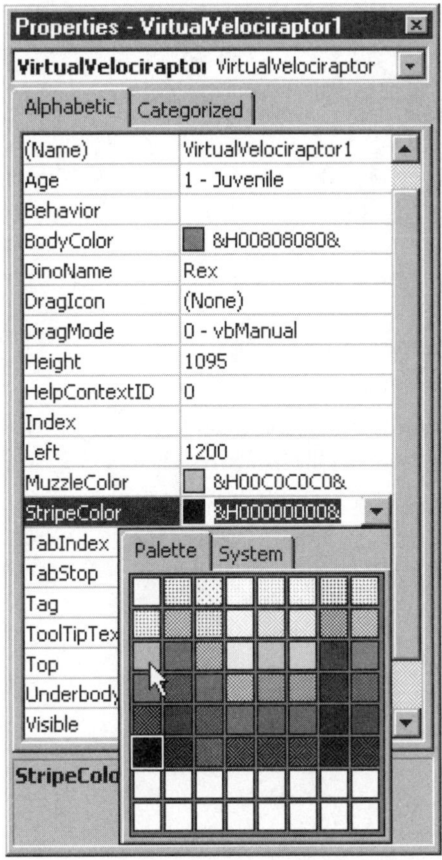

As Figure 10.5 shows, the Color page displayed by the Property Pages dialog box for the VirtualVelociraptor control has a list box containing the four color properties of the control.

Figure 10.5 A standard property page showing multiple properties

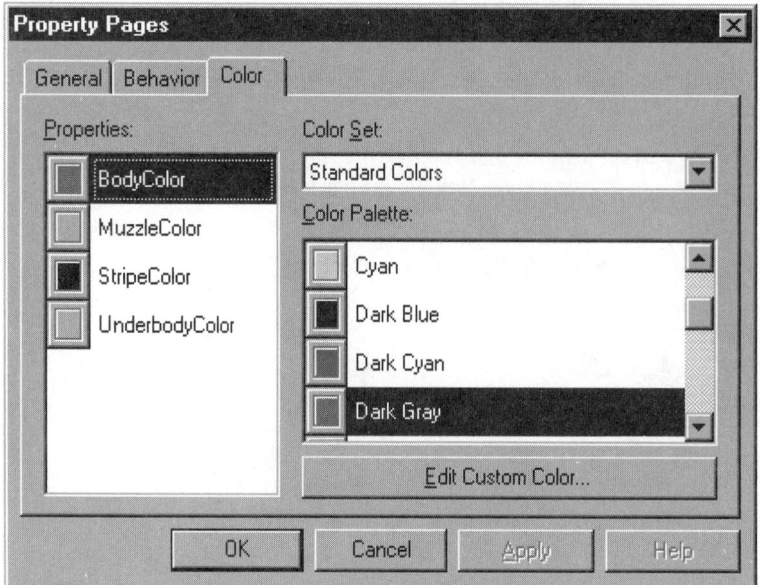

Figure 10.5 also shows that the Property Pages dialog box uses a very different format than that used by the Properties window.

> **Note** When a standard property page displays multiple properties, the ApplyChanges event is raised each time the user selects a different property from the list.

The following code fragment shows how the StripeColor property of the hypothetical VirtualVelociraptor control should be declared in order to work with the Properties window and Property Pages dialog box:

```
Private mStripeColor As OLE_COLOR

Public Property Get StripeColor() As OLE_COLOR
   StripeColor = mStripeColor
End Property

Public Property Let StripeColor( _
      ByVal NewColor As OLE_COLOR)
   mStripeColor = NewColor
End Property
```

For More Information See "Adding Properties to Controls" in Chapter 9, "Building ActiveX Controls."

Property Page Design Guidelines

You may find the following guidelines helpful in designing property pages that are professional-looking and easy to use.

- When the property pages for your control are shown, focus should be on the first field of the first tab. To do this, give the first control on each PropertyPage the lowest TabIndex number for the page.
- If properties are arranged in multiple columns on a page, tab order should usually be top to bottom in the first column, then move to the top of the next column.
- Provide access keys (keyboard shortcuts) for all the fields on a property page.

  Note The letter "A" is not available as an access key, because the Property Pages dialog box uses it for the Apply button.

- Place standard property pages for fonts, colors, and pictures at the end of the list of property pages for a control.
- Group similar properties together — for example, all properties that affect a control's appearance should go on the same page.
- Use a uniform size for your property pages. When the Property Pages dialog box displays multiple pages, it uses the same width and height for all of them.

  Tip The standard pages for fonts, colors, and pictures are all the same size. If you use these pages, set your other property pages to this standard size. A quick way to set the standard size is to set the StandardSize property of the PropertyPage to Large at design time.

- For ease of use, keep the number of tabs to a minimum. For example, don't add a tab for your control's About box.
- Most control components (.ocx files) that provide more than one control have a page with the caption "General" which contains items that are common to many controls.
- Keep your pages simple and fast. Your users will generally be developers employing your control to get a job done — animation and fancy graphics will just get in their way.
- The Property Pages dialog box will show a Help button if you've used the General tab of the Project Options dialog box to add a Help file to your project. You can set the HelpContextID properties of your property pages and of the controls they contain.
- When you add labels to your property pages, make sure you include the property name in the label. You may want to localize your control for international use, or add user-friendly captions for the benefit of desktop tools such as Microsoft Office, but remember that the user must be able to identify the actual property names in order to write code for them, or look them up in your Help file.

- When you create strings for the named constants in an enumeration, always include the actual constant name, because that's what the person using your control will have to use when programming.
- If you plan to localize your control component for international use, make sure that combo boxes, text boxes, and so on are wide enough to accommodate translated strings. If you plan to localize for locales — such as Japan — that use DBCS characters, make sure the font you're using is available on DBCS systems, and that the height of your text boxes will accommodate DBCS characters.
- Avoid showing dialog boxes from property pages. (The File Open dialog is an exception to this rule.)
- Cross-tab property dependencies. If two properties interact — for example, if setting the value of one property limits the valid values for another property — place the properties on the same page.

For More Information Rules for layout that simplify localization can be found in Chapter 16, "International Issues," in the *Microsoft Visual Basic* 6.0 *Programmer's Guide.*

CHAPTER 11

Building ActiveX Documents

This chapter covers the issues involved in building an ActiveX document-based solution. Some of the topics correspond to the sequence of development tasks presented in Chapter 5, "Creating an ActiveX Document."

Contents

What Is an ActiveX Document?

The word "document" in "ActiveX document" is somewhat misleading. While the genesis of ActiveX documents reveals that a Microsoft Visual Basic ActiveX document is analogous to a Word document, when you create a Visual Basic ActiveX document, the distinction between a "document" and an application becomes genuinely blurred. While a traditional document (such as a Word document) is static, ActiveX documents need not be. Using Visual Basic, you can create a complete application with the semantics of a traditional document. In other words, you have the functionality of the application, but the flexibility of a document's behavior — when a user opens an ActiveX document, she will not only have the full functionality of an application, but the ability to persist and distribute "copies" of the data intrinsic to the application. Thus, the "document" is truly active.

An Analogy: Word Document = ActiveX Document

ActiveX documents are not an entirely new concept. You are probably already familiar with Word documents. As you know, a Word document is not the same as the Word application — the Word document (with the extension .doc) contains the actual content, whereas the Word application (Winword.exe) is used to create the document.

You may also know that a Word document can be viewed in other containers. In that case, the Word application supplies the objects that enable another ActiveX container (such as Internet Explorer) to view and activate the document. And this same mechanism works for ActiveX documents created with Visual Basic.

As Figure 11.1 shows, when you create an ActiveX document-based project, you are creating a Visual Basic "document" that can be contained in an ActiveX container (such as Internet Explorer). Compiling the ActiveX document creates both a Visual Basic Document file (with the extension .vbd) and its corresponding server — which can be an ActiveX .dll, or ActiveX .exe file. In other words, the .vbd file is to the .exe or .dll file what the .doc file is to the Winword.exe file.

Figure 11.1 Word Documents and ActiveX Documents Compared

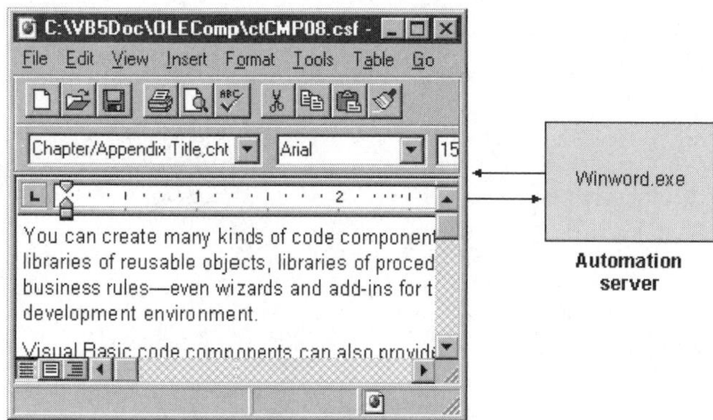

The actual document

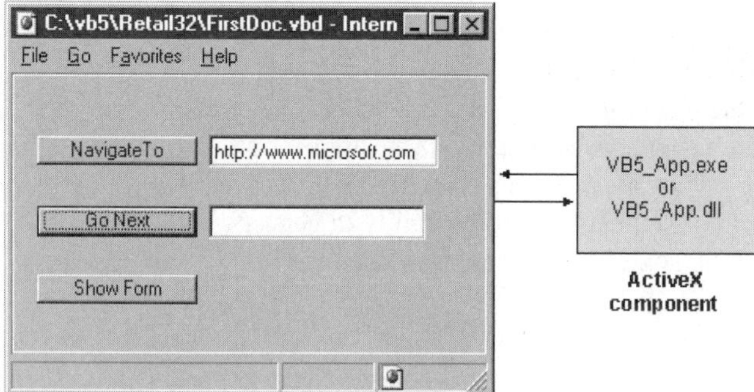

The Visual Basic ActiveX document

- ActiveX Document Advantages
- ActiveX Document Creation Basics
- Parts of an ActiveX Document
- Converting Existing Applications into ActiveX Documents
- ActiveX Document Similarities to ActiveX Controls
- Key Events in the Life of an ActiveX Document

ActiveX Document Advantages

The advantages of creating and deploying ActiveX documents are:

- You can leverage your knowledge of Visual Basic. If you are skilled in programming Visual Basic, you already have the knowledge to reach your goals — you do not have to learn another programming language (as you do to create an HTML page).
- You can leverage the Visual Basic programming environment. The full development environment is available to you, including the Visual Basic code window, debugger, and compiler.
- Ability to create ActiveX documents that run in Internet Explorer. For all intents and purposes, an ActiveX document is a Visual Basic application that is now accessible in a widely used container.
- Execution on a local machine. The ActiveX component can contain all the necessary code to deliver the results of complex calculations.
- Immediate visual feedback about layout of elements. Placing TextBox and CommandButton controls on an ActiveX document gives you immediate feedback about how the document will look. In contrast, coding an HTML document takes practice and guesswork.
- Support for the Hyperlink object, which allows an ActiveX document to request that the container (if it is Hyperlink-aware) navigate to another ActiveX document, or a Web site.
- Support for the AsyncRead method. The method begins an asynchronous transfer of data, allowing other code to execute while the data is retrieved.

  Note There is one control that cannot be placed on an ActiveX document: the OLE Container Control. Also note that embedded objects, such as an Microsoft Excel or Word documents, are not allowed on ActiveX documents.

ActiveX Document Creation Basics

Creating an ActiveX document has great similarities to creating an ActiveX control. Just as with ActiveX controls, you are not necessarily in control of the host application — you are a cog in somebody else's machine. Therefore, much of your code must be defensive — allow your application to gracefully exit when necessary. And, as when developing an ActiveX control, you can expose methods, events and properties that can be used by other components.

The topics in this chapter provide the basic facts and concepts you need to create ActiveX documents. First, however, is a recap of the process of ActiveX document creation.

The Process in a Nutshell

The process of creating an ActiveX document is like creating any other project in Visual Basic:

1. Begin by starting a new project and selecting either ActiveX Document EXE or ActiveX Document DLL. By default, these template projects contain a single UserDocument. Each UserDocument is the core object for an ActiveX document.
2. Add controls to the UserDocument, and add code for the controls.
3. Add a Help menu to the UserDocument.
4. Add other forms, code modules, or more UserDocument objects to the project.
5. Test and debug the ActiveX document by running the project and viewing the document in the target container (the container application you will eventually use to view the document — for example, Internet Explorer).
6. Compile the project as either an in-process component, or an out-of-process component. A .vbd file (required when you use a browser such as Internet Explorer to view an ActiveX document) is also created.
7. Deploy the ActiveX document(s).

The .exe or .dll file contains the actual compiled code. Initially, the .vbd file contains the class ID of the .exe or the .dll file. If you elect to allow users to save data (using the PropertyBag), the data will also be stored in the .vbd file. Users can view your ActiveX document by opening the .vbd file in a host application.

For More Information Deployment of ActiveX documents is covered in "Building Internet Applications." For more information about the difference between the in-process and out-of-process components, see "In-Process and Out-of-Process ActiveX Documents." Details about the .vbd file are covered in "Parts of an ActiveX Document."

Parts of an ActiveX Document

An ActiveX document created with Visual Basic is always composed of a UserDocument object, code, code modules, and controls that you place on the UserDocument.

Project Files

Like Visual Basic forms, UserDocument objects have code modules and visual designers, as shown in Figure 11.2.

Figure 11.2 UserDocument designer and code window

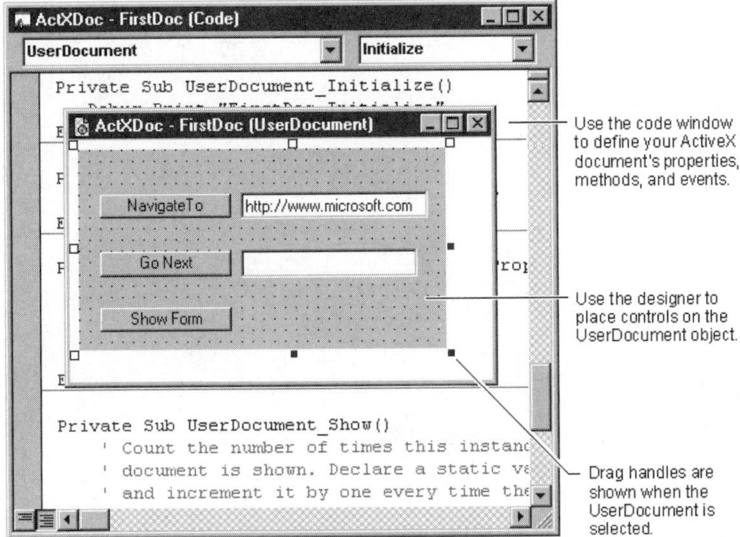
ActXDoc - FirstDoc (Code)
UserDocument
Initialize
Private Sub UserDocument_Initialize()
ActXDoc - FirstDoc (UserDocument)
NavigateTo
http://www.microsoft.com
Go Next
Show Form
Private Sub UserDocument_Show()
' Count the number of times this instanc
' document is shown. Declare a static va
' and increment it by one every time the
Use the code window to define your ActiveX document's properties, methods, and events.
Use the designer to place controls on the UserDocument object.
Drag handles are shown when the UserDocument is selected.

Like forms, UserDocument objects are stored in plain text files that contain the source code and property values of the UserDocument and the controls placed on it. Visual Basic uses the extension .dob for these source files.

If a UserDocument contains controls that use graphical elements which cannot be stored as plain text, such as bitmaps, Visual Basic stores those elements in a .dox file. This is analogous to the .frx files used to store graphical elements used in forms.

The .dob and .dox files completely define an ActiveX control's appearance and interface (properties, events, and methods). A compiled ActiveX document will then consist of either an ActiveX .exe or .dll and an accompanying .vbd file. In a browser such as Internet Explorer, the user must navigate to the .vbd file to open the ActiveX document.

Compiled Files

An ActiveX document can be built as an out-of-process component (an .exe file) or an in-process component (a .dll file). In both cases, when you run or compile the project, in addition to creating an .exe. or a .dll file, Visual Basic creates a Visual Basic Document file, which has the extension ".vbd." When you compile an .exe or .dll, the .vbd file will be placed in the same directory as the compiled component.

The .vbd file is actually an OLE structured storage — this basically means that data in the file can be accessed and manipulated via standard OLE interfaces. Other Microsoft applications, such as Word and Excel, save data in this manner.

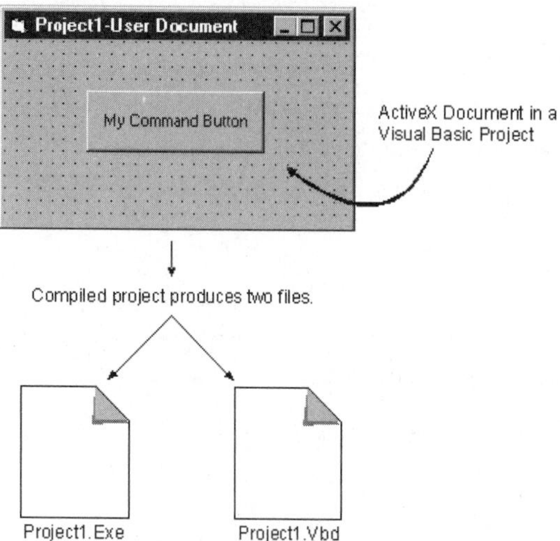

Note When you run an ActiveX project from the Visual Basic IDE, a temporary .vbd file will be created in the directory where Visual Basic has been installed. The temporary .vbd file will have the same name as the UserDocument with the "vbd" extension. If a .vbd with the same name exists (in the Visual Basic directory), that .vbd file will be moved to a temporary file location. When the project stops running, the original file will be restored. While the project is running, however, you can navigate to the temporary file (from a browser or other application).

To view the ActiveX document in a container application, such as Internet Explorer or Microsoft Office Binder, you must navigate to the .vbd file. For example, if you created an ActiveX document named "DocObject1.vbd," and it is in the default directory of the Visual Basic program, you might type the following URL in the Address box of Internet Explorer:

```
file://c:\Program Files\VB\DocObject1.vbd
```

Note This path will vary depending on which version of Visual Basic you have installed. If Visual Basic has been installed as part of Microsoft Visual Studio, for example, the URL shown above may instead be `file://c:\Program Files\Microsoft Visual Studio\VB\DocObject1.vbd`.

You can also use the Hyperlink object's NavigateTo method, from within an ActiveX document, to open another ActiveX document, as shown:

```
Private Sub cmdGoNext_Click()
   UserDocument.Hyperlink.NavigateTo _
      "c:\Program Files\VB\DocObject1.vbd"
End Sub
```

Note Once you have compiled your ActiveX document, you can change the extension of the .vbd file. In other words, instead of having users navigate to "Nice.vbd," you can have them navigate to "Nice.dog."

For More Information To learn how to navigate between ActiveX documents in a browser, see "Using the HyperLink Object with ActiveX Documents," later in this chapter.

Converting Existing Applications into ActiveX Documents

You may have several existing applications that are candidates for conversion into ActiveX documents. If so, you can use the ActiveX Document Migration Wizard to ease the transition.

Note The OLE Container control and embedded objects (for example, Microsoft Word or Microsoft Excel documents) cannot be placed on an ActiveX document, and will be removed.

To use the ActiveX Document Migration Wizard

1. Open the project you wish to convert.
2. On the **Add-Ins** menu, click **Add-In Manager**.
3. Highlight **VB ActiveX Document Migration Wizard**, click the desired behaviors in Load Behavior, and then click **OK**.
4. On the **Add-Ins** menu, click **ActiveX Document Migration Wizard**.
5. Follow the directions until the Wizard has finished its task.

What the Wizard Does

The Wizard performs the following tasks:

- Copies form properties to a new UserDocument.
- Copies all controls from the form to the UserDocument, and retain their names.
- Copies all code behind the form to the UserDocument.

- Comments out all illegal code such as `Me.Left` and `End`.
- Switches the project type to ActiveX EXE or DLL.
- Where there is an exact counterpart on the UserDocument, copy event handlers to the UserDocument, replacing "Form" with "UserDocument." For example, "Form_Click()" becomes "UserDocument_Click()." In cases where there is no counterpart, the event handler is copied over leaving the "Form" part intact. These are copied to the General section of the code window, and can then be called as procedures. In other words, if you need to invoke code from the Form_Load event, simply call it from an appropriate event:

```
Private Sub UserDocument_Show()
   Form_Load
End Sub
```

> **Note** The Form object's Load event doesn't have a direct counterpart in the UserDocument. You place Load event procedures in the Show event handler, but you should be aware that the Show event gets called every time the user navigates to the ActiveX document (in a Web browser). To prevent Load event procedures from running every time the Show event occurs, use a module-level variable as a flag — if the flag has been set, don't run the procedures. Code for this technique is shown in "Determining the ActiveX Document's Container Programmatically," later in this chapter.

ActiveX Document Similarities to ActiveX Controls

In many ways, ActiveX documents resemble ActiveX controls. Knowing how they are similar can be of some benefit, as the programming techniques, caveats, and strategies apply to both.

Here are a few of the relevant similarities:

- Like an ActiveX control, an ActiveX document can't exist without a container. Whereas an ActiveX control is contained in a form, UserDocument, or UserControl, the ActiveX document is contained in a container such as Internet Explorer or Microsoft Binder.
- The author of a control cannot know for sure which development environment the control will eventually be used in. Likewise, the developer of an ActiveX document cannot know which container will be used to view the ActiveX document.
- The UserDocument object also features several events that are also found on the UserControl object. The common events include: Initialize, InitProperties, ReadProperties, EnterFocus, ExitFocus, WriteProperties, and the Terminate event.

Because of the great similarity between ActiveX documents and ActiveX controls, much of what is written in Chapter 9, "Building ActiveX Controls," also applies to building ActiveX documents. The following sections are of particular relevance:

- "The UserControl Object," discusses the core document for ActiveX controls. This object has great similarities to the UserDocument object.
- "Controls You Can Use As Constituent Controls" discusses the controls that can be placed on a UserControl. These same points can generally be applied to an ActiveX document.
- "Object Models for Controls" discusses a strategy of dealing with complex controls, which can also be applied to ActiveX documents.
- "Adding Internet Features to Controls" explains, in detail, the AsyncRead method, the AsyncReadComplete event, and the Hyperlink object. These same features are available for ActiveX documents.
- "Adding Properties to Controls" and "Adding Methods to Controls" show you how and why to add public properties and methods to controls. The same methods apply (in part) to ActiveX documents.
- "Creating Robust Controls" gives a thorough list of do's and don'ts for creating robust controls. Many of the principles apply to ActiveX Documents as well.

Key Events in the Life of an ActiveX Document

The design of an ActiveX document depends greatly on the application(s) you are targeting. All containers are not created equal, and this is especially evident when considering events. However, before examining the events, read the two following notes, which affect the availability and behavior of key events.

A Note on Siting

Like an ActiveX control, an ActiveX document cannot exist by itself. It must be placed in a container. The process of hooking an ActiveX document up to its container is called *siting* — that is, assigning the ActiveX document a *site* in the container.

It's only after an ActiveX document has been sited that the properties of the container become available to it. For example, the UserDocument object's Parent property (which returns a reference to the container) is not available until the ActiveX document is sited. The Hyperlink object is also unavailable until the document has been sited.

For More Information Because of the similarity of ActiveX document creation to ActiveX control creation, you may wish to peruse "Control Creation Terminology" in Chapter 9, "Building ActiveX Controls."

A Note on Saving Properties

If a container application supports the PropertyBag, you can easily save and retrieve data to a file — whether it saves to the .vbd file or not depends upon the application. For example, Internet Explorer saves data to the .vbd file, but Office Binder saves all data to the .obd (Office Binder Data) file. However, once data has been saved, the InitProperties will not occur; instead, the ReadProperties event will replace it. Similarly, the WriteProperties event will not occur until the user saves a property.

For More Information To find out how to save properties with the PropertyBag, see "Persisting ActiveX Document Data," later in this chapter.

Key UserDocument Events

The meanings of the key events in the life of a UserDocument object are as follows:

- The Initialize event occurs every time an instance of your document is created or recreated. It is always the first event in an ActiveX document's lifetime.
- The InitProperties event occurs only as long as none of the ActiveX document properties have been saved using the PropertyBag. Once a property value has been saved, this event will be replaced by the ReadProperties event.
- The ReadProperties event occurs instead of the InitProperties event only after a property has been saved using the PropertyBag. You must add code to actually read the property.
- The EnterFocus event occurs when any object, including the ActiveX document, receives focus.
- The ExitFocus event occurs when no object on the ActiveX document, including the document itself, has focus any longer.
- The Resize event occurs every time a container is resized.
- The Scroll event occurs whenever the user clicks on the container's scrollbar or the scrolling region of the container, or if the user drags the scrollbar. Note: Scrollbars appear on the container only when the container's Viewport is sized smaller than the MinWidth or MinHeight of the UserDocument.
- The WriteProperties event occurs immediately before the Terminate event, when, during the life of the ActiveX document, at least one property value has changed. To notify the container that a property has changed, use the PropertyChanged statement. This is covered in greater detail in "Persisting ActiveX Document Data," later in this chapter.
- The Terminate event occurs when the ActiveX document is about to be destroyed. You can use the Termination event to clean up any object references by setting all global object references to Nothing.

Note In Internet Explorer 4.0, the ActiveX document will be terminated as soon as the user navigates away from the document. In Internet Explorer 3.0, an ActiveX document is stored in a cache of four documents. When the user loads or navigates to a fifth document, the ActiveX document will be terminated.

Opening an ActiveX Document Before Saving Properties

When the user opens an ActiveX document on which no properties have been saved, the following events will occur.

Event	What Gets Done
Initialize	Document created but not sited in container yet.
InitProperties	Default values for properties are set.
Show	The document is shown in the container. The document has been sited in the container, therefore container properties become available.
EnterFocus	The document gets focus.

Opening an ActiveX Document After Saving Properties

If the user has saved any property, the ReadProperties event will occur instead of the InitProperties event.

Event	What Gets Done
Initialize	Document created but not sited in container yet.
ReadProperties	Properties are read through the PropertyBag object's ReadProperties method.
Show	The document is shown in the container.
EnterFocus	The document gets focus.

Show and Hide Events

Possibly, the two most important events for an ActiveX document are the Show and Hide events.

These events are especially important for these reasons:

- The Show event occurs whenever the user navigates to the document (in a browser). You can use this event to check for global object references set by other ActiveX documents.
- The Show event occurs after the ActiveX document is fully sited in the container (unlike the Initialize property). Because you can't count on the InitProperties event to always occur, the Show event can be used as another event to verify the container. See "Determining the ActiveX Document's Container Programmatically" in this chapter for an example.

- The Hide event occurs whenever the user navigates off the document (in a browser). The event also occurs immediately before the Terminate event. Use the event to destroy any global object references before navigating to another document.

  Note In Internet Explorer 3.0, an ActiveX document is stored in a cache of four documents. When the user loads or navigates to a fifth document, the ActiveX document will be terminated. The Hide event will occur when the user navigates off the ActiveX document to another document, or when Internet Explorer 3.0 is terminated while the document is being viewed or is still within the cache of active documents.

For More Information "Life Cycle of a UserDocument," one of the step-by-step procedures in Chapter 5, "Creating an ActiveX Document," demonstrates the key events in the life of an ActiveX document.

Design Considerations for ActiveX Documents

Before designing an ActiveX document, you must be aware of a few considerations.

- ActiveX documents are not stand-alone applications.

  An ActiveX document can only exist in a container. Because containers vary, you can't always predict the capabilities and limitations of your ActiveX document environment. At best, you can target a particular container or set of containers, and degrade gracefully in all others.

- For ActiveX projects that need to exchange data between multiple ActiveX documents, you must implement global object variables and object references.

  Global object references, however, come with some overhead: you must track them to ensure they aren't overwritten inadvertently, and you must be sure that they are released. This is covered in more detail in "Ensuring Communication Among ActiveX Documents" in this chapter.

- Navigation, or how to get from one ActiveX document to another, may vary from one container to another.

  For example, to show another ActiveX document in the Visual Basic development environment, you must use the CreateToolWindow function — which doesn't require the .vbd file. In contrast, to show a second ActiveX document in Internet Explorer, you must use the Hyperlink object's NavigateTo method with the .vbd file.

- To enable one ActiveX document to pass data to another, you must implement public properties or methods.

- You cannot place an OLE Container control or embedded objects (such as Microsoft Word or Microsoft Excel documents) on a UserDocument.

- In-Process and Out-of-Process ActiveX Documents

In-Process and Out-of-Process ActiveX Documents

When you create an ActiveX document, you are creating an ActiveX component, and as such, the component can be either *in-process* or *out-of-process*.

For More Information For a detailed description about the difference between in-process and out-of-process components, see "In-Process and Out-of-Process Components," in Chapter 6, "General Principles of Component Design."

The Case for DLLs

There are a few reasons why you may want to create your ActiveX document as an in-process component (.dll file).

1. The performance of an in-process component, or .dll file, will surpass the performance of the same component compiled as an .exe.

2. Multiple clients accessing the same .exe can overwrite global data. For example, imagine a suite of ActiveX documents being used by two different instances of Internet Explorer. Also imagine that the suite uses a global object variable to store a numeral, such as an interest rate. If the value of the variable is changed by one set of documents, the other set will begin using the new value with no indication that it has changed.

Targeting an ActiveX Document Container

ActiveX documents, like ActiveX controls, cannot be used alone. ActiveX documents must exist in a *container*, which is itself an object. Most ActiveX documents, however, will be viewed in an application that provides an object that is the actual container of the ActiveX document. Throughout this document, we will therefore refer to these applications as *container applications*, or applications that can contain an ActiveX document.

Here are three containers, and their advantages:

- **Microsoft Internet Explorer** (version 3.0 or later) — Using Internet Explorer, an ActiveX document can be a familiar version of an existing application with added Internet capabilities. For example, an existing application can be enhanced with Web links (using the Hyperlink object). You can also deploy the ActiveX document over the Internet, allowing users to get the latest version of your application.

  Note The deployment of ActiveX documents differs slightly depending on the version of Internet Explorer that you are targeting. For more information on deploying ActiveX documents, see "Manually Deploying ActiveX Components" in Part 5, "Building Internet Applications."

- **Microsoft Office Binder 1.0** (or later) — The Microsoft Binder is an electronic "paper clip" that can hold several disparate documents, such as Word and Excel documents. Use an ActiveX document to add database programming or multimedia display capabilities to binders. For example, a repair manual assembled as a binder of Word documents could be enhanced by the addition of a Visual Basic ActiveX document that displayed video clips of repair procedures.
- **Visual Basic Development Environment Tool Window** — The Visual Basic Environment Tool Window is an object created by the CreateToolWindow function. Using this function, you can create a dockable window in the Visual Basic development environment. This window can then contain ActiveX documents that provide additional user interface capabilities to the development environment. For instance, you could create a resource editor or menu editor using the Visual Basic Extensibility Object Model.

Issues for Containers

Because the capabilities of an ActiveX document can depend on the host application, you should consider the following questions:

- Will this document depend on the features of a particular host application?

  For example, if you are creating an ActiveX document that will run in Internet Explorer, you may want to exploit its ability to show an ActiveX document in one frame, and HTML documents in another.
- Will I be creating a suite of documents that work together?

  For example, if the document is a simple calculator, it will probably not demand more than a single ActiveX document, and the answer is "no."

If the answer to either of these is "yes," then you will need to investigate the capabilities of the target application(s). Specifically, you will want to know how to navigate from one ActiveX document to another (if you are creating a suite of documents), or how to access the features of the host application. Other than documentation from the creator of the container application, the only way to discover the object model is by using the Object Browser.

One Example: One Goal, Two Containers

To illustrate this, let's examine a multidocument scenario. Imagine you have created two ActiveX documents, and want to open the second by clicking on a button on the first.

If the host application is Internet Explorer, you must use the Hyperlink object's NavigateTo method to get from one document to another, as shown in the following code:

```
Private Sub cmdGoTo_Click()
   ' Assuming the name of the
   ' destination is AxDoc2.vbd.
   UserDocument.HyperLink.NavigateTo _
      "file://c:\docs\AxDoc2.vbd"
End Sub
```

On the other hand, Microsoft Binder operates on an entirely different metaphor. Instead of navigating to another document, you must add a section to the Binder. An example of the code is shown in the following:

```
Private Sub cmdAddSection_Click()
   ' Use the same document: AxDoc2.
   UserDocument.Parent.Parent.Sections. _
   Add , "c:\docs\AxDoc2.vbd"
End Sub
```

Looking into the Target Application's Object Model

From the preceding two different methods shown, it becomes apparent that you cannot count on one method to get from one ActiveX document to another in every container. The question then becomes, "How do I discover the method for a target host application?"

One way (besides documentation) to discover an application's methods is to use the Object Browser. For example, to explore the object model of Microsoft Binder, follow these steps:

To discover the objects and methods of Microsoft Binder

Note You must have Microsoft Office Binder 1.0 or later, which can be installed with Microsoft Office.

1. On the **Project** menu, click **References**.
2. In the scrolling list of available references, click **OLE Automation Binder 1.0 Type Library** (or **Microsoft Binder 8.0 Object Library** for Office '97).
3. Click **OK**.
4. Press F2 to open the **Object Browser**.
5. Click the **Project/Library Box**, and then click **Office Binder**.
6. In the **Classes** List, click **Sections**.
7. In the **Members of** List, click **Add**. You will now see the syntax of the Add method, which you can use to add the ActiveX document to the Sections collection.

Navigating Through the Object Model

You may have noticed that the Object Browser hasn't given you a complete guide to the object model. Compare the code:

```
UserDocument.Parent.Parent.Sections.Add _
, "c:\docs\AxDoc2.vbd"
```

with the information found in the Object Browser. The difference lies in the addition of "UserDocument.Parent.Parent" to the code.

The discrepancy arises because the ActiveX document is itself "buried" lower within the object model. To Office Binder, the ActiveX document is just one more Section object in a Sections collection. Thus the code `TypeName(UserDocument.Parent)` returns "Section," while `TypeName(UserDocument.Parent.Parent)` returns "Binder."

In order to navigate through the hierarchy to the top of the object model, the code uses the reference returned by the Parent property. However the code must navigate one final level — again using the Parent property. This results in the `Parent.Parent` code. The code then navigates back down to the Sections collection, culminating in the Add method.

For More Information To learn about the Object Browser, see "Finding Out about Objects," in Chapter 9, "Programming with Objects," in the *Microsoft Visual Basic 6.0 Programmer's Guide*. For details about navigating through the Object Model, see "Navigating Object Models" in Chapter 10, "Programming with Components," in the *Microsoft Visual Basic 6.0 Programmer's Guide*.

The Microsoft Binder as an ActiveX Container

The Microsoft Office Binder is an electronic "paper clip" — you can add several disparate kinds of documents to the Binder that have some relation to each other. "Documents" can include:

- Word documents
- Excel documents
- PowerPoint presentations

This topic covers the basics of using the Binder as a container of ActiveX documents.

Adding an ActiveX Document

There are two ways to add an ActiveX document to a Binder:

- Add an ActiveX document as a section.
- Add an ActiveX as a file.

Adding the ActiveX Document as a Section

When you add an ActiveX document as a section, the Binder adds the document using its ProgID. When an ActiveX document is added this way, it's akin to adding a blank Word document — the document is a "blank" document. To identify the "blank" document, Binder looks for the *ProgID* of the ActiveX document. In brief, the ProgId (or *programmatic ID*) is the class name and the component name separated by a period. For example, the ProgID of an ActiveX document with no changes to the default settings would be "Project1.UserDocument1."

> **Note** When you add a new section, you are creating a new object from the ActiveX document class. Thus the InitProperties event will always occur (instead of the ReadProperties event).

For More Information For details about Programmatic IDs, see "Adding Classes to Components," in Chapter 6, "General Principles of Component Design."

To add an ActiveX document as a section

1. Start Microsoft Binder.
2. On the **Section** menu, click **Add** to open the **Add Section** dialog box.
3. From the scrollable list of ProgIDs, double-click your ActiveX document.

Adding the ActiveX Document as a File

When you add an ActiveX document as a file, you can select a particular .vbd file that you may have saved earlier.

> **Note** If you have created an ActiveX document that persists data (through the PropertyBag), and you have saved data to the file, adding that .vbd file will cause the ReadProperties event to occur. But if you did not write code to persist data, the InitProperties event will fire instead. For details on persisting data, see "Persisting ActiveX Document Data" in this chapter.

To add an ActiveX document as a section

1. Start Microsoft Binder
2. On the **Section** menu, click **Add from File** to open the **Add from File** dialog box.
3. Navigate to your .vbd file, and click **Add**.

Saving an ActiveX Document in the Binder

As with any other document in the binder, you can save the ActiveX document as one of a group of documents. When you save the ActiveX document in this way, the WriteProperties event will fire. However, to actually persist data in the document, you must have written the proper code in the WriteProperties event.

To save an ActiveX document in the Binder

1. Add the ActiveX document, either as a section or a file.
2. On the **File** menu, click **Save Binder** to open the **Save Binder As** dialog box.
3. Type the name of the Binder and click **Save**.

Programming the Binder

You can create ActiveX documents that programmatically manipulate other sections. In order to do this, you must know the object model of the Binder.

The Binder's object model is built around a collection of Section objects, the Sections collection. And each Section object can contain a Microsoft Excel, Word, PowerPoint, or Visual Basic ActiveX document. Using this knowledge, it's possible to walk through the Sections and get a reference to each document. Using that reference, you can then manipulate the document's objects. This is easier to explain in a simple procedure.

Example: Manipulating an Excel Spreadsheet

The following scenario is necessarily simple: add an Excel worksheet and an ActiveX document to the Binder, and using an ActiveX document, retrieve a value from the worksheet.

To retrieve a value from an Excel worksheet

1. In Visual Basic, on the **File** menu, click **New Project**. Then click the ActiveX Document DLL icon.
2. In the Project Explorer window, double-click **UserDocument1** to show its designer.
3. Draw a TextBox control on the designer, and change its name to "txtCell."
4. Draw a CommandButton control on the designer, and change its caption to "Get Value."
5. On the **Project** menu, click **References** to show the **References** dialog box.
6. From the scrolling list of references, click the **OLE Automation Binder 1.0** Type Library checkbox.
7. Double-click the **CommandButton** to show its code window.
8. Add the following code to the Command1 click event.

```
Private Sub Command1_Click()
   Dim i As Integer ' Counter
   Dim objX As Sections ' Object variable
   Set objX = UserDocument.Parent.Parent.Sections
   For i = 1 to objX.Count
      If TypeName(objX.Item(i).Object) = _
         "Worksheet" Then
```

```
        txtCell = objeX.Item(i).Object.Range. _
           ("A1").Value
        End If
     Next i
  End Sub
```

9. Press F5 to run the project.
10. Minimize the Visual Basic instance.
11. Start Microsoft Binder.
12. On the **Section** menu, click **Add Section**.
13. Double-click **Microsoft Excel Worksheet**. A blank worksheet is now added to the Binder.
14. Type a distinctive number or text into cell A1 (it's already selected for you, so you can simply begin typing).
15. On the **Section** menu, click **Add Section**.
16. Double-click **Project1.UserDocument1**.
17. Click **Get Value**. The text or number you just typed into the spreadsheet will appear in the textbox.

The Code Explained

Because we want to early-bind the object variable, step 6 instructs you to add a reference to the OLE Automation Binder Type Library. Thus in the code, we declare the object variable of type Sections. The code then sets the variable to the Binder's Sections collection.

Once we have a reference to the collection, we can iterate through its members using the For statement. Within the For look, we then use the TypeName function to return the type of each object in the section. If the TypeName function returns "Worksheet," we know that it's the Excel worksheet in the collection. Having determined that, the code simply returns the contents of cell A1 to the TextBox control.

Another Example: Adding a Second ActiveX Object

Adding another ActiveX document to the Binder is also accomplished using the Sections collection. This time, however, we use the Add method of the Sections collection.

```
Option Explicit
Private mMyDoc2 As axdDoc2 ' Module level variable

Private Sub AddDoc_Click()
   Dim objX As Sections ' Object variable
   Set objX = UserDocument.Parent.Parent.Sections
   Set mMyDoc2 = objX.Add( , "c:\axdDoc2.vbd")
End Sub
```

The preceding code again uses the Sections collection, but instead uses the Add method to add a second ActiveX document to the binder. You may have noticed that the code also declares a module-level variable as type axdDoc2 (assuming that is the name of the second document). The code sets the object variable to the reference returned by the Add method. With that reference, you can then access the public properties and methods of the second document, as shown:

```
txtName.Text = mMyDoc2.Name
   ' Assuming there's a public property called Name.
mMyDoc.MyMethod ' Assuming a public function exists.
```

The Visual Basic IDE as an ActiveX Document Container

Using the Extensibility object model and add-ins, you can greatly extend the Visual Basic development environment. You can also create ActiveX documents to extend the Visual Basic IDE. Develop your ActiveX document as you would any other, but use the CreateToolWindow function to create a tool window in the IDE which will contain the ActiveX document.

> **Note** This topic assumes you have some knowledge of add-ins — what they are, and how to create them. If you are unfamiliar with add-ins, see "Creating a Basic Add-In," in Chapter 1, "Add-Ins Overview," in Part 3: "Extending the Visual Basic Environment with Add-Ins."

Using the CreateToolWindow function has the following advantages over other add-ins:

- The CreateToolWindow function returns a dockable window.
- The window correctly follows window minimize and maximize semantics without any coding. For example, tool windows will "remember" where they were last placed or docked.

The CreateToolWindow Function

The CreateToolWindow function is a method of the Windows collection. The function creates a tool window — a container for the ActiveX document — and returns a reference to the window. The following series of steps outline what happens in a typical scenario:

1. On the **Add-Ins** menu, the user clicks **AddIn Manager**, and a list of all available add-ins appears.
2. From the list, the user clicks "MyActiveXAddIn."
3. As the add-in is created, the OnConnect event occurs.

4. In the OnConnect event, the code invokes the CreateToolWindow function, creating the tool window.
5. The function call returns a reference to the newly created tool window that contains the ActiveX document.
6. Using the reference, the code can manipulate tool window properties. For example, to show the tool window, the **Visible** property is set to **True**.

To create a simple Add-in using an ActiveX document

1. On the **File** menu, click **New Project** to open the **New Project** dialog box. Double-click the AddIn icon to create a new Add-in project.
2. Click the **Project** menu, then click **Add UserDocument** to open the **Add UserDocument** dialog box. Double-click the UserDocument icon to add a UserDocument to the project.
3. In the Properties window, double-click **Name**, and change the name of the UserDocument to "axdUserDoc."
4. In the Project Explorer window, double-click the Connect icon to open the class module's code window. There is already a fair amount of code written in the template, and we will just add a bit to it. Look at the Declarations section, and modify it to resemble the following code:

```
Implements IDTExtensibility

Public FormDisplayed     As Boolean
Public VBInstance        As VBIDE.VBE
Public mcbMenuCommandBar As Office.CommandBarControl
Dim frmAddIn             As New frmAddIn
Public WithEvents MenuHandler As CommandBarEvents

' Add the following declarations for the
' CreateToolWindow function:
Private mWin As Window
Private mobjDoc As axdUserDoc
Const guidMyTool$ = "(4244B234-E45F-12dg-803f-04884)"
```

   The code you added declares the necessary object variables for the CreateToolWindow function. The Window variable "mWin" will be set to the reference returned by the function; you can then use this reference to show or hide the window. The second variable, "mobjDoc," will be set to reference the UserDocument. You can then use this reference to manipulate the ActiveX document. Finally, the constant "guidMyTool" is used by the function to identify the window instance; for every tool window you create, this string must be unique.

5. In the code window, scroll down to the OnConnection event. We will add code to this event, but to avoid confusion, select all of the code in the event, and delete it. Then add the following code:

```
Private Sub IDTExtensibility_OnConnection(ByVal VBInst As Object,
➥ ByVal ConnectMode As VBIDE.vbext_ConnectMode,
➥ ByVal AddInInst As VBIDE.AddIn, custom() As Variant)
   Set mWin = AddInInst.VBE.Windows. _
      CreateToolWindow(AddInInst, _
      "MyAddin.axdUserDoc", _
      "ActiveX Caption", guidMyTool, mobjDoc)
   mWin.Visible = True
End Sub
```

This code uses the Set statement to set the Window variable "mWin" to a reference to the window created by the function. This reference is then used to set the Visible property of the window to True.

6. Press CTRL+G to view the Immediate window.
7. Type "AddToIni" and press RETURN. You have just added the progID of the project to the VBAddIn.ini file, a necessary step when creating an Add-in.
8. Press F5 to run the project.
9. Minimize the Visual Basic window. This will prevent confusion as you will start another Visual Basic instance.
10. Start another instance of Visual Basic.
11. When the **New Project** dialog box appears, press ENTER to start a new Standard .exe project.
12. On the **Add-Ins** menu, click **Add-In Manager** to display the **Add-In Manager** dialog box.
13. From the list of available add-ins, click **My Add-In**, then click **OK**. The ActiveX document you just created will now appear as a part of the Visual Basic development environment.
14. After viewing the document, you will want to shut it down. To do this, open the **Add-in Manager** dialog box again, and clear the **MyAddIn** checkbox, then click **OK**.

Adding a Second Window

Having an understanding of the mechanics of the function allows us to create a more complex scenario: creating a second window, containing a second ActiveX document, from the first.

To add a second ActiveX document

1. If you haven't already, quit the second instance of Visual Basic.
2. On the **Project** menu, click **Add UserDocument** and add a second UserDocument to the project.

3. Change the name of the UserDocument to "axdUserDoc2."
4. Add a TextBox control to the UserDocument.
5. Double-click the designer, and add the following code:

```
Public Property Get Text () As String
   Text = Text1.Text
End Property

Public Property Let Text(ByVal newText As String)
   Text1.Text = newText
End Property
```

   The preceding code creates a public property, which you will set when you create the window for the document.

6. In the Project Explorer window, double-click AddIn to open the code module. Add the following code to the Declarations section.

```
Public gAddIn As vbide.Addin
```

   The new line declares a global variable that will be set with a reference to the add-in instance.

7. In the Project Explorer window, double-click Connect to open the class module. Look at the OnConnect event, and modify it to resemble the following code:

```
Private Sub IDTExtensibility_OnConnection(ByVal _
VBInst As Object, ByVal ConnectMode As _
VBIDE.vbext_ConnectMode, ByVal AddInInst As _
VBIDE.AddIn, custom() As Variant)
   Set mWin = AddInInst.VBE.Windows. _
      CreateToolWindow(AddInInst, _
      "MyAddin.axdUserDoc", _
      "ActiveX Caption", guidMyTool, mobjDoc)
   mWin.Visible = True

   ' Add this new code:
   Set gAddIn = AddInInst
End Sub
```

   The new line sets the global variable to the add-in instance, making it available to create more windows.

8. In the Project Explorer Window, double-click **axdUserDocument** to bring its designer forward.
9. On the Toolbox, double-click the CommandButton icon to add a CommandButton control to the UserDocument.
10. Change the caption of the button to "Show Next."

11. Double-click the designer to open its code window, and add the following code:

```
Private mWin2 As Window
Private mDoc2 As axdUserDoc2
Const guidMyTool$ = "Xiang19X67Hangzhou4/27"

Private Sub Command1_Click()
   set mWin2 = gAddIn.VBE.Windows. _
      CreateToolWindow(gAddIn, _
      "MyAddin.axdUserDoc2", _
      "Second ActiveX Document", _
      guidMyTool, mDoc2)
   mWin2.Visible = True
   mDoc2.Text = "This is the second document."
End Sub
```

12. Press F5 to run the project.
13. Run another instance of Visual Basic.
14. When the **New Project** dialog appears, press ENTER to start a new Standard .exe project.
15. On the **Add-Ins** menu, click **Add-In Manager** to display the **Add-In Manager** dialog box.
16. From the list of available Add-ins, select the **My Add-In** checkbox, then click **OK**. The ActiveX document you just created will now appear as a part of the Visual Basic development environment.

Determining the ActiveX Document's Container Programmatically

The characteristics of your user's target application have a large impact on your ActiveX document design. Consequently, your code should verify which container is being used in order to react appropriately. For example, if you intend your document to be viewed in the Visual Basic Development Environment Tool Window, your code should check the container before accessing extensibility objects (which are unavailable in Internet Explorer).

To determine the container of the ActiveX document, use the TypeName statement with the Parent property of the UserDocument. A simple example of this is shown:

```
Dim strContainer As String
strContainer = TypeName(UserDocument.Parent)
```

The following table shows the three possible strings returned by Internet Explorer, Microsoft Binder, and the window created by the CreateToolWindow function in the Visual Basic development environment:

Container	Return String
Internet Explorer	IwebBrowserApp
Microsoft Binder	Section
Window	Window

Defensive Programming

Because you may never know which container the user will actually use to view an ActiveX document, you should prepare for the "wrong" container (a container which lacks the features your ActiveX document needs to function optimally). Although the TypeName function will not return the version of the container, it will at least allow you to determine if the container is unequivocally "wrong." In that case, you may inform the user that some functionality is not available with the container, and that she should use the "right" container to view the document.

Because the Show event occurs when an ActiveX document is sited on the container, it is the best event for determining the container. Be aware, however, that the Show event occurs whenever the document is shown (and this behavior varies according to the container application). To sidestep this problem, declare a module level variable to function as a flag. After verifying the container, the flag is reset. Subsequent Show events will then check the flag, and avoid redundantly checking the container again.

```
Option Explict
Private mblnSHOWN As Boolean

Private Sub UserDocument_Show()
   If Not mblnSHOWN Then
      Dim strContainer As String
      strContainer = TypeName(UserDocument.Type)
      ' Use the Select Case statement to test.
      Select Case strContainer
         Case "IwebBrowserApp"
      ' Supported container: continue to open app.
         Case "Section"
      ' Supported container: continue to open app.
         Case Else ' Handle other unknown containers.
      ' Unsupported container: exit gracefully.
         MsgBox "Sorry, please open this " & _
         "document with Internet Explorer " & _
         "3.0 or later."
         End Select
      mblnSHOWN = True ' Reset the flag
   End If
End Sub
```

Note You can't use the Initialize event to test the container because when that event fires the document is not yet sited. For an explanation of when the document is sited, see "Key Events in the Life of a UserDocument," earlier in this chapter.

Designing the User Interface for ActiveX Documents

Designing an ActiveX document's User Interface has some similarities, and some major differences, to designing the User Interface for a standard application. Similarities include the ability to add forms and menus to the project. However, the differences result from one overwhelming fact: The ActiveX document is always viewed in a container. In other words, the User Interface of your ActiveX document will always be viewed within the context of another application. The following topics explain what you should consider as you design a User Interface for an ActiveX document.

- **Menu Design for ActiveX Documents** Add menus to your ActiveX documents with the Menu Editor.
- **ActiveX Document Viewport** The container's Viewport determines the size of the window an ActiveX document is being viewed in. This topic shows you how to control what is shown in the ViewPort.
- **Adding Forms and Modules to ActiveX Document Projects** Add forms to your ActiveX document project as you would with any other. The topic also covers the NonModalAllowed property.

Menu Design for ActiveX Documents

You can create your own menus for your ActiveX designer by using the Visual Basic Menu Editor. Containers that support ActiveX documents will also automatically merge any Help menu you create with the container's Help menu.

Tell Them Who You Are

When a user comes across your document — whether through a browser, binder, or other application — she may not immediately recognize it. For this reason, it is highly recommended that you always add an "About" menu to every ActiveX document you create.

You should also be aware that some containers will not display their menus correctly unless the ActiveX document merges a Help menu with the container's Help menu.

To merge an About box with the container's Help menu

1. On the **Project** menu, click **Add Form**.
2. In the **Add Form** dialog box, double-click the **AboutBox** with SysInfo icon to add an About Box form to the project.
3. Set the **Caption** property of the form and Label controls appropriate to your ActiveX document.
4. In the Project Explorer window, double-click your UserDocument to bring its designer forward.
5. Click the UserDocument designer to select it, and on the **Tools** menu, click **Menu Editor** to display the menu editor dialog box.
6. Click the **Caption** box and type **&Help**.
7. Click the **Name** box and type **mnuHelp**.
8. Click the **NegotiatePosition** box, and click **Right**.
9. Click the **Next** button to create a new menu item.
10. In the **Caption** box type "About" and the name of your ActiveX document.
11. In the **Name** box type **mnuAbout**.
12. Click the right-facing arrow button to indent the menu item.
13. Click **OK**.
14. Double-click your ActiveX designer to bring its **Code** window to the front.
15. Add the following code to the mnuAbout Click event:

```
Private Sub mnuAbout_Click()
   frmAbout.Show vbModal
End Sub
```

ActiveX Document Viewport

An ActiveX document cannot be viewed as a stand-alone application — it must be viewed in a container application. The area in the container application through which the document is visible is also known as the *Viewport*. The following Figure illustrates the Viewport of Internet Explorer.

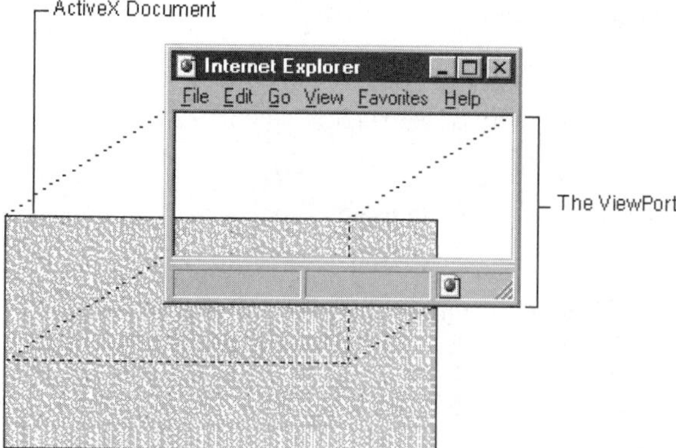

Naturally, the Viewport can be resized by the user, and the developer has no control over this. However, using the SetViewPort method, you can manipulate which part of an ActiveX document is shown in the Viewport. First, however, let's examine other Viewport features, as understanding them will make it easier to the SetViewPort method.

The ViewPortTop, ViewPortLeft, ViewPortHeight, and ViewPortWidth Properties

The ViewPortHeight, ViewPortWidth, ViewPortLeft, and ViewPortTop properties are read-only properties. They return the coordinates of the Viewport relative to the ActiveX document. The following Figure shows Internet Explorer overlaying the ActiveX document. The Viewport properties are called out. Notice that in this case the ActiveX document is larger than the Viewport. In reality, when the Viewport is too small to show the entire document, scrollbars will appear. (The scrollbars, however, can be turned off by setting the ScrollBars property to False. Note that this is a read-only property, and must be set at design time).

The following figure shows the Viewport properties after the user has scrolled to see the other parts of the document; notice that only the ViewPortLeft and ViewPortTop properties have changed:

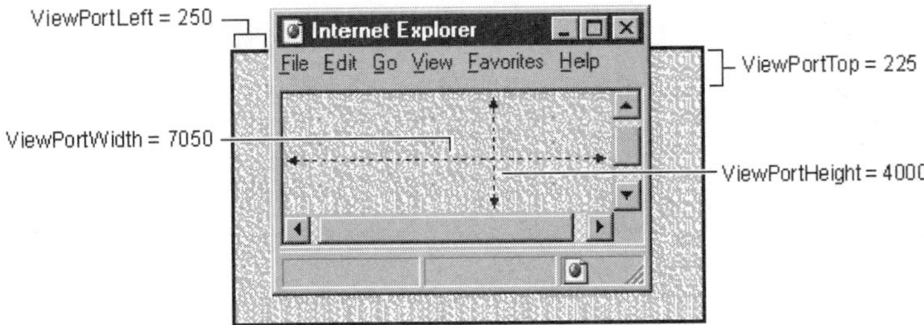

Finally the following figure shows the Viewport properties after the user has resized the Viewport. Notice that the ViewPortHeight and ViewPortWidth have now changed:

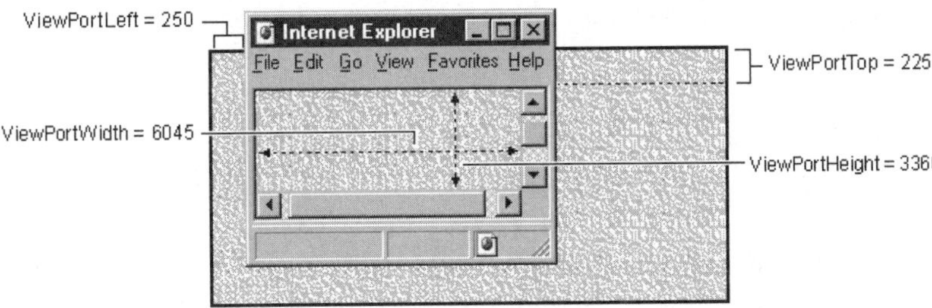

The MinHeight, MinWidth Properties

Because an ActiveX document is contained by another application, you will have no control over how much space the container application gives to your ActiveX document. However, you will be able to specify the minimum space your ActiveX document needs before scrollbars appear by setting the MinHeight and MinWidth properties.

When you design an ActiveX document, the Height and Width of the UserDocument designer become the default settings for the MinHeight and MinWidth properties. Also, the MinHeight and MinWidth properties are always set to the ScaleMode of the UserDocument.

In the following figure, the ActiveX document is smaller than the Viewport. In this case, the container has no scrollbars, and the "empty" part of the Viewport is filled with the BackColor of the ActiveX document. However, if the user resizes the container so that the Viewport is smaller than the ActiveX document, scrollbars will appear.

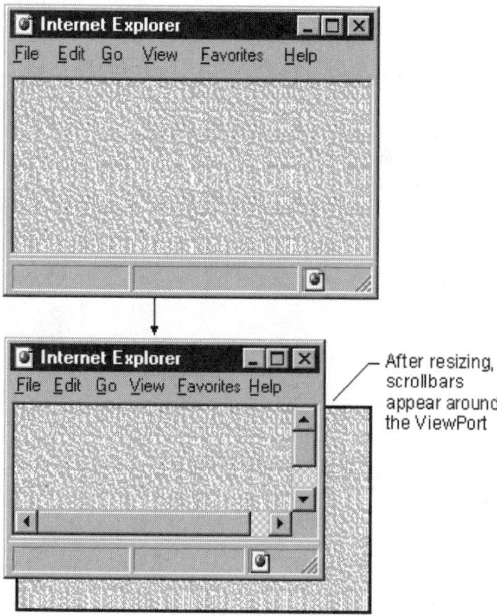

The MinHeight and MinWidth properties are settable. In other words, you can cause scrollbars to appear on the container by simply setting the MinHeight and MinWidth properties to be larger than the Viewport properties. For example, imagine an ActiveX document that allows the user to insert any image into an PictureBox control, and that the control resizes automatically to the size of the image. By setting the MinHeight and MinWidth properties to always be larger than the control, you can assure that scrollbars will always appear to let the user see the entire image:

```
Private Sub Picture1_Resize()
   UserDocument.MinHeight = _
      Picture1.Height + 100
   UserDocument.MinWidth = _
      Picture1.Width + 100
End Sub
```

Using the SetViewPort Method to Scroll

You can cause the Viewport to scroll to a specific coordinate by using the SetViewPort method. The method requires two arguments, the Top and Left arguments. For example, by setting these arguments to the Left and Top properties of a TextBox placed on the document, you can programmatically ensure that the TextBox with the focus always appears in the top left corner of the ActiveX document. This is illustrated:

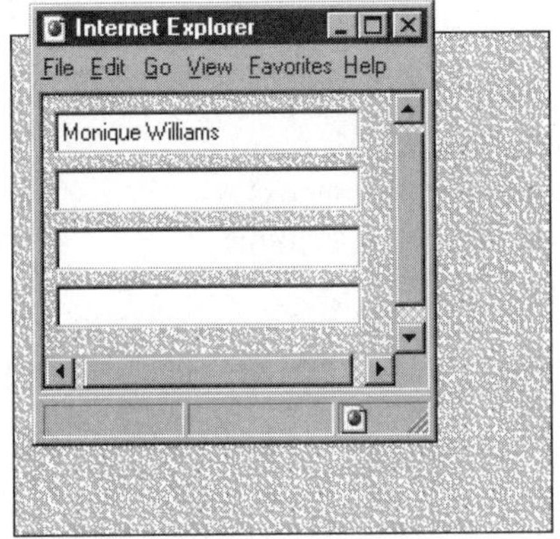


```
Private Sub Text1_GotFocus (Index As Integer)
  UserDocument.SetViewPort _
    Text1(Index).Left, Text1(Index).Top
End Sub
```

The HScrollSmallChange and VScrollSmallChange Properties

The HScrollSmallChange and VScrollSmallChange properties function like the SmallChange property (of the HScolllBar and VScrollBar controls).

> **Note** There is no "HScrollLargeChange" or "VScrollLargeChange" property because the Viewport handles this for you automatically. The "LargeChange" value is determined by the current height and width of the Viewport.

Adding Forms and Modules to ActiveX Document Projects

When you create a Visual Basic project, you are used to starting with a standard Form. When you create an ActiveX document, you are by no means limited to using only ActiveX documents: You can add standard forms and modules to your project, as you would to any other project.

Modeless Dialog Boxes Sometimes Aren't Allowed

When you create an ActiveX DLL, you'll have one limitation: Depending on the container, modeless dialog boxes may or may not be displayed. For example, imagine that you've created an ActiveX DLL that includes an ActiveX document that shows a modeless form. If you view the document in Office Binder, showing the modeless form will present no problems. On the other hand, if you view the same document in Internet Explorer, attempting to display the same modeless form will raise an error.

> **Note** With Internet Explorer 4.0 or later, the ability to show modeless forms is dependent on the threading model. This is discussed in "Apartment-Model Threading in Visual Basic" in Chapter 8, "Building Code Components."

Avoid the Problem Using the NonModalAllowed Property

However, the problem of not being allowed to display a modeless dialog box can be sidestepped. Using the NonModalAllowed property, you can check before displaying a form, and react appropriately. In short, the NonModalAllowed property (a read-only property), returns True or False, depending on whether or not the App object allows modeless forms to be displayed. Simple code can then be written as in the following example:

```
Private Sub cmdShowMe_Click()
      If App.NonModalAllowed Then ' Show the form
                                  ' modeless.
   frmModeless.Show vbModeless, Me
      Else ' Show the form modally.
   FrmModeless.Show vbModal, Me
   EndIf
End Sub
```

For More Information For more details about displaying forms, see "Displaying Forms from Code Components" in Chapter 6, "General Principles of Component Design."

Adding Internet Features to ActiveX Documents

ActiveX documents allow you to take advantage of the Internet through use of the Hyperlink object, and the ability to download data asynchronously.

- **Downloading Data Asynchronously** Asynchronously download data using the AsyncRead method in conjunction with the AsyncReadComplete event.
- **Using the Hyperlink objects with ActiveX Documents** Using the properties and methods of the Hyperlink object, your ActiveX document can request a hyperlink-aware container, such as Microsoft Internet Explorer, to jump to a given URL.
- **Saving State Across Pages with Get Property / Put Property** You can use Internet Explorer's GetProperty and PutProperty methods to save data and even pass it between objects.

Downloading Data Asynchronously

Asynchronous downloading is like the process of having a pizza delivered to your home. You first make a call to a pizza place and place an order. You then go about your business while others make the pizza. When the pizza is ready, a delivery person knocks on your door and informs you that your dinner has arrived.

With the UserDocument, the equivalent of the phone call is the AsyncRead method. Consequently, the AsyncReadComplete event is the equivalent of the pizza delivery person's knock on your door. This may be easier to understand in a simple scenario: loading a text file into a TextBox control.

To asynchronously load a Picture object into a PictureBox control

1. Press CTRL+N to begin a new project.
2. Click **ActiveX Document DLL** to start a new ActiveX DLL project.
3. In the Project Explorer window, double-click the UserDocument1 icon to open its designer.
4. On the Toolbox, click the TextBox control icon and draw a TextBox control on the designer. Set the MultiLine property to True.
5. Double-click the UserDocument designer to open its code window.
6. Add the following code to InitProperties event:

```
Private Sub UserDocument_InitProperties()
   Dim strPath As String ' file path
      ' Change the path to a different text file if you
      ' wish. If you are on an intranet, you can
      ' also set the path to another computer on
      ' which you have access privileges.
   strPath = "c:\Windows\Readme.txt"
      ' Now invoke the AsyncRead method. Set the
      ' type to vbAsyncTypeFile (a file), and the
      ' name of the property to Pizza.
   UserDocument.AsyncRead strPath, _
      vbAsyncTypeFile,  "Pizza"
End Sub
```

   The preceding code is the "Pizza call." We gave the third argument (the property name argument) a distinctive name.

7. Add the following code to the designer. This code is the "knock on the door." It informs you that your "pizza" has arrived, and you should deal with it:

```
Private Sub UserDocument AsyncReadComplete _
(AsyncProp As VB.AsyncProperty)
   Dim FileNum as Long

      ' Use a Select Case statement to determine which
      ' property is being delivered.
   Select Case AsyncProp.PropertyName
      Case "Pizza"

         ' Open the file and read the contents
         ' into the TextBox
         FileNum = FreeFile
         Open AsyncProp.Value For Input As FileNum
         Text1.Text  = Input(LOF(FileNum), FileNum)
         Close Filenum
   End Select
End Sub
```

8. Press F5 to run the project.
9. Internet Explorer (or your default browser) will open and display your .vbd file. If you have used a file on your own computer, the call will happen too quickly for you to perceive any delay. However, if you have access to a larger file on a remote computer, the effect may be more noticeable.

To take our pizza delivery example one step further, imagine that there is a guarantee that the pizza will be delivered within 30 minutes or it's free. In this case, you might be very interested in the progress of the pizza delivery person. You can check on the progress of your "pizza" by adding code to the AsyncReadProgress event:

```
Private Sub UserDocument AsyncReadProgress _
(AsyncProp As VB.AsyncProperty)
   ' Use a Select Case statement to read the StatusCode
   Select Case AsynchProp.StatusCode
      Case vbAsynchStatusCodeSendingRequest
         MsgBox "Attempting to connect"
      Case vbAsynchStatusCodeEndDownloadData
         MsgBox "Download complete"
      Case vbAsynchStatusCodeError
         MsgBox "Error - aborting transfer"
         CancelAsynchRead "Pizza"
   End Select
End Sub
```

Now when you run the project, the code in the AsyncReadProgress event will display two message boxes: first when an attempt is made to connect to the file, and then when the transfer is complete. If you set a breakpoint on the Select Case statement and step through the code, you'll notice that the vbAsynchStatusEndDownloadData status code is returned before the AsyncReadComplete event is fired. This gives you one last chance to cancel or redirect the file (akin to refusing to answer the door when your "Pizza" arrives).

If an error occurs during the transfer (for example, losing a network connection) the vbAsyncStatusCodeError status code is returned, allowing you to call the CancelAsyncRead method to cancel the transfer and avoid a run-time error.

To see a list of possible status codes returned by the AsyncReadProgress event, look at the AsyncStatusCodeConstants in the Object Browser.

For More Information For an in-depth look at the AsyncRead method and the AsyncReadComplete and AsyncReadProgress events, see "Adding Internet Features to Controls" in Chapter 9, "Building ActiveX Controls." Although the topic covers the UserControl object, the mechanics are identical.

Using the HyperLink Object with ActiveX Documents

If you target a Web browser as your container application, and you create more than one ActiveX document, you must use the HyperLink object to navigate between the different documents.

The Hyperlink object gives your documents access to ActiveX hyperlinking functionality. Using the properties and methods of the Hyperlink object, your ActiveX document can request a hyperlink-aware container, such as Microsoft Internet Explorer, to jump to a given URL.

The NavigateTo Method

The NavigateTo method executes a hyperlink jump to the target specified in the URL argument. The URL can be set to an HTML, Word, or Excel document as well as a .vbd file. For example, the following code navigates to the www.microsoft.com Web page:

```
Private Sub cmdGoTo_Click()
   UserDocument.Hyperlink.NavigateTo _
      "http://www.microsoft.com"
End Sub
```

To jump from one ActiveX document to another, you can use the same method, as shown.

```
Private GoNextDoc_Click()
   ' Assuming the next ActiveX document is named
   ' MyDoc2.vbd
      UserDocument.Hyperlink.NavigateTo _
      "file://c:\ActXDocs\MyDoc2.vbd"
```

Dynamically Constructing an Absolute Path

When you compile an ActiveX project with multiple ActiveX documents, Visual Basic creates the .vbd files in the same directory as the ActiveX .dll or .exe. However, if you move the .vbd files into another directory, you must give the NavigateTo method a fully qualified path for every .vbd file. However, because you cannot determine where a user will place the .vbd files, you must be able to dynamically create the absolute path.

The following code dynamically constructs the path of a .vbd file by parsing the LocationName property of Internet Explorer which returns the absolute path of the document currently displayed by Internet Explorer. The code parses this path, and discards the name of the current .vbd file. The code then appends the name of a second ActiveX document to the remainder of the path.

```
Dim strPath As String     ' String to be parsed
Dim strAbsPath As String ' Result of parsing
Dim intI As Integer       ' Character position counter

' Return the path of the current ActiveX document.
strPath = Trim$(UserDocument.Parent.LocationName)

' Find the position of the last separator character.
For intI = Len(strPath) To 1 Step -1
   If Mid$(StrPath, intI, 1) = "/" Or _
      Mid$(StrPath, intI, 1) = "\" Then Exit For
Next intI

' Strip the name of the current .vbd file.
strAbsPath = Left$(StrPath, intI)

' Navigate to the second ActiveX document.
UserDocument.Hyperlink.NavigateTo _
strAbsPath & "MyDoc2.vbd"
```

Automatically Starting a Browser

If the NavigateTo method is invoked from an ActiveX document contained in an application that supports the Hyperlink object (such as Internet Explorer), the same application instance will be used to "go" to the target document. If the application does not support hyperlinking (Microsoft Binder, for example), then an application that does (determined by the registry) will be started to handle the request. In other words, if the method is invoked from within an application that doesn't support hyperlinking, another that does will be started.

Navigating Between ActiveX Documents

The NavigateTo method can be used to jump from one ActiveX document to another; in fact, it is the only way to start another document in a browser. Thus, if you create a suite of ActiveX documents, and your target container application is a browser that supports the Hyperlink object, you must use the NavigateTo method to open the next document. For example, the following code will cause the second (in a suite) document to appear in the Internet Explorer when the user clicks the cmdGoNext button on the first document:

```
Private Sub cmdGoNext_Click()
   ' The second ActiveX document's file is named _
   ' "ActiveDoc2.vbd"
   UserDocument.HyperLink.NavigateTo _
   "file://c:\ActiveX\ActiveDoc2.vbd"
End Sub
```

The NavigateTo method also includes a second argument, the FrameName argument, that specifies a particular frame in the document to jump to.

The GoBack and GoForward Methods

The GoBack and GoForward methods execute a jump forward or backward to the next document in the browser's history list. These methods only work with hosts that are Hyperlink aware (such as Internet Explorer 3.0 and later).

When implementing the GoForward or GoBack method, be sure to use error checking in case there is no document in the history list to jump to. An example is shown:

```
Private Sub cmdGoForward_Click()
   On Error GoTo noDocInHistory
   UserDocument.Hyperlink.GoForward
   Exit Sub
noDocInHistory:
   Resume Next
End Sub
```

Saving State Across Pages with Get Property / Put Property

As an alternative to saving property values to the built-in PropertyBag object, you can use the facilities of Internet Explorer to save the state of an ActiveX Document. The Internet Explorer object model exposes two methods useful for saving and restoring an object's state PutProperty and GetProperty.

When the user moves away from the page containing your ActiveX document, you can use the PutProperty method to store data. You can then use the GetProperty method when the user returns to the page — or from any other page. This allows you to pass data from one ActiveX document to another, from an ActiveX document to an ActiveX control, or vice versa. You can even pass objects (such as the ActiveX document itself) from one page to another.

> **Note** The PropertyPut and PropertyGet methods can also be used with ActiveX controls created in Visual Basic.

The following code stores a value ("MyProperty") for an ActiveX document named MyUserDoc:

```
Private Sub UserDocument_Hide()
   Dim varValue as Variant

   varValue = MyUserDoc.MyProperty
   MyUserDoc.Parent.PutProperty "MyProperty", varValue
End Sub
```

The PutProperty takes two arguments: a String to reference the property name, and a Variant to hold the value. Because the value argument is a Variant, it can also be used to store an object (in this case the document itself):

```
Private Sub UserDocument_Hide()
   MyUserDoc.Parent.PutProperty "MyUserDoc", Me
End Sub
```

To restore a property, you would use the following code:

```
Private Sub UserDocument_Show()
   Dim varValue as Variant

   varValue = MyUserDoc.Parent.GetProperty("MyProperty")
   MyUserDoc.MyProperty = varValue
End Sub
```

Persisting ActiveX Document Data

Data persistence is the ability of a component to store and retrieve data. How an ActiveX document persists data depends greatly on the container application in which the document appears. Some applications allow you to persist data by writing to an interface of the application. For example, the Internet Explorer 3.0 (and higher) and Microsoft Office Binder allows you to write to a file using the PropertyBag. Other applications, however, do not provide any such intrinsic method of storing data. In those cases, you must use another method, such as writing data to files. Let's start with the PropertyBag.

Note Internet Explorer also allows you to save and restore data using its PutProperty and GetProperty methods. For more information, see "Saving State Across Pages with Get Property / Put Property" in "Adding Internet Features to ActiveX Documents," earlier in this chapter.

The PropertyBag

The PropertyBag is an object that allows you to save data to a file. The file can be either the .vbd, .obd, or some other kind of file — it depends on the application. The PropertyBag has two methods, the WriteProperty method, and the ReadProperty method. The PropertyBag object is exposed as part of the WriteProperties and ReadProperties event declaration.

Saving Data with the WriteProperty Method

The process of saving data is outlined:

1. In an event that occurs when a property has changed, invoke the PropertyChanged method. The method notifies the container that a property has changed.
2. In response to the PropertyChanged method, the container is "dirtied." And before the container terminates, the WriteProperties event occurs.
3. In the WriteProperties event, use the WriteProperty method to save the property to the .vbd file.

The following code shows a simple illustration of this process:

```
Private Sub Text1_Change()
   PropertyChanged "Text"  ' Notify container a
                           ' property has changed.
End Sub

Private Sub UserDocument_WriteProperties _
   (PropBag As VB.PropertyBag)
   ' Write the Property to the Property Bag.
   UserDocument.WriteProperty "Text1", Text1.Text, _
      "Hello"
End Sub
```

Reading Properties

The next time the ActiveX document is opened, the ReadProperties event occurs. The PropertyBag is available in the event, and you can retrieve the persisted data using the ReadProperty method. The following code retrieves the data stored in the preceding code:

```
Private Sub UserDocument_ReadProperties _
   (PropBag As VB.PropertyBag)
   ' Read the property back into the TextBox control.
   Text1.Text = ReadProperty("Text1", "Hello")
End Sub
```

Saving a Default Value

You may have noticed that two code samples included an extra argument: the default value "Hello." Why provide a default when saving the property value? Before saving the value, the WriteProperty method compares the property value with this default. If they are the same, the property value doesn't have to be saved, because default values will be set automatically when the control is reloaded. This keeps the data file from being cluttered with hundreds of default entries.

Saving Binary Data

It's also possible to write and read binary data to the PropertyBag. This becomes useful if you have data that is stored in binary form. For example, you may have a graphics file that is stored in a custom format.

The process of saving binary data differs slightly from that of saving control properties:

1. Declare a module-level byte array.
2. In an appropriate event, use the ReDim statement, and store the binary data in the array.

3. Invoke the PropertyChanged method.
4. In the WriteProperties event, save the byte array using the WriteProperty method.

These steps are shown in the following simple implementation:

```
Private mbytMyData() As Byte ' Declare byte array.

Private Sub cmdSavePic_Click()
   ReDim mbytMyData(1 to 5000)
   ' Code to move data into byte array not shown.
   PropertyChanged
End Sub

Private Sub UserDocument_WriteProperties(PropBag As _
   VB.PropertyBag)
   PropBag.WriteProperties "myPic", mbytMyData
End Sub
```

Persisting Data Using the Open Statement

If you are using a container that does not support the PropertyBag, or if you are saving User Defined Type (UDT) data, use the Open statement to read and write the data to disk. Instructions on using the Open statement can be found in "Using Sequential File Access" in Chapter 14, "Processing Drives, Folders, and Files," of the *Microsoft Visual Basic 6.0 Programmer's Guide*.

For More Information To learn the do's and don'ts of adding properties to components, see "Adding Properties and Methods to Classes," in Chapter 6, "General Principles of Component Design."

Ensuring Communication Among ActiveX Documents

Designing ActiveX documents requires a different mindset. Not only are you bereft of QueryUnload and similar events, but you don't even know when your ActiveX document may be invoked: In an ordinary application, you might have a user navigate through three forms to get to a particular point in your application, but if those forms are ActiveX documents, the user could place the last one in her Favorites list, and come back to it after a week, without going through the intermediate forms! This topic explains how you can control this behavior.

A Little Play: Socrates and Plato

The key to determining whether the user has come to an ActiveX document "cold" (for example, from the Favorites list), or from a known ActiveX document is in setting up a signaling system of some kind. The known ActiveX document must have some way of declaring itself to another ActiveX document in the same suite, and when the second document receives that signal, it can proceed.

One way to set up a signal is to use a global variable. When the global variable is set by a known document, the second document can detect it by using the Is Nothing statement. To illustrate, imagine that the global variable is an envelope that is being passed between two people, Socrates and Plato. Whenever Socrates wants to send a message to Plato, he stuffs the envelope with the message, and leaves it on a pedestal where Plato always passes. When Plato passes the pedestal, he always picks up the envelope, opens it, and checks for a message from Socrates. If there is a message, Plato executes the instructions. Otherwise, he goes on his way.

To implement this metaphor, we need three "actors":

- Socrates: played by UserDocument1
- Plato: played by UserDocument2
- The Envelope: played by global variable named "gEnvelope" in a code module named "Module1."

In order to create a global variable, we must first declare it in a code module (Module1):

```
Public gEnvelope As UserDocument1
```

Now imagine that UserDocument1 has a single button on it named "cmdGoPlato." The code for it is:

```
Private Sub cmdGoPlato_Click()
   Set gEnvelope = Me ' Stuff the envelope.
   Hyperlink.NavigateTo "c:\pedestal\UserDocument2"
End Sub
```

The stage is now set. When the user clicks the button, the "envelope" is stuffed, and, using the Hyperlink object, sent to UserDocument2.

UserDocument2, meanwhile, has code in the Show event that will check the envelope. It does this by first checking if the global variable **is not** set to Nothing. If it is not set to Nothing, then the "envelope" is filled, and the code can proceed. Otherwise, it displays a message that requests the user to open UserDocument1 and click the "Go Plato" button.

```
Private Sub UserDocument_Show()
   If Not gEnvelope Is Nothing Then' proceed normally.
      ' Set properties using the object reference etc.

      ' VERY IMPORTANT! Set the variable to Nothing.
      ' Otherwise the object reference will keep the
      ' object in existence!
      Set gEnvelope = Nothing
Else
      MsgBox "Sorry, please open UserDocument1 first."
      ' If you're really feeling agressive about this,
```

```
        ' you can even hyperlink the user to Socrates:
        Hyperlink.NavigateTo _
        "c:\pedestal\UserDocument1.vbd"
    End If
End Sub
```

Tracking Your Object References

You may notice that the preceding code sets the object reference to Nothing after the first document hyperlinks to the second. It's very important that you set all such global object references to Nothing. Because as long as the object exists, it continues to use resources and memory. A more complete discussion of this can be found in "Object References and Reference Counting," in Chapter 9, "Programming With Objects," of the *Microsoft Visual Basic 6.0 Programmer's Guide*.

Debugging ActiveX Documents in Internet Explorer

When you are creating an ActiveX document, you have the full Visual Basic development environment at your disposal, including all debug tools.

Debugging with Internet Explorer

If you switch back to Visual Basic and attempt to stop the project while your ActiveX document is being displayed in Internet Explorer, Visual Basic will alert you that stopping the project will cause an error in the application hosting the ActiveX document. You should avoid doing this by clicking No, then switch back to Internet Explorer and force it to release the reference to the ActiveX document using one of the following methods:

- Quit Internet Explorer.
- Navigate to a different document (this can be either an HTML document or another ActiveX document).

> **Note** Internet Explorer 3.0 keeps a cache of the four most recently viewed documents, including references to ActiveX documents. The reference to the ActiveX document is released after navigating to the fourth document.

After Internet Explorer releases its reference, you can switch back to Visual Basic, stop the project, and modify it as you wish. When you are ready to view the document again, run the project, switch back to Explorer, and select the address of the project from the drop-down list of addresses.

CHAPTER 12

Creating Data Sources

A data source is an object that binds other objects to data from an external source. The foundation for a data source object is a data-aware class module, which is essentially a class module that exposes interfaces to an external source of data. Data-aware classes are covered in depth in Chapter 9, "Programming with Objects," in the *Microsoft Visual Basic 6.0 Programmer's Guide.*

Data-aware classes can also be used as the basis for ActiveX components. One common example of a data-aware component is the ADO Data control, which provides a visual interface for binding controls to a database through ADO. Although you could create a data-aware class that does the same thing as the ADO Data control, sharing that class between multiple applications or multiple programmers could prove difficult.

A much better approach would be to create an ActiveX component that duplicates or expands on the functionality of the ADO Data control. As with any ActiveX component, this could take any one of several forms: an ActiveX control, an ActiveX DLL, or an ActiveX EXE. In any case, your ActiveX data source can be easily shared, simplifying access to data regardless of where that data resides: in a local database like Access, in a remote database such as SQL Server, or even in a private OLE DB data store.

The series of step-by-step procedures in this chapter will demonstrate two different approaches to creating data source components. First we'll build an ActiveX data source control, MyDataControl, which emulates the ADO Data control. Next we'll bind the MyDataControl to other controls using both simple and complex binding. Finally, we'll create an ActiveX DLL, MyData, that demonstrates binding to a private data store in an OLE DB simple provider.

The procedures for creating the data source components build on each other. The sequence in which you perform the procedures is therefore important. You should already be familiar with the basics of building ActiveX components before proceeding with this example.

Contents

- Adding Data Handling Code
- Running the MyDataControl Project
- Creating the MyData Component Project
- Creating the MyOSPObject Class
- Creating the MyDataSource Class
- Testing the MyData Component
- Data Sources Recap

Sample Application: Axdata.vbg

Provides a prebuilt example of the data source project discussed in this chapter. In addition, the bitmaps and text file needed for the sample are located in the same directory as the Axdata.vbg sample, which is listed in the Samples directory.

These procedures will be easier to follow if you set up your Visual Basic development environment to show the necessary windows.

Before You Begin

1. On the **View** menu, click **Toolbox** to open the Toolbox.
2. On the **View** menu, click **Project Explorer** to open the Project Explorer window. The Project Explorer window will be used extensively to switch between project files.
3. If the Project Explorer window is in Folder view, click the **Toggle Folders** button on the Project Explorer window toolbar to turn the folders off.
4. On the **View** menu, click **Properties Window** to open the Properties window.
5. On the **View** menu, click **Immediate Window** to open the Immediate window. You will need this window open at design time, in order to demonstrate the control's code running at design time.
6. On the **Tools** menu, click **Options** to open the **Options** dialog box.

   Select the **Editor** tab, and make sure the **Require Variable Declaration** box is selected. This makes it much easier to catch typing errors.

   Select the **Environment** tab. Make sure **Prompt To Save Changes** is checked, then click **OK**. This will make it easy to save the changes to the project as you go along.

For More Information See "Creating Data-Aware Classes" in Chapter 9, "Programming with Objects" in the *Microsoft Visual Basic 6.0 Programmer's Guide.*

Creating the MyDataControl Project

The MyDataControl control will be compiled into an .ocx file in a later step in this chapter, so it can be used in other projects. Thus the MyDataControl project will be created as an ActiveX control project.

To create the MyDataControl project

1. On the **File** menu, click **New Project** to open the **New Project** dialog box. (This will close your current project or project group; you will be prompted to save any changes you have made.) Double-click the ActiveX Control icon to create a new project.

   Visual Basic automatically adds a UserControl designer to the project. The default name, UserControl1, appears as the caption of the designer.

2. On the **Project** menu, click **Project1 Properties** to open the **Project Properties** dialog box. In the **General** tab, fill out the information shown in the table below, and then click **OK**.

Property	Setting
Project Name	MyDataControl
Project Description	ActiveX data source control demo.

3. Double-click **UserControl1** in the Project Explorer window to bring the designer to the front.

4. In the Properties window, double-click the **Name** property and change the name of the user control to MyData. The new name appears in the title bar and in the Project Explorer window.

5. In the Properties window, double-click the **DataSourceBehavior** property to change its value to 1 – vbDataSource. The DataSourceBehavior property allows the control to act as a data source; setting it also adds a GetDataMember event to the control.

6. On the **File** menu, click **Save Project** to save the project files. Name them as shown in the following table. Visual Basic will provide the indicated extensions automatically.

File	File name	Extension
User control	MyData	.ctl
Project	MyDataControl	.vbp

   Binary information in a control — such as bitmaps — will be saved in a binary file with the same name and an extension of .ctx.

For More Information See "Setting Up a New Control Project and Test Project" and "Debugging Controls," in Chapter 9, "Building ActiveX Controls."

Drawing the MyData Control

A data control needs a user interface to allow the user to move back and forth through the data. In this case, we'll duplicate the functionality and appearance of the familiar Data control using four CommandButtons and a Label control, with a PictureBox to act as a container.

To add constituent controls to the MyData control

1. In the Project Explorer window, double-click **MyData** to open its designer.
2. In the **Toolbox**, double-click the **PictureBox** control to place a PictureBox control on the MyData designer. Move it near the upper left-hand corner of the designer.
3. In the Properties window, set the following property values for the PictureBox control:

Property	Value
BackColor	&H80000005 (Window Background)
Width	4500

4. With the PictureBox control selected, select the **CommandButton** control in the **Toolbox** and draw a CommandButton control on top of Picture1. Repeat the process to add a total of four CommandButton controls (but don't create a control array).
5. In the Properties window, set the following property values for the CommandButton controls. Where multiple values are shown, values represent settings for Command1 through Command4; otherwise, the value applies to all four CommandButton controls:

Property	Values
(Name)	cmdFirst; cmdPrev; cmdNext; cmdLast
Caption	(Empty)
Picture	First.bmp; Prev.bmp; Next.bmp; Last.bmp
Style	1 – Graphical
Width	300

Note The bitmaps for the Picture property can be found in the same directory as the AXData sample application.

6. In the **Toolbox**, select the **Label** control draw a label on top Picture1. In the Properties window, set the following property values for the Label control:

Property	Value
(Name)	lblCaption
BackStyle	0 – Transparent
Caption	MyData

7. Rearrange the Shape and Label controls to look similar to the example shown below. Don't worry about precise placement because the code in the Resize event will take care of that. Select the MyData control and use the grab handles to resize it slightly larger than the area containing the controls.

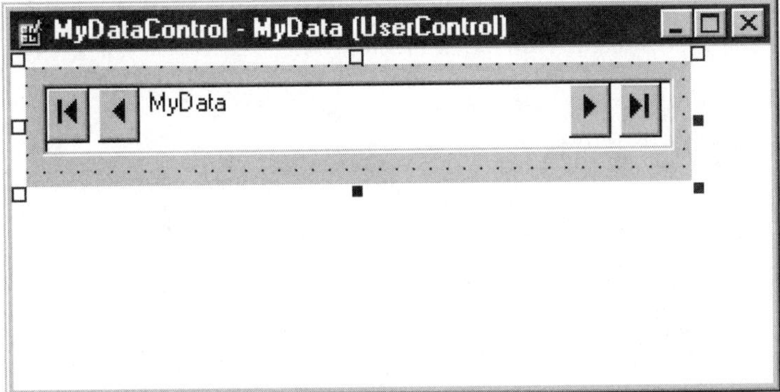

8. Double-click the **MyData** designer to bring the code window to the front, and add the following code to the UserControl_Resize event procedure:

```
Private Sub UserControl_Resize()
   Picture1.Move 0, 0, Width, Height
   cmdFirst.Move 0, 0, cmdFirst.Width, Height - 60
   cmdPrev.Move cmdFirst.Left + cmdFirst.Width, 0, _
      cmdPrev.Width, Height - 60
   cmdLast.Move (Width - cmdLast.Width) - 60, 0, _
      cmdLast.Width, Height - 60
   cmdNext.Move cmdLast.Left - cmdNext.Width, 0, _
      cmdNext.Width, Height - 60

   lblCaption.Height = TextHeight("A")
   lblCaption.Move cmdPrev.Left + _
      cmdPrev.Width, ((Height - 60) _
      / 2) - (lblCaption.Height / 2), _
      cmdNext.Left - (cmdPrev.Left _
      + cmdPrev.Width)
End Sub
```

This code will execute when the MyData is initialized or whenever it is resized to rearrange the constituent controls and provide a consistent appearance.

9. Add a pair of Property Let / Property Get procedures to expose the Caption property of lblCaption:

```
Public Property Get Caption() As String
   Caption = lblCaption.Caption
End Property
```

```
Public Property Let Caption(ByVal NewCaption As String)
   lblCaption.Caption = NewCaption
   PropertyChanged "Caption"
End Property
```

10. In the **Object** box, select (**General**). In the **Procedure** box, select (**Declarations**) to position yourself at the top of the code module. Add the following code:

```
Option Explicit

' Enumerations for the BOFAction Property.
Public Enum BOFActionType
   adDoMoveFirst = 0
   adStayBOF = 1
End Enum

' Enumerations for the EOFAction Property.
Public Enum EOFActionType
   adDoMoveLast = 0
   adStayEOF = 1
   adDoAddNew = 2
End Enum

' Declare object variables for ADO connection
' and Recordset objects.
Private cn As ADODB.Connection
Private WithEvents rs As ADODB.Recordset

' Default Property Values:
Const m_def_RecordSource = ""
Const m_def_BOFAction = BOFActionType.adDoMoveFirst
Const m_def_EOFAction = EOFActionType.adDoMoveLast
Const m_def_ConnectionString = ""

'Property Variables:
Private m_RecordSource As String
Private m_BOFAction As BOFActionType
Private m_EOFAction As EOFActionType
Private m_ConnectionString As String
```

11. In the **Object** box, select **UserControl**. In the **Procedure** box, select the **InitProperties** event. Add the following code to the UserControl_InitProperties event procedure:

```
Private Sub UserControl_InitProperties()
   m_RecordSource = m_def_RecordSource
   m_BOFAction = m_def_BOFAction
   m_EOFAction = m_def_EOFAction
   lblCaption.Caption = Ambient.DisplayName
   m_ConnectionString = m_def_ConnectionString
   Set UserControl.Font = Ambient.Font
End Sub
```

12. Before we move on, now would be a good time to save your changes. Choose **Save Project** from the **File** menu to save your project.

For More Information See "Drawing the ShapeLabel Control" and "Adding an Event to the ShapeLabel Control" in Chapter 4, "Creating an ActiveX Control."

Adding the AXDataSource Project

In order to test the MyData control, you need a test project. To allow debugging of in-process components, Visual Basic allows you to load two or more projects into a *project group*. In addition to enabling in-process debugging, the project group makes it easier to load your .ocx project and test project.

To add a test project to the project group

1. On the **File** menu, click **Add Project** to open the **Add Project** dialog box.

   Important Do not click Open Project or New Project, as these will close your control project.

2. Double-click the Standard EXE icon to add an ordinary .exe project. You can now see both projects in the Project Explorer window, and the caption of the Project Explorer window shows the default project group name.
3. Right-click Project1 in the **Project Explorer** and choose **Set as Start Up**. The Project Explorer window identifies the Startup project by displaying its name in bold type.
4. Select the designer for the MyData control and press CTRL+F4 to close it.
5. Select the **MyData** control in the **ToolBox** and add it to Form1. If the code in the UserControl_Resize event executes correctly, your form should look like this:

6. On the **File** menu, click **Save Project Group** to save the test project and the project group. Name the files as shown below. Visual Basic will provide the indicated extensions automatically.

File	File name	Extension
Form	DataSourceTest	.frm
Project	DataSourceTest	.vbp
Project group	AXData	.vbg

For More Information Test projects for ActiveX controls are discussed in more detail in "Debugging Controls" in Chapter 9, "Building ActiveX Controls."

Adding Data Handling Code

In order to turn the MyData control into a data source, you'll need to add some code to handle connecting to the data and moving through the records. You'll also need to expose a number of properties to allow a developer using the control to select a data source at design time.

To add data handling code to the MyData control

1. In the Project Explorer window, click **MyData** to select it, then press F7 or click the **Code** button on the Project Explorer window toolbar, to open the Code window.
2. Select **References** from the **Project** menu to open the **References** dialog box. Add a reference to the **Microsoft ActiveX Data Objects 2.0 Library**.
3. Add the following Property Let / Property Get procedures to expose design-time properties:

```
' read only
Public Property Get RecordSet() As ADODB.RecordSet
   Set RecordSet = rs
End Property

Public Property Get RecordSource() As String
   RecordSource = m_RecordSource
End Property

Public Property Let RecordSource(ByVal New_RecordSource As String)
   m_RecordSource = New_RecordSource
End Property

Public Property Get BOFAction() As BOFActionType
   BOFAction = m_BOFAction
End Property
```

```
Public Property Let BOFAction(ByVal New_BOFAction As BOFActionType)
   m_BOFAction = New_BOFAction
End Property

Public Property Get EOFAction() As EOFActionType
   EOFAction = m_EOFAction
End Property

Public Property Let EOFAction(ByVal New_EOFAction As EOFActionType)
   m_EOFAction = New_EOFAction
End Property

Public Property Get ConnectionString() As String
   ConnectionString = m_ConnectionString
End Property

Public Property Let ConnectionString(ByVal New_ConnectionString _
      As String)
   m_ConnectionString = New_ConnectionString
End Property
```

4. In the **Object** box, select **cmdFirst**. In the **Procedure** box, select the **Click** event. Add the following code to the cmdFirst_Click event procedure to move to the first record in a recordset:

```
Private Sub cmdFirst_Click()
   If rs Is Nothing Then Exit Sub
   rs.MoveFirst
End Sub
```

5. In the **Object** box, select **cmdLast**. In the **Procedure** box, select the **Click** event. Add the following code to the cmdLast_Click event procedure to move to the last record in a recordset:

```
Private Sub cmdLast_Click()
   If rs Is Nothing Then Exit Sub
   rs.MoveLast
End Sub
```

6. In the **Object** box, select **cmdPrev**. In the **Procedure** box, select the **Click** event. Add the following code to the cmdPrev_Click event procedure to move backwards through a recordset:

```
Private Sub cmdPrev_Click()
   If rs Is Nothing Then Exit Sub

   If rs.BOF Then
      Select Case m_BOFAction
         Case BOFActionType.adDoMoveFirst
            rs.MoveFirst
```

```
            Case BOFActionType.adStayBOF
               Exit Sub
            Case Else
               Exit Sub
         End Select
      Else
         rs.MovePrevious
      End If
   End Sub
```

7. In the **Object** box, select **cmdNext**. In the **Procedure** box, select the **Click** event. Add the following code to the cmdNext_Click event procedure to move forward through a recordset:

```
Private Sub cmdNext_Click()
   If rs Is Nothing Then Exit Sub

   If rs.EOF Then
      Select Case m_EOFAction
         Case EOFActionType.adDoAddNew
            rs.AddNew
         Case EOFActionType.adDoMoveLast
            rs.MoveLast
         Case EOFActionType.adStayEOF
            Exit Sub
         Case Else
            Exit Sub
      End Select
   Else
      rs.MoveNext
   End If
End Sub
```

8. In the **Object** box, select **UserControl**. In the **Procedure** box, select the **Terminate** event. Add the following code to the UserControl_Terminate event procedure to ensure that the objects created by the control are shut down properly:

```
Private Sub UserControl_Terminate()
   On Error Resume Next

   If Not rs Is Nothing Then
      rs.Close
      Set rs = Nothing
   End If

   If Not cn Is Nothing Then
      cn.Close
      Set cn = Nothing
   End If
```

```
    Err.Clear
End Sub
```

9. In the **Object** box, select **UserControl**. In the **Procedure** box, select the **WriteProperties** event. Add the following code to the UserControl_WriteProperties event procedure to save the property values that are entered at design time:

```
Private Sub UserControl_WriteProperties(PropBag As PropertyBag)
    'Write property values to storage
    Call PropBag.WriteProperty("Caption", _
        lblCaption.Caption, Ambient.DisplayName)
    Call PropBag.WriteProperty("RecordSource", _
        m_RecordSource, m_def_RecordSource)
    Call PropBag.WriteProperty("BOFAction", _
        m_BOFAction, m_def_BOFAction)
    Call PropBag.WriteProperty("EOFAction", _
        m_EOFAction, m_def_EOFAction)
    Call PropBag.WriteProperty("ConnectionString", _
        m_ConnectionString, m_def_ConnectionString)
End Sub
```

10. In the **Object** box, select **UserControl**. In the **Procedure** box, select the **ReadProperties** event. Add the following code to the UserControl_ReadProperties event procedure to save the property values that are entered at design time:

```
Private Sub UserControl_ReadProperties(PropBag As PropertyBag)
    'Load property values from storage
    lblCaption.Caption = PropBag.ReadProperty("Caption", _
        Ambient.DisplayName)
    m_RecordSource = PropBag.ReadProperty("RecordSource", _
        m_def_RecordSource)
    m_BOFAction = PropBag.ReadProperty("BOFAction", m_def_BOFAction)
    m_EOFAction = PropBag.ReadProperty("EOFAction", m_def_EOFAction)
    m_ConnectionString = PropBag.ReadProperty("ConnectionString", _
        m_def_ConnectionString)
End Sub
```

11. In the **Object** box, select **UserControl**. In the **Procedure** box, select the **GetDataMember** event. Add the following code to the UserControl_GetDataMember event procedure to connect to the data specified in the ConnectionString and RecordSource properties:

```
Private Sub UserControl_GetDataMember(DataMember As String, _
        Data As Object)
    Dim conn As String

    On Error GoTo GetDataMemberError
```

```
    If rs Is Nothing Or cn Is Nothing Then
        ' make sure various properties have been set
        If Trim$(m_ConnectionString) = "" Then
            MsgBox "No ConnectionString Specified!", _
                    vbInformation, Ambient.DisplayName
            Exit Sub
        End If

        If Trim$(m_RecordSource) = "" Then
            MsgBox "No RecordSource Specified!", _
                vbInformation, Ambient.DisplayName
            Exit Sub
        End If

        If Trim$(m_ConnectionString) <> "" Then
            ' Create a Connection object and establish
            ' a connection.
            Set cn = New ADODB.Connection
            cn.ConnectionString = m_ConnectionString
            cn.Open

            ' Create a RecordSet object.
            Set rs = New ADODB.RecordSet
            rs.Open m_RecordSource, cn, adOpenKeyset, adLockPessimistic
            rs.MoveFirst
        Else
            Set cn = Nothing
            Set rs = Nothing
        End If
    End If

    Set Data = rs

    Exit Sub

GetDataMemberError:

    MsgBox "Error: " & CStr(Err.Number) & vbCrLf & vbCrLf & _
        Err.Description, vbOKOnly, Ambient.DisplayName
    Exit Sub
End Sub
```

12. Save your work before going on to the next step.

In the next step we'll run our project to see the results.

Running the MyDataControl Project

In the previous topic, we added the code that allows the MyData control to provide data to other objects. In this step we'll connect the MyData control to an ADO source and bind to it using both simple and complex binding.

To test the MyData control

1. If it's still open, close the MyData designer and open the designer for Form1.
2. Select the **MyData** control and switch to the Properties window.
3. Double-click the **ConnectionString** property and enter the DSN connection string for the Northwind database. It should look something like this: DSN = Northwind.

   Important If you haven't previously created a DSN for the Northwind database, you'll need to create one first. The procedure for creating a DSN is discussed in "Connection Objects" in Chapter 3, "About the Data Environment Designer," in the *Data Access Guide*.

4. Double-click the **RecordSource** property and enter Customers. This specifies the Customers table in the Northwind database; you could also enter a SQL statement here in order to filter the data.
5. Select a **TextBox** control in the **Toolbox** and add it to Form1, then switch to the Properties window.
6. Select the **DataSource** property and choose MyData1 from the drop-down list.
7. Select the **DataField** property. The drop-down list should contain a list of the fields in the Customers table. Select the CompanyName field.
8. Select **Start** from the **Run** menu to run the project.

   As you click the buttons on the MyData control, names from the CompanyName field should appear in the TextBox. Try editing a name in the TextBox, then move forward and back to the same record. You'll notice that your change has been saved to the database. The TextBox is simple-bound to the Northwind database by way of the MyData control.

9. Stop the project (by selecting **End** from the **Run** menu), then select the form.
10. Choose **Components** from the **Project** menu to open the **Components** dialog. Check the **Microsoft Data Grid 6.0** to add it to your project, then click **OK**.
11. Select the **DataGrid** in the **Toolbox** and add it to Form1, then switch to the Properties window.
12. Select the **DataSource** property and set it to MyData1.

13. Select **Start** from the **Run** menu to run the project.

    The grid should contain all of the data from the Customers table. As you click the buttons on the MyData control, the selected row in the grid changes to match the data in the TextBox, scrolling as necessary. As with the TextBox, you can edit data in the grid and the changes are saved in the database. The DataGrid is complex-bound to the Northwind database by way of the MyData control.

14. Stop the project (by selecting **End** from the **Run** menu), then select the MyData control on Form1.

15. In the Properties window, double-click the ConnectionString property and enter an OLE DB connection string, such as Provider=Microsoft.Jet.OLE DB.3.51;Data Source=c:\northwind.mdb.

    > **Important** If you haven't previously created a OLE DB connection for the Northwind database, you'll need to create one first. The procedure for creating a DSN is discussed in "Creating the Northwind OLEDB Data Source" in Chapter 7, "Using Visual Basic's Standard Controls," in the *Microsoft Visual Basic 6.0 Programmer's Guide.*

16. Select **Start** from the **Run** menu to run the project.

    You'll see that the data looks and acts exactly like it did before. The data is now being accessed through an OLE DB interface rather than a ODBC interface, and all you had to do was change the connection string!

As long as you have the project open, take some time to play around with other property settings such as BOFAction and EOFAction to see their behavior.

In the next few steps, we'll build a ActiveX DLL and connect our form to an OLE DB Simple Provider.

Creating the MyData Component Project

The MyData component is an ActiveX DLL that acts as a data source. In this example, we'll use it to provide data through an OLE DB Simple Provider — it could just as easily be used as an ODBC or OLE DB data source. First we'll need to add another project to the AXData project group.

To add a test project to the project group

1. On the **File** menu, click **Add Project** to open the **Add Project** dialog box.

    > **Important** Do not click Open Project or New Project, as these will close your control project.

2. Double-click the ActiveX DLL icon to add a DLL component project. This will add a new project, Project 2, and a new class module, Class1, to the Project Explorer window.

3. Select **Project2** in the **Project Explorer**, then double-click the Name property in the Properties window and change the Name to MyDataComponent.
4. Choose **MyDataComponent Properties** from the **Project** menu to display the **Project Properties** dialog. Set the properties for the MyDataComponent project as follows:

Property	Setting
Project Description	Sample OLE DB Simple Provider Component

5. Select **References** from the **Project** menu. Add the following references in the **References** dialog box:

Reference	Purpose
Microsoft Data Source Interfaces	Allows the component to act as a data source.
Microsoft OLE DB Simple Provider 1.5 Library	Used to access data sources through the OLE DB Simple Provider interface.
OLE DB Errors Type Library	Provides error messages.

6. Select **Save Project Group** from the **File** menu to save your changes before moving on to the next step.

In the next step, we'll create a class that implements the OLE DB Simple Provider interface.

Creating the MyOSPObject Class

In the previous topic, we added an ActiveX DLL project to the AXData sample. In this step, we'll create a class that implements the OLE DB Simple Provider (OSP) interfaces to access data stored in a text file.

To create the MyOSPObject class

1. In the Project Explorer, select **Class1** from the MyDataComponent project. In the Properties window, set the properties for Class1 as follows:

Property	Setting
(Name)	MyOSPObject

   You may have noticed that the DataSourceBehavior is set to none. If this component is to act as a data source, shouldn't the DataSourceBehavior be set to another value? Don't worry — we'll add another class in a later step that provides the data source capability for the component.

2. Double-click **MyOSPObject** in the **Project Explorer** to open its code window.

3. In the **Object** box, select (**General**). In the **Procedure** box, select (**Declarations**) to position yourself at the top of the code module. Add the following code:

```
Option Explicit
Implements OLEDBSimpleProvider
Dim MyOSPArray()
Dim RowCount As Integer
Dim ColCount As Integer
Dim colListeners As New Collection
Dim ospl As OLEDBSimpleProviderListener
Public FilePath As String
```

   Note the use of the Implements keyword for OLEDBSimpleProvider. Remember, Implements is like a contract — it means that you'll need to implement all of the interfaces of the OLEDBSimpleProvider class.

4. Add the following procedures to read and write data from a file:

```
Public Sub LoadData()
   ' This procedure loads data from a semi-colon
   ' delimited file into an array.
   Dim GetLine As Variant
   Dim Spot As Integer, Position As Integer
   Dim Row As Integer, Col As Integer

   On Error GoTo ErrorTrap
   Open FilePath For Input Lock Read Write As #1
   Position = 1
   Row = 0
   Line Input #1, GetLine
   Spot = InStr(1, GetLine, ";")
   RowCount = val(Left$(GetLine, Spot))
   ColCount = val(Right$(GetLine, Len(GetLine) - Spot))
   ReDim MyOSPArray(RowCount + 1, ColCount + 1)
   While Not EOF(1)
      Line Input #1, GetLine
      Col = 1
      Spot = InStr(1, GetLine, ";")
      While Spot <> 0
         MyOSPArray(Row, Col) = Left$(GetLine, Spot - 1)
         Col = Col + 1
         GetLine = Right$(GetLine, Len(GetLine) - Spot)
         Spot = InStr(1, GetLine, ";")
      Wend
      If Len(GetLine) <> 0 Then
         MyOSPArray(Row, Col) = GetLine
      End If
      Row = Row + 1
   Wend
   Close #1
   Exit Sub
```

```
ErrorTrap:
   Err.Raise (E_FAIL)
End Sub

Public Sub SaveData()
   ' This procedure writes data from an array to a semi-colon
   ' delimited file
   Dim PutLine As Variant
   Dim iRow As Integer, iCol As Integer

   On Error GoTo ErrorTrap
   Open FilePath For Output Lock Read Write As #1
   Print #1, RowCount & ";" & ColCount

   For iRow = 0 To RowCount
      For iCol = 1 To ColCount
         PutLine = PutLine & MyOSPArray(iRow, iCol) & ";"
      Next iCol
      Print #1, PutLine
      PutLine = ""
   Next iRow
   Close #1
   Exit Sub

ErrorTrap:
   Err.Raise (E_FAIL)
End Sub
```

5. In the **Object** box, select **Class**. In the **Procedure** box, select the **Terminate** event. Add the following code to the Class_Terminate event procedure to save the data when the class is terminated:

```
Private Sub Class_Terminate()
   On Error Resume Next
   ' Call the SaveData method
   SaveData
End Sub
```

To implement OLEDBSimpleProvider

Since the MyOSPObject class implements the OLEDBSimpleProvider class, we have to implement all of its interfaces, even if we aren't going to use them:

1. In the **Object** box, select **OLEDBSimpleProvider**. In the **Procedure** box, select the **addOLEDBSimpleProviderListener** function. Add the following code to the function procedure to add listeners that will notify the class when data changes:

```
Private Sub OLEDBSimpleProvider_addOLEDBSimpleProviderListener _
   (ByVal pospIListener As OLEDBSimpleProviderListener)
   ' Add a listener to the Listeners collection.
   If Not (pospIListener Is Nothing) Then
      Set ospl = pospIListener
      colListeners.Add ospl
   End If
End Sub
```

2. In the **Object** box, select **OLEDBSimpleProvider**. In the **Procedure** box, select the **deleteRows** function. Add the following code to the procedure to delete a row of data from a file:

```
Private Function OLEDBSimpleProvider_deleteRows _
   (ByVal iRow As Long, ByVal cRows As Long) As Long
   Dim TempArray()
   Dim listener As OLEDBSimpleProviderListener
   Dim v As Variant

   ' Make sure iRow is in the correct range:
   If iRow < 1 Or iRow > RowCount Then
      Err.Raise (E_FAIL)
   End If

   ' Set cRows to the actual number which can be deleted
   If iRow + cRows > RowCount + 1 Then
      cRows = RowCount - iRow + 1
   End If

   ' Establish a Temporary Array
   cNewRows = RowCount - cRows
   ReDim TempArray(cNewRows + 1, ColCount + 1)

   ' Notify each listener:
   For Each v In colListeners
      Set listener = v
      listener.aboutToDeleteRows iRow, cRows
   Next

   ' Copy over the first rows which are not being deleted
   For Row = 0 To iRow - 1
      For Col = 0 To ColCount
         TempArray(Row, Col) = MyOSPArray(Row, Col)
      Next Col
   Next Row
```

```
    ' Copy the last rows which are not being deleted
    For Row = iRow + cRows To RowCount
       For Col = 0 To ColCount
          TempArray(Row - cRows, Col) = MyOSPArray(Row, Col)
       Next Col
    Next Row

    ' Re-allocate the array to copy into it
    ReDim MyOSPArray(cNewRows + 1, ColCount + 1)

    ' Set the real row count back in
    RowCount = cNewRows

    ' Copy over the rows
    For Row = 0 To cNewRows
       For Col = 0 To ColCount
          MyOSPArray(Row, Col) = TempArray(Row, Col)
       Next Col
    Next Row

    ' Clear the temporary array
    ReDim TempArray(0)

    ' Notify each listener
    For Each v In colListeners
       Set listener = v
       listener.deletedRows iRow, cRows
    Next

    ' Return number of deleted rows
    OLEDBSimpleProvider_deleteRows = cRows
End Function
```

3. In the **Object** box, select **OLEDBSimpleProvider**. In the **Procedure** box, select the **find** function. Add the following code to the procedure to find data within a file:

```
Private Function OLEDBSimpleProvider_find(ByVal iRowStart As Long, _
   ByVal iColumn As Long, ByVal val As Variant, _
   ByVal findFlags As OSPFIND, ByVal compType As OSPCOMP) As Long

   Dim RowStart As Integer, RowStop As Integer
   If (findFlags And (OSPFIND_UP Or OSPFIND_UPCASESENSITIVE)) _
      <> 0 Then
      RowStart = RowCount + 1
      RowStop = 0
      StepValue = -1
   Else
      RowStart = 0
      RowStop = RowCount + 1
      StepValue = 1
   End If
```

```
If (findFlags And (OSPFIND_CASESENSITIVE Or _
   OSPFIND_UPCASESENSITIVE)) <> 0 Then
   CaseSens = 1'Use a Text Compare not Case Sensitive
Else
   CaseSens = 0'Not Case Sensitive use Binary Compare
End If

If VarType(val) = vbString Then
   StringComp = True
Else
   StringComp = False
End If

iAnswerRow = -1
For iRow = RowStart To RowStop Step StepValue
   If StringComp Then
      CompResult = StrComp(MyOSPArray(iRow, iColumn), _
         val, CaseSens)
      Select Case (compType)
         Case OSPCOMP_DEFAULT, OSPCOMP_EQ:
            If CompResult = 0 Then
               iAnswerRow = iRow
               Exit For
            End If
         Case OSPCOMP_GE
            If CompResult >= 0 Then
               iAnswerRow = iRow
               Exit For
            End If
         Case OSPCOMP_GT
            If CompResult > 0 Then
               iAnswerRow = iRow
               Exit For
            End If
         Case OSPCOMP_LE
            If CompResult <= 0 Then
               iAnswerRow = iRow
               Exit For
            End If
         Case OSPCOMP_LT
            If CompResult < 0 Then
               iAnswerRow = iRow
               Exit For
            End If
         Case OSPCOMP_NE
            If CompResult <> 0 Then
               iAnswerRow = iRow
               Exit For
            End If
```

```
            End Select
         Else
            Select Case (compType)
               Case OSPCOMP_DEFAULT, OSPCOMP_EQ:
                  If MyOSPArray(iRow, iColumn) = val Then
                     iAnswerRow = iRow
                     Exit For
                  End If
               Case OSPCOMP_GE
                  If MyOSPArray(iRow, iColumn) >= val Then
                     iAnswerRow = iRow
                     Exit For
                  End If
               Case OSPCOMP_GT
                  If MyOSPArray(iRow, iColumn) > val Then
                     iAnswerRow = iRow
                     Exit For
                  End If
               Case OSPCOMP_LE
                  If MyOSPArray(iRow, iColumn) <= val Then
                     iAnswerRow = iRow
                     Exit For
                  End If
               Case OSPCOMP_LT
                  If MyOSPArray(iRow, iColumn) < val Then
                     iAnswerRow = iRow
                     Exit For
                  End If
               Case OSPCOMP_NE
                  If MyOSPArray(iRow, iColumn) <> val Then
                     iAnswerRow = iRow
                     Exit For
                  End If
            End Select
         End If
      Next iRow
      OLEDBSimpleProvider_find = iAnswerRow
   End Function
```

4. In the **Object** box, select **OLEDBSimpleProvider**. In the **Procedure** box, select the **getColumnCount** function. Add the following code to the procedure to return the number of fields within a file:

```
Private Function OLEDBSimpleProvider_getColumnCount() As Long
   OLEDBSimpleProvider_getColumnCount = ColCount
End Function
```

5. In the **Object** box, select **OLEDBSimpleProvider**. In the **Procedure** box, select the **getEstimatedRows** function. Add the following code to the procedure to return the estimated number of rows of data within a file:

```
Private Function OLEDBSimpleProvider_getEstimatedRows() As Long
   OLEDBSimpleProvider_getEstimatedRows = RowCount
End Function
```

6. In the **Object** box, select **OLEDBSimpleProvider**. In the **Procedure** box, select the **getLocale** function. Add the following code to the procedure:

```
Private Function OLEDBSimpleProvider_getLocale() As String
   OLEDBSimpleProvider_getLocale = ""
End Function
```

   Note that in this case the function simply returns a null value. Even though it doesn't do anything, the function has to be added — since this class implements OLEDBSimpleProvider, all of its interfaces have to be included.

7. In the **Object** box, select **OLEDBSimpleProvider**. In the **Procedure** box, select the **getRowCount** function. Add the following code to the procedure to return the number of rows of data within a file:

```
Private Function OLEDBSimpleProvider_getRowCount() As Long
   OLEDBSimpleProvider_getEstimatedRows = RowCount
End Function
```

8. In the **Object** box, select **OLEDBSimpleProvider**. In the **Procedure** box, select the **getRWStatus** function. Add the following code to the procedure to set the Read/Write status by column — in this case, the first column will be read-only while the remaining columns will be read-write:

```
Private Function OLEDBSimpleProvider_getRWStatus _
   (ByVal iRow As Long, ByVal iColumn As Long) As OSPRW
   If iColumn = 1 Then
      ' Make the first column read-only
      OLEDBSimpleProvider_getRWStatus = OSPRW_READONLY
   Else
      ' Make the column read-write
      OLEDBSimpleProvider_getRWStatus = OSPRW_READWRITE
   End If
End Function
```

9. In the **Object** box, select **OLEDBSimpleProvider**. In the **Procedure** box, select the **getVariant** function. Add the following code to the procedure to return data stored in a specific row and column:

```
Private Function OLEDBSimpleProvider_getVariant _
   (ByVal iRow As Long, ByVal iColumn As Long, _
   ByVal format As OSPFORMAT) As Variant
   OLEDBSimpleProvider_getVariant = MyOSPArray(iRow, iColumn)
End Function
```

The getVariant function also accepts a format argument which can be used to determine the formatting of the data returned.

10. In the **Object** box, select **OLEDBSimpleProvider**. In the **Procedure** box, select the **insertRows** function. Add the following code to the procedure to insert a new row of data into a file:

```
Private Function OLEDBSimpleProvider_insertRows _
   (ByVal iRow As Long, ByVal cRows As Long) As Long
   Dim TempArray()
   Dim listener As OLEDBSimpleProviderListener
   Dim v As Variant

   ' Establish a temporary array
   cNewRows = RowCount + cRows
   ReDim TempArray(cNewRows + 1, ColCount + 1)

   ' If inserting past the end of the array, insert at
   ' the end of the array
   If iRow > RowCount Then
      iRow = RowCount + 1
   End If

   ' Notify listener
   For Each v In colListeners
      Set listener = v
      listener.aboutToInsertRows iRow, cRows
   Next

   ' Copy over the existing rows
   For Row = 0 To iRow
      For Col = 0 To ColCount
         TempArray(Row, Col) = MyOSPArray(Row, Col)
      Next Col
   Next Row

   ' Copy the last rows which follow the inserted rows
   For Row = iRow + 1 + cRows To cNewRows
      For Col = 0 To ColCount
         TempArray(Row, Col) = MyOSPArray(Row - cRows, Col)
      Next Col
   Next Row

   ' Re-allocate the array to copy into it
   ReDim MyOSPArray(cNewRows + 1, ColCount + 1)

   ' Copy over the rows
   For Row = 0 To cNewRows
      For Col = 0 To ColCount
```

```
            MyOSPArray(Row, Col) = TempArray(Row, Col)
         Next Col
      Next Row

      ' Clear the temporary array
      ReDim TempArray(0)

      ' Set the real row count back in
      RowCount = cNewRows

      ' Notify listeners
      For Each v In colListeners
         Set listener = v
         listener.insertedRows iRow, cRows
      Next

      ' Return number of inserted rows
      OLEDBSimpleProvider_insertRows = cRows
   End Function
```

11. In the **Object** box, select **OLEDBSimpleProvider**. In the **Procedure** box, select the **isAsynch** function. Add the following code to the procedure to determine if the OSP can return data asynchronously:

```
Private Function OLEDBSimpleProvider_isAsync() As Long
   OLEDBSimpleProvider_isAsync = False
End Function
```

12. In the **Object** box, select **OLEDBSimpleProvider**. In the **Procedure** box, select the **removeOLEDBSimpleProviderListener** function. Add the following code to the procedure to remove a listener:

```
Private Sub OLEDBSimpleProvider_removeOLEDBSimpleProviderListener _
   (ByVal pospIListener As OLEDBSimpleProviderListener)
   ' Remove the listener
   For i = 1 To colListeners.Count
      If colListeners(i) Is pospIListener Then
         colListeners.Remove i
      End If
   Next
End Sub
```

13. In the **Object** box, select **OLEDBSimpleProvider**. In the **Procedure** box, select the **setVariant** function. Add the following code to the procedure to retrieve data from a particular row and column and to designate a listener to provide notification that data has changed:

```
Private Sub OLEDBSimpleProvider_setVariant(ByVal iRow As Long, _
   ByVal iColumn As Long, ByVal format As OSPFORMAT, _
   ByVal Var As Variant)
   Dim listener As OLEDBSimpleProviderListener
   Dim v As Variant

   For Each v In colListeners
      Set listener = v
      listener.aboutToChangeCell iRow, iColumn ' Pre-notification
   Next

   MyOSPArray(iRow, iColumn) = Var

   For Each v In colListeners
      Set listener = v
      listener.cellChanged iRow, iColumn       ' Post-notification
   Next
End Sub
```

14. In the **Object** box, select **OLEDBSimpleProvider**. In the **Procedure** box, select the **stopTransfer** function. Add the following code to the procedure:

    ```
    Private Sub OLEDBSimpleProvider_stopTransfer()
       ' Do nothing because we are already populated
    End Sub
    ```

    Note that there is no code in this procedure, but the procedure must be included because this class implements OLEDBSimpleProvider. You could add code here that would allow you to cancel loading during a long transfer.

15. Choose **Save Project Group** from the **File** menu to save your changes. When prompted for a file name for the Class module, choose the default (MyOSPObject.cls). When prompted for a file name for the Project, choose the default (MyDataComponent.vbp).

Whew! If that seemed like a lot of code, there's a good reason for it — the MyOSPObject class provides much of the functionality that you might find in a database. With OSP, you can use almost any file as you might have used a database in the past.

In the next step, we'll create another class that acts as the data source to the MyOSPObject class.

Creating the MyDataSource Class

In the previous topic, we created a class that implements an OLE DB Simple Provider. In this step we'll create another class that will provide data from the MyOSPObject class to other objects.

To create the MyDataSource class

1. Select the **MyDataComponent** project in the **Project Explorer**.
2. Select **Add Class Module** from the **Project** menu, then choose **Class Module** from the **Add Class Module** dialog box.
3. Select the Properties window and set the following properties for the new class module:

Property	Setting
(Name)	MyDataSource
DataSourceBehavior	2 – vbOLEDBProvider

4. In the **Object** box, select **Class**. In the **Procedure** box, select the **GetDataMember** event. Add the following code to the Class_GetDataMember event procedure:

```
Private Sub Class_GetDataMember(DataMember As String, Data As Object)
   ' Declare an instance of the MyOSPObject class
   Dim MyOSP As New MyOSPObject

   ' Make sure the DataMember is valid
   If DataMember = "" Then
       Err.Raise (E_FAIL)
   End If

   ' Set the FilePath property
   MyOSP.FilePath = DataMember

   ' Call the LoadData method to populate the class
   MyOSP.LoadData

   ' Set MyDataSource's data to MyOSPObject's data
   Set Data = MyOSP
End Sub
```

5. Choose Save Project Group from the **File** menu to save your changes. When prompted for a file name for the Class module, choose the default (MyDataSource.cls).

As you may have noticed, this class is much simpler than the MyOSPObject class. In fact, if you go back and compare it with the GetDataMember event, you'll see that it's doing essentially the same thing. The main difference here is that we're using a class that we created rather than the pre-existing ADODB class.

In the next step, we'll convert the form that we created earlier to use our new data source object, and we'll test it to see the results.

Testing the MyData Component

In the previous topics, we created an ActiveX DLL containing two classes, MyOSPObject and MyDataSource. In this topic we'll use the MyDataComponent object as a data source for the form that we created in an earlier topic.

To test the MyData control

1. Select **Project 1 (DataSourceTest.vbp)** in the **Project Explorer**.
2. Select **References** from the **Project** menu to open the **References** dialog. Add a reference to **MyDataComponent**.
3. Add a reference to the **Microsoft Data Adapter Library**. The Data Adapter object acts as an intermediate layer between OLE DB and OSP.
4. Double-click **Form1** in the **Project Explorer** to open its designer.
5. Select **DataGrid** in the **ToolBox** and add a second DataGrid to Form1. You don't need to set any properties for DataGrid2.
6. Double-click **Form1** to open its code window. In the **Object** box, select (**General**). In the **Procedure** box, select (**Declarations**) to position yourself at the top of the code module. Add the following code:

```
Option Explicit
Dim da As New DataAdapter
Dim ds As New MyDataSource
```

7. In the **Object** box, select **Form**. In the **Procedure** box, select the **Load** event. Add the following code to the Form_Load event procedure to initialize the MyDataComponent object and assign it to the controls:

```
Private Sub Form_Load()
   ' Set the Object property of the Data Adapter
   ' to the MyDataSource object
   Set da.Object = ds

   ' Set the DataMember property
   DataGrid2.DataMember = App.Path & "\Customer.txt"
   ' Set the DataSource to the DataAdapter
   Set DataGrid2.DataSource = da
End Sub
```

Note The above code assumes that the Customer.txt file is located in the same directory as your application. If you have the Customer.txt file in a different location, change the path accordingly. A copy of the Customer.txt file is included with the AXData sample application.

8. Select **Start** from the **Run** menu to run the project.

   Notice that the second DataGrid contains the same data as the first; like the first, you can edit data in the second grid and the changes will be saved. The big difference between the two is that the first DataGrid is bound to a database, but the second DataGrid isn't — it's bound to a text file through the OLE DB Simple Provider interface.

That does it for the data sources example. Of course, you could easily expand on this. For example, you might add methods to the MyOSPObject class to navigate through the records, or perhaps methods that validate content or formatting for a particular field. You can take it as far as you want.

Data Sources Recap

The preceding topics demonstrated how easy it is to create data source components — first as an ActiveX control, then as an ActiveX DLL. Those aren't the only options either. You could just as easily create an ActiveX EXE data source, or simply use a data-aware class as a data source. So how do you decide? There aren't any hard and fast rules, but here are a few suggestions:

- Use a data-aware class when you don't anticipate that you'll need to reuse a data source — for example, to access data that keeps track of scores for a game.
- Use an ActiveX DLL when you need a data source that doesn't require a visual interface and that runs in-process. An example of this might be a component that supplies stock quotes to be displayed in another control or in a spreadsheet. Such a component can easily be reused in different applications.
- Use an ActiveX EXE for a data source that needs to run out-of-process, such as a middle-tier component that enforces business rules against a back-end database. An ActiveX EXE can also be reused in different applications.
- Use an Active X control when you need a visual interface for your data source. The obvious example for this is the Data control; however, you might also want to combine the display interface as a part of your data source by using a grid, chart, or group of text boxes. Of course, ActiveX controls can also easily be shared and distributed.

In addition to choosing the type of data source, you also have a lot of flexibility when it comes to choosing a data interface. As demonstrated in the preceding topics, you can easily switch between OLE DB and ODBC data source using just about any database as a back-end.

Perhaps the most intriguing option is the OLE DB Simple Provider. The example demonstrated the use of a simple text file as a data source, but that's just the tip of the iceberg. With OSP, you have complete control over how and where the data is stored. You can create your own custom file formats, storing data in a binary format that only your component can read. You could even use an OSP component to store and retrieve objects.

With all the possibilities, one thing is certain — data source components elevate data binding to a whole new level.

APPENDIX A

ActiveX Component Standards and Guidelines

Your component will be easier to use if your object model is similar in style to those of other components, and if the methods and properties of your objects have the same names as methods and properties that provide the same functionality for objects provided by other components.

This appendix includes the following topics relating to these issues.

Contents

For More Information Chapter 9, "Programming with Objects," and Chapter 10, "Programming With Components," in the *Microsoft Visual Basic 6.0 Programmer's Guide,* contain information you may find helpful in understanding these issues.

Object Naming Guidelines

When selecting names for objects, properties, methods, and events, choose names that can be easily understood by the users of your component. These elements comprise the programming interface of your component — the more clear you make their names, the more usable your code will be.

The rules in this topic apply to names for:

- Objects.
- The properties, methods, and events that comprise the interfaces of your objects.
- Named arguments of properties, methods, and events.

Use Entire Words or Syllables Whenever Possible

It is easier for users to remember complete words than to remember whether you abbreviated Window as Wind, Wn, or Wnd. The following table lists two examples of recommended naming conventions.

Use	Don't use
Application	App
SpellCheck	SpChk

When you need to abbreviate because an identifier would be too long, try to use complete initial syllables. For example, use AltExpEval instead of either AlternateExpressionEvaluation or AltExpnEvln.

Use Mixed Case

All identifiers should use mixed case, rather than underscores, to separate the words in the identifier. The following table lists two examples of recommended naming conventions.

Use	Don't use
ShortcutMenus	Shortcut_Menus, Shortcutmenus, SHORTCUTMENUS, SHORTCUT_MENUS
BasedOn	basedOn

Use Consistent Terminology

Use the same word you use in the interface; don't use identifier names like HWND, which are based on Hungarian notation. Remember that this code will be accessed by other users, so try to use the same word your users would use to describe a concept.

Use the Correct Plural for Collection Class Names

Using plurals rather than inventing new names for collections reduces the number of items a user must remember. It also simplifies the selection of names for collections. The following table lists some examples of collection class names.

Use	Don't use
Axes	Axiss
SeriesCollection	CollectionSeries
Windows	ColWindow

For example, if you have a class named Axis, a collection of Axis objects is stored in an Axes class. Similarly, a collection of Vertex objects is stored in a Vertices class. In rare cases where the same spelling is used for both singular and plural, append the word "Collection" — for example, SeriesCollection.

> **Note** This naming convention may not be appropriate for some collections, especially where a set of objects exists independently of the collection. For example, a Mail program might have a Name object that exists in multiple collections: ToList, CcList, and so forth. In this case, you might specify the individual name collections as ToNames and CcNames.

Use a Prefix for Your Constants

Select a three- or four-letter, lowercase prefix that identifies your component, and use it on the names of constants your component provides in its type library, as well as on the names of the Enums that define those constants.

For example, a code component that provides loan evaluations might use "levs" as its prefix. The following Enum for loan types uses this prefix. (In addition, the constants include the upper-case characters "LT" to indicate the enumeration they belong to.)

```
Public Enum LoanType
   levsLTMortgage = 1
   levsLTCommercial
   levsLTConsumer
End Enum
```

Using a prefix reduces the chance that the constants for your component will have name conflicts with constants for other components. Name conflicts of this type can cause difficult bugs for your users.

The shorter the constant name, the more important this rule becomes. In the worst case — constant names that are common words, like the names of colors — such conflicts become almost inevitable.

Verb/Object vs. Object/Verb

If you create method names that combine a verb with the name of the object it acts on, you should be consistent about the order. Either place the verb before the object in all cases, as with InsertWidget and InsertSprocket, or always place the object first, as with WidgetInsert and SprocketInsert.

Both schemes have their advantages. Verb/object order creates names that are more like normal speech, and thus show the intent of the method better. Object/verb order groups together all the methods that affect a particular object.

It doesn't matter which order you choose, but mixing the two orders will confuse the users of your component.

ActiveX Component Shutdown

To create a well-behaved component, you have to give up control over your component's lifetime. Your component is started automatically when a client requests an object. It should shut down when all clients have released the objects they were using — and not a moment sooner.

The reason for this is that the objects your component provides become integral parts of the client applications that use them. A client that uses one of your objects must be able to count on the object existing until the client is done with it.

By the same token, if clients have released all references to the objects your component provides, your component should shut down and release the memory and resources it was using.

Therefore, in designing a well-behaved component the two most important guidelines are:

- Don't force your component to shut down while client applications have references to your objects.
- Don't force your component to remain in memory when all object references have been released.

Visual Basic provides a great deal of assistance in following these basic guidelines. This topic explains how you can do your part.

Don't Force Your Component to Shut Down

This means that you should never use the End statement to shut down your component, as long as client applications are holding references to your objects.

This guideline is easy to follow for in-process components, because Visual Basic prevents the use of the End statement in ActiveX DLL and ActiveX control projects. If you include the End statement in your code, an error will occur when you make the compiled component.

> **Note** Visual Basic doesn't allow the End statement in an in-process component because executing it would also terminate the client.

Out-of-Process Components

If you shut down an out-of-process component with the End statement, client applications are left holding references to objects that no longer exist. When they attempt to invoke the properties and methods of those objects, they will receive errors.

In addition, your component may not shut down correctly, because your objects never receive their Terminate events. This is because the End statement halts execution of your component abruptly, releasing objects and freeing memory. *No further Visual Basic code is executed*, including code you have placed in the QueryUnload and Unload events of forms, and in the Terminate events of forms and classes.

If you observe the four rules Visual Basic uses to determine when to shut your component down, as described in "Visual Basic Component Shutdown Rules," you should never need to force your component to shut down.

Don't Force Your Component to Remain Loaded

Visual Basic will automatically unload your component according to the shutdown rules enumerated In "Visual Basic Component Shutdown Rules." As you'll see from the discussion of those rules, it's possible to keep your component loaded after clients have released their references to its objects.

Generally speaking, this is a bad idea. Your component goes on taking up memory, even when it's not supplying objects. In fact, an out-of-process component that refuses to shut down may go on taking up memory long after all clients have terminated.

> **Note** You can't force an in-process component to remain loaded beyond the termination of its client. When the client closes, the component is unloaded regardless of any outstanding object references, open forms, and so on. This includes references the client may have obtained, and then passed to other client processes.

Reasons to Keep a Component Loaded

What rule is without exceptions? There are two important circumstances in which you may want to keep your component in memory deliberately:

- If your component is a stand-alone desktop application that also provides objects, the way Microsoft Excel does, and it's been started by the end user, then it's inappropriate for it to close when the last client releases its last reference.

  > **Note** Visual Basic helps you with this, by not shutting down an out-of-process component that has a loaded form, as described in "Visual Basic Component Shutdown Rules" under Rule 2: Forms.

- If you're designing a component to work with a particular client — for example, if client and component are parts of a larger system — and the client frequently releases all of its references to objects the component provides, you may want to keep the component running to avoid the delay caused by reloading it into memory.

  > **Note** You can keep your component loaded in this situation using the information in "Visual Basic Component Shutdown Rules," under Rule 1: References and Rule 2: Forms.

In either of these special cases, forcing your component to remain loaded means that you must find some other way to determine when it should unload.

Visual Basic Component Shutdown Rules

The rules Visual Basic uses to determine when to shut down are different for in-process and out-of-process components.

Rule	In-process component	Out-of-process component
References	There are no references — internal or external — to the component's *public* objects.	No out-of-process clients have references to the component's *public* objects.
Forms	The component has no forms *visible.*	The component has no forms *loaded.*
Code	No code in the component's modules is currently executing, or in the calls list waiting to be executed.	Same as in-process.
Startup	The component is not in the process of being started, in response to a client request for an object.	Same as in-process.

Rule 1: References

When determining whether to shut down a component, Visual Basic considers only the references to *public* objects. References to objects created from classes whose Instancing property is Private *will not count toward keeping a component running.*

> **Important** Classes in the VB type library are also private, and references to objects of these classes *will not* keep a component loaded. Classes in the VBA type library are public. (To view the classes in each of these libraries, select the library of interest in the Project/Library box on the Object Browser.)

In-Process Components

For in-process components, the References rule has additional consequences in two areas: private objects and internal references to public objects.

> **Note** A client application written in Visual Basic may not attempt to unload an in-process component immediately after the last reference is released. The frequency of attempts depends on how frequently idle time becomes available. Two minutes is a good rule of thumb.

Invalid References to Private Objects May Be Fatal to In-Process Clients

Suppose your in-process component passes a client a reference to a private object, and the client subsequently releases its last reference to your public objects. Your component may unload at any point thereafter — because the reference to the private object doesn't prevent shutdown — leaving the client with an invalid reference to the private object.

If the client attempts to use this invalid reference, a program fault will occur, and the client will terminate abruptly. If the client rarely takes a code path in which it attempts to use the invalid reference, such program faults may appear random and difficult to debug.

Important Private objects — that is, objects from classes in the VB library, or objects from classes whose Instancing property is Private — are usually private for a reason. If you need to pass an instance of one of your private classes to a client, you should do the work to make the object safe for public use, and then change the Instancing property of the class to PublicNotCreatable.

Internal References to Public Objects Prevent DLL Unloading

For in-process components, Visual Basic has no way to distinguish between external references to public objects (that is, references held by a client) and internal references to public objects (that is, references in object variables within your in-process component).

Therefore, if your in-process component is holding a reference to one of its own public objects, Visual Basic will not unload it. Any objects your component is holding references to will continue taking up memory and resources.

The most common causes of such internal references are global object variables — for example, a global collection — and circular references. Circular references arise when two objects keep references to each other, as discussed in "Dealing with Circular References," in Chapter 6, "General Principles of Component Design." The sample application for Chapter 6 explores workarounds to global collections and circular references.

Multiple In-Process Components May Keep Each Other Loaded

If several in-process components are in use, and they obtain references to each other's public objects, the object references will keep Visual Basic from shutting the components down.

Out-of-Process Components

For an out-of-process component, Visual Basic keeps separate counts of external and internal references to public objects. Only external references — that is, references held by clients — will keep your component running. This is in contrast to the counting rule for in-process components.

Note In contrast to in-process components, Visual Basic's marshaling rules prohibit out-of-process components from passing private object references to clients.

Avoid Keeping Internal References

Internal references to public objects — global object variables, global collections, or circular references — should still be avoided. Although internal references will not keep an out-of-process component running, they may keep orphaned objects from being destroyed.

For example, suppose an out-of-process component is being used by two clients, and that client A releases all of its object references before client B does. If the component is holding internal references to the objects client A was using, they will go on taking up memory and resources until the component shuts down — which will not happen until client B releases the last of its objects.

If in the meantime a third client begins using objects provided by the component, orphaned objects from both client A and client B may go on taking up memory and resources.

References Held by In-Process Components Don't Count

Your out-of-process component may be using objects provided by an in-process component, running in the out-of-process component's process space. The out-of-process component may pass references to its public objects to the in-process component, or the in-process component may independently request an object from the out-of-process component.

Regardless of how they are obtained, references held by an in-process component will not keep the out-of-process component from unloading when out-of-process clients have released all their object references.

Rule 2: Forms

It may seem odd that Visual Basic takes forms into account when determining whether it's safe to close a component. To understand the logic of this, consider applications like Microsoft Excel, which can be started by the person who uses the computer, and can also provide objects to client applications.

If it's wrong to pull your component out from under client applications that are using its objects, it's even worse to pull a user's spreadsheet, perhaps representing hours of painstaking labor, out from under the user just because client applications have released all the objects they were using.

In other words, the person using the user interface (if your component has one) is also a client.

How Visual Basic Interprets the Forms Rule

In-process components depend on their clients in a different way than out-of-process components do, so Visual Basic interprets the Forms rule differently for the two cases.

A visible form will keep an in-process component in memory, even if the client has released all object references; an invisible form will not.

> **Note** In-process components can be kept running in this fashion only until the client application closes. At that time, all forms are forced to unload. Forms unloaded at this time do not receive QueryUnload events, and the *cancel* argument of the Unload event is ignored.

By contrast, any loaded form will keep an out-of-process component running past the point at which all references have been released — even past the termination of all clients.

Visual Basic makes this distinction because an out-of-process component may be a standalone desktop application, and the fact that its forms are invisible may be only a temporary state.

Controlling Form Lifetime

In general, forms should be unloaded when the object that created them terminates. For example, your component may use a hidden form to hold a Timer control. You can put code to unload the form in the Terminate event procedure of the object that creates and loads the form.

> **Tip** If multiple objects are sharing the same form, you can create a UseCount property for the form. Increment and decrement the UseCount property in the Initialize and Terminate events of the objects, and unload the form when the UseCount reaches zero.

Components That Are Desktop Applications

If your component is also a stand-alone desktop application, its main form will keep your component running even if no client applications are using your objects. When the user chooses Exit from your File menu, or clicks the close box on your main form, you should simply unload the form, along with any hidden forms that are loaded, such as frequently used dialog boxes.

As far as the user is concerned, your application has closed. However, if client applications still have references to your objects, Visual Basic keeps your component running in the background.

When Client Applications Can Manipulate the User Interface

The most difficult shutdown case is for a component that provides objects that control its user interface. For example, you might create a Window class that controls the MDI child forms in your application's main form. If the user closes your main window, should you hide the main form even though client applications have child windows visible?

Questions like this keep user interface designers awake at night. You have many options. For example, the QueryUnload event of your main form has an *unloadmode* argument you can test to determine if the form is closing because the user clicked the close box, or because your program code is trying to unload it.

You can unload the child forms that the user opened through your application's menus and toolbar buttons, hide the main form, and set the Visible property of your Application object to False. Client applications can set the Visible property to True again if necessary.

Alternatively, you can unload all the user's forms, and leave the remaining child forms visible in your main window. You may want to show the user a message indicating what you're doing, and perhaps provide the option of hiding the main window anyway, because the computer user is generally regarded as the ultimate owner of the visual interface.

There are no right answers. Your best bet is to do lots of usability testing.

Rule 3: Code Executing

Visual Basic will not unload your component if it is currently executing code. This includes the case where your component has called a routine in another component, a function in a DLL, or a Windows API function. While the external routine is executing, the procedure that made the call is waiting in the calls list, and Visual Basic will not close your component.

There are no actions you need to take — or refrain from — in regard to this shutdown condition. Like external object references, Visual Basic manages it for you.

Rule 4: Startup

The last condition is a special case that covers the awkward gap between the time your component to starts up because a client application has requested one of your objects, and the moment when your component returns the object reference. There may be moments in the startup sequence when there are no forms loaded and no code executing, and there certainly aren't any external object references.

As with the code execution condition, you don't need to take any action because Visual Basic handles this case for you.

Summary of Guidelines for Component Shutdown

The following guidelines summarize what you need to remember about component shutdown.

- A well-behaved component does not control its own lifetime.
- Don't shut an out-of-process component down forcibly using the End statement.

  As a corollary to this, don't implement a Quit method. Releasing a component by releasing all references to its objects is good programming practice. Educate users of your component by explaining in your Help file that this is the correct way to release your component. Don't encourage bad programming practices by giving developers a shortcut that could disrupt other clients.
- Don't prolong the life of your component needlessly by keeping a form loaded but hidden when there are no objects using it.
- Avoid circular references that artificially prolong the life of your component, such as an object that holds a reference to a form that in turn holds a reference to the object. Circular references are discussed in "Dealing with Circular References," in Chapter 6, "General Principles of Component Design."
- If your component is a stand-alone desktop application that also provides objects, remember that the computer user is one of your clients.

Most of the work of being a good component is done for you by Visual Basic. You can go a long way by simply letting it do its job.

Object Model Creation Guidelines

As discussed in "Organizing Objects: The Object Model," in Chapter 6, "General Principles of Component Design," the hierarchy you use to organize the objects in your component can range in complexity from none at all — that is, only independent externally creatable objects with no dependent objects — to a large structure with many dependent objects.

Guidelines for Creating Collection Classes

A collection provides a way to connect a group of dependent objects with an object that "contains" them. For example, an Invoice object might have a collection of LineItem objects.

As discussed earlier in "Naming Guidelines," the name of a collection should be the plural of the name of the object it contains. Thus an Invoice object might have a LineItems collection to contain its LineItem objects.

Implementing Collections

Visual Basic provides a generic Collection class for managing groups of objects, as discussed in "The Visual Basic Collection Object," in Chapter 9, "Programming with Objects," in the *Microsoft Visual Basic 6.0 Programmer's Guide*.

You can implement collections for your component's object model by wrapping a private Collection object in a class module, thus defining a *collection class* from which you can create instances as needed. This is explained in "Creating Your Own Collection Classes," in Chapter 9, "Programming with Objects," in the *Microsoft Visual Basic 6.0 Programmer's Guide*.

In addition to describing the steps you need to take, "Creating Your Own Collection Classes" includes code examples that show why collection classes are the most robust way to use the Collection object.

A robust implementation is critical to the successful reuse of component code. Other programmers will rely on the robustness of the objects you create. Don't take shortcuts.

Collection Class Properties and Methods

The following table shows properties and methods you should implement for collection classes.

Method or property	Description
Add	Adds an item to a collection. If used for object creation, the method should return a reference to the newly created object.
Count (property)	Returns the number of items in the collection.
Item	Returns a reference to a single item from the collection. The argument may be a numeric index or a key value. This is usually the default property.
Remove	Removes an item from a collection. The argument may be a numeric index or a key value.
NewEnum	Returns the IUnknown interface of an enumerator object that For Each … Next can use to iterate over the items in a collection. Should be hidden in the type library. Must have a Procedure ID value of –4 to work with For Each … Next.

Implementing an Add or Insert Method

One of the keys to creating a robust collection class is implementing your own Add method. Your Add method can delegate to the Add method of a Visual Basic Collection object, while providing type safety or controlling access to the collection.

Type safety is very easily implemented, as shown in the following code fragment for the Add method of a hypothetical Widgets collection class:

```
Public Sub Add(ByVal NewWidget As Widget, _
      Optional ByVal Key As String = "")
   If String = "" Then
      mcolWidgets.Add NewWidget
   Else
      mcolWidgets.Add NewWidget, Key
   End If
End Sub
```

All the work of maintaining the collection and generating error messages is delegated to a private instance of the Visual Basic Collection class, a reference to which is kept in `mcolWidgets`. The Add method of the private Collection object, which can accept objects of any type, is shielded by the declaration shown above, which can accept only Widget objects.

> **Note** Many existing collection implementations use Add as the name of a method that creates a new element within a collection. You may want to name a method like that shown above — which puts an externally created object into a collection — "Insert" instead of "Add."

You can use the Add method to control access to a collection by making the class of objects the collection contains PublicNotCreatable. In this way, the Add method becomes the only way to create new objects within the collection. If you implement your Add method in this fashion, it should return a reference to the newly created object.

The Add method is a good place to call Friend functions that set the values of read-only properties such as the Parent property.

Examples and Utilities

"Creating Your Own Collection Classes" provides sample code for a collection class implemented according to these guidelines, and explains how to make Item the default method; how to hide NewEnum in the type library; and how to give NewEnum the correct Procedure ID.

The Class Builder utility, included in the Professional and Enterprise Editions of Visual Basic, creates collection class source code that follows these guidelines. You can customize this source code with your own events, properties, and methods.

For More Information See "Add Method," "Remove Method," "Item Method," or "Count Property" in the *Microsoft Visual Basic 6.0 Language Reference* in the *Microsoft Visual Basic 6.0 Reference Library* or "The Visual Basic Collection Object" in Chapter 9 "Programming with Objects," in the *Microsoft Visual Basic 6.0 Programmer's Guide*.

Guidelines for Creating Root Objects

As the name implies, a *root object* is at the base of an object model. Thus it can be thought of as the object that contains all the other objects in the object model. Root objects are usually externally creatable — that is, clients can create instances of the root class using the New operator or the CreateObject function.

For example, the root object of a billing system might have, as one of its properties, an Invoices collection. Each Invoice object in the collection might contain a LineItems collection, so that you could access a particular LineItem object in this fashion:

```
Dim li As LineItem
Set li = <root object>.Invoices(1138).LineItems(3)
```

Naming the Root Object

The name of the root object will vary, depending on the type of component. If your component is a stand-alone desktop application that also provides objects, the way Microsoft Excel does, then "Application" might seem like a logical name for your root object.

On the other hand, if your component runs in process, providing objects to clients but having no user interface of its own, "Application" is probably not an appropriate name for the root object. Use a name that suggests the functionality of your component, or that is similar to your component's type library name.

> **Tip** So many object models use "Application" as the name of their root object that it has become a source of global name space pollution. That is, in order to get the right Application object, you frequently have to qualify it with the type library name. Be original. Find a name that suggests the unique character of your component's root object.

Note Although "Application" is generally recognized as the prototypical root object name, the code examples in this topic use "Root" instead — simply because "Application" is so thoroughly overused.

Root Object Properties and Methods

A root object is the logical place to define properties and methods that affect the entire component. For example, a root object might have a read-only Version property. By definition, a root object will also contain collections or object properties for objects at the next level of the hierarchy.

Global Root Objects and Global Helper Objects

It's fairly common for a root object to be a global object. You can do this in your component by setting the Instancing property of your root object's class module to GlobalMultiUse, as described in "Global Objects," in Chapter 8, "Building Code Components." This makes the properties and methods of the root object appear to be global procedures, the way the members of the VB and VBA libraries are.

If your root object is global, you can allow users to start an instance of your component simply by referring to the root object in code. Provide the root object with a read-only property of the same name, which returns a self-reference. The following code fragment shows how this might look for a root object named "Root."

```
Public Property Get Root() As Root
   Set Root = Me
End Sub
```

This sounds self-referential, but it works — when a client refers to Root in code, the global object is created before the Property Get is called.

Backing Your Root Object with a Global Object

For some components, it may not be appropriate to have all of the properties and methods of your root object dumped willy nilly into the global name space. In this case, don't make your root object global. Instead, create a class named Globals, and set its Instancing property to GlobalMultiUse.

You can add to this Globals class those properties and methods you want to have in the global name space. In those cases where you want to expose the root object's methods, add methods with the same arguments to the Globals class, and delegate to the method of the same name on the root object.

You can still allow users to start your component simply by referring to its root object in code; simply add a property such as the following to the Globals class:

```
Public Property Get Root() As Root
   If gRoot Is Nothing Then
      Set gRoot = New Root
   End If
   Set Root = gRoot
End Property
```

This example assumes your root object is named “Root,” and that you keep a reference to it in the global variable `gRoot`.

The Globals class is a good place to put general-purpose procedures you want your users to be able to access globally.

> **Tip** Implement any object properties you add to the Globals class using Property Get procedures, rather than with public object variables. Property Get defines a read-only property, whereas users may accidentally set public object variables to Nothing.

The GetObject Function

Chapter 10, “Programming with Components,” in the *Microsoft Visual Basic 6.0 Programmer’s Guide*, describes the use of the GetObject function to get a reference to a running instance of a component, or to test to see if one is running. A client application cannot automatically use the GetObject function to obtain a reference to an existing instance of a class defined in a Visual Basic component.

You can do the work yourself, by putting your root object in the *Running Object Table* (ROT). COM provides the ROT as a location for running objects to register themselves, so that functions like GetObject can be used to locate them.

An alternative technique is to make your root object PublicNotCreatable, so that clients can’t create instances directly. Instead, you can provide a MultiUse Connector object which clients can create. The Connector object can provide a property (generally with the same name as your root object) that returns a reference to a single shared root object.

This technique is described in “Asynchronous Call-Backs and Events” in Chapter 8, “Building Code Components,” and demonstrated in the sample applications for that chapter.

> **Tip** A Globals object, described earlier in this topic, can provide the same functionality as a Connector object, in an unobtrusive fashion.

For More Information The ROT is explained in many books about COM, such as *Inside OLE, 2nd Edition*, by Kraig Brockschmidt.

Instancing for Root Objects

The functionality your root object provides depends heavily on which value you choose for the Instancing property of its class module: PublicNotCreatable, SingleUse, GlobalSingleUse, MultiUse, or GlobalMultiUse.

PublicNotCreatable Root Objects

If your root object is marked PublicNotCreatable, client applications cannot create instances of it using the New operator or the CreateObject function. While this may seem somewhat upside down — most people will expect the root object to be a way to get at all the other objects in your object model — in conjunction with a global object or a Connector object, as described earlier in this topic, it can be a way to allow clients to share a single instance of your root class.

In order to give clients access to the root object in this case, you must give your public creatable objects (such as the Connector object or the Globals object) a property that returns a reference to the root object, as shown here:

```
Property Get Root() As Root
   Set Root = gRoot
End Property
```

Note that this does not create circular references, because the dependent objects are not holding actual references to the Root object; they are only using Property Get to return a global reference.

You can also implement a global object with such a property, as described earlier in this topic.

SingleUse Root Objects

If the class that defines your root object is has the Instancing property settings SingleUse or GlobalSingleUse, a client application will start a new running instance of your component every time it uses the New operator or the CreateObject function to create a root object.

In its Initialize event procedure, your root object might set a global reference to itself that other objects can use to gain access to it, as shown in the following code fragment:

```
Private Sub Class_Initialize()
   ' Variable gRoot is declared Public in a standard
   '   module.
   Set gRoot = Me
   ' ...additional initialization code...
End Sub
```

If you don't keep a global reference to the root object, and the client releases its reference — while keeping references to one or more dependent objects — your component can get into a state in which the dependent objects exist without the root.

> **Note** Because a SingleUse root object causes a new instance of your component to be loaded for each client request, keeping a global reference doesn't result in orphaned objects (as described in "ActiveX Component Shutdown"), unless clients pass each other references to root objects.

SingleUse Root Objects and Exclusive Use of Components

Depending on whether you mark additional class modules as externally creatable, marking your root object SingleUse can also give each client application exclusive use of a copy of your component.

If the only externally creatable class in your component is the root object, every client application will have its own instance of your component. Because Visual Basic classes do not support the use of the GetObject function to obtain references to existing objects, there is no way another client can get access to a running copy of your component.

The disadvantage of this is that every client must start an instance of your component, which will use more memory and system resources. If you need to give each client application exclusive use of a copy of your component, you may find it more efficient to write an in-process component.

SingleUse Root Objects and Shared Components

If you mark other classes in your component MultiUse or GlobalMultiUse, clients can create objects from those classes without first creating a root object.

This is similar to the way Microsoft Excel's externally creatable objects work. If you create a Microsoft Excel Application object, you start a new running instance of Microsoft Excel. If you create a new Sheet or Chart object, however, they will be provided by a previously running instance of Microsoft Excel, if there is one.

To handle additional externally creatable objects, the Initialize event procedures for all externally creatable objects should test for the existence of the root object, and create it if it doesn't yet exist:

```
' Code fragment from any externally creatable class.
Private Sub Class_Initialize()
   If gRoot Is Nothing Then
      Set gRoot = _
         CreateObject("MyComponent.Root")
   End If
   ' ...more initialization code for this object...
End Sub
```

It's important to use the CreateObject function to create the root object, rather than the New operator. Otherwise a client can create another root object in the same instance of the component at a later time. For more details, see "Scalability Through Multiple Processes: SingleUse Objects" and "How Object Creation Works in Visual Basic Components" in Chapter 8, "Building Code Components."

> **Tip** Why not create the root object in your Sub Main procedure? For one thing, creating objects in Sub Main is not a good idea. It can lead to deadlocks and object creation time-outs. Furthermore, if your component is starting in response to a request from a client, you cannot tell what object is being created. If you create the SingleUse root object in Sub Main when a client has requested the root object, the client's request will fail.

Note Marking multiple classes in your component SingleUse or GlobalSingleUse may produce unexpected results, as discussed in "Scalability Through Multiple Processes: SingleUse Objects" in Chapter 8, "Building Code Components."

MultiUse Root Objects

If you mark your root class MultiUse or GlobalMultiUse, each client that will get its own root object, but all the instances may come from the same running instance of your component.

The implementation decision you face is this: Should all those instances share the same collections of dependent objects, or should each root object have its own collections? This depends entirely on what use you intend for your component. If it's an out-of-process component that's also a stand-alone desktop application, you may want each of the root class instances to act like an Application object — in which case they should all share global collections of dependent objects.

Independent Root Objects

On the other hand, if each root object and the dependent objects it contains represent a unit of functionality, and you want clients to be able to use more than one unit, then the root class instances should be independent of each other, each with its own collections of dependent objects.

You can still back your root objects with a Globals object, as described earlier in this topic, only in this case the Globals object would need to contain a collection of root objects instead of a single instance.

Data that's global to the running instance of your component, such as version number, could also be exposed using read-only properties of the Globals object.

Creating Interfaces for Use with the Implements Statement

When you create interfaces for use with the Implements statement, you can use Visual Basic or any tool that creates type libraries, such as the MkTypLib utility or the Microsoft Interface Definition Language (MIDL) compiler.

Most classes created in Visual Basic define interfaces that work with Implements. When you create an interface by defining a class in Visual Basic, simply make sure that none of the properties or methods have underscores in their names.

Interfaces created with tools other than Visual Basic must follow certain restrictions in order to work with Implements. The following list includes most of these restrictions.

- Interface methods cannot have underscores in their names.
- Only [in] and [in,out] params are allowed — [out] only params are not allowed, and [lcid] parameters are not allowed.
- Method return types must be HRESULT, in order for errors to be propagated. You will not see the HRESULT in Visual Basic, as it is translated into an exception (raised error). To create a method that will have a return type when used in Visual Basic code, you must use [out, retval] on the final parameter.
- Only Automation data types may be used:

VB Data Type	MIDL Equivalent
Integer	short
Long	long
Single	float
Double	double
Byte	unsigned char
Boolean	boolean or VARIANT_BOOL
String	BSTR
Variant	VARIANT
Date	DATE
Currency	CURRENCY or CY
Object	IDispatch
IUnknown	IUnknown

- SAFEARRAY parameters containing any of the simple data types from the list above are allowed.
- Enum parameters are allowed.
- Dispinterface interface pointers are allowed as parameters.
- Dual interface pointers are allowed as parameters.
- CoClass parameters are allowed.

- If you're creating a type library in order to make a system interface usable with Implements, you must not use the [oleautomation] or [dual] attributes. Type libraries must be registered before you can add them to the Visual Basic References dialog box, and registering a type library with the [oleautomation] attribute will overwrite information required to remote the system interface. THIS WILL CAUSE OTHER APPLICATIONS ON THE SYSTEM TO FAIL. The [dual] attribute must not be used because it implies [oleautomation].

  Note It may be useful to specify [oleautomation] while creating the typelib, in order to enforce correct types, but the type library must be built without the attribute before you reference it through the Visual Basic References dialog box.

- Unsigned long and unsigned short parameters are not included in the data type table, and are not allowed.
- User-defined data types (structures) are not allowed as parameters.
- Interfaces must be based on IUnknown or IDispatch. The full vtable (after IUnknown/IDispatch) must be described in a single interface.
- Restricted vtable entries are ignored and do not prevent the Implements statement from working.
- Most pointers cannot be passed as [in] parameters. (For example, as a remoting optimization, a C++ interface can declare a parameter as [in] VARIANT* pVar. This will not work with Implements.) An [in] parameter can be a BSTR, a pointer to an interface (for example, IDispatch*), or a SAFEARRAY pointer (SAFEARRAYs are always passed as pointers). An [in,out] parameter can be a pointer to an Automation type, or a double pointer to an interface (for example, IDispatch**). (Note that 'ByVal As String' in Visual Basic maps to [in] BSTR. You cannot use [in] BSTR* with Visual Basic.)
- Implements does not work with dispinterfaces.

For more information See "Polymorphism," in "Programming with Objects" in the *Microsoft Visual Basic 6.0 Programmer's Guide*, and also "Providing Polymorphism by Implementing Interfaces," in Chapter 6, "General Principles of Component Design" in Part 2, "Creating ActiveX Components," in this book.

PART 3

Extending the Visual Basic Environment with Add-Ins

The Microsoft Visual Basic development environment comes with a fixed level of functionality and a select set of tools. You may find that you require some functionality or a tool that doesn't exist in Visual Basic's Integrated Development Environment (IDE), or find yourself repeatedly doing a simple task. To solve this dilemma with prior versions of Visual Basic, you might have purchased pre-fabricated controls or toolsets to augment the IDE. Now, you can elect to create your solutions from within Visual Basic using its extensibility object model.

Objects from this model can be programmatically used to construct *add-ins* — modular ActiveX components that connect to the IDE and provide it additional functionality. In many cases, if the functionality is generic enough, these ActiveX components can even be used in other applications (that can use ActiveX components).

Add-ins can be constructed to work inside or outside the IDE, or both. They can automate repetitive tasks, monitor the IDE for the occurrence of certain events, act upon those events, or perform complex tasks. Add-ins can be activated through menu commands, toolbar buttons, or through Windows events.

One variation of add-in is a Wizard. A Wizard is a step-by-step instructive program you can create to lead users of your applications through a particularly difficult procedure.

With add-ins and the extensibility model, you are now able to tailor the Visual Basic IDE to your unique needs with applications that do exactly what you want them to do.

Chapter 1 Add-Ins Overview

Explains extensibility and how it's implemented in Visual Basic in the form of add-ins, and provides a step-by-step procedure for creating a simple, working add-in.

Chapter 2 Extensibility Model Objects and Structure

Provides a map to the objects you can use to create and connect add-ins, along with links to more detailed reference information on each.

Chapter 3 How to Build an Add-In

Offers in-depth discussion of the steps and issues associated with creating add-ins to automate programming tasks. Uses code from a sample application included with Visual Basic.

Chapter 4 Connecting and Exposing Add-Ins

Covers add-in essentials and illustrates methods for connecting and exposing your add-ins in the Visual Basic environment.

CHAPTER 1

Add-Ins Overview

Consider, for a moment, a socket wrench.

By attaching different sockets to it, you can use it for different tasks. Add-ins are to the Microsoft Visual Basic development environment what sockets are to a socket wrench; they provide it additional and interchangeable functionality. Unlike a socket wrench, though, you can attach several add-ins to Visual Basic at the same time, among other things.

In the following topics, you'll discover exactly what add-ins are, what they can do to help you program in Visual Basic, and how you can create and use them.

Contents

What Is Extensibility?

Extensibility is the capacity to extend or stretch the functionality of the development environment — to add something to it that didn't exist there before. Extensibility is not a new concept to development environments. Some language development packages give you the ability to add functionality to their user environments. However, the extent of control provided to you can be limited, or difficult to understand and implement.

Visual Basic provides you with a powerful, easy-to-understand modular system for customizing its environment through a programming interface known as the Extensibility object model. Its sole purpose is to allow you to "hook into" the workings of Visual Basic and create extensions known as add-ins.

The Visual Basic extensibility model consists of six related groups of individual code objects which control each major facet of the Visual Basic IDE. Each functional group enables you to create tools to customize the Visual Basic development environment and help you accomplish your programming tasks more quickly and easily. These groups are:

- Form manipulation objects
- User-interface manipulation objects

- Event response objects
- Add-in management objects
- Project and component manipulation objects
- Code manipulation objects

Each group consists of one or more collections and objects which together contribute to a particular purpose. For example, the primary function of the forms object group is to allow you to programmatically manipulate forms in your Visual Basic projects. One object in this group is the CommandBar object, which allows you to manipulate menus and toolbars. Another is the CodePane object, which allows you to display code contained in an object.

Other groups contain objects which allow you to manipulate and maintain the projects themselves, their source code, how they respond to events, and so forth.

What does all this mean to you? This means that you don't have to settle for the constraints of the programming environment or rely on third-party extensions that don't do exactly what you want them to do. You might, for example, create add-ins to:

- **Customize the Visual Basic user interface.** For example, you can create an enhanced version of the Project Explorer window where you can customize views, add or delete folders, navigate and view project elements, and so on.
- **Control projects.** You can design an add-in that loads a group of projects, one after another.
- **Programmatically edit code.** You can use an add-in to automatically add comments to certain lines of code.
- **Control forms.** You can create an add-in that closes all currently open forms, or one that adjusts all open forms to the same size.

These are just a few ideas. Add-ins give you the freedom to create custom programming solutions to save you time and help you become more productive. Just think of the possibilities!

For more information See "What is an Add-In?" for information on different kinds of add-ins.

What Is an Add-In?

You can use the Visual Basic extensibility object model to ease development through add-ins. *Add-ins* are tools that you create programmatically using objects and collections in the extensibility model to customize and extend the Visual Basic environment. In a sense, add-ins "snap on" to the Visual Basic integrated development environment (IDE).

Whether created in Visual Basic or Visual C++, the primary goal of an add-in is to enable you to automate something in the development environment that is difficult, or tedious and too time-consuming to accomplish manually. Add-ins are time- and labor-saving automation tools for the Visual Basic programming environment.

Note When using C++ to develop add-ins, whenever you get a pointer from Visual Basic using Automation, you must call "release" when you are finished using it. Visual Basic follows the standard reference counting rules. For example, when you get a pointer out of Visual Basic by calling _NewEnum, you must call release through that pointer. Also, when you use `pDispatch = m_ourMenuItems.Item(pszCaption)`, you must also use `pDispatch->Release()`.

There are four types of add-ins: add-ins, Wizards, utilities, and builders.

- *Add-in* is the generic term for a program you create that performs task(s) within the IDE, often in response to certain events (such as a mouse click or a form opening). Its actions may or may not be visible to the user.
- A *Wizard* is a special type of add-in which leads a user step-by-step through a task, often an especially complex or tricky one. Although they can be constructed any way you like, Microsoft implements its Wizards in a specific manner. A Microsoft Wizard consists of a number of frames, each frame containing an image in the upper left corner, a label description to the right of the image which may also contain instructions, and an optional area near the bottom in which other controls (such as ListBox or CommandButton controls) can be placed. To help you create Wizards, we've included an add-in called the Wizard Manager.

  For more information about wizards, see "Wizards and the Wizard Manager" in Chapter 3, "How to Build an Add-In."
- A *utility* is an add-in, sometimes a rather large one, which doesn't necessarily require Visual Basic to run. This means that it is compiled as an ActiveX executable, but it retains the ability to also be called as an add-in in the Visual Basic IDE. VisData is an example of a utility.
- A *builder* is a type of add-in which helps a user to view or set properties of a control, or properties that several controls have in common. However, builders aren't normally created as add-ins anymore because Visual Basic gives you many builder-like capabilities at design time through the PropertyPage object.

Chapter 3, "How to Build an Add-In," discusses the specifics of creating these add-ins.

Most add-ins that you've seen or used before were probably visually-based; that is, they appeared as commands in menus or as buttons on toolbars in the Visual Basic IDE. Now, add-ins don't necessarily have to be visible — they can sit hidden in the background and respond to events such as the sizing of a form or control. Or they may be invisible and do something like reset a timer control when a certain project loads, or they may be entirely visual; for example they may size a group of like objects by sizing only one of the objects.

Creating a Basic Add-In

Building an add-in consists mainly of creating a class module that handles events specific to add-ins and any events you want to specify, along with your support modules and forms. Unless you need to have multiple instances of an add-in running in the same IDE, all class procedures should be declared Private to prevent other routines from inadvertently referencing them.

Once the add-in code is complete, you must compile it as an ActiveX .dll or .exe file, since add-ins must be ActiveX components. For various reasons, it's generally best to create add-ins as ActiveX .dll files.

To create the AddInProject add-in

1. On the **File** menu, click **New Project** to open the **New Project** dialog box. (This will close your current project or project group; you will be prompted to save any changes you have made.) Double-click the ActiveX DLL icon to create a new project.

2. Click the **Project** menu, then click **References**. Select the **Microsoft Visual Basic Extensibility** and **Microsoft Office 8.0 Object Library** check boxes.

   This gives you access to the extensibility objects and collections that you need to create add-ins.

3. Click the **Project** menu, then click **Add Module**. In the **Add Module** dialog box, double-click the Module icon to create a new module.

   Note that there is an icon for an AddIn template. The template includes some of the code necessary for beginning an add-in.

   Enter the following code in the new module:

   ```
   Declare Function WritePrivateProfileString& Lib _
   "kernel32" Alias "WritePrivateProfileStringA" _
   (ByVal AppName$, ByVal KeyName$, ByVal _
   keydefault$, ByVal FileName$)
   Sub AddToINI()
   Dim rc As Long
      rc = WritePrivateProfileString("Add-Ins32", _
      "AddInProject.AddInClass", "0", "VBADDIN.INI")
      MsgBox _
         "Add-in is now entered in VBADDIN.INI file."
   End Sub
   ```

4. In the Project Explorer window, double-click the Class module Class1 to bring it to the front. Set its **Name** property to "AddInClass" and make sure that its **Instancing** property is set to "5 – MultiUse."

5. Add the following line of code to the Class module:

   ```
   Implements IDTExtensibility
   ```

   This adds a reference to the IDTExtensibility object to your project.

6. Click IDTExtensibility in the **Object** box.

   Notice that four new events appear in the **Procedure** box: OnConnection, OnDisconnection, OnStartupComplete, and OnAddInsUpdate.

7. Click each of the events in the **Procedure** box to add their procedures to your Class module.

   While you can enter the procedure syntax manually, it's strongly recommended that you click the event name in the box to add the procedures to the Class module to ensure that all names and arguments are entered correctly. Plus, it's faster!

   All four of these event procedures must be present in your Class module for add-ins to work correctly. Also, if one or more of the event procedures has no code in it, it will be removed upon compilation, so it's important that you add at least a comment to each of the four events to ensure that they remain in the Class module when you compile.

8. Now that you have all four events added, add the following code to them:

   ```
   Private Sub IDTExtensibility_OnConnection(ByVal _
   VBInst As Object, ByVal ConnectMode As _
   VBIDE.vbext_ConnectMode, ByVal AddInInst As _
   VBIDE.AddIn, custom() As Variant)
      MsgBox "Add-in is now connected"
   End Sub

   Private Sub IDTExtensibility_OnDisconnection(ByVal _
   RemoveMode As VBIDE.vbext_DisconnectMode, _
   Custom () as Variant)
      MsgBox "Add-in is now disconnected"
   End Sub

   Private Sub IDTExtensibility_OnStartupComplete _
   (custom() As Variant)
      ' Comment to prevent procedure from being
      ' deleted on compilation.
   End Sub

   Private Sub IDTExtensibility_OnAddInsUpdate _
   (custom() As Variant)
      ' Comment to prevent procedure from being
      ' deleted on compilation.
   End Sub
   ```

9. On the **Project** menu, click **Project1 Properties**, then enter **AddInProject** in the **Project Name** box. Click **OK**.
10. On the **File** menu, click **Save Project** to save the project files. Name them as shown in the following table. Visual Basic will provide the indicated extensions automatically.

File	File name	Extension
Basic module	AddIn	.bas
Class module	AddInClass	.cls
Project	AddInProject	.vbp

To test the AddInProject add-in

1. Click the **File** menu, then click **Make AddInProject.dll**. In the **Make Project** dialog box, click **OK**.

   This will register the add-in in the system registry.
2. In the **Immediate** window, enter `AddToINI` and press RETURN. You get a message box that says "Add-in is now entered in VBADDIN.INI file."
3. On the **File** menu, click **New Project** to open the **New Project** dialog box. (This will close AddInProject.vbp; you will be prompted to save any changes.) Double-click the Standard EXE icon to create a new project.
4. Click the **Add-Ins** menu, then click **Add-In Manager**. Notice that a new entry, "AddInProject.AddInClass," appears in the list.
5. Select the **AddInProject.AddInClass** check box, then click **OK**.

   At this point, you should get the following dialog box:

6. Click **OK**. Clear the **AddInProject.AddInClass** check box, then click **OK**.

   You should get the following dialog box:

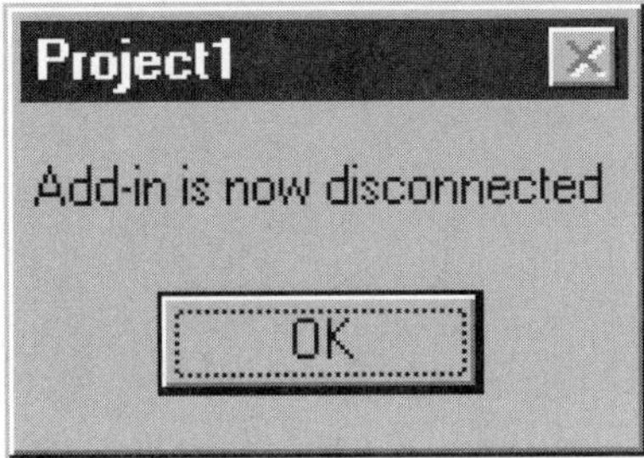

What Just Happened?

The purpose of this add-in is to demonstrate the components and behavior of an essential component of an add-in — its Class module. Let's go through each of the previous steps and discuss what it did, and more importantly, how and why it was done the way it was.

- The AddToINI procedure has only one purpose in life: to add an entry for your new add-in to a file in the Windows directory called Vbaddin.ini. Why do this? So that it is recognized by Visual Basic as an available add-in. You can add this entry any way you like, but the Windows WritePrivateProfileString API function call works well for this.

  This brings up an important point: When you distribute an add-in to other users, either you or they must run this function (or use some alternative method) on their machines to update the Vbaddin.ini file before they'll be able to use your add-in. If you don't do this, Visual Basic won't know that the add-in is available, and the add-in won't appear in the list of add-ins in the Add-In Manager.

  You can put such a procedure in a basic module (as was done here) and instruct the user to run the function, but a more elegant solution is to do it for the user in a setup program that you supply to install the add-in.

- The Class module is the heart of an add-in. It is the place where the add-in responds to events. In this example, it admittedly doesn't do very much — it just puts up message boxes when you connect and disconnect the add-in — but you could design an add-in that responded to literally hundreds of events!

  Although the main Class module is useful, it's best not to put all of the code in it, unless it's brief. You can put other code in basic modules or other Class modules and call the procedures from the main Class module. Just follow your normal procedural programming guidelines.

- The act of compiling the DLL registers it in the system registry.

- Running the AddToINI procedure in the Immediate window creates an .ini file entry for the add-in in Vbaddin.ini. For more information on how to add this reference, see "Adding an Add-In Reference to the Vbaddin.Ini File" in Chapter 4, "Connecting and Exposing Add-Ins."
- The rest of the steps show how you can now activate the add-in in another project as well as demonstrate how it appears and behaves in the Add-In Manager. Also, they show how selecting and clearing the add-in entries in the Add-In Manager triggers the OnConnection and OnDisconnection events.

CHAPTER 2

Extensibility Model Objects and Structure

When driving through an unfamiliar city, it's usually helpful to have a road map to find your way around. Consider this chapter your road map to the extensibility model. Studying and becoming familiar with it will make it quicker and easier for you to program that perfect add-in that does exactly what you need it to do.

Many objects in the model relate to each other for specific functional purposes, such as manipulating source code or connecting and using add-ins. In the diagram in "The Extensibility Model Objects," in this chapter, these related objects are grouped together by similar boxes. This makes it easier for you to locate the objects you need to accomplish the tasks you want to perform.

The group of objects, "Objects that Extend the User Interface," is documented in this book. Objects in that group, such as the CommandBar object, are documented in an online topic. In that topic, you'll be able to see a detailed description of the CommandBar object, plus all the properties, events, and methods that apply to it.

This chapter presents the overall structure of the Visual Basic extensibility object model — the "big picture." In addition, it shows each functional group of objects, along with descriptions of all the objects in each group.

Contents

The Extensibility Model Objects

Here is an overview diagram of the extensibility object model:

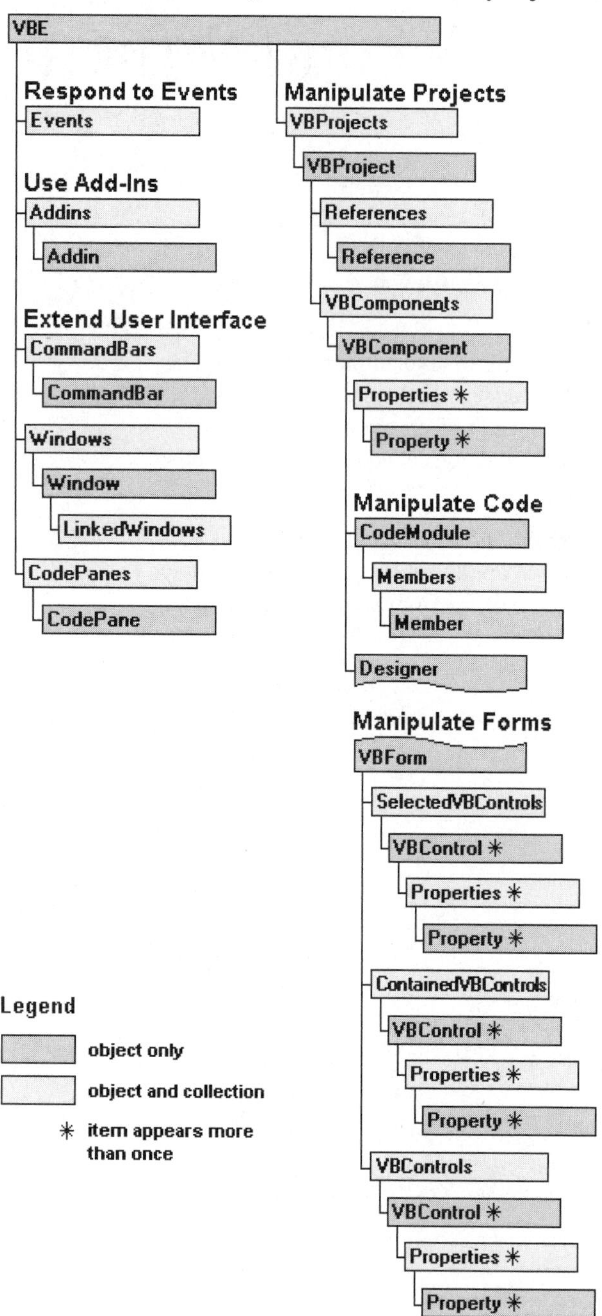

Objects That Extend the User Interface

This group of objects helps you customize the Microsoft Visual Basic user interface.

Using these objects, you might:

- Add a new button or command to an existing *command bar*. (A command bar is a menu or toolbar in Visual Basic.)
- Create an entirely new menu or toolbar for your add-in.
- Open, close, move, and alter the size of user interface windows.
- Use the CodePanes collection and CodePane object to display code and determine what code a user has selected.

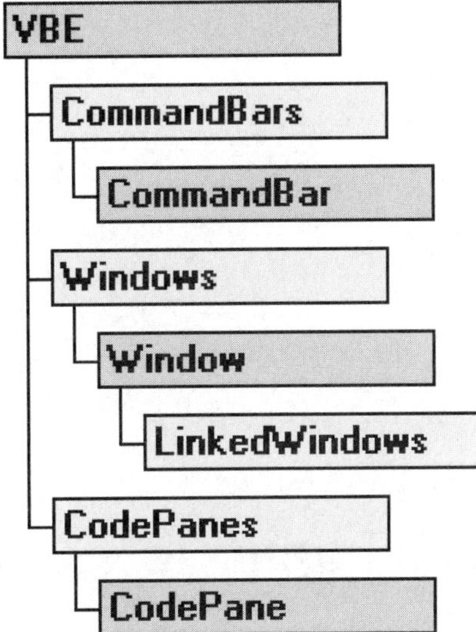

Objects That Allow You to Manipulate Projects

This group of objects helps you control and manipulate projects in Visual Basic.

Using these objects, you might:

- Select one project out of several to operate on, or select several for group project operations.
- Remove all other projects in Visual Basic and start a new project.
- Add new projects to the current Visual Basic session.

- Notify yourself or react in a certain manner when particular projects are loaded or unloaded.
- Display project names elsewhere, such as in a combo box.
- Change project options.
- Add and remove components.

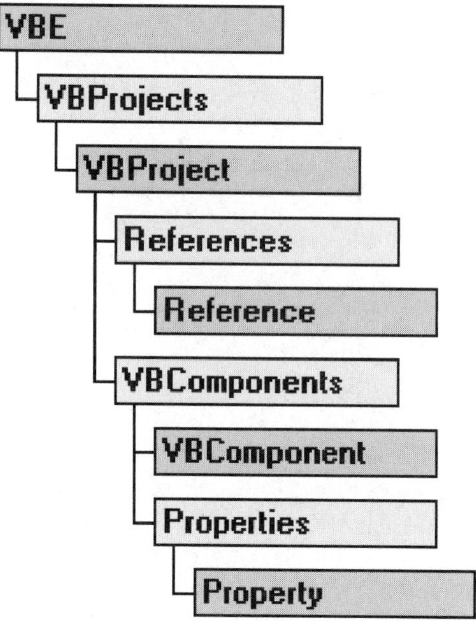

Objects That Allow You to Manipulate Forms

This group of objects helps you control and manipulate designers in Visual Basic.

Using these objects, you might programmatically manipulate the designers for a form, control, property page, or ActiveX document in order to:

- Add a designer.
- Add code and controls.
- Hide or unhide the designer.
- Position controls.
- Change the designer's properties.

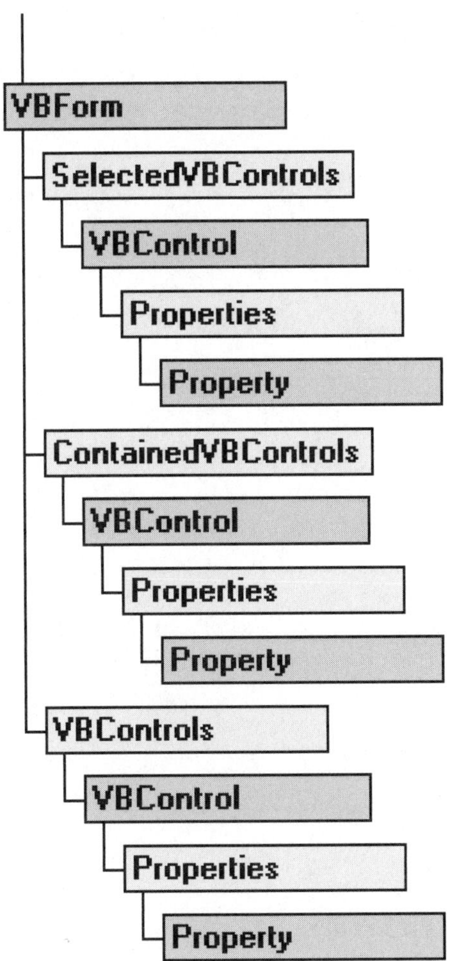

Objects That Allow You to Respond to Events

This group of objects helps you respond to events that occur in Visual Basic. The VBA object can be either the Visual Basic environment, in design view, or the program that you create, at run time.

Events also occur on the following collections:

- VBProjects
- VBComponents
- VBControls
- References

Using these objects, you might monitor and/or intercept and handle events that occur in the Visual Basic interface, such as when a form is added to the project, or when a project is added.

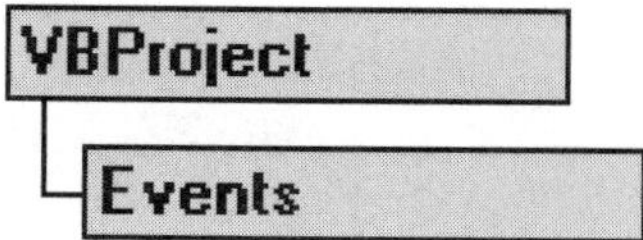

Objects That Allow You to Manipulate Code

This group of objects helps you programmatically control and manipulate code in Visual Basic.

Using these objects, you might:

- Select, add, or delete lines of code.
- Search and replace occurrences of certain strings.

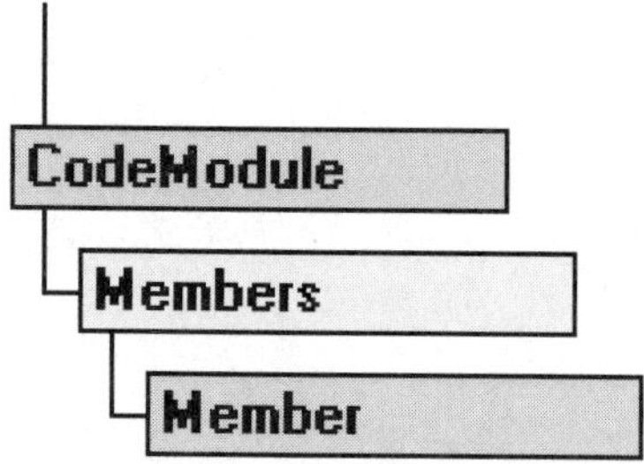

Objects That Allow You to Use Add-Ins

This group of objects helps you control and manipulate add-ins in Visual Basic.

Using these objects, you connect and disconnect add-ins, and access objects provided by add-ins.

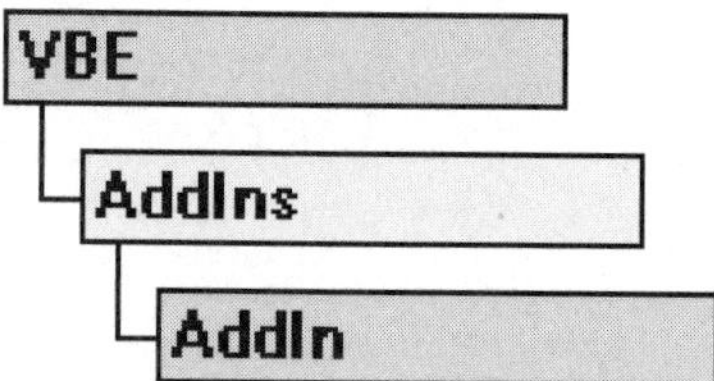

CHAPTER 3

How to Build an Add-In

In this chapter, you'll learn the basics of building add-ins. We'll show you how to program each functional group of objects in the extensibility model, as well as how to use the Wizard Manager to easily create professional-looking Wizards. You'll also learn about the Add-In toolbar — a great place to place add-ins and Wizards for quick and easy user access.

Contents

Add-In Creation Basics

Every add-in project shares some common elements, and there are some decisions you should make before you get started with creating your add-in. This section is an overview of these elements.

Add-In Essentials

All add-ins, regardless of what they do, require that you reference the items discussed in this topic. When you begin an add-in project, selecting the add-in template that comes with Visual Basic will provide a project containing code for all of the items listed in this topic. The template is described in this topic.

All add-ins you create with Visual Basic require the following:

- **Root Object** The top-most, or "root" object in the extensibility model is the VBE object. The VBE object represents the Visual Basic environment. It hosts all of the extensibility objects and collections, which in turn have a number of properties, methods, and events which expose its functionality.

For More Information See "Visual Basic Instance Variable" in this chapter for information on using the VBE object.

- **IDTExtensibility Interface** An interface named IDTExtensibility is provided to give you quick access to necessary events in the extensibility model. These interface methods are meant to be contained in a class module in your add-in. To expose the interface's methods, use the Implements statement in a class module's Declaration section. The syntax is:

  ```
  Implements IDTExtensibility
  ```

  The IDTExtensibility interface contains four methods for handling add-in events:

  - OnConnection
  - OnDisconnection
  - OnStartupComplete
  - OnAddInsUpdate

  Although these are methods to the IDTExtensibility interface, to you as a programmer, they act exactly like events, triggering when an event occurs.

  The IDTExtensibility interface speeds up the process of creating these four essential procedures and eliminates problems with add-ins due to entry errors in the parameter list, or other procedure syntax errors.

  When you click the Objects drop-down box in the code window for the class module, you'll see IDTExtensibility. When you select IDTExtensibility, the four required add-in event procedures appear in the Procedures drop-down box. Simply click the name of each procedure to add it to the class module.

  Since add-ins require that all members of an interface be implemented, the class module must contain all four procedures. You can add as many other procedures to the class module that you want, but you must have those four at a minimum for your add-in to work.

  > **Note** One important caveat is that each of the four procedures must contain at least one line of code, such as a statement, procedure call, comment, and so on. If the procedure is empty, it will be removed by the compiler. If you don't have any particular code you want to put in these procedures, just insert a comment.

For More Information Add-in events are also covered in Chapter 4, "Connecting and Exposing Add-Ins" in the section "Connecting or Disconnecting Add-Ins." Other events that you'll want to handle are covered in this chapter under the section "Responding to Events with Add-Ins."

- **Visual Basic Instance Variable** Each collection and object in the extensibility model requires a variable to store and reference the current instance of Visual Basic. An instance is a dynamic identification variable for the current session of Visual Basic. Since you can conceivably have more than one session of the Visual Basic IDE running at any given time, the instance variable differentiates one Visual Basic session from another.

To declare a Visual Basic instance variable in the declarations section of a module or class module, you might enter:

```
' The variable VBInst is set to the current instance ' of Visual Basic.
Global gVBInst As VBIDE.VBE
```

For More Information "Creating a Basic Add-In," in Chapter 1, "Add-Ins Overview," steps you through creating a simple add-in and provides a brief illustration of the items presented here at work together.

Add-In Template

Visual Basic's add-in template contains the basic, necessary code that all add-ins require. To use the add-in template to create a new add-in project, choose Add-In in the New Project dialog box. This template contains the essentials:

- A basic module which declares global variables, such as a Visual Basic instance variable, plus an AddToIni procedure, which writes the name of the add-in to the Vbaddin.ini file.
- A class module with pre-created IDTExtensibility interface procedures

The template also includes these other useful features:

- A CommandBar event handler
- Rudimentary error-handling code
- Code to access the add-in as a button on the Standard toolbar

The add-in template is a great starting point for your add-in projects.

Design Considerations for Add-Ins

Before creating an add-in, you should decide what the goal you want your add-in to accomplish and how you want it to work. Two factors that have an impact on this decision are usage of the CreateToolWindow function, and choosing a project compile type.

CreateToolWindow Function

While not a required add-in feature, the CreateToolWindow function is a feature you may want to consider using for many add-ins. When you create an add-in, any forms it uses are Visual Basic forms by default. While this is fine for most applications, some programmers may desire that the add-in window act as other windows in Visual Basic do and dock with other IDE windows. The way to create windows like this is to use ActiveX documents and the CreateToolWindow function.

A UserDocument window inside a ToolWindow creates an ActiveX document which can dock with existing windows and act like other windows in the Visual Basic IDE. Writing your add-ins to use CreateToolWindow will also aid you in migrating your add-ins to future versions of Visual Basic.

For an example of how CreateToolWindow is used in an add-in, see the following code fragment, taken from the TabOrder sample application (in the \vb\samples\CompTool\AddIns\TabOrder directory):

```
Dim docTabOrderObject As Object  'user doc instance
' The guidMYTOOL$ constant is the unique registry
' identifier for your add-in.
Const guidMYTOOL$ = "{B7AFC8D0-EBE5-11cf-A497- _
   00A0C911E8B0}"
Set winWindow = _
gVBInstance.Windows.CreateToolWindow(gVBInstance. _
Addins("TabOrder.Connect"), "TabOrder.docTabOrder", _
LoadResString(10), guidMYTOOL$, docTabOrderObject)
```

The code above creates a Tool Window to hold an ActiveX document.

You can generate your own values for the GUID string constant using a tool called Guidgen.exe, which is located in the \tools\idgen directory of Visual Basic.

Choosing a Project Type

Before getting too involved writing an add-in, you should decide how you want to compile the project.

In most situations, you'll likely want to create and compile your add-ins as ActiveX DLL projects, which are in-process components. As in-process components, they provide better overall performance in Visual Basic.

You may want to compile your add-in as a .dll file if:

- The add-in will always be used in conjunction with the Visual Basic IDE (or other programming environment that can use Visual Basic-created add-ins).
- The add-in contains references to certain properties that are available only in Visual Basic.
- The add-in must run as quickly as possible. ActiveX out-of-process components may perform more slowly than in-process components due to the time involved in marshaling across process boundaries.

You might, however, choose to compile an add-in as an ActiveX .exe file if you want the add-in to be able to run on its own — independent of Visual Basic — as well as in the Visual Basic environment.

When you use the Add-In template to create your add-in (which is recommended), your project type defaults to ActiveX EXE. You can change the project type on the General tab of the Project Properties dialog box.

Programming in the Extensibility Model

Once you have a framework in place for your add-in, you can begin to attach code to manipulate and/or extend Visual Basic. As mentioned in Chapter 2, "Extensibility Model Objects and Structure," the extensibility model can be broken down into a number of functional groups, each affecting a major portion of Visual Basic.

Note Many of the example code fragments below are included to demonstrate how the various collections and objects, and their properties, methods, and events, are used in a real-world program. As such, they may contain references to variables, controls, and such that aren't fully explained in this text. For example, many of the samples reference a variable named "vbi," which is a variable to reference the current instance of Visual Basic. (For more information on this, see "Visual Basic Instance Variable" in "Add-In Essentials.") The important thing to realize is that these examples should act as a basis for your own exploration of the extensibility model, not as complete, free-standing programs. To gain a good feel for the entire feature set, we recommend that you examine the VBIDE library in the Object Browser. We also urge you to examine the TabOrder sample application in the \vb\samples\CompTool\AddIns\TabOrder directory for more examples of programming add-ins.

Manipulating the IDE with Add-Ins

Several objects in the extensibility object model allow you to manipulate and extend the Visual Basic IDE. The code in this topic illustrates a few examples.

Commandbars Collection and CommandBar Object

These allow you to manipulate command bars, which are a meld of toolbars and menu bars. You can do nearly anything to a CommandBar object, including creating new ones, deleting existing ones, and changing their size, location, and icons.

Here is an example of how to manipulate command bars:

```
Dim mcbMenuCommandBar As Office.CommandBarControl

' Make sure the Standard toolbar is visible.
gVBInstance.CommandBars("Standard").Visible = True
' Add as button to the Standard toolbar.
' This adds the button to the right of the Toolbox
' button.
Set mcbMenuCommandBar = _
gVBInstance.CommandBars("Standard").Controls.Add _
(1, , , gVBInstance.CommandBars("Standard") _
.Controls.Count)
' Set the caption of the button.
mcbMenuCommandBar.Caption = "My Test"
' Copy an icon to the clipboard.
```

```
Clipboard.SetData LoadPicture("c:\windows\circles.bmp")
' Paste the icon on the button.
mcbMenuCommandBar.PasteFace

' Handle the CommandBarEvents object.
Set Me.MenuHandler = _
gVBInstance.Events.CommandBarEvents _
(mcbMenucommandBar)
```

For More Information For additional information on using CommandBars, see "Creating a Toolbar Button for Add-In Activation" in Chapter 4, "Connecting and Exposing Add-Ins."

Windows Collection and Window Object

These allow you to create and delete windows, as well as move and size windows open in the IDE. All windows are contained in the Windows collection. This means that these windows are never really closed, but rather their visibility is altered with the Visible property.

Note that while you can use the Window object to manipulate a window frame itself, you cannot use it to manipulate the objects contained in a window (such as controls). To do that, you must reference the appropriate object.

The following code fragment demonstrates how to reference the Window object and Windows collection:

```
' Toggle window visibility. Assumes ordering of
' windows in lists matches ordering of windows in
' collection. A better method is to look up window by
' caption and type.
Private Sub cmdToggle_Click()
   Dim w As Window
   Dim sw As String

   sw = Combo1.Text
   If sw <> "" Then
      If sw = "MainWindow" Then
         Set w = vbi.MainWindow
      Else
         Set w = vbi.Windows(Combo1.ListIndex)
      End If
      w.Visible = Not w.Visible
      RefreshWindows
   End If
End Sub
```

LinkedWindows Collection

This contains all of the panes in a given LinkedWindowFrame. A "linked window" is defined as two or more windows which are docked together into a single, joint window surrounded by a frame known as a "LinkedWindowFrame." Each sub-window in the LinkedWindowFrame is known as a "pane." LinkedWindowFrames exist around all windows that can be linked or docked together, with the exception of code windows, designer windows, the Object Browser window, and the Search and Replace window.

If you remove all panes from a LinkedWindowFrame, it is deleted. (The sole exception is the Main window.)

Only windows of type LinkedWindowFrame have a LinkedWindows collection. For other window types, this collection is **Nothing**.

The code fragment below demonstrates how to reference the LinkedWindows collection:

```
' Unlink or undock window if it is linked or docked.
Private Sub cmdUnlinkWindow_Click()
   Dim w As Window
   Dim sw As String

   sw = Combo1.Text
   If sw = "" Then Exit Sub
   If sw = "MainWindow" Then
      Set w = vbi.Windows.MainWindow
   Else
      Set w = vbi.Windows(Combo1.ListIndex)
   End If
   If Not w.LinkedWindowFrame Is Nothing Then
      w.LinkedWindowFrame.LinkedWindows.Remove w
   End If
   RefreshWindows
End Sub
```

CodePane Object

This is a window provided by an object which visually displays the object's code. You cannot create or destroy CodePane objects in the IDE, but you can manipulate their height, width, and location. You can also insert or delete lines of code (using the InsertLines and DeleteLine methods), as well as select certain lines and make the highlight visible or not. You can use the GetSelection method to copy selected code into the Windows clipboard.

While the CodePane object allows you to visually examine or select existing code, it doesn't allow you to alter it. To do this, you must use the CodeModule object, as described in "Manipulating Code with Add-Ins" in this chapter.

The following code fragment demonstrates how to reference the CodePane object:

```
' Scroll codepane using scrollbar.
Private Sub sclCodePane_Change()
   Dim p As VBProject
   Dim c As VBComponent
   Dim cp As CodePane
   Dim sc As String
   Dim sp As String

   sp = cmbProj.Text
   sc = cmbComp.Text
   If sp <> "" And sc <> "" Then
      Set c = _
         vbi.VBProjects.Item(sp). _
         VBComponents.Item(sc)
      Set cp = c.CodeModule.CodePane
      cp.TopLine = sclCodePane.Value + 1
   End If
End Sub
```

Manipulating Projects with Add-Ins

This group of objects allow you to manipulate projects — that is, add or remove projects to or from an existing project group. Also, you can add or remove VBComponents to or from projects. A VBComponent is any object that can be added to a Visual Basic project, such as forms, controls, code modules, and so forth.

The following code fragments demonstrate how to reference the VBProject object and VBProjects collection, as well as other extensibility objects:

```
' Create new project.
Private Sub cmdCreateNew_Click()
   Dim p As VBProject
   Set p = vbi.VBProjects.Add _
      (cmbProjKind.ItemData(cmbProjKind.ListIndex))
   If txtProjName.Text <> "" Then
      p.Name = txtProjName.Text
   End If
End Sub

' Activate component.
Private Sub cmdActivate_Click()
   Dim sc As String
   Dim sp As String
   Dim c As VBComponent

   sp = cmbProj.Text
   sc = cmbComp.Text
```

```
    If sp <> "" And sc <> "" Then
        Set c = _
            vbi.VBProjects.Item(sp).VBComponents.Item(sc)
        c.Activate
    End If
End Sub

' Create new component of the type indicated in the
' cmbCompKind combo.
Private Sub cmdCreateNewVBComponent_Click()
    Dim p As VBProject
    Dim c As VBComponent
    Dim sp As String
    sp = cmbProj.Text
    If sp <> "" Then
        Set p = vbi.VBProjects.Item(sp)
        Set c = p.VBComponents.Add _
            (cmbCompKind.ItemData(cmbCompKind.ListIndex))
    End If
End Sub

' Get the text from the code module and display in text
' control.
Private Sub cmdGetText_Click()
    Dim i As Long
    Dim str As String
    Dim p As VBProject
    Dim c As VBComponent
    Dim sc As String
    Dim sp As String

    Screen.MousePointer = vbHourglass
    sp = cmbProj.Text
    sc = cmbComp.Text
    If sp <> "" And sc <> "" Then
        Set c = _
            vbi.VBProjects.Item(sp).VBComponents.Item(sc)
        txtDisplay.Text = ""  ' Clear the text control
        For i = 1 To c.CodeModule.CountOfLines
            str = str & c.CodeModule.Lines(i, 1) & CRLF
        Next i
        txtDisplay.Text = str
        SynchCodePaneScroll
    End If
    Screen.MousePointer = vbDefault
End Sub

' Refresh the list of projects. Called from events in
' the main object.
```

```
Public Sub RefreshProjects()
   Dim p As VBProject
   Dim tempIndex As Long

   Screen.MousePointer = vbHourglass
   If cmbProj.ListCount > 0 Then
      tempIndex = cmbProj.ListIndex
      ' Temp index to restore prior selection.
   End If
   cmbProj.Clear
   For Each p In vbi.VBProjects
      cmbProj.AddItem p.Name
   Next p
   ' Restore prior selection.
   If cmbProj.ListCount > 0 Then
      If tempIndex <= cmbProj.ListCount - 1 Then
      cmbProj.ListIndex = tempIndex
      Else
         cmbProj.ListIndex = 0
      End If
   End If
   Screen.MousePointer = vbDefault
End Sub
```

Manipulating Forms and Controls with Add-Ins

A *designer* is a base on which you create your visual interface. You can think of it in the extensibility model as an empty socket in which you can plug in different designer types.

From its beginnings, Visual Basic used one kind of designer. Now, however, Visual Basic can host other kinds, including UserDocuments and UserControls that allow you to create ActiveX documents and ActiveX controls that can be used not only in Visual Basic, but in Microsoft Office applications such as Microsoft Word or Microsoft Excel.

The following code fragments demonstrate how to reference the VBForms object, as well as other extensibility objects:

```
' Add controls to form. Type of controls to add is
' based on the type of control selected in ComboBox.
Private Sub cmdAddControl_Click()
   Dim c As VBComponent
   Dim p As VBProject
   Dim vbc As VBControl
   Dim vbc2 As VBControl
   Dim vbf As VBForm
   Dim sc As String
   Dim sp As String
   Dim svbc As String
   Dim pid As String
```

```
    sp = cmbProj.Text
    sc = cmbComp.Text
    svbc = cmbControls.Text
    If sp <> "" And sc <> "" And svbc <> "" Then
       Set p = vbi.VBProjects.Item(sp)
       Set c = p.VBComponents.Item(sc)
       If c.Type = vbext_ct_VBForm Then
          Set vbf = c.Designer
          Set vbc = vbf.VBControls.Item(svbc)
          pid = vbc.ProgId
          Set vbc2 = vbf.VBControls.Add(pid)
       End If
    End If
End Sub

' Refresh the list of controls on a form. Sub is called
' from event handler in the main object when controls
' are added.
Public Sub RefreshControls()
    Dim c As VBComponent
    Dim p As VBProject
    Dim vbc As VBControl
    Dim vbf As VBForm
    Dim sc As String
    Dim sp As String
    Dim tempIndex As Long

    Screen.MousePointer = vbHourglass
    If cmbControls.ListCount > 0 Then
       tempIndex = cmbControls.ListIndex
       ' Temp index to restore prior selection
    End If
    sp = cmbProj.Text
    sc = cmbComp.Text
    If sc <> "" And sp <> "" Then
       cmbControls.Clear
       Set p = vbi.VBProjects.Item(sp)
       Set c = p.VBComponents.Item(sc)
       If c.Type = vbext_ct_VBForm Then
             c.Activate
             Set vbf = c.Designer
             For Each vbc In vbf.VBControls
                cmbControls.AddItem _
                vbc.Properties("name")
             Next vbc
          Else
             cmbControls.Text = "No Form Selected"
          End If
          ' Restore the prior selection.
```

```
            If cmbControls.ListCount > 0 Then
                If tempIndex <= cmbControls. _
                ListCount - 1 Then
                    cmbControls.ListIndex = tempIndex
                Else
                    cmbControls.ListIndex = 0
                End If
            End If
        End If
        Screen.MousePointer = vbDefault
    End Sub

    ' Remove control from form
    Private Sub cmdRemoveControl_Click()
        Dim c As VBComponent
        Dim p As VBProject
        Dim vbc As VBControl
        Dim vbf As VBForm
        Dim sc As String
        Dim sp As String
        Dim svbc As String

        sp = cmbProj.Text
        sc = cmbComp.Text
        svbc = cmbControls.Text
        If sp = "" Or sc = "" Or svbc = "" Then Exit Sub
        Set p = vbi.VBProjects.Item(sp)
        Set c = p.VBComponents.Item(sc)
        If c.Type = vbext_ct_VBForm Then
            Set vbf = c.Designer
            Set vbc = vbf.VBControls.Item(svbc)
            vbf.VBControls.Remove vbc
        End If
    End Sub
```

Responding to Events with Add-Ins

As a Visual Basic programmer, you're accustomed to handling events such as a mouse move, a mouse click, the selection of an item in a ComboBox, and so on. In the Visual Basic version extensibility model, you are given an additional level of control — the ability to respond to events that occur in the IDE itself, such as when a user selects a project in the Project Explorer window or highlights code in a module. The Events object is your gateway to these events.

The Events object, which is referenced directly from the root VBE object, supplies methods that allow add-ins to connect to all events in the extensibility model. (Note that events can also occur in each object.)

The Events object contains the following objects:

- CommandBarEvents
- FileControlEvents
- ReferencesEvents
- SelectedVBControlsEvents
- VBComponentsEvents
- VBControlsEvents
- VBProjectsEvents

Each of these objects allows you to respond to events that pertain to that object. For example, the CommandBarEvents object allows you to respond to events that occur to CommandBar objects, such as when a command bar is clicked. The SelectedVBControlsEvents objects allows you to respond to events that occur to any currently selected Visual Basic controls, and so on.

The WithEvents keyword exposes these events. For example, the VBComponentsEvents object has the ItemAdded event, which occurs when a component is added to a project, the ItemRemoved event, which occurs when a component is removed from a project, and so on.

Here's an example of how to declare such an object in a class module:

```
Private WithEvents evtVBProjects As VBProjectsEvents
```

In order to gain access to these events, however, the object must be referenced. Let's examine and reference one such object, the VBControlsEvents object, which is a property of the VBIDE.Events object. It has three events: ItemAdded, ItemRemoved, and ItemRenamed, and two parameters, VBProject, and VBForm.

In order to gain access to the ItemAdded, ItemRemoved, and ItemRenamed events, you must first reference the VBControlEvents object using the Set statement in the Declarations section of the main class module:

```
' Expose the Events.
Public WithEvents CtrlHandler As VBControlsEvents

' Gain access to the events by referencing the object.
Set Me.CtrlHandler = gVBInstance.Events.VBControlsEvents(Nothing, Nothing)
```

You now have programmatic access to the ItemAdded, ItemRemoved, and ItemRenamed events, and you now can build an add-in that can respond when a user adds, removes, or renames a control in a project. How it responds to these events is up to you and the code you place in the event procedures.

The arguments in the previous Set statement are set to Nothing. This means that we are not referring to a specific form in a project, but rather to any form in any project. You can consider the Events objects' arguments as a sort of filter which determines which events in a project, component, or control you're interested in monitoring. If you specify a particular project and form when setting an instance to a VBControlsEvents object, for example, control events are raised only for that particular form in that particular project. If you set both values to Nothing, however, all control events for all forms in all associated projects are raised. In other words, you are not filtering any of the control events.

Manipulating Code with Add-Ins

The Visual Basic extensibility model provides you with the ability to view and manipulate code in Visual Basic projects through the CodeModule object. Using the CodeModule object, you can programmatically add or remove code to or from a project, search through code, or alter it. You can browse code to find out how many total lines it has, or in a particular procedure, what the starting and ending lines are, and so on. You can also add, delete, or replace lines of code.

> **Important** You should realize the distinction between the CodeModule and CodePane objects. The CodePane object only allows you to view code, but not alter it. The CodeModule object allows you to alter code, but not view it. The two objects work together to allow you to both view and alter code.

The Members object allows you to view and manipulate code and attributes for procedures in a given module. The attributes pertaining to each procedure change depending on the type of module and procedure you're viewing. To see the attributes of a procedure, choose Procedure Attributes from the Tools menu.

A designer is not an object per se; it's really a base on which you create your visual interface. You can think of it in the extensibility model as an empty socket in which you can plug in different designers. For example, if you are using Visual Basic forms, whenever you create or edit a form, you use the Visual Basic forms designer. If you are creating or editing a UserDocument, you are using the UserDocument designer. When creating or editing a UserControl, you are using the UserControl designer. While designers are programmatically different from each other, though, they may or may not have any visual differences to the user.

The following code fragments demonstrate how to reference the CodeModule object:

```
' Clear the code module of all text
Private Sub cmdClearText_Click()
   Dim p As VBProject
   Dim c As VBComponent
   Dim sc As String
   Dim sp As String

   Screen.MousePointer = vbHourglass
```

```
   sp = cmbProj.Text
   sc = cmbComp.Text
   If sp <> "" And sc <> "" Then
      Set c = _
         vbi.VBProjects.Item(sp).VBComponents.Item(sc)
      c.CodeModule.DeleteLines 1, _
         c.CodeModule.CountOfLines
      SynchCodePaneScroll
   End If
   Screen.MousePointer = vbDefault
End Sub

' Insert text into code module.
Private Sub cmdInsertText_Click()
   Dim p As VBProject
   Dim c As VBComponent
   Dim sc As String
   Dim sp As String

   Screen.MousePointer = vbHourglass
   sp = cmbProj.Text
   sc = cmbComp.Text
   If sp <> "" And sc <> "" And txtDisplay.Text _
      <> "" Then
      Set c = _
         vbi.VBProjects.Item(sp).VBComponents.Item(sc)
      c.CodeModule.AddFromString txtDisplay.Text
      SynchCodePaneScroll
   End If
   Screen.MousePointer = vbDefault
End Sub

' Sync up the position of the scrollbar control with
' current CodePane position.
Private Sub SynchCodePaneScroll()
   vbi.VBProjects.Item(sp).VBComponents.Item(sc)
   Dim cp As CodePane
      Set cp = GetCodePane
      sclCodePane.Max = cp.CodeModule.CountOfLines
      sclCodePane.Value = cp.TopLine - 1
End Sub
```

Manipulating Add-Ins

The AddIns collection contains references to AddIn objects and is accessed directly from the root VBE object. Every add-in listed in the Add-In Manager dialog box in an instance of Visual Basic has an AddIn object in this collection. The AddIn object provides information about an add-in to other add-ins.

Using the AddIns collection and AddIn object, you can manipulate add-ins — connect and disconnect them programmatically, add or remove them with the Update method, and so forth.

Experimenting with the Extensibility Model

Once you become more familiar with the extensibility model, it can help to experiment with the various properties, methods and events contained in it. The following is one way to do this:

1. Start Visual Basic and choose Addin as the project type in the New Project dialog.
2. In the Visual Basic Project window, double click on the Connect class module to view its code.
3. Use Find from the Edit menu to search for OnConnection. This should place the cursor in the IDTExtensibility_OnConnection procedure.
4. There is a comment 3 or 4 lines into the procedure suggesting that the following statement is a good place to put a breakpoint for testing code. Place a breakpoint on the suggested line.
5. Place your cursor in the Immediate window, type `AddToIni`, then press ENTER to execute that procedure. (AddToIni is a procedure in the module Addin.Bas.)
6. Press F5 to put the Addin into Run mode.
7. Start another instance of Visual Basic. Choose the default (Standard EXE) from the initial dialog, then choose Add-In Manager from the Add-Ins menu.
8. Check My Addin-In on the list of Available Add-Ins. Press OK in the Add-In Manager dialog. The IDTExtensibility_OnConnection is called in the first instance of Visual Basic, and execution is suspended at the breakpoint that you set in step #4.
9. Use Step Into from the debug menu to execute the line:

   ```
   Debug.Print VBInst.FullName
   ```

   Notice that the path and name of the current instance of Visual Basic is printed in the Immediate window.

10. You can now use **VBInst** as the object for the example code. Simply replace the dummy object **Application.VBE** with the Visual Basic object **VBInst** before executing the example lines in the Immediate window.

For example, you can modify the example:

```
Print Application.VBE.VBProjects(1).VBComponents.Count
```

to read as follows:

```
Print VBInst.VBProjects(1).VBComponents.Count
```

When you press ENTER on the latter line in the Immediate window, the number of Visual Basic components is printed on the next line.

You now can experiment with various methods and properties in the Immediate window.

Wizards and the Wizard Manager

A Wizard is a tool which leads a user step-by-step through an unusually long, difficult, or complex programming task. If you want to create Wizards that look and act similarly to those used in Microsoft products, you can use the Wizard Manager.

First, let's clarify what the Wizard Manager does *not* do. It does not automatically create complete, functional Wizards. This makes sense, because it's up to you, the programmer, to decide what your Wizard will do. What it *will* do for you is create a framework of steps in your Wizard, and help you manage the order in which they will appear when the Wizard is run. You add your code to the framework to perform the actual tasks. The resulting Wizards look and operate like other Wizards.

How the Wizard Manager Works

Programmatically, a Wizard is a form which contains a variable number of frames (or "steps"), each of which comprises a step to completing a Wizard's task. For example, one step of a Wizard might allow the user to choose a style for an output report, such as Classic, Modern, and so on, while the next screen might allow the user to decide how and where to display fields on the report.

The Wizard Manager uses only one form for the entire Wizard. This form (which must be named "frmWizard") has a visible area that is the same size as each step frame. When a step is presented, its Left property is set to that of the visible area of the form, making it visible to the user. The Left properties of steps not in use are set away from the visible area of the form. You can think of it like viewing a stack of pictures from a nearby table, where you place one picture at a time in front of you to view it, then return it to the stack on the table when you're done. In similar fashion, the current step is moved to the visible area, then moved away to the "storage" area when you move to another step.

All About Steps

When you first start the Wizard Manager, you're provided you with a preset "stack" of steps as a starting point. These steps are: **Introduction**, **Step x**, and **Finished!**.

- The **Introduction** step, which usually contains a graphic of some sort, is used for informing the user about the name and function of the Wizard, or any other information you want to impart.
- The **Step x** steps are a set of four generic, template-like steps that you can replicate or delete as many times as needed. These steps form the bulk of the Wizard and are where questions are asked, input gathered, calculations made, properties changed, and so forth. Four identical generic steps are initially provided for your use. You may require more or less steps, depending on what you want your Wizard to do.
- The **Finished!** step, which contains a picture of a checkered flag, is the last step of the Wizard and is normally displayed when all of the steps of the Wizard are complete, alerting the user that they've completed the task.

Each step provided by the Wizard Manager consists of three areas:

- **An Image control** The Image control is located in the upper left corner of the step and is used to display a graphic for that step, if desired.
- **A Label control** The Label control is located in the upper right corner of the step and is normally used to display instructions to the user about what to do in that step.
- **A TextBox control** The TextBox control is located in the bottom half of the step and is normally used to display additional information to the user. Alternatively, it can be deleted and other controls placed there instead.

The Add-In Toolbar

While you can give users access to your add-in nearly anywhere in Visual Basic (this is covered in detail in Chapter 4, "Connecting and Exposing Add-Ins"), you might want to consider putting them on the Add-In toolbar.

The Add-In toolbar is provided with Visual Basic as a sort of "one-stop shopping" for all of your add-ins and Wizards. It's a site where you can place your add-ins and Wizards as buttons for easy access. Also, the add-in or Wizard is not loaded until a user clicks the button. It saves the user from the task of going into the Add-In Manager, clicking the box of an add-in that they want, then clicking OK. If you place your add-in on the Add-In toolbar, it appears as a button. To invoke and load the add-in, simply click its button. Very convenient!

Note You can place Wizards on the Add-In Toolbar as well as add-ins.

To start the Add-In toolbar, choose "VB Add-In Toolbar" in the Add-In Manager. You should see a small toolbar appear beneath the Standard toolbar:

The first button on the left (the "+/-" button) allows you to add or remove items from the toolbar. To add it, browse for your add-in, check its box in the **Available Add-Ins** list, then click **OK**. Your add-in (or Wizard) should appear on the Add-In toolbar. For more information on the **Add-In toolbar** dialog box, search the Visual Basic documentation.

Of course, you're also given programmatic control of the Add-In toolbar, since it's probably impractical to visit the computer of every person you give your add-in to make sure it's showing on their Add-In toolbar.

The Add-In toolbar object model has an object known as the Manager object. It contains two methods:

- AddToAddInToolbar
- RemoveAddInFromToolbar

These methods allow you to programmatically place and remove buttons to and from the Add-In toolbar.

This code is an example of how to programmatically add an add-in to the Add-In toolbar and ensure that the Add-In toolbar is automatically loaded the next time Visual Basic is started:

```
Sub Main()
   dim x as Object
   Set x=CreateObject("AddInToolbar.Manager")
      x.AddToAddInToolbar ("C:\VB\MyAdd.DLL", _
      "MyAddIn.Connect", "MyAddIn Title", True, True)
End Sub
```

This code is an example of how to remove an add-ins button from the Add-In toolbar:

```
Sub Main()
   dim x as Object
   Set x=CreateObject("AddInToolbar.Manager")
   x.RemoveAddInFromToolbar sAddInName:="MyAddIn Title"
End Sub
```

The registry location for the Add-In toolbar is (HKEY_CURRENT_USER\Software\Microsoft\VBA\ Microsoft Visual Basic\AddInToolbar).

CHAPTER 4

Connecting and Exposing Add-Ins

This chapter covers the essentials of what every add-in you build requires. It also gives you some methods and ideas for connecting and exposing your add-ins in the Microsoft Visual Basic environment.

Contents

Registering Add-Ins

As an ActiveX component, an add-in must be properly registered in the system registry before it can be recognized or used by any Windows program, including Visual Basic. The process of compiling the add-in in Visual Basic automatically registers it on your system, but anyone who intends to use your add-in on another system must register it there before they can use it.

This means that if the add-in is an in-process component (.dll file), you (or your customer) must use a utility such as Regsvr32.exe to register it on their system. For ease of use to the customer, you would normally do this in the add-in's setup program.

If the add-in is an out-of-process component (.exe file), running the .exe file registers it. If you'd rather register the add-in without running it, add the `/regserver` parameter to the .exe file's command line, such as when you're creating a setup:

```
MyAddIn /regserver
```

When the add-in reference is written to the system registry, the registered name is the programmatic ID — comprised of the name of your add-in project (as shown in the Project Name box on the General tab of the Project Properties dialog box) plus the name of the class module that contains the add-in's connect and disconnect event-handling code.

For example, if you create an add-in using the Visual Basic default names — Project1 for the project name and Class1 for the class module name — then the registered name of the add-in will be Project1.Class1.

Adding an Add-In Reference to the Vbaddin.ini File

Once an add-in is registered in the system registry, you must add an entry to the `[Add-Ins32]` section of the Vbaddin.ini file in the Windows directory in order for Visual Basic to recognize it and make it available for connection through the Add-In Manager. You can do this any way you like, but the most often used programmatic method is through the Windows API function WritePrivateProfileString. Here is example code demonstrating how to do this (the function's arguments are described after the example):

```
Declare Function WritePrivateProfileString& Lib _
"kernel32" Alias "WritePrivateProfileStringA" _
(ByVal AppName$, ByVal KeyName$, ByVal _
keydefault$, ByVal FileName$)
Sub AddToINI()
Dim rc As Long
   rc = WritePrivateProfileString("Add-Ins32", _
   "MyAddInProject.MyAddInClass", "0", _
   "VBADDIN.INI")
   MsgBox "Add-in is now entered in VBADDIN.INI file."
End Sub
```

What Do the Arguments Mean?

The first argument of `WritePrivateProfileString` is the name of the section of the .ini file in which to place the information. In the case of add-ins, this should always be `"Add-Ins32"`.

The second argument is the programmatic ID, which consists of the names of your project and class, separated by a dot. The project name is entered in the **Properties** dialog box in the **Projects** menu. The class name is entered in the **Name** property of the class module. (Note that the name of the module plays no part in this.)

The third argument is a value for the add-in's entry in the Vbaddin.ini file — in this case, 0. Setting the entry to 1 means that the add-in will be loaded (that is, selected in the Add-In Manager) at IDE startup. Setting the entry to 0 means that it will not be loaded at IDE startup, but it will be included in the list of available add-ins in the Add-In Manager.

The fourth and final argument is the name of the file to apply the setting to. In the case of add-ins, this is the Vbaddin.ini file.

A More Friendly Name

While the name format of project.class (its programmatic ID) looks fine in the .ini file, it might be a bit confusing for users seeing it in the Add-In Manager's add-in list. You can change this to a more friendly name.

To change the add-in name that appears in the Add-In Manager

1. In Visual Basic, click the **View** menu, then click **Object Browser**.
2. In the **Classes** list, right-click the name of the class which handles your add-in's OnConnection and OnDisconnection events, then click **Properties**.
3. In the **Member Options** dialog box, enter your friendly name in the **Description** box. Click **OK**.

The text you enter will be saved along with the add-in, so users will see the same description in their Add-In Manager once it's installed on their system.

Connecting or Disconnecting Add-Ins

Once an add-in is registered in the system registry and referenced in the Vbaddin.ini file, it can be connected to the IDE. The connection allows the add-in to respond to events and perform activities. You can connect or disconnect an add-in either manually or programmatically.

Handling the OnConnection and OnDisconnection Events

Whether you manually or programmatically connect an add-in, the add-ins IDTExtensibility_OnConnection event procedure is called. When you disconnect it, the IDTExtensibility_OnDisconnection event is called.

The example in Chapter 3, "How to Build an Add-In," inserted event handlers for both events in a class module called Connect:

```
Private Sub IDTExtensibility_OnConnection(ByVal _
VBInst As Object, ByVal ConnectMode As _
VBIDE.vbext_ConnectMode, ByVal AddInInst As _
VBIDE.AddIn, custom() As Variant)
   MsgBox "Add-in is now connected"
End Sub
Private Sub IDTExtensibility_OnDisconnection(ByVal _
RemoveMode As VBIDE.vbext_RemoveMode, _
Custom () as Variant)
   MsgBox "Add-in is now disconnected"
End Sub
Private Sub IDTExtensibility_OnStartupComplete _
(custom() As Variant)
   ' Comment to prevent procedure from being
   ' deleted on compilation.
End Sub
```

```
Private Sub IDTExtensibility_OnAddInsUpdate _
(custom() As Variant)
    ' Comment to prevent procedure from being
    ' deleted on compilation.
End Sub
```

In this case, the only thing the program does is display a message box to notify you when the add-in was connected or disconnected. The last two event procedures are not used in this example, but must be present for the add-in to work correctly.

What Do the Parameters Mean?

The VBInst parameter in the OnConnection event procedure is an object reference to the current instance of Visual Basic. This object is the means through which you can access the Visual Basic extensibility object model.

The ConnectMode parameter notifies Visual Basic as to how the add-in was invoked. It has three possible settings:

vbext_cm_AfterStartup	Add-in was connected after startup of development environment.
vbext_cm_Startup	Add-in was connected on standard startup of development environment.
vbext_cm_ExternalStartup	Add-in was connected by something other than the Visual Basic development environment.

The RemoveMode parameter in the OnDisconnection event procedure notifies Visual Basic as to how the add-in was disconnected.

Manually Connecting and Disconnecting Add-Ins

The primary (and simplest) way to connect an add-in to Visual Basic is to manually select its check box in the Add-In Manager, available from the Visual Basic Add-Ins menu. The primary way of disconnecting an add-in is to clear the check box.

Note that an add-in isn't truly connected or disconnected until you click the Add-In Manager's OK button. When you select an add-in and then click OK, Visual Basic immediately attempts to create an instance of the add-in. If it can do so, the add-in becomes active. If for some reason Visual Basic cannot create an instance of the add-in, you'll get an error message. (See "Add-In Troubleshooting" in this chapter for probable causes and solutions to this.) When you disconnect the add-in, the memory the add-in occupied is released.

This is important to remember. If you close only the visible portions of an add-in — by double-clicking its system menu or by clicking its close button, for example — its forms disappear from the screen, but the add-in is still present in memory. While it is possible to write code in the form's Unload event to release certain handles and pointers to free up some memory, the add-in object itself will always stay resident in memory until the add-in is disconnected through the Add-In Manager dialog box.

Programmatically Connecting and Disconnecting Add-Ins

Another way that you can connect a previously unconnected add-in — programmatically and behind the scenes — is to set the Connect property of the AddIns collection to True, then use the Update method on the Addins collection in the OnAddInsUpdate event procedure.

Changing the AddIns collection's Connect property to True sets the add-in's connection flag from 0 to 1 (meaning that it is connected at IDE startup). This change triggers the OnAddInsUpdate event, which occurs whenever changes are made to any add-in listed in the Add-In Manager (or Vbaddin.ini file entries). Using the Update method on the AddIns collection forces the Add-In Manager to re-read the list of add-in entries in the Vbaddin.ini file. When this occurs, since the flag is now set to True, the add-in is connected.

In this following example, Visual Basic iterates through the Addins collection to check whether the given add-in's programmatic ID matches a programmatic ID in the list of available add-ins. This is done only to certify that the index number of the add-in that will be passed to the Connect property actually exists. You cannot directly enter the add-in's programmatic ID as a parameter for the AddIns collection's Connect property. Once the programmatic ID is ascertained as valid, the add-in's Connect property is set to 1 (connected).

Alternatively, you may elect to insert the number of the add-in, but this is not recommended because the add-in's number may change if it is stopped and re-started.

> **Note** This example assumes that you've already set up the requisite variables for a basic add-in, such as a variable for the Visual Basic instance (here called "vbi.") These requisites are covered later in this chapter. You must also replace `"proj.class"` with the programmatic ID of the add-in you wish to activate.

```
Sub ConnectAddIn()
   For Each x In vbi.AddIns
   ' Go through each add-in in the collection.
      If x.ProgId = "proj.class" Then x.Connect = True
      ' If any of the progIDs match that of the given
      ' add-in, set its Connect flag to True.
   Next x
   ' Continue iterating through the collection.
End Sub
```

If you then perform an Update method on the AddIns collection, the collection is updated. Visual Basic then notices that the add-in is marked for connection, and connects it. To perform this update, add the following line of code to the OnAddInsUpdate event procedure in the class module:

```
vbi.AddIns.Update
' Perform an Update on the AddIns collection.
```

This method forces Visual Basic to re-read the Vbaddin.ini file. Since the flag on the add-in you want to start has been set to 1, or connect, the add-in is connected.

To programmatically disconnect an add-in, follow the same procedure, only set the Connect property of the AddIns collection to False.

Exposing Add-Ins to the Visual Basic Environment

Once you've connected your add-in, you'll likely want to expose it in the IDE. Of course, add-ins don't necessarily have to be initiated from the IDE or even have a visible user interface. You can activate them behind the scenes through events and they can work unnoticed in the background. Most add-ins, however, are activated through either a menu command or toolbar button.

You must decide how the add-in will be initiated — by a menu command, a toolbar button, or by the occurrence of an event. Since chances are good that most add-ins you create will be visible in the development environment, you'll want to be able to control when they're active and when they're not.

There are five ways to control an add-in's operation:

- Create a menu command for it.
- Create a button for it on a toolbar (such as the Add-In toolbar).
- Start or stop it with events.
- Have the add-in present a non-modal form with which the user interacts.

Command Bars: A Replacement for Menus and Toolbars

Even though menus are differentiated from toolbar buttons because they look different from each other, to Visual Basic they are in essence the same kind of object. Internally, Visual Basic considers menus, menu commands, toolbars, and toolbar buttons as command bars.

A *command bar* unifies the concept of menus and toolbars into a single common visual and programmatic object. As command bars, menus contain menu commands which can have icons and captions and exhibit button-like behavior while remaining in the familiar menu format. Some toolbar buttons have drop-down arrows, similar to ComboBox controls. A command bar object can contain other command bar objects, depending on its type.

While a discussion of the command bar object model is beyond the scope of this book, here are a few basics to help you place your add-in where you want it.

There are three types of command bars:

Pop-up	A Pop-up command bar is equivalent to a menu item on a menu bar.
ComboBox	A ComboBox command bar is similar to a ComboBox control. That is, a toolbar button with a drop-down arrow next to it (like the Add Project toolbar button). When you click the arrow, it displays more menu commands with icons.
Button	A Button command bar is equivalent to a standard toolbar button. That is, a button with an icon displayed on it.

Getting to Command Bars Through Code

The concept of command bars is important to you really only as a programmer, since the interface acts more or less the same as it did in previous versions of Visual Basic. Programmatically, however, it is quite different. You can gain access to and explore the various command bar objects in the Object Browser by selecting the Microsoft Office 8.0 Object Library check box in the References dialog box.

Since menus and toolbars are in the same object library, they're referred to through the CommandBarControl object. For example, to declare the basic object for use in your code, you would enter:

```
Dim mcbMenuCommandBar As Office.CommandBarControl
```

Every toolbar, menu, or context menu in the development environment is a command bar. It helps to understand command bars if you think of them as containers that hold other command bars. Therefore, a menu bar command bar can contain several menu items, each of which is itself a command bar, and each menu item can contain several menu commands, each of which is also a command bar.

Getting Your Bearings Among the Command Bars

This model makes placing your add-in in the development environment easy. You simply refer to the command bar in which you wish your add-in to appear. You refer to the command bars from top to bottom and left to right. In the example below, we expose our new add-in as a command on the Tools menu. Here's an example of how to do this:

```
Set mcbMenuCommandBar = _
VBInst.CommandBars(1).Controls(8).CommandBar. _
Controls.Add(1, , , 3)
```

The code above installs a pop-up command bar before the third menu command from the top. What's in this code?

- The first reference to command bars is `CommandBars(1)`. (Note that because Item is the CommandBars collection's default property, the code here is the same as if we used `CommandBars.Item(1)`.) The first reference to command bars is the toolbar itself. The first toolbar is always the menu bar. So when we say `CommandBars(1)` we're talking about the menu command bar.
- The second reference is `Controls(8)`. This means the eighth control from the left on that command bar, which is the Tools menu.
- The next two references are `CommandBar.Controls`. This means that we're affecting the Tools command bar.
- The last reference is `Add(1, , , 3)`. Using the Add method, we add a new command bar (in this case a menu command) to the Tools menu. You can view the parameters for the Add method by examining the CommandBarControls object in the Object Browser.

Working with the Model's Flexibility

Note, however, that command bar controls can be moved by users to any location within a menu or toolbar, which means you cannot rely on them to always remain in the same numeric position. Additionally, if you support localized versions of Visual Basic, you cannot rely on the command bar control captions to always remain the same.

However, there is a method that allows you to always obtain a specific menu item, regardless of its location. The name of the CommandBar object of the menu item is not localized; thus, you can always specify this name in the top-level CommandBars collection to refer to a menu item. For example, to obtain a reference object to the command bar representing the Add-Ins menu, you could use the following statement:

```
Set cmdBar = VBInst.CommandBars("Add-Ins")
```

This works regardless of the location of the menu item or the caption name. You obtain the CommandBar object of a particular menu item, then use its Controls collection to add an item to the menu.

Creating a Menu Command for Activating Add-Ins

In some cases, you may want to provide access to your add-in through a menu command. In this example, we'll place a menu command for our new add-in on the Tools menu.

The following procedure is designed to build on example code presented in "Creating a Basic Add-In," in Chapter 1, "Add-Ins Overview."

To place a menu command for an add-in on the Tools menu

1. Make sure that "Microsoft Office 8.0 Object Library" is selected in the **References** dialog box. This allows you access to the Office command bar objects.
2. Add the following code to the General Declarations section of the class module:

```
Public VBI As VBIDE.VBE
   ' VBI is assigned a pointer to the current IDE's
   ' VBA object which is later passed as a parameter
   ' to the OnConnection procedure. It's retained
   ' because you need it later for disconnecting the
   ' add-in. Other procedures may have a need for it
   ' as well.
Private mcbMenuCommandBarCtrl As _
   Office.CommandBarControl
   ' This will be set to the new command bar control.

Private WithEvents MenuHandler As CommandBarEvents
   ' This is the event handling procedure for
   ' the click event of the new command bar control.
```

3. The following procedure is called when the add-in is connected in the Add-In Manager. It adds a new menu command to the **Tools** menu called "My New Add-In." In the IDTExtensibility_OnConnection procedure, remove the MsgBox line and add the following:

```
Private Sub IDTExtensibility_OnConnection _
   (ByVal VBInst As Object, _
   ByVal ConnectMode As VBIDE.vbext_ConnectMode, _
   ByVal AddInInst As VBIDE.AddIn, _
   custom() As Variant)
   ' Save the current instance of Visual Basic.
   Set VBI = VBInst
   ' Add a menu command to the Tools menu.
   Set mcbMenuCommandBarCtrl = _
   VBI.CommandBars("Tools").Controls.Add(before:=3)
   ' Place a separator bar before the new
   ' menu command.
   mcbMenuCommandBarCtrl.BeginGroup = True
   ' Set the title for the add-in.
   mcbMenuCommandBarCtrl.Caption = "My New Add-In"
   ' Copy an icon bitmap to the clipboard.
   Clipboard.SetData _
   LoadPicture("c:\windows\triangles.bmp")
   ' Copy the icon from the clipboard to the menu
   ' command's icon.
   mcbMenuCommandBarCtrl.PasteFace
   ' Connect the event handler to receive the
   ' events for the new command bar control.
   Set MenuHandler = _
   VBI.Events.CommandBarEvents _
   (mcbMenuCommandBarCtrl)
   ' Place a separator bar after the new
   ' menu command.
   VBI.CommandBars("Tools").Controls(4).BeginGroup _
   = True
End Sub
```

4. The next procedure is called whenever the add-in is disconnected. The `mcbMenuCommandBar.Delete` line ensures that the menu command in the **Tools** menu is removed once the add-in is disconnected. Add the following lines to the IDTExtensibility_OnDisconnection procedure. (You can also remove the MsgBox line from the original code if you wish):

```
Private Sub IDTExtensibility_OnDisconnection _
(ByVal VBInst As Object, ByVal LoadMode As _
Long, ByVal AddInInst As VBIDE.AddIn, custom() _
As Variant)
   ' Delete the new menu command from the Tools
   ' menu.
   mcbMenuCommandBarCtrl.Delete
End Sub
```

5. The MenuHandler_Click event is called whenever you click the new menu command on the **Tools** menu. The optional message box function is here only to signal that the Click event was correctly intercepted. Add the following procedure to the add-in's class module by using the drop-down to insert the event handler:

```
Private Sub MenuHandler_Click(ByVal _
CommandBarControl As Object, handled As Boolean, _
CancelDefault As Boolean)
   MsgBox "You clicked the new menu command."
End Sub
```

6. Save and then compile the project (as an ActiveX component).
7. Start a new project and activate the add-in through the Add-In Manager.
8. Look in the **Tools** menu. Notice that there is now a **My New Add-In** menu command.
9. Click the new menu command. You should get a message box confirming that you clicked the menu command.
10. Disconnect the add-in in the Add-In Manager. Notice that the menu command is removed from the **Tools** menu.

To summarize, you now have an add-in which:

- Adds a command to the Tools menu when connected to Visual Basic.
- Demonstrates that it handles an event when the menu command is clicked.
- Removes the command from the Tools menu when disconnected.

Creating a Toolbar Button for Add-In Activation

As explained earlier, a toolbar is simply another form of command bar object. So to convert our example add-in from appearing as a menu entry to appearing as a button on a toolbar, make the following code changes:

```
' This line puts a command bar as a button on the
' toolbar before the 20th item, in this case, the
' form coordinates box.
Set mcbMenuCommandBarCtrl = _
VBInst.CommandBars("Standard").Controls.Add(1, , , 20)
```

If you want to put the add-in on the Add-In toolbar rather than the Standard toolbar, first activate the Add-In toolbar in the Add-In Manager, then change the reference name of the CommandBar object. The following code adds a button in the first position (leftmost side) of the Add-In toolbar.

```
' This line puts a command bar as a button on the
' Add-in toolbar.
Set mcbMenuCommandBarCtrl = _
VBInst.CommandBars("Add-Ins").Controls.Add(1)
```

Starting and Stopping an Add-In Using Events

What should you do if you want to control start and stop an add-in without user intervention?

The answer is to control it through events. Add-ins don't require menu commands or toolbar buttons to activate them. Clicking a command bar object (such as a menu command or toolbar button) triggers the Click event of that object (in our example, the MenuHandler_Click event).

So to control an add-in without using a UI, simply program your own events in a class module.

Add-In Troubleshooting

If you get an error when creating or activating your add-in, check the following:

- Make sure that the add-in was created as an ActiveX DLL or ActiveX EXE project.
- Make sure the add-in component is registered on the machine on which you are going to use it

  For more information about registering your add-in, see "Registering Add-Ins" earlier in this chapter.

- Make sure that Microsoft Visual Basic Extensibility is selected in the References dialog box. (In Visual Basic, click the Project menu, then click References.) This is because the VBIDE collection and VBA object are part of that type library. If it's not active, references to extensibility (add-in) objects cannot be resolved properly, and you'll get errors at compile time.
- If your add-in uses command bars, make sure that Microsoft Office 8.0 Object Library is selected in the References dialog box. This gives your program access to the command bar objects, collections, properties, and events.
- Make sure that the project name written to the Vbaddin.ini file add-in entry *exactly* matches the name of your project.

  You can view or set the project name by clicking the Project menu, then clicking *project name* Properties. Enter the project name in the Project Name box.
- Make sure that the Name property of your class module that exposes the IDTExtensibility interface matches the name written to the Vbaddin.ini file entry.
- Make sure that the Visual Basic run-time DLL and any other necessary files are on file paths that are available to your add-in. (This shouldn't be an issue if you run the Visual Basic setup program.)
- Make sure that your add-in's class module contains procedures for the OnConnection, OnDisconnection, OnStartupComplete, and OnAddInsUpdate events. Add-ins require that these four event procedures be present, even if they contain only a comment. The procedures must contain at least one line of code, otherwise the compiler will remove the empty procedures from the class module, and the add-in will not work correctly.

PART 4

Accessing DLLs and the Windows API

How to access the Windows API through Visual Basic by calling functions in dynamic-link libraries (DLLs). Through DLLs, you can access the thousands of procedures that form the backbone of the Microsoft Windows operating system, as well as routines written in other languages.

Chapter 1 Accessing DLLs and the Windows API

How to access the Windows API through Visual Basic by calling functions in dynamic-link libraries (DLLs).

CHAPTER 1

Accessing DLLs and the Windows API

When you need capabilities that go beyond the core language and controls provided with Microsoft Visual Basic, you can make direct calls to procedures contained in *dynamic-link libraries* (DLLs). By calling procedures in DLLs, you can access the thousands of procedures that form the backbone of the Microsoft Windows operating system, as well as routines written in other languages.

As their name suggests, DLLs are libraries of procedures that applications can link to and use at run time rather than link to statically at compile time. This means that the libraries can be updated independently of the application, and many applications can share a single DLL. Microsoft Windows itself is comprised of DLLs, and other applications call the procedures within these libraries to display windows and graphics, manage memory, or perform other tasks. These procedures are sometimes referred to as the Windows API, or application programming interface.

DLLs or Automation?

Another way to bring more power into Visual Basic is through Automation (formerly called OLE Automation). Using Automation is simpler than calling routines in a DLL, and it doesn't create the same level of risk that you'll hit when going straight to the Windows API. By using Automation, you can get programmatic access to a wide range of objects exposed by external applications.

For more information For additional information on Automation, see Chapter 10, "Programming with Components," in the *Microsoft Visual Basic 6.0 Programmer's Guide.*

Contents

- Passing User-Defined Types to a DLL Procedure
- Passing Function Pointers to DLL Procedures and Type Libraries
- Passing Other Types of Information to a DLL Procedure
- Converting C Declarations to Visual Basic

Using a DLL Procedure in Your Application

Because DLL procedures reside in files that are external to your Visual Basic application, you must specify where the procedures are located and identify the arguments with which they should be called. You provide this information with the Declare statement. Once you have declared a DLL procedure, you can use it in your code just like a native Visual Basic procedure.

> **Important** When you call any DLLs directly from Visual Basic, you lose the built-in safety features of the Visual Basic environment. This means that you increase the risk of system failure while testing or debugging your code. To minimize the risk, you need to pay close attention to how you declare DLL procedures, pass arguments, and specify types. In all cases, save your work frequently. Calling DLLs offers you exceptional power, but it can be less forgiving than other types of programming tasks.

In the following example, we'll show how to call a procedure from the Windows API. The function we'll call, SetWindowText, changes the caption on a form. While in practice, you would always change a caption by using Visual Basic's Caption property, this example offers a simple model of declaring and calling a procedure.

Declaring a DLL Procedure

The first step is to declare the procedure in the Declarations section of a module:

```
Private Declare Function SetWindowText Lib "user32" _
Alias "SetWindowTextA" (ByVal hwnd As Long, _
ByVal lpString As String) As Long
```

You can find the exact syntax for a procedure by using the API Viewer application, or by searching the Win32api.txt file. If you place the Declare in a Form or Class module, you must precede it with the Private keyword. You declare a DLL procedure only once per project; you can then call it any number of times.

Calling a DLL Procedure

After the function is declared, you call it just as you would a standard Visual Basic function. Here, the procedure has been attached to the Form Load event:

```
Private Sub Form_Load()
   SetWindowText Form1.hWnd, "Welcome to VB"
End Sub
```

When this code is run, the function first uses the hWnd property to identify the window where you want to change the caption (Form1.hWnd), then changes the text of that caption to "Welcome to VB."

Remember that Visual Basic can't verify that you are passing correct values to a DLL procedure. If you pass incorrect values, the procedure may fail, which may cause your Visual Basic application to stop. You'll then have to reload and restart your application. Take care when experimenting with DLL procedures and save your work often.

> **Note** Very few API calls recognize the default Variant data type. Your API calls will be much more robust if you declare variables of specific types and use Option Explicit.

Accessing the Microsoft Windows API

You can gain access to the Windows API (or other outside DLLs) by declaring the external procedures within your Visual Basic application. After you declare a procedure, you can use it like any other language feature in the product.

The most commonly used set of external procedures are those that make up Microsoft Windows itself. The Windows API contains thousands of functions, subs, types, and constants that you can declare and use in your projects. These procedures are written in the C language, however, so they must be declared before you can use them with Visual Basic. The declarations for DLL procedures can become fairly complex. While you can translate these yourself, the easiest way to access the Windows API is by using the predefined declares included with Visual Basic.

The file Win32api.txt, located in the \Winapi subdirectory of the main Visual Basic directory, contains declarations for many of the Windows API procedures commonly used in Visual Basic. To use a function, type, or other feature from this file, simply copy it to your Visual Basic module. You can view and copy procedures from Win32api.txt by using the API Viewer application, or by loading the file in any text editor.

> **Note** The Windows API contains a vast amount of code. To find reference information on the procedures and other details included in this API set, refer to the Win32 SDK, included on the Microsoft Developer Network Library CD.

Using the API Viewer Application

The API Viewer application enables you to browse through the declares, constants, and types included in any text file or Microsoft Jet database. After you find the procedure you want, you can copy the code to the Clipboard and paste it into your Visual Basic application.

Figure 1.1 The API Viewer application

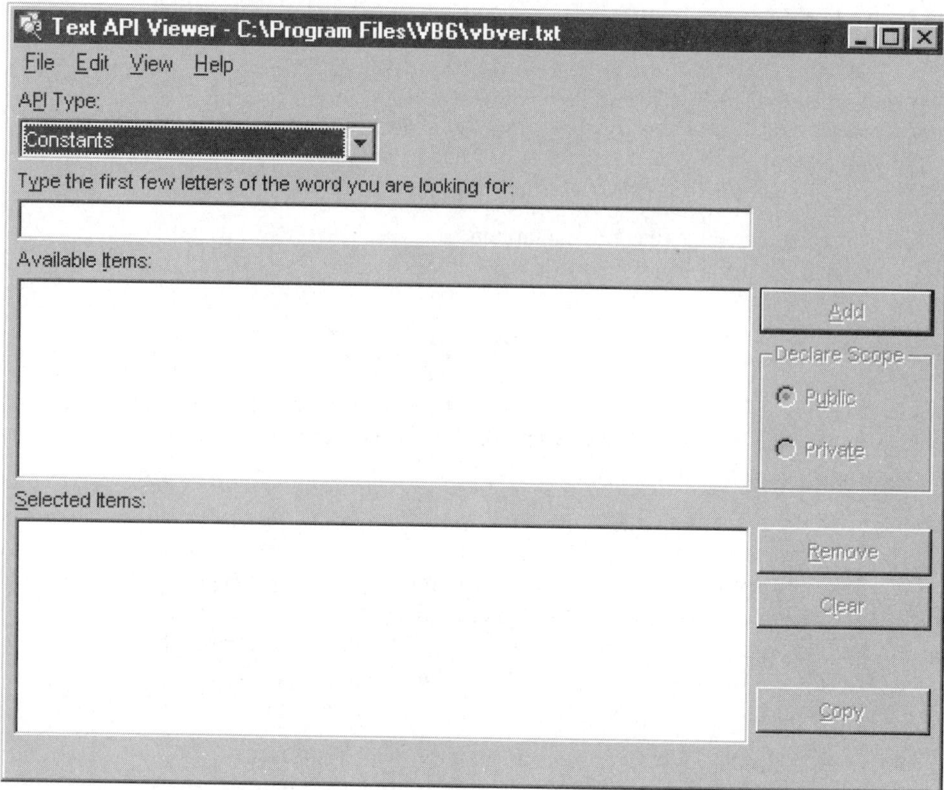

To load the Win32api.txt file, choose Load Text File from the File menu. After the file is loaded, you can view entries in the Available Items list box by selecting Declares, Constants, or Types in the API Type drop-down list box. To search for specific items in the file, use the Search button.

To load a Jet database API file, choose Load Database File from the File menu. You can then search for specific items in the database by typing the first letter of the item you want to find.

Adding Procedures to Your Visual Basic Code

Once you have found a procedure you want, choose the Add button to add the item to the Selected Items box. You can add as many items as you like. To remove an entry from the Selected Items box, select the item, then choose the Remove button.

To copy the items from the Selected Items list box to the Clipboard, choose the Copy button. All of the items in the list will be copied. You can then open your Visual Basic project and go to the module in which you want to place the API information. Position the insertion point where you want to paste the declarations, constants, and/or types, and then choose Paste from the Edit menu.

Converting Text Files to Jet Database Files

To optimize speed, you can convert the Win32api.txt file into a Jet database file, because it is much faster to display the list when opening a database than when opening a text file.

To convert the text file, start the API Viewer application, then choose the Load Text File command from the File menu and open the .txt file. A message will appear asking if you want to convert the .txt file to a database file. Choose Yes to confirm the conversion. If you choose No, you can still convert the file later by choosing the Convert Text to Database command from the File menu.

Loading an API File Automatically from the Command Line

You can specify a text or database file on the command line for Apilod32.exe so that the file is automatically loaded when you start API Viewer. Use the following syntax to load the file you choose when you start the API Viewer application:

```
Apilod32.exe {/T|/D} filename
```

Argument	Description
/T	API Viewer will load the file as a text file. /T must be uppercase.
/D	API Viewer will load the file as a database file. /D must be uppercase.
Filename	The path of the file you want to open.

There must be a space between /T or /D and the *filename* argument. An error message will be displayed if the file is not found. If you specify a file that is not a database or text file, an error message will be displayed when you try to load the file.

Viewing the Win32api.txt file with a Text Editor

You can also load the Win32api.txt file in a text editor, such as Microsoft Word or WordPad, to locate the procedures you want to use. Again, you just copy the procedures from the file to a Visual Basic module to use them in your application.

> **Tip** Don't load the Win32api.txt file into a module. This is a large file, and it will consume a lot of memory in your application. You will generally use only a handful of declarations in your code, so selectively copying the declarations you need is much more efficient.

Using Procedures from Other Sources

If you are attempting to call a procedure in a DLL that is not part of the operating system, you must determine the proper declaration for it. The topic "Declaring a DLL Procedure" explains the syntax of the Declare statement in detail.

Note If you use Visual C++ (or a similar tool) to create DLLs that will be called by Visual Basic, use the __stdcall calling convention. Do not use the default calling convention (_cdecl).

Declaring a DLL Procedure

Even though Visual Basic provides a broad set of predefined declares in the Win32api.txt file, sooner or later you'll want to know how to write them yourself. You might want to access procedures from DLLs written in other languages, for example, or rewrite Visual Basic's predefined declares to fit your own requirements.

To declare a DLL procedure, you add a Declare statement to the Declarations section of the code window. If the procedure returns a value, write the declare as a Function:

Declare Function *publicname* **Lib** "*libname*" **[Alias** "*alias*"**] [([[ByVal]** *variable* **[As** *type***] [,[ByVal]** *variable* **[As** *type***]]...])] As Type**

If a procedure does not return a value, write the declare as a Sub:

Declare Sub *publicname* **Lib** "*libname*" **[Alias** "*alias*"**] [([[ByVal]** *variable* **[As** *type***] [,[ByVal]** *variable* **[As** *type***]]...])]**

DLL procedures declared in standard modules are public by default and can be called from anywhere in your application. DLL procedures declared in any other type of module are private to that module, and you must identify them as such by preceding the declaration with the Private keyword.

Procedure names are case-sensitive in 32-bit versions of Visual Basic. In previous, 16-bit versions, procedure names were not case-sensitive.

For More Information See "Declare Statement" in the *Microsoft Visual Basic 6.0 Language Reference* volume of the *Microsoft Visual Basic 6.0 Reference Library.*

Specifying the Library

The Lib clause in the Declare statement tells Visual Basic where to find the .dll file that contains the procedure. When you're referencing one of the core Windows libraries (User32, Kernel32, or GDI32), you don't need to include the file name extension:

```
Declare Function GetTickCount Lib "kernel32" Alias _
"GetTickCount" () As Long
```

For other DLLs, the Lib clause is a file specification that can include a path:

```
Declare Function lzCopy Lib "c:\windows\lzexpand.dll" _
(ByVal S As Integer, ByVal D As Integer) As Long
```

If you do not specify a path for *libname*, Visual Basic will search for the file in the following order:

1. Directory containing the .exe file
2. Current directory
3. Windows system directory (often but not necessarily \Windows\System)
4. Windows directory (not necessarily \Windows)
5. Path environment variable

The following table lists the common operating environment library files.

Dynamic Link Library	Description
Advapi32.dll	Advanced API services library supporting numerous APIs including many security and Registry calls
Comdlg32.dll	Common dialog API library
Gdi32.dll	Graphics Device Interface API library
Kernel32.dll	Core Windows 32-bit base API support
Lz32.dll	32-bit compression routines
Mpr.dll	Multiple Provider Router library
Netapi32.dll	32-bit Network API library
Shell32.dll	32-bit Shell API library
User32.dll	Library for user interface routines
Version.dll	Version library
Winmm.dll	Windows multimedia library
Winspool.drv	Print spooler interface that contains the print spooler API calls

Working with Windows API Procedures That Use Strings

When working with Windows API procedures that use strings, you'll need to add an Alias clause to your declare statements to specify the correct character set. Windows API functions that contain strings actually exist in two formats: ANSI and Unicode. In the Windows header files, therefore, you'll get both ANSI and Unicode versions of each function that contains a string.

For example, following are the two C-language descriptions for the SetWindowText function. You'll note that the first description defines the function as SetWindowTextA, where the trailing "A" identifies it as an ANSI function:

```
WINUSERAPI
BOOL
WINAPI
SetWindowTextA(
   HWND hWnd,
   LPCSTR lpString);
```

The second description defines it as SetWindowTextW, where the trailing "W" identifies it as a wide, or Unicode function:

```
WINUSERAPI
BOOL
WINAPI
SetWindowTextW(
   HWND hWnd,
   LPCWSTR lpString);
```

Because neither function is actually named "SetWindowText," you need to add an Alias clause to the declare to point to the function you want to reference:

```
Private Declare Function SetWindowText Lib "user32" _
Alias "SetWindowTextA" (ByVal hwnd As Long, ByVal _
lpString As String) As Long
```

Note that the string that follows the Alias clause must be the true, case-sensitive name of the procedure.

> **Important** For API functions you use in Visual Basic, you should specify the ANSI version of a function, because Unicode versions are only supported by Windows NT — not Windows 95. Use the Unicode versions only if you can be certain that your applications will be run only on Windows NT–based systems.

Passing Arguments by Value or by Reference

By default, Visual Basic passes all arguments *by reference*. This means that instead of passing the actual value of the argument, Visual Basic passes a 32-bit address where the value is stored. Although you do not need to include the ByRef keyword in your Declare statements, you may want to do so to document how the data is passed.

Many DLL procedures expect an argument to be passed *by value*. This means they expect the actual value, instead of its memory location. If you pass an argument by reference to a procedure that expects an argument passed by value, the procedure receives incorrect data and fails to work properly.

To pass an argument by value, place the ByVal keyword in front of the argument declaration in the Declare statement. For example, the InvertRect procedure accepts its first argument by value and its second by reference:

```
Declare Function InvertRect Lib "user32" Alias _
"InvertRectA" (ByVal hdc As Long, _
lpRect As RECT) As Long
```

You can also use the ByVal keyword when you call the procedure.

> **Note** When you're looking at DLL procedure documentation that uses C language syntax, remember that C passes all arguments except arrays by value.

String arguments are a special case. Passing a string by value means you are passing the address of the first data byte in the string; passing a string by reference means you are passing the memory address where another address is stored; the second address actually refers to the first data byte of the string. How you determine which approach to use is explained in the topic "Passing Strings to a DLL Procedure" later in this chapter.

Nonstandard Names

Occasionally, a DLL procedure has a name that is not a legal identifier. It might have an invalid character (such as a hyphen), or the name might be the same as a Visual Basic keyword (such as GetObject). When this is the case, use the Alias keyword to specify the illegal procedure name.

For example, some procedures in the operating environment DLLs begin with an underscore character. While you can use an underscore in a Visual Basic identifier, you cannot begin an identifier with an underscore. To use one of these procedures, you first declare the function with a legal name, then use the Alias clause to reference the procedure's real name:

```
Declare Function lopen Lib "kernel32" Alias "_lopen" _
(ByVal lpPathName As String, ByVal iReadWrite _
As Long) As Long
```

In this example, `lopen` becomes the name of the procedure referred to in your Visual Basic procedures. The name `_lopen` is the name recognized in the DLL.

You can also use the Alias clause to change a procedure name whenever it's convenient. If you do substitute your own names for procedures (such as using `WinDir` for `GetWindowsDirectoryA`), make sure that you thoroughly document the changes so that your code can be maintained at a later date.

Using Ordinal Numbers to Identify DLL Procedures

In addition to a name, all DLL procedures can be identified by an *ordinal number* that specifies the procedure in the DLL. Some DLLs do not include the names of their procedures and require you to use ordinal numbers when declaring the procedures they contain. Using an ordinal number consumes less memory in your finished application and is slightly faster than identifying a procedure in a DLL by name.

Important The ordinal number for a specific API will be different with different operating systems. For example, the ordinal value for GetWindowsDirectory is 432 under Win95, but changes to 338 under Window NT 4.0. In sum, if you expect your applications to be run under different operating systems, don't use ordinal numbers to identify API procedures. This approach can still be useful when used with procedures that are not APIs, or when used in applications that have a very controlled distribution.

To declare a DLL procedure by ordinal number, use the Alias clause with a string containing the number sign character (#) and the ordinal number of the procedure. For example, the ordinal number of the GetWindowsDirectory function has the value 432 in the Windows kernel; you can declare the DLL procedure as follows:

```
Declare Function GetWindowsDirectory Lib "kernel32" _
Alias "#432" (ByVal lpBuffer As String, _
ByVal nSize As Long) As Long
```

Notice that you could specify any valid name for the procedure in this case, because Visual Basic is using the ordinal number to find the procedure in the DLL.

To obtain the ordinal number of a procedure you want to declare, you can use a utility application, such as Dumpbin.exe, to examine the .dll file. (Dumpbin.exe is a utility included with Microsoft Visual C++.) By running Dumpbin on a .dll file, you can extract information such as a list of functions contained within the DLL, their ordinal numbers, and other information about the code.

For More Information For more information on running the Dumpbin utility, refer to the Microsoft Visual C++ documentation.

Flexible Argument Types

Some DLL procedures can accept more than one type of data for the same argument. If you need to pass more than one type of data, declare the argument with As Any to remove type restrictions.

For example, the third argument in the following declare (`lppt As Any`) could be passed as an array of POINT structures, or as a RECT structure, depending upon your needs:

```
Declare Function MapWindowPoints Lib "user32" Alias _
"MapWindowPoints" (ByVal hwndFrom As Long, _
ByVal hwndTo As Long, lppt As Any, _
ByVal cPoints As Long) As Long
```

While the As Any clause offers you flexibility, it also adds risk in that it turns off all type checking. Without type checking, you stand a greater chance of calling the procedure with the wrong type, which can result in a variety of problems, including application failure. Be sure to carefully check the types of all arguments when using As Any.

When you remove type restrictions, Visual Basic assumes the argument is passed by reference. Include ByVal in the actual call to the procedure to pass arguments by value. Strings are passed by value so that a pointer to the string is passed, rather than a pointer to a pointer. This is further discussed in the section "Passing Strings to a DLL Procedure."

Passing Strings to a DLL Procedure

In general, strings should be passed to APIs using ByVal. Visual Basic uses a String data type known as a BSTR, which is a data type defined by Automation (formerly called OLE Automation). A BSTR is comprised of a header, which includes information about the length of the string, and the string itself, which may include embedded nulls. A BSTR is passed as a pointer, so the DLL procedure is able to modify the string. (A *pointer* is a variable that contains the memory location of another variable, rather than the actual data.) BSTRs are Unicode, which means that each character takes two bytes. BSTRs typically end with a two-byte null character.

Figure 1.2 The BSTR type (each box represents two bytes)

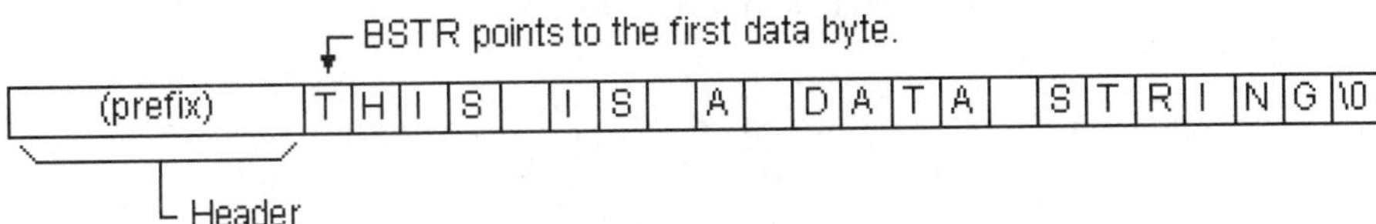

The procedures in most DLLs (and in all procedures in the Windows API) recognize LPSTR types, which are pointers to standard null-terminated C strings (also called ASCIIZ strings). LPSTRs have no prefix. The following figure shows an LPSTR that points to an ASCIIZ string.

Figure 1.3 The LPSTR type

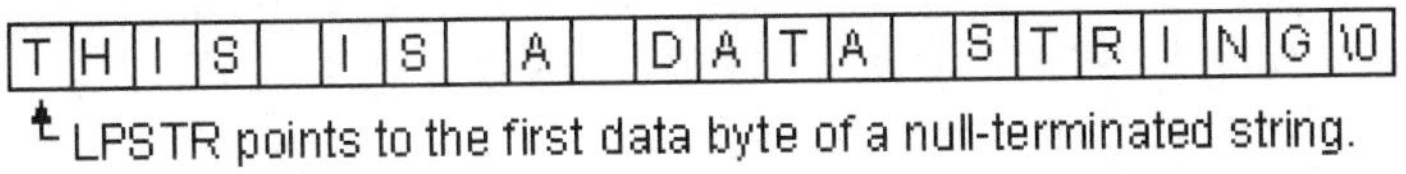

T H I S I S A D A T A S T R I N G \0

LPSTR points to the first data byte of a null-terminated string.

If a DLL procedure expects an LPSTR (a pointer to a null-terminated string) as an argument, pass the BSTR by value. Because a pointer to a BSTR is a pointer to the first data byte of a null-terminated string, it looks like an LPSTR to the DLL procedure.

For example, the sndPlaySound function accepts a string that names a digitized sound (.wav) file and plays that file.

```
Private Declare Function sndPlaySound Lib "winmm.dll" _
Alias "sndPlaySoundA" (ByVal lpszSoundName As String, _
ByVal uFlags As Long) As Long
```

Because the string argument for this procedure is declared with ByVal, Visual Basic passes a BSTR that points to the first data byte:

```
Dim SoundFile As String, ReturnLength As Long
SoundFile = Dir("c:\Windows\System\" & "*.wav")
Result = sndPlaySound(SoundFile, 1)
```

In general, use the ByVal keyword when passing string arguments to DLL procedures that expect LPSTR strings. If the DLL expects a pointer to an LPSTR string, pass the Visual Basic string by reference.

When passing binary data to a DLL procedure, pass a variable as an array of the Byte data type, instead of a String variable. Strings are assumed to contain characters, and binary data may not be properly read in external procedures if passed as a String variable.

If you declare a string variable without initializing it, and then pass it by value to a DLL, the string variable is passed as NULL, not as an empty string (""). To avoid confusion in your code, use the vbNullString constant to pass a NULL to an LPSTR argument.

Passing Strings to DLLs That Use Automation

Some DLLs may be written specifically to work with Automation data types like BSTR, using procedures supplied by Automation.

Because Visual Basic uses Automation data types as its own data types, Visual Basic arguments can be passed by reference to any DLL that expects Automation data types. Thus, if a DLL procedure expects a Visual Basic string as an argument, you do not need to declare the argument with the ByVal keyword, unless the procedure specifically needs the string passed by value.

Some DLL procedures may return strings to the calling procedure. A DLL function cannot return strings unless it is written specifically for use with Automation data types. If it is, the DLL probably supplies a type library that describes the procedures. Consult the documentation for that DLL.

For More Information For information on Automation data types, see the *OLE 2 Programmer's Reference,* published by Microsoft Press.

Procedures That Modify String Arguments

A DLL procedure can modify data in a string variable that it receives as an argument. However, if the changed data is longer than the original string, the procedure writes beyond the end of the string, probably corrupting other data.

You can avoid this problem by making the string argument long enough so that the DLL procedure can never write past the end of it. For example, the GetWindowsDirectory procedure returns the path for the Windows directory in its first argument:

```
Declare Function GetWindowsDirectory Lib "kernel32" _
Alias "GetWindowsDirectoryA" (ByVal lpBuffer As _
String, ByVal nSize As Long) As Long
```

A safe way to call this procedure is to first use the String function to set the returned argument to at least 255 characters by filling it with null (binary zero) characters:

```
Path = String(255, vbNullChar)
ReturnLength = GetWindowsDirectory(Path, Len(Path))
Path = Left(Path, ReturnLength)
```

Another solution is to define the string as fixed length:

```
Dim Path As String * 255
ReturnLength = GetWindowsDirectory(Path, Len(Path))
```

Both of these processes have the same result: They create a fixed-length string that can contain the longest possible string the procedure might return.

> **Note** Windows API DLL procedures generally do not expect string buffers longer than 255 characters. While this is true for many other libraries, always consult the documentation for the procedure.

When the DLL procedure calls for a memory buffer, you can either use the appropriate data type, or use an array of the byte data type.

Passing Arrays to a DLL Procedure

You can pass individual elements of an array the same way you pass a variable of the same type. When you pass an individual element, it will be passed as the base type of the array. For example, you can use the sndPlaySound procedure to play a series of .wav files stored in an array:

```
Dim WaveFiles(10) As String
Dim i As Integer, worked As Integer
   For i = 0 to UBound(WaveFiles)
      worked = sndPlaySound(WaveFiles(i), 0)
   Next i
```

Sometimes you may want to pass an entire array to a DLL procedure. If the DLL procedure was written especially for Automation, then you may be able to pass an array to the procedure the same way you pass an array to a Visual Basic procedure: with empty parentheses. Because Visual Basic uses Automation data types, including SAFEARRAYs, the DLL must be written to accommodate Automation for it to accept Visual Basic array arguments. For further information, consult the documentation for the specific DLL.

If the DLL procedure doesn't accept Automation SAFEARRAYs directly, you can still pass an entire array if it is a numeric array. You pass an entire numeric array by passing the first element of the array by reference. This works because numeric array data is always laid out sequentially in memory. If you pass the first element of an array to a DLL procedure, that DLL then has access to all of the array's elements.

As an example, consider how you can use an API call to set tab stops within a text box There are internal tab stops in multiple-line (but not single-line) text box controls: If the text in the text box contains tab characters (character code 9), the text following the tab character is aligned at the next tab stop. You can set the position of these tab stops by calling the SendMessage function in the Windows API and passing an array that contains the new tab stop settings.

```
Private Declare Function SendMessageSetTabs Lib _
"user32" Alias "SendMessageA" (ByVal hwnd As Long, _
ByVal wMsg As Long, ByVal wParam As Long, _
lParam As Any) As Long
Const EM_SETTABSTOPS = &HCB

Sub ChangeTabs(anyText As TextBox, tabcount As Integer)
Dim i As Integer
Dim alngTabs() As Long
Dim lngRC As Long
ReDim alngTabs(tabcount - 1)
   For i = 0 To UBound(alngTabs)
      alngTabs(i) = (i + 1) * 96
      ' Set value to specify tabs in "dialog units."
   Next i
   ' Call with null pointer to empty existing
   ' tab stops.
   lngRC = SendMessageSetTabs(anyText.hwnd, _
   EM_SETTABSTOPS, 0, vbNullString)
   ' Pass first element in array; other elements
   ' follow it in memory.
   lngRC = SendMessageSetTabs(anyText.hwnd, _
   EM_SETTABSTOPS, tabcount, alngTabs(0))
   anyText.Refresh
End Sub
```

When you call this procedure, you specify the name of the text box and the number of tab stops you want to use for the indent. For example:

```
Private Sub Command1_Click()
   ChangeTabs Text1, 4
End Sub
```

This approach will also work for string arrays. A DLL procedure written in C treats a string array as an array of pointers to string data, which is the same way Visual Basic defines a string array.

For More Information For more information on SAFEARRAYs and other Automation data types, see the Microsoft Press book, *OLE 2 Programmer's Reference*.

Passing User-Defined Types to a DLL Procedure

Some DLL procedures take user-defined types as arguments. (User-defined types are referred to as "structures" in C and as "records" in Pascal.) As with arrays, you can pass the individual elements of a user-defined type the same way you would pass ordinary numeric or string variables.

You can pass an entire user-defined type as a single argument if you pass it by reference. User-defined types cannot be passed by value. Visual Basic passes the address of the first element, and the rest of the elements of a user-defined type are stored in memory following the first element. Depending on the operating system, there may also be some padding.

For example, several procedures in the operating environment DLLs accept a user-defined type for a rectangle, which has the following structure:

```
Type RECT
   Left As Long
   Top As Long
   Right As Long
   Bottom As Long
End Type
```

Two of the procedures that accept a rectangle are DrawFocusRect, which draws a dotted outline around the specified rectangle, and InvertRect, which inverts the colors of the specified rectangle. To use the procedures, place these declarations in the Declarations section of a standard module:

```
Declare Function DrawFocusRect Lib "User32" Alias _
"DrawFocusRect" (ByVal hdc As Long, _
lpRect As RECT) As Long

Declare Function InvertRect Lib "User32" Alias _
"InvertRect" (ByVal hdc As Long, _
lpRect As RECT) As Long

Dim MouseRect As RECT
```

Now you can use the following Sub procedures to call the DLLs:

```
Private Sub Form_MouseDown (Button As Integer, _
Shift As Integer, X As Single, Y As Single)
   ScaleMode = 3
   If Button And 1 Then
      MouseRect.Left = X
      MouseRect.Top = Y
      MouseRect.Right = X
      MouseRect.Bottom = Y
   End If
End Sub

Private Sub Form_MouseUp (Button As Integer, _
Shift As Integer, X As Single, Y As Single)
   ScaleMode = 3
   If Not (Button And 1) Then
      MouseRect.Right = X
      MouseRect.Bottom = Y
      InvertRect hDC, MouseRect
   End If
End Sub
```

```
Private Sub Form_MouseMove (Button As Integer, _
Shift As Integer, X As Single, Y As Single)
   ScaleMode = 3
   If Button And 1 Then
      DrawFocusRect hDC, MouseRect
      MouseRect.Right = X
      MouseRect.Bottom = Y
      DrawFocusRect hDC, MouseRect
   End If
End Sub
```

User-defined types can contain objects, arrays, and BSTR strings, although most DLL procedures that accept user-defined types do not expect them to contain string data. If the string elements are fixed-length strings, they look like null-terminated strings to the DLL and are stored in memory like any other value. Variable-length strings are incorporated in a user-defined type as pointers to string data. Four bytes are required for each variable-length string element.

> **Note** When passing a user-defined type that contains binary data to a DLL procedure, store the binary data in a variable of an array of the Byte data type, instead of a String variable. Strings are assumed to contain characters, and binary data may not be properly read in external procedures if passed as a String variable.

Passing Function Pointers to DLL Procedures and Type Libraries

If you're familiar with the C programming language, function pointers may be familiar to you. If you're not, the concept merits some explanation. A *function pointer* is a convention that enables you to pass the address of a user-defined function as an argument to another function you've declared for use within your application. By using function pointers, you can now call functions like EnumWindows to list the open windows on the system, or EnumFontFamilies to catalog all of the current fonts. You can also use them to gain access to many other functions from the Win32 API that have not previously been supported in Visual Basic.

For Visual Basic, several limitations apply to the use of function pointers. For details, see "Limitations and Risks with Function Pointers" later in this part.

Learning About Function Pointers

The use of function pointers is best illustrated with an example. To start, look at the EnumWindows function from the Win32 API:

```
Declare Function EnumWindows lib "user32" _
(ByVal lpEnumFunc as Long, _
ByVal lParam as Long ) As Long
```

EnumWindows is an enumeration function, which means that it can list the handle of every open window on your system. EnumWindows works by repeatedly calling the function you pass to its first argument (lpEnumFunc). Each time EnumWindows calls the function, EnumWindows passes it the handle of an open window.

When you call EnumWindows from your code, you pass a user-defined function to this first argument to handle the stream of values. For example, you might write a function to add the values to a list box, convert the hWnd values to window names, or take whatever action you choose.

To specify that you're passing a user-defined function as an argument, you precede the name of the function with the AddressOf keyword. Any suitable value can be passed to the second argument. For example, to pass the function MyProc as an argument, you might call the EnumWindows procedure as follows:

```
x = EnumWindows(AddressOf MyProc, 5)
```

The user-defined function you specify when you call the procedure is referred to as the *callback function*. Callback functions (or "callbacks," as they are commonly called) can perform any action you specify with the data supplied by the procedure.

A callback function must have a specific set of arguments, as determined by the API from which the callback is referenced. Refer to your API documentation for information on the necessary arguments and how to call them.

Using the AddressOf Keyword

Any code you write to call a function pointer from Visual Basic must be placed in a standard .BAS module — you can't put the code in a class module or attach it to a form. When you call a declared function using the AddressOf keyword, you should be aware of the following conditions:

- AddressOf can only be used immediately preceding an argument in an argument list; that argument can be the name of a user-defined sub, function, or property.
- The sub, function, or property you call with AddressOf must be in the same project as the related declarations and procedures.
- You can only use AddressOf with user-defined subs, functions, or properties — you cannot use it with external functions declared with the Declare statement, or with functions referenced from type libraries.
- You can pass a function pointer to an argument that is typed As Any or As Long in a declared Sub, Function, or user-defined type definition.

  Note You can create your own call-back function prototypes in DLLs compiled with Visual C++ (or similar tools). To work with AddressOf, your prototype must use the __stdcall calling convention. The default calling convention (_cdecl) will not work with AddressOf.

Storing a Function Pointer in a Variable

At times, you may need to store a function pointer in an intermediate variable before passing it to the DLL. This is useful if you want to pass function pointers from one Visual Basic function to another. It's required if you are calling a function like RegisterClass, where you need to pass the pointer through an argument to a structure (WndClass), which contains a function pointer as one of its elements.

To assign a function pointer to an element in a structure, you write a wrapper function. For example, the following code creates the wrapper function FnPtrToLong, which can be used to put a function pointer in any structure:

```
Function FnPtrToLong (ByVal lngFnPtr As Long) As Long
   FnPtrToLong = lngFnPtr
End Function
```

To use the function, you first declare the type, then call FnPtrToLong. You pass AddressOf plus your callback function name for the second argument.

```
Dim mt as MyType
mt.MyPtr = FnPtrToLong(AddressOf MyCallBackFunction)
```

Subclassing

Subclassing is a technique that enables you to intercept Windows messages being sent to a form or control. By intercepting these messages, you can then write your own code to change or extend the behavior of the object. Subclassing can be complex, and a thorough discussion of it is beyond the scope of this book. The following example offers a brief illustration of the technique.

> **Important** When Visual Basic is in break mode, you can't call vtable methods or AddressOf functions. As a safety mechanism, Visual Basic simply returns 0 to the caller of an AddressOf function without calling the function. In the case of subclassing, this means that 0 is returned to Windows from the WindowProc. Windows requires nonzero return values from many of its messages, so the constant 0 return may create a deadlock situation between Windows and the Visual Basic, forcing you to end the process.

This application consists of a simple form with two command buttons. The code is designed to intercept Windows messages being sent to the form and to print the values of those messages in the Immediate window.

The first part of the code consists of declarations for the API functions, constant values, and variables:

```
Declare Function CallWindowProc Lib "user32" Alias _
"CallWindowProcA" (ByVal lpPrevWndFunc As Long, _
   ByVal hwnd As Long, ByVal Msg As Long, _
   ByVal wParam As Long, ByVal lParam As Long) As Long

Declare Function SetWindowLong Lib "user32" Alias _
"SetWindowLongA" (ByVal hwnd As Long, _
ByVal nIndex As Long, ByVal dwNewLong As Long) As Long

Public Const GWL_WNDPROC = -4
Global lpPrevWndProc As Long
Global gHW As Long
```

Next, two subroutines enable the code to hook into the stream of messages. The first procedure (Hook) calls the SetWindowLong function with the GWL_WNDPROC index to create a subclass of the window class that was used to create the window. It then uses the AddressOf keyword with a callback function (WindowProc) to intercept the messages and print their values in the Immediate window. The second procedure (Unhook) turns off subclassing by replacing the callback with the original Windows procedure.

```
Public Sub Hook()
   lpPrevWndProc = SetWindowLong(gHW, GWL_WNDPROC, _
   AddressOf WindowProc)
End Sub

Public Sub Unhook()
   Dim temp As Long
   temp = SetWindowLong(gHW, GWL_WNDPROC, _
   lpPrevWndProc)
End Sub

Function WindowProc(ByVal hw As Long, ByVal uMsg As _
Long, ByVal wParam As Long, ByVal lParam As Long) As _
Long
   Debug.Print "Message: "; hw, uMsg, wParam, lParam
   WindowProc = CallWindowProc(lpPrevWndProc, hw, _
   uMsg, wParam, lParam)
End Function
```

Finally, the code for the form sets the initial hWnd value, and the code for the buttons simply calls the two subroutines:

```
Private Sub Form_Load()
   gHW = Me.hwnd
End Sub
```

```
Private Sub Command1_Click()
   Hook
End Sub

Private Sub Command2_Click()
   Unhook
End Sub
```

Limitations and Risks with Function Pointers

Working with function pointers can be unforgiving. You lose the stability of Visual Basic's development environment any time you call a DLL, but when working with function pointers, it can be especially easy to cause the application to fail and to lose your work. Save often and back up your work as necessary. Following are notes on some areas that require special attention when working with function pointers:

- **Debugging**. If your application fires a callback function while in break mode, the code will be executed, but any breaks or steps will be ignored. If the callback function generates an exception, you can catch it and return the current value. Resets are prohibited in break mode when a callback function is on the stack.
- **Thunks**. *Thunking* is the way that Windows enables relocatable code. If you delete a callback function in break mode, its thunk is modified to return 0. This value will be correct most of the time — but not all of the time. If you delete a callback function in break mode and then type it again, it's possible that some callees will not know about the new address. Thunks aren't used in the .exe — the pointer is passed directly to the entry point.
- **Passing a function with the wrong signature**. If you pass a callback function that takes a different number of arguments than the caller expects, or mistakenly calls an argument with ByRef or ByVal, your application may fail. Be careful to pass a function with the correct signature.
- **Passing a function to a Windows procedure that no longer exists**. When subclassing a window, you pass a function pointer to Windows as the Windows procedure (WindowProc). When running your application in the IDE, however, it's possible that the WindowProc will be called after the underlying function has already been destroyed. This will likely cause a general protection fault and may bring down the Visual Basic development environment.
- **"Basic to Basic" function pointers are not supported**. Pointers to Visual Basic functions cannot be passed within Visual Basic itself. Currently, only pointers from Visual Basic to a DLL function are supported.
- **Containing errors within a callback procedure**. It is important that any errors within a callback procedure not be propagated back to the external procedure that initially called it. You can accomplish this by place the On Error Resume Next statement at the beginning of the callback procedure.

Passing Other Types of Information to a DLL Procedure

Visual Basic supports a wide range of data types, some of which may not be supported by the procedures in certain dynamic-link libraries. The following topic describes how to handle some of the special cases you may find when using Visual Basic variables with DLL procedures.

Passing Null Pointers

Some DLL procedures may sometimes expect to receive either a string or a null value as an argument. If you need to pass a null pointer to a string, declare the argument As String and pass the constant vbNullString.

For example, the FindWindow procedure can determine if another application is currently running on your system. It accepts two string arguments, one for the class name of the application, and another for the window title bar caption:

```
Declare Function FindWindow Lib "user32" Alias _
"FindWindowA" (ByVal lpClassName As String, _
ByVal lpWindowName As String) As Long
```

Either of these arguments can be passed as a null value. Passing a zero-length string ("") does not work, however, as this passes a pointer to a zero-length string. The value of this pointer will not be zero. You instead need to pass an argument with the true value of zero. The easiest way to do this is by using the constant value vbNullString for the appropriate argument:

```
hWndExcel = FindWindow(vbNullString, "Microsoft Excel")
```

Another way to handle this situation is to rewrite the declare to substitute a Long data type for the argument that you want to pass as null, and then call that argument with the value 0&. For example:

```
Declare Function FindWindowWithNull Lib "user32" -
Alias "FindWindowA" (ByVal lpClassName As Long, _
ByVal lpWindowName As String) As Long

hWndExcel = FindWindow(0&, "Microsoft Excel")
```

Passing Properties

Properties must be passed by value. If an argument is declared with ByVal, you can pass the property directly. For example, you can determine the dimensions of the screen or printer in pixels with this procedure:

```
Declare Function GetDeviceCaps Lib "gdi32" Alias _
"GetDeviceCaps" (ByVal hdc As Long, _
ByVal nIndex As Long) As Long
```

You can also pass the hDC property of a form or the Printer object to this procedure to obtain the number of colors supported by the screen or the currently selected printer. For example:

```
Private Sub Form_Click ()
Const PLANES = 14, BITS = 12
   Print "Screen colors ";
   Print GetDeviceCaps(hDC, PLANES)* 2 ^ _
   GetDeviceCaps(hDC, BITS)
   Print "Printer colors ";
   Print GetDeviceCaps(Printer.hDC, PLANES) * _
   2 ^ GetDeviceCaps(Printer.hDC, BITS)
End Sub
```

To pass a property by reference, you must use an intermediate variable. For example, suppose you want to use the GetWindowsDirectory procedure to set the Path property of a file list box control. This example will not work:

```
ReturnLength = GetWindowsDirectory(File1.Path,_
Len(File1.Path))
```

Instead, use the following code to set the property:

```
Dim Temp As String, ReturnLength As Integer
Temp = String(255, 0)
ReturnLength = GetWindowsDirectory(Temp, Len(Temp))
Temp = Left(Temp, ReturnLength)
File1.Path = Temp
```

Use this technique with numeric properties if you want to pass them to DLL procedures that accept arguments by reference.

Using Handles with DLLs

A *handle* is a unique Long value defined by the operating environment. It is used to refer to objects such as forms or controls. The operating environment DLL procedures make extensive use of handles — handles to windows (hWnd), handles to device contexts (hDC), and so on. When a procedure takes a handle as an argument, always declare it as a ByVal Long. DLL functions that return a handle can be declared as Long functions. Handles are identifier (ID) numbers, not pointers or numeric values; never attempt mathematical operations on them.

The hWnd property of forms and nongraphical controls and the hDC property of forms and picture box controls supply valid handles that you can pass to DLL procedures. Like any other property passed to a DLL procedure, they can be passed only by value.

Passing Variants

Passing an argument of type Variant is similar to passing any other argument type, as long as the DLL procedure uses the Automation VARIANT data structure to access the argument data. To pass Variant data to a argument that is not a Variant type, pass the Variant data ByVal.

Converting C Declarations to Visual Basic

The procedures in DLLs are most commonly documented using C language syntax. To call these procedures from Visual Basic, you need to translate them into valid Declare statements and call them with the correct arguments.

As part of this translation, you must convert the C data types into Visual Basic data types and specify whether each argument should be called by value (ByVal) or implicitly, by reference (ByRef). The following table lists common C language data types and their Visual Basic equivalents for 32-bit versions of Windows.

C language data type	In Visual Basic declare as	Call with
ATOM	ByVal *variable* As Integer	An expression that evaluates to an Integer
BOOL	ByVal *variable* As Long	An expression that evaluates to a Long
BYTE	ByVal *variable* As Byte	An expression that evaluates to a Byte
CHAR	ByVal *variable* As Byte	An expression that evaluates to a Byte
COLORREF	ByVal *variable* As Long	An expression that evaluates to a Long
DWORD	ByVal *variable* As Long	An expression that evaluates to a Long
HWND, HDC, HMENU, etc. (Windows handles)	ByVal *variable* As Long	An expression that evaluates to a Long
INT, UINT	ByVal *variable* As Long	An expression that evaluates to a Long
LONG	ByVal *variable* As Long	An expression that evaluates to a Long

(continued)

(continued)

C language data type	In Visual Basic declare as	Call with
LPARAM	ByVal *variable* As Long	An expression that evaluates to a Long
LPDWORD	*variable* As Long	An expression that evaluates to a Long
LPINT, LPUINT	*variable* As Long	An expression that evaluates to a Long
LPRECT	*variable* As *type*	Any variable of that user-defined type
LPSTR, LPCSTR	ByVal *variable* As String	An expression that evaluates to a String
LPVOID	*variable* As Any	Any variable (use ByVal when passing a string)
LPWORD	*variable* As Integer	An expression that evaluates to an Integer
LRESULT	ByVal *variable* As Long	An expression that evaluates to a Long
NULL	As Any or ByVal *variable* As Long	ByVal Nothing or ByVal 0& or vbNullString
SHORT	ByVal *variable* As Integer	An expression that evaluates to an Integer
VOID	Sub *procedure*	Not applicable
WORD	ByVal *variable* As Integer	An expression that evaluates to an Integer
WPARAM	ByVal *variable* As Long	An expression that evaluates to a Long

PART 5

Building Internet Applications

Visual Basic offers several possibilities for how you can move your applications onto the Internet or a corporate intranet.

Chapter 1 Introduction to Internet Applications

Introduces the developmental approach for creating applications for the Internet using Dynamic HTML and Internet Information Server technology.

Chapter 2 Developing DHTML Applications

Explains how to create, test, and deploy client-based Internet applications using Dynamic HTML.

Chapter 3 Developing IIS Applications

Explains how to create, test, and deploy server-based Internet applications using Internet Information Server.

Chapter 4 Downloading ActiveX Components

Explains how to package and deploy ActiveX controls, components, and user documents on the Web, through Internet Component Download.

CHAPTER 1

Introduction to Internet Applications

Microsoft Visual Basic lets you create applications for the Internet or a corporate intranet in several different ways. Using the new Internet programming features in Visual Basic, you can make use of your skills as a Visual Basic programmer to produce dynamic, powerful Internet applications with little effort. You can produce applications that run on the client or the server, present HTML pages inside a forms-based application, or use ActiveX components on the Web. In addition, you can quickly and easily set up your applications for Internet component download and deployment.

Contents

What is an Internet Application?

Simply put, an Internet application is an interactive, compiled application that can be accessed through a corporate intranet or through the Internet. Internet applications can perform complex business processes on either the client or the server. In a server-based Internet application, the application uses the HTTP Internet protocol to receive requests from a client, typically a Web browser, process associated code, and return data to the browser.

In Visual Basic Internet programming, you can add active content to Web pages with little effort. Visual Basic Internet applications link Visual Basic code to one or more HTML pages and handle events raised in those pages by interacting with programs on either a client or a server. There are two types of Internet applications in Visual Basic: server-based IIS applications and client-based DHTML applications.

The user interface in a Visual Basic Internet application can be a series of HTML pages, a mix of HTML pages and Visual Basic forms, or a Visual Basic form that makes use of special components such as the WebBrowser control to take advantage of some of the power of the Internet. Regardless of the type of user interface, the application handles events, calls methods, and sets and retrieves properties based on elements in the HTML page.

The Web pages that make up the user interface for Visual Basic Internet applications are generally produced by a Web designer, rather than a developer. If you prefer to create your own HTML pages you can, but you do not have to. Instead, you can focus on your talents as a Visual Basic programmer by writing Visual Basic code that interacts with and uses HTML. Using your skills as a developer, you can easily produce dynamic, powerful applications for the Web.

For example, using Visual Basic Internet technology, you might create an application that can be used entirely on the browser to let salespeople track their status on the road, then link up to the central server when they return to the office. Or, you might create a sophisticated database-driven system that presents a catalog of selections to your end users, through their browser. Users could choose products from the catalog and your application would run associated Visual Basic code to retrieve product detail from a database recordset and send that information to the user.

For More Information More about Internet protocols is available on the World Wide Web.

Understanding Internet Basics

You can program for the Web, using your skills as a Visual Basic programmer, no matter what your level of experience with Internet technology. If you are new to the Internet or unfamiliar with its technology, Visual Basic allows you to quickly and easily produce functional applications. If you are more experienced with Internet technology, you can work at a more advanced level.

From one perspective, Internet technology simply provides another area for your development efforts. When you deploy Internet applications on the Web, you may go about it differently — incorporating HTML pages with your Visual Basic code, providing security features, and so on — but you're still calling methods, setting properties, and handling events. In this way, all of your knowledge as a Visual Basic developer can be carried into the Internet arena.

From another perspective, applying Internet technology enables you to extend your development skills in exciting new ways. For example, writing Visual Basic code that manipulates HTML pages allows you to decrease deployment costs, reduce client maintenance problems, and reach the broad audience of the Internet.

Internet Clients and Servers

A common way to think about Internet development is in terms of client/server relationships. In this case, the client is the browser, and the server is the Web server. Most interactions on the Internet or an intranet can be thought of in terms of requests and responses. The browser makes a request to the Web server (usually to display a page the user wants to see) and the Web server returns a response (usually an HTML page, an element, or an image) to the browser.

Internet vs. Intranet

The Internet encompasses two categories: the Internet and the intranet. The Internet is a global, distributed network of computers operating on a protocol called TCP/IP. An intranet is also a network of computers operating on the TCP/IP protocol, but it is not global. Generally, intranets are restricted to a particular set of users and are not accessible by the outside world. For example, many corporations use a corporate intranet to provide information to their employees, and run another Internet site for external users. Users within the company can access both the intranet sites and the Internet, but users outside the company can access only the company's Internet sites.

HTML Pages

HTML (HyperText Markup Language) is a language that allows you to display documents in a Web browser. You use HTML to create .htm files that are displayed in a browser. When you create an Internet application in Visual Basic, your user interface is usually made up of HTML pages rather than forms. In many ways, an .htm file (which allows you to display HTML pages) is similar to a Visual Basic .frm file (which allows you to display a Visual Basic form).

> **Note** While the user interface is generally made up of HTML pages, it can also contain a mix of Visual Basic forms and HTML pages.

An .htm file is a text document that contains a series of tags that tell the browser how to display the file. These HTML tags supply information about the page's structure, appearance, and content. The following figure shows the relationship between page in the browser and its HTML tags:

HTML Page and Source HTML

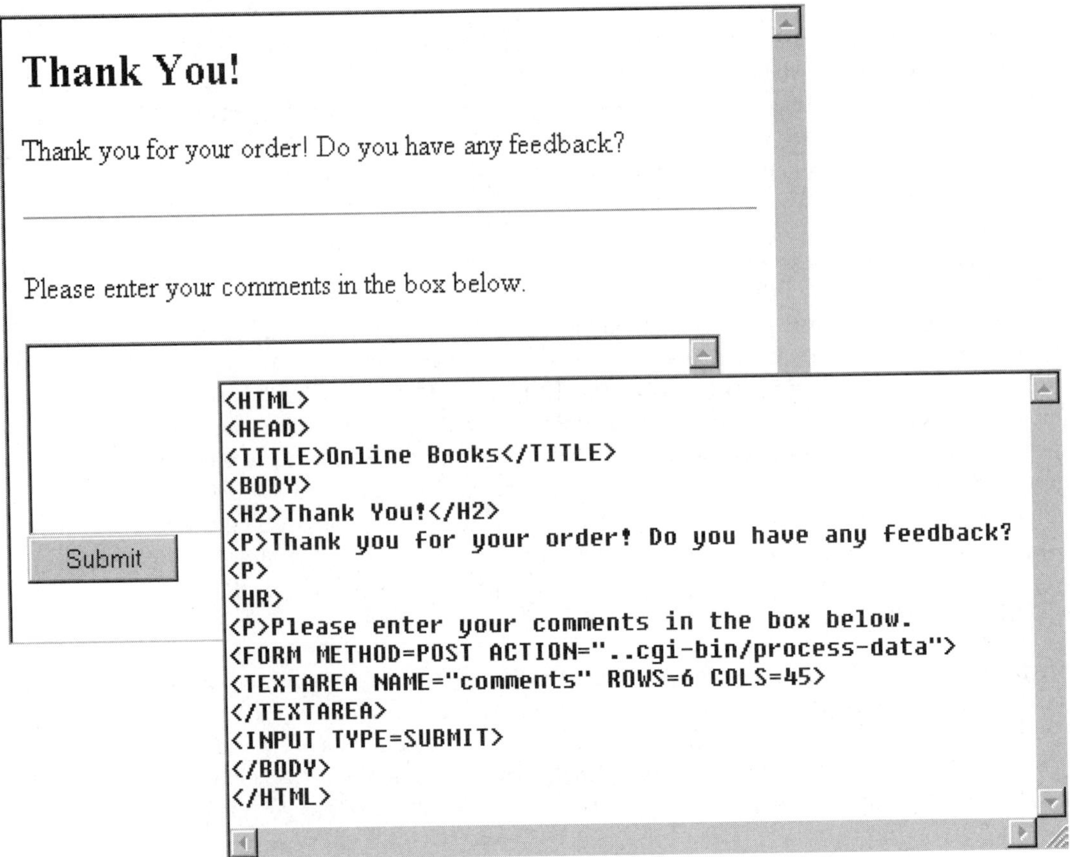

In addition to describing the structural relationships among page elements, some HTML tags also contain attributes. Attributes provide details about a particular tag. For example, the tag that inserts an image onto a page contains an attribute that specifies the name of the file to insert. The tag is shown below.

HTML Tags and Attributes

```
<img src="logo.gif">
 tag     attribute
```

Internet Object Models

You use the concepts of object-oriented programming in your Visual Basic Internet applications just as you do in forms-based Visual Basic applications. In Visual Basic Internet applications, you use Internet-related object models to access and manipulate information and controls on your HTML pages.

There are two types of Visual Basic Internet applications: IIS applications and DHTML applications. In IIS applications, you make use of the Active Server Pages (ASP) object model to retrieve information from the user, send information to the browser, and maintain information about the current session. In DHTML applications, you use the Dynamic HTML (DHTML) object model to manipulate the elements on an HTML page.

The important point to remember is that you access the information on your HTML pages through objects, regardless of whether the objects themselves are ASP or DHTML. The object models are explained in much greater detail in the chapters describing each type of application.

For More Information See the next section, "A History of Development on the Internet," for more information on the differences between IIS and DHTML applications. See Chapter 2, "Developing DHTML Applications," for more information on using Dynamic HTML objects. See Chapter 3, "Developing IIS Applications," for more information on using ASP objects. See the MSDN Web site at http://www.microsoft.com/msdn for details on using HTML and Internet technologies.

A History of Development on the Internet

Visual Basic programming technology represents a new set of approaches to Web technology, focused on the Visual Basic developer. This section offers a brief history of the Web's evolution from linked static content to the dynamic, compiled environment of Visual Basic Internet applications.

Static Content

The first applications on the Internet consisted of static pages that delivered their content to the browser and did not react dynamically to any actions the user performed. Although this model provides ready access to nicely formatted pages of information for your employees or potential customers, it provides limited interaction between the user and the Web server — and the static pages have to be manually edited to update their content.

Dynamic Content Through Gateway Programming

The development of gateway interfaces such as Common Gateway Interface (CGI), Internet Server Application Programming Interface (ISAPI), and others allowed users to add dynamic content to the Web. With dynamic content, a browser can send a request for information. The server, instead of returning a static page, runs a script or application and returns HTML that reflects up-to-date, accurate information.

The disadvantage of gateway programs is that they are difficult to create and change. Gateway programs are not integrated into HTML files; in fact, they require an entirely different design process than do HTML files. In addition, all processing in a gateway program happens entirely on the server. This can increase server load and lead to backlogs in processing.

Scripting

Scripting enables dynamic content by embedding executable scripts directly in an HTML page. Rather than querying the server for an executable, the browser can process scripts as it loads the HTML page. These scripts can be processed on either the client or the Web server. The most common languages for client-side scripting are VBScript and JavaScript. A common framework used for server-side scripting is called Active Server Pages, or ASP.

In the ASP scripting model, HTML development and scripting development are part of the same process. This translates into tangible benefits, enabling Web providers to provide interactive business applications rather than merely publishing content. For example, a travel agency can go beyond just publishing flight schedules; it can use ASP scripting to enable customers to check available flights, compare fares, and reserve a seat on a flight.

With ASP scripting, you can use any scripting language for which an appropriate scripting engine is available. ASP supplies scripting engines for Microsoft Visual Basic Scripting Edition (VBScript) and Microsoft JScript. You can incorporate sophisticated functionality using ActiveX components to process data and generate useful information.

Visual Basic Internet Applications

Visual Basic Internet technology takes the process one step further by allowing you to link standard Visual Basic code to a user interface of HTML pages. This provides an extremely powerful mechanism for associating programming functionality with your Web pages, while allowing you to create dynamic, interactive content. With Visual Basic Internet technology, you can perform complex business operations while avoiding some of the intricacies of gateway programming or scripting. You can also enjoy all the benefits of working in Visual Basic, such as using class modules, controls, and designers, and debugging your code.

There are two main types of Visual Basic Internet applications: IIS applications and DHTML applications:

- IIS applications, named for Microsoft Internet Information Server, reside on a Web server and are used to process incoming requests from a browser. IIS applications process the requests, run associated Visual Basic code, and return responses to the user. All processing for an IIS application happens on the server.
- DHTML applications, named for Dynamic HTML, can take one of two forms: an application that is downloaded to a user's computer and runs there, or an HTML-based application that runs within a form, using the WebBrowser control. In either case, a DHTML application lets you write code that handles events on an HTML page. Most processing in a DHTML application can happen on the browser computer, although the application can make calls to the server if necessary.

DHTML applications require the end user to have Microsoft Internet Explorer version 4.0 or later, while IIS applications are browser- and operating system — independent to the end user. Because of this, IIS applications are the appropriate choice when you want to develop an application that reaches a broad audience. DHTML applications may be the more appropriate choice for intranet applications or applications that need to support remote or offline usage.

There are also other types of applications you can create in Visual Basic that make use of the Internet. For example, you can create ActiveX components that can be used on the Internet. These include ActiveX controls that can be used on Web pages, ActiveX documents that can run in a browser, and ActiveX code components that can be deployed on a Web server for behind-the-scenes processing. In addition, you can use the WebBrowser control to use HTML pages within a forms-based application.

For More Information See "Other Internet Technologies in Visual Basic" for more information on incorporating ActiveX components into your Internet applications. For information on using the WebBrowser control, see the *Internet Client SDK* on the MSDN Library CD, under the heading "SDK Documentation."

Advantages of Visual Basic Internet Applications

There are many ways to develop applications for the Internet. Prior to Visual Basic 6.0, developers relied on CGI programs, on ActiveX functionality, or on Active Server Pages to create dynamic, interactive Internet applications. Internet application development in Visual Basic offers several key advantages over those approaches:

- You can greatly reduce the cost of deployment per user. End users of an IIS Internet application can run the application using only a browser; no special software aside from the appropriate browser needs to be installed on their computers. End users of a DHTML Internet application need only the appropriate browser and the Visual Basic run-time on their computers. These necessary pieces are installed automatically.
- You can leverage your knowledge of Visual Basic and use the Visual Basic programming environment. You do not have to learn scripting or manipulate HTML tags to develop a highly functional Web-based application.

- You can separate designing the user interface from writing the code for a form or page. In previous Web-based applications, developers had to insert their script directly into an HTML document that was also used to generate the user interface. The end result was code that could be difficult to read and maintain.
- In IIS applications, you can reuse pages in different contexts. Unlike HTML, where information to move from page to page must be embedded in the HTML itself, navigation information for a page in a Visual Basic Internet application is stored separately from the page itself. This allows you to reuse the page in several places in your application, changing the navigation each time depending on the context.
- You can lessen download time and therefore reduce your network load, because the system does not need to download large components to run the application.
- You can easily maintain application state, such as the user's name or account number, between client requests. Depending on the type of application, you can manage state on the client, the server, or both.
- You can debug your IIS and DHTML applications using Visual Basic's standard debugging tools. Script and CGI-based Internet applications, on the other hand, can be very difficult to debug.

Security and Internet Applications

This section briefly introduces security issues for your Visual Basic Internet applications.

Security for DHTML Applications

DHTML applications are affected by security in the following ways:

- You may encounter zone security in Internet Explorer 4.*x* when you attempt to download your DHTML application to a client. For an explanation of security zones, see the Internet Client SDK, available on your MSDN CD.
- When you deploy your DHTML application, you must make sure the deployment files are properly signed and licensed. For more information, see Chapter 4, "Downloading ActiveX Components."

Security for IIS Applications

IIS applications face the same restrictions listed for DHTML applications in the section above. In addition, IIS applications have additional security options based on the fact that all IIS applications use an Active Server Page (ASP) as the entry point into the application. You can secure an ASP page in several ways:

- You can set permissions on the virtual directory on your Web server that contains the ASP page.
- You can set file access permissions, if you are using the Windows NT File system (NTFS) to determine which users can access the ASP page.
- You can use client certificates through two protocols known as Secure Sockets Layer (SSL) 3.0 or through Private Communications Technology (PCT). A *client certificate* is an encrypted number the browser sends to the server when it requests the ASP page.

For More Information See "An Introduction to Webclasses" in Chapter 3, "Developing IIS Applications," for more information on the relationship between IIS applications and ASP pages.

System Requirements for Internet Applications

System requirements vary depending on whether you're developing DHTML applications or IIS applications.

DHTML Application Requirements

System requirements for DHTML applications vary for the development computer and the end-user's computer.

The Development Computer

In order to create and test client intranet applications, you must have Internet Explorer 4.01 SP1 or later installed on your computer. In addition, you may want the HTML editor of your choice and other programs you use to create Web pages, such as image editors, and any supplemental programs your DHTML application will use, such as database programs.

The End-User Computer

End-users of a DHTML application must have Internet Explorer 4.0 or later. The first time end users download a DHTML application, they must download the Visual Basic run-time (Msvbvm50.dll) if it is not already on their computer. For subsequent applications, they do not need to download this file again. In addition, if the application uses ActiveX components, the end user must download those as well. You should be certain to include all necessary components in your download files.

IIS Application Requirements

System requirements for IIS Applications vary for the development computer, the deployment computer, and the end-user's computer.

The Development Computer

To create and test IIS applications, you need to have Internet Explorer 4.0 and a Web server installed on your development computer that is capable of running Active Server Pages. You can use any of the combinations in the table below for development purposes:

Operating System	Web Server
Windows NT Server 4.0 or later	Internet Information Server 3.0 or later, with Active Server Pages
Windows NT Workstation 4.0 or later	Peer Web Services 3.0 or later, with Active Server Pages
Windows 95 or later	Personal Web Server 3.0 or later, with Active Server Pages

Important If you are using Windows NT Server or Windows NT Workstation, you must have Service Pack 3.0 installed.

The Deployment Computer

For deployment purposes, you must have Microsoft Internet Information Server, along with any supplemental system such as database applications that are needed by your application.

The End-User Computer

End users of an IIS application must have a browser installed. Although Internet Explorer 4.0 or later is recommended, any browser can act as the front end of an IIS application.

For More Information See Chapter 2, "Developing DHTML Applications," for more information on creating, testing, and deploying intranet applications. See Chapter 3, "Developing IIS Applications," for more information on creating, testing, and deploying IIS applications.

Other Internet Technologies in Visual Basic

In addition to DHTML applications and IIS applications, there are other types of Internet functionality you can add to your projects in Visual Basic, including:

- ActiveX components that can be used on HTML pages, either as part of an IIS or DHTML application or not. ActiveX components include controls, code components, and ActiveX documents. Using some or all of these solutions, you can create highly functional Internet solutions for your business needs.
- Internet extensions for Visual Basic applications. You can use special controls that provide some Internet-related functionality. These include the Internet Transfer control, the WebBrowser control, and the WinSock Control.

ActiveX Controls

ActiveX controls enliven and add power to your HTML pages. In addition to creating your own controls, you can use the Internet controls provided with the Professional and Enterprise editions of Visual Basic to extend standard applications with Internet technology. For example, you can use ActiveX controls on a Web page to add customized menus to your web pages, add a scrolling banner you can use to present advertisements or important announcements, or add animated effects.

Using HTML and VBScript, you can include ActiveX controls on an HTML page, set their properties, call their methods, and handle their events.

For More Information See Chapter 9, "Building ActiveX Controls," in Part 2: "Creating ActiveX Components," for information on developing ActiveX controls for your Visual Basic applications.

ActiveX Code Components

You can use ActiveX code components (.dll or .exe files) to add functionality to an HTML page on either the client or server. Code components on the client can offer an increase in speed, since users' commands do not need to be routed back to the server. Server components also have the benefit of being able to show user interface elements.

For More Information See Chapter 2, "Creating an ActiveX DLL," Chapter 3, "Creating an ActiveX EXE Component," or Chapter 8, "Building Code Components," in Part 2: "Creating ActiveX Components," for information on developing ActiveX components for your Visual Basic applications.

ActiveX Documents

ActiveX documents integrate tightly with the other elements of your Internet or intranet site. You can use ActiveX documents in conjunction with DHTML applications, IIS applications, or HTML pages that are not associated with a Visual Basic Internet application. You can deploy these components so that users can navigate transparently between ActiveX documents and other pages in your application or Web site.

You might use ActiveX documents within your Internet applications for two reasons:

- If you need to use the Visual Basic programming model rather than the programming model used in DHTML or IIS applications.
- If you want to have control over the whole frame of the browser window, rather than just a part of it. When you display a Web page in the browser, the HTML you write to display the page lets you specify the appearance of only the page itself. You cannot write HTML to control the menu, the scroll bar, or any other part of the browser window. When you use an ActiveX document, you can control additional pieces of the window: You can add menus, toolbars, scroll bars, and other items. For example, if you want one page of your DHTML application to contain a custom menu, you might use an ActiveX document.

As is the case with the elements of an HTML page, ActiveX documents that are not installed on users' computers can be automatically downloaded when users navigate to them — and upgraded automatically if the versions on the server are more recent.

For More Information See Chapter 11, "Building ActiveX Documents," in Part 2: "Creating ActiveX Components," for information on creating an ActiveX document.

Internet Extensions for Standard Applications

The Professional and Enterprise Editions of Visual Basic also include controls designed specifically to encapsulate Internet-related technology. These include:

- Internet Transfer Control — Packages three common Internet protocols: HyperText Transfer Protocol (HTTP), File Transfer Protocol (FTP), and Gopher.
- WinSock Control — Allows you to connect to a remote computer and exchange data using either the User Datagram Protocol (UDP) or the Transmission Control Protocol (TCP).

In addition, a WebBrowser control that is available when you install Internet Explorer 4.*x* allows you to run Web pages as part of a Visual Basic form.

For More Information For information about the Internet Transfer control and the WinSock control, see Part 1: "Using ActiveX Controls." For information on using the WebBrowser control, see the *Internet Client SDK* on the MSDN Library CD, under the heading "SDK Documentation."

CHAPTER 2

Developing DHTML Applications

A DHTML application is a Visual Basic application that uses a combination of dynamic HTML and compiled Visual Basic code in an interactive, browser-based application. A DHTML application resides on the browser machine, where it interprets and responds to actions the end user performs in the browser.

In its simplest form, a DHTML application can be a single HTML page that uses Visual Basic code and the Dynamic HTML object model to instantly respond to actions that occur on the page. This could involve responding to user-initiated actions such as mouse movements and clicks, or responding to actions the browser itself performs, such as opening the page or loading a picture. These are just a few of the things you could do with a more complicated DHTML application:

- Retrieve data from the page and use it to query a database.
- Update the page's appearance and behavior.
- Create HTML elements and insert them onto a page in response to user requests.

DHTML applications use Visual Basic code to perform much of the same processing you might have previously done with script, CGI processing, and other methods of Internet application development — and much of it can be done without transferring processing to the server.

DHTML applications are named for dynamic HTML, a technology extension of Internet Explorer 4.*x* that allows developers and end users to interact with Web pages in new ways. DHTML applications must be run on Internet Explorer 4.*x*.

This chapter assumes that you are familiar with some basic Internet concepts that are covered in Chapter 1, "Introduction to Internet Applications." See it for more information on Internet technologies in general, including HTTP, the Internet development environment, and models of Web browser and Web server interaction.

Contents

Sample Applications: DhShowMe.vbp and PropBag.vbp

DhShowMe.vbp demonstrates several techniques for incorporating Dynamic HTML functionality into the Web pages you create for DHTML applications and into your Visual Basic code. The pages in this application demonstrate how you can use Dynamic HTML to change the styles, layout, and elements on your Web pages, and how you can use the object model to handle events at multiple levels of the page. If you installed the sample applications, you will find DhShowMe.vbp in the \Program Files\Microsoft Visual Studio\Common Files\Samples\VB\DhShowMe directory.

PropBag.vbp demonstrates how to use the GetProperty and PutProperty functions to save state between your Web pages in a DHTML application. If you installed the sample applications, you will find PropBag.vbp in the in the \Program Files\Microsoft Visual Studio\Common Files\Samples\VB\PropBag directory.

What is a DHTML Application?

A DHTML application is a group of HTML pages that work together to perform a business process. You write Visual Basic code to handle events that occur when these pages are viewed in the browser. You can respond to events that occur on any element on the page — from clicking a button to loading an image to passing the mouse over a certain part of the page.

Most of the processing associated with a DHTML application occurs on the client computer, although the application can make calls to the server. However, performing the majority of processing on the client (in this case, the browser) allows your applications to respond quickly to user actions without making time-consuming trips to the server. In addition, corporations can lower the cost of training and support associated with their applications by presenting commonly used information and applications through the browser.

The end user views a DHTML application with Internet Explorer 4.0 or later. DHTML applications are designed to work most optimally on intranets. An *intranet* is a Web site or series of Web sites that belong to an organization and can be accessed only by the organization's members. Many corporations use an intranet, rather than the Internet, to offer their employees easy access to corporate information, such as customer order information, sales data, or performance figures, while preventing outside access to that data.

In addition to writing Visual Basic code to hook up to a Web page, you can use a special designer in Visual Basic to create Web pages that act as the user interface of your application. You can also pull an existing Web page into Visual Basic and modify it. This allows you to tailor the process to your preferences — if you are familiar with HTML and want to create your own pages you can do so using the DHTML Page designer. If not, you can have an experienced Web developer create the pages and simply add them to your application.

Note See Chapter 1, "Introduction to Internet Applications," for more information on Internet technologies in general, including HTTP, the Internet development environment, and models of Web browser and Web server interaction.

Important You must use Internet Explorer version 4.01 or later if you want to create or run a DHTML application in Visual Basic.

Web Pages vs. Forms

DHTML applications are structured differently than forms-based Visual Basic applications. In a DHTML application, the user interface consists of a series of HTML pages rather than forms. An HTML page is like a form in that it contains all the visual elements that make up your application's user interface. You can place the some of the same items into a page as you do a form, including text, buttons, checkboxes, and radio buttons.

An HTML page is stored in an .htm file that is analogous to a .frm file, in that it is used to render and display the form to the end user. You can create these pages yourself, or a Web designer or a developer can create the pages and you can then link the finished pages into your project.

The following table sums up the differences between forms-based applications and Web-based applications:

	Forms-based application	Web-based application
User interface	Visual Basic forms	HTML pages
UI elements (for example, text boxes, buttons, images)	controls	elements
File format	.frm files	.htm or .html files, or generated from Visual Basic code
Creator	developer	Web designer or developer
Run time	Visual Basic run-time DLL, msvbvm50.dll	Web browser or Web browser control, with msvbvm50.dll

Structure of DHTML Applications

DHTML applications are made up of the following pieces:

- One or more HTML pages.
- Visual Basic code that handles the events generated from the HTML pages.
- A run-time component that hosts the page in the Web browser or Web browser control.
- A project DLL that contains your Visual Basic code and is accessed by the run-time component, generated automatically when you debug or compile.

There is a one-to-one relationship between the designers and the HTML pages in your project. For each page in your application, there is a page designer.

Advantages of DHTML Applications

Building a DHTML application in Visual Basic provides several advantages over other methods of Internet development. DHTML applications give you:

- **Dynamic HTML**. When you create a DHTML application, you have full access to the richness of Dynamic HTML, integrated with the power of Visual Basic code and controls. See "Dynamic HTML in Visual Basic" for more information about the Dynamic HTML features you can access.
- **Lessened server load**. DHTML applications conserve server resources because each request or user action does not have to be routed through the Web server.

- **Fewer refreshes, faster responses**. When an end user's actions initiate changes to a typical Web page, the browser must refresh the page from the server. In a DHTML application, the browser can process user data, make changes to the page's layout and appearance, and process code all without refreshing the page.
- **Dynamic interaction**. Visual Basic code on a Web page can directly manipulate any element on the page and create and manage new elements on the fly, allowing for truly dynamic user interfaces.
- **Improved state management**. Typically, HTML pages are *stateless* — that is, no information about an HTTP request is maintained after the response is received from the server. Visual Basic DHTML applications allow you to store state between requests, without using the server. Therefore, multiform or multipage applications are possible without requiring server interaction, complex URL-based state, or cookies.
- **Offline capability**. For a DHTML application, users can browse to and use a DHTML application on their corporate intranet. Later, when disconnected, the same users can still make use of their Web-based application through the browser's cached storage.
- **Code security**. When you embed scripts within an HTML page, anyone can access your page, read the script, and make changes to it. Using Visual Basic to develop your DHTML application, your code is compiled, is not part of the HTML page itself, and cannot be tampered with as easily.

For More Information For more information about HTTP, see "Understanding Internet Basics" in Chapter 1, "Introduction to Internet Applications."

Key Events in DHTML Applications

Your DHTML application goes through several main events during its lifetime. There are three objects involved in the life of the application:

- The **BaseWindow object** represents an instance of the browser and is used to display the Document object.
- The **Document object** represents the HTML page the end user views in the Web browser or Web browser control. You use events in the Document object to access the Dynamic HTML object model and handle user actions in the browser. The Document object, in turn, contains the DHTMLPage object.
- The **DHTMLPage object** is contained by the document object, and represents a run-time utility that hooks up the page to its Visual Basic code when the application runs. The DHTMLPage object provides functionality such as a load, unload, initialize, and terminate events for your HTML pages. You cannot access the DHTMLPage object directly through the Document object.

The following figure shows how these objects work together:

Page Designer Top-Level Objects

```
BaseWindow Object
 │
 │ displays
 └Document Object
   │
   │ contains
   └DHTMLPage Object
```

The DHTMLPage object manages the lifetime of your HTML pages with the following sequence of events:

1. The Initialize event occurs early in the loading process, whenever the run-time DLL for the application is created or recreated by the system. It is always the first event in a DHTML application. When the Initialize event is fired, not all objects on the page have been loaded, so object references may not be valid. Because of this, you should not use the Initialize event to reference and set properties for elements on the page.
2. The Load event occurs later in the loading process, after the Initialize event. If your page is loading asynchronously, the Load event is fired after the first element on the page has been created. If your page is loading synchronously, the Load event is fired after all of the elements have been created. You can use the Load event to set information on the page.
3. The Unload event occurs when the end user moves to another page referenced by the DHTMLPageDesigner object or closes the application. During unload, all of the objects on the HTML page still exist. This is therefore a good time to do any state management, cleanup, or other processing that needs to reference items on the page.
4. The Terminate event occurs when the HTML page is about to be destroyed. None of the objects on the page exist in memory during the terminate event, so you cannot use this event to reference items on the page for state management or other processing.

For More Information See "Document Object Model" in the "Dynamic HTML" section of the *Internet Client SDK* for a full list of the properties, methods, and events available for the Document object. For information on how to use the Dynamic HTML object model in Visual Basic, see "Writing Code with Dynamic HTML" in this chapter.

Dynamic HTML in Visual Basic

Dynamic HTML is an extension of HTML that allows Web authors and developers to create pages that dynamically update their content and interact with the user without relying on scripts or server-side processing. When you create a DHTML application, the resulting pages use the Dynamic HTML technology in Internet Explorer 4.*x*. Dynamic HTML's object model allows you to interact with HTML pages in new ways — for example, manipulating their properties, methods, and events, and exercising finer control over the layout of the pages.

A summary of key features of Dynamic HTML is presented in the following topics:

- Element Appearance in DHTML Applications
- Element Positioning in DHTML Applications
- Event Bubbling in DHTML Applications

HTML Elements As Objects

An HTML page consists of a series of objects that are called elements. Elements on a page can include simple items such as headings, paragraphs of text, and images, or more complicated items such as form fields, or tables and their rows, columns, and cells. On the surface, the page's elements correspond very closely to the items in a Visual Basic form. However, in past versions of HTML you could not access properties and events on all of these objects: only certain elements were available to be programmed.

With Dynamic HTML, you can now access and manipulate every element on a Web page. This allows you to treat an HTML page much like a form — you can change the attributes for any element, write code or script that performs actions on it, and access its methods and events.

For More Information See "The Dynamic HTML Object Model in Visual Basic," later in this chapter, for more information on the objects available in DHTML applications. See "Dynamic HTML" in the *Internet Client SDK* for more information on features of Dynamic HTML. See Chapter 9, "Programming with Objects," in the *Microsoft Visual Basic 6.0 Programmer's Guide,* for more information on the basics of object programming.

Element Appearance in DHTML Applications

Dynamic HTML allows you to create richer, more interactive user interfaces by allowing you to:

- Use additional measurement units, for finer control over the positioning of page elements.
- Create elements that wrap around other elements, nest within them, or act as blocks.
- Have finer control over tables.
- Support additional types of graphics, including *.mpg files* (movie clips) and *.png files* (portable network graphics designed to address some of the shortcomings of .gif files), and other media types registered with the browser.

In addition, you can make use of dynamic styles and dynamic content to fine-tune the appearance of your page.

Dynamic Styles

Originally, HTML was intended to provide a way to separate the structure and content of a Web page from its presentation. That is, the HTML code that defined a page's content and structure was not intended to also define the physical appearance of elements on the page. In earlier version of HTML, this separation was not possible. The only way to allow users to control the formatting of page elements was to introduce tags such as bold <B> and italic <I> and a variety of attributes that controlled such things as font style and size.

With Dynamic HTML, the original intent of HTML is realized in that you can use *cascading style sheets* (CSS) to format your page elements. The code controlling the appearance of page elements can be stored in a style sheet. This style sheet is kept separate from the HTML code controlling the page's content and structure.

A style sheet is a collection of properties that control the appearance of elements on a Web page. Style sheets can apply a style to a group of elements, or to a single element. In addition, you can apply multiple styles to each element on the page. There are three main types of styles you can use in your DHTML applications:

- *Inline styles* are styles applied to a single element and applied within the element's HTML tag. This is the least flexible way to use styles.
- *Global style sheets* are defined at the beginning of an HTML file and set and apply styles for all elements within the page. This is a flexible way to set all styles for a single page.
- *Linked style sheets* are stored in a separate file and can apply to multiple pages. This is the most powerful and flexible way to set styles for an application that uses more than one page.

The advantage of using style sheets is that it is very easy to make changes to a page's appearance without writing code. That is, you can change a single line of code in the style sheet — such as increasing the font size of an element — and have that change be reflected in multiple locations throughout your page or in multiple pages. In previous version of HTML, you would have had to make the same change in each location where you wanted to alter the page's appearance. Because of this, it is preferable to avoid using inline styles as much as possible, and store your style information in either a global or a linked style sheet.

> **Note** To define global style sheets in your DHTML applications, you need to edit your application's HTML pages in an external editor, as Visual Basic does not provide a way to define styles sheets within the designer. However, if you use the designer to open a page that references a style sheet, the styles for that document appear in the toolbar.

For More Information For more information on using style sheets in your applications, see "Dynamic Styles" in the "Dynamic HTML" section of the *Internet Client SDK.*

Dynamic Content

Dynamic content means that you can customize or replace the contents of a page after the page has been loaded, without making a trip to the server. In past version of HTML, any change to a page's contents required the browser to submit a request to the Web server and then wait for a new version of the page to be sent. Customization required more processing time, and it was often difficult to retain context for the page's contents.

Using the properties and methods provided in Dynamic HTML, you can easily add new elements with events or remove existing elements. In addition, you can change portions of existing elements by inserting new content within them.

For More Information For more information on using style sheets in your applications, see "Dynamic Content" in the "Dynamic HTML" section of the *Internet Client SDK.*

Element Positioning in DHTML Applications

Several features of Dynamic HTML give you detailed control over the position and behavior of elements on an HTML page. You can control where an object is placed, and work with special effects such as animation, transitions and filters, and automatic resizing.

Positioning and Animation

Positioning is the ability to place an HTML element at a specific point in a page by assigning an x- and y-coordinate and a z-plane to that element. This means you can place elements exactly where you want them and achieve special, overlapping effects by defining how elements should be stacked on top of one another.

Because the object model gives you access to styles and style sheets, you can set and change the position of an element as simply as you set and change its color. This makes it especially easy to change the position of elements based on how the user is viewing the page, or to animate the elements. For animation, all you need is to slightly modify the position of an element at some regular interval.

For More Information For more information on positioning effects, see "Positioning in the Dynamic HTML" section of the *Internet Client SDK.*

Automatic Resizing and Scrolling

In a standard Visual Basic application, you have to write code that tells the system how to respond when a user resizes a form. In a Web page built with Dynamic HTML, the Web browser automatically handles the resize event and adjusts the user interface accordingly. In Dynamic HTML, percentages can be used as sizes for elements. In addition, you can anchor elements at a particular place in the flow of text. This enables a page to resize flawlessly.

In addition, you can now create bottomless, scrollable forms. Forms in Visual Basic do not scroll and have a set size. HTML pages, however, always include a scroll bar and can be considered bottomless because the user can continue scrolling as long as there are elements to view.

Filters and Transitions

Internet Explorer 4.0 enables you to specify filters and transitions using cascading style sheet, or CSS, properties. *Filters* are effects (such as text drop shadows) that can be applied to content on Web pages. *Transitions* are effects that can be applied when changing the display of an element — switching from one image to another, for example. Both transitions between pages and transitions on specific elements within a page are supported.

In addition to the set of standard filters and transitions included in Internet Explorer 4.0, the standard filters and transitions can be supplemented by additional third-party filters and transitions.

For More Information For more information on filters and transitions, see "Filters and Transitions" in the "Dynamic HTML" section of the *Internet Client SDK.*

Event Bubbling in DHTML Applications

Unlike standard Visual Basic programming, where each object must have its own unique event handler, objects in Dynamic HTML can share event handlers. When an event occurs on a child object, the event can travel up the chain of hierarchy within the page until it encounters an event handler to process the event. This process is called event bubbling.

The following figure shows the process of event bubbling.

Event Bubbling Process

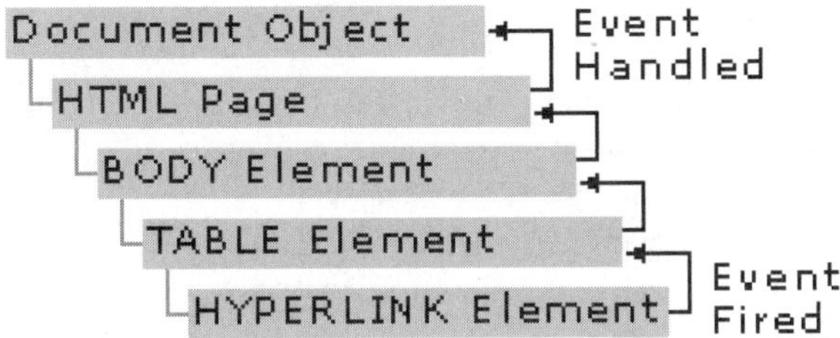

In this picture, the diagram displays a portion of the structure of an HTML page within a DHTML application. The top level is the Document object, which contains the HTML page. The Body element is the top-level tag in the HTML page. Within the body is a table, and within the table is a hyperlink. In a sense, the hyperlink can be said to be the child of the table, which is in turn a child of the body tag, and so forth.

When the hyperlink event fires, Visual Basic can bubble that event up the hierarchy until it finds an event handler. If it does not find an event handler in the hyperlink, it looks in the table, then the body, then the DHTMLPage object, and finally in the document. The event stops bubbling the first time it finds an event handler.

> **Note** The hierarchy through which events bubble up is determined by the position of elements in the HTML stream. This order does not necessarily correspond to the order of items you view on the screen. For example, in the picture above, the Hyperlink element appears beneath the table in the HTML stream. If you use position attributes on the Hyperlink to move it so that it appears elsewhere when it is displayed in the browser, its events will still bubble up to the table because its position in the HTML stream is unchanged.

Event bubbling can reduce the amount of code you need to write. For example, suppose you want a second set of options to become available when a check box is selected. Rather than writing a click event procedure for each check box on your form, you can write the procedure on the form itself. When one of the check boxes is selected, the event will automatically bubble up to the parent form and be processed there.

You can cancel event bubbling on an element if you do not want the element's events to bubble up the hierarchy. You stop bubbling by setting the cancelBubble property of the event object to true in any event handler. After the handler returns, the event stops bubbling and comes to an immediate end.

For More Information For more detailed information on how to bubble events or cancel bubbling, see "Understanding the Event Model" in the "Dynamic HTML" section of the *Internet Client SDK.*

Design Considerations for DHTML Applications

There are several factors you should keep in mind when creating a DHTML application. These include deciding how you want your application to load in the Web browser or Web browser control, and making decisions about the layout and structure of the pages you create. You must make sure that the elements on your page are properly named and that your pages do not contain any references that would prevent the application from locating related files.

General Considerations

- **Follow principles of good Web design**. The HTML pages you develop for your application should follow principles of good Web design that are described in most HTML style references. For example, you should remember that end users sometimes view Web pages with the pictures turned off. This can make your application difficult or impossible to use if you embed key information in images. Keep this in mind as you design your interface, and provide backup mechanisms for any crucial information presented in a picture.
- **Only elements with an ID attribute can be programmed**. If you create your HTML pages outside of Visual Basic and then import them into the page designer, be sure to give all of the elements for which you want to handle events a unique ID attribute so that you can manipulate them easily in your Visual Basic code.
- **All IDs must be unique when you use Dynamic HTML in Visual Basic**. In a Visual Basic project, all of the names and IDs you give to forms, their elements, and associated modules must be unique. Dynamic HTML used outside of Visual Basic does not have this same restriction — multiple items on an HTML page created outside of Visual Basic can be given the same ID. If you use a page with duplicate IDs in Visual Basic, the page designer appends numbers to the duplicate IDs to make them unique. When you use an external page, be aware that some IDs may be changed.
- **Use relative URLs**. Your application and its HTML pages can be deployed onto a Web server with a different directory structure than the one on the development computer. Because of this, it is best to use relative URLs in your HTML pages rather than absolute URLs. *Absolute URLs* indicate the exact drive and directory in which your HTML page will expect to find any related images or other files it references. *Relative URLs* give the name of the file to locate and indicate its location in relation to your project directory, specifying how many directories up or down to move to find the reference.

- **Use style sheets whenever possible**. Rather than accessing the style property of an individual element to set an element's physical appearance, use global or linked style sheets as much as possible. Global or linked style sheets allow you to take full advantage of the flexible nature of Dynamic HTML. For more information on styles in Dynamic HTML, see "Element Appearance in DHTML Applications," earlier in this chapter.
- **Not all properties cascade**. In Dynamic HTML, most properties that you set for a page can cascade down to the page's children through style sheets. For example, if you set a font for the page, paragraphs, buttons, and other elements with text will inherit that font setting and use the same font. When you set a background color, however, it does not cascade down to any of the object's children.
- **Some objects cannot be moved once you place them on the page**. Some Visual Basic controls, such as the common dialog or the sysinfo control, are invisible at run time. If you add one of these objects to your HTML page, you cannot select it and move it around within the page after you initially draw it. You can, however, select the control in the treeview and either delete it or access its properties.
- **You cannot use the page designer in a single-threaded DLL.** To create a DHTML application, you must set your project to be apartment-threaded. You set this on the General tab of the Project Properties dialog box.

Asynchronous Loading Considerations

When the system loads a Visual Basic form, the entire form is loaded and then displayed. When the system loads an HTML page into a Web browser or Web browser control, some parts of the page that load more quickly are displayed first, while the browser finishes loading and displaying other portions of the page. This process is called *asynchronous loading* and presents some unique challenges for a Web application. Users may have access to some parts of your user interface before other, dependent elements appear. For example, if the code behind a command button references an event on an image control, an error can occur if the user selects the button before the image is loaded.

> **Note** By default, asynchronous loading is turned off for your HTML pages. If you want to change this setting, you can set the AsyncLoad property for page to True.

To lessen the effects of asynchronous loading in your application:

- **When possible, leave AsyncLoad set to False**. To prevent the browser from displaying any part of the page until the entire page is loaded, set the AsyncLoad property on the page designer to False. This makes the browser wait to run any Visual Basic code until all elements and events are loaded. False is the default setting of this property.

- **When you must use asynchronous loading, check for the existence of an object before you reference it**. When you must use asynchronous loading, it is best to not write code that crosses object boundaries by referencing one object on the page from within another object. There are times, however, when crossing object boundaries will be necessary. In these cases, include code that checks to see whether the object exists, or provide error handling that tells the system how to react when the referenced object does not exist.
- **Don't rely on backward references to avoid trouble**. *Backward referencing* means using references to only those elements on the page that appear above the current item. The assumption is that the page will load in an orderly, top-to-bottom fashion. This is not the case. Elements on an HTML page can load in a random order.

DHTML Application Development Process

The process of creating a DHTML application is similar to creating any other project in Visual Basic. The overall process is presented below. Details for each step in the process can be found in later topics in this chapter.

These are the steps you perform to create a DHTML application. For more information on the individual steps in the process, see the following sections.

1. Start a new project and select DHTML Application as the project type.
2. From the Project Explorer window, open the designer.
3. If you are designing your user interface from scratch, add HTML elements and ActiveX controls to your page and arrange them as desired.
4. If you want to edit an existing page, use the Properties dialog box to reference an external HTML file, then make any necessary changes to the page's contents and appearance.
5. Add code for any elements on the page for which you want to handle user actions.
6. If necessary, add other pages to the project, add elements to them, and write code.
7. Test and debug the application by running the project and viewing the document in Internet Explorer 4.01 Service Pack 1 or later.
8. Compile the project.
9. Deploy the application using the Package and Deployment Wizard.

Beginning Your DHTML Application Project

When you begin a DHTML application, you select a special type of project called a *DHTML Application* project. A DHTML Application project is an ActiveX DLL project that automatically sets the correct references you need to access the designer for your HTML pages and the appropriate toolbox tab and controls.

Visual Basic automatically inserts a designer into the project and displays it on the screen when you open this project type. The designer corresponds to a single HTML page and acts as the base on which you create its user interface. If you want to include more than one HTML page in your application, you can insert additional designers into your project.

The application you create runs as an in-process component in the Web browser or Web browser control. For more information on in-process components, see "In-Process and Out-of-Process Components," in Chapter 6, "General Principles of Component Design," in Part 2, "Creating ActiveX Components."

To begin your DHTML application

1. Start a new project and select **DHTML Application** as your project type.
2. In the Project Explorer window, open the Designers folder, then double-click on **DHTMLPage1** to display it in the main window.

To add additional DHTML pages to your project

1. On the **Project** menu, click **Add DHTML Page** and Visual Basic adds a new page designer to your project.

   Note The first four kinds of ActiveX designers loaded for a project are listed on the **Project** menu. If more than four designers are loaded, the later ones will be available from the **More ActiveX Designers** submenu on the **Project** menu.

2. In the **DHTMLPage Properties** dialog box, choose how you want to save your HTML pages, then click **OK**.

Save Options for Pages and Designers

When you add pages to the project, you must make decisions about how your page will be saved and whether you will create a new page or edit an existing HTML page from your hard drive. There are two ways you can save your page:

- Save it within the designer file. This method allows you to easily share files between developers or move your development project from machine to machine without worrying about paths to any external pages. However, saving your page in this way prevents you from using the Launch Editor feature to edit it in an external HTML or text editor.
- Save the page to a location on your computer. This method creates external HTML files that are referenced in the designer's SourceFile property by an absolute path. When you save to an external file, you can use the Launch Editor feature to edit the page in an external HTML or text editor. However, moving your file from machine to machine may cause the path you entered for your source file to become invalid.

The SourceFile property for the designer reflects the save method you choose. When you save within the designer, the SourceFile property is blank. When you specify an external file, the SourceFile property reflects the full path to the file you selected.

The save options you choose apply only until the project is built. At that time, the system generates external HTML files for the pages in your project and stores them in the location you specify.

Specifying Save Options for a Page

To access the DHTMLPage Properties dialog box

- Select the page designer and then click the Properties toolbar icon.

To save your HTML page within the designer files until the project is built

- Click **Save HTML inside the designer** in the **.DHTMLPage Properties** dialog box.

To create a new page and save it to a location on your computer

1. Click **Save HTML in an external file** in the **.DHTMLPage Properties** dialog box.
2. Click **New**, enter a file name for your page, and click **OK**.

To import an existing page and save it to a location on your computer

1. Click **Save HTML in an external file** in the **.DHTMLPage Properties** dialog box.
2. Click **Open**, choose the file you want to edit, and click **OK**.

To import an existing page but save it within the designer

1. Click **Save HTML in an external file** in the **.DHTMLPage Properties** dialog box.
2. Click **New**, choose the file you want to import, and click **OK**.
3. Click **Apply** to import the page.
4. Click **Save HTML within the designer**.
5. Click **OK** to return to the page designer.

   Visual Basic sets the value of the SourceFile property to reflect the choices you made.

   > **Note** You can edit the SourceFile property directly to make the same choices. Enter a path and file name in the Properties window to import a file or save to an external file, or clear the contents of the SourceFile property to save the page within the designer.

Designing Pages for DHTML Applications

There are three ways you can create the user interface of your DHTML application:

- You can create pages from scratch, adding HTML elements from the toolbox and arranging them as desired.
- You or a Web developer can create pages in an external HTML editor, then you can reference them in the page designer.
- You can use a combination of both methods.

Page Design: Visual Basic vs. HTML Editors

When you create pages in Visual Basic, you add HTML elements to the designer and arrange them on the page. You do not need to know any HTML tags to build a page in this way, because Visual Basic creates the tags and attributes for each element for you. This method of design is quick and easy and allows you to create functional pages without learning the details of HTML.

However, Visual Basic is not designed to be an advanced HTML editor and does not contain some of the features you will find in many HTML editors. For example, you cannot view the source code for your page, and you cannot easily work with advanced features such as animation. It is best to create your pages in Visual Basic when your application's user interface will be relatively simple and you do not want to work in the HTML source code.

If you are more familiar with HTML or you want to incorporate more advanced features into your pages, you should create your pages in an external editor and then import them into Visual Basic. Creating pages externally gives you several advantages:

- You can use the editor of your choice, with any advanced features it includes. This may give you finer control over the appearance and layout of the page.
- You can access the source code for the HTML page and perform fine-tuning that you cannot do in the page designer.
- You can have a graphic designer or another person create the pages if you prefer not to create them yourself.

You can use a variety of external programs to create your HTML pages, including editors such as Microsoft FrontPage, a word processing program such as Microsoft Word, or Notepad.

In addition to using Visual Basic or an external program to create your pages, you can use a combination of both methods. You can create the preliminary page layout in Visual Basic, then open the page in an editor to do any fine-tuning, or you can create the page in an editor and rearrange and fine-tune elements in Visual Basic.

Using Existing HTML Pages in the Page Designer

You can use existing HTML pages for your application's user interface rather than designing the pages in Visual Basic. This is useful if you prefer not to design the user interface yourself, or if you want to design it using another tool and then bring it into your Visual Basic application. Using an external program can give you access to the source HTML, rather than just a visual representation of the page, and may give you more advanced functionality when you design the page. You can design your interface in any HTML editor, word processor, or text program.

To use an existing HTML page, you reference it as the source for the page by setting the SourceFile property. Visual Basic loads the file and displays it in the rightmost pane of the designer window. You can then tailor the page's appearance, if necessary, by changing properties or adding, deleting, or rearranging elements on the page.

When the designer loads the page, it also checks to see what elements exist on the page. It displays all elements in the leftmost pane of the designer window, in the treeview.

To reference an existing HTML page

1. If necessary, add a new designer to your project by clicking **Add DHTML Page** from the **Project** menu.

   Note Remember that there is a one-to-one relationship between pages and designers. Each time you want to add a new page to your application, you must first add a designer from the Project menu.

2. In the **DHTMLPage Properties** dialog box, click **Open**, then choose the HTML page you want to import and click **OK**.

   Visual Basic loads the HTML page when you close the dialog box and displays it in the designer window.

For More Information See "Understanding the Page Designer Treeview," later in this chapter, for more information on the treeview and what it displays in the page designer.

Creating New HTML Pages in the Page Designer

You can design HTML pages in Visual Basic, using the DHTML Page designer. The designer allows you to create your application's user interface without explicitly writing any HTML code. Instead, you add HTML elements to the designer's drawing surface, arrange them as desired, and set properties that control their appearance. Visual Basic writes the HTML code for each element behind the scenes, storing it either in an HTML file whose location you specify, or saving it within the designer itself.

It is best to design your pages within Visual Basic when you are creating a relatively simple user interface. Visual Basic does not give you direct access to the source HTML, and it does not contain some of the advanced features you will find in HTML editing programs. If your interface is more complex or you prefer greater control over the HTML source code, you can create your pages in an external program and then link them to your project.

Visual Basic provides a set of HTML elements that you can add to the page when you design HTML pages in Visual Basic. These include the most common HTML elements, such as buttons, text boxes, option buttons, checkboxes, and images. You cannot use intrinsic Visual Basic controls such as the text box or checkbox on your pages; instead you must use the special HTML controls. These controls, called elements, appear automatically on an HTML tab in the toolbox when you add a page to your project.

There are four ways you can add elements to your page:

- You can select the element from the toolbox, then draw it on the detail pane.
- You can double-click the toolbox icon for the element.

- You can drag and drop the element from the toolbox onto the designer's detail pane.
- You can type text directly onto the designer's detail pane to create paragraphs, headings, and other text elements, then set properties to change them to the appropriate style.

In addition to the HTML elements in the toolbox, you can add any ActiveX control to your page. For example, you can use Visual Basic to define an ActiveX control, add it to your toolbox, and insert it on any HTML page.

> **Note** Some Visual Basic controls, such as the common dialog or the sysinfo control, are invisible at run time. If you add one of these objects to your HTML page, you cannot subsequently select it in the drawing surface and move it around within the page. To manipulate one of these controls after you have added it to the page, select it in the treeview.

For More Information For an explanation of the relationship between the elements on an HTML page and the HTML source code, see "Understanding Internet Basics" in Chapter 1, "Introduction to Internet Applications."

To create an HTML page from scratch

1. If necessary, add a new designer to your project by clicking **Add DHTML Page** from the **Project** menu.
2. Add the elements you need to the page:
   - To add text, labels, or headings to your page, click on the page, press ENTER until you reach the location at which you want the text to appear, and then type the text.
   - To add an HTML element to your page, click the appropriate icon from the HTML tab of the toolbox and then draw the element on the page.
   - To add an ActiveX control to your page, switch to the standard tab of the toolbox, select the ActiveX control, and draw the control on the page.

     Note You may need to use the Components dialog box to add the ActiveX control you want to your project before you will see it in the toolbox.
3. Resize and position your elements as you would for any standard Visual Basic project. See "Positioning Elements," later in this chapter, for information on moving HTML elements.
4. Set any default properties to control the appearance of the page.
   - To set properties for the page, such as background color, select the **Body** element in the Properties window list, then set properties.
   - To set properties for an element, select the element in the designer, then set its properties.

   Tip Some HTML elements have a very large number of properties available. It is simplest to work on the Categorized panel when you access the Properties window for these elements. The primary properties (such as ID) appear under the Misc category, while properties dealing with appearance and styles appear under the Style category.

Positioning HTML Elements

After you add elements to your page, you may want to rearrange and fine-tune their positioning. There are several things you should know about positioning elements on the page:

Move text elements with the keyboard. Text elements such as headings, paragraphs, and labels are positioned independently of other elements on the page. You can move text elements by using the ENTER or BACKSPACE keys. Moving a text element in this way does not affect the other elements around it — that is, all of the text elements on your page will move down a line if you press ENTER at the top of the page, but buttons and other visual elements will not be moved.

> **Tip** You can also move align text elements using the toolbar alignment icons.

Move nontext elements with the mouse. You can move elements such as buttons, images, and checkboxes by clicking on them, selecting the gray border around the element, and moving the element to its new location.

> **Note** You must select the border of an element in order to move or delete it. When you select the body of an element, the border shows a series of diagonal lines. When you select the border of an element, the border shows gray fill. You can move an element when the gray fill is visible.

Elements without a run-time interface cannot be repositioned once they are added to the page. Some Visual Basic controls, such as the common dialog or the sysinfo control are invisible at run time. If you add one of these to the page, you cannot select it or reposition it. You can delete the item by selecting it from the treeview and using the shortcut menu option to remove it.

Elements in an HTML page can be layered. In addition to arranging your elements on the page in two-dimensional space, you can layer elements on top of and behind each other by using the Order toolbar options.

There are two positioning modes: absolute and relative. These modes determine how the system interprets your actions as you add elements to the page. It is important to understand the ramifications of choosing between these two modes.

Absolute and Relative Positioning

When you are designing or editing pages in the designer window, you can work in one of two modes: absolute mode or relative mode:

- In absolute positioning mode, all items you drag onto or move on the page are placed at the exact location where you release the cursor. Visual Basic writes information to the HTML for each element that indicates the exact position of the item.

- In relative positioning mode, each new item you drag onto the screen is placed in the next available cursor position. If you have not used the cursor to add any paragraph <P> tags to the page, the elements you drop on the page are positioned in the next available space, moving left to right across the screen, regardless of where you drop the element on the page.

The following screen shows how Visual Basic positions three buttons that are dropped at varying locations on the drawing surface in absolute mode:

Buttons Positioned in Absolute Mode

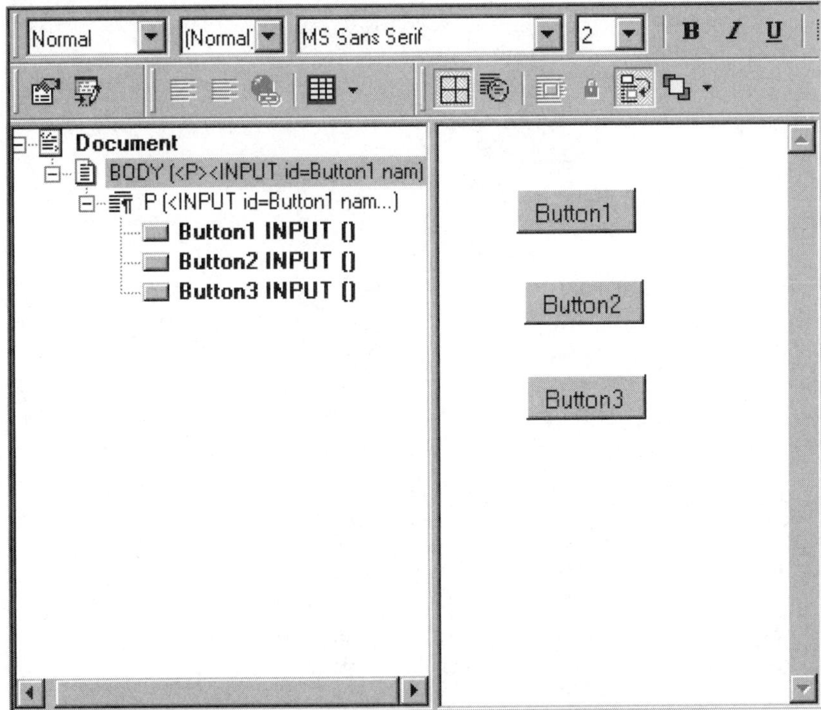

If you were not working in absolute mode and dropped those three buttons onto the screen, they would be positioned as shown in the following screen:

Buttons Positioned in Relative Mode

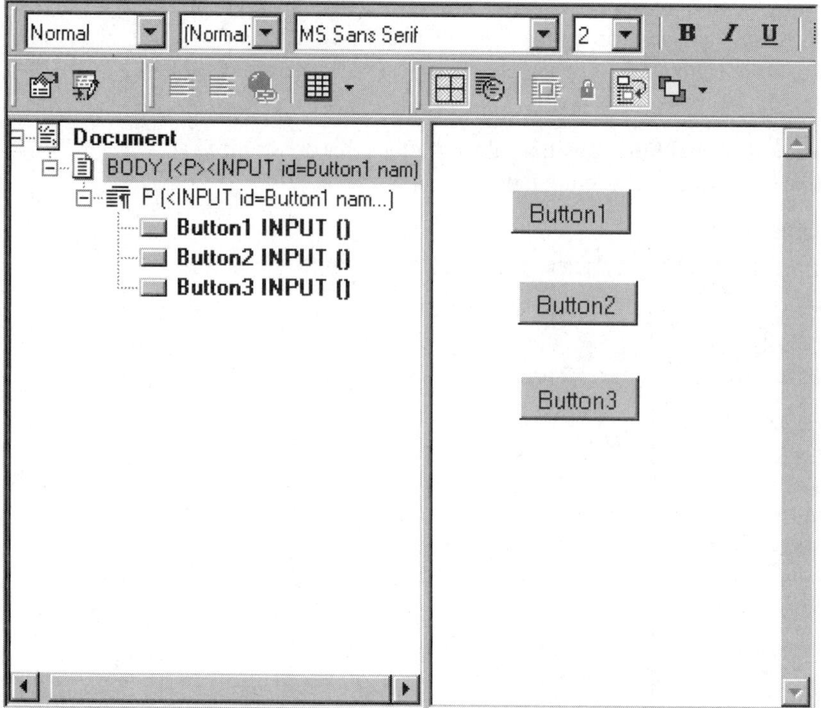

Absolute and relative mode have advantages and disadvantages. Absolute mode allows you finer control over the layout of your page but is not as flexible as relative positioning. With relative positioning, the page can easily adjust to end users with different viewing environments. For example, if the browser screen is small or the computer's resolution is much lower than that on the development machine, only a portion of your absolutely positioned page may appear to the end user. In relative positioning, the page would dynamically wrap its elements and adjust to the browser's screen space.

To change from absolute mode to relative mode, you select or deselect the Absolute Positioning icon on the toolbar. This sets the mode for the entire page.

> **Note** You can also turn on Absolute Positioning for select items on the page, rather than the whole page itself, by using the Absolute Positioning toolbar icon. Selecting this button affects both the selected element and all subsequently created elements on the page unless you deselect it. It does not affect elements already placed on the page.

Layering Elements

You can layer elements on top of and behind each other using z-order properties. Z-order assigns a sequence number to elements that indicates how elements are layered. For example, the following screen shows three layered buttons.

Buttons Arranged in Layers

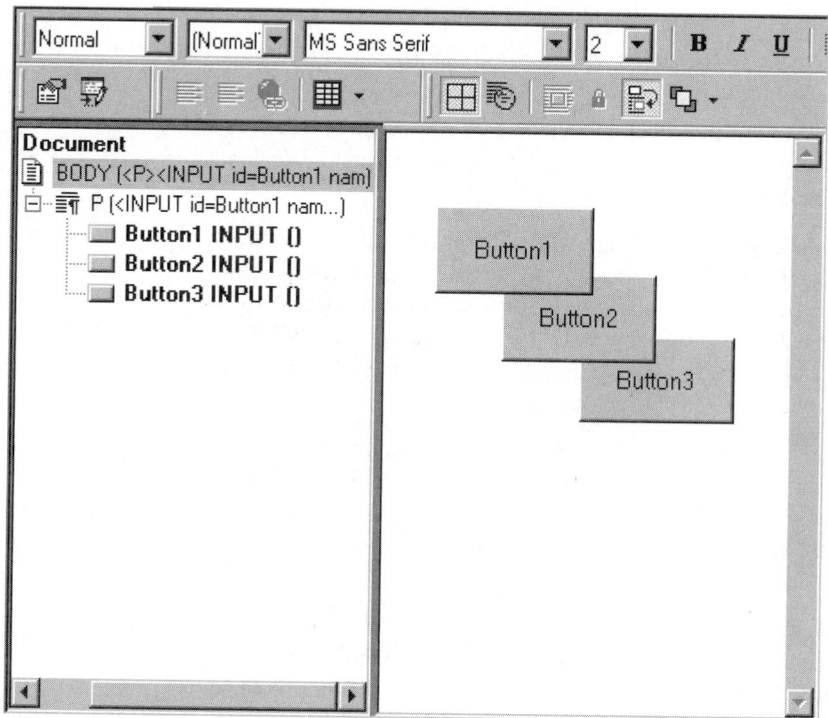

In this screen, three buttons have been arranged so that they overlap. Button1 is in the foreground, with Button2 placed behind it and Button3 placed in the back.

You can manipulate the layering of elements that occupy the same space by selecting the element you want to move forwards or backwards and selecting the Order icon on the toolbar for the page.

Z-ordering in DHTML applications is recorded differently than z-ordering in forms. On an HTML page, the body element, or page surface, is considered to have a z-order value of zero. Items that are layered on top of the body have a positive z-order value, and items that are layered behind the body have a negative z-order value.

Locking Elements

It is easy to accidentally move an element on your HTML page by clicking on it and moving the mouse. You can prevent an element from being moved by locking it. Any absolutely positioned element can be locked in place with the Lock icon on the toolbar.

Grouping HTML Elements

You group sections of an HTML page when you want to perform an action on multiple elements. For example, you might group a series of paragraphs in order to apply a single style to the entire section, instead of to each paragraph individually. You use the HTML tags DIV and SPAN to group your elements in this way:

- DIV is used to group a series of elements into a larger group. For example, you can group multiple paragraphs and headings or several elements on a form together using the DIV tag. DIV is used to offset a group of elements; that is, when you insert a DIV tag in a page, the DIV tag adds a paragraph break after its closing tag. DIV should not be used within a paragraph of text for this reason.
- SPAN is used within an element to group a part of it that is too small to capture with regular HTML tags. For example, you can use the SPAN tag to group a few sentences from within a paragraph, so you can perform actions that affect only that text. SPAN does not make formatting changes to the document as does the DIV tag, and is therefore better suited for use within paragraphs and in other elements where you do not want to introduce more white space.

You can add DIV and SPAN tags to the page designer by highlighting the elements you want to group, then choosing the DIV or SPAN icon from the toolbar. Visual Basic automatically inserts the appropriate opening and closing tags in the HTML for your page. The resulting DIV and SPAN elements appear in the treeview, and you can assign IDs and write code for them.

Grouping elements in DIV and SPAN tags can be an important part of your coding efforts, because it allows you to manipulate precise portions of the page. The following HTML code shows an example of DIV and SPAN tags used to manipulate parts of a Web page:

```
<DIV id="client-fullname" class="client">
<SPAN class="client-lastname">Last name:</SPAN>
<SPAN class="client-firstname">First name:</SPAN>
</DIV>
```

In this example, a DIV tag with the ID “client-fullname” groups the fields that specify the client’s first and last name. Each label is part of a SPAN tag. If you wanted to perform an operation on all of the fields on the form, you could use the DIV tag to do so. If you wanted to perform an operation on just one item in the form, you could use the appropriate SPAN tag.

To add a DIV or SPAN tag to your page

1. Select the elements on your HTML page that you want to enclose in a DIV or SPAN tag.

   Note You can highlight the elements in either the drawing surface or in the treeview.

2. Click the Wrap Selection in <DIV>...</DIV> toolbar icon to add a DIV tag, or the Wrap Selection in <SPAN>...</SPAN> toolbar icon to add a SPAN tag.

   Visual Basic inserts opening and closing tags around your selection.

3. If you want to program the DIV or SPAN elements, add a unique ID for each element by selecting it in the treeview panel, then setting its **ID** property in the Properties window.

For More Information For more information on DIV and SPAN tags, see the W3C documentation at http://www.w3.org.

Creating Hyperlinks in the Page Designer

A hyperlink is an HTML feature that lets you make a piece of text or an image into a jump that, when selected, opens another Web page or moves to another location within the current page. You can create hyperlinks easily when you are designing an HTML page in the page designer.

There are two ways to create a hyperlink:

- If you want to turn existing text into a hyperlink, you can use the Make Selection Into Link toolbar icon.
- If you want to create a new hyperlink, you can use the Hyperlink icon on the HTML panel of the toolbox.

To create a hyperlink from existing text

1. Highlight the text or image on your HTML page that you want to make into a hyperlink.

   Note You can highlight the elements in either the drawing surface or in the treeview.

2. Click the Make Selection Into Link icon on the toolbar.

   The page designer inserts opening and closing tags around your selection and formats it as a hyperlink.

To create a new hyperlink

- Drag and drop the **Hyperlink** from the toolbox onto the detail panel, then position and format it accordingly.

  Important A hyperlink element is part of the text stream on your HTML page and must be repositioned using the keyboard rather than the mouse. To move a hyperlink element, place your cursor before the hyperlink and press ENTER.

Working with Tables in the Page Designer

You can easily create tables when designing an HTML page from scratch or working with an existing page. The designer toolbar provides options that allow you to easily insert a table of the size and shape you need. In addition, you can add, delete, and manipulate the rows, columns, and cells in existing tables.

Note You can use the Show Borders icon in the toolbar to display or hide the borders of a table for which the Border property is set to zero. When a tables Border property is zero, no borders appear in the designer, and the table will be borderless when displayed in the browser for the end user. You can use the Show Borders icon to temporarily view the borders in the designer, making it easier to manipulate the table.

To add a table

- Click the **Table Operations** drop-down icon from the toolbar, then click **Insert Table**.

  Note By default, Visual Basic inserts a table with two columns and two rows. You can position your cursor in any cell and type in contents for that cell, or you can fill in table rows programmatically.

To add a row or column to the table

- Position your cursor in the row above which you want to add a column or row, then click the **Table Operations** drop-down icon from the toolbar and click **Insert Row** or **Insert Column**.

To delete a row or column from the table

- Place your cursor in the row or column, then click the **Table Operations** drop-down icon from the toolbar and click **Delete Row** or **Delete Column**.

To add table cells

- Position your cursor in the cell to the left of which you want to add a new cell, then click the **Table Operations** drop-down icon from the toolbar and click **Insert Cell**.

To delete table cells

- Place your cursor in the cell, then select **Delete Cell** from the **Table Operations** submenu.

Working with Lists in the Page Designer

There are two types of lists you can add to a DHTML page: a List element and a Select element. The List element is a scrolling list. The Select element creates a combo box much like the one you add to Visual Basic forms.

Adding items to HTML lists works very differently from the process of adding items to a list box or combo box on a Visual Basic form. You cannot use the List property or the AddItem method to add items to an HTML element. Instead, there are two ways you can populate your list:

- To populate the list at design time, you can edit the HTML in an external editor and enter the appropriate values.
- To populate the list at run time, you can use a method of the Document object in Dynamic HTML.

When you first add a list to an HTML page in the designer, the HTML for the list element looks like this:

Element	Original HTML When Element is Created

List	`<select name="List1" id="List1" value="List1">`
	`<option value="List">`
	`</select>`

Select	`<select name="Select1" id="Select1" value="Select1">`
	`<option selected value="Select">Select`
	`</select>`

Note If you edit your HTML using FrontPage, you may see closing </option> tags in the code shown above. Either usage is acceptable.

To populate a list element

1. Click the **Launch Editor** button from the designer toolbar.
2. In your HTML or text editor, view the source code for the list element.
3. Copy the <option value="list"> line and paste it between the opening and closing <select> tags once for each list item you want to add. For example, if you are adding four list items, there would be four instances of <option value="list"> in your HTML code.
4. Type the list item you want to add after each <option> tags. Your resulting HTML will look something like this:

```
<select name="List1" id="List1" value="List1">
   <option value="List">First list item
   <option value="List">Second list item
   <option value="List">Third list item
</select>
```

5. Save your changes and return to the designer. When prompted to refresh the changed file, click **OK**.

To populate a select element

1. Click the **Launch Editor** button from the designer toolbar.
2. In your HTML or text editor, view the source HTML code for the list element.
3. Copy the <option selected value="Select"> line and paste it between the opening and closing <select> tags once for each list item you want to add. For example, if you are adding four list items, there would be four instances of <option selected value="Select">.
4. Edit the tags you have copied so that only one line says "option selected value="Select". The other lines should only say "option value="Select". For example, if you have added three lines, your HTML would now look like this:

```
<select name="Select1" id="Select1" value="Select1">
   <option selected value="Select">Select
   <option value="Select">Select
   <option value="Select">Select
</select>
```

5. Type the list item you want to add after each <option> tags, replacing the word "Select." Your resulting HTML will look something like this:

```
<select name="Select1" id="Select1" value="Select1">
   <option selected value="Select">Default list item
   <option value="Select">Second list item
   <option value="Select">Third list item
</select>
```

6. Save your changes and return to the designer. When prompted to refresh the changed file, click **OK**.

Populating a List or Select Element at Run Time

You can also populate list elements at run time. For example, suppose you have an HTML page with a list, a text field, and a button. You want the end user to be able to enter a value in the text field, then press a button to make that value appear in the list. The following picture shows the HTML page:

HTML Page with List Elements

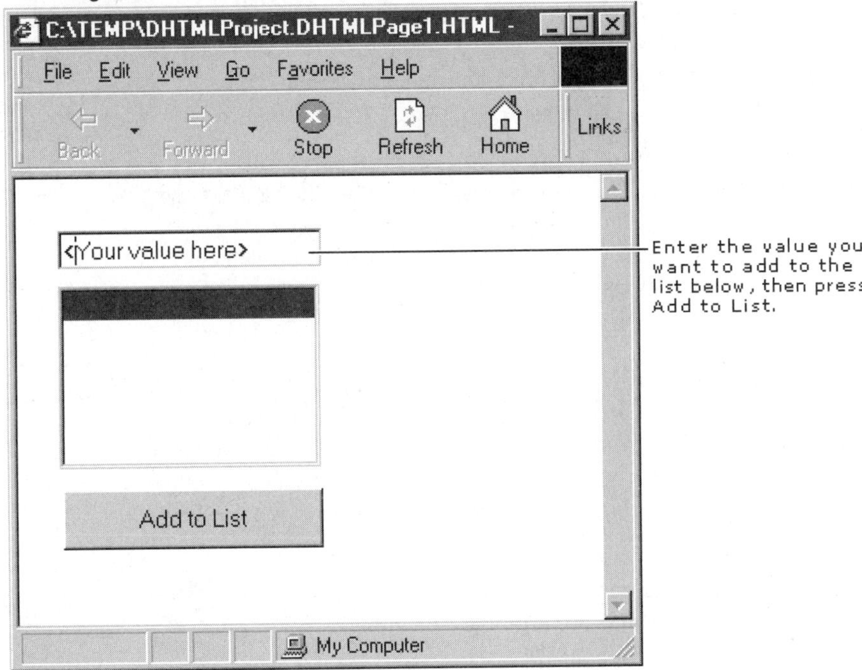

The button code can use a method of the DHTML Document object called CreateElement to add list items to the list. The code would be as follows:

```
Private Function Button1_onclick() As Boolean
   Dim e as HTMLOptionElement
   Set e = Document.createElement("OPTION")
   e.Text=TextField1.Value
   e.Value="ListItemValue"
   List1.Options.Add e
End Function
```

> **Note** The CreateElement method can be used only for Select elements, such as the list and select elements in the toolbox, and for IMG elements. You cannot use it to create a new element of any other type.

Understanding the Page Designer Treeview

The designer window for your DHTML applications consists of two parts — the detail panel, on the right and the treeview panel, on the left. The detail panel shows the HTML page as it will appear in the browser and is the area you use to draw and manipulate your page's appearance. The treeview is used to show the elements that make up the HTML page and their relationship to the overall object model for the application. When you first begin a project for a DHTML application, the treeview contains three elements — the Document, the Body, and a paragraph, or <P>, tag.

After you reference an existing HTML page or begin creating your own in the page designer, the treeview displays a listing for each tag on the HTML page. This includes all visible elements on the page, such as buttons, text, images, checkboxes, and options boxes, and a series of tags, such as text formatting tags for bold, italic, and underline, organizational tags such as DIV and SPAN, and other tags.

Although all elements on a page are displayed in the treeview, you can only write code for those elements that contain an ID attribute. The treeview displays in bold the elements with ID attributes. For each element, the page designer lists the ID, if one exists; the type of element; and in some cases the beginning of the content for that element. If an element does not have an ID, you can assign one to it in the Properties window.

The treeview provides three valuable shortcuts:

- When you select an item in the treeview, Visual Basic highlights the appropriate item in the detail panel and in the Properties window. This can help you determine at a glance the correspondence between elements in the treeview and on the page. Note that this works in reverse as well: When you select an element on the detail panel or in the Properties window, Visual Basic highlights the corresponding element in the treeview and scrolls the treeview accordingly.
- You can double-click an element in the treeview to open the Code Editor window for that element. The system selects the default event for the element.
- For ActiveX controls that do not have a visible user interface at run time (such as the common dialog control), the treeview is the only way you can select and manipulate these elements after adding them to your page.

For More Information See "Making Page Elements Programmable" in this chapter for more information on how to work with element IDs.

Launching an HTML Editor from the Page Designer

If you have saved your HTML page to an external file, you can launch an HTML editor from within Visual Basic and view your page within it. You might do this if you want to fine-tune the appearance of your page, or if you want to work in the HTML source code. When you launch an external editor from Visual Basic, Visual Basic saves your current project and any changes you have made to the page, then opens the page in the default HTML editor for your system. If you do not have an HTML editor installed, the system opens Notepad and displays the HTML source.

> **Note** You can set the default editor that Visual Basic will open on the Advanced panel of the Options dialog box.

You can launch an external editor for only those files that were saved to a location on your hard drive, rather than stored within the designer. If you want to edit a file you initially stored within the designer, you must specify a save location for it by filling in the SourceFile property for the page.

Note If you specify a different source file after one has already been set, Visual Basic prompts you to save your current HTML page before switching to the newly specified file. This will save your changes to the old file name before opening the new file.

Any changes you make to the page in an external editor appear in Visual Basic as soon as you save in the editor. However, changes you make in Visual Basic may not automatically be updated in the editor, depending on the editor you choose to use. Be careful to avoid conflicts when you have an HTML page open in both Visual Basic and another program. In general, it is best to make changes to the document in only one location at a time. The steps for editing a document should be:

1. Launch the editor from Visual Basic.
2. Edit your HTML.
3. Save your changes and close the editor.
4. Choose "Yes" at the prompt in Visual Basic asking if you want to refresh the page.

Note In addition to watching for changes when you launch an external editor, Visual Basic watches for changes to the page's source file any time you have the page open in Visual Basic. If the source file changes, a prompt appears that asks if you want to reload your page.

To edit your HTML page outside of Visual Basic

- Click the **Launch Editor** button in the designer window. The default HTML editor appears.

Important If you select the Launch Editor button when the SourceFile property has not been set, the system will not launch the editor. Set the SourceFile property, then click the Launch Editor button again. Be aware that this will change the save options for your page. For more information, see "Beginning your DHTML Application Project," earlier in this chapter.

Writing Code Using Dynamic HTML

When you create a DHTML application in Visual Basic, you use the Dynamic HTML object model to access and manipulate anything within the page. The HTML elements in the page are available as individual objects, which means you can examine and modify an element and its attributes by reading and setting properties and by calling methods.

The object model also makes user actions — such as clicking, double-clicking, or right-clicking an element, pressing keys, and loading forms — available as events. You can intercept and process these and other events by creating event procedures in your Visual Basic code.

For a Visual Basic programmer, there are many aspects of the Dynamic HTML object model that are unfamiliar. The following sections present an overview of some of the key differences between Visual Basic's programming model and the Dynamic HTML object model. The following table explains some of the areas where you may encounter differences and lists the sections to which you can go for more information.

If you need help	See
Understanding the object model	"The Dynamic HTML Object Model in Visual Basic"
Understanding what Visual Basic events the events in Dynamic HTML correspond to	"Events in Dynamic HTML"
Making elements on your page programmable	"Making Page Elements Programmable"
Working with styles	"Setting and Retrieving Properties for a Web Page" or "Dynamic HTML in Visual Basic"
Working with text elements in your pages	"Handling Text in the Page Designer"
Retrieving data from a form or other elements within an HTML page	"Retrieving Data from an HTML Page"
Navigating among pages	"Navigating in DHTML Applications"
Creating elements on the fly and inserting them, with events, onto the HTML page	"Dynamically Creating Elements and Events"
Storing and retrieving state information	"Managing State in DHTML Applications"

The Dynamic HTML Object Model in Visual Basic

Using the Dynamic HTML object model, you can access and manipulate anything within your application's HTML pages. The HTML elements in a page are available as individual objects, meaning you can examine and modify elements and their attributes by reading and setting properties and by calling methods. The text in elements is available through the elements' properties and methods.

The object model also makes user actions, such as pressing a key and clicking the mouse, available as events. You can intercept and process these and other events by creating event procedures in your Visual Basic code.

The following figure shows the major objects in the Dynamic HTML object model.

Dynamic HTML object model

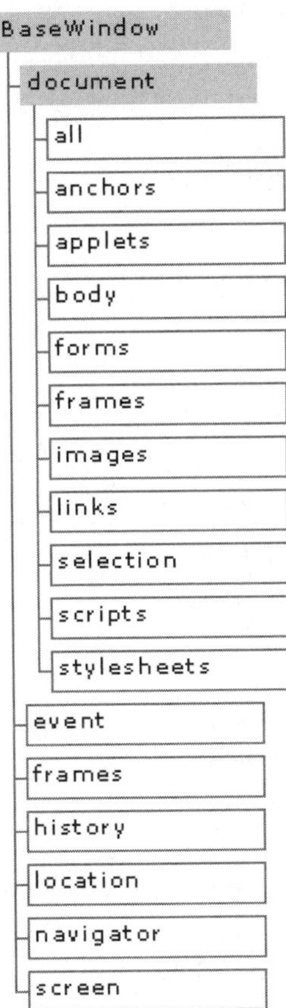

> **Note** The BaseWindow object used by Visual Basic in the picture above corresponds to the topmost Window object in the Dynamic HTML object model.

The two main objects in the object model, for the purposes of Visual Basic, are the BaseWindow object and the Document object.

- The **BaseWindow object** represents an instance of the browser and is used to display the Document object.
- The **Document object** represents the HTML page you view in the browser. You use events in the Document object to access the Dynamic HTML object model and handle user actions in the browser.

Events in Dynamic HTML

Most events in the Dynamic HTML object model are similar to the events in the Visual Basic programming model. Event names, however, are often slightly different. All event names in Dynamic HTML are preceded by the word "on." You can locate most common events by looking for them under this prefix. For example, the Visual Basic click event corresponds to onclick, load corresponds to onload, and so on.

For More Information See "Document Object Model" in the "Dynamic HTML" section of the *Internet Client SDK* for a full list of the properties, methods, and events available in an HTML page through the Dynamic HTML object model.

Visual Basic Events vs. Dynamic HTML Events

The sections below list some of the more commonly used events in Visual Basic, their counterparts in Dynamic HTML, and any additional information needed for you to use them.

Keyboard Events

Keyboard events in Dynamic HTML correspond very closely to keyboard events in Visual Basic. The following table lists the common Visual Basic keyboard events and their Dynamic HTML counterparts:

Visual Basic Event	DHTML Event	Comments
Keydown	onkeydown	Fires when a key is pressed.
Keypress	onkeypress	Fires when a user's keyboard input is translated to a character.
Keyup	onkeyup	Fires when a user releases a key.

When a keyboard event occurs, the keycode property of Dynamic HTML's event object contains the Unicode keycode of the corresponding key. The altKey, ctrlKey, and shiftKey properties specify the state of the ALT, CTRL, and SHIFT keys. You can change which key is associated with the event by either changing the value of the keycode property or returning an integer value. You can cancel the event by returning zero or false.

Mouse Events

Mouse events in Dynamic HTML correspond closely to mouse events in Visual Basic. The following table lists the common Visual Basic mouse events and their Dynamic HTML counterparts:

Visual Basic Event	DHTML Equivalent	Comments
Click	onclick	In addition to occurring when a user clicks on an element, this event also fires when the user presses ENTER on an element that can receive focus, such as a button.
Doubleclick	ondblclick	This event works similarly to its Visual Basic counterpart.
Mousedown, mouseup, mousemove	onmouseout, onmousedown, onmouseup, onmousemove, onmouseover	When moving between elements, the onmouseout event fires first to indicate that the mouse has left the original element. Next the onmousemove event fires, indicating that the mouse has moved. Finally, onmouseover fires to indicate that the mouse has entered the new element.

When a mouse event occurs, the button property of the event object identifies which mouse button (if any) is down. The x and y properties specify the location of the mouse at the time of the event. For the onmouseover and onmouseout events, the toElement and fromElement properties specify the elements the mouse is moving to and from.

Focus and Selection Events

Focus and selection events in Dynamic HTML differ slightly from their Visual Basic counterparts. In particular, focus events are called only from certain elements, and selection and dragging are handled differently. The following table lists the common Visual Basic focus and selection events and their Dynamic HTML counterparts:

Visual Basic Event	DHTML Equivalent	Comments
Gotfocus	onfocus	Fires when the user moves to an element capable of receiving input, such as a button or form element.
Lostfocus	onblur	Fires when you move out of an element that is capable of receiving input.
Selchange	onselectstart onselect	The onselectstart event fires when a selection is first initiated — for example, when the user clicks a character or object in the document. Onselect fires when the user changes the selection — for example, by moving the mouse over a portion of the document while holding down the mouse button.
Dragdrop, dragover	ondragstart	Fires when the user first begins to drag the selection. The default action is to prepare the selection to be copied to another element.

Note Onblur and onfocus fire whether you move between elements in the page, between frames, or even between applications on the desktop. For example, if a page element has focus and the user switches to another application, the onblur event fires for that element. When the user switches back, onfocus fires.

Other Events

Visual Basic Event	DHTML Equivalent	Comments
Change	onchange	Onchange fires when the user tabs off or presses ENTER on an element, moving out of it. In Visual Basic, the change event fires as soon as the user performs any action within the control.
Close	-	No direct equivalent exists for this event.
Error	onerror	Fires when an error occurs loading an image or other element, or when a scripting error occurs.
Initialize	onready statechange	Fires when the page changes from initializing to interactive, and from interactive to loaded. A page is interactive as soon as the user can interact with it by scrolling or clicking on anchors or elements. A page is loaded when all the content has been downloaded.
Load	onload	Fires after the document is loaded and all the elements on the page have been completely downloaded.
Paint	-	No direct equivalent exists for this event.
Resize	onresize	This Dynamic HTML event functions similarly to its Visual Basic counterpart; however, you do not need to write code to handle resizing of an HTML page as you do a Visual Basic form. Resize in HTML happens automatically.
Scroll	onscroll	Fires whenever the scroll box for the page or any element within it is repositioned.
Terminate	-	No direct equivalent exists for this event. You can perform terminate-type actions in the onunload event. A terminate event does exist for the DHTMLPage object. This object is not part of the Dynamic HTML object model, and is unique to Visual Basic.
Unload	onunload	Fires immediately prior to the document being unloaded (when navigating to another document).

Events Unique to Dynamic HTML

In addition, there are some events in Dynamic HTML that do not have equivalents in Visual Basic. A few of the more interesting of these are shown in the following table:

DHTML Event	Usage
Onabort	Fires when the user aborts the download of an image or page element by pressing the Stop button.
Onreset	Fires when the user selects a Reset button on a form.
Onsubmit	Fires when the user selects a Submit button on a form. Can be used to perform validation of data on the client before sending it to the server.

For More Information See "Events" in the "Document Object Model References" section of the *Internet Client SDK* for more information on Dynamic HTML events.

Making Page Elements Programmable

Elements on a page in a DHTML application are capable of being handled programmatically — that is, you can respond to events for the elements and write code that tells the system what to do when an event is fired. You choose which elements can be programmed by ensuring that those elements for which you want to write code have unique IDs. Only elements with IDs can be programmed.

> **Note** Some elements are automatically assigned an ID when you add them to a page. For those that are not, you must add the ID yourself by entering a value for the ID property.

An ID is an attribute of an HTML tag that provides a unique identifier for an element on the page. For example, you may have multiple paragraph elements in your document, each marked with the standard <P> HTML tag. Without an ID, there is no way to tell one of these elements from another. Suppose you want to perform an operation on a single paragraph in your page, such as turning all of the text in that paragraph blue, but you do not want to apply that change to any other paragraphs in the page. Without an ID attribute, you cannot specify that the operation should affect any one <P>, or paragraph. However, if you assign a unique ID to the paragraph you want to change, you can reference just that paragraph in your code.

> **Note** For Visual Basic, all of the IDs on a page must be unique. This is not true of HTML pages outside of Visual Basic, so it is possible that you may import a page that contains duplicate IDs. Visual Basic will automatically append numbers to the end of any nonunique IDs during the import process.

After you add an ID to an element, it appears in bold in the treeview. This shows you at a glance the elements that are currently programmable in your page. You can double-click on any programmable element in the treeview or detail panel to move to the Code Editor window for that element.

Name vs. ID

In forms-based Visual Basic applications, the Name property acts as the main identifying property for controls on the page. For HTML elements, the ID property is the value that uniquely identifies the element in code. In most cases, the Name property does not play an important role in the life of elements on an HTML page.

There is one situation in which the Name property is useful for HTML page elements: making a set of option buttons mutually exclusive. For example, suppose you have three option buttons that are intended to identify how the user is going to pay for an order: with cash, with a credit card, or with a check. In a forms-based application, you would make these elements part of a control array, thus allowing the user to select only one of them. In a DHTML application, you use the Name property to produce the same result. For each option button you want to group together, you set the Name property to the exact same value. For example, you might set the Name property for these three options to "PaymentOptions." This makes the option buttons function as a group — when one is selected, the other two are automatically deselected.

> **Note** Even though you assign the same Name property to the three option buttons in this example, they must still have unique ID values. The value of the ID property must always be unique in Visual Basic.

To make an element programmable

1. In either the treeview or the detail panel, click the element for which you want to assign an ID.
2. In the Properties window, enter a value for the **ID** property, then press ENTER.

   The system adds the element to the Object list in the Code Editor window, and makes the name of the element bold in the treeview.

To access the Code Editor window for a programmable element

- Double-click on the element in the designer's treeview or detail panel.

Enabling the Default Action for an Element

Many elements on an HTML page have a default action. For example, the default action for a hyperlink is to launch the specified Web page when clicked. When you write Visual Basic code for an object on the page, you must include a statement that enables the default action to occur after your procedure is processed.

In Internet Explorer 4.*x*, when you attach an event to any object, the system returns a True or False value when the event is fired. A return value of True allows the default action to occur, and a value of False prevents the action from occurring. Visual Basic always defaults booleans to False, so by default, any event procedure the system runs prevents the default action from occurring. To avoid this problem, you must include a line of code that returns a value of True in order for the action to occur.

For example, suppose you have the following hyperlink on your HTML page:

```
<a href = "http://www.microsoft.com">Go to Microsoft</a>
```

You want to write additional code that intercepts this request and performs a procedure before the link is followed to the Microsoft site. The following code shows the correct way to do this:

```
Private Function Hyperlink1_onclick() as Boolean
   ' Your event procedure code here
   ' Send a true value to the system to request default processing
   Hyperlink1_onclick = True
End Function
```

If you leave out the line of code that sends the True value, the system will process the code you've written, but will not open the Web site specified in the hyperlink tag.

Setting and Retrieving Properties for a Web Page

Using Visual Basic and Dynamic HTML, you can easily change the styles of elements on the pages that make up your application's user interface. You do by manipulating the properties of page elements.

Setting and retrieving properties for elements on an HTML page works differently than it does for controls on a form. In a form, you access the properties of a control directly by referencing the name of the control and the name of the property you want. For most elements in a Web page, you must use a secondary object known as the Style object to access properties for an element.

Working with Physical Properties on Page Elements

When you want to set a physical property such as background color, you use a collection called Style to access the appropriate property. The following table shows how you set and retrieve properties in standard Visual Basic applications and in DHTML applications. In this example, properties are being set and retrieved for a command button with the ID "Button1."

Setting and Retrieving Property Values

	Setting a Property	Retrieving a Property Value
In Visual Basic	`Button1.BackColor = vbBlue`	`Dim Color as String` `Color = Button1.backcolor`
In Dynamic HTML	`Button1.style.backgroundColor = "blue"`	`Dim Color as String` `Color = Button1.style.backgroundColor`

Note Color names in DHTML applications are different from the color names you use in forms-based Visual Basic applications. When you specify a color for a page element, you must either specify an RGB value (such as #5F9EA0) or a color label as specified by Internet Explorer 4 (such as "cadetblue"). A full list of the color names supported by Internet Explorer 4 can be found in the Color Table topic in the Dynamic HTML section of the *Internet Client SDK*.

Working with Physical Properties on the Document Object

The only element within an HTML page to which the Style object syntax does not apply is the document itself. You do not use the style property to set the background color or other physical properties for the document. Instead, you access those properties directly as shown in the following code:

```
Document.bgcolor = "lightyellow"
Document.fgcolor = "slateblue"
```

The following code shows how you retrieve the RGB value for the background color for the Document object:

```
Dim Color as string
Color = Document.bgcolor
```

> **Note** The fgcolor property sets the color for the page's text elements only.

Common Styles for HTML Elements

The style properties you use to set the physical appearance of an HTML element are named differently than their corresponding properties in Visual Basic. The following table lists a few of the more frequently used styles and explains their use.

DHTML Style	Purpose
backgroundcolor	Setting the background color of all elements except the Document object, which represents the body of the page. For the page itself, the property is called *bgcolor*.
border	Setting a border around any element. All elements on an HTML page can have a border, including paragraphs of text.
color	Setting the foreground color for all elements except the Document object, which represents the body of the page. For the page itself, the property is called *fgcolor*.
font	Setting the font for the element. A series of related properties (fontfamily, fontsize, fontstyle, etc.) are used to fine-tune the appearance of the font.
margin	Controlling the distance between the border of the element and the edge of the page. This property can be set to control all of the element's margins, or you can set the top, bottom, left, and right margins independently through a series of related properties.
padding	Controlling the distance between the inner text of the element and its border. This property can be set to control the padding space on all sides of the elements, or you can set the padding of the top, bottom, left, and right sides independently through a series of related properties.
textdecoration	Formatting text within an element. You use this property to make the text blink, or to display it with a strikethrough, underline, or overline.

For More Information For more information on the Style collection, any of the properties listed above, or other style-related properties in Dynamic HTML, see "Dynamic HTML" in the *Internet Client SDK*, available on your MSDN CD.

Retrieving Data from an HTML Page

You can retrieve data from elements on an HTML page using Dynamic HTML. This allows you to retrieve and manipulate data without making trips to the server for processing. Using properties of the objects on the page, you can gather data, perform calculations on it in your Visual Basic code, and display responses without ever transferring processing from the client to the server, which can increase your response time to user actions and requests.

For example, suppose you are working with an application that allows users to query books from a database by entering the author's name, the title of the book, or the call number of the book in text fields on a search page. The text fields are named Author, Title, and CallNo. When a query is submitted from the application's search page, the application must retrieve the value from these text fields.

The following code shows how you could use variables to retrieve the values from these fields:

```
Private function cmdSearch_onclick() As Boolean
   'Create variables to contain the search criteria.
   Dim sAuthor as String
   Dim sTitle as String
   Dim sCallNo as String

   'Retrieve criteria from the page.
   sAuthor=Me.author.Value
   sTitle=Me.title.Value
   sCallNo=Me.callno.Value

   'Code here to process the data and return the query.
End Function
```

This code uses the Value property of the HTML text fields to retrieve the fields' data. Your code would open a database connection, create a recordset, and return the appropriate records. This data could then be sent to the user.

Handling Text in the Page Designer

Text replacements are a frequent operation in many Visual Basic applications. Often you want to change the text displayed in a form element in response to a user event. In forms-based Visual Basic applications, you usually do this by setting the Text property of the control in question.

For the HTML pages in a DHTML application, text replacements are handled differently than they are on forms. It is important to remember that a standard text element in an HTML page consists of both a set of tags and of text that is embedded between them. For example, the following is the HTML for a typical heading element on a page:

```
<H3 ID=Subhead1>My Heading</H3>
```

The <H3> and </H3> tags tell the browser how to format and display the text "My Heading." The ID=Subhead1 portion is an attribute that assigns a unique ID to the heading and makes it programmable.

When you want to make changes to text on an HTML page, you must specify whether you are replacing it with straight text or text that includes additional HTML tags. Additionally, you must indicate whether the original tags for the element should be affected by the replacement. You do this with two sets of properties: innerText and outerText, and innerHTML and outerHTML.

Changing Text Within HTML Tags

To change text within HTML tags, use the innerText or innerHTML properties. These properties both replace the existing text without changing the tags around the text. They differ in how the system processes them:

- **innerText** provides changes that the system inserts as straight text, without performing any parsing.
- **innerHTML** provides text replacements and additional HTML tags that must be parsed and inserted between the original tags.

The following table shows how you would use the innerText and innerHTML properties to change an element:

	Using innerText	**Using innerHTML**
Original HTML for the element	<H3 ID=Subhead1>My Heading</H3>	<H3 ID=Subhead1>My Heading</H3>
Replacement code	Subhead1.innerText="Heading One"	Subhead1.innerHTML="<I>Heading One</I
Resulting HTML	<H3 ID=Subhead1>Heading One</H3>	<H3 Subhead1><I>Heading One</I></H3>
Element displayed in browser	**Heading One**	**Heading One**

Replacing Text and Tags

To change both the text and the original tags around an element, you can use two properties called outerText and outerHTML. Both properties replace the text enclosed in the HTML for a specific element and the element tags themselves. Like innerText and innerHTML, they differ in terms of how the system processes them:

- **outerText** provides changes that the system inserts as straight text, without performing any parsing. This text replaces the entire original element, including its HTML tags.
- **outerHTML** provides text replacements and additional HTML tags that must be parsed and inserted in place of the original tags.

The following table shows how you would use the outerText and outerHTML properties to replace the original element with text alone or text and tags:

	Using outerText	**Using outerHTML**
Original HTML for the element	<DIV><H3 ID=Subhead1>My Heading</H3></DIV>	<H3 ID=Subhead1>My Heading</H3>
Replacement code	`Subhead1.outerHTML=Heading Two`	`Subhead1.outerHTML= <P ID=Newpar><U>Heading Two</U></P>`
Resulting HTML	Heading Two	<P ID=Newpar><U>Heading Two</U></P>
Element displayed in the browser	Heading Two	Heading Two

If you use OuterHTML to change the ID for an element, any Visual Basic code you wrote for events on the old element ID will no longer work. You must either copy your old code to the appropriate procedures for the new element ID, or leave the ID unchanged.

> **Note** In addition to replacing text, you can append text to an existing element with the insertAdjacentHTML property.

For More Information See "Properties" in the Document Object Model section of the *Internet Client SDK* for more information on how to use innerText, outerText, innerHTML, outerHTML, and insertAdjacentHTML.

Navigating in DHTML Applications

You can write code in your DHTML application to allow the end user to move from one page to another. If you have multiple page designers in your application, you can move from one page to another within your application, or you can navigate to an external Web site outside of the application.

There are two main ways you can allow for navigation:

- Program a hyperlink to move to the desired location by setting its HREF property.
- Program another element, such as a button, to move to a new page when activated.

Navigating with Hyperlinks

You can easily provide navigation to another page by including a hyperlink element in your page. You add the hyperlink to your page, then set a property called HREF that tells the system where to go when the link is selected.

After you add the hyperlink to your page, you indicate the location to which it should jump by setting the HREF property for the element. You can type in a full or relative location to another page on the Web site, whether that page is part of your application or not.

> **Note** It is best to use relative references to the pages to which you want to jump unless those pages are located on external Web sites. If they are pages that you intend to deploy with the application, make sure that your directory structure on the development machine mimics the structure on the site to which you will deploy, then use a relative path to the file. For Web pages on external sites, use a direct reference to the exact location.

To navigate using a hyperlink

1. In either panel of the designer window, click the hyperlink you want to use to navigate.
    - If you need to add a new hyperlink to your page, drag the Hyperlink icon from the toolbox to the page.
    - To convert existing text to a hyperlink, highlight the text and click the Make Selection into Link icon from the designer toolbar.
    - If you want to use an existing hyperlink on the page, select the hyperlink and make sure that its ID property is set.
2. In the Properties window, enter a full or relative path to another page in the HREF property.

    > **Note** To use an absolute reference, enter your link in the following format:
    >
    > **http://***www.server.com/directory/page.htm*

    Test your link by running the project.

Navigating Programmatically

In addition to using the HREF property on the Hyperlink element, you can programmatically allow any other element to navigate to another page. The most common example of this would be to create a button which, when clicked, moves users backwards or forwards in your application.

Note While it is possible to use other elements in addition to the button or the hyperlink to move from page to page, it may not be intuitive to your users that elements are being used in this way. Use principles of good design when determining what navigational features you want to include in your application.

After you add the element to your page, you can write code for it that tells the system how to respond when the element is activated. In this case, your code will tell the browser to navigate to another page.

The following code shows an example of how you would use a button to move from the current page in your application to another called DHTMLPage2:

```
Private Function Button1_onclick() As Boolean
   BaseWindow.navigate "Project1.DHTMLPage2.html"
End Function
```

In this code the navigate method of the BaseWindow object is used to move to the desired location. Project1.DHTMLPage2.html is the name assigned to the page when the project is compiled.

To navigate using an element other than a hyperlink

1. In the page designer, click the element you want to use to navigate.
   - If you need to add a new element to your page, drag the appropriate icon from the toolbox to the page.
   - If you want to use an existing element on the page, select the element in either panel of the designer window.
2. Verify that the element has an ID, by checking the contents of the **ID** property in the Properties window. If the element does not have an ID, add a value for this property.
3. Access the Code Editor window for the element, and select the appropriate event from the Event list.
4. Write your code as shown in the example above.
5. Compile your project and test.

Dynamically Creating Elements and Events

In addition to laying out your page elements in the page designer, you can create HTML elements and insert them on the page from code. You might do this if you want to create a page in response to a user's actions. For example, you might dynamically create a page and its contents in response to a query. You create and insert an HTML element by writing HTML in your code, using the DHTML object model's insertAdjacentHTML method.

Example: Retrieving Customer Information

Suppose you are building an application in which a search button launches a database query that returns a customer's last name and order number. You want to create page elements on the fly to contain your query results.

The first thing the code must do in this example is retrieve the user's search criteria from two text fields on the page. These fields have the IDs "custLN," for the last name for which the user wants to search, and "orderNO" for the order number. In this case, you could use two variables to retrieve the search criteria from these fields:

```
Private Function cmdSearch_onclick() As Boolean
    Dim sLastName As String
    Dim sOrderNum As String
    Dim divCustInfo as HTMLDivElement
    'Retrieve the search criteria and store it in the variables
    SLastName = Me.custLN.Value
    SorderNum = Me.orderNO.Value
End Function
```

Example: Creating Elements and Replacing Contents

After you retrieve the values from the query page, you will perform the query and send the results to the user by creating and populating a DIV tag on a results page. There are a series of steps you need to perform in this process:

1. Retrieve the query results from a database.
2. Check to make sure the DIV to contain the results does not already exist. If the query has previously been run, the DIV tag may already exist on the page. If the query has not been run before, you must create the DIV tag in your code.
3. If necessary, create the DIV tag and other necessary elements.
4. Insert your results set into the DIV tag on the results page.

The following code shows how you would check for the DIV tag as part of the function begun in the previous section.

```
Private Function cmdSearch_onclick() As Boolean
    'Code here to Dim variables and retrieve search criteria
    'Check for a DIV tag called custinfo.
    Set divCustInfo = Me.Document.All("custinfo")
    'Create three sets of HTML elements if the DIV tag is not
    'found: a separator line, a DIV with text, and a programmable
    'DIV to contain the query results.
```

```
    If divCustInfo Is Nothing Then
       Me.Document.body.insertAdjacentHTML "BeforeEnd", _
         "<DIV><HR SIZE=2></DIV>"
       Me.Document.body.insertAdjacentHTML "BeforeEnd", _
         "<DIV CLASS=custhead>Customer Information</DIV>
       Me.Document.body.insertAdjacentHTML "BeforeEnd", _
         "<DIV id=custinfo>"
       'Run the query using a CustomerQuery function and insert the
       'results in the custinfo DIV tag.
       If sLastName <> "" Then
          Me.Document.body.insertAdjacentHTML "BeforeEnd", _
            CustomerQuery(sLastName)
       EndIf
       'Create and insert the closing tag for the programmable DIV
       'element.
       Me.Document.body.insertAdjacentHTML "BeforeEnd", "</DIV>"
    'If the DIV tag already exists, run the CustomerQuery function and
    'replace the element with the query results.
 Else
       DivCustInfo.innerHTML = CustomerQuery(sLastName)
    EndIf
 End Function
```

Managing State in DHTML Applications

Typically, Internet applications are *stateless,* in that the protocol that passes requests and responses between the browser and Web server is not capable of maintaining information between each request. Therefore, the protocol does not "remember" any information from previous requests when it receives a new request. This is also generally true of DHTML applications, in that the browser does not usually store detailed information between actions.

Because the protocol itself cannot maintain state, you must use other means to store information you want the application to remember between requests. In a DHTML application, you use the GetProperty and PutProperty functions to store and retrieve data. These functions store data as long as the end user's Web browser window is open.

> **Note** The GetProperty and PutProperty functions are part of the modDHTML module that is added to your project when you create a new project using the DHTML Application template.

You store information using the PutProperty function. In this function, you identify the name of the property in which you want to store information, and the value to store. The browser stores the indicated data in a *property bag*. A property bag is a file that is used to temporarily store information.

You retrieve information using the GetProperty function. In this function, you identify the name of an existing property that you want to retrieve from the property bag. You can assign this value to fields on the page, or use it in your calculations.

Example: Saving and Retrieving State

For example, suppose you want to build a simple application that will store and retrieve data across page boundaries. The application will consist of two pages: one to store values, and one to retrieve them.

The first page in the application contains a text field into which the end user can enter a value, and a button that stores the value to the property bag. The code for the button, called StoreButton1, would look like this:

```
Private Function StoreButton1_onclick() As Boolean
   PutProperty "Property1", TextField1.Value
End Function
```

The second page in the same application contains a button that, when clicked, retrieves the property from the property bag. The code for that button, called "GetButton1", would look like this:

```
Private Function GetButton1_onclick() As Boolean
   MyValue.innerText = "The value of the property is " & _
      GetProperty("Property1")
End Function
```

This function uses the innerText property of Dynamic HTML to replace the contents of a DIV tag, called "MyValue," with a sentence which contains the retrieved property.

Testing Your DHTML Application

When you debug a DHTML application, you have the full Visual Basic development environment at your disposal. You can use all the tools available in Visual Basic — breakpoints, watch variables, debug statements, and so on — to debug your project.

> **Note** A file named VB6DEBUG.DLL enables you to debug your DHTML application across processes. Do not delete this file or you will not be able to test your application.

The settings in the Debugging tab of the Project Properties dialog box determine whether the system waits for you to tell it what to do when you go into run mode or automatically starts a page designer you specify, displaying its page in the browser. You can also indicate whether to open a new instance of Internet Explorer or use an existing instance.

When Visual Basic runs the application, it inserts an OBJECT tag into the body of each HTML page used in your application. The OBJECT tag is used to download the HTML page when the application is deployed. The tag includes a classID used to include of find the page in the Windows registry, an ID used to reference the page in the run-time DLL, and a CODEBASE tag used to tell the browser where to find the page if it's not already on the client's computer.

For More Information See Chapter 13, "Debugging Your Code and Handling Errors," in the *Microsoft Visual Basic 6.0 Programmer's Guide* for more information on how to test and debug your applications.

Building Your DHTML Application

DHTML applications are compiled the same way any Visual Basic project is compiled — by choosing Make from the File menu. A DHTML application must be built as an in-process component, or a DLL file.

Project Files in DHTML Applications

Like standard Visual Basic projects, DHTML application projects have code modules and visual designers — in this case, the DHTML Page designer. Visual Basic creates a page designer for each HTML page in your application. For each page designer, Visual Basic stores the following:

- A .dsr file *.Dsr files* are plain text files that contain the source code for the designer and references to the HTML pages they contain.
- A generated *.dsx file* that contains binary information about the designer.
- The HTML pages associated with an application are saved to the location you specify.

Any files associated with the HTML pages are also a part of your project, in that they must be deployed with the project. For example, if your HTML page references a series of images, the image files themselves must be deployed with the project. See "Deploying Your DHTML Application," later in this chapter, for more information.

Compiled Files in DHTML Applications

When you compile a DHTML application, Visual Basic creates a DLL containing the page designer and its code. The HTML pages and their associated files are stored separately from the DLL and must be deployed with it.

During compile, Visual Basic creates several additional files. These include your project file, a .vbw file that contains layout information on your project, an .exp file, and a library file.

To build your DHTML application

1. If the project is still in run mode, click the End button to return to design mode.
2. Set the **BuildFile** property to the full path and file name to which you want to build the project.

   Note By default, the **BuildFile** property is set to the value of the **SourceFile** property.

3. On the File menu, click **Make *Project*.dll** to open the **Make Project** dialog box. Click **OK** to make the DLL file.

Deploying Your DHTML Application

You package and deploy your DHTML application using the Visual Basic Package and Deployment Wizard. The Package and Deployment Wizard packages your project .dll files and all associated files into a "cabinet" or .cab file. The wizard can then deploy this cabinet file and its associated support files to a location you indicate on a Web server.

> **Note** The .cab files you generate for your DHTML applications should be digitally signed prior to deployment. See "Digital Signing for ActiveX Components" in Chapter 4, "Downloading ActiveX Components," for an explanation of how to sign your files.

Files to Deploy

The application files that must be deployed include:

- The .dll files for the project — including the Visual Basic run-time DLL and the .dsr and .dsx files for the project. These are automatically packaged into the .cab file when you run the Package and Deployment Wizard.
- The HTML page or pages associated with the project. The Package and Deployment Wizard does not package these into the .cab file, but it copies them to the indicated location on the Web site when you deploy the .cab file.
- Any files referenced by the HTML pages, such as images. The Package and Deployment Wizard does not automatically recognize these dependencies, but you can add them to the list of additional files to deploy.

The files end users need to download for a DHTML application vary depending on whether or not they have previously downloaded an application or not. If the end user is downloading for the first time, he must download the Visual Basic run-time DLL and the page designer run-time DLL in addition to the files associated with the application. If he has previously downloaded a DHTML application, the user does not need to download the run-time components again.

The Deployment Process

These are the steps in deploying your DHTML application to the Internet:

1. Debug and compile your application.
2. Use the Package and Deployment Wizard to build a .cab file that contains the necessary files for your application.
3. Digitally sign your .cab file and rebuild.
4. Use the Package and Deployment Wizard to deploy your application to the Web server you want to use.
5. Manually copy any files associated with your application's HTML pages, such as images, to the necessary location on your Web server.

   Note You can also use the Package and Deployment Wizard to perform this step.
6. Test the pages in your application to make sure that all the links to associated files still work. If not, you may have to adjust the location of your files on the Web server to match the URLs in the HTML pages.

For More Information See Chapter 17, "Distributing Your Applications," in the *Microsoft Visual Basic 6.0 Programmer's Guide,* for instructions on using the Package and Deployment Wizard to distribute your DHTML application.

CHAPTER 3

Developing IIS Applications

An IIS application is a Visual Basic application that uses a combination of HTML and compiled Visual Basic code in a dynamic, browser-based application. An IIS application resides on a Web server, where it receives requests from a browser, runs code associated with the requests, and returns responses to the browser.

In its simplest form, you can use an IIS application to intercept a user request and return an HTML page to the browser. These are just a few of the things you can do with more advanced IIS applications:

- Query databases in response to a user's request, writing information to and from records.
- Retrieve HTML pages and replace portions of them with dynamic content before sending them to the browser.
- Dynamically create HTML elements and generate events for them on the fly, at run time.

With these or other advanced uses of IIS applications, you can perform complicated processing based on the actions users perform in the browser. IIS applications can use Visual Basic code to perform much of the same processing you might have previously done with script, CGI processing, and other methods of Internet application development.

IIS applications are named for Microsoft Internet Information Server, the Web server you use to run your IIS applications. IIS applications can run in any browser, on the Internet or an intranet, and therefore make it easy to reach a broad audience.

This chapter assumes that you are familiar with some basic Internet concepts that are covered in Chapter 1, "Introduction to Internet Applications." See it for more information on Internet technologies in general, including HTTP, the Internet development environment, and models of Web browser and Web server interaction.

For More Information See "System Requirements for IIS Applications," later in this chapter, for more information on the system configuration needed to develop and test IIS applications.

Contents

Sample Application: Wcdemo.vbp

Wcdemo.vbp demonstrates several key features of webclass programming in Visual Basic. In this application, you can see examples of how to fire template and custom events, how to dynamically generate pages in response to user requests, how to use custom webitems, and how to use the URLData property to store state information between requests. Wcdemo.vbp is listed in the Samples directory.

What Is an IIS Application?

An IIS (Internet Information Server) application is a Visual Basic application that lives on a Web server and responds to requests from the browser. An IIS application uses HTML to present its user interface and uses compiled Visual Basic code to process requests and respond to events in the browser.

To the user, an IIS application appears to be made up of a series of HTML pages. To the developer, an IIS application is made up of a special type of object called a *webclass*, that in turn contains a series of resources called *webitems*. The webclass acts as the central functional unit of the application, processing data from the browser and sending information to the users. You define a series of procedures that determine how the webclass responds to these requests. The webitems are the HTML pages and other data the webclass can send to the browser in response to a request.

IIS Applications vs. ASP Applications

IIS applications bear a superficial resemblance to Active Server Pages applications. Both types of applications present dynamic Web sites and perform their processing on the server rather than the client. However, each has its unique advantages. Active Server Pages are for script developers interested in authoring Web pages, and offer the unique capability of intermingling script with HTML. IIS applications are for Visual Basic developers building Web-based applications, rather than Web pages. IIS applications allow for complicated business processing and easy access from almost any browser or platform.

IIS Applications vs. DHTML Applications

An IIS application is also similar to another type of Internet application you can create in Visual Basic — a DHTML application. Like IIS applications, DHTML applications also allow you to respond to events in an HTML page. However, there are several key differences between the two types of applications:

- Dependency — DHTML applications are intended for use on intranets, and are dependent on Internet Explorer 4.0 or later, while IIS applications can be used on the Internet or an intranet. End users of an IIS application do not need a specific operating system or browser.
- Object model — DHTML applications use a different object model than IIS applications to access and work with the elements on an HTML page. While IIS applications use the Active Server Pages object model, DHTML applications use the Dynamic HTML object model.
- Location of processing — IIS applications are designed to perform most of their processing on the Web server, but DHTML applications perform most of their processing on the browser machine. You do not create any Web server components when you create a DHTML application.

For More Information See “A History of Development on the Internet” in Chapter 1, “Introduction to Internet Applications,” for more information on the differences between IIS applications and DHTML applications.

Advantages of IIS Applications

Building a server-side Internet application in Visual Basic gives you several advantages over other methods of Internet development, including:

- Reduced cost of deployment per user. End users of an IIS application can run the application using only a browser; no special software needs to be installed on their computers for the application to work.
- A familiar development environment and model. You can leverage your knowledge of Visual Basic by using the Visual Basic programming environment and standard, compiled Visual Basic code. In addition, you can add classes, modules, or any Visual Basic ActiveX component to your project.

- Access to a broad audience. IIS applications work with a wide variety of browsers and operating systems, so you can easily reach a wide audience.
- An object model that gives you direct access to the resources of the Internet Information Server. The Active Server Pages framework provides an object model that allows you to directly manipulate the objects at the core of IIS. This allows you to retrieve information from a browser, send information to it, and perform complex operations on the contents of a Web page. For more information on the object model, see "The Object Model for IIS Applications," later in this chapter.
- Reusable components. Once you have created a webclass, you can easily access it in another webclass. For more information, see "Navigating Between Webclasses," later in this chapter.
- Separation of code and HTML. Unlike scripting, your code is not embedded in the HTML document, so you can separate the process of designing the application's user interface from writing, testing, and debugging its code.
- State management across multiple interactions with the client. You can manage state using objects or a database, or you can shuttle state between the client and the server. For more information, see "State Management in IIS Applications," later in this chapter.
- Streamlined processing. You do not have to create the HTML template files your application sends to the browser, if you do not want to. In Visual Basic Internet application development, the process of designing your user interface is separated from the process of developing and coding your application. You can have a designer create the template files you want to use.

System Requirements for IIS Applications

System requirements for IIS applications vary for the development computer, the deployment computer, and the end-user's computer.

The Development Computer

To create and test IIS applications, you need to have Internet Explorer 4.0 and a Web server installed on your development computer that is capable of running Active Server Pages. You can use any of the combinations in the table below for development purposes:

Operating System	Web Server
Windows NT Server 4.0 or later	Internet Information Server 3.0 or later, with Active Server Pages
Windows NT Workstation 4.0 or later	Peer Web Services 3.0 or later, with Active Server Pages
Windows 95 or later	Personal Web Server 3.0 or later, with Active Server Pages

Important If you are using Windows NT Server or Windows NT Workstation, you must have Service Pack 3.0 installed.

The Deployment Computer

For deployment purposes, you should have Internet Information Server (with Active Server Pages) installed on your Web server, along with any supplemental system such as database applications that are needed by your application.

The End-User Computer

End users of an IIS application must have a browser installed. Although Internet Explorer 4.0 or later is recommended, any browser can act as the front end of an IIS application.

Note If your webclass is set to stay alive between requests, the end user must have a browser that supports cookies and cookies must be enabled. For more information, see "Moving State Between the Browser and the Web Server," later in this chapter.

An Introduction to WebClasses

A webclass is a Visual Basic component that resides on a Web server and responds to input from the browser. When you create an IIS application, you create its webclasses using the Webclass Designer. Webclasses typically contain webitems and the code that delivers those webitems to a client.

Note There is a one-to-one relationship between the Webclass Designer and the webclass. If you want to add additional webclasses to your application, you must add additional designers.

A webclass is associated with one and only one client for its entire life cycle. Visual Basic creates a logical instance of the webclass for each client that accesses it. However, for each client, the webclass is capable of maintaining state between requests.

For More Information See "State Management in IIS Applications," later in this chapter, for more information about maintaining state in a webclass.

Webclasses and .ASP Files

Each webclass in an IIS application has an associated .asp (Active Server Pages) file that Visual Basic generates automatically during the compile or debug process. The .asp file hosts the webclass on the Web server. In addition, it generates the webclass's run-time component when the application is first started and launches the first event in the webclass's life cycle.

The following figure shows the relationship between .asp files, webclasses, and webclass contents.

Relationship between .asp files and webclasses

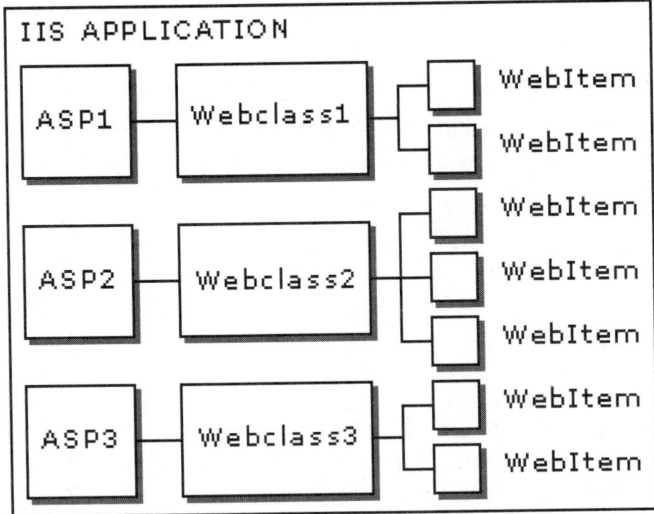

As shown in this picture, there is a one-to-one relationship between webclasses and .asp files — each webclass has its own ASP. In turn, a webclass can have many webitems associated with it.

The path to the ASP acts as the *base URL* for the webclass and its webitems. A *URL* is a standard way of indicating the location of a document or other item that is available electronically. (For example, http://www.microsoft.com is a URL.) When you want to go to a page on the Web, you enter the URL for the page and the browser retrieves and displays it. You can indicate the URL directly, by typing it into the location line of your browser, or indirectly, by selecting a link that tells the browser the correct URL to which it should go. A *base URL* refers to the webclass itself, and can act as an entry point into the application.

For example, suppose you have a project called Project 1, that contains a webclass called CustomerInquiry. Visual Basic creates an Active Server Page called Project1_CustomerInquiry.asp for the webclass when you compile the project, and stores it in the specified directory, called CustomerSupport, on the Web server you specify: www.mycompany.com. The base URL for your webclass would be the following:

```
http://www.mycompany.com/CustomerSupport/Project1_CustomerInquiry.asp
```

To start your IIS application, the user accesses this URL with their browser.

> **Note** You can specify the name of the ASP file for your webclass by setting the NameinURL property to the name you want to use.

Webclass Contents: Templates and Custom Webitems

A webclass typically contains webitems that it uses to provide content to the browser and expose events. A webitem can be one of two things:

- An HTML template file — HTML template files are HTML pages that you associate with your webclass. When the webclass receives a request, it can send the HTML pages to the browser for display. Templates differ from regular HTML pages only in that they often contain replacement areas the webclass can process before sending the page to the browser. This allows you to customize your response.
- A custom webitem — Custom webitems do not have an associated HTML page they can return to the user. Instead, a custom webitem is a programmatic resource that consists of one or more event handlers that are logically grouped together to help organize your Web application. These event handlers are called from the browser, either when the page loads or when a user selects an HTML element. The event handlers can generate a response to the browser or pass processing to another of the webclass's webitems.

Templates and custom webitems both expose events that the webclass processes when certain actions occur in the browser. You can write event procedures for these events using standard Visual Basic code, thus linking the actions that occur on a Web page to Visual Basic processing.

Each webclass can contain multiple templates and webitems. In most cases, you will need only one webclass in your application, but you might want to use multiple webclasses if you want to break up your application into parts that can be reused in other applications.

For More Information See "Webclass Events," later in this chapter, for more information on template and custom webitem events. See "Adding HTML Templates to the Webclass" for more information on template webitems. See "Adding Custom WebItems to a Webclass," later in this chapter, for more information on custom webitems.

IIS Applications vs. Traditional Visual Basic Applications

IIS applications are structured differently than standard, forms-based Visual Basic applications. In an IIS application, the user interface consists of a series of HTML pages rather than traditional Visual Basic forms. An HTML page is like a form in that it contains all the visual elements that make up your application's user interface. You can place some of the same items into a page as you do a form, including text, buttons, check boxes, and option buttons.

An HTML page referenced in an IIS application is saved to an .htm or .html file that is analogous to a .frm file, in that it is used to render and display the page to the end user. Visual Basic creates the .htm file from the original HTML page when you save or debug your application, or when you use the Edit HTML Template menu command.

In an IIS application, you do not use Visual Basic to create the HTML pages that make up the application's user interface. A Web designer or a developer creates the pages using an HTML editor, a word processing package, or a text editor, and you link the finished pages into your webclass.

The following table sums up the differences between forms-based applications and Web-based applications:

	Forms-based application	Web-based application
User interface	Visual Basic forms	HTML pages
UI elements (for example, text boxes, buttons, images)	Controls	Elements
File format	.frm files	.htm files
Creator	Developer	Web designer with a developer, or the developer alone
Run time	Visual Basic run time	Web browser

Structure of IIS Applications

An IIS application consists of the following pieces. Many of these are generated for you automatically when you build your project. The pieces include:

- One or more webclasses, which are generated automatically when you create a webclass project.
- One or more HTML templates and their events.
- One or more custom webitems and their events.

  Note A webclass may contains a mixture of templates and custom webitems, only templates, or only custom webitems. You do not necessarily have to have both templates and custom webitems in your webclasses.

- An .asp (Active Server Pages) file used to host the webclass in Internet Information Server (IIS). The .asp is generated automatically when you create a webclass project.
- A webclass run-time component, MSWCRUN.DLL, that helps process requests.
- A project DLL (generated automatically on compile) that contains your Visual Basic code and is accessed by the run-time component.

The following figure shows how the server portions of an IIS application work together:

Structure of IIS applications

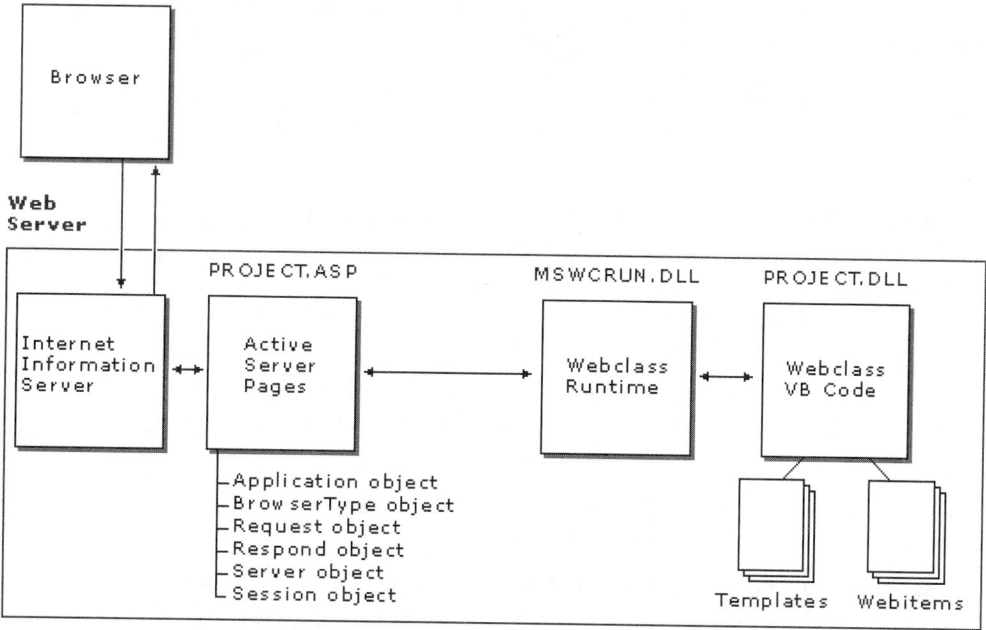

Like other Visual Basic applications, an IIS application has code modules and a visual designer. IIS application objects are stored in plain text files that contain the source code of the webclass, events and property settings, and the webitems for the webclass. Visual Basic uses the extension .dsr for these files. In addition to the .dsr file, Visual Basic generates a .dsx file that contains a binary version of the application.

Design Considerations for IIS Applications

There are several factors you should keep in mind when creating an IIS application. These include deciding on a consistent directory structure, using paths that will make your deployment work smoothly, and considering the unique navigational considerations of Web applications.

General Considerations

- **Use relative URLs to images and related files.** Your application and its HTML pages can be deployed onto a Web server under a different parent directory than the one on the development computer. Because of this, it is best to use relative URLs in your HTML pages rather than absolute URLs. *Absolute URLs* indicate the exact drive and directory in which your HTML page will expect to find any related images or other files it references. *Relative URLs* give the name of the file to locate and indicate its location in relation to your project directory, specifying how many directories up or down to move to find the reference.

- **Anticipate your Web server directory structure**. During design, think about the Web server directory structure you will use when you deploy your application, and use the same directory structure on your development machine. Your project files — including the designer, its DLL, any template files, and any additional files the templates reference (such as .gifs) — must be stored in the project directory or in subdirectories below it. For more information, see "Managing your Project Files," later in this chapter.
- **Use generated URLs**. Use generated URLs whenever possible to move to other webitems or pages, rather than typing a manual URL (http://www.myserver.com/mypage.htm) into your webclass templates or code. For more information, see "Specifying URLs for Webitems" in this chapter.
- **Gather request resources with BeginRequest**. Use the BeginRequest event to gather expensive server-side resources that the webclass should not hold longer than the duration of a request. Release those resources with the EndRequest event.
- **Use ADO data features**. When working with databases in your webclass code, use ODBC connection pooling and ADO disconnected recordsets. For more information, search the MSDN library for ActiveX Data Objects.
- **Review your state management options carefully**. When planning your application, it is important to read through the information on state management and choose the most appropriate method for your needs. For more information, see "State Management in IIS Applications," later in this chapter.
- **Be careful when using wcRetainInstance**. When keeping a webclass alive between requests, be aware that Visual Basic creates apartment-model objects that it places into the Session objects. This causes IIS to bind the client to a particular thread. This may cause difficulties for your application. This may also be an issue if you put Visual Basic classes into the Session or Application objects. For more information, see "State Management in IIS Applications" in this chapter.
- **Do not use HTML pages that contain forms with the GET method**. If you use an HTML template file that contains forms that use the GET method, you will not be able to successfully connect events and run the application. You need to make sure that all template files you use in your webclass use the POST method for any forms.

Navigational Considerations

It is difficult to predict the exact way in which users are going to interact with a browser-based application. Unlike a forms-based application, where navigation from form to form is generally fixed, users in a browser-based application can move backward and forward at any time, can jump randomly, or can close the application without completing their current process. Because of this inherent flexibility, there are several things you should keep in mind:

- **Close database transactions**. Try to avoid holding open database transactions across request boundaries, because there is no guarantee that the user will return to the transaction after the initial request is made. Holding a transaction open on a database consumes expensive resources and locks a part of the database from other users. Instead, consider committing database changes at the end of every request.
- **Allow for open navigation**. Structure your application so that users can navigate freely among the application's webitems, rather than assuming a fixed navigation path. You can do this by including navigational buttons and other aids that allow a user to return to the starting point from any place in the application, or including other cues that help the user figure out the appropriate navigational choice from each screen.
- **Anticipate re-submits**. Consider how you will handle out-of-sequence navigation caused by use of the browser's back button and history menu. This can be particularly important in the case of applications that use HTML forms. In these situations, the user might complete a transaction and then use the back button to return to a data entry form thinking they can make a correction and resubmit.
- **Refill data structures when a user moves backwards**. Any internal data structures you use in the application must be filled appropriately. For example, suppose your startup screen in the application asks for a user name and password, which you then store in member variables. If a user is in the middle of your application and navigates back to the startup screen, you must reset the variables to their original state.

IIS Application Development Process

The process of creating an IIS application is similar to creating any other project in Visual Basic. The overall process is presented below. Details for each step in the process can be found later in this chapter.

The overall process for creating IIS applications is:

1. Start a new project and select IIS Application as the project type.
2. Save the project.

   Note Unlike forms-based Visual Basic applications, you must save an IIS application before you add HTML template webitems to it.

3. Add as many HTML template webitems and custom webitems to the webclass as needed.
4. Add any custom events to the project.
5. Write code for all standard, template, and custom events in the project.

   Note Make sure you write code for the Start event, or your application will not run unless the user specifies a webitem in the base URL. For more information, see "Setting the Start Event" in this chapter.

6. Add other code modules or webclass objects to the project.

7. Test and debug the application by running the project and viewing the application in the browser. It is recommended that you test all browsers you plan to support before releasing the application to end-users.
8. Compile the project.
9. Deploy the application.

Beginning Your IIS Application Project

When you begin an IIS application, you select a special type of project called an IIS Application. An *IIS Application* project is an ActiveX DLL project type that automatically includes an instance of the appropriate ActiveX designer. The designer, called a *WebClass object*, acts as the base on which you create your application.

The Webclass designer corresponds to a single webclass in your application, but it can contain multiple HTML templates and webitems. If you want to include more than one webclass in your application, you can insert additional designers into your project.

There are several properties that you should always set for the webclass.

- **StateManagement** — This property, available for the webclass object in the Properties window, determines whether your webclass stays alive between browser requests or is destroyed at the completion of each request.
- **Public** — Your webclass must be set to public in order for the application to run. This is controlled by the Public property, available for the webclass object in the Properties window. By default, the Public property is set to True.
- **Unattended Execution** — This option, available in the Project Properties dialog box for your IIS applications, allows instances of a DLL class to be allocated on any thread. This ability is necessary to IIS in order to avoid having all webclass instances allocated to a single thread.
- **Retained in Memory** — This option, available in the Project Properties dialog box for your IIS applications, allows the Visual Basic project to keep its run-time support state permanently loaded on the server's threads, allowing server programs that load Visual Basic projects to run significantly faster.

To begin your IIS application

1. Start a new project and select **IIS Application** as your project type.
2. In the Project Explorer window, open the Designers folder, then double-click on the designer to display it in the main window.

To add additional webclass designers to your project

- On the **Project** menu, click **Add Webclass** and Visual Basic adds it to your project.

  Note The first four kinds of ActiveX designers loaded for a project are listed on the **Project** menu. If more than four designers are loaded, the later ones will be available from the **More ActiveX Designers** submenu on the **Project** menu.

For More Information See "State Management in IIS Applications," later in this chapter, for more information on setting the StateManagement property for your webclass. Also see "Public Property" in the *Microsoft Visual Basic 6.0 Language Reference* volume of the *Microsoft Visual Basic 6.0 Reference Library.*

Adding HTML Templates to the Webclass

You add HTML templates to your IIS application to enable your webclass to send HTML pages to the browser in response to user requests. When you add a template to your webclass, you choose an HTML page you want to associate with it. Visual Basic then scans that file and looks for HTML tags that are capable of launching a request to the server. Such tags include form elements, image tags, hyperlinks, and most other tags that contain an URL reference.

> **Note** Although a webclass can contain multiple template webitems, each template webitem can represent only one HTML page. You must add additional templates for each HTML page you want to include in your application.

Tags in the HTML page can contain attributes that launch a server request. For example, in an IMG tag, the SRC attribute is used to specify a URL location from which to retrieve a file. This attribute, and others like it that call the server, can become events in your IIS application. Visual Basic lists each of these tags and attributes in the right panel of the designer window. The name of each tag is taken from the ID attribute for that tag, if one exists. An *ID attribute* is an optional HTML attribute that you add to the .htm file itself. For each HTML tag in the file, you can assign a unique ID that can be used to identify that tag in script or code.

> **Note** You can use Visual Basic to assign the name of the webclass or its templates, but you cannot use the Properties window to assign an ID to the selected tag.

If your HTML template file contains a tag that does not have an ID, the designer assigns it an ID based on its position in the HTML page. For example, the third <A> tag without an ID would be named Hyperlink3. This ID is not permanent; if you do not connect any of the tag attributes to events or webitems, the ID is not stored in the HTML page. However, when you connect one of the tag's attributes, the ID becomes permanent and is stored in the .dsr file for the page.

You must save your project before you can add a template to it. After you add the template, Visual Basic does one of the following things:

- If the .htm file you chose for the template was located outside the project directory, Visual Basic makes a copy of the template file and places it in the project directory.
- If the .htm file you chose for the template came from the project directory or if there is another .htm file there with the same name, the system creates a copy of the .htm file but appends a number to its name. For example, a file called OrderForm.htm would be changed to OrderForm1.htm.

The action of copying the .htm file occurs when you save or debug the project, or when you use the Edit HTML Template menu command.

> **Important** From this point on, the .htm file in the project directory acts as the source file for your project. If you want to make changes to the HTML page's appearance, you do so in this copy of the HTML page.

If your HTML template file references any additional files, such as images, you must copy those files into the project directory or a subdirectory of it. You can do this before you add the template to the webclass or after, but you must do it before debugging or running the project.

In addition, if you import an HTML page for which a similarly named .htm file already exists in the project directory, VB appends a number to the .htm file it creates for the new file. This prevents Visual Basic from overwriting an existing .htm file if you reuse a template in more than one webclass. For example, suppose you have an HTML page called feedbk.htm. The first time you add this to a webclass, Visual Basic generates a file in the project directory with the name feedbk.htm. If you add this same file to another webclass in the application, the new .htm file Visual Basic creates is named feedbk1.htm.

For more Information For more information on the directory structure you should use for your projects, see "Managing your Project Files," later in this chapter. For more information on tags and attributes, see "Understanding Internet Basics" in Chapter 1, "Introduction to Internet Applications."

To add an HTML template to an IIS application

1. In the Webclass Designer window, click the **Add HTML Template WebItem** button on the Webclass toolbar.
2. In the **Add HTML Template** dialog box, select the HTML page you want, then click **OK**.
3. If the template file you chose references any additional files, such as .gif or .jpg files, copy those files to the project directory or a subdirectory beneath it.

   > **Note** If the template file contains absolute references to the previous locations of those files on the development computer, you need to make changes to the .htm file to reflect the location the files will have when deployed to the server. See "Managing Your Project Files," later in this chapter, for more information on using relative and absolute paths in your template files.

Removing a Template from a Webclass

You can remove a template from a webclass if you no longer want to send that template file to the browser in response to requests. You cannot replace one template with another; instead you must remove the first template file and add a link to a new file. If the template files have the same name, any event procedures you wrote for the former template will be available to the new template.

For example, suppose you are working with a catalog application and want to change the order form your application uses. You delete a template file called OrderForm, then add another HTML page with the same name that contains a different order entry form. All event procedures associated with the original OrderForm file, such as OrderForm_Respond, are immediately associated with the new file.

To remove a template from the webclass

- Right-click the template webitem and click **Delete**.

Editing the HTML for a Template

After you have inserted an HTML template file, you can use the HTML editor of your choice to make changes to the page's content and layout. You do so by selecting the Edit HTML Template option from the context menu for a template. Visual Basic opens the .htm file from the project directory. After you finish editing, the designer displays a prompt asking if you want to refresh the file. You must refresh the file if you want to see the changes you made.

By default, Visual Basic displays either your default HTML editor or Notepad when you edit your template. Visual Basic automatically detects your default HTML editor by looking at the system registry.

> **Note** You can determine the program that opens when you edit your template by making an entry in the External HTML Editor field found on the Advanced tab of the Project Options dialog box.

To edit your HTML webitem

1. In the left panel of the Designer window, right-click the template for which you want to edit the HTML, then select **Edit HTML Template**.
2. Make your changes to the .htm file, save, and return to Visual Basic.
3. If you have made any changes to the event tags in the file, right-click the webitem and select **Refresh HTML Template**, or respond to the prompt to refresh.

   Visual Basic parses the file.

Saving Changes to Your Template

If you want to update the webclass with changes you have made to the .htm file, you refresh the link between your template and its external file. When you refresh the template, Visual Basic checks to see whether the events currently listed for the template still exist, and whether any new attributes should be added. The program adds any new attributes and processes any changes for existing events. If an event for the template no longer exists in the .htm file, Visual Basic removes it from the webclass. Any procedures you wrote for the event are not removed — you must clean up the event procedures yourself.

If another user makes changes to an .htm file used in your webclass, you receive a prompt asking whether you want to refresh the template. This message appears each time a user saves the .htm file in an editor.

To save changes to the .htm file you've referenced

- In the left panel of the designer window, right-click the template for which you want to refresh your import, then select **Refresh HTML Template**.

  Visual Basic parses the file.

For More Information See "Connecting Events in a Webclass," later in this chapter, for more information on connecting and disconnecting events for a webitem.

Adding Custom Webitems to the Webclass

You add custom webitems to your webclass to specify programmatic resources, rather than file-based resources, for your application. Unlike template webitems, which are linked to and manipulate HTML pages, custom webitems are containers that generally group a set of code procedures you want the webclass to be able to access from multiple places in the application.

There are several ways in which custom webitems are useful:

- Custom webitems can help you produce more modular or structured code. For example, suppose you have several HTML template files in your webclass that all contain a single image, called logo.gif, that is stored in a database. Rather than writing a separate procedure to retrieve and display this image for each IMG tag event in the webclass, you can add a custom event to a custom webitem and define the image retrieval procedure there. Each webitem can then access the custom webitem's event, using the URLFor method, instead of handling the procedure itself.
- Custom webitems can provide a good way to encapsulate code in your IIS application that produces a frequently used HTML response, such as a standard header or a table.
- Custom webitems can allow you to send a response to the browser at times when a template file is not a good solution or when a template is not available. For example, if you want to dynamically generate a page in response to a search request, you could do this by using a template file and parsing replacements, or you could generate the entire page within a custom webitem's Respond event.

To add a custom webitem to a webclass

1. In the Webclass Designer window, click the **Add Custom WebItem** button on the toolbar. A webitem appears in the treeview, beneath the **Custom WebItems** folder.
2. To rename the webitem, use the **Properties** window to specify a name.

To remove a custom webitem from the webclass

- Right-click the webitem and click **Delete**.

For More Information See "Webclass Events," later in this chapter, for more information on custom events. See "Specifying URLs for Webitems," later in this chapter, for more information on using the URLFor method.

Managing your Project Files

When you edit an HTML template file, save your project, or debug the application, Visual Basic saves the webclass and its associated template .htm files to the directory you specify. When you debug the project, Visual Basic uses this directory as the IIS virtual directory the webclass needs to run. A *virtual directory* is a directory outside your Web server's home directory that appears to browsers as a subdirectory of the home directory. A virtual directory allows you to publish contents to the Web from directories outside the home directory structure.

> **Note** All of the project files — including the designer and any files the templates reference — should be located either in the project directory or in a subdirectory beneath it. The .htm files for the templates must be in the main project directory.

You can think of your project directory for an IIS application as a "mirror" of the directory structure you will use on the Web server when you deploy the application. You should arrange the files for your project in the directory structure you plan to use. For example, if you plan to use a separate graphics directory on the Web server, you should use a similar subdirectory beneath your project directory.

Relative vs. Absolute URL Paths

After you link a template file to a webclass, you must make sure that the references it contains to images and other files will work correctly when you deploy your application to the server. In most cases, you can ensure this by using relative paths in the URLs that reference these images and other files.

For example, suppose you have an HTML page that references two images on your local drive, using *absolute URLs* — that is, URL paths that indicate the drive and directory in which to find an associated file. When you deploy the template file to the Web, these references are no longer valid. Instead, you should replace these absolute references with *relative URLs* — that is, URL paths that indicate the location of an item relative to the current directory, without giving a specific drive or root directory. As long as the directory structure you use on your development computer mimics the directory structure you use on the Web site, your links will resolve correctly after deployment.

There are two situations in which you can safely use absolute URL paths:

- If your HTML template file references an image or other file that has a permanent home on a Web server, you do not need to replace an absolute reference to this image with a relative image. Absolute references to server locations will resolve correctly after you deploy your application.
- References to external sites (such as www.microsoft.com) can be referenced with absolute URL paths.

Example: Setting Up Directories for a Simple Webclass

Suppose you have a project called feedback.vbp. The webclass in this project uses a single template file: thankyou.htm. This HTML page references two image files: a corporate logo called logo.gif and a decorative picture called banner.gif. The following table shows the original locations of the files in this project:

File	Original Location
feedback.vbp	c:\vb98\myproject\
thankyou.htm	c:\front page\
logo.gif	c:\front page\images\
banner.gif	c:\front page\images\

After you add the template to the webclass and save the project, Visual Basic creates a copy of the HTML page and stores it in the project directory. The following table shows the changes to your directory structure after adding the template. These changes happen automatically when you add the template.

File	Interim Location
feedback.vbp	c:\vb98\myproject\
thankyou.htm	c:\vb98\myproject\
logo.gif	c:\front page\images\
banner.gif	c:\front page\images\

The final step is to move the .gif files into the project directory or a subdirectory beneath it. Suppose you plan to use a separate graphics directory on the Web server to contain your images. You need to use this same structure on your development computer, so you would create a graphics subdirectory under c:\vb98\myproject\ for your images, then manually copy the files to that location. The following table shows the final directory structure for your file, before deployment. You would make these changes manually by copying the files to the project directory.

File	Final Location
feedback.vbp	c:\vb98\myproject\
thankyou.htm	c:\vb98\myproject\
logo.gif	c:\vb98\myproject\graphics\
banner.gif	c:\vb98\myproject\graphics\

Example: Using Relative Paths

After copying the graphics files to the subdirectory as shown above, you must make sure that your references to these images in the .htm file and in your Visual Basic code use relative paths that accurately reflect the files' location after deployment. For example, in the .htm file any references to the logo graphic should be:

```
images/logo.gif
```

This is considered a *relative URL* because it does not provide the full server and directory path to the file. Instead, it indicates that the file can be found in a graphics subdirectory of the Web server directory from which the current page was drawn.

For More Information See the HTML reference of your choice for more information on relative and absolute paths.

Using Frames with Webclasses

HTML has a feature _that allows you to divide the display area in a browser into two or more sections. These sections are called *frames*. Each frame can display content from a different Web page. For example, suppose you are working with a catalog application. You might use frames to display a list of all items in the catalog in one frame and detail for the selected item in a second frame.

Frames are created from an HTML page that contains tags known as FRAMESET tags. The FRAMESET tags indicate how many frames the page should contain, their size and position, and the HTML pages that should be displayed in each frame. The browser accesses the page containing the frameset information, processes the tags, and shows the resulting information to the user.

If you want to use frames with a webclass application, the simplest way to do it is to use an HTML template file to contain modified frameset information, add it to your webclass, then link webitems or events to each frame. The following HTML code shows how you might create a template file with frameset information.

```
<FRAMESET frameBorder=0 cols=30%,70% TARGET=Right MARGINHEIGHT=0>
   <FRAME id=Left>
   <FRAME id=Right>
</FRAMESET>
```

Normally, you would need to include information telling the browser what content to display in each frame. However, in a webclass application, you do not need to do this because you can link webitems or custom events to each frame and use the processing defined for those items to tell the webclass what to do. The following figure shows how the .htm file shown above would display in the page designer prior to connecting any events:

Frame document in the Webclass Designer

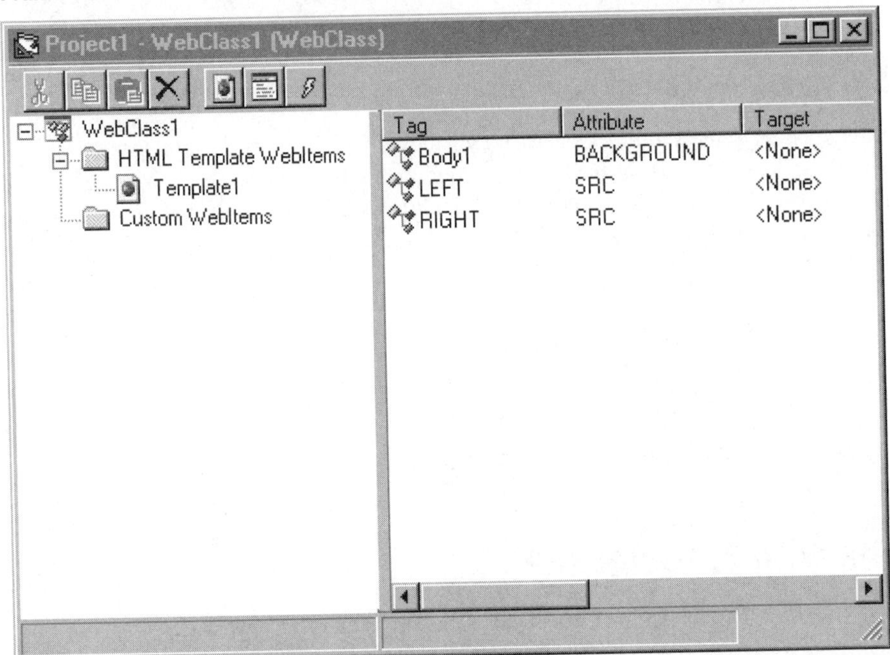

For the frames above, you might link a custom event called ShowList to the first frame, and a custom event called ShowDetail to the left frame. You would define processing for ShowList that writes a list of the items in your catalog to the leftmost frame. You would define processing for ShowDetail that displays detail information for the first item in the list. When the browser opens the frameset template file, it parses these two events and displays the results. The user can then work with the data in the list and detail frames.

For More Information See "Frameset" in the *Internet Client SDK* for more information on the frameset tags.

Webclass Events

Every webitem in the webclass contains a series of events. There are three kinds of webclass events: standard events, template events, and custom events. The following table summarizes the main differences between these three events.

Event	Originates	Appears	Applies to	Example
Standard event	Predefined.	Only in the Code Editor window's Procedure list.	Templates and custom webitems.	Respond, ProcessTag
Template event	Event candidates are generated by Visual Basic when it parses an HTML template file.	In the Designer window, and in the Code Editor window after connecting.	Templates.	Img1 SRC, Form1
Custom event	Added by the developer.	In the Designer window, and in the Code Editor window.	Custom webitems or templates.	VerifyUser, DisplayChart

The end user of an IIS application initiates the process that fires an event by clicking on an element in the browser — for example, a hyperlink — that makes a request to the server. The webclass intercepts this request and takes one of the following actions:

- If an event is specified in the request, the webclass fires the Visual Basic event by matching the request up to the appropriate webitem and event procedure.
- If the event specified in the request does not correspond to any existing webclass event, the webclass fires the UserEvent event for the template.
- If there is no event specified in the request, the webclass fires the Respond event for the template.
- If no webitem or event is specified in the request, the system launches the ASP for the application and fires the webclass's Start event.

For More Information See "Responding to Events in IIS Applications," later in this chapter, for more information on writing code to process your events.

Standard Webclass Events

By default, each template and webitem you add to a webclass has a set of standard events that automatically appear in the Code Editor window. There are three standard events for any webitem:

- Respond — Sets the default action a webitem takes when activated by a user request.
- ProcessTag — Processes specific tags in a template file and replaces their content with data you specify. The tags to process are identified by the TagPrefix property for the webitem.
- UserEvent — Processes webclass events created at run time.

The most commonly used of these is the Respond event. This is the default event for templates and webitems. The webclass fires the Respond event in two situations: when the webitem is first activated, or when it receives a request from the browser that does not correspond to a template event. The webitem can be activated from the client or the server. A client-side activation occurs when a request contains a reference to the next webitem that should be called. A server-side activation occurs when the NextItem property is set. In either scenario, the Respond event processes the request and sends a response to the browser.

For example, if a user accesses a customer inquiry application and submits a query about whether an order has been shipped, the Respond event might retrieve the request data, process the request by reading a database and retrieving the order detail, then write a reply back to the client that contains the retrieved information.

> **Note** Unlike template events and custom webitem events, the Respond event does not appear in the designer's Detail panel. You access it from the code window's Procedure drop-down list along with other standard events that are not exposed through an external file or from a user's action in the designer.

Events in an IIS application are fired by actions that occur in the browser. These actions might be initiated by the user selecting an element that contains a URL, or they might be caused by the browser loading a page. For example, when the browser loads a page containing an IMG tag, it fires the event corresponding to that tag when it attempts to resolve the URL for the image and display it. Alternately, a user can select an item such as a hyperlink and manually fire an event. In both cases, the event is fired because the browser accesses a URL that calls the server.

For More Information See "Transitioning Between WebItems," later in this chapter, for more information on the NextItem property. See "Respond Event," "ProcessTag Event," "TagPrefix Property," and "UserEvent Event" in the *Microsoft Visual Basic 6.0 Language Reference*. For information on using the ProcessTag event to process text replacements, see "Performing Text Replacements in a Webclass," later in this chapter. For information on using the UserEvent event to process dynamically created events, see "Defining Webclass Events at Run Time," later in this chapter.

Template Webitem Events

Tags within an HTML template file can act as event sources if the browser calls the server when the user selects their corresponding HTML elements. Elements call the server if their HTML tags have attributes that contain a URL. For example, when the user selects a hyperlink, the browser sends a URL request to the server to display another page. The hyperlink tag can therefore be treated as an event source in the webclass, because the webclass can intercept this request and process Visual Basic code for it.

When you add a template, Visual Basic scans the file and makes note of each tag within it that can make a server request. The designer displays the attributes of these tags in the right panel. Most tags have only one attribute that can call the server, but some tags, such as the IMG tag, have multiple attributes that can do so. There are three steps to setting up template webitem events:

1. You choose which of the tag attributes displayed in the Detail panel you want to treat as events.
2. You perform a process known as "connecting" for each attribute you want to process.
3. You write code for each connected event.

Connecting an attribute means that you are activating it, or enabling the attribute to be treated as an event. Until an attribute is connected, it does not appear in the Code Editor window for the webclass and you cannot write procedures for it. After the tag attribute is connected, it appears in the Procedure drop-down list in the Code Editor window with the other standard events. You can select the template event and write code for it like you would any Visual Basic event.

A template event differs from a standard event in two main ways:

- Template events are generated from an .htm file. A standard event is predefined and appears automatically for every template in the webclass. Because template events are generated from the HTML, you can have a different set of template events for each template file.
- Template events must be connected before they can be programmed. Standard events are always available in the Code Editor window.

For More Information See "Adding HTML Templates to the Webclass," earlier in this chapter, for information on adding a template file to the Webclass and viewing the tags that can act as events. See "Connecting Events in a Webclass," later in this chapter, for instructions on connecting tags to events and webitems.

Custom Webitem Events

You can add custom events to webitems in order to provide additional event handling for them. When you create a custom event, you associate it with the template or custom webitem for which it will be fired, then define the code to determine the action Visual Basic takes when the event fires.

Custom events can be fired directly from the browser through the URLFor method. For example, you can access a custom event by using the URLFor method to reference the custom webitem and event name, as shown in the following code:

```
Response.Write "<A HREF=""" & URLFor(CustomWebItem1,"CustomEventName") _
& """></A>"
```

When the user selects this hyperlink in the browser, the webclass intercepts the request and fires the specified custom event on the server.

To add custom events to a custom webitem

1. In the left panel of the designer window, right-click the custom webitem to which you want to add an event.
2. Click **Add Custom Event**. An event appears in the right panel of the designer window.
3. Write code for the event.

For More Information See the next section, "Firing Custom Events," and "Specifying URLs for Webitems," later in this chapter, for more information on the URLFor method, or see "URLData Property" in the *Microsoft Visual Basic 6.0 Language Reference*.

Firing Custom Events

Unlike template events, which are fired when the user selects an element in the browser, custom events do not automatically correspond to an element in the browser. To fire these events, you must first use the URLFor method to associate the custom event with an element in the browser. The URLFor method does this by creating a URL that references the custom event. When the user selects the element associated with the URL (for example, a hyperlink), the custom event fires.

For example, suppose you add a custom event named RetrieveAuthorBio to your project, and associate it with a custom webitem called AdditionalInfo. The following screen shows the project.

Sample Project

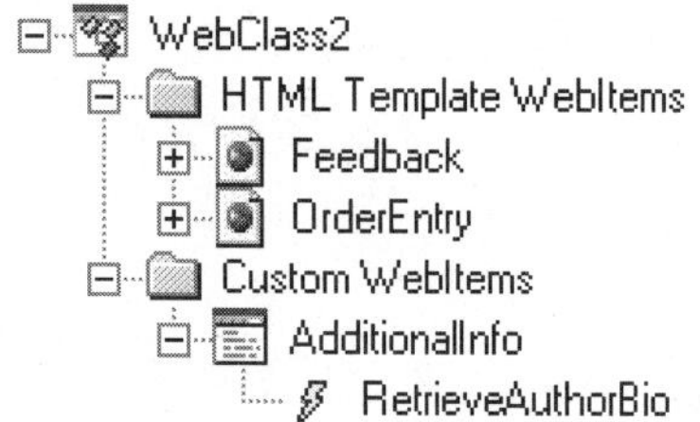

Suppose you want to fire the RetrieveAuthorBio event from another page in your application. The following code shows how you would use the URLFor method to include a link to this event:

```
Response.Write "<A HREF=""" & URLFor(AdditionalInfo,"RetrieveAuthorBio") _
& "" ">Retrieve</A>"
```

This code inserts a hyperlink onto the page that, when selected, activates the AdditionalInfo webitem and fires its RetrieveAuthorBio event.

For More Information See "URLFor Method" in the *Microsoft Visual Basic 6.0 Language Reference* for more information on syntax and arguments for this method. See "Webclass Events" in this chapter for more information on custom events.

The Webclass Life Cycle

Like a form-based application, a webclass is initialized and destroyed, although these events are fired differently than they are for a form. In addition, a webclass has several other events that mark stages in its life, indicating when the browser displays the first webitem and when requests are received and processed.

These are the key events in the life of a webclass:

1. The Initialize event occurs when an end user accesses the .asp (Active Server Pages) file that acts as the host for your IIS application. In the Initialize event, the webclass is created as an object. This is always the first event in the webclass's lifetime.

   Note If the StateManagement property for the webclass is set to wcNoState, the webclass fires the Initialize event each time it receives an HTTP request. See "State Management in IIS Applications," later in this chapter, for more information about setting the StateManagement property.

2. The BeginRequest event is the next event called after the Initialize event when the user starts the application, and is also fired each time the webclass receives a subsequent request from the browser. This event marks the beginning of processing for an HTTP request. You might use this event to perform processing required for every request the webclass will perform. For example, you could use BeginRequest to retrieve state information from a database or to verify user information before processing a request.

3. The Start event generally occurs the first time BeginRequest is fired in the application. It is not fired on subsequent requests. This event is generally used to send an initial response to the browser, launching the Respond event for the specified webitem.

   Note If the end user specifies a webitem and event in the initial URL they use to launch the application, the webclass does not fire the Start event. In this case, the specified event would be the first event fired. See "Setting the Start Event," later in this chapter, for more information.

4. The EndRequest event occurs when the webclass has finished processing an HTTP request and has returned a response to the client. The processing of an event might require the webclass to process several templates or webitems and their associated event procedures before a response is returned to the client.

5. The Terminate event tells the run-time DLL to destroy the instance of the webclass.

   Note If the StateManagement property for the webclass is set to wcNoState, the webclass fires the Terminate event each time it sends a response to the browser. If the StateManagement property for the webclass is set to wcRetainInstance, the webclass fires the Terminate event only after it calls the ReleaseInstance method. See "State Management in IIS Applications," later in this chapter, for more information about setting the StateManagement property.

There are no Load and Unload events for an IIS application. Instead, the BeginRequest or EndRequest events can perform some of the same functions as the Load and Unload event did — these events can be used to initialize values your application needs to run, and clean up state and other values at the end of a request. Begin and EndRequest are unique events for a webclass. A webclass may receive multiple requests throughout its life. These events allow the webclass to process each request as a unique entity.

Connecting Events in a Webclass

Responding to Events in IIS Applications

HTML template files are made up of HTML tags, tag attributes, and text. HTML tags tell the system how to format and display the information on the page. Attributes provide additional detail about a specific item on the page. For example, for a picture in an HTML page, a tag called an IMG tag tells the system to format and display a picture. An attribute of that tag tells the system where to retrieve the picture from on the server.

When Visual Basic first adds a template to your webclass, it parses the file and lists all the tags for which one or more attributes can be treated as events. These attributes are not actual events, however, until they go through a process known as *connecting*. Prior to connection, it is more accurate to think of the tag attributes listed in the designer as event candidates.

You can connect an attribute in two ways:

- You can connect the attribute to an event if you want to write code that tells the webclass how to respond when the element is processed by the browser. Elements are processed on the browser when the user selects the element or when the page processes them automatically, such as when it loads the page.
- You can connect the attribute to a webitem if you want the element to activate a webitem and fire its Respond event when the element is processed in the browser.

For More Information See "Webclass Events," earlier in this chapter, for more information on adding events to a webclass and the types of events a webclass can process. See "Responding to Events in IIS Applications," later in this chapter, for more information on writing code to process your events.

Connecting Attributes to Events

The template events in a webclass generally correspond to attributes of HTML tags in the template file. For example, an image event corresponds to an attribute of the IMG tag in the HTML page, and a hyperlink event corresponds to an A tag attribute in the HTML page. However, the association between attributes and events is not automatic — you must connect to events those tag attributes that you want to treat as events.

Connecting an attribute to an event enables the webclass to launch an event procedure when the end user selects the HTML element the tag attribute represents. For example, suppose you are working with a template called FeedbackPage. When you add this template to the webclass, Visual Basic parses the file and discovers that there are two elements within it capable of submitting requests to the server: a Submit hyperlink and a Home hyperlink. It lists the tags and attributes for these two elements in the designer's Detail panel. You can connect the attributes to events if you want them to fire events in your application.

Only connected events can be programmed. That is, after you connect an event, it appears in the Procedure drop-down list in the Code Editor window, and you can write procedures for it. Disconnected events do not appear in this list.

The Webclass Designer indicates the events that have not been connected in two ways:

- Tags that have not yet been connected for the selected template appear in the Detail panel. After you connect an attribute, Visual Basic also displays the event in the Treeview panel, under the template to which it belongs, and displays the yellow lightning bolt icon for the event.
- The Target column displays the word "<None>" for any disconnected tags. Once the tag has been connected to an event, the designer displays the name of the event in the Target column.

After you connect an attribute to an event, you can either write code for it in the Code Editor window, rename the event to which it is connected, or disconnect it. You might disconnect an event if you want to connect it to a webitem instead of to an event, or if you do not want it to function as an event. See the next section, "Connecting Attributes to a Custom WebItem," for information on connecting to a webitem rather than an event.

To connect an attribute to an event

1. In the left panel of the **Webclass Designer**, click the template that contains the attribute you want to connect.
2. In the right panel of the **Webclass Designer**, right-click the attribute you want to connect, then select **Connect to Event**.

   Visual Basic changes the text in the Target column to indicate that the attribute has been connected, and it displays the event in the tree view beneath the appropriate template.

To disconnect an attribute from an event

- Right-click the event in the right panel of the **Webclass Designer**, then click **Disconnect**.

Connecting Attributes to a Webitem

When you connect an attribute to a webitem rather than an event, you tell the webclass to activate that webitem when the HTML element the tag attribute represents is selected in the browser. When Visual Basic activates the webitem, it fires the webitem's Respond event. You must choose the specific webitem to which you want to connect the attribute.

For example, you might connect the attributes from a template file's IMG tag to a custom webitem that references an image stored on the server. When the user selects the element corresponding to the tag, it makes a call to the server that the webclass intercepts. The webclass tells Visual Basic to launch the associated webitem and fire its Respond event, which in turn retrieves the image from the database and returns it to the browser.

Visual Basic indicates that an attribute has been connected to a webitem in the Target column. Before you connect an attribute to a webitem, the word <None> appears in the Target column. After connection, the Target column displays the name of the webitem to which you connected the tag.

After you connect an attribute to a webitem, you can disconnect it and either leave it disconnected or connect it to another webitem. See "Connecting Attributes to Events" for more information on connecting to events.

To connect an attribute to a webitem

1. In the left panel of the **Webclass Designer**, click the template that contains the tag you want to connect.
2. In the right panel of the **Webclass Designer**, right-click the attribute you want to connect, then select **Connect to Webitem**.
3. In the **Connect to WebItem** dialog box, select the webitem to which you want to connect your tag attribute, then click **OK**.

   Visual Basic displays the name of the webitem to which the attribute has been connected in the Target column.

To disconnect an attribute from a webitem

- Right-click the event in the right panel of the **Webclass Designer**, then click **Disconnect**.

Manually Adding Event Notation to an .HTM File

When Visual Basic saves the .htm file for a webclass template, it makes changes to it. For each tag attribute you connect to an event or a webitem, Visual Basic replaces a portion of the element's HTML with notation unique to the webclass. This allows the webclass to access the HTML page and determine the webitem and event that should be fired when the user selects the element. You can modify the .htm file manually to include this notation if you want to connect events without using the designer.

Note You do not have to perform the process described in the sections below if you are connecting events from within the Webclass Designer; the designer automatically modifies the HTML file.

Manual Notation to Connect an Attribute to an Event

If you want to manually modify an .htm file to include a reference to a webitem and event, you use different notation than what Visual Basic includes automatically. For example, suppose you have an HTML template file that contains the following code:

```
<form method=post>
```

If you want to manually hook up this tag to an event, you could modify the HTML as follows:

```
<form action=www.myserver.com/Project1_MyWebclass.asp?WCI=webitem1 _
?WCE=eventname method=post>
```

This notation indicates that the form tag should activate the webitem called “webitem1” and launch its FormSubmit event. The notation contains the following parts:

- *www.myserver.com* is the server on which your webclass resides.
- *Project1_MyWebclass.asp* is the name of the Active Server Pages (ASP) file associated with your webclass. The ASP is created when you run the project, and the name is set equal to the value of the NameinURL property for the webclass.
- WCI=*webitem1* identifies the webitem being referenced.
- WCE=*eventname* tells the webclass the event in the webclass to which this tag corresponds. When the user selects the element for this tag in the browser, the webclass can read this notation and determine the event that it should fire.

Manual Notation to Connect an Attribute to a WebItem

When you connect an attribute to a webitem instead of an event, you do not use the WCE=*Eventname* syntax in your .htm file. Instead, you would use the WCI=*Webitemname* argument only, as shown in the following code:

```
<form action=www.myserver.com/Project1_MyWebclass.asp?WCI=webitem1 method=post>
```

This notation indicates that the form tag should activate the webitem called “webitem1” and launch its default event. The notation contains the following parts:

- *www.myserver.com* is the server on which your webclass resides.
- *Project1_MyWebclass.asp* is the name of the Active Server Pages (ASP) file associated with your webclass. The ASP is created when you run the project and has the same name as your webclass.
- WCI=webitem1 identifies the webitem being referenced.

For More Information See “Connecting Events in a Webclass,” earlier in this chapter, for more information on connecting attributes to events and webitems.

The Object Model for IIS Applications

IIS applications are hosted by an .asp (Active Server Pages) file and make use of several of the objects in the Active Server Pages object model. The webclass uses these objects to access and manipulate information from an HTML page. The ASP objects that a webclass can use include:

- **Request** — Receives requests from end users in the browser.
- **Response** — Sends information to the browser in order to display it to the user.
- **Session** — Maintains information about the current user session and stores and retrieves state information.
- **Application** — Manages state that is shared across multiple webclass instances.
- **Server** — Creates other objects and determines server-specific properties that might influence the webclass's processing.
- **BrowserType** — Determines the capabilities of the user's browser and makes processing decisions based on that information.

The ASP Request Object

You use the Request object to retrieve information from or about the current user. The Request object gives you access to all of the information passed in any HTTP request. HTTP requests contain information about the current user, any data they entered prior to making the request, and arguments that tell the Web server how to process and respond to the request.

Most frequently, you use the Request object to retrieve information from an HTML form. For example, you might retrieve all of the form elements passed back in a Submit event. The following example shows how you might use the Request object to gather information from the browser:

```
Private Sub Webitem1_Submit
   'Define variables to hold information retrieved from the request
   Dim first as String
   Dim last as String
   'Retrieve form information and assign it to the variables, using
   'the Request object and its Form collection.
   First = Request.Form("Firstname")
   Last = Request.Form("Lastname")
End Sub
```

You can use the Request object's associated collections to access information. These collections include:

- QueryString — Retrieves the values of additional arguments in a URL when a request is passed using the GET method. GET is used by the Web server to retrieve objects and, in some cases, to send information from an HTML form.
- Form — Retrieves the value of form elements passed in an HTTP request when the request is passed using the POST method. POST is a method used by the Web browser to send the information from an HTML form.

  Note POST is the more common method used to send form information. You can use the Request object to access any of this data. You should not use the GET method in your HTML template files.
- Cookies — Retrieves the data contained in cookies sent with the form request. Cookies are small parcels of information used to store data about the current user. These can be passed between the browser and the Web server.
- ServerVariables — Retrieves information such as header values, logon name, or server protocols in use.
- ClientCertificate — Retrieves information stored in certificate fields when the browser sending the request supports client certificates. Certificates identify a user to the Web server.

For More Information See "Getting Information from a User," in the *Active Server Pages Scripting Guide,* for more information on the Request object and its collections.

The ASP Response Object

You use the Response object to return information to the browser. For example, you might use the object's Respond event to write HTML to the browser. There are several methods you can use with the Response object:

- Use the Write or BinaryWrite method to send information directly to a browser.
- Use the Redirect method to direct the user to a different URL than the one the user requested, such as a different webclass or an external page.
- Use the Cookies collection to set cookie values to return to the browser and store these values for future use. A *cookie* is a set of information about the user that can be passed between the client and the server, identifying the user to either system.
- Use the Buffer property to postpone a response while the entire page is processed.
- Use the AddHeader method to add http headers to a response.

The following example shows how you might use the Response object to write a few lines of HTML code to the browser:

```
With Response
   'Indicate the beginning of the HTML page
   .Write "<HTML>"
   'Indicate the beginning of the body section
   .Write "<BODY>"
   'Send a line with heading two style followed by
   'a paragraph break
   .Write "<H2>Feedback Form</H2><P>"
   'Send a paragraph of text
   .Write "Please enter your comments below:<P>"
   'other write statements to present form elements
   'and close the HTML document.
End With
```

For More Information See "Sending Information to a User," in the *Active Server Pages Scripting Guide,* for more information on the Response object and its collections.

The ASP Session and Application Objects

The Session and Application objects both store state information about the webclass's end users. The Session object can store information about a single user in the current session. The Application object can store information about multiple users.

You use the Session object to maintain information about the current user session and to store and retrieve state information. For example, suppose you have an application that uses two main pages: one that summarizes customer information, and one that allows the user to order products. You want to ensure that the customer only sees the information page once, regardless of how many transactions they enter. In order to do this, the webclass must be able to determine whether the user has seen the customer information when it processes each new order. You can do this by using the Session object to retain information about where the user has already been.

You use the Application object to store information about multiple users. For example, suppose you want to keep track of the number of users who access a webclass and access that statistic online. You can do this by storing a count in the Application object and incrementing it each time a user accesses a part of the webclass.

For More Information See "State Management in IIS Applications," later in this chapter, for a code example of storing state in the Session and Application objects.

The ASP Server Object

You use the Server object to create objects and determine server-specific properties that might influence the webclass's processing. For example, suppose you have a library of business objects that are used during event processing. One of these objects must be kept alive throughout the session in order to maintain internal state. You can do this using the Server and Session objects.

In this case, you could choose to store the object as a Session property, using Server.CreateObject to create an instance of it. This is necessary so that IIS can detect the threading model of the object and optimize subsequent request processing.

The following code shows how you would do this in your event procedure:

```
Dim BusObj as SomeBusinessObject
Set BusObj = Server.CreateObject("OurCompany.SomeBusinessObject.1")
'Code here to call methods of the object
Set Session("BusObjInstance") = BusObj
```

The ASP BrowserType Object

You use the BrowserType object to determine the capabilities of the user's browser and make processing decisions based on that information. For example, suppose you have an application that contains a button called CheckInventory. This button allows the user to check available inventory before placing an order. You provide two versions of the event procedure for this button in your webclass — one using HTML and one using JavaScript. You might do this if the JavaScript procedure provides a better user experience — for example, it might not cause a page transition, where the HTML procedure would.

In this scenario, you could use the BrowserType object to determine which procedure to use by determining if the user's browser supports JavaScript. The following code shows how you would use the BrowserType object to make this choice:

```
Private Sub OrderForm_ProcessTag(ByVal TagName As String, TagContents As String, SendTags
as Boolean)

   'If the browser supports Javascript, generate HTML to call a method on an applet.
   'If it does not, generate HTML to fire an event on the webclass.

   If TagName = "WC@FORMTAGSTART" Then
      If BrowserType.javascript And BrowserType.javaapplets Then
         TagContents = "<FORM onsubmit=""JavaScriptHandler()"">"
      Else
         TagContents = "<FORM ACTION=" & URLFor(OrderForm _
         "OrderForm_Submit") & " METHOD=POST>"
      End If
   End If
   SendTags = False
End Sub
```

Responding to Events in IIS Applications

Most of the processing that occurs in an IIS application occurs in the event procedures for the application's webitems. You use these events to tell Visual Basic what to do when it receives a request from the browser for a particular element on a page. Visual Basic matches requests it receives to webitem events and runs any code it finds for the event procedures.

You use Visual Basic code to tell the webclass how to process requests. These are just a few of the things you can do in your event procedures:

- Write the contents of an HTML template to the browser, or generate your own HTML.
- Redirect to another page in the application and display it, or move to another webitem and process its default event.
- Open a database connection, create recordsets, and manipulate the data to be returned to the user.
- Perform replacements on text within your HTML templates.
- Retrieve user data for processing.

Setting the Start Event

Before you can respond to user requests, you must, in most cases, write code that tells the webclass what to do when the application is first started. You can do this using the Start event.

The Start event occurs when the user first accesses your application by navigating to the .asp file that forms the base URL for your application. For example, if you have a webclass called Project1_OrderEntry.asp on a Web server called www.mycatalog.com, the base URL to fire the Start event for your application would be:

```
http://www.mycatalog.com/Project1_OrderEntry.asp
```

In most cases, you should write code for the Start event in order for Visual Basic to successfully run your webclass. You use the Start event to navigate to the first webitem in your application. The following code shows how you might do this:

```
Private Sub Webclass_Start()
   Set NextItem = Webitem1
End Sub
```

This code uses the NextItem property to navigate to the first webitem in the webclass, named Webitem1.

There are situations in which the Start event does not fire when the application is first launched. If the user specifies a webitem in the base URL, the webclass does not launch the Start event — instead, it launches the specified event for the webitem or the webitem's default event. For example, if the user knew they wanted to open a webitem called Form1 in the Project1_OrderEntry webclass, they could enter the following base URL to launch the application:

```
http://www.mycatalog.com/Project1_OrderEntry.asp?WCI=Form1
```

The notation WCI=Form1 tells the run-time DLL to open a webitem, called Form1 when it starts the application. In this case the Start event does not fire when the run-time DLL starts the application.

For More Information See "The Webclass Life Cycle," earlier in this chapter, for more information on the Start event in IIS applications. See "Transitioning Between WebItems," later in this chapter, for more information on the NextItem property.

Sending HTML to the Browser

When the webclass processes a request from the browser, it must send the browser a response. Generally, that response is a stream of HTML that the browser displays to the user. You can return HTML to the browser in two ways:

- You can send the contents of an HTML template file directly to the browser using the WriteTemplate method.
- You can produce the HTML stream with Visual Basic code.

Sending HTML from a Template

The WriteTemplate method is the simplest way to send HTML to the browser in response to a user action. When the webclass launches an event procedure for a template event that contains this method, it sends the template's HTML back to the browser. The resulting page appears to the user.

> **Note** If the template that you want to send to the browser contains any replacement indicators, the webclass fires the ProcessTag event before it sends the response. This happens automatically as part of WriteTemplate method processing.

The following code shows an example of how you would use this method in code:

```
Private Sub OrderSearch_Respond()
   OrderSearch.WriteTemplate
End Sub
```

In this code, a webitem named OrderSearch has an HTML template file associated with it. When Visual Basic fires the Respond event for this webitem, it writes the contents of that template to the browser, which displays it to the end user.

Note The WriteTemplate method does not fire the Respond event if called from an event in another webitem. In order to keep the webclass code organized, you will often want to invoke the WriteTemplate method within a Respond event.

The WriteTemplate method can take one optional argument called Template that allows you to specify a different template file to return to the browser. This is helpful when you need to choose from a group of templates with common events. For example, you may have a set of news articles that are formatted similarly and contain a common series of hyperlinks and other tag elements, no matter what the story content. These articles are stored in template files available to a webclass. You can hook up the appropriate tag elements to events in your webclass, but then use the Template argument in a WriteTemplate call to specify the appropriate template file to retrieve for a user request.

For More Information See "Performing Text Replacements in a Webclass," later in this chapter, for more information on the ProcessTag event and its processing as part of a Respond event. See "WriteTemplate Method," in the *Microsoft Visual Basic 6.0 Language Reference,* for more information on using the WriteTemplate method and its arguments.

Sending HTML from Code

If you know HTML well, you can also write HTML line by line in your event procedures and send it to the browser using the Response object. This is a more complicated way of sending HTML than the WriteTemplate method, but it is useful in situations where you do not have a template to work with (such as if you are working with a custom webitem) or in which you want to generate a customized response.

The following sample shows how you use the Response object's Write method to send HTML to the browser. In this procedure, the webclass retrieves user information from a database and writes it to an HTML table:

```
Private Sub CustomerList_Respond()
   With Response
      'Write the HTML header information and start a table
      .Write "<HTML>"
      .Write "<BODY>"
      .Write "<TABLE BORDER CELLSPACING=1 CELLPADDING=7>"

      'Fill in cells until the end of file is reached in the recordset
      Do While rs.EOF = False

         'Write the user's name and address to a row in the table
         .Write "<TR>"
         .Write "<TD>" & rs("lastname") & "," & rs("firstname") & "</TD>"
         .Write "<TD>" & rs("address") & "</TD>"
         .Write "<TD>" & rs("city") & "</TD>"
         .Write "<TD>" & rs("state") & "</TD>"
         .Write "<TD>" & rs("zipcode") & "</TD>"
         .Write "</TR>"
```

```
        'Move to the next record in the recordset, then loop
            rs.MoveNext

        Loop

        'End the table, then write closing tags for the page.
        .Write "</TABLE>"
        .Write "</BODY>"
        .Write "</HTML>"
    End With
End Sub
```

A few notes on using the Write method:

- Items to be sent to the browser must be enclosed in quotes. This includes both text and HTML tags. For example: "</TD></TR>", or "<P>Please enter your name.</P>" If you want to insert a quotation mark as part of your response, you must use two quotation marks together. For example, "" inserts a quotation mark. Three quotation marks (""") insert a quotation mark and open or close another set of quotation marks.
- You might find it simpler to use the With statement, as shown above, when writing HTML in code.
- You do not need to break your Write statements as shown above. You can put all of your HTML in a single Write statement, or break them into separate statements for easier readability.

For More Information See "The Object Model for IIS Applications," earlier in this chapter, for more information on using ASP objects in your webclass code.

Retrieving Information from an HTML Form

You can use the Request object to retrieve the information a user enters on an HTML form. Submitting a form can fire an event within your webclass, if you have connected the FORM ACTION tag attribute to an event; if so, you can use this event to gather and manipulate information. You use the Request object's Form collection to retrieve named fields from the form and set their value equal to variables in the webclass. For example, the following code shows how you would retrieve information from a book request form in an order entry application:

```
Private Sub BookList_Search()
    ' declare variables for form information
    Private sTitle as String
    Private sAuthor as String
    Private sPublisher as String

    ' retrieve form arguments and assign to variables
    sTitle = Request.Form("title")
    sAuthor = Request.Form("author")
    sPublisher = Request.Form("publisher")
```

```
    ' further code here to process this information,
    'open the database, find the book, and return it.
End Sub
```

When you add a template that contains a form to a webclass, you might notice that the form elements, such as buttons and text areas, do not appear in the Detail panel and event candidates. You can have the webclass respond to events that occur on these form elements by connecting the parent Form for the elements to an event. Then write code for the parent form that uses the Request object's Form collection to determine which element was selected.

For More Information See "The Object Model for IIS Applications," earlier in this chapter, for more information on using ASP objects in your webclass code.

Performing Text Replacements in a Webclass

Text replacements are useful in situations where you are generating some parts of your HTML page on the fly. For example, you might want to personalize a Web page with the user's name, as entered on a previous page in your application. You could insert a replacement indicator in the .htm file, then replace it at run time with the user's name.

In a more complex example, suppose you want to populate a table with the results of a database query. You can use replacement indicators in the HTML for the table to mark where information should go, then replace these indicators with the retrieved information after your query runs.

The process of performing text replacements involves scanning a webclass template file for special indicator tags and replacing them or their contents with custom content. The webclass processes these indicators automatically when it responds to the WriteTemplate method in an event procedure. WriteTemplate sends the contents of an HTML template file to the browser, after any replacements are finished.

The tags processed on the server have the following format:

- A tag prefix, usually a set of characters used to indicate to the webclass that a replacement operation is necessary. For example, you might use WC@ as your tag prefix. The tag prefix is the same for each location in the template where a replacement operation must occur. You define the tag prefix by setting the TagPrefix property for each template. WC@ is the default tag prefix in Visual Basic.
- A tag name, usually a descriptive word, that identifies the replacement area. This is usually different for each location in the template where a replacement operation must occur. If you want to perform the same replacement in several locations, use the same tag name.
- Tag contents, which represent the current contents of the tag before replacement. You can use arguments in the ProcessTag event to replace either the tags and their content, or just the content.

Together, these elements provide the webclass with the information it needs to process the tag. You insert these indicators at each location in the file where you want the system to process replacements.

For More Information See "Sending HTML to the Browser," earlier in this chapter, for more information on the WriteTemplate method and its processing. See "ProcessTag event" in the *Microsoft Visual Basic 6.0 Language Reference*.

Modifying a Template File to Use Replacements

In order to perform text replacements, you must first define a tag prefix for the template, in the Webclass Designer, then use an editor to insert those tags prefixes into the file wherever you want a replacement to occur. You can indicate as many replacement areas in a file as you want.

For example, suppose you have a template in your webclass called FeedbackPage. On this page, you want to perform a replacement in two areas: you want to insert the user's name and the date on which the user's order will be shipped. You have defined the tag prefix for this webitem to be WC@.

> **Note** The tag prefix must begin with an alphabetical character and should contain a unique character to provide for optimal processing.

Suppose that your FeedbackPage file looks like this before you add the replacement tags:

```
<HTML>
<BODY>
<P>Thank you for your order. We estimate that your order will be shipped on the following
date: xxx.
<P>
</BODY>
</HTML>
```

In order to indicate replacement areas for the name and date, you would modify the file as shown below:

```
<HTML>
<BODY>
<P>Thank you for your order, <WC@customer>firstlast</WC@customer>. We estimate that your
order will be shipped on the following date: <WC@shipdate>shipdate</WC@shipdate>.
<P>
</BODY>
</HTML>
```

The following figure identifies the pieces of the replacement area in the previous code:

Replacement indicators

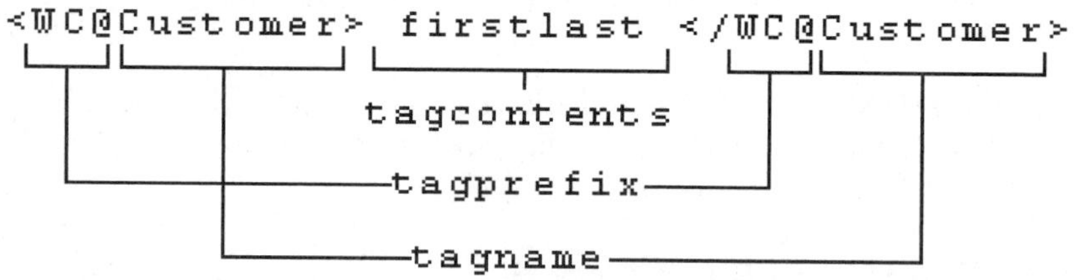

<WC@Customer> firstlast </WC@Customer>

tagcontents

tagprefix

tagname

Writing Code to Process a Replacement Area

You write all of the code to replace text in your file within the ProcessTag event. If you have a template file that contains several replacement areas and you need to treat them differently in your procedures, you would use a conditional statement such as If or Select Case to specify the different actions to take for each tag prefix on the page.

The order of processing for a file with tag prefixes is:

1. Visual Basic processes user code and calls the WriteTemplate method from an event handler in the application. Typically, the event handler is for the Respond event.
2. The webclass processes and replaces all prefixed tags in the file, according to the code you wrote for the ProcessTag event.
3. The webclass writes the template file to the Response object.
4. The WriteTemplate method sends the template file to the browser.

   Note The ProcessTag event cannot be fired automatically from the user's actions in the browser. It is called by the WriteTemplate method from within another event procedure.

For example, in the example in the previous section, you modified an .htm file to include two replacement areas: one called "customer" and one called "shipdate." The following event procedure could be used to process those replacements:

```
Sub FeedbackPage_ProcessTag(ByVal TagName as String, TagContents as _
String, SendTags as Boolean)
   'Work with previously defined variables FirstName, LastName,
   'and ShipDate
   If TagName = "wc@customer" Then
      TagContents = FirstName & "" & LastName
   EndIf
   If TagName = "wc@shipdate" Then
      TagContents = ShipDate
   EndIf
   SendTags = False
End Sub
```

In this code, the webclass retrieves information from several member variables that were previously set to values the user entered. These values correspond to the user's first name, last name, and a calculated date for shipment. The values from these three variables are inserted onto the page, which is then displayed to the user.

When the ProcessTag event is fired, the TagContents argument retrieves the current value of the text between the tags in the .htm file. For example, in the following line of HTML code, "customer" is the current value of the TagContents argument.

```
<P>Thank you for your order, <WC@customer>customer</WC@customer>.
```

You set new values for the TagContents in your ProcessTag event procedure. You can use the existing contents to help retrieve the new values. For example you could use a database key as your TagContents, then reference that value in your ProcessTag event procedure to retrieve a record from the database.

To perform text replacements for a webitem in your application

1. In the **Webclass Designer**, click the template for which you want to define text replacements, then set the value of the **TagPrefix** property in the **Properties** window to the prefix you want to use.

   Note The tag prefix must begin with an alphabetical character.

2. Open the .htm file for the template in the editor of your choice, then insert replacement indicators anywhere you want to replace text, using this format:

   <tagprefix tagname>tagcontents</tagprefix tagname>

Argument	Definition
tagprefix	The tag prefix you defined in the Properties window, for this template.
tagname	A unique identifier by which you will reference this replacement area in code. For example, for a tag prefix that will be used to insert the customer's order number, you might use the tagname "orderno."
tagcontents	A placeholder for the content you will insert. This argument can also be used to provide information about what the content should be, or to hold information that will be needed when processing the replacement, such as a database key.

3. In the **Webclass Designer**, right-click the template and click **View Code**.

4. Write code for the ProcessTag event for the webitem, using an If or Select Case statement to work through each replacement area in the file.

Rescanning for Replacement Areas

In normal replacement processing, the webclass automatically scans the .htm file once to find all tag prefixes in the file when the webclass processes the WriteTemplate event. After finding these replacement areas, the webclass processes the tags and replaces them as indicated in code. However, your code might indicate that the webclass should insert additional tag prefixes when it replaces one of the original tags. In this situation, the webclass must search the replacement area again for these new replacement indicators and process them as well.

You can tell the webclass to search again by setting the ReScanReplacements property for the webitem. The ReScanReplacements property causes the webclass to make an additional pass through the replacement tags during the ProcessTag event. You must write code for any additional replacement areas you generate in order for the ProcessTag event to work through them.

> **Note** The ReScanReplacements property tells the webclass to make another search during the ProcessTag event only. You cannot use this property to scan for replacement areas during other events.

To enable the webclass to recursively check the file for new tag prefixes

- In the **Properties** window, select the webclass and set the **ReScanReplacements** property to **True**.

Working with Lists in Webclasses

One common scenario you might want to enable is to populate the contents of a list or select element at run-time, using text replacement. List elements and select elements produce elements on your HTML page that are similar to the list box and combo box controls you use on Visual Basic forms.

Prepopulating Select Elements

Select elements in HTML have the following syntax:

```
<select name="List1" id="List1" value="List1">
   <option value="List">First list item
   <option value="List">Second list item
   <option value="List">Third list item
</select>
```

This select element is prepopulated with the list items indicated between the <select> and </select> tags.

Populating a List Element in Code

Select elements have a restriction that only <option> tags may appear between the opening and closing <select> tags. Therefore, to populate such an element at run time using text replacements, you would do the following:

- Modify your HTML to remove the select element and put text replacement tags in its place.
- Write code in the ProcessTags event procedure that would insert the select element and its option tags when the tag prefix is process.

Your resulting HTML code might look like this:

```
<WC@SelectElement></WC@SelectElement>
```

Your code in the ProcessTags procedure would take the form:

```
If TagName = "wc@SelectElement" Then
      'Code here using Response.Write to add a select element and it's
      'contents to the page.
EndIf
```

For More Information See "Performing Text Replacements in a Webclass," earlier in this chapter, for more information on tag prefixes, the ProcessTags procedure, and replacing elements in your templates.

Specifying URLs for WebItems

You use the URLFor method to easily create hyperlinks that jump to other webitems in your application. When the webclass displays a webitem in the browser, it must first locate the template file for that webitem on the server. You might not know the exact location to which you will deploy the application when you write the code. URLFor provides a convenient shortcut for you to use in these situations.

> **Note** In addition to specifying the location of the webitem, the URLFor method can also fire a specified event. The event argument is optional.

The following code shows how you might use URLFor to create a link to a webitem:

```
Private Sub ThankYouForm_Respond
   With Response
      .Write "<HTML>"
      .Write "<BODY>"
      .Write "Thank you for completing our survey. <P>"
      .Write "To return to the order inquiry page, select the _
following  link: <P>"
      .Write  "<A HREF=""" & URLFor(CustomerOrder) & """ & Return</A>"
      .Write "</BODY>"
      .Write "</HTML>"
   End With
End Sub
```

In this code, the developer creates a simple HTML page by using the Response object's Write method to create the HTML line by line. One of the elements created is a hyperlink that moves to another webitem called "CustomerOrder." The code for this hyperlink uses the URLFor method rather than specifying the exact location of the webitem on the server. No event is specified for the CustomerOrder webitem, so by default the run-time DLL launches the webitem's Respond event.

For More Information See "Firing Custom Events," earlier in this chapter, for more information on using the URLFor method to fire events.

Transitioning Between WebItems

You use the NextItem property to shift processing from one webitem to another on the server. You might do this if there are several processes you want to perform before returning a response to the browser. Normally, the webclass performs these steps when it receives a request:

1. Intercepts the request and matches it to a webitem in the application.
2. Identifies the proper event to fire on the webitem, then fires it.
3. Processes any code for that event.
4. Returns a response to the browser.

NextItem is used to add an extra step to this process. After the webclass processes the code for the event it matches to the request, the NextItem property can pass processing along to another webitem. This allows the application to perform additional processing before returning a response to the user. The process is now this:

1. Intercepts the request and matches it to a webitem in the application.
2. Identifies the proper event to fire on the webitem, then fires it.
3. Processes any code for that event.
4. Processes the NextItem property and shifts processing to another webitem and fires its Respond event.
5. Returns a response to the browser.

> **Note** No matter where the NextItem property occurs in the event procedure, Visual Basic finishes processing that procedure before it shifts processing to the indicated webitem. This is the main difference between setting the NextItem and directly calling an event subroutine in another webitem.

The following code shows NextItem used in a Respond event:

```
Private Sub Feedback_Respond()
    ' Code to process the contents of the feedback form
    ' inserted here.
    ' Transition:
    Set NextItem = Thankyou
End Sub
```

This procedure is fired when the user submits the contents of a page containing a feedback form. In response, Visual Basic transitions to another webitem containing a thank-you page.

There are three situations in which the webclass ignores the NextItem property. If you use the property in event procedures for the following events, the webclass will not process the NextItem property:

- EndRequest
- ProcessTag
- FatalErrorResponse

For More Information See "NextItem Property" in the *Microsoft Visual Basic 6.0 Language Reference*.

Navigating Between Webclasses

On occasion, you may want to create an application that has more than one webclass. You might do this if you want to encapsulate certain functionality within one webclass and reuse it in other locations. For example, you might want to use a webclass to handle customer order processing, then access this application from another webclass that also must perform these same processes.

If you are working in an IIS application with multiple webclasses, you can use the Redirect method to navigate from one webclass to another. A redirect is generally placed in the Respond event for a webitem. When a redirect is called in an event procedure, the run-time DLL suspends processing on the current webclass, shifts focus to the indicated webclass, and launches its BeginRequest event. Control can be returned to the original webclass by using another redirect.

> **Note** Each webclass in your project has its own .asp file, generated when you test or compile your project. You should specify the full path to this file in your redirect statement.

The following code shows an example of a redirect. The code in this example responds to the Click event for a button named "SearchForm" on a template called "OrderSearch." The webclass checks to see whether the action was fired as a result of a search request. If so, it uses the Request object to retrieve information from the form. If not, the server redirects to the first page in the application.

```
Private Sub OrderSearch_SearchForm()
   'if a search was initialized, retrieve form arguments
   If Request.Form("ACTION") = "Search" Then
      sCustMun = Request.Form("custNO")
      sOrderNum = Request.Form("orderNO")
      sLastName = Request.Form("custLN")
      'Navigate to an order status page
      Set NextItem = OrderStatus
   Else
      'if not, redirect to the opening page
      Response.Redirect "http://www.myserver.com/mydirectory/
      Project1_Welcome.asp"
   End If
End Sub
```

For More Information See "An Introduction to Webclasses," earlier in this chapter, for more information about how an ASP page is used in a webclass.

Using Databases with Webclasses

You can use the ADO features of Visual Basic to retrieve and manipulate information stored in a database in response to user requests. Using webclasses in this way can help you create a powerful application. With ADO, you can open a connection to the database, build recordsets, retrieve data, and update information in the database.

> **Note** If you are working with a database, you must have the appropriate database program on your Web server. In addition, you should make use of ODBC connection pooling and ADO disconnected recordsets when accessing a database. For more information on these features, see the ActiveX Data Objects documentation in your MSDN library.

There are multiple ways you might use databases in your applications. For example, you might create an application in which a series of images for a catalog are stored in a database. When users in your IIS application select a link from the catalog table of contents, the webclass can intercept that link, open a connection to the database, retrieve the image, and return it to the browser. Or you might use a search page to query a database for matching items and display the results in a generated table.

You can use the Respond event or another event for the appropriate webitem to handle your database connection and processing. For example, the following code shows how you would open a connection to an ADO database, create a recordset, and retrieve information from it:

```
Private Sub AuthorList_Respond()

   'Declare object variables for the database connection and recordset
   Dim cn As New ADODB.Connection
   Dim rs As New ADODB.Recordset
```

```
'Open the database connectioncn.ConnectionString =
"DSN=csmith;UID=sa;PWD=sa;DATABASE=pubs"cn.Open
'Create the recordsetrs.Open "select * from customer", cn, adOpenStatic, adLockReadOnly

   'Write resulting information to a table, record by record
   With Response
      .Write "<HTML>"
      .Write "<BODY>"
      .Write "<TABLE BORDER CELLSPACING=1 CELLPADDING=7>"

      Do While rs.EOF = False
         .Write "<TR><TD>"
         .Write rs("authorlast") & ", " & rs("authorfirst")
         .Write "</TD><TD>"
         .Write rs("title")
         .Write "</TD><TD>"
         .Write rs("publisher")
         .Write "</TD><TR>"
         rs.MoveNext
      Loop
      .Write "</TABLE>"
      .Write "</BODY>"
      .Write "</HTML>"

   End With

   'Close the recordset and the database connection
   rs.Close
   cn.Close

End Sub
```

For More Information For more information on ADO processing, search for "ActiveX Data Objects" in the MSDN Library.

Defining Webclass Events at Run Time

In addition to handling events that exist in the webclass at design time, you can create events at run time and process them dynamically. The ability to generate events at run time is useful in cases where you generate part or all of your user interface dynamically, by writing HTML in your response to the browser.

You generate user events at run time using the URLFor method, which takes two arguments: the name of a webitem in your webclass, and the name of an event. To create a user event, you pass this function the name of an event that was not defined at run time.

Processing for these run-time events is handled by the UserEvent event. In the procedure for this event, you write code that tells the webclass how to process all its dynamically generated events. If there is more than one of these events, you must use a conditional statement such as If or Select Case to tell the webclass how to respond to each of them.

Example: Dynamic Events in a Search Page

Suppose you have an application that consists of two pages:

- A search page that looks up last names in a database. The interface for this page is fixed: it contains a few elements that are used to launch the search request.
- A results page that displays the results in a table and provides a hyperlink for each to find more information. The interface for this page changes based on the number of records found in the database.

The following figure shows two possible outcomes of the search.

Tables with Dynamically Generated Events

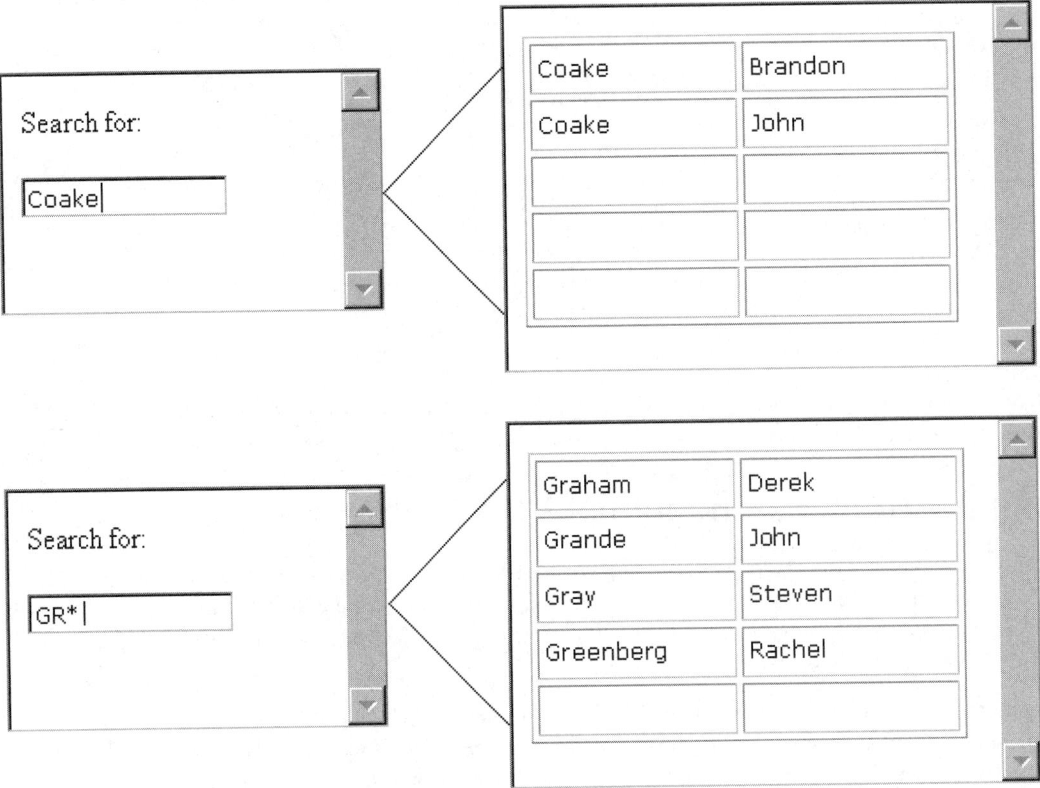

Suppose that for each row the search returns, you want to generate a hyperlink the user can select to receive more information. These hyperlinks can act as events for the webclass, but you cannot handle these events at design time because they are created dynamically when the search is executed. Therefore, you must generate these events at run time.

The following shows some of the Visual Basic code you would use to generate the table and create user events for it.

```
With Response

  'Begin a table
  .Write "<TABLE BORDER CELLSPACING=1 CELLPADDING=7>"

  'For each record in the result set, generate a row.
  Do While rs.EOF = False
    'Start a row and cell
    .Write "<TR><TD>"

    'Insert a hyperlink calling the lastname field,which represents
    'a database key into the database record, for the Response webitem
        .Write  "<A HREF=""" & URLFor(Response, rs("lastname") & """>"

    'Make the text of the hyperlink the person's name.
    .Write rs("lastname") & ", " & rs("firstname")
    .Write </A>"
    .Write "</TD></TR>

    'Move to the next record and loop
    rs.MoveNext
  Loop

  'End the table
  .Write "</TABLE>"

End With
```

To handle the events for the response page, you would define code for the Response webitem's UserEvent event.

Coding User Events

You handle all user events for a webitem within a single UserEvent procedure. If you have a page that contains several user events and you need to treat them differently in your procedures, you would use a conditional statement such as If or Select Case to specify the different responses for each dynamic event name on the page.

> **Note** In the case of the table generated in the previous section, you would not use an If or Select Case statement because you want to perform the same operation for each row — retrieve the database key from the table, then look up the record and display more information.

The webclass fires the UserEvent event when it receives a request from the browser that references a user event. The following code shows the procedure you might define for the events in the table shown in the section above:

```
Private Sub Response_UserEvent(ByVal EventName As String)

   'Set a previously-defined variable to a new recordset
   rs = New Ado.recordset

   'Retrieve the key
   rs.GetPerson EventName

   'Code here to display a page with all of the information
   'for the retrieved record.
End Sub
```

In this code, the developer creates a new recordset and retrieves the value for the specified key. You would replace the word Key with the appropriate key value.

State Management in IIS Applications

Typically, Internet applications are *stateless,* in that the protocol that passes requests and responses between the browser and Web server is not capable of maintaining information between each request. Therefore, the protocol does not "remember" any information from previous requests when it receives a new request.

Because the protocol itself cannot maintain state, you must use other means to store information you want the application to remember between requests. There are several ways you can store state for a Web-based application:

- Use the WebClass object or other objects on the server to store state information between client requests.
- Use a database to store state information between requests.
- Move state information back and forth between the server and the browser on each request, using cookies, the URLData property, or hidden HTML fields.

  Note You can use a combination of these methods. For example, you might store information in a database and use cookies to send the database keys to the client.

Each approach has its own advantages and disadvantages. Storing state in objects is easy, but it may affect the scalability of your applications because the server must keep the object instantiated across requests and locate the same object each time it makes a subsequent request. Using databases is more scalable, but requires you to manage connections and recordsets. Moving state back and forth between client and server allows you to avoid storing information in either location but does increase the bandwidth of each request, has capacity limitations, and is potentially less secure.

Storing State in Objects

One of the easiest ways to store state information for an IIS application is to store it in an object. When you store state in an object, you use properties or variables within the object to hold the information you want to retrieve. There are several approaches you can take to use objects in this way for your IIS applications:

- If your webclass is set up to stay instantiated between requests, you can store state information in member variables of the WebClass object.
- You can store information in the Active Server Pages' Application and Session objects.
- You can create your own Visual Basic objects that are designed to work on the Web server and store information within them. The objects you create must stay instantiated between requests in order to maintain state. You can make the objects stay instantiated in two ways: by storing them in the Session or Application objects, or by referencing them in member variables of the webclass itself, if the webclass's StateManagement property is set to wcRetainInstance. If the webclass's StateManagement property is set to wcNoState, you must use the Session or Application objects to store your Visual Basic objects.

Regardless of which approach you use, you write code in your webclass that writes information to the appropriate object upon receiving a request, retrieves information as necessary from the objects, and manipulates the stored state information.

> **Note** If your webclass is set to stay alive between requests, the end user must have a browser that supports cookies and cookies must be enabled. For more information, see "State Management in IIS Applications," earlier in this chapter.

Storing State in the WebClass Object

Normally, the webclass run time creates an instance of the webclass each time a request is made, then destroys it after the response has been sent to the browser. However, you can use a webclass property called StateManagement to alter this behavior.

Using StateManagement, you can keep the instance of the webclass instantiated, or alive, between requests. If you choose to keep the webclass alive between requests, the run-time DLL instantiates the webclass when the first request occurs and does not destroy it until the application terminates. This enables you to use variables within the webclass to store some information between browser requests. However, this solution will affect the scalability of your application because webclasses that stay alive are stored in the Active Server Pages Session object. As a result, subsequent requests must be routed to the same Web server and the ASP must take actions to ensure that the correct thread is used to process the request.

> **Note** You can use the ReleaseInstance method to terminate an instance of a webclass you have kept alive across requests. When you use this method in a procedure, the run-time DLL terminates the instance of the webclass at the end of the procedure.

If you choose not to keep the webclass alive, the run-time DLL creates and destroys the webclass for each request. You can still maintain state information if you select this option, but you cannot store it in the WebClass object. Instead, you need to use other methods to maintain your state. Some of these methods include using objects, databases, cookies, or the URLData property to manage your state.

To keep the webclass alive across requests

- In the **Properties** window, click the name of the webclass, then set the **StateManagement** property to **2 – wcRetainInstance**.

To terminate an instance of a webclass you have previously kept alive

- In the event procedure from which you want to terminate the webclass, call the **ReleaseInstance** method.

Storing State in the Session Object

You can use the Session object to maintain state information about a single webclass user. The Session object is part of the Active Server Pages object model and is treated as a property of the WebClass objects in your IIS application.

> **Note** Using this method does not require you to set the webclass's StateManagement property to wcRetainInstance — you can store state in the Session object even if your webclass is set to store no state.

Both the Session object and the WebClass object allow you to store state on the webclass level in session-specific, server-side state. However, storing information directly in the Session object rather than that WebClass object allows you to share state with other webclasses or Active Server Pages. In addition, Visual Basic objects (such as the WebClass object) are apartment-threaded and bind all requests to a particular thread in IIS, so using the Session object is more optimal.

Suppose you want to ensure that a user in your application sees a page called CustomerInfo only once. The following code shows how you can set a Session object property during processing to record the fact that the user has seen this page:

```
Sub CustomerInfoForm_Submit

    'Code to process the form here

    'Set the value of the session variable accordingly.
    Session("CustomerInfoDisplayed") = True

End Sub
```

This code sets the value of a Session object variable to True when the user clicks a button on the CustomerInfo page. This tells the webclass that the user has been to the page in question.

Once that information is recorded, the webclass must use this information to make processing decisions. The following code shows how the webclass accesses the Session object property to determine whether or not to display the customer information form at another critical point in the application:

```
Sub PlaceOrder_Click

   'If the session variable is not set then customer info
   'page has not yet been displayed, so return it to the user

   If Session("CustomerInfoDisplayed")= "" Then
      Set NextItem = CustomerInfoForm
   Else
      Set NextItem = OrderForm
   EndIf
End Sub
```

In this code, the webclass checks a Session object property to see whether the customer information page has already been displayed. If so, it displays the order form. If not, it displays the customer information.

Storing State in the Application Object

You can use the Active Server Pages Application object to maintain state information about one or more users for the webclass. The Application object is part of the Active Server Pages object model, and is treated as a property of the WebClass objects in your IIS application. This object allows you to track more information than can be recorded in the Session object.

Suppose you want to count the number of times all users in your application access a certain page. The following code shows an event procedure you would use to store this count in the Active Server Pages Application object:

```
Private Sub MyWebclass_Start

   'Create a variable to store the number of users
   Dim Counter as Long

   'Temporarily lock the application, then increment
   'the count by one.
   Application.Lock
   Counter = Application("MyWebClassAccessCounter")
   Counter = Counter + 1

   'Store the value
   Application("MyWebClassAccessCounter") = Counter

   'Unlock the application
   Application.Unlock
```

```
    'Begin the application
    Set NextItem = WebItem1

End Sub
```

Storing State in Databases

You can use Visual Basic's ActiveX Data Objects (ADO) technology to store state information for your IIS application in a database. When you store state information in a database, you write records to a database table each time you receive a request from the browser, and retrieve information from those records as needed. This is useful when you have a webclass that is not set up to stay instantiated between requests.

Storing state information in a database involves several things:

- Opening a connection to the database and writing information to a record there when you want to store your information.
- Opening a connection to the database, retrieving records, and manipulating their data when you want to retrieve the state information.

Database state storage can allow you to retain information for long periods of time. For example, suppose you are working in an IIS application that manages the transactions and processing associated with an online bookstore. You have a series of pages in your application that gather information about the buyer. You could use databases to store the buyer information offline and save it for future visits by the same user. When a previous user shows up for a subsequent session, even if the next visit is weeks or even months later, the webclass can retrieve the user information from the database by using the login name and password the user supplies.

In addition, you can use the databinding properties of Visual Basic to manage some state. Because webclasses are Visual Basic objects, they can expose properties that can be bound to a database using the DataBinding and DataFormat objects. This means that property values can be transferred between the webclass and the database automatically through getting and setting those properties.

For More Information For more information on ADO processing, search for "ActiveX Data Objects" in the MSDN Library.

Moving State Between the Browser and the Web Server

A simple way of maintaining state information involves making the information a part of the requests and responses you send between the browser and the Web server. There are three ways to do this:

- Using cookies to store information on the client and send it to the Web server in requests.
- Using the webclass's URLData property to move information between the client and the server without permanently storing it in either location.
- You can use hidden fields to store small pieces of data between the client and the server.

Each approach has its advantages and disadvantages. Cookies can sometimes allow you to send more information than URLData or hidden fields, but some browsers may not allow cookie functionality. URLData ties information to a specific page, which can be useful. Hidden fields bind information to a specific form on a specific page, and are best when you want to send a small amount of data.

Passing State Information with Cookies

You can use cookies to maintain some state information within a session. A *cookie* is a small packet of information that the server sends to the browser and which the browser stores for subsequent transactions with that server. The cookie includes information about the current user and a range of URLs for which the state is valid. When the browser makes another HTTP requests within that range, it includes the cookie in the request data. This allows you to maintain information about server requests and transport it between the client and the server.

Most frequently, cookies are used to store a database key on the client that the server then uses to retrieve state information. In this scenario, you write the database key to the cookie and pass it to the client, where it is stored. The next time the browser sends a request to the same Web site, it includes the cookie. The Web site then uses the cookie value to retrieve the appropriate information from a database table.

There are limits to the number of cookies you can send and the number that can be issued by a single site. It is recommended that you use a small number of cookies in your application and don't use them to send large amounts of data. Due to their size limitations, cookies are ideally suited for sending small pieces of information such as the user's ID.

> **Note** Remember that users can turn off the ability to support cookies in their browsers, and that cookies can be temporary or not supported at all.

Cookies store information for a specific server, rather than for a specific page in your application. If you want to assign unique state information for a particular page, use the URLData property to manage your state information. See "Passing State Information with the URLData Property," below, for more information.

For More Information See the HTML reference of your choice for more information on using cookies.

Passing State Information with the URLData Property

You can use the URLData property to transfer information between the browser and the Web server. The URLData property appends information to specific URLs that the webclass sends to the browser. When the browser submits another request using one of these URLs, the information can be passed back to the Web server for further processing. In this way, you can send and retrieve state information without storing it in either location.

The URLData property offers several advantages:

- It can be used with browsers that do not support cookies.
- It stores state data on the page itself. Therefore, if the user uses the back button and resubmits the page, the webclass receives the same state data that was originally sent with the page.

There are two main disadvantages to URLData. First, URLData is restricted in the amount of data it can send. The size limitation varies from browser to browser, but most browsers can handle about 2K of data in the URL. You should test the URL length you are planning to use in your application. Second, URLData is not a feasible way of sending information if you are using a form with the GET method in Internet Explorer 4.*x*. Use the POST method in this situation, or use another means to transmit your state.

The URLData property can add information to URLs in the webclass's responses in two cases:

- When the webclass calls a WriteTemplate method.
- When the webclass calls a URLFor method.

In the WriteTemplate scenario, the webclass generates a response that typically involves formatting a template file to send to the browser. The URLData property tells the webclass to perform additional processing on the template — it must append the specified information to each URL in the template file that contains a parameter called WCU.

> **Note** The webclass adds the WCU parameter to your template each time you connect a tag attribute to a webitem or event. You can also add this notation manually if you are working without a template.

This method of state management is particularly useful when you have selected wcNoState as the StateManagement property setting for your webclass. When wcNoState is selected, you cannot store information within the WebClass object on the server.

Setting State Information for a URLData Response

To set state information to use with URLData, you simply assign a value to the URLData property in your event procedure. Processing differs depending on whether or not you are using a template:

- If you are working without a template, using Response.Write to send HTML to the browser, the webclass's URLFor method returns a URL to the browser that contains the URLData property's value as a parameter.
- If you are using a template file, the webclass processes adds your URLData property value to any location in the template where the WCU parameter appears.

  Note When the webclass assigns the URL data to the WCU parameters, it scans the file for all occurances of &WCU and ?WCU, and assigns the value of the URLData property to them in the format &WCU=*Your URL data.* If, for some reason, you want the letters ?WCU or &WCU to appear as part of your template's text and you want the webclass to ignore this text when it parses the file, enter the text as ?WCUWCU or &WCUWCU. When the webclass runtime finds such as string, it will strip out the extra WCU and leave the text as you intended. This extra level of encoding is only necessary if you assign a value to URLData.

For example, the following code shows how you might set state data within a custom event called "Set" for a webitem called "Item2":

```
Private Sub Item2_Set()
   'Set the value of the URLData property.
   URLData = "CustomerID: 77788"

   'Use the URLFor function to launch a response.
   Response.Write "<A HREF=""" & URLFor(Item3) & """>Go to Item 3</A>"

End Sub
```

Retrieving State Information from a URLData Request

If you have previously set the URLData property for a response, the information you sent to the browser will be returned to you when the webclass processes the URL that contains the data. You can retrieve the value of the URLData property in order to manipulate and process the state information on the Web server.

For example, the following code shows how you might retrieve state data within the Respond event for a webitem called "Item2":

```
Private Sub Item2_Respond()

   'Retrieve state information and use it to customize a response.
   Response.Write "Welcome back," & FetchNameFromDatabase(Me.URLData)

End Sub
```

For More Information See "Handling Sequencing in Webclasses" in this chapter for information on using the URLData property to set a navigational sequence in your application. See "URLData Property" in the *Microsoft Visual Basic 6.0 Language Reference*.

Using Hidden Fields

You can use the HTML HiddenField control on one of your Web pages and use that field to store information for the current page. This method of state management only works on HTML pages that contain a form.

Hidden fields are good for maintaining state for specific forms and are easily accessible from cookies or other client-side scripts. The main disadvantages of using hidden fields are that the information they transmit is bound to a form and is available in the HTML source view for the page, so anyone who can access the HTML source can view the data. You may want to encrypt your data when using this method.

For More Information See the HTML reference of your choice for more information on using hidden fields.

Handling Sequencing in Webclasses

Normally, you cannot control the way that users move through your IIS application. Unlike in a forms-based application where navigation from form to form is generally fixed, Web-based applications present a unique challenge because users can select the Back button, items from the History list, or other navigational aids to move in ways that you cannot predict.

If you want to ensure that users move in a set path through your application, you can use the URLData property to include sequencing information with the requests and responses the webclass handles. For example, suppose you have a webclass with three webitems. Item one is an introductory page, item two is a customer order form, and item three is a summary page that gives information about the current order. You want to prevent the user from moving directly from item one to item three.

The URLData property enables you to set a sequence number for each webclass request. When the property is set, the run-time DLL automatically parses the data object and appends the value you assigned to the property to each URL it finds embedded in a response. For example, if you have a URL that reads:

```
WCI=webitem1?WCE=event1
```

and you use the following code to set the URLData property:

```
Me.URLData=01
```

the run-time DLL will append the value of the URLData property to the URL, using a WCU indicator. The resulting HTML looks like this:

```
WCI=webitem1?WCE=event1&WCU=01
```

This argument is passed to the client and stored there. On the next request, the browser includes the argument, telling the server that this request is the next in sequence after response 01.

At this point in your code, you would increment the value of the URLData property by one to indicate that a second response has been sent. You would do that with the following code:

```
Me.URLData=02
```

When the webclass encounters this setting, it parses the response again and appends this number to all URLs. The number 02 is then sent to the browser and stored, to be returned on the next request that contains the URL.

You can ensure proper sequencing by writing code that determines whether the URLData argument received with each request is valid. For example, you would store the value of the argument after each request, using either a variable or an external store such as a database, then compare each new request to see if the correct number has been used. The following example shows the code you might use to ensure sequence on the second request:

```
If URLData = 02 Then
   WebItem2.WriteTemplate
Else
   'Code here to send an error to the browser
   'and redirect to the previous page.
EndIf
```

Building Your IIS Application

IIS applications are compiled the same way any Visual Basic project is compiled — by choosing Make from the File menu. An IIS application must be built as an in-process component, or a DLL file.

When you run or compile the project, Visual Basic creates the following files:

- A DLL file Visual Basic uses to run the project.
- An .asp file that hosts the application in the browser and creates its run-time component.
- An .exp file generated by the linker when the project is compiled and linked.
- A .vbw file that contains the windows layout information for the project.

When you run or compile the project, you should place the DLL file in the same directory as your project files, for easiest deployment.

To compile your IIS application

1. If the project is still in run mode, click the End button to return to design mode.
2. On the File menu, click **Make *Project*.dll** to open the Make Project dialog box. Click **OK** to make the DLL file.

Debugging Your IIS Application

You debug an IIS application in the same way you do any other Visual Basic application — by entering run mode from Visual Basic. Visual Basic loads the webclass run time, creates the virtual root from which to run the .asp file for the application, if necessary, and launches the system's default browser with an HTTP reference to the .asp file. The .asp file, in turn, launches the webclass.

> **Note** Although you can view the .htm files associated with your application in the browser by opening them from the browser's File menu, this is not debugging your application. You must use the Start option from Visual Basic to enter debugging mode.

When you debug, you have the full Visual Basic development environment at your disposal. You can use all the tools available in Visual Basic — breakpoints, watch variables, debug statements, and so on — to debug your project.

Visual Basic prompts you when you debug that it is going to create a virtual directory for your project. A *virtual directory* is a directory outside your Web server's home directory that appears to browsers as a subdirectory of the home directory. It allows you to publish contents to the Web from directories outside the home directory structure. You cannot change the location of the virtual directory Visual Basic creates for the webclass.

The Project Properties dialog box's Debugging panel settings determine whether the system waits for you to tell it what to do when you go into run mode or automatically starts the webclass you specify. When you choose to automatically start the webclass, Visual Basic launches Internet Explorer, navigates to the URL for your application, and fires the webclass's BeginRequest event.

Visual Basic deletes all temporary files when it comes out of run mode. In addition, it destroys the instance of the Webclass Designer and restarts the designer in design mode.

For More Information See Chapter 13, "Debugging Your Code and Handling Errors," in the *Microsoft Visual Basic 6.0 Programmer's Guide* for more information on how to test and debug your IIS application.

Errors in Webclasses

You can use Visual Basic's error-handling features in your IIS applications to trap errors and take corrective action. When an error occurs, Visual Basic sets the various properties of the error object, Err, such as an error number or a description. You can use the Err object and its properties in an error-handling routine so that your application can respond intelligently to an error situation.

In addition to standard error handling, IIS applications allow you to use two special features to handle errors:

- You can use the Trace method to debug your application on the production computer.
- You can use the FatalErrorResponse event to respond to serious run-time errors.

For More Information The basics of error handling are discussed in Chapter 13, "Debugging Your Code and Handling Errors," in the *Microsoft Visual Basic 6.0 Programmer's Guide*. For information specific to ActiveX projects, see "Generating and Handling Errors in ActiveX Components," in Chapter 7, "Debugging, Testing, and Deploying Components," in Part 2, "Creating ActiveX Components."

Using the Trace Method

You can use the Trace method to help identify errors during the debug process and to track performance and statistical data. The Trace method sends a specified string to the Win32 OutputDebugString API. The string can then be captured to a suitable debugging tool such as DBMON.

Using the Trace method can allow you to debug on your production server computer and record useful information such as information about the execution of the application, error messages that occur, and any other information you need.

For More Information See "Trace Method" in the *Microsoft Visual Basic 6.0 Language Reference* for more information on using this method in your error handling.

Handling Fatal Errors

A fatal error on a webclass is one from which the application cannot recover or restore the appropriate webitem. For example, a fatal error might be an unhandled error within a webclass event, a structural error, or an unexpected error within the run-time DLL. Following such an error, the webclass run time fires the FatalErrorResponse event. The application is terminated and the instance of the webclass is destroyed.

When a fatal error occurs, the application can write a message to the Response object in the handler for the FatalErrorResponse event. This message can be one that you write, or it can be the default message for the .asp file associated with the webclass. To write your own message, use the Response object, then set the *senddefault* argument of the FatalErrorResponse event to False. To use the default error message, leave the senddefault argument set to True.

> **Note** The webclass run time provides an Error property that is only available from within the FatalErrorResponse event. This property returns an object that describes the error that caused the webclass to terminate.

The webclass run time also logs fatal errors to the NT event log. You can disable fatal error logging by changing the LogErrors registry value under HKEY_LOCAL_MACHINE\SOFTWARE\Microsoft\Visual Basic\6.0\WebClass from 1 to 0.

> **Note** On Windows 95 systems, the run-time DLL creates a log file in the Windows directory and logs the error there.

For More Information See "FatalErrorResponse Event" in the *Microsoft Visual Basic 6.0 Language Reference* for more information on handling non-recoverable errors.

Deploying Your IIS Application

You package and deploy your IIS application using the Visual Basic Package and Deployment Wizard. The Package and Deployment Wizard packages your project .dll files and all associated files into a "cabinet" or .cab file. The wizard can then deploy this cabinet file and its associated support files to a location you indicate on a Web server.

> **Note** Although IIS applications are deployed to a Web server and not to the client computer, you still must package them into a cabinet file and deploy them to the Web site. The .cab file is then unpacked on the Web server and the necessary components are installed and registered.

You must either deploy to an existing virtual directory on the server or manually create a virtual directory before you deploy your .cab file to it. To create a virtual directory, you define a directory on the Web server, then use the Internet Server Manager in Internet Information Server to define this directory as a virtual directory and set an alias for it. See your Microsoft Internet Information Server product documentation for further details on creating virtual directories.

The application files that must be deployed include:

- The .dll files for the project — including the WebClass object and the Visual Basic run time, and the .dsr and .dsx files for the project. These are automatically packaged into the .cab file when you run the Package and Deployment Wizard.
- The HTML page or pages associated with the project. The Package and Deployment Wizard does not package these into the .cab file, but it copies them to the indicated location on the Web site when you deploy the .cab file.
- Any files referenced by the HTML pages, such as images. The Package and Deployment Wizard does not automatically recognize these dependencies, but you can add them to the list of dependency files the wizard displays.

These are the steps in deploying your IIS application to the Internet:

1. Debug and compile your application.
2. Use the Package and Deployment Wizard to build a .cab file that contains the necessary files for your application.
3. Use the Package and Deployment Wizard to deploy your application to the Web server you want to use.

For More Information See Chapter 17, "Distributing Your Applications," in the *Microsoft Visual Basic 6.0 Programmer's Guide*, for instructions on using the Package and Deployment Wizard to package and deploy your IIS application.

CHAPTER 4

Downloading ActiveX Components

Visual Basic lets you use ActiveX technology to create components that can be used on HTML pages or as alternatives to an HTML page. These components can include controls (.ocx files), code components (.exe and .dll files) that run on the client, or ActiveX documents (.vbd files) that function much like an HTML page. Using these solutions, you can create highly functional Internet solutions to your business needs. Internet component download delivers these ActiveX solutions to users through an Internet browser. This section offers information on how to package and download your ActiveX controls, code components, and ActiveX documents.

> **Note** In addition to ActiveX controls, code components, and ActiveX documents, you can create Internet applications using ActiveX designers. Information about deploying these Internet applications, called DHTML applications and IIS applications, can be found in their respective chapters. This chapter covers downloading of other ActiveX components; however, much of the information contained here will help you understand the process of deploying Internet applications in more detail.

Delivering software on the Internet raises new issues in software distribution. For example, you cannot predict the scope of the audience that will download your software or the configuration of their computers. In addition, the process of downloading a component is often a passive process that occurs without a specific request from the user. Internet component download helps address these issues.

For More Information See Chapter 2, "Developing DHTML Applications," for information on deploying DHTML Internet applications. See Chapter 3, "Developing IIS Applications," for information on deploying IIS applications.

Contents

For More Information See http://support.microsoft.com/support/inetsdk for a collection of information about Internet component download. See Microsoft Developer Network Online on the Microsoft Web site at http://www.microsoft.com/msdn/ for the latest news on ActiveX, Visual Basic, and other Microsoft technologies.

Steps to Prepare Your Component for Download

When you prepare ActiveX components for Internet download, you must package them into a file that can be delivered to the user's browser. In addition, you must perform a few precautionary steps to ensure users who download your components that your software will not harm their computers.

There are five general steps to take in preparing your ActiveX control, code component, or ActiveX document for Internet download. The following table indicates the steps and the types of ActiveX components to which each step applies.

Step	ActiveX Controls (.ocx files)	Code Components (.exe/.dll files)	ActiveX Documents (.vbd files)
Digitally sign the software to be distributed.	X	X	X
Verify the software's safety levels.	X	X	X
Arrange licensing of items that require it.	X		
Package the item for download.	X	X	X
Test your download.	X	X	X

Digital Signing for ActiveX Components

Internet Explorer's default security settings require that any software available for download must have a digital signature before download can occur. A digital signature provides a way to verify:

- The contents of a file.
- That the file comes from a responsible source.

Signatures verify content by providing a means of ensuring that a file's contents have not been altered since it was first made available for download. A digital signature verifies the source by identifying the legal entity that created the software. When you include a signature with a piece of downloadable software, you are the legal entity. The legal entity may be held responsible for any destruction caused by signed software when it is downloaded or run.

Software That Should Be Signed

There are five types of files to which you can apply a digital signature:

- .exe files
- .cab files
- .dll files
- .ocx files
- .vbd files

If you are providing one of these types of files for download, you should establish a digital signature for it.

> **Note** Normally, it is sufficient to sign only the .cab file in which your components are packaged. However, if you intend to distribute an .ocx, .exe, .vbd or .dll without packaging it in a .cab file, you should sign the component itself.

You provide a digital signature by purchasing a certificate from a *certificate authority*. A certificate authority is a company that validates your identity and issues a certificate to you. The certificate contains your digital signature and is a verification of your credentials. In the event of any problems, the certificate authority becomes a witness to your identity.

Public Keys and Private Keys

You use a technology called *Authenticode* when working with digital signatures. The goal of Authenticode is to deter the distribution of potentially harmful code by creating accountability. Authenticode verifies the publisher of a piece of code to Internet end users who are downloading it. In addition, Authenticode ensures users that the code has not been altered after the signature was applied.

Authenticode technology is derived from public key signature technology. Public key signature technology uses what are known as *key pairs* to encrypt data. Key pairs are used to encrypt and decrypt files. In public key technology, a public key and a private key ensure the privacy of files. A *public key* is used to encrypt the data, and a *private* key is used to decrypt it. While this is a successful means of protecting smaller files such as e-mail messages, the process is time consuming for larger files. Authenticode is the modified form of this technology, designed for use with larger files.

Authenticode and Signing

The following steps occur in the Authenticode process:

1. When the developer signs the file, a number called a *hash* is calculated. The hash number represents the total bytes in the file. This number is encrypted using a private key and inserted into the file. The developer then packages and deploys the file to a Web server.

2. When a user downloads or installs the file, their computer calculates a second hash number and compares it to the original. If the numbers match, the content is verified.

3. The browser uses the public key to determine your identity and the certificate authority that provided the digital signature.

4. The certificate authority verifies the source's identity and issues a certificate that contains the source's name encrypted with the private key.

5. The browser uses the private key to decrypt the file. Installation proceeds.

The Authenticode software utility you need to apply a digital signature can be found in the ActiveX SDK, available for download from Microsoft's Internet site. The digital signature must be obtained from an issuing authority such as GTE or VeriSign, Inc.

For More Information See the *Internet Client SDK* on your MSDN Library CDROM, or at http://www.microsoft.com/workshop/prog/inetsdk/ for more information on how to download the *ActiveX SDK*. For more information on public and private encryption, search the Internet for RSA or public-key signatures.

Safeguarding Your Certificate

It is very important to keep your certificate safe because your firm guarantees any file signed with the certificate, regardless of whether the signature was authorized or not. You should keep the certificate with the certificate authority that issued it and send files there for signing or, if you keep the certificate on site, strictly control access to it.

For More Information See the Authenticode link on the Microsoft Security Advisor table of contents on the Microsoft Web site at http://www.microsoft.com/security to learn the latest about security and digital signing.

How to Sign Your Code

You can sign any .ocx, .exe, .dll, .vbd or .cab file you intend to distribute. There are two main steps to perform when you sign code. First, you must apply for a certificate, then you sign your code.

To sign your code

1. Apply for a certificate from a certificate authority. For instructions on obtaining a certificate see http://www.microsoft.com/workshop/prog/security/authcode/certs.htm .

2. Get the latest version of the ActiveX SDK from http://www.microsoft.com/workshop/prog/sdk/. This contains the tools you need to sign your code.

3. Prepare you files to be signed. If you are signing any .exe, .ocx, .vbd or .dll file, you do not need to do anything special. If you are signing a .cab file, you must add the following entry to your .ddf file and remake your .cab file:

   ```
   .Set ReservePerCabinetSize=6144
   ```

4. Sign your files using the tools in the ActiveX SDK. The following is an example of how you might sign a file:

```
Signcode -prog myfilename -name displayname -info http://www.mycompany.com - spc
mycredentials.spc -pvk myprivatekey.pvk
```

5. Test your signature:

   - To test a signed .exe, .dll, .vbd or .ocx file, run chktrust *filename* where *filename* is the name of the file you signed.

   - To test a signed .cab file, run chktrust -c *cabfilename*.cab where *cabfilename* is the name of the .cab file you signed.

If your signing process was successful, either of these tests will display your certificate.

Safety Settings for ActiveX Components

Safety settings are used to guarantee users that an ActiveX control will interact safely with their computer and its data. When you distribute ActiveX controls for Internet component download, you must assign safety levels to them. If you do not, and your controls damage users' computers or corrupt their data, you can be held legally accountable if the controls were signed.

You can help prevent these problems by verifying that your code is safe and marking it as such. There are two levels to safety in Internet component download:

- Safe for initialization
- Safe for scripting

Note Safety settings apply only to components downloaded in Internet Explorer.

Safe for Initialization

When you mark a control safe for initialization, you guarantee that it will not perform harmful actions on the end user's computer, no matter what data or scripts are used in its initialization. A control that is safe for initialization does not write or modify any registry entries, .ini files, or data files as a result of initialization parameters. Safe for Initialization makes no claims about the safety of the control's methods, run-time properties, or the information it makes available to a script writer.

By default, Internet Explorer displays a warning and does not download controls that have not been marked safe for scripting and initializing. You can designate your software as safe for scripting and initialization when you use the Visual Basic Package and Deployment Wizard to package it for Internet distribution.

Safe for Scripting

When you mark a control safe for scripting, you guarantee that no script can cause the control to damage the users' computers or data. Controls marked safe for scripting should not be able to obtain unauthorized information from the users' computers or corrupt their systems.

Before you mark a control safe for scripting, you must verify that it does not perform any illegal activities or allow openings that could be used to cause damage. In general, controls that can automatically obtain any information about the user and expose that information to a script writer are not safe for scripting. Such seemingly innocent activities can be considered criminal acts in some countries.

In particular, a control should not perform the following actions as a result of scripting:

- Insertion or retrieval of custom, script-defined registry and .ini file information. In other words, users should not be able to specify through a script which registry or .ini file information to insert.
- Insertion or retrieval of variable registry and .ini file information that is not owned by the control.

  Note It is acceptable for a control to insert and retrieve registry and .ini file information that is predefined when the control is distributed, belongs only to the control, and exists for the purpose of helping the control manage its internal functions.

- Reading a file from a hard drive with a name specified by scripting.

There is a fine line between safe and unsafe actions. For example, an ActiveX control that always writes information to its own registry entry may be safe, but a control that lets you name that entry is unsafe. A control that creates a temporary file without using any initialization or scripting value may be safe, but a control that allows the name of the temporary file to be assigned at initialization or by scripting is unsafe.

Prior to marking a control safe for scripting, it is advisable to create documentation recording the justification, taking the same type of care due any legal contract. This documentation can be included in the .inf file for your control. Your documentation might include:

- A review by an expert, external developer who understands both the source code and VBScript.
- A table listing all exposed methods, events, and properties of the controls.
- A table listing all the files opened, API calls used, and the information retrieved or written.

If there are any dependencies or data transfer between the elements of these two tables, then the control is probably not safe for scripting.

Note Determining whether a control is safe is not a trivial exercise. To understand what type of functionality you should not implement for your control, you might begin by noting the API calls and commands not implemented in VBScript. See http://www.microsoft.com/vbscript/ for information on the API calls and commands not implemented in VBScript.

Limitations of the Safety Flags

A control marked safe for scripting and safe for initialization is not necessarily safe to use. The previous two sections list actions that the control cannot perform as a result of initialization or scripting, but a control could still perform these unsafe actions at other times.

For example, suppose you create an ActiveX control that could reformat your hard-drive after 10 uses. This action does not occur as a result of scripting or initialization, so you can mark the control as safe. Of course, the person who writes such a control is liable for the usual penalties reserved for virus writers.

Responsibility for ensuring that adequate safeguards are in place belongs to the developer, not to end users or to HTML authors. If you as the developer fail to include adequate safeguards, you can be held legally responsible.

The bottom line in ensuring the safety of your software is to always have your code independently reviewed by a seasoned developer who understands the issues well. You may want to include information about this review in the .inf file for your download.

For More Information See "Designing Controls for Use With HTML" in Chapter 9, "Building ActiveX Controls," for guidelines for making your controls safe for scripting and initialization. See "Advanced Customization for Internet Component Download" in this chapter for more information on including information in the .inf file.

Setting Safety Levels for ActiveX Components

There are two ways you can set safety levels for your downloadable components. The easiest way is to use the Package and Deployment Wizard to mark your .cab files as safe. The other option is to use the IObjectSafety interface to tell the client machine that your code is safe.

Note IObjectSafety is an advanced coding topic that requires an understanding of the Implements interface and is intended for experienced programmers. For information on this interface, see "Polymorphism" in Chapter 9, "Programming with Objects," in the *Microsoft Visual Basic 6.0 Programmer's Guide.*

Using the Package and Deployment Wizard

If you do not implement the IObjectSafety interface on your objects, the Package and Deployment Wizard will present you with the opportunity to set safety flags on your download package. You can select the Safe for Scripting flag, the Safe for Initialization flag, or both.

> **Note** If you have used the IObjectSafety interface for an object, it will not appear in the safety settings screen of the Package and Deployment Wizard.

For More Information See Chapter 17, "Distributing your Applications," in the *Microsoft Visual Basic 6.0 Programmer's Guide* for more information on using the Package and Deployment Wizard to package your controls.

Using IObjectSafety

IObjectSafety is an interface that exposes functionality to Internet Explorer's Safe for Scripting and Safe for Initialization security features. IObjectSafety should be implemented for objects that have interfaces that support untrusted clients — or those clients for which specific functionality cannot be predicted or safe usage cannot be guaranteed — such as scripts. The interface allows you to specify which parts of the object need to be protected from use.

Using IObjectSafety, you can mark your object and its parts in three ways:

- Safe for Automation with untrusted Automation clients or scripts
- Safe for initialization with untrusted data
- Safe for running untrusted scripts

There are three possible scenarios to consider for your objects:

1. All properties and methods on your object are always safe for scripting. In this scenario, you can notify the client that your object is safe for scripting by not returning an error in the IObjectSafety_SetInterfaceSafetyOptions interface method. This allows your object to be successfully created and run.
2. Your object is never safe for scripting. In this case, you can notify the client that your object is not safe by returning an error, E_Fail, in the IObjectSafety_SetInterfaceSafetyOptions interface method. This prevents the client from accessing any methods or properties through script.
3. Some but not all of the properties and methods on your object are unsafe for scripting. In this case you can either notify the client that your entire object is unsafe, or notify the client that your object is safe, but disable the properties and methods that are unsafe.

For More Information See the Internet Client SDK at http://www.microsoft.com/msdn/sdk/inetsdk/help/compdev/safety.htm for more information on the IObjectSafety interface. An IObjectSafety sample application can be found in the \Program Files\Microsoft Visual Studio\Common Files\Samples\VB\IobjSaf directory.

Licensing for ActiveX Components

When you add an ActiveX control to a Web page, you are distributing it to any users who download the control from the page. Unless you license the control, there is little to prevent an end user from taking your control and using it in their own applications. The license acts as a kind of copyright for your control, preventing unauthorized use.

Licensing ActiveX controls for use on the Internet is a complex subject. An expression in a license such as "used on one computer" has a totally different meaning on the Internet when the "one computer" may be an HTTP server that is hosting 200 different IP addresses. The software may be in-use (running in memory) on thousands of anonymous computers and never in use on the computer for which it was licensed. These issues should be reviewed before you license your ActiveX controls for use on the Internet.

This section explains Microsoft's current licensing scheme, how to implement it with Visual Basic, and how HTML authors can use it on their pages. A general discussion of some licensing issues is also included.

For More Information See the *Internet Client SDK* at http://www.microsoft.com/workshop/prog/inetsdk/ for detailed information on the licensing model and the .lpk file.

Microsoft's Licensing Scheme

Visual Basic implements a licensing scheme that uses a mechanism that contains methods the computer uses to retrieve a control's licensing information and create instances of objects. This is the most common licensing scheme in use.

The basics of licensing through this scheme are:

- Each HTML page using one or more licensed controls requires a license file (.lpk) that contains the license strings for each control.
- Each HTML page can use only a single .lpk file, but a single .lpk file can be used for more than one page.
- The .lpk file must be on the same server as the HTML page it covers.
- The .lpk file must contain a plain text copyright notice to dissuade casual copying of .lpk files.

The License File

The *license file* is an .lpk file you associate with one or more HTML pages. It contains license strings for each ActiveX control on the pages to which it refers. You use the License Package Authoring Tool to create an appropriate license file for their pages. This tool, which is available in the Tools directory, presents you with a list of controls you can include in you license file.

A sample license file is shown below:

```
LPK License Package
////////////////////////////////////////////////////////
// WARNING: The information in this file is
// protected by copyright law and international
// treaty provisions. Unauthorized reproduction or
// distribution of this file, or any portion of it,
// may result in severe criminal and civil penalties,
// and will be prosecuted to the maximum extent
// possible under the law. Further, you may not reverse
// engineer, decompile, or disassemble the file.
////////////////////////////////////////////////////////
{3d25aba1-caec-11cf-b34a-00aa00a28331}
AQWWF/QT0BG9ewCg0QKOmo=
BQAAAA=yhtrFpw/zxGAdURFU1QAACkAAAB
DAG8AcAB5AHIAaQBnAGgAdAAgACgAYwApACAAMQA5ADkANQAsACAAMQA5ADkANgAg
AE0AYQBjAHIAbwBtAGUAZABpAGEALAAgAEkAbgBjAC4A=
```

Important The License Package Authoring Tool won't create an entry in the .lpk file for your ActiveX control unless you check the Required License Key checkbox in the Project Options dialog of your control project.

The License Manager

You must embed an object called the *license manager* in the Web page from which a user will download your ActiveX controls. The license manager uses an OBJECT tag to reference the control's .lpk file. If you use the Package and Deployment Wizard to create your download, it produces the license manager and inserts it in the file for you.

The following is a sample of the license manager:

```
   <!--  If any of the controls on this page require licensing, you must create a license
   package file. Run LPK_TOOL.EXE in the Tools directory to create the required .lpk file.
-->
<OBJECT CLASSID="clsid:5220cb21-c88d-11cf-b347-00aa00a28331">
   <PARAM NAME="LPKPath" VALUE="LPKfilename.LPK">
</OBJECT>
```

Note You must replace the LPKPath and LPKfilename.LPK parameters in the example above with the path and name of your license file.

This HTML code identifies the .lpk file as an object with the class ID shown above.

For More Information See "Licensing ActiveX Controls" in the ActiveX Controls section of the *Internet Client SDK* at http://www.microsoft.com/workshop/prog/inetsdk.

Other License Models

There are other licensing models besides Microsoft's scheme. One requires a key that varies with time. In this approach, the following steps occur:

1. The browser makes a call to an HTTP server that examines the URL of the HTML page making the call.
2. The server examines the user's IP location for run-time licenses, then returns a license key.

There are also other licensing mechanisms possible. For example, if run-time licenses are required, then Basic authentication, NT authentication, or other authentication may be required before the license file may be obtained.

For More Information See the "Authentication and Security for Internet Developers" white paper at http://www.microsoft.com/workshop/server/asp/feature/security-f.htm for more information on basic text authentication and NT security.

Internet Component Download

Downloading applications or components from the Internet is significantly different from installing a standard Visual Basic application. In standard applications, the user uses a setup program to install the software. On the Web, users download the application after accessing a Web page from which it is available. The browser, rather than a setup program, is responsible for copying all the needed files to the user's computer.

End users use Internet component download to automatically download and install Internet applications and ActiveX components from Web pages. You can use the Package and Deployment Wizard to prepare your software for Internet component download. The Package and Deployment Wizard creates a cabinet (.cab) file that contains all of the information necessary to download, install, and register your software.

The benefits of Internet component download include:

- File compression for faster download.
- A single file for your component and an .inf file that describes other files required.
- Dependency files, such as Msvbvm50.cab, will only be downloaded as necessary — thus minimizing download time.
- Easier updating when new versions of your component are created.
- Automatic installation performed when the control is downloaded.

For More Information See the "Code Download Training Site" at http://support.microsoft.com/support/inetsdk for a collection of information about Internet component download. See "File Packaging with the Package and Deployment Wizard," later in this chapter, for more information about the concepts in Internet component download.

How Internet Component Download Works

In Internet component download, you first package the components you want to download into a .cab file so that the browser can download them intelligently. The Package and Deployment Wizard's packaging process builds an HTML page that refers to this cabinet file through an OBJECT tag. When a user opens this Web page, the browser reads the OBJECT tag and retrieves the necessary files for the download.

As part of the .cab file creation process, the Package and Deployment Wizard creates an .inf file that contains information about the download. You can customize this file if you need to include additional information.

> **Note** If you update the .inf file, you must rebuild your .cab file.

For More Information See "File Packaging with the Package and Deployment Wizard," later in this chapter, for a full list of the files created with the .cab file.

The OBJECT Tag

The following HTML fragment shows the OBJECT tag for a .cab file called MyContrl.cab:

```
<OBJECT
   CLASSID="clsid:25BDF09D-EC8B-11CF-BD97-00AA00575603"
   CODEBASE="/Controls/MyContrl.cab#version=1,0,0,0"
   ID=MyContrl>
</OBJECT>
```

The OBJECT tag shown above contains three attributes:

- CLASSID — contains the class ID used to register the control in the Windows registry.
- CODEBASE — points to a location from which to download the .cab file and specifies the version number of the control contained in the .cab file.
- ID — specifies the name to use when scripting the component.

The Download Process

The system performs the following actions when downloading a .cab file's contents onto a client machine:

1. The browser checks the registry for the class ID in the OBJECT tag. If it fails to find it, it processes the CODEBASE attribute. If the browser does find the class ID, it checks the file referenced in the registry entry to see if it is current and proceeds with the download if it is not.
2. The browser downloads and unpacks the appropriate .cab file.
3. The browser processes the .inf file associated with the .cab file.

4. Internet Explorer makes registry settings, including those related to the component's status as safe for scripting or safe for initializing, if appropriate.
5. The browser checks to see whether you have any necessary files or components already installed. If you do, it checks to see whether the files or components are current. If they are current, the browser makes no changes to them. If they are not current, the browser replaces them with a new copy that it downloads and extracts.
6. The browser installs and registers your component.

Checklist for Component Download

The following checklist shows the steps that you should follow to create a fully signed, safe Internet component download for an ActiveX control.

> **Note** If you are creating a download for another type of ActiveX component, you would not perform the steps involving safety settings.

1. Design the software, specifying the intended software safety level.
2. Create the software and test. If you are using the IObjectSafety interface, implement the appropriate safety settings on your objects.
3. Create a document showing the object is safe.
4. Get an independent review.
5. Recreate the .cab using the Package and Deployment Wizard, and set the appropriate safety flags if you did not use the IObjectSafety interface.
6. Modify the .inf file as required to add readme information and other files.
7. If you modified the .inf in step 6, recreate the .cab file using Makecab.exe.
8. Digitally sign the .cab file.
9. Test the final .cab file with each platform on which it may run.

Resources for Component Download

The following resources may be needed to create and test your packages for Internet component download. Most of the resources are part of Visual Basic.

pdaddin.dll or pdcmdln.exe	Package your components for download using the Package and Deployment Wizard, either from within Visual Basic (pdaddin.dll) or as a stand-alone executable (pdcmdln.exe).	Visual Basic installation
lpk_tool.exe	Create the license for any controls.	Visual Basic Tools directory

(continued)

(continued)

Resource	Purpose	Source
makecab.exe	Build cabinet files.	Visual Basic installation
signcode.exe	Manage digital signatures	ActiveX SDK
Authenticode certificate	Identify the developer	Verisign Inc., GTE, or another vendor that provides signatures
Internet Explorer	Test download and installation	www.microsoft.com
regsvr32.exe	Register and unregister software for testing	Visual Basic Tools directory

File Packaging with the Package and Deployment Wizard

You can use the Visual Basic Package and Deployment Wizard to quickly and easily package your ActiveX components for Internet component download. The Package and Deployment Wizard packages your components into a file that the browser can recognize, and creates a Web page from which the user can download the page. You then deploy the resulting materials to a Web server where users can access it.

> **Note** Before using the Package and Deployment Wizard to package your own ActiveX control for Internet component download, you should become familiar with several important concepts, including component safety and digital signatures.

Files Created by the Package and Deployment Wizard

The Package and Deployment Wizard creates two main sets of files when it packages code for Internet component download: distribution files and support files. Distribution files are located in the directory you specify when you begin the wizard. This directory typically contains the .cab file and any .htm files associated with it.

> **Note** If you make any changes to the project after you build the .cab file, such as modifying the list of files to include with the download or digitally signing the components, you may need to rebuild the .cab file.

The wizard creates a directory for support files and places the input file (.inf file) for the .cab in this directory. In addition, the support files directory contains the Diamond Directives (.ddf) file, and other files needed for the download.

The following table lists all the file types created by the wizard:

Extension	Description
.cab	Windows setup file or "cabinet" file that contains the .ocx file, the .inf file and other dependent files. You can digitally sign this file to prevent tampering.
.htm	HTML file used to display a Web page. This file contains a link to the .cab file and is used to launch the download process.
.ddf	Diamond Directives file. This is the project file for creating the .cab files.
.inf	Code download information file. This file includes information on how the control should be installed. It permits customization of installation.
.ocx	ActiveX control. You can digitally sign this file to prevent tampering.
.dll	ActiveX document or code component.

HTML Created by the Package and Deployment Wizard

The following fragment from an .htm file illustrates what the Package and Deployment Wizard produces in a typical Internet component download.

```
<HTML>
<!--  If any of the controls on this page require licensing,
➥ you must create a license package file.
   Run LPK_TOOL.EXE in the tools directory to create the required LPK file.

<OBJECT CLASSID="clsid:5220cb21-c88d-11cf-b347-00aa00a28331">
   <PARAM NAME="LPKPath" VALUE="LPKfilename.LPK">
</OBJECT>
-->
<OBJECT
   classid="clsid:F651BF93-239B-11D0-8908-00A0C90395F4"
   id=ShapeLabel
   codebase="ControlDemo.CAB#version=1,0,0,1">
</OBJECT>
</HTML>
```

Examine the second Object tag in the example above. This tag contains a reference to a control with the ID ShapeLabel. It has a class ID of F651BF93-239B-11D0-8908-00A0C90395F4. Each ActiveX control you create will have a different class ID. The class ID is used to create an instance of the control on the HTML page, similar to the process of placing a control on a Visual Basic form.

Internet Explorer uses the class ID to check the registry to see if the control exists. When it does not exist or when the version number of the control is less than the version specified in the CODEBASE attribute, Internet Explorer downloads and installs the specified file.

The important parts of the Object tag include:

Tag Attributes	Description
CLASSID	Class identifier, contains the class ID for the component.
ID	Name of the component. Used in scripting, this is equivalent to the Name property of a control on a Visual Basic form.
CODEBASE	Minimum version number of the control required and the location of an installation point.

For More Information See Chapter 17, "Distributing your Applications," in the *Microsoft Visual Basic 6.0 Programmer's Guide,* for instructions on using the Package and Deployment Wizard to package your controls. See http://www.w3c.org for more information about the OBJECT tag and its use. See http://www.microsoft.com/workshop/prog/cab/ for more information on .cab files.

Testing your Internet Component Download

Testing your download file is more complex than testing a conventional setup program because the software does not install unless one of two things is true:

- The software does not already exist on the user's computer.

  – or –

- The software being downloaded is newer than any version that already exists on the user's machine.

Because of this, you must be careful when you test your download to ensure that you test both scenarios. As a developer, you should test your application on multiple machines with varying configurations. At a minimum, you should test the download on both your development machine and on a machine that does not have Visual Basic installed, and on multiple operating systems. In addition, you must check your safety levels.

> **Note** If you do not have a machine without Visual Basic installed, you can simulate one. See "Testing Component Download on Clean Machines," later in this chapter, for instructions.

Setting Safety Levels Prior to Testing

Before testing your download, be sure the safety level in Internet Explorer is set to Medium. If the safety level is set to High, the required files will not get downloaded. If you set the safety level to None, all of the missing components will be installed without warning.

When the safety level is set to Medium, the following warnings occur:

- The browser warns you that an installation attempt is being made and prompts you to install the .cab file. If you choose to continue, the browser downloads and expands the .cab.
- The browser asks if you want to install any dependency files, such as Microsoft Automation or the Microsoft Visual Basic run-time library. The Authenticode screen displays information about these components. If you choose to continue, the browser installs these files.
- If you are downloading an ActiveX document in a version of Internet Explorer prior to 4.0, a script warning appears warning you that the Web page contains scripting code. This code is necessary in order to view your ActiveX document. If you choose to continue, the download proceeds. This warning does not appear in Internet Explorer 4.0 or later.

These warnings are all part of the Internet Explorer's safety mechanisms. If you do not receive all of these warnings, do not be alarmed. You may not receive a warning if a necessary component is already installed on the client machine or a security level option in Internet Explorer is set to something other than the defaults.

To check the safety level in Internet Explorer 4. *x*

1. Click **Internet Options** from the **View** menu.
2. From the **Options** dialog box, click the **Security** tab.
3. Click the appropriate safety level, then click **OK**.

To check the safety level in Internet Explorer 3.*x*

1. Click **Options** from the **View** menu.
2. From the **Options** dialog box, click the **Security** tab.
3. Click the **Safety Levels** button.
4. Click the appropriate safety level, then click **OK**.
5. Click **OK** to return to the browser.

Testing Safety Levels

You can check safety levels by creating additional .cab files and HTML pages for testing, as suggested in the following table:

To test pages with	Create a page that hosts a control with
No initialization or scripting	No PARAM values or other variables set by the control.
Initialization only	PARAM values assigned to a control.
Scripting only	PARAM values set by VBScript only.
Scripting and initialization	Initial PARAM values set and then modified by VBScript.

Testing Component Download on Development Machines

You can test your component download on your development machines to make sure that the download file installs correctly. However, because your development machines are likely to have some of the necessary components or files already installed, you may not experience the same download as your end users will. In addition to testing on your machines, it is important to also test your installation on a machine that does not have Visual Basic installed.

> **Note** If you do not have a machine without Visual Basic installed, you can simulate one. See "Simulating a Clean Machine" for instructions.

Testing Installation of the Component on the Development Machine

The simplest way to check your download is to remove the software registration from the registry, then access the page generated by the wizard.

> **Note** The procedures in this section require a copy of regsvr32.exe to be installed on your machine. If it is not, you can find it on the Visual Basic installation CDROM.

To test installation on the development machine

- Unregister the component:
  - If you are using Internet Explorer 4.0 or later, access the **Downloaded Program Files** folder in either the Windows or the Winnt40 directory, right-click the control, and select **Remove**. The system automatically removes and unregisters the item and any of its dependencies.
  - If you are using a version of Internet Explorer prior to 4.0, run Regsvr32 to unregister the component, as in the following example:

    ```
    regsvr32 /u controldemo.ocx
    ```

    Note If regsvr32.exe is not in your path, provide the full path to the file in your statement. Access the Web page the Package and Deployment Wizard created. The component should download.

    Remember to select Binary Compatibility in your Visual Basic project settings to prevent multiple, different class IDs for your software.

    If you leave the `DestDir=` line in the .inf file blank, the component file should appear in your Occache or Downloaded Program Files directory. You may find other copies in subdirectories called conflict directories, such as Occache\Conflict.2. The date and time of each file will differ, indicating different builds of the control and different class IDs. Care must be taken to ensure that the Class ID remains the same between the builds.

For More Information See "Version Compatibility in ActiveX Documents," in Chapter 7, "Debugging, Testing, and Deploying Components," in Part 2, "Creating ActiveX Components," for more information on binary compatibility.

Testing the Installation of Support Files on the Development Machine

In addition to removing the component registry, you should test that all of the necessary support files also install and register correctly. To do so, temporarily unregister everything in your system directory and your Occache or Downloaded Program Files directories.

> **Note** The procedures in this section require a copy of regsvr32.exe to be installed on your machine. If it is not, you can find it on the Visual Basic installation CD-ROM.

To test installation of support files on the development machine

1. Unregister the support files:
   - If you are using Internet Explorer 4.0 or later, access the Downloaded Program Files folder in either the Windows or the Winnt40 directory, right click the file, and select Remove. The system automatically removes and unregisters the item and any of its dependencies.
   - If you are using a version of Internet Explorer prior to 4.0, run Regsvr32 to unregister the files. Use the following command line in each applicable directory to unregister the necessary files:

     ```
     for %f in (*.ocx *.dll) do regsvr32 /u /s %f
     ```

2. Once all of the support files have been unregistered, access the Web page the Package and Deployment Wizard created. The component should download.

To reregister support files after testing

- Use the following command to restore the original entries:

  ```
  for %f in (*.ocx *.dll) do regsvr32 /s %f
  ```

Testing Component Download on Clean Machines

By testing your download on a clean machine — one that does not already have Visual Basic installed — you get an accurate look at the download experience your users are likely to encounter. This is an essential part of the testing process. You can simulate a clean machine by removing certain files and registry settings from one of your development machines, then restoring those files and settings after you have finished testing.

> **Note** The procedures in this section require a copy of regsvr32.exe to be installed on your machine. If it is not, you can find it on the Visual Basic installation CD-ROM.

Simulating a Clean Machine

One of the systems you test should be a machine that does not have Visual Basic or the Visual Basic Run-time Library installed — a "clean machine." If you do not have access to this type of machine, you can simulate one by following the instructions in this section. These steps may also be taken to clean a client machine that has been exposed to one or more of the files in the download.

> **Warning** Removing, renaming, or unregistering files as described below can impact other programs on your machine. Before deleting, renaming, or unregistering any files, it is advisable to copy these files to a safe alternate location from which you can restore them.

This process requires a copy of Regsvr32.exe. This file may be installed onto your development machine; if it is not, it may be found on the Visual Basic installation CD-ROM.

To simulate a clean machine

1. From the **Start** menu, click **Run**.
2. In the **Run** dialog box, type in the following command;

   ```
   Regsvr32.exe /U <Path to Windows folder>\System\Msvbvm50.dll
   ```

   > **Note** If you are running on a Windows NT machine, the Msvbvm50.dll is installed into the Windows\System32 folder.

3. From the **Start** menu, click **Find**, and then select **Files or Folder**.
4. Delete or rename the following two files, located in either your System or System32 directory:

   Msvbvm50.dll
   Asycfilt.dll

   Important Do not delete other versions of these files in alternative locations.

5. Unregister and delete or rename the item to be downloaded and any remaining dependency files installed on the client machine:

   - If you are using Internet Explorer 4.0 or later, access the Downloaded Program Files folder in either the Windows or the Winnt40 directory, right click the control, and select Remove. The system automatically removes the item and any of its dependencies.
   - If you are using a version of Internet Explorer prior to 4.0, use the following syntax:

     Regsvr32.exe /U <PATH>\System*file*

     where *file* is the name of the file to unregister.

Note Most controls install into the Windows\System, Windows\System 32, Windows\OCCache, or the Downloaded Program Files folders. However, some downloaded controls are not visible in Explorer's file view after download. It is necessary for these files to open a DOS window, navigate to the Downloaded Program Files folder, then run regsvr32 for those .ocx files to unregister them. You can then delete them at the DOS prompt.

Tip For a list of dependency files, open the .inf file created by the Package and Deployment Wizard and look in the Add.Code section. If you are uncertain whether a file needs to be unregistered, you can run REGSVR32.EXE with the /U switch. If you receive an error, the file does not need to be unregistered.

To test your download on a simulated clean machine

- Once all of the dependency files have been unregistered and renamed or deleted, access the Web page the Package and Deployment Wizard created. The component should download.

Restoring Your Simulated Clean Machine

You can reverse all the changes you made when you simulated a clean machine, if necessary. Normally, you do not need to do this because downloading the component you were testing should install and register the necessary files. However, if something goes wrong during download, you can restore the files yourself.

There are two steps to restoring your machine: You must rename or restore any files you deleted or renamed, and you must re-register the files you removed from the registry. When you restore, you must rename or restore any file you deleted or renamed.

To retrieve a file you deleted

- Retrieve it from the Windows Recycle Bin.

  – or –

- Obtain a fresh copy from the Visual Basic CD-ROM, if it was originally obtained as part of your installation.

  – or –

- Obtain a fresh copy from the appropriate third party, if the file did not come from the Visual Basic installation.

Once the necessary files have been restored, you can run Regsvr32.exe to register those files that you unregistered. For example, to register the Visual Basic Run-time Library, execute the following command from the run dialog:

```
Regsvr32 <Path to Windows>\System\Msvbvm50.dll
```

To register a file you unregistered

- Use the Regsvr32.exe program to register the file, as shown in the previous example.

Troubleshooting your Internet Component Download

A few of the more common problems in Internet Component Download and their solutions are listed in this section. These include:

- You receive an error deleting or renaming the Visual Basic run-time library when simulating a clean machine.
- You receive the error message "The Dynamic Link Library could not be found in the specified path."
- You receive the error message "An error has occurred copying MSVBVM50.DLL. Ensure the location specified below is correct."
- Internet Explorer prompts "Opening file xxx.VBD. What would you like to do with this file? Open it or save to disk?"
- You receive the error message "Internet Explorer is opening a file of unknown type: xxx.VBD."

Errors Deleting or Renaming the Visual Basic Run Time

You can receive these errors when you attempt to rename or delete the Visual Basic runtime (MSVBVM50.DLL) when simulating a clean machine. In most cases, these errors occur because the file is in use. You cannot delete the Visual Basic run time when Visual Basic is running. In addition, this error may occur if the browser is viewing an ActiveX document or has currently done so.

To fix this error, close Visual Basic or close your browser and try to delete the file again.

Error: "The Dynamic Link Library could not be found in the specified path."

This error generally occurs during testing when the ActiveX document you have been trying to download is still present on the machine.

To fix this problem, delete the ActiveX document from either the OCCache folder or the Downloaded Program Files folder, then restart your download.

Error: "An error has occurred copying Msvbvm50.dll. Ensure the location specified below is correct:"

This error typically occurs when there is insufficient disk space on the machine to which you are attempting to download. To fix this error, free up disk space and restart your download.

Prompt: "Opening file *DocumentName*.VBD. What would you like to do with this file? Open it or save it to disk?"

This error occurs when the Visual Basic run-time library (MSVBVM50.DLL) is not installed. Generally, this occurs when the safety level in Internet Explorer is set to High. To correct this, you must set the safety level in Internet Explorer to Medium or None.

Error: "Internet Explorer is opening file of unknown type: *DocumentName*.VBD from..."

This error can occur when you download an ActiveX document. The most common of these are listed below, with information on how to solve the problem.

Cause	Solution
You are using the wrong .vbd file	Make sure you are using the .vbd file provided by the Package and Deployment Wizard.
You are using an outdated .vbd file	The CLSID of your .vbd and .exe files may be out of synch. To preserve CLSIDs across builds in your projects, select Binary Compatibility on the Components tab of the Project Property dialog box.
Your actxprxy,dll is missing or not registered	Use regsvr32 to register the file, or try recompiling your project.
The Visual Basic runtime is not registered or not in the path	Use regsvr32 to register the file, or add it to your system path.
Your ActiveX document is not signed or safe for scripting	Set the browser safety settings to Medium.
There is a run-time error in the ActiveX document's initialization code, particularly in the Initialize or InitProperties procedures	Do a run-time error check on your project.
.cab files are not being downloaded	Make sure you are not distributing Visual Basic's core-dependent .cab files, which are not signed, onto a machine with browser security set to High. – or – Select "Use alternate locations" from the Run-Time Components window.

Other solutions you can try include:

- Turn on version numbering in your ActiveX document project and put the version number in a field so it displays on the main form of your downloaded page. This lets you check to find out if your project downloaded or if you are seeing an older version.
- Always close and reopen the browser between download attempts to clear the cache.
- Make sure you are using the latest versions of the controls and DLLs that ship with Visual Basic in your ActiveX document.

For More Information For more information on troubleshooting the download of ActiveX documents, see Article Q167380 in the Microsoft KnowledgeBase at http://premium.microsoft.com/support/kb/ARTICLES/.

Advanced Customization for Internet Component Download

There are several things you can do to customize your file download, including:

- Modifying an .inf file for the project. You might do this if you want to include information about your security settings, or to include an outside review of your component.
- Modifying the .ddf file for the project. You need to do this if you have added any additional files to your download, or if you have changed your .inf file.
- Manually rebuilding the .cab file. You need to do this if you have modified your .inf or .ddf files in any way.

The following sections provide more information on making these changes.

Modifying the .inf File

You can customize the installation process by modifying the .inf file. The modified file can then be included in a manually rebuilt .cab file (using the .ddf project file), or it can be directly referenced by the CODEBASE attribute of the OBJECT tag.

> **Note** An .inf file can be used in the CODEBASE attribute, but this should be avoided. Since an .inf file cannot have a digital signature, using it here would require you to digitally sign any compiled files (for example, .ocx files) to which it refers. This may require you to sign and deploy several executables individually, rather than signing one .cab file that packages all of them.

Typical modifications to an .inf file include:

- Adding a license agreement.
- Adding a readme file.
- Adding additional documentation.

Note As an ActiveX control developer, you can modify your Internet component download files, but you should be aware that doing so may place a potential liability on yourself or your firm if the modifications are done incorrectly. Some changes indicate that you guarantee, assure, or warranty that the changes are correct and truthful. Attempts to avoid these liabilities by citing "as is" or "suitability" clauses in a license agreement may be ruled invalid by many courts.

Sample .inf File

Here is an example of an .inf file:

```
;inf file for ControlDemo.ocx
;DestDir can be 10 for Windows directory, 11 for Windows\System(32) directory, or left
blank for the Occache or the Downloaded Program Files directory.

[version]
signature=$CHICAGO$

[Add.Code]
CONTROLDEMO.OCX=CONTROLDEMO.OCX
MSVBVM50.DLL=MSVBVM50.DLL

[CONTROLDEMO.OCX]
file-win32-x86=thiscab
RegisterServer=yes
clsid={F651BF93-239B-11D0-8908-00A0C90395F4}
DestDir=
FileVersion=1,0,0,1

[MSVBVM50.DLL]
hook=MSVBVM50.cab_Installer
FileVersion=5,1,43,19

[MSVBVM50.cab_Installer]
file-win32-x86=http://activex.microsoft.com/controls/vb5/MSVBVM50.cab
InfFile=MSVBVM50.inf
```

Important Only the original developer may legally mark a control as safe. There are *no* circumstances where you should ever mark someone else's control as safe. Changing the safety of a control can result in both a copyright infringement and criminal charges.

Adding Version Information to the .inf File

You can use the .inf file to specify the version of your component. The .inf file should have a file section that specifies a version and the same class ID specified in the <OBJECT> tag.

As illustrated in the example below, this file version specifies the version of the ActiveX control to be downloaded:

```
[circ3.ocx]
; The lines below specify that the specified Circ3.ocx (clsid,
; version) needs to be installed on the system. If it doesn't exist
; already, can be downloaded from the given location (a .cab).
NOTE:
; If "thiscab" is specified instead of the file location, it is
; assumed that the desired file is present in the same .cab cabinet
; that the .inf originated from. If the location pointed to
; is a different .cab, that cabinet is also downloaded and
; unpacked in order to extract the desired file.

file=http://www.code.com/circ3/circ3.cab
clsid={9DBAFCCF-592F-101B-85CE-00608CEC297B}

; Note that the {}s are required when entering the CLSID in the .inf
; file. This is slightly different from the HTML syntax for inserting
; CLSIDs in an <OBJECT> tag.

FileVersion=1,0,0,143
```

Modifying the .ddf File

You need to modify the project's .ddf file if you modify the .inf file or digitally sign your control in the Support directory. You also need to verify that any files added to the .inf file have also been added to the .ddf file, or they will not be available for installation.

Here is an example of a .ddf file created by the Package and Deployment Wizard:

```
.OPTION EXPLICIT
.Set Cabinet=on
.Set Compress=on
.Set MaxDiskSize=CDROM
.Set ReservePerCabinetSize=6144
.Set DiskDirectoryTemplate=
.Set CompressionType=MSZIP
.Set CompressionLevel=7
.Set CompressionMemory=21
.Set CabinetNameTemplate="ControlDemo.cab"
"C:\Website\Cabfiles\ControlDemo.inf"
"C:\ControlDemo\ControlDemo.ocx"
```

The following entries in the .ddf file should not be changed:

Entry	Description
MaxDiskSize=CD-ROM	This allows the .cab file to be as large as needed.
ReservePerCabinetSize=6144	This reserves space for a digital signature.

Manually Building .cab Files

You need to rebuild the .cab file every time you modify the .inf or .ddf file associated with it. To rebuild the .cab file, you need Microsoft's Cabinet Builder, Makecab.exe. This file is usually located in \VB\Setupkit\kitfil32.

The simplest way to rebuild the .cab file is to use the existing .ddf file for the project with the following command:

```
makecab /f yourcontrolname.ddf
```

The Cabinet Builder generates two additional informational files, setup.inf and setup.rpt.

For More Information For more information on modifying files associated with a .cab file, see to the Microsoft Developer's Network. For detailed information about .inf files, see the documentation included with Microsoft's Visual C++ and on the MSDN Library CD-ROM.

Manually Deploying ActiveX Components

In addition to using the Package and Deployment Wizard to package your components for download, you can also manually prepare your files for Internet download. This approach requires more effort on your part than using the Package and Deployment Wizard. In most cases, you will want to use the wizard to package and deploy your controls. However, you may want to manually package your components if you want to include custom information not supported by the Package and Deployment Wizard.

The following sections explain the basics of manually preparing your controls, ActiveX documents, and code components for download:

- Manually Deploying ActiveX Controls
- Manually Deploying Code Components
- Manually Deploying ActiveX Documents

Manually Deploying ActiveX Controls

You perform these steps to manually deploy ActiveX controls on an HTML page:

1. Create an HTML page the users can access to download your control.
2. On the HTML page, use the OBJECT tag to provide a means for the browser to download, register, and reference the ActiveX control. The object tag includes the control's class ID, an ID attribute used to reference the control, the CODEBASE tag, and parameters to set properties. The following shows an example of the HTML you might use:

```
<OBJECT
   classid="clsid:2F390484-1C7D-11D0-8908-00A0C90395F4"
   codebase="http://www.mysite.com/controls/label.ocx
   #version=1,0,0,0"
   id="Catalog"
   width="150"
   height="20"
   align="center"
   vspace="0"
>
   <PARAM NAME="Caption" value="Our Catalog">
   <PARAM NAME="FontName" value="News Gothic MT">
   <PARAM NAME="FontSize" value="11">
   <PARAM NAME="FontBold" value="1">
   <PARAM NAME="ForeColor" value="000000">
</OBJECT>
```

3. Use VBScript to handle click events so that clicking each control will load a specific .htm file in a specific HTML frame. The following code shows an example:

```
<SCRIPT LANGUAGE="VBScript">
Sub Welcome_Click
   Parent.Parent.Frames(1).Location.Href="Welcome.htm"
   Welcome.ForeColor = 000000
End Sub
</SCRIPT>
```

Manually Deploying Code Components

Code components are .exe or .dll files, rather than .ocx files. For client-side deployment, you can reference and script ActiveX components with the same kinds of HTML and VBScript code you might use for ActiveX controls. You perform the following steps to deploy a code component to a client:

1. Use HTML to create a page containing an element to launch the display of the component. For example, you might create a button that would launch the component. Include a name for the element to use in script, a type to show on the page, and a "value" — similar to the Caption property of a command button in Visual Basic.

   The following code shows a sample of what your HTML might look like for a button that references a Login dialog box:

```
<FORM NAME="LoginButton">
   Click here to log in:
   <INPUT NAME="cmdLogin" TYPE="Button" VALUE="Log in…">
</FORM>
```

2. Use the OBJECT tag to provide a means for the browser to download, register, and reference the ActiveX component. The OBJECT tag includes the component's class ID, a unique identifier used to reference the component, and a CODEBASE attribute to tell the browser where to find the component.

   Note See "Manually Deploying ActiveX Controls," earlier in this chapter, for an example of the OBJECT tag.

3. Use VBScript to show the component. The following shows an example of how you would do this for a login dialog component:

```
<SCRIPT LANGUAGE="VBScript">
' Create variables for the HTML form containing the
' button, and for the object exposing the method that
' shows the dialog box.
Dim dlgLogin
Dim TheForm
Set TheForm = ActiveX document.LoginButton
' Include a procedure that shows the dialog box
' when the button is clicked.
Sub cmdLogin_onClick
   Set dlgLogin = Login
   dlgLogin.ShowDialog
End Sub
</SCRIPT>
```

In this example, the component itself would include code that forms the login string and sends it to the server for validation.

Manually Deploying ActiveX Documents

The process for deploying ActiveX documents manually differs depending on whether you are deploying for Internet Explorer 3.*x* or 4.*x*.

Deploying ActiveX Documents in Internet Explorer 3.*x*

You perform these steps to deploy an ActiveX document manually in Internet Explorer 3.*x*:

1. Create an HTML page that will be used to download the ActiveX document.

2. In an existing HTML page from your application or Web site, create a link to the page you just created.

3. In the HTML page used to download the ActiveX document, use the OBJECT tag to provide a means for the browser to download, register, and navigate to the ActiveX document.

   Note See "Manually Deploying ActiveX Controls," earlier in this chapter, for an example of the object tag.

4. In the download page, insert VBScript that instructs Internet Explorer to navigate immediately to the ActiveX document through its .vbd file. The following code shows an example:

```
<HTML>
<OBJECT ID="SampleDoc1"
CLASSID="CLSID:11111111-1111-1111-1111-111111111111"
CODEBASE="Project1.CAB#version=1,0,0,0">
</OBJECT>
<SCRIPT LANGUAGE="VBScript">
Sub Window_OnLoad
   Location.Href = "SampleDoc1.VBD"
End Sub
</SCRIPT>
</HTML>
```

   In this code fragment, only the name of the .vbd file is given, rather than a fully qualified path. Internet Explorer looks for it in the same directory as the .htm file containing the VBScript.

Downloading ActiveX Documents in Internet Explorer 4.*x*

If you want to manually set up an ActiveX document for deployment on systems using Internet Explorer 4.0 or later, you can use a tool called the CodeBase Fixup Utility. CodeBase Fixup Utility is a tool that adds codebase information to a .vbd file or other ActiveX documents. The code information specifies the version number of the ActiveX document and the URL of the server used to download it. This approach presents several advantages:

- You no longer need a separate HTML page to launch your download.
- You can now mail the URL to the .vbd file and users can select it to view the ActiveX document in the browser.
- The browser can automatically download the latest version of the ActiveX document if it is not installed on the user's machine.

The Package and Deployment Wizard automatically configures your ActiveX documents using the CodeBase Fixup Utility. If you are using the wizard to package your components for download, you do not need to perform this procedure.

For More Information For instructions on how to use the CodeBase Fixup Utility tool, see the Readme.txt file installed with the tool in the Tools directory, or on the Visual Basic owner's Web site at http://www.microsoft.com/vstudio.

Index

B

D

E

J

K

L

M

P

R

S

T

U

V

W

Z

Register Today!

Return this
Microsoft® Visual Basic® 6.0 Reference Library
registration card today

OWNER REGISTRATION CARD **1-57231-864-3**

Microsoft® Visual Basic® 6.0 Reference Library

FIRST NAME MIDDLE INITIAL LAST NAME

INSTITUTION OR COMPANY NAME

ADDRESS

CITY STATE ZIP

E-MAIL ADDRESS ( ) PHONE NUMBER

U.S. and Canada addresses only. Fill in information above and mail postage-free.
Please mail only the bottom half of this page.

start
faster
go
farther